The Guide to the
American Revolutionary War
In Pennsylvania, Delaware, Maryland,
Virginia, and North Carolina

The Guide to the American Revolutionary War In Pennsylvania, Delaware, Maryland, Virginia, and North Carolina

Battles, Raids, and Skirmishes

Norman Desmarais

Busca, Inc.
Ithaca, New York

Busca, Inc.
P.O. Box 854
Ithaca, NY 14851
Ph: 607-546-4247
Fax: 607-546-4248
E-mail: info@buscainc.com
www.buscainc.com

BUSCA = SEARCH

Copyright © 2011 by Norman Desmarais
All rights reserved. No part of this book may be reproduced or transmitted in any form or by any means, electronic or mechanical, including photocopying, recording, or by any information storage or retrieval system, without permission in writing from the copyright owner.

First Edition

Printed in the United States of America

ISBN: 978-1-934934-05-0

Publisher's Cataloging-In-Publication Data
(Prepared by The Donohue Group, Inc.)

Desmarais, Norman.
  The guide to the American Revolutionary War in Pennsylvania, Delaware, Maryland, Virginia, and North Carolina : battles, raids and skirmishes / Norman Desmarais. -- 1st ed.

     p. : ill., maps ; cm. -- (Battlegrounds of freedom ; [5])

  Includes bibliographical references and index.
  Release date supplied by publisher.
  ISBN: 978-1-934934-05-0

  1. United States--History--Revolution, 1775-1783--Campaigns--East (U.S.) 2. United States--History--Revolution, 1775-1783--Battlefields--East (U.S.) 3. East (U.S.)--History, Military--18th century. I. Title. II. Series: Battlegrounds of freedom ; [5].

E230.5.E27 D47 2012
973.3/3

All maps Copyright © 2011 DeLorme (www.delorme.com) Street Atlas USA®.
Reprinted with permission.

Photography: author unless otherwise noted

Composition: P.S. We Type ♦ Set ♦ Edit

The author has made every effort to ensure the accuracy of the information in this book. Neither the publisher nor the author is responsible for typographical mistakes, other errors, or information that has become outdated since the book went to press.

This volume is part of the BATTLEGROUNDS OF FREEDOM series.

To the men and women of our armed forces who go in harm's way to preserve the freedoms our ancestors have secured for us.

Contents

List of Illustrations ix

Acknowledgments xi

Foreword by Mark Hurwitz... xiii

Preface..xv
    Strategic Objectives xvi; Nomenclature xvii; Conventions and Parts of This Book xix

1. Pennsylvania.. 1
    Beaver 2; Beaver Creek 2; Fort McIntosh 2; Pittsburgh and vicinity 4; Fort Pitt 4; Economy 4; Logstown 4; Kittanning 5; Fort Armstrong 5; Conemaugh River between Torrance and Bolivar 5; Goshen; Susquehanna River 6; Westmoreland County 6; Wyoming Valley 6; Fort Hand 7; Penn Valley 8; Lycoming County 8; Chillisquaque 12; Centre Township, Columbia County 13; Nazareth 13; Thompson's Island, upper Allegheny River 13; Fishing Creek 14; Bedford 15; Northampton County 16; West Buffalo Township 16; Northumberland County 16; Montour County 17; Fort Mead 17; Conyngham 18; Catawissa 19; Philadelphia and vicinity 19; Washington Crossing 19; Whitemarsh 22; Chester 27; Chadd's Ford 27; Chestnut Hill 31; Frazer 33; Near Valley Forge 34; Road to Philadelphia 34; Malvern 35; Phoenixville 36; Norristown 38; Frankford 38; Germantown 40; Philadelphia 43; Gray's Ferry Road, below Philadelphia 46; Delaware River near Philadelphia 47; Carpenter's Island, near Philadelphia 51; Near Darby (Gray's Ferry) 52; Fort Mifflin (Mud Fort) 53; Falls of the Schuylkill 57; Near Philadelphia 60; Fairhill, John Dickinson's residence 60; Black Horse Tavern (also known as Bryn Mawr, Harrington House, or Rebel Hill) 61; Smithfield 66; Spring House 67; Smithfield 67; Marcus Hook 68; Barren Hill 68; North Wales 72; Biles Island 72

2. Delaware 73
    Lewes 75; Near Cape Henlopen 75; Wilmington 76; Dover 80; Newark 80; New Castle 82; Bombay Hook 83; Kenton 84; Jordan's Island, Chester River 85; Duck Creek, Kent County 85; Off the Delaware Capes 86

3. Maryland.. 87
    Near Hagerstown 87; Swan Point, Chesapeake Bay 88; Sandy Point 89; Hopkins Island 92; Cedar Point, Chesapeake Bay 92; Holland Straits 94; Spesutie Island, Chesapeake Bay 94; Off Weltch Point, Elk River 94; Elkton 94; Perryville 96; Princess Anne County 96; Priests Town 96; Benoni Point, Choptank River 96; Vienna 97; Annapolis 98; Port Tobacco 98

4. Virginia 100
    Hampton 102; Poquoson, near Hampton 106; Norfolk 107; Kempsville 111; Jamestown 112; Burwell's Ferry 112; James River 114; Great Bridge 115; Cobham 117; Mulberry Island 118; Elizabeth River 118; Isle of Wight County 119; Hobb's Hole (Tappahannock) 119; Wallops Island 119; Gwynn's Island, Chesapeake Bay 120; Eastern Shore 122; Brent's House, Potomac River 123; Tangier Island, Chesapeake Bay 124; Off Willoughby's Point 124; Off Cape Henry 124;

Portsmouth 126; Portsmouth–Great Bridge Road 127; Suffolk 128; Henry's Point 128; Charles City Courthouse 130; Bland's Mills 130; Near Smithfield 131; Chesapeake Bay Shore 131; Bermuda Hundred 132; Shirley 132; Spencer's Ordinary (tavern) 133; Green Spring 134; South Quay 136; Pungoteague 136; Six Mile Ordinary, near Williamsburg 137; Yorktown 138; Chesapeake Bay 141; Siege of Yorktown 142; Little Fox and Great Fox Islands 152; Abingdon 156; Washington County 156; Augusta County 156; City Point 157; Hood's Farm 157; Petersburg 161; Osborne's (Osburn's) 163; Chesterfield County 165; Point of Fork 166; Raid on Charlottesville 167; New London and Bedford 167

5. North Carolina 169
Brunswick, Cape Fear and vicinity 170; Fayetteville and vicinity 177; Currie 178; Ocracoke Bar 181; Outer Banks 183; Roanoke Inlet 183; Cape Lookout, Ocracoke Inlet 184; North Carolina coast 184; Cape Hatteras 185; Currituck Inlet 186; Wilmington and vicinity 186; Halifax 192; Colson's Mill 193; Anson County 194; Mask's Ferry (also known as William Mast's Ferry) 194; Yadkin River 194; Richmond Town 195; Shallow Ford 195; Great Swamp, Bladen County 200; Hillsborough and vicinity 200; Danbury 206; Winston–Salem 206; Chatham County 207; Summerfield 212; Speedwell Furnace or Iron Works 215; Burlington vicinity 216; Alamance River 218; Fletcher's Mill 222; Wetsell's (Wetzell's, Weitzell's, Whitsell's or Whitsall's) Mill 222; Greensboro 224; Moncure 233; Stewards (Stewart's, Stuart's) Creek, southeastern North Carolina 233; Sanford 234; Stantonsburg 235; Swift Creek and Fishing Creek 235; Clinton 235; Wallace 236; Kenansville 237; Edenton 238; Southern Pines 239; New Bern 240; Wyanoke Ferry 242; Pittsboro 242; Drowning Creek 243; Kingston 245; Robeson's Plantation, Cape Fear River 245; Fanning's Mill 245; Elizabethtown 246; Raft Swamp (McPhaul's or McFall's Mill, Burnt Swamp) 247; Livingston's Creek 249; Clarkton 249; Beck's Ford 250; Kirk's Farm 250; Brush Creek 251; Cumberland County 251; Leonard Creek 252; Seven Creeks 252; Carthage 253; Beaufort 253; Morganton 254; Franklin 256; Western North Carolina 257; French Broad River 257; Salisbury and vicinity 258; Lincolnton 261; Laurel Hill, Lincoln County 267; Gilbert Town 268; Charlotte and vicinity 269; Cornelius 272; Torrence's (Tarrant's or Torrance's) Tavern 273; Webster 274; Mount Airy 275; Boone, Ashe County 275; Mill's Station 276

Notes 277

Glossary 311

Index...315

Please see the Busca website **www.buscainc.com** for more Resources on the volumes by Norman Desmarais including complete chronological and alphabetical lists of battles, raids, and skirmishes; a complete Bibliography for all sources used and cited in the creation of these volumes; and photos.

List of Illustrations

Maps

Pennsylvania 3
Philadelphia and vicinity 20
Maryland and Delaware 74
Virginia east 103
Virginia west 155
North Carolina east 171
North Carolina west 255

Photos

Cover   Commemoration of the 225th anniversary of the surrender at Yorktown

PA-1.   Durham boats 21
PA-2.   Raft for ferrying horses and cannons 22
PA-3.   Hope Lodge, Whitemarsh 23
PA-4.   Mather Mill 24
PA-5.   Emlen house 24
PA-6.   General Washington's headquarters, Brandywine 28
PA-7.   General Lafayette's headquarters, Brandywine 28
PA-8.   Paoli massacre site 35
PA-9.   British grenadiers 37
PA-10.   Cliveden, Chew mansion, site of the Battle of Germantown 41
PA-11.   Tomb of the Unknown Soldier of the American Revolution 44
PA-12.   Gundalow 45
PA-13.   Chevaux-de-frise 48
PA-14.   Grape shot 49
PA-15.   Mortar 51
PA-16.   Frigate or man-of-war 54
PA-17.   Merion Meeting House 61
PA-18.   Anthony Wayne Inn 62
PA-19.   Pont Reading, Joshua Humphreys's house 63
PA-20.   Grave of Oneida warriors 69

DE-1.   Reenactors portraying soldiers of the Delaware Regiment 73
DE-2.   Whaleboat with swivel gun 79
DE-3.   Monument commemorating the Battle of Cooch's Bridge 81
DE-4.   Longboat 83

MD-1.   Elk's Landing, Elkton 95

VA-1.   St. John's Episcopal Church, Richmond 101
VA-2.   Bomb or shell 104

VA-3.	Ropewalk	109
VA-4.	Wall gun	116
VA-5.	Earthen embrasure	121
VA-6.	Pinnace	125
VA-7.	Henry's Point	129
VA-8.	Site of Powell Creek/Bland's Mills	131
VA-9.	Shirley Plantation	132
VA-10.	Nelson House, Yorktown	139
VA-11.	Moore House, Yorktown	140
VA-12.	Surrender field	141
VA-13.	Redoubt # 9	143
VA-14.	Fusiliers' Redoubt	144
VA-15.	French hussar	147
VA-16.	Zigzag communicating trench	149
VA-17.	Surrender at Yorktown, commemoration	151
VA-18.	City Point	157
VA-19.	Trunnion	160
VA-20.	Markers at the Blandford Cemetery, site of the Battle of Petersburg	161
VA-21.	Osborne's Landing	164
NC-1.	Old Mother Covington and her daughter	179
NC-2.	Grasshopper	198
NC-3.	Cox's Mill	208
NC-4.	Alston house or House in the Horseshoe	210
NC-5.	Bruce family cemetery	213
NC-6.	Alamance battleground	218
NC-7.	Clapp's Mill monument	219
NC-8.	Millstone, Clapp's Mill	219
NC-9.	Stuart monument	225
NC-10.	Turner monument	226
NC-11.	Hoskins/Wyrick House	227
NC-12.	Site of the battle of Ramsour's Mill	262
NC-13.	Warlick Monument	263
NC-14.	Millstones from Ramsour's Mill	264
NC-15.	Tomb of six captains	264
NC-16.	Tarleton's Tea Table	265

ACKNOWLEDGMENTS

I would like to express my gratitude to Jack Montgomery, acquisitions librarian at the University of Western Kentucky, Bowling Green, for igniting the spark to write this book, for his encouragement through the project, and for introducing me to Connie Mills, the Kentucky Library Coordinator at the Kentucky Library and Museum who provided valuable assistance in locating primary sources for the Kentucky chapter. Michael Cooper, my publisher fanned the flame, nurtured the idea, and brought it to fruition.

I also wish to thank Providence College, my employer, for providing research and faculty development funds as well as time to pursue research. That research began with one sabbatical and extended beyond another. The staffs at the Phillips Memorial Library of Providence College and the other academic libraries in Rhode Island were very helpful in obtaining and providing much material.

Edward Ayres, Historian for the Jamestown-Yorktown Foundation, based at the Yorktown Victory Center in Yorktown, Virginia provided valuable assistance in locating Revolutionary War era maps. Michael Cobb, curator of the Hampton History Museum in Hampton, Virginia, graciously guided me through his museum collection—both the public display and the storage area and helped me locate sites in southern Virginia. Peggy Haile-McPhillips, City Historian at the Norfolk (Virginia) Public Library, helped greatly in identifying and locating places in the Norfolk area that had changed names and had long ago disappeared.

I also want to thank Norm Fuss for his help in researching and mapping the location of Tompkins Bridge.

David Loiterstein, Marketing Manager at Readex, also deserves my gratitude. He arranged for me to review the Early American Imprints Series I: Evans, 1639–1800 and the Early American Newspapers Series I, 1690–1876 and Series II, 1758–1900. The review periods coincided with important stages in my research. This undoubtedly made for better, more thorough, reviews; and it provided me with access to a wealth of primary sources that opened new avenues of research.

The members of the Brigade of the American Revolution (B.A.R.), the Continental Line, and the British Brigade generously give of themselves to help re-create the era of the American War for Independence. Some of these people work at musea or at historical sites. Some are members of their town historical societies or even historians for their city or town. Many are amateur historians who know a great deal about the Revolutionary War in their area. They provided enormous insight into events and the location of sites. Special thanks go to Bob Winowitch and David Clemens who guided me around Long Island to ensure that I visited all the relevant sites there. They also provided historical material and referred me to important sources for further information.

Other B.A.R. members, including Reinhard Batcher III, Todd Braisted, Todd Harburn, Thomas F. Kehr, Lawrence McDonald, Alan Morrison, Thaddeus J. Weaver, and Vivian Leigh Stevens read portions of the manuscript, suggested corrections and/or identified sources of additional information.

Many of the photographs were taken at various re-enactments. Without the efforts of the members of the B.A.R., these photos would not have been possible. Marshall Sloat,

Scott Dermond, Daniel O'Connell, Todd Harburn, Paul Bazin, and Deborah Mulligan deserve credit for providing additional photographs.

There's a certain serendipity to research. During the 225th anniversary re-enactment of the march to Yorktown, Virginia, as the troops crossed the Hudson River in whaleboats, I overheard B.A.R. member Daniel Hess talking about an engagement in which one of his ancestors had fought. I had been trying to locate documentation for that event; so I asked him about it after disembarking. He later sent me a copy of his ancestor's pension application which not only described the event which I had been trying to document but also identified two other events unknown to me.

DeLorme's Street Atlas USA software was very valuable in creating and annotating all the maps. GPS devices are useful for locating known places with addresses. They are not so useful for getting to a general location such as a particular hill or field. Maps are more useful for this purpose; but it takes a specially trained eye to identify changes in terrain that may cover earthworks or fortifications. Marshall Sloat has such an eye and I am grateful to him for accompanying me on some research trips, both as a companion and navigator. He helped me locate landmarks, monuments, and other physical features that would elude the common person. He also helped document the visits with photographs.

John A. Robertson has done a yeoman's job in creating interactive maps to complement this series. The maps can be viewed as a Google or Yahoo cartographic or topographical map with cartographic, aerial, or hybrid views. Google Earth maps can be zoomed to a variety of detail levels. Below an altitude of 200 feet, the maps turn to ground level view and allow taking a virtual tour of the landscape with a 360 degree view. One can toggle easily between aerial and ground level views. There's also a facility to add place marks or create polygons to modify the map to one's liking, add images, record a tour, or show sunlight across the landscape. A ruler makes it easy to measure distance between locations. Google Earth also has many photos that can be viewed with a single mouse click. These can sometimes provide a virtual tour of the better known sites.

Moving the cursor over each marker on the map displays the abbreviation for the state and the location name. Clicking on the marker reveals the dates of the action(s) there in mmddyy format along with an abbreviation for the volume which covers them and the page numbers. There's also an option to enter one's address or zip code to get driving directions.

The maps can be accessed at: http://gaz.jrshelby.com/desmarais/.

I wish to extend special thanks to my wife, Barbara, for her patience and support during the long periods of research and writing. She also accompanied me on many research trips and read maps and gave me directions as we drove to sites. She visited more forts and battlefields than she cares to remember.

Mark Hurwitz proofread the entire text and provided valuable feedback and suggestions. He also wrote the foreword. June Fritchman kindly offered some help with corrections and revisions of prior manuscripts in this series.

FOREWORD

by
Mark Hurwitz
Commander
Brigade of the American Revolution

To paraphrase Historian Geoffrey C. Ward, "the American War for Independence was fought from the walls of Quebec to the swamps of Florida, from Boston, to the Mississippi River." Now, if a shot was fired in anger, Norman Desmarais has documented it in this landmark study and guide, *The Guide to the American Revolutionary War*. It is a worthy successor to his *Battlegrounds of Freedom* (2005).

This comprehensive guide to the famous and unknown sites is groundbreaking. Beyond Lexington, Concord, Trenton, Brandywine, Saratoga, Monmouth, and Yorktown, Norman has fretted out the smaller actions and skirmishes which make up the eight year conflict, 1775–1783. Amazingly, Norman has found sites where settlers were scalped on the frontier to ships exchanging cannon fire on the high seas.

Norman Desmarais's passion for history comes as no surprise to me. After corresponding with Mr. Desmarais on an earlier multimedia CD-ROM project (*The American Revolution.—American Journey: History in Your Hands* series.—Woodbridge, CT: Primary Source Media, 1996), I finally got to meet him in November, 1995, when he attended a Brigade of the American Revolution (B.A.R.) event at Fort Lee Historic Park, Fort Lee, NJ. At that time, I had the opportunity to introduce him to Carl Becker, Commander of the 2nd Rhode Island Regiment, from his native state. Carl recruited him on the spot, and Norman, the academic historian, began his career as a re-enactor.

Becoming a "living historian" allows one to have laboratory to work in, wearing the uniforms, feeling the sweat, handling the weapons, experiencing the linear tactics, hearing the field music, smelling the smoke, which gives real perspective to the study of this period of history. This experience even goes beyond the "Staff Rides" of historic battlefields that the U.S. Army conducts with its officers.

The B.A.R. and the 2nd R.I. Regiment gave Norman the opportunity to visit many of the historic battle sites and get to see them "from the inside" and with the eye of a common soldier. This travel fueled his love for research and launched his encyclopedic study of Revolutionary War battle sites covering all of North America.

As a re-enactor, I have been studying the American War of Independence for nearly 35 years. Reading Desmarais's manuscript, I made discoveries both near and far.

- Being brought up and currently residing in my hometown of Springfield, NJ, I knew of the famous Battle of Springfield, June 23rd, 1780. Norman's research uncovered the following precursor, among many other actions there: "The militia killed and wounded 8 or 10 Waldeckers near Springfield on Sunday morning, January 19, 1777. They captured the rest of the party, 39 or 40, including 2 officers without suffering any casualties." (*The Pennsylvania Evening Post*, January 23, 1777)
- Meanwhile he found, west of the Mississippi: "St. Louis, Missouri—A small marker at 4th & Walnut Streets in downtown St. Louis which commemorates

the action that occurred on May 26, 1780." Desmarais's detailed entry then illuminates this unique action.
- Then at the end of the War for Independence, Savage Point, GA (Savage Point is located at a bend in the Ogeechee River at Richmond Hill State Park.): "Gen. Wayne suffered 5 men and horses killed and 8 wounded. He captured a British standard, 127 horses, and a number of packs." (*The Pennsylvania Packet or the General Advertiser.* 11:924 (August 15, 1782) p. 3)

I hope that readers can use this guide to find for themselves that history truly "happened here" as they travel the breadth of America and Canada.

PREFACE

The Guide to the American Revolutionary War in Pennsylvania, Delaware, Maryland, Virginia, and North Carolina: Battles, Raids, and Skirmishes is the fourth volume of a six-volume geographic history of the American War for Independence. The idea for the project came at a re-enactment of a 225th anniversary event when I overheard some of my fellow interpreters commenting about the several events on the calendar that summer that they knew nothing about. There had been no guidebooks published about the Revolutionary War since the nation's bicentennial in 1975. Moreover, those guidebooks and most of the history textbooks only cover the major, better known battles such as Lexington and Concord, Bunker Hill, Trenton and Princeton, Saratoga, Camden, Guilford Courthouse, and Yorktown.

Battlegrounds of Freedom: A Historical Guide to the Battlefields of the War of American Independence[1] served the purpose of an overview. It covered all the major battles and several of the minor ones, along with the winter encampments at Morristown and Valley Forge. It also included a chapter on re-enacting to make it distinctive from other guidebooks. The success of that volume encouraged me to continue the project.

This continuation of the *Battlegrounds of Freedom* series covers the battles and, much more specifically, the raids and skirmishes of the Revolutionary War, many of which do not get covered even in the most detailed history books. The series intends to provide comprehensive, if not exhaustive, coverage of the military engagements of the American War for Independence. It also aims to serve as a guide to the sites and the military engagements. It does not intend to cover specifically naval battles; but it does include naval actions in which one of the parties was land-based. British ships fired frequently on shore installations, ship-building industries, towns, houses, or troops on land. Such actions usually provoked a hostile response, even if a weak one. These minor clashes also illustrate the dangers faced by coastal residents and by troops moving within sight of enemy ships. Actions on inland lakes or bays are considered along with land actions as are attacks on enemy watering parties or other landing parties.

The work also covers engagements between French or Spanish troops and Crown forces as well as raids by Native Americans instigated or led either by British officers and agents or by Congressional forces. It does not attempt to cover raids on the cabins of western settlers that would have occurred regardless of the war, even though the residents retaliated.

Francis B. Heitman's *Historical Register of Officers of the Continental Army during the War of the Revolution, April 1775 to December 1783*[2] provides an alphabetical list of 420 engagements. This list seems to have been adopted as the U.S. Army's official list of battles and actions. Howard Henry Peckham's *The Toll of Independence: Engagements & Battle Casualties of the American Revolution*[3] expands this list to 1,330 military engagements and 220 naval engagements. He gives a brief description of the actions arranged chronologically, but his concern is primarily to tally the casualties. My research started with Peckham's work for the list of engagements, as his is comparatively the most extensive.

The multiple *Guide to the American Revolutionary War* volumes almost triple the number of engagements (more than 3,000) found in Peckham. They correct some of the entries and provide documentary references. The lack of primary source materials makes some actions very difficult to discover and document. The problem is most evident in "neutral territory," such as Elizabethtown, New Jersey, and Staten Island, New York, where conflict pretty much became part of everyday life. Sometimes, military actions occurred in several places during the same expedition or as part of a multi-pronged effort. Rather than repeat a narrative in several different places, we refer the reader to the main or a related account through *See* and *See also* references. However, each volume of the series is intended to be self-contained as much as possible with respect to the others.

Mark Mayo Boatner's *Encyclopedia of the American Revolution*[4] and his *Landmarks of the American Revolution: A Guide to Locating and Knowing What Happened at the Sites of Independence*[5] have long been considered the Bible for Revolutionary War aficionados and re-enactors. These works appeared in a new edition in 2007.[6] This is an excellent source to begin research on the Revolutionary War together with *The Encyclopedia of the American Revolutionary War: A Political, Social, and Military History*.[7]

Each volume in the *Battlegrounds of Freedom* series covers its respective states affected by the war and each location where an engagement occurred. It follows a hybrid geographical/chronological approach to accommodate various audiences: readers interested in American history, re-enactors, tourists, and visitors. The states are arranged from north to south and east to west. Within each state, the engagements appear chronologically. Locations with multiple engagements also appear chronologically so readers can follow the text as a historical sequence or "story" of a site before proceeding to the next one. For example, the treatment of the events at Whitemarsh, Pennsylvania covers engagements dating from February 19, 1777 to May 20, 1778 before proceeding to the Battle of the Brandywine (September 11, 1777). Cross references have been added as necessary.

The text identifies the location of the sites as best as can be determined, provides the historical background to understand what happened there, indicates what the visitor can expect to see there, and identifies any interpretive aids. It is not meant to replace the guides produced for specific sites and available at visitor centers. These guides usually provide more details about the features of a particular site. Also, monographs devoted to specific engagements or campaigns will be more detailed than what we can present here.

Strategic Objectives

The presence of large numbers of troops in an area gave residents cause for concern. The soldiers were always short of food and constantly searching for provisions. It took a lot of food to feed an army. While troops were allotted daily rations, they rarely received their full allocation.

A soldier's typical weekly ration would consist of:
- 7 pounds of beef or 4 pounds of pork
- 7 pounds of bread or flour sufficient to bake it
- 3 pints of peas or beans
- ½ pound of rice
- ¼ pound of butter[8]

This would translate to the following weekly rations for an army of 1,000 men:
- 3½ tons of beef or 2 tons of pork
- 3½ tons of bread or flour sufficient to bake it
- 94 bushels of peas or beans
- 1¾ tons of rice
- 250 pounds of butter

The threat of a foraging expedition caused residents to hide their cattle and the expedition usually elicited an attack from the enemy. As one side tried to obtain food and supplies, the other tried to prevent them from doing so or to re-capture the stolen goods along with the enemy's baggage and supplies. While most of these actions were militarily insignificant, they often had the effect of reducing both forces. Crown forces were harder to replace because they usually had to come from overseas.

Military objectives not only included the capture of enemy forts, strongholds, and armies but also the control of important crossroads, rivers, and ferries. The rivers were the 18th-century highways and made travel and transportation much quicker than the unpaved roads. Controlling these strategic points either facilitated or blocked troop movements and supply lines.

Nomenclature

The two sides in the American War for Independence are generally referred to as the British and the Americans. However, this is a gross oversimplification. While it is a convenient way to refer to both sides, it is often inaccurate, particularly when discussing engagements in the South where most of the actions were between militia units or armed mobs with very few, if any, regular soldiers. For example, Major Patrick Ferguson was the only British soldier at the Battle of Kings Mountain (South Carolina). Many actions in the South seem to have been occasions for people to settle grudges with their neighbors in feuds that resemble that between the Hatfields and the McCoys. In a sense, the war in the South was very much a civil war. In other areas, it took on the nature of a world war.

Moreover, the provincials were British citizens—at least until they declared their independence on July 4, 1776. Prior to that date, the provincials believed their grievances were with Parliament and not the King. Most of the citizens did not favor independence but rather hoped for redress of their grievances and the re-establishment of relations with Parliament. However, when King George III sided with Parliament and declared the colonies in rebellion on August 23, 1775, the provincials realized that their hopes were dashed. After the news reached the colonies on October 31, 1775, they began to see independence as their only recourse.

The Declaration of Independence made a definite break between England and her American colonies; but it took a while for those ideas to become widely accepted. In fact, it took 18 months after the outbreak of the war to enunciate that objective; and it took eight years to win the war that secured the independence of the United States of America. Even though England officially recognized the new country with the signing of the Treaty of Paris in 1783, it often continued to act as though it still controlled the colonies. This was one of the factors that led to the War of 1812.

While the provincials called themselves Americans, to refer only to those who favored independence as Americans is too broad, as they were less than a majority of the population. Although all the provincials were British citizens until the signing of Declaration of Independence and their effective independence at the end of the war, to refer to them as Americans confuses a political position with hegemony. That would be comparable to referring to Republicans or Democrats as Americans, implying that the other party is not American. Similarly, to refer to them as Patriots implies that those who remained loyal to the King were less patriotic when they fought to maintain life as they knew it.

Consequently, we refer to the supporters of independence as Rebels, Whigs, or Congressional troops. We also distinguish between the local militias and the regular soldiers of the Continental Army ("Continentals") as narratives allow further distinction. We also refer to Allied forces to designate joint efforts by Congressional forces and their foreign allies, primarily French and Spanish.

Similarly, the "British" armies were more complex than just English troops. They certainly consisted of Irish, Scot, and Welsh troops. We sometimes refer to them by regiment, e.g. 71st Highlanders, Black Watch, Royal Welch Fusiliers, when individual regiments are prominent in an engagement. They are also referred to generically as Regulars or Redcoats. (Some derogatory references call them lobsterbacks or bloodybacks because of the flesh wounds from whipping—a common form of punishment at the time.)

While British troops are often called Redcoats, not all wore red coats. The artillerymen wore dark blue coats. While some of the dragoons wore red, others such as Tarleton's Legion, wore green coats. There are instances where the two sides confused each other because of the similarity of the coats. For example, Major General Henry "Light-Horse Harry" Lee (1756–1818) and his legion tried to surprise Lieutenant Colonel Banastre Tarleton (1744–1833) on the morning of February 25, 1781. The front of Lee's Legion encountered two mounted Loyalists who mistook them for Tarleton's Legion. The Loyalists were taken to General Lee who took advantage of their mistake by posing as Tarleton. He learned that Colonel John Pyle had recruited about 400 Loyalists and that they were on their way to join Tarleton. Lee and his men continued the ruse, surrounded the Loyalists, and captured them all, depriving General Charles Cornwallis of badly needed troops at Yorktown.

Loyalist troops were issued both red and green uniforms with a wide variety of facings. Those who wore the green coats were sometimes referred to as Green Coats or simply as the Greens. Some authors refer to the Loyalists as Tories, a term which has taken on derogatory significance.

Moreover, King George III, who was of German origin, arranged to reinforce his armies with large numbers of German troops. They wore coats of various shades of blue, as well as green with red facings. Many of these soldiers came from the provinces of Hesse Hanau and Hesse Kassel and became known as Hessians. Other regiments were known by their provinces of origin (e.g., Braunschweiger or Brunswick and Waldeck) or by the name of their commander (von Lossberg, von Donop, etc.).

We use the terms Crown forces, King's troops, Royal Navy to refer to these combined forces or the regiment name, commanding officer, or group designation (e.g. Hessians, Loyalists) to be more specific.

People of color fought on both sides. We use the currently politically correct terminology of African Americans, even though not all of them came from Africa, and Native Americans as the generic terms. We also use the specific tribal name, if known: Iroquois, Mohawk, Oneida, Cherokee, etc. Mulattoes referred to people of mixed race. Quotations retain the terminology used by the original writer.

The Native American tribes tended to support the Crown because they realized that the settlers coveted their land and presented a greater threat than the British Army. Great Britain had fewer troops in the West (west of the Appalachians) than in the East (along the East Coast and east of the Appalachians), so it needed their support. More than 1,200 Delawares, Shawnees, and Mingoes lived in the Ohio valley. North of them, 300 Wyandots, Hurons, and 600 Ottawas and thousands of Chippewas inhabited southern Michigan and the shores of Lake Erie. Several hundred Potawatomis extended toward the southern end of Lake Michigan. The area north and east of Fort Pitt was occupied by the Senecas, and several hundred Miamis lived along the Maumeee and upper Wabash rivers. The Weas, Piankeshaws, Kickapoos, and other tribes settled on the Wabash and west toward the Mississippi, while an unknown number of Foxes, Sauks, and Mascoutens lived beyond the Great Lakes.

The Native American tribes were unreliable and not great assets as combatants. Sometimes, they were even a liability. For example, the murder of Jane McCrea by her Native American escorts during the Saratoga campaign brought new recruits to the Congressional forces and deterred Loyalists from actively supporting the Crown troops. British commanders often found it impossible to determine whether the Native Americans would fight and for how long. When they did fight, they usually did so in small groups and for limited periods. They were also often divided by rivalries among themselves, easily frightened by any show of strength, and usually unwilling to leave their families for long campaigns. Without the support of the Native Americans, however, Crown forces had no hope of controlling the West. The Crown forces provided the tribes with gifts every year to insure their continued support. These gifts included a large supply of ammunition and clothing as well as gifts for the chief warriors.[9]

Nobody knows how many provincials remained loyal to King George III during the American War for Independence. Many history books credit John Adams with estimating that one-third of the population favored the Revolution, one-third were against it, and another third leaned to whichever side happened to control the area. The quotation reads:

> I should say that full one-third were averse to the revolution. These, retaining that overweening fondness, in which they had been educated, for the English, could not cordially like the French; indeed, they most heartily detested them. An opposite third conceived a hatred of the English, and gave themselves up to an enthusiastic gratitude to France. The middle third, composed principally of the yeomanry, the soundest part of the nation, and always averse to war, were rather lukewarm both to England and France.[10]

On another occasion, Mr. Adams noted that the colonies had been nearly "unanimous" in their opposition to the Stamp Act in 1765 but, by 1775, the British had "seduced and deluded nearly one third of the people of the colonies."[11]

In the first quotation, Ray Raphael[12] notes that Adams was writing about the political sentiments of Americans toward the conflict between England and France in 1797; but the two quotations somehow blended together in popular historiography to refer to the American War for Independence. So Adams has become the definitive contemporary source on the political allegiance of the period.

Conventions and Parts of This Book

Cognizant that one may begin a tour anywhere, the first occurrence of a person's name in a section identifies him or her as completely as possible with the full form of the name with birth and death dates, if known. Some readers will probably find this awkward or cumbersome as they read several sections. We hope that those who consult a specific section will find this helpful.

Most chapters begin with a map of the sites in that state to facilitate orientation, and additional maps face the beginning of their respective sections. Some chapters with many actions are subdivided north to south and east to west, and these divisions are reflected with references to their respective maps. These maps have pointers to engagement locations and are printed on regular paper like the photos.

Engagements are then listed chronologically within their subdivisions along with the corresponding map. Locations with multiple engagements group those events in chronological order under the same heading to provide a historical sequence or "story" of a site before proceeding to the next one. Cross references have been added as necessary.

Each site begins with the name of the city or town (or the most commonly known name of the engagement), and the name (and alternate names) of the battle or action. The location names are followed by the dates, in parentheses, of significant actions discussed in the text. Specially formatted text identifies the location of the site, indicates what the visitor can expect to see, and identifies any interpretive aids. Historical background to understand what happened at a site follows. In any case, this book does not mean to replace more-detailed tourist guides for specific sites that are available at visitor centers.

Events are marked with a bullet character (★) for easy identification and to dispel confusion.

Travelers should take care to map their route for most efficient travel as many sites are not along main roads. Sometimes, one must backtrack to visit a place thoroughly. Travelers should also be aware that some locations in a particular state may be farther than other locations in a neighboring state. Consulting maps allows the visitor to proceed from one location to another with the least amount of backtracking. It also offers options for side trips as desired. Consult the appendices at the publisher's web site (**www.buscainc.com**) to see how battle sites are grouped and keyed to major cities or locations. Interactive maps for this series are available at **http://gaz.jrshelby.com/desmarais/**.

One of the appendices gives a chronological list of battles, actions, and skirmishes. History books often present events in purely chronological order. However, that is not a good approach for a guidebook to follow, as events can occur simultaneously great distances apart. For example, the powder alarm in Williamsburg, Virginia occurred on the same day as the battles of Lexington and Concord in Massachusetts. The web site also features a comprehensive state-by-state alphabetical list of locations where actions (battles, raids, or skirmishes) took place.

Other books take a thematic approach, covering campaigns or specific themes like the war on the frontier. This technique, while more focused, often ignores information relevant to a site that properly belongs to another theme. For example, a theme covering Major General John Burgoyne's (1722–1792) campaign of 1777 may not cover the capture of Fort Ticonderoga in 1775 or its role in the Seven Years War (also known as the French and Indian War).

The many photographs, with descriptive captions and keyed to the text, are important for identifying details of historic buildings, monuments, battlefields, and equipment. Many of the photos are of battle and event re-enactments. All photos, except otherwise identified, are by the author. Full-color photos of some of the images in this and other volumes are on the publisher's web site (**www.buscainc.com**).

Another feature that modern readers and visitors will find useful are URLs for web sites of various parks and tourist organizations. These URLs are correlated with various battle sites and sometimes events. Visitors may want to consult these web sites ahead of time for important, updated information on special events, hours, fees, etc. These URLs were active and accurate at the time this book went to press.

The Glossary provides definitions for some 18th-century military and historical terms. There are also scholarly reference Notes for sources used in this book and an

Index. The full Bibliography of the sources consulted for the *Battlegrounds of Freedom* series is on the publisher's web site (**www.buscainc.com**).

Most of the sites described in this book are reconstructions or restorations. Many buildings were damaged during the War for Independence or fell into disrepair over the years. They were refurbished, for the most part, for the nation's bicentennial in 1975–1976. Battlefield fortifications were sometimes destroyed after a battle so they could not be re-used by the enemy at a later time. For example, the hornworks and siege trenches at Yorktown, Virginia were destroyed after the surrender of General Charles Cornwallis so the Crown forces could not re-use them for a subsequent assault. They were, however, rebuilt and used again during the War of Rebellion (Civil War). There are many houses and structures still standing that demonstrate what life was like in the 18th century. Only those related to the battles are covered.

Many of the sites have been obliterated by urban development and have nothing to see or visit. Houses and other construction have supplanted them. One battlefield is covered by a shopping mall; another has been submerged under a man-made lake; others were destroyed by high-rise apartment or office buildings. Many are remembered only with a roadside marker. Some don't even have that.

Many sites have little importance to the outcome of the war. Some actions were mere skirmishes or raids lasting only a few minutes. For example, some actions consisted of a single volley. After one of the forces fired, it fled. Yet, some important events, such as the capture of Fort Kaskaskia by George Rogers Clark in Illinois and the capture of Fort Ticonderoga by Benedict Arnold, Ethan Allen, and the Green Mountain Boys were effected without firing a single shot. The battle at Black Mingo Creek, South Carolina lasted only 15 minutes. Other engagements, particularly those involving Lieutenant Colonel Francis Marion, known as the Swamp Fox, were fought in the swamps of South Carolina and are hard to find.

Some sites remain undeveloped and virtually ignored. This is not necessarily bad. While erosion, neglect, and plant or tree growth slowly undermine earthworks, they do significantly less damage than the rapid deterioration resulting from bikers and walkers.

One cannot easily cover all the sites of the American War for Independence. However, one can visit all the sites and events that affected the outcome of the war. One can also visit enough locally significant spots to get an understanding of what the war was like for the people of that region. This book tries to cover the extant battle sites and hopes to serve as a companion on the voyage of discovery.

Norman Desmarais
normd@providence.edu

1
Pennsylvania

Pennsylvania was situated roughly in the center of the American colonies. This made it a convenient location for delegates from the North and South to meet. Pennsylvania was also a transition zone between the plantation societies of the South and the northern and middle colonies. The Seven Years War (French and Indian War) (1756–1763) brought conflict to the frontier of the Quaker colony. Members of the Quaker majority in the provincial assembly yielded power to non-Quakers who were allies of the Society of Friends who could authorize defensive measures and to attempt to dislodge the French from the Ohio Valley.

Philadelphia was the site of the First and Second Continental Congresses; but the government moved to York when the British occupied the city on Friday, September 26, 1777 until June 1778. The Constitutional Convention met in Philadelphia in 1787 and Pennsylvania became the second state.

Pennsylvania's military zeal emerged when hostilities broke out at Lexington and Concord, Massachusetts. Many companies of eager but inexperienced Pennsylvanians converged on Cambridge, Massachusetts in the late spring of 1775, as General George Washington (1732–1799) formed the various militias into the Continental Army. Pennsylvania contributed 33,035 men to General Washington's army—7,357 militia and 25,678 in the Continental Army. Some Pennsylvanians joined Benedict Arnold (1741–1801) on his march through Maine to besiege Quebec. Others went with General Richard Montgomery (1737–1775) to attack Quebec from the west. Others defended the territories closer to home, particularly the New Jersey seacoast and the Hudson River valley, when the British withdrew from New England to the middle colonies which they perceived as more friendly.

Pennsylvanians fought for a variety of reasons. Workers and tradesmen tried to keep the power they had gained through the Committees of Correspondence. They wanted a more egalitarian government that would enforce fair trade. Others hoped for relief from imperial trade restrictions.

Pennsylvania had a large population of Quakers, particularly in Bucks and Chester counties, who refused to fight at all. There were also several settlements of Moravians and Mennonites whose religious principles also opposed warfare. Philadelphia had a large Loyalist population.

Much of the German population in central Pennsylvania fought to demonstrate their equality with their English-speaking neighbors. Others saw the war as an opportunity to gain political recognition that would put them on par with eastern Pennsylvanians.

Settlers in the Juniata Valley and along the western frontier were preoccupied with fighting the Native Americans, regardless of whether they were friendly or hostile. The Native Americans, in turn, retaliated against the settlers to avenge their losses and to protect their land. Some were prompted by British promises of security and arms. They tended to attack in small raiding parties, but sometimes they would join Loyalists in large forces to overwhelm the settlers.

> The Pennsylvania Historical and Museum Commission (PHMC) (phone: 800-747-7790) is the state's official agency for the preservation of its historic heritage. It manages the state's more than 1,800 historic markers and publishes the *Guide to the Historical Markers of Pennsylvania*. The Pennsylvania Historical and Museum Commission (website: **www.phmc.state.pa.us**; (phone: 866-PA-TRAIL) maintains more than 50 state historic properties, state historical musea, and landmarks administered by independent state commissions.

See the map of Pennsylvania.

Beaver
Beaver Creek (ca. July 25, 1776)
Fort McIntosh (July 30, 1779)

> The Beaver River flows from New Castle to the Ohio River at Beaver, near Fort McIntosh. Raccoon Creek runs roughly parallel to the Ohio River which is about 5 miles east of it, northwest of Pittsburgh and south of Fort McIntosh. Howard Peckham places this event at Beaverdam Creek in Georgia. Beaverdam Creek begins in Riverdale, Georgia, near the intersection of routes GA 85 and GA 138W, about 15 miles south of Atlanta and flows into the Flint River, farther south in Riverdale. However, the location of George Baker's house on the dividing ridge between the Ohio River and Raccoon Creek would place this action near Fort McIntosh in Pennsylvania.
> There are two Raccoon Creeks in Georgia. One runs north to south, west of Summerville, about 18 miles northwest of Rome. The other is about 37 miles southeast of Rome and flows north from the Paulding Forest Wildlife Management Area in Rockmart to the Etowah River in Cartersville. However, the Ohio River does not come anywhere near Georgia.
> Fort McIntosh was the second largest fort on the frontier after Fort Pitt. It was built on a high bluff, 130 feet above the Ohio River and a little less than a mile below the mouth of the Beaver River. Contemporary drawings indicate the fort was composed of buildings of laid up logs forming an irregular square or a trapezoid, about 150 feet on each side, with raised bastions. At least two of the bastions mounted iron cannon and the fort may have had four cannons. Log walls or palisades connected the bastions, and a 15-foot-wide ditch protected three sides of the fort. The 130-foot slope to the Ohio River protected the other side. The gate at the north end was probably protected by a semi-lunette or a ravelin. A covered way provided access to water in case of attack. Inside were three barracks, warehouses, the commandant's house, officer's quarters, a forge, kitchen, and powder magazines. Nothing remains of the original fort. About one-third of the site is now a park and the rest is occupied by private residences.[1]

Two men reaping near the mouth of the Beaver River went to George Baker's (1732–1802) house on the dividing ridge between the Ohio River and Raccoon Creek to find the house destroyed and Baker, his wife and five children missing. A party of six men went scouting to the mouth of Raccoon Creek and saw six Cherokees crossing in a canoe near the mouth of the Beaver River. They returned to report that they saw the Baker family tied with bark at the place where they crossed the river. Captain John Pulliam (1757–1813) and a party of 15 men set out in pursuit. They skirmished with the

Pennsylvania 3

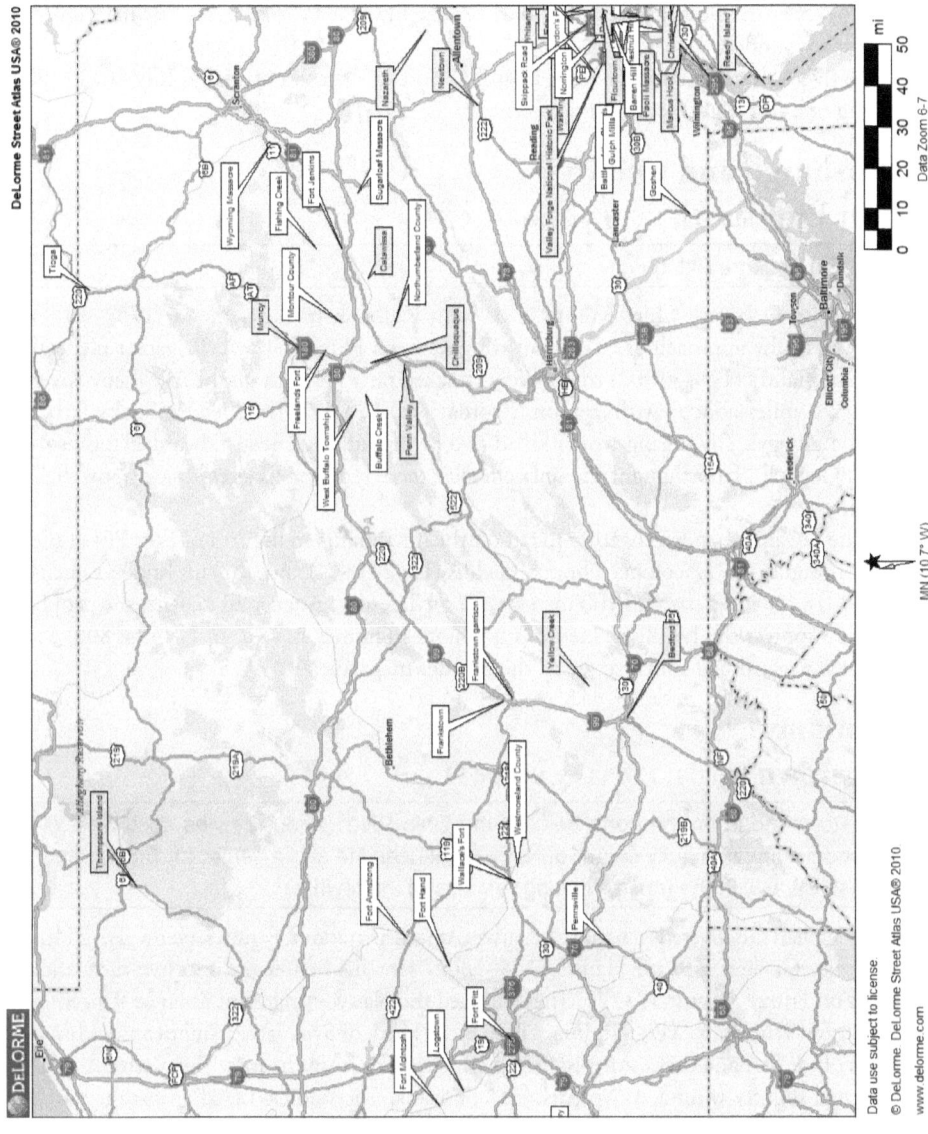

Pennsylvania: Map for The Guide to the American Revolutionary War in Pennsylvania, Delaware, Maryland, Virginia, and North Carolina © 2011 *DeLorme (www.delorme .com) Street Atlas USA®*

Cherokees at the Beaver River around Thursday, July 25, 1776 and lost one man killed and one wounded.[2]

★ Native Americans fired on the garrison at Fort McIntosh on Friday, July 30, 1779, killing one and slightly wounding another.[3]

Pittsburgh and vicinity
Fort Pitt (June 21, 1777; Aug. 26–27, 1777)

> Fort Pitt became Pittsburgh.

Despite Delaware Chief Killbuck's or John Killbuck Jr. Gelelemend (1737–1811) warning of the approach of a band of Mingoes from Pluggy's Town, Brigadier General Edward Hand's (1744–1802) troops were attacked near Fort Pitt on the Allegheny River about 20 miles above Pittsburgh on Saturday, June 21, 1777. Chief Killbuck's father led the Pluggy's Town gang which killed two of Brigadier General Edward Hand's soldiers. General Hand thought the only effective remedy was a counter attack upon their town.[4]

★ The Loyalists banded together to cut off the inhabitants in the area of Fort Pitt at the end of August 1777. Colonel Thomas Gaddis (1742–1834) and Captain Enoch Enochs (1750–1835) and a party of 100 men set out on Tuesday, August 26 to assist the people and to suppress the Loyalists. Lieutenant Colonel Thomas Brown, Jr. (1738–1800) assembled a guard of 15 men to guard the powder magazine.[5]

Economy
Logstown (Aug. 1, 1777; Oct. 20, 1777)

> Logstown stood on the north bank of the Ohio River, about 2 miles southwest of Economy. It was a busy center of Native American life and a center for French and British trade with the tribes. Nothing remains of the town.

Spies had discovered a band of Native Americans about 8 miles below Fort Pitt. Brigadier General Edward Hand (1744–1802) sent his lieutenant and five men after them on Friday, August 1, 1777. They pursued the Native Americans as far as Wheeling Fort (now Wheeling, West Virginia). They met a party of five Native Americans within 3 miles of the fort and had a skirmish less than 300 yards from the fort. The Native Americans had slightly wounded two African Americans. The soldiers killed and scalped one Native American and captured "A good Rifle Gun and his Accuterments and a famous Neet-made Ware Club his scalp was ellegantly Adornd with Three fine Rows of Tassels and Feathers."[6]

★ Captain John Lucas's (1749–1836) company of Virginia militia left Pittsburgh at 10 PM on Sunday, October 19, 1777 and stopped at Logstown the following morning. There, they met with two or three Native Americans who fired on the militiamen, killed one and wounded another and fled. The militiamen were so alarmed that Captain Lucas could not get a single man to help him surround a cornfield where he thought the Native Americans were hiding.[7]

Kittanning
Fort Armstrong (Aug. 19, 1777)

> Fort Armstrong stood within the manor of Kittanning which was 2 miles south of the present town of Kittanning. Kittanning is a Delaware word, corrupted from Kit-han-nink, which means the main stream.[8]

★ Whig Captain Samuel Moorhead or Morehead (1749–1814) sent out party of men to drive cattle to Fort Armstrong on Tuesday evening, August 19, 1777. A considerable party of Native Americans fired on them a little way from the fort. They killed and scalped three soldiers.[9]

Conemaugh River between Torrance and Bolivar
Westmoreland County (Sept. 2 or 9, 1777)

> The boundaries of Virginia and Pennsylvania were not yet definitely determined in the mid–18th century. Both Virginia and Pennsylvania claimed the territory on the Ohio and between the Ohio and the Monongahela rivers. When the dispute was finally settled, this territory went to Pennsylvania and became an important part of Westmoreland County. The location of this event may have occurred on the Conemaugh River between Torrance and Bolivar about 40 miles east of Pittsburgh.[10]

★ A band of Native Americans attached to the British Army attacked Captain Andrew Van Swearingen (1747–1824), of the 8th Pennsylvania, and a small party of men on the Conemaugh River somewhere between Torrance and Bolivar on Tuesday, September 9, 1777. (Some accounts give the date as September 2.) They captured Captain Van Swearingen, a lieutenant and 20 privates. British Brigadier General Simon Fraser's (1729–1777) "batman" (one who takes care of his officer's horse) rescued Captain Van Swearingen from the Native Americans and took him to the general who interrogated him concerning the strength of the Continental Army. Van Swearingen only told him that it was commanded by Major Generals Horatio Gates (1728–1806) and Benedict Arnold (1741–1801). General Fraser then returned him to join the other prisoners with directions not to be ill treated.[11]

Goshen (Sept. 16, 1777)

> Goshen is about 19 miles south-southeast of Lancaster and about 4.75 miles east of Benton on the Susquehanna River.

The Crown forces sent their sick and wounded to Wilmington after the Battle of Brandywine (see page 27). The rest of the army marched to Goshen in two columns on Tuesday, September 16, 1777. Along the way, they received intelligence that the enemy was advancing on the Lancaster Road and were within 5 miles of Goshen. The two columns advanced to attack the Congressional forces. General Charles Cornwallis (1738–1805) took his column by Goshen Meetinghouse while Lieutenant General Wilhelm von Knyphausen (1716–1800) went by the road to Downing Town.

A violent rain began to fall as the two columns advanced and continued the entire day and night without intermission which made an attack impracticable. The 1st light infantry, at the head of Lord Cornwallis's column encountered an advanced guard of Congressional troops about a mile outside Goshen and dispersed them, killing 12 and wounding more, without losing a man.

At about the same time, the chasseurs in front of Lieutenant General von Knyphausen's column fell in with another party and killed an officer and five men and took four officers prisoners. They lost three men wounded.

The Congressional forces, now apprised of the Crown army's approach, marched the entire night of the 16th and arrived at Yellow Springs the following morning. All their small ammunition was damaged by the rain.[12]

Susquehanna River
Pine Creek (Dec. 23, 1777)
Great Island (Jan. 1, 1778)

> The mouth of Pine Creek is at its confluence with the West Branch Susquehanna River between the boroughs of Avis (in Clinton County, to the west) and Jersey Shore (in Lycoming County, to the east). Great Island is an island formed at the junction of Eagle Creek and the West Branch Susquehanna River about 7 miles west of the mouth of Pine Creek.

A man was tomahawked near the mouth of Pine Creek on Tuesday, December 23, 1777. A party of 11 Native Americans killed another man 2 miles north of the Great Island about Thursday, January 1, 1778. Colonel Philip Frederic Antes (1730–1801) pursued them. The light snow made it easy to track them. When the militiamen caught up with the Native Americans, they killed two. The rest fled and the militiamen followed them for a long distance but could not overtake them.[13]

Westmoreland County
Wallace's Fort (April 28, 1778)

> Wallace's Fort, erected on the farm of Richard Wallace, contained about half an acre of ground and had a good blockhouse. It was located a short distance south of Blairsville, between the old Forbes road and the Conemaugh River and 16 or 20 miles from Fort Ligonier.

A large party of Native Americans raided Wallace's Fort, garrisoned by militia, on Tuesday, April 28, 1778. They killed nine militiamen and slightly wounded their captain, Captain Hopkins. They also captured nine guns.[14]

Wyoming Valley
Wyoming Massacre (July 3–4, 1778)

> The Wyoming Massacre site is on Wyoming Avenue (Route PA 11 and Susquehanna Avenue) in Wyoming, Pennsylvania.
> The remains of 166 victims from the massacre were buried in a mass grave in the fall of 1778. A 63-foot granite monument, erected in the 1840s, at 4th Street and

> Wyoming Avenue marks the grave site. The inscription lists the names of some 40 survivors. The two guns that stand guard date from the Civil War and were mounted in the casemates of Fort Hancock at Sandy Hook, New Jersey and used in the defenses of New York Harbor. The Bloody Rock is preserved in a small memorial down the road on 8th Street. Urbanization has obliterated the pine woods, swamps, and fields, leaving no reminder of the bloody events that occurred around present Wyoming Avenue and the surrounding area.
>
> With the outbreak of the American War for Independence, the Wyoming Valley's importance as a granary led to a number of attacks by Loyalist and Native American forces. Connecticut and Pennsylvania both claimed land in the area and attempted to secure their claims in bloody conflicts. Both sides reorganized and aligned themselves with the Loyalists or the Whigs when the war began.

Colonel John Butler (1728–1796), the 53-year-old Loyalist leader, led 200 British troops, 200 Loyalists, and 700 Native Americans, mainly Senecas and Cayugas, to the Wyoming Valley at the end of June 1778. They marched 200 miles from Fort Niagara and appeared near the settlements about Friday, June 26. There were several skirmishes over the next few days but Colonel Butler was unable to learn anything about the number or force of the enemy. He led a general assault against 300 confused Pennsylvania militiamen and 60 Regulars about a mile north of Forty Fort, which was 3 miles from Kingston, on Friday, July 3, 1778. They routed the defenders and essentially wiped them out in an engagement that lasted one or two hours. Only 60 men were able to escape. This left the settlements of the Wyoming Valley unprotected. Two prisoners who managed to escape told the story of a Native American woman killing 14 prisoners at a site now known as "The Bloody Rock."

The following day, July 4, the Seneca and Cayuga warriors traveled through the valley in a series of raids, looting, killing 300 people, and destroying more than 1,000 homes. Butler also took a large quantity of livestock. Some accounts report that the Seneca and Cayuga warriors chased the survivors as they tried to escape through the swamps and woods along the river as they fled to Forty Fort. Reports of the massacre of men, women, and children, including the torture and burning to death of many of the Whigs, spread up and down the valley. The incident became known as the Wyoming Massacre.

Other accounts claim that John Butler did his best to limit punishment only to those who had actively resisted. Still others say that the Loyalists in the Wyoming Valley seized an opportunity to take revenge for the treatment they had received from the Whigs. The survivors accepted John Butler's terms of surrender the next day in which they agreed to lay down their arms for the remainder of the war, destroy their fortifications, and stop persecuting their Loyalist neighbors.

Major General John Sullivan (1740–1795) led an expedition up the Susquehanna River in reprisal. His army destroyed their farms and orchards so thoroughly that the Seneca and Cayuga were forced to move to Fort Niagara and live off British charity for the rest of that year and most of the next. They never recovered from this devastation.[16]

Fort Hand (July 7, 1778; April 26, 1779; June 15, 1779)

> Fort Hand was at Kittanning to the south side of the Kiskiminetas in Westmoreland County. A four-ton boulder on a corner of the old foundation of the fort bears a bronze tablet identifying the location of Fort Hand.

Captain Samuel Miller (d. 1778), of the 8th Pennsylvania Regiment, was ordered from Valley Forge to Westmoreland County on a recruiting mission on February 10, 1778. He and a party of nine men, chiefly Continental soldiers, were bringing grain from a farm near the Kiskiminetas to Fort Hand, about 14 miles north of Hannastown. On their return, on Tuesday, July 7, 1778, they were surprised by a party of Native Americans who laid an ambush for them. Captain Miller and seven of his men were killed. Their bodies were found, scalped, and stripped.[17]

★ Native Americans fired on two men plowing near Fort Hand on Monday, April 26, 1779. They escaped into the fort; but the Native Americans killed the horses and oxen used for plowing as well as all the cows and sheep. The fort, commanded by Captain Samuel Moorhead or Morehead (1749–1814), had only 17 soldiers inside. The Native American force was estimated at more than 100, including some white renegades. The few women inside the fort melted their pewter spoons and dishes to make bullets for the men when lead ran out. The siege lasted from 1 PM on the 26th to about noon the next day. The Native Americans killed one and wounded two and set fire to an empty building near the fort during the night. They left around mid-day the following day, probably fearing reinforcements were on the way.[18]

★ Captain Brady (1756–1795), of the 8th Pennsylvania Regiment, a young Delaware chief, and 20 white men, all painted like Native Americans, set out to meet a party of Senecas on their way to attack the Sawickly settlements around mid-June 1779. However, the Native Americans passed them and killed a soldier between Fort Crawford and Fort Hand.

At the Sawickly settlements, the Native Americans killed a woman and four children and took two children prisoners. Captain Brady pursued the party and caught up with seven of them about 15 miles north of Kittanning. The Native Americans had chosen an advantageous situation. Nonetheless, Captain Brady attacked them immediately, killing their leader and badly wounding several others. He re-took six horses, the two children, the scalps and all the plunder, including all their guns, tomahawks and coats.[19]

Penn Valley (ca. July 24, 1778)

★ Captain John Finley's (1750–1780) company of the 8th Pennsylvania Regiment had a skirmish with some Native Americans in Penn Valley around Friday, July 24, 1778. They lost two men killed.[20]

Lycoming County

Canton (Sept. 26, 1778)

Muncy (Sept. 26, 1778; July 3, 1779; July 11, 1779)

Freelands Fort (autumn 1778; April 11, 1779; April 16, 1779; April 26, 1779; July 21, 1779; July 28, 1779)

Warrior Run (July 28, 1779)

Tioga Point (Sept. 26, 1778)

Tioga (Aug. 17, 1779)

> Freelands Fort was about 17 miles north of Sunbury on Warrior Run which flows from north to south from Muncy. Muncy was about 7 miles north of Freelands Fort. Tioga is now Athens, on the Susquehanna River in northern Pennsylvania, just south of the New York state line near Elmira.

A band of about 400 volunteers and 17 horsemen under the command of Lieutenant Henry Carberry proceeded to Fort Muncy on an expedition against the Native Americans. They intended to penetrate the Sheshequin path to Tioga, at the junction of the Cayuga and the main northeast branch of the Susquehanna. They met at Muncy on Friday, September 18, 1778. When they mustered, they found they numbered only 200 men. They deemed the number small and presumed the Native Americans had not discovered their plans. They hoped to make a good diversion, if nothing more, while the inhabitants were sowing their grain on the frontiers.

After some necessary delay, Colonel Thomas Hartley (1748–1800) moved his small army out from Fort Muncy at 4 AM on Monday, September 21 with two boxes of spare ammunition and twelve days' of provisions. They proceeded north up Lycoming Creek and followed the Sheshequin Trail across into the upper North Branch Valley. They encountered great rains and large swamps, mountains, defiles, and rocks along the route that impeded their march and they had to clear the way as they proceeded. They waded or swam the Lycoming River more than 20 times. They had their first contact with the foe, near present Canton in Bradford County on the 25th. From that point on, the work had to be done quickly because their presence was no longer a secret. They moved rapidly to LeRoy, then Sheshequin, where fifteen prisoners were rescued and numerous cattle of the Wyoming settlements were recaptured.

An advance party of 19 men met with an equal number of Native Americans on the path on the morning of the 26th. As they approached each other, the militiamen fired first and killed and scalped an important chief. The rest of the Native Americans fled. A few miles further, they discovered the camp site where more than 70 warriors spent the night on their march toward the frontier settlements. Panic spread and they fled with the other warriors.

The volunteers advanced toward Sheshequin and took 15 prisoners in the neighborhood. They learned that a man had deserted from Captain Simon Spalding's or Spaulding (1742–1806) company at Wyoming after the men departed from there. That man notified the Native Americans of the intended expedition against them.

Colonel Hartley and his volunteers, with the horsemen and some infantrymen in front, hastened to Queen Esther's village at Tioga Point, now near Athens, and put it to the torch on the 26th. The Native Americans having been warned, vacated the place as the men approached the town near dark. The men were tired and could not proceed any further that night.

They captured another prisoner and learned that the Native Americans knew of their plan for several days and that the Native Americans headed to the German Flats (in New York) and had taken eight scalps and 70 oxen intended for the garrison at Fort Stanwix. They also learned that Walter Butler (ca.1752–1781) commanded the Native Americans and 300 Loyalists who intended to attack Wyoming and the settlements on the West Branch again as they withdrew toward Chemung and to engage the Whigs in battle in the defiles nearby.

The Whigs reached Wyalusing at midnight on the 28th. The force was here organized into three divisions. Captain James Murray (1736–1816) commanded the third. The leading parties of the Native Americans caught up with them here. Just out of Wyalusing, the Native Americans tried to delay the column's advance by attacking its front. Colonel Hartley knew the main body would soon catch up and his men must keep moving. His men outflanked the Native Americans in front and put them to flight but they launched a strong attack against the rear of the column about 2 PM. Colonel Hartley acknowledged that the Native Americans were driven off by clever maneuvering, remarkable teamwork and by the grace of God. His force suffered four killed and 10 wounded but killed more than 10 Native Americans and wounded an unknown number.

The expedition continued down the river, through Wyoming, and reached Sunbury on October 5. In all they marched over 300 miles, much of it through pure wilderness. They fought several battles; they rescued 16 white prisoners; they brought in 50 head of cattle, 28 canoes and much plunder. They destroyed the villages at Sheshequin, Tioga and Wyalusing and they did it with relatively small loss. In his official report, Colonel Hartley acknowledged the work of Captain Murray and his company as follows: "from his knowledge of Indian affairs, and their mode of fighting, was serviceable. His Men were Marksmen and were useful."[21]

★ Sometime in the autumn of 1778, Mrs. Elizabeth Gillen McKnight (d. 1807), wife of James McKnight (1753–1828), and Mrs. Margaret Wilson Durham, wife of James Durham (1753–1801), mounted on horseback with small children in their arms, departed from Freelands Fort to go to Northumberland with a number of men on foot. They met with no interruption until they got 1 mile below the mouth of Warrior Run, when they were unexpectedly fired upon by a party of Native Americans. Mrs. McNight's horse suddenly wheeled and galloped back.

She came near losing her child but caught it by the foot and held it firmly, dangling by her side, until the frightened horse brought her back to the fort. Mrs. Durham's infant was shot in her arms when she fell from the horse. She was immediately scalped and left for dead. Peter and Elias Williams found her and carried her to Dr. William Plunket (1734–1791) in Sunbury, where she was treated for her injuries. She survived for 50 more years and had other children.

When they heard the alarm, two of Mrs. McNight's young sons ran and tried to hide under the bank of the river. However, the Native Americans found their hiding place and captured them. James Durham was also taken to Canada at the same time. All three survived and returned home after the peace treaty was signed in 1783.[22]

★ Captain John Brady (1733–1779), ordered from the Continental Army to remain at home to assist in guarding the frontier, was active as a ranger and was detested by the Native Americans. He took a wagon and a few men and proceeded to Fort Muncy to get supplies on Sunday, April 11, 1779. As he returned home, he rode some distance behind the wagon and guard. When they got a short distance from his home, Brady took a shorter road than the one taken by the wagon and guard. When he came to a small stream, known as Wolf Run, about 1 mile west of Muncy, three Native Americans fired. Brady fell from his horse, dead with two balls in his back. The frightened animal galloped away but one of Brady's companions caught it by the bridle, jumped on its back and rode to Fort Brady in a few minutes. The occupants of the fort heard the gunfire and became alarmed. Several people, including Mrs. Brady, rushed out of the fort and inquired where Captain Brady was. The wagon guard and several others quickly returned to the place where the firing occurred and found Captain Brady lying dead in the road. However, the Native Americans, in their haste, did not scalp him or take any of his effects.[23]

★ A party of about 30 or 40 Native Americans captured and killed seven militiamen who were stationed at Freelands Fort on Friday, April 16, 1779. They also took two or three inhabitants who went in search of their horses about 4 or 5 miles from Fort Muncy. A large party of Native Americans fired upon them and captured or killed all but one man. When he heard the firing, Captain Andrew Walker (1756–1845), commander of

Freelands Fort, turned out with 34 Continental troops and went to the place where they heard the firing. They found four men killed and scalped and assumed the rest were taken prisoners.[24]

★ James McKnight (1753–1828), whose property was only a short distance from Freelands Fort, asked for a guard to go with him and his parents to milk their cows on Monday, April 26, 1779. (James McKnight was one of Northumberland County's representatives to the Pennsylvania Assembly at this time.) Lieutenant Jacob Spees and a dozen or so of his militia company from the Middle Creek Valley got the assignment. A band of thirty or forty Native Americans surprised them as they milked. They killed and scalped James McKnight's parents, William and Elizabeth, and three of the soldiers. They also took several soldiers captive. Some accounts say that James McKnight was also captured, as Colonel Samuel Hunter (1732–36 to 1784) reported to the Executive Council. Other accounts say that James personally carried the bodies of his parents to the Chillisquaque cemetery and buried them himself.[25]

★ A band of Native Americans killed three men and took two prisoners near Lycoming on Saturday, July 3, 1779. On Thursday, the 8th, they burned widow Smith's mills and killed one man. Three days later, on the 11th, they killed two men and took three prisoners near Fort Brady. They burned Starret's mills and all the principal houses in Muncy township the same day.[26]

★ About the end of June 1779, the soldiers of the 11th Regiment pulled out of the local forts in order to cooperate with an expedition being prepared at Wyoming. The Native Americans lost no time in taking advantage of the situation. A band of them, apparently the advance party of a force of at least 100 Loyalists and 200 Senecas under the command of Captain John McDonald of the British Army first went to Fort Muncy. When they found that the settlers had evacuated the fort and fled down-river to Sunbury, they stealthily approached Freelands Fort. They attacked a group of men working in a cornfield outside the fort on Wednesday, July 21, 1779. They killed three of them and carried away two others.[27]

★ Captain John McDonald and Hiokatoo (b. 1708), a Seneca chief, and the husband of Mary Jemison (Deh-he-wä-mis) (1743–1833), together with about 200 Senecas and 100 Loyalists dressed in red regimentals came down Lycoming Creek and dispersed over the valley to burn and destroy everything they could find. They found Fort Muncy evacuated, but they burned all the woodwork.

A scouting party in the Muncy Valley, just ahead of the main body, captured several families. Captain McDonald, enraged that the settlers had escaped, ordered his forces to scour the Muncy Valley and burn every cabin, house, outbuilding, barn, and haystack they could find. They then moved rapidly over Muncy Hill toward Freelands Fort. They arrived before dawn on Tuesday, July 28, 1779. The fort contained about 20 men and 50 women and children. The attack began just after sunrise and the firing continued quite briskly for a time. Captain McDonald offered terms of surrender at about 8:30. The defenders believed that, if they refused, they would all be put to death. They signed the capitulation about 9 AM.

Captain Hawkins Boone (d. 1779) heard the firing over at Boone's Fort and quickly raised a relief force of thirty-three of his neighbors. They moved as quickly and quietly as possible and arrived at Freelands Fort just after the surrender but were unaware of the capitulation. They saw a gathering of Senecas and fired a volley into it, causing numerous casualties. However, Boone's men were outnumbered and soon found themselves surrounded. The fight became desperate and finally ended about 2 PM with Boone and

17 of his men dead. A few escaped and several were taken prisoners. Four others had been killed during the battle for the fort and a total of 25 were marched off to Canada. Four old men and the 50 women and children were allowed to head down-river to Fort Augusta at Sunbury. Captain McDonald's forces then set the neighboring houses on fire. Some prisoners who escaped reported that Captain Boone's and 11 other scalps were brought to the fort in a handkerchief.

Captain McDonald's forces then took their prisoners and headed quickly back in the direction from which they came. Approximately 500 militiamen from Lancaster and Cumberland Counties gathered in Sunbury and went in pursuit of Captain McDonald's forces on August 5. They soon realized that it was impossible to catch them, so they gave up the chase and returned home.[28]

★ Major General John Sullivan (1740–1795) led his division of 2,300 men toward Tioga on Saturday, July 31, 1779. Brigadier General Edward Hand (1744–1802) led one of the brigades. Brigadier General William Maxwell (1733–1796) and Brigadier General Enoch Poor (1736–1780) led the other brigades of Continentals. Sullivan wrote to the President of Congress on August 15:
> [The] enemy encamped a mile above Tioga, Gen. Hand advanced. . . They decamped with such precipitation as to leave their blankets, etc., behind them. He then moved with a design to possess . . . an advantageous hill, . . . his advance party was attacked in a desultory manner by them . . . he immediately ordered his men to dislodge them with their bayonets, this they readily effected as the enemy did not wait the charge.[29]

★ Six soldiers of the 11th Pennsylvania Regiment went in search of horses at Tioga on Tuesday, August 17, 1779. A band of Native Americans attacked them, killed one and wounded another.

The troops then entered the Iroquois town of Chemung (New York), destroyed the houses and crops of the area and returned to Tioga. Another force of 1,400 Continentals joined them there. The combined forces proceeded up the Chemung River on August 26 with General Hand at the head of the main force. Strong flanking parties moved parallel to the main body of troops to uncover and repulse any Native American and Loyalist attacks. Hand's scouts reported on August 29 that the Loyalists and Native Americans obstructed their path with logs at Newtown. Sullivan and his forces crossed the creek and engaged the enemy at the battle of Newtown (New York).[30]

★ A party of 500 men began to destroy Fort Sullivan at Tioga at 8 AM Sunday, October 3, 1779. Six pounds of flour were issued to each man for their march to Wyoming at 6 AM the following day. The artillery, stores and other baggage were put on board the boats as were the sick, the lame and men without shoes.[31]

Chillisquaque (Nov. 8, 1778; Oct. 14, 1782)

Chillisquaque is about 2.5 miles north-northwest of the junction of Routes PA 147 and PA 405 and about 3 miles east of the South Branch of the Susquehanna River. Liberty Township, about 2 miles east of Pottsgrove.

Colonel Thomas Hartley's (1748–1800) expedition accomplished much, but it did not get rid of all the Native Americans. On Monday, November 9, 1778, he reported a force of 70 of them heading for the forks of the Chillisquaque. The report was that the Native Americans burned numerous plantations along their route and took several prisoners, but few specific names and locations were recorded. The Native Americans apparently took pains to by-pass Fort Bosley, which was still garrisoned by some of Colonel Hartley's 11th Regiment troops. They did not, however, ignore Freelands Fort.[32]

★ A band of eight Native Americans came into the area of the Chillisquaque on Monday, October 14, 1782. They attacked John Martin (d. 1782) and his family near Colonel James Murray's (1736–1816) place in what is now Liberty Township. They murdered John's wife and scalped her and severely wounded and scalped him also, leaving him to bleed to death. They took his daughter, Susan, and an eight-year-old granddaughter, Ann McNeal (1774–late 1860s). John's other two sons, Roger and Hays, were both engaged away from the house at the time.

The Native Americans took their captives and headed for New York. Ann McNeal's aunt, also taken prisoner, supposedly made a pair of moccasins for the barefooted Susan and created a sling, from the bottom of her long dress, to carry Ann. Susan was released at the end of the war, after about a year in captivity. She returned and married John Davis and lived in Limestone Township until her death. Ann remained a captive for about eight years. When she was released, she was taken to Pittsburgh for repatriation with many others who suffered similar experiences. Her uncle Roger had great difficulty to identify her and brought her back home. Ann lived a long life, dying in the late 1860s. She bore the scars of her captivity the entire time.[33]

Centre Township, Columbia County
Fort Jenkins (April 11, 1779)

> Fort Jenkins was on the north bank of the North Branch of the Susquehanna River in Centre Township about midway between Berwick and Bloomsburg in Columbia County.

A band of Native Americans attacked the inhabitants living near Fort Jenkins on Sunday, April 11, 1779 and took two or three families prisoners. The garrison was alarmed and about 20 men turned out of the fort, but the Native Americans drove them back to the safety of the fort with the loss of three killed and four badly wounded. The Native Americans burned several houses near the fort, killed cattle, and drove off a number of horses.[34]

Nazareth (June 26, 1779)

Sentries at Nazareth spotted two Native Americans on Friday night, June 25, 1779 and fired at them, but they escaped. The following day, a scalping party routed a family between Nazareth and Easton, about 10 miles from Easton. They took three women prisoners and a boy about 14 years old and scalped and tomahawked them.[35]

Thompson's Island, upper Allegheny River (Aug. 15, 1779)
Sullivan–Clinton Expedition (May to Nov. 1779)
Brodhead Expedition (Aug. 11 to Sept. 14, 1779)

> The skirmish at Thompson's Island occurred on the Allegheny River in Warren County. The site is marked on U.S. 62, 9 miles southwest of Warren and 15 miles south of the New York State line.

General George Washington (1732–1799) planned a campaign to punish the Iroquois nations for a series of raids in 1778, including the Wyoming Valley massacre. He appointed Major General John Sullivan (1740–1795) to command the main body of troops. General Sullivan began assembling his troops at Easton, Pennsylvania in early May but did not begin to march until June 18 and did not leave the Wyoming Valley until July 31. He proceeded up the Susquehanna Valley and reached Tioga on Tuesday, August 10, 1779. Meanwhile, Brigadier General James Clinton (1733–1812) led a smaller column through the Mohawk Valley (New York). The two columns joined forces at Tioga on Thursday, August 19.

The army of about 4,000 men proceeded through the Genessee Valley and through the Finger Lakes region destroying Iroquois villages, farms and crops that were almost ready to harvest. They returned to Wyoming on October 8th, and to Easton on the 15th.

See individual towns for the accounts: **Newtown, Catherine's Town, Appletown, Kindaia, Cayuga Lake, Canandaigua, Geneseo** in New York and **Tioga** in Pennsylvania.

In conjunction with Sullivan's expedition, Colonel Daniel Brodhead (1736–1809) marched up the Allegheny Valley from Pittsburgh.

★ Major General John Sullivan (1740–1795) sent Colonel Daniel Brodhead (1736–1809) on a punitive expedition against the Seneca and Muncie tribes on the Allegheny River which lasted from August 11 to September 14, 1779. The troops burned 40 Native American towns in Pennsylvania and New York and destroyed all their corn (estimated at 160,000 bushels) and large quantities of other articles. They overran and destroyed the whole country of the Senecas and other tribes of the Six Nations, forcing them to flee to Fort Niagara for security. The army lost fewer than 40 men killed, wounded, and captured, including those who died natural deaths. General Brodhead and his army of 605 men, most of them from his own 8th Pennsylvania Regiment, marched from Fort Pitt on Wednesday, August 11, 1779 with one month's provisions.[36]

★ When General Brodhead reached the mouth of Mahoning Creek (near modern Templeton), he was detained four days by heavy rain. He headed inland "through a country almost impassable by reason of stupendous heights and frightful declivities" and returned to the Allegheny about 15 miles above Venango (today's Franklin). The route then got worse.

The expedition followed what is now U.S. 62, a route recommended for its scenic beauty. Then, it was "a continued narrow defile, allowing us only the breadth of an Indian path to march upon." About 30 to 40 Native Americans landed their canoes opposite Thompson's Island on Sunday, August 15, 1779, in the only attempt to block Brodhead's advance.

Lieutenant Jonathan Hardin, in command of the advance guard of 14 whites and eight Delawares, attacked before the braves could get organized. The militiamen killed five warriors. The others abandoned their canoes and fled into the woods "with the utmost horror and precipitation." Others swam the river, probably to Thompson's Island. Hardin had only three men slightly wounded.

The expedition continued without opposition and burned 10 Mingo, Muncie, and Seneca villages (a total of 165 dwellings) situated nearly 200 miles above Fort Pitt, and 500 acres of corn. They also confiscated articles valued at $3,000. On their return trip, the expedition found "a creek [Oil Creek] about 10 miles above Venango, remarkable for an oily liquid which oozes from the sides and bottom of the channel and the adjacent springs, much resembling British oil, and if applied to a woolen cloth burns instantly."[37]

Fishing Creek (late March 1780)

Fishing Creek is about a mile northwest of Jonestown.

A party of Senecas appeared at Fishing Creek, not far from what is now Lightstreet, in late March 1780. They killed two Van Campen brothers and a pre-teen son of one of them. They also carried off another son of each brother (both boys were named Moses Van Campen) and another man named Peter Pence (1742–1812). These three freed themselves of their bonds during the night, killed nine of their ten captors, and escaped. This attack frightened the residents of the Mahoning settlement, causing them to seek shelter at Colonel William Montgomery's (d. 1781) house, which he had reportedly fortified and which was called Fort Montgomery. Captain Thomas Gaskins's company was also re-called into service.[38]

Bedford

Bedford Purchase (before April 22, 1780; May 4, 1781; June 2, 1781; June 3, 1781)

> Bedford is in Bedford County. Yellow Creek is about 12 miles northeast of Bedford. In 1781, Frankstown referred to the area now occupied by the town of Canan (or Canan Station) situated in the general vicinity of the mouth of Sugar Run where it joins the Mill Run. It is located about 31 miles north of Bedford and about 4 miles south of Altoona. The "Frankstown garrison" was a stockaded structure, probably on Michael Fetter's (1725-1790) property, about a mile west of the present-day borough of Hollidaysburg and about 2.5 miles south of Frankstown.[39]

A band of Native Americans killed 25 people on Yellow Creek, near Bedford before Saturday, April 22, 1780. General Daniel Brodhead (1736–1809) and a considerable body of Continental troops and militiamen prepared for a speedy expedition against the Native Americans destroying the settlements on the Pennsylvania frontier.[40]

★ A band of Native Americans came into Bedford County on Friday, May 4, 1781 and killed a man, a woman and two children. They also took a man prisoner less than a mile from Colonel John Pipers's (1729–1816) house on Yellow Creek.[41]

★ A party of volunteers from Bedford were going to Frankstown when a band of Native Americans attacked them on Saturday morning, June 2, 1781. The attackers killed 30 people and only seven escaped to the garrison at Frankstown.[42]

★ A party of eight rangers under Captain John Boyd (1750–1832) or (1736–1807) and 25 volunteers under Captain John Moore (1737–1801) or (1761–1854) and Lieutenant Smith of the Bedford County Militia had an engagement with a large party of Native Americans about 2.5 miles northwest of the Frankstown garrison on Sunday, June 3, 1781. Some of the rangers ran into the garrison and notified Captain James Young (d. 1816) who commanded 75 Cumberland militiamen there. When he learned what had happened, Captain Young immediately sent out a party and brought in seven prisoners, five of them wounded. The other two escaped to Bedford. Eight others were killed and scalped. Captains Boyd, Moore, and James Dunlap (1740–1781) and six others were missing. Captain Young, expecting that the large number of enemies would surround his garrison, immediately sent an express to Lieutenant George Ashman (1740–1811), of the Bedford County Militia. However, before Lieutenant Ashman could muster a sufficient number of volunteers to march to Frankstown, the attackers had withdrawn over Allegheny Hill. Heavy rains swelled the rivers and creeks, making it impossible to pursue them. The Cumberland militia was low on ammunition and was due to be discharged two days later.[43]

Northampton County (May 12, 1780)

> Northampton County includes the Lehigh Valley. Nazareth is located in the center of the county.

On Friday, May 12, 1780, Lieutenant Colonel William Bond (1734–1776) received intelligence of a person who called himself Captain Land who was recruiting for the Native Americans in Northampton County. Captain Land concealed his recruits at Tottamy's Gap on the Blew Mountains. Colonel Bond raised a party of 10 men and set an ambush along the roads which he expected them to travel. That evening, Captain Land and his party headed to join the Native Americans and fell into the ambush about 8 PM. A smart skirmish ensued. The force of recruits was weaker than expected and soon gave way. Captain Land escaped after receiving some wounds, leaving his hat, knapsack, gun and a large quantity of blood on the ground. Colonel Bond's men could only find two of Captain Land's party and took them prisoners. One of them was slightly wounded.[44]

West Buffalo Township
French Jacob's Mill (May 18, 1780)

> Some people date this event as occurring on May 8, 1780.

Jacob Groshong (1725–1800?) (christened Johann Jacob Grosjean) moved to Buffalo Township, Northumberland County, Pennsylvania (now West Buffalo Township, Union Co.) on January 8, 1773 and purchased 75 acres in the Buffalo Valley and on the north side of Buffalo Creek. Native Americans habitually made harassing attacks on the populace in the area and structures such as a mill would draw extra attention. Jacob had a hiding place in his mill near a big spring where he would go and stay until the Native Americans retreated. He would then return to normal activities and continue to work his mill until the next attack. Apparently, he was on good terms with the Native Americans, as it is said he did a brisk trade with them.

Companies of soldiers protected the citizenry during the late 1770s. Bi-weekly patrols of five men scouted for signs of trouble and would alert others to assemble and repel the opposition. One such patrol regularly billeted at Jacob Groshong's mill. The patrol was washing clothes and drying them on the boulders near the mill on Thursday, May 18, 1780, when a band of Delawares fired on them. Taken completely by surprise, the soldiers scrambled for the mill. Four of them were killed instantly. The fifth probably would have been killed also if he had not stumbled and fallen just before reaching the door. Bullet holes in the door frame indicate he would have been hit directly in the head. Neighbors heard the shots and alerted others. They quickly assembled and chased the Delawares away. The old mill was torn down in later years and the lumber reused. Carpenters made sure the timbers with bullet holes in them were left exposed for all who passed through to see.[45]

Northumberland County (summer 1780)

> Northumberland County extends east of Sunbury and west of Mount Carmel.

There were at least 15 documented attacks throughout Northumberland County during the spring and summer of 1780. There were a total of 23 killed, 3 wounded and

19 captured, including women and children. Only a few women and children managed to escape before they were to be carried off to New York and Canada.[46]

Montour County (June 19 or July 15, 1780)

> Montour County is north of Northumberland County. An attack in Montour County in 1780 is reported as having occurred on both June 19 and July 15, 1780. It occurred near where Lieutenant Robert Curry (1741–1780) was killed on July 9, 1780. The McMahan farm is located in Liberty Township along present Route 45, just before crossing the Chillisquaque heading toward Montandon.

A Native American and a Loyalist named Captain Caldwell (d. 1780), wearing war paint, surprised Captain James McMahan (1736–1816) in the woods a short distance from the stockade he had erected on his farm. They captured him, tied his wrist with bark and headed toward what is now Milton. The Native American left him in Captain Caldwell's care while he ran off to meet the rest of their party. Captain McMahan freed himself and broke his rifle over Captain Caldwell's head, killing him. He escaped just before the Native American returned.[47]

Fort Mead (July 9, 1780)

> Fort Mead was constructed in the summer of 1778 on the North Branch of the Susquehanna River, midway between Northumberland and the Mahoning settlement (now known as Danville). It was at the foot of a ravine which was the pass over the mountain and the Indian trail from Canada to the Susquehanna Valley.

First Lieutenant Robert Curry (1741–1780), of the 7th Company of the First Battalion of Northumberland County militia thought it best to leave his farm on the north side of Montour Ridge and move his family over the mountains for safety in the spring of 1780. They took shelter in Fort Mead, which was under the command of Captain Thomas Gaskins (d. 1813) and where Lieutenant Curry was second in command. Curry would cross the mountain frequently to look after his crops and things which he had left behind. His wife Jane would accompany him on many of these trips.

Robert and Jane (1750–1825) were returning to the fort after one such trip on horseback late Friday afternoon, June 9, 1780. As they came over the mountain, they descended the path and were less than a mile from the fort when three Senecas fired their muskets from their hiding place and killed both horses. Jane started to run toward the fort. She stopped to see what had become of her husband and saw a Seneca standing over him, striking him with his tomahawk. He did not take time to scalp his victim, but cut off the whole top of the head with a tomahawk.

Another Seneca ran after Jane, took her prisoner and hurried toward the mountains, suspecting that the occupants of the fort heard the shots and would come after them. They crossed the mountain, passed the Curry farm, and traveled about a mile further into the forest where they built their campfire. Before the Senecas laid down for the night, they tied their prisoner securely and soon fell asleep, with one on each side of her. Jane Curry (1750–1825) succeeded in getting her scissors from a pocket under her dress and cut the cords which bound her. It began to rain in the early evening; so the sound of the rain on the leaves masked the sounds of her walking. She had only gone a short distance when the Senecas awoke and pursued her.

Jane hid herself in a hollow log while the Senecas searched the forest for her for a long time. They even stood on the very log in which she was concealed. The Senecas had a little dog which Jane had befriended during her brief captivity. When the dog found her in the log, he did not betray her by barking. After a long and thorough search, the Senecas returned to their campfire and fell asleep.

Jane emerged from her hiding place and headed to the fort for help. She became confused and lost her direction in the darkness and groped her way through the woods. At one point, she put her hand in the stream to see which direction the current ran. She reached the other side of the mountain by daybreak. She related the account to Captain Gaskins who walked with her to the spot where her husband's body lay. Jane took the handkerchief from her neck and tied it around his crownless head.

The body was retrieved and brought to the fort. The next day, it was taken up the river in a canoe, to Montgomery's Landing (now Danville), while a scouting party walked along the bank. Lieutenant Robert Curry (1741–1780) was buried with the honors of war in the Mahoning graveyard (now Memorial Park on Bloom Street)—the very ground he had helped purchase for that purpose less than five years before.[48]

Conyngham
Sugarloaf Massacre (Sept. 11, 1780)

> The Sugarloaf Massacre occurred near the village of Conyngham, Sugar Loaf township (Nescopeck or Nusquepack, Scotch Valley). The site is near Route PA 93, just beyond the town of Conyngham, about 5 miles northwest of Hazleton. There's a marker at the intersection of Route PA 93 and Hidden Creek Court, 0.2 miles west of Main St., to commemorate the event.

After the attack on Fort Rice (now in West Virginia) and the destruction of Bosley's mills, a fortified station near Washingtonville, and the destruction of Fort Jenkins and surrounding buildings which occurred between September 6 and 10, 1780, Captain Thomas Robinson (1729–1811) and his company were ordered to bring in the Loyalists on the North Branch of the Susquehanna River at a place called Catawissa and on Fishing Creek. These Loyalists were suspected of giving the Native Americans information about the activities of the whites which probably resulted in the loss of several militiamen who strayed from the camps.

A party of about 80 Senecas and Loyalists (some accounts say they numbered 250 to 300) proceeded up the river to Berwick on Friday, September 8, 1780, crossed the river and followed the path until they arrived about 7 or 8 miles from Nescopeck Falls in Scotch Valley, where they lay in ambush awaiting Captain Daniel Klader or Clader (1750–1780) and a platoon of 40 to 50 militiamen from Captain Johannes Van Etten, Sr.'s (1730–1815) company from Northampton County. They traveled north from the Lehigh Valley along a path known as "Warrior's Trail" (present-day Route PA 93). They headed north and got as far as present-day Conyngham when they were ambushed by Roland Montour, son of the legendary Queen Esther, and members of the Seneca tribe and Loyalist militiamen near the Little Nescopeck. Captain Klader's militiamen stacked their arms and scattered about noon on Monday, September 11, many of them gathering grapes when they were surrounded and attacked. Captain Klader was left dead where he fell fighting. His lieutenant, John Moyer (1760–1812), was taken prisoner but later escaped. Moses Van Campen (1757–1849) reported that all but three, who escaped, were killed, and one other, Ensign James Scobey (1745–1819), was taken a prisoner to Niagara.

Lieutenant Colonel Stephen Balliett (1753–1821), who commanded another detail to bury the dead reported "we found ten of our soldiers dead, scalped, stripped naked and in a most cruel and barbarous manner tomahawked, their throats cut, etc." The militiamen killed four to seven Native Americans. Col. Samuel Roy, in a letter dated Mount Bethel, October 7, 1780, notes that, according to Colonel Balliett, 20 men returned. He says only 16 are accounted for and that 10 were dead and buried, and six escaped or were taken prisoners.

Moses Van Campen was later ordered to take a detail to bury the dead. He said:
> Never shall I forget the impression made on my mind on coming in sight of the slain bodies of my countrymen. Several days had elapsed since the time they had met such terrible deaths, and the bodies had been exposed to beasts of prey and vultures. It was a scene that could only be looked upon by those accustomed to the horrors of war.[49]

Catawissa (July 26, 1782)

> Catawissa is on the Susquehanna River, about 3.5 miles south of Bloomsburg. The farm on which this engagement occurred was on the north side of the river, across from Catawissa.

Robinson's Ranging Company rebuilt Fort Muncy early in 1782 to serve as a rendezvous for scouting parties. Forts Bosley and Rice (in what is now West Virginia) also continued as strongholds for local defense. Yet, the Native Americans continued to terrorize the area. A party of Native Americans murdered and scalped John Furry (1735–1782) along with his wife and two daughters on Friday, July 26, 1782. They took John's son, Henry, prisoner and sold him to a Frenchman in Canada.[50]

Philadelphia and vicinity

See the map of Philadelphia and vicinity.

Washington Crossing (Dec. 25, 1776)

> Washington Crossing Historic Park (website: **http://www.portal.state.pa.us/portal/server.pt/community/military_history_trail/20268/washington_crossing_historic_park/963353**) is a 500-acre park divided into two areas. The Thompson's Mill section is 1.5 miles southeast of New Hope via Route PA 32. The McConkey's Ferry section is 5 miles farther south on Route PA 32. A bridge connects the park with New Jersey's Washington Crossing State Park. (See also Washington Crossing in the New Jersey volume.)
>
> The Continental Army camped at Bowman's Hill, about 4 miles north of the site of the actual crossing. A memorial flagpole marks the graves of the troops who died during the encampment. A visitors center and several 18th-century buildings dominate the site of the crossing. One of these is the brown fieldstone McConkey's Ferry Inn where General Washington dined before the crossing.
>
> Another is the Durham Boat House which houses replicas of the boats the troops used to cross the river. The boats (see photo PA-1) were first built in 1750 to carry iron ore and pig iron down the Delaware River to Philadelphia. They remained in operation until about 1860 with as many as 300 boats, manned by more than 2,000 men, carrying iron ore, iron, whiskey, and grain from Easton to Philadelphia during their peak years. The boats varied in length from 40 to 60 feet. An empty boat had a draft of about 5 inches. Fully loaded with 15 tons, it could float in only 30 inches

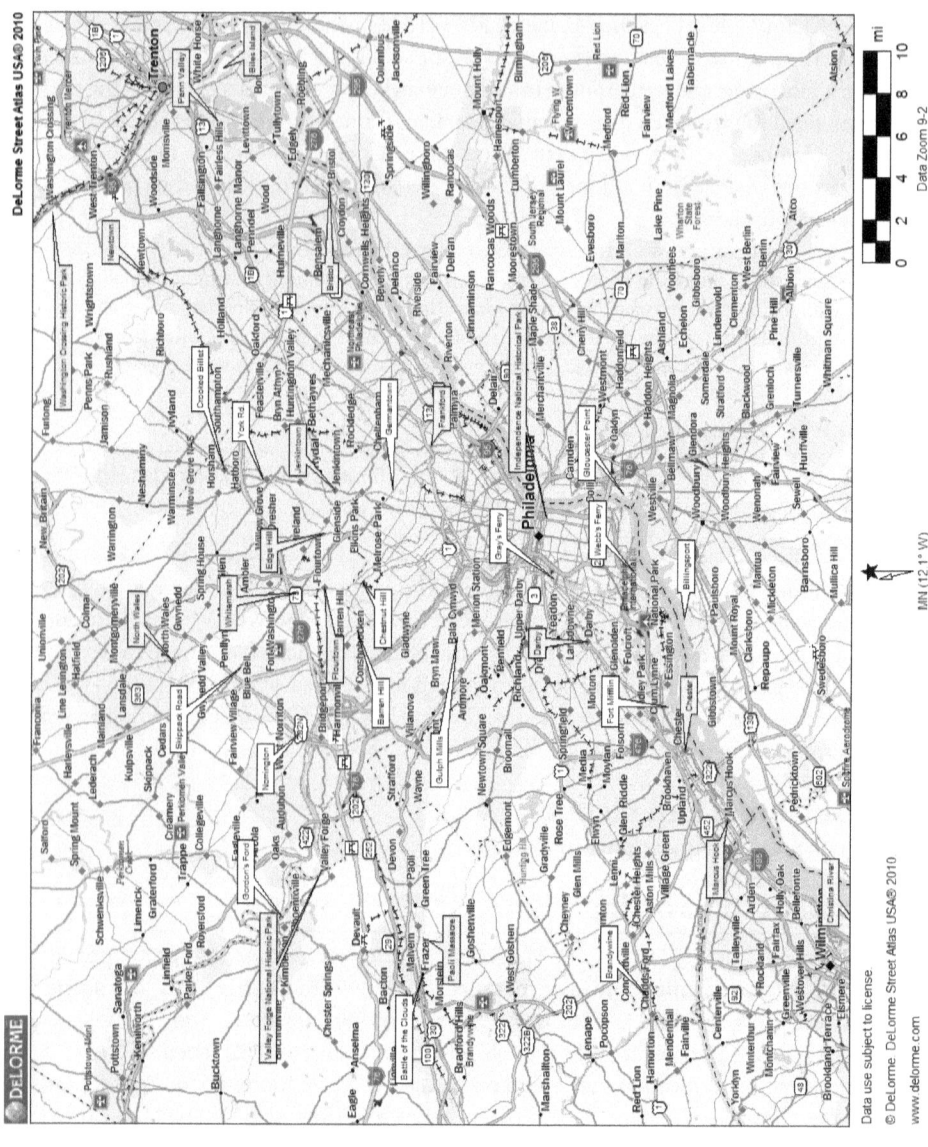

Philadelphia and vicinity: Map for The Guide to the American Revolutionary War in Pennsylvania, Delaware, Maryland, Virginia, and North Carolina © 2011 DeLorme (www.delorme.com) Street Atlas USA®

of water. The Durham boats depended on the current to travel downstream. A crew of six men and a captain used poles and oars to travel against the current and through the rapids. A stern-sweep oar, 25 to 30 feet long, guided the boats.

General George Washington (1732–1799) formulated a bold plan to strike the Hessian garrisons at Trenton and Bordentown (New Jersey) by surprise on Christmas night 1776 when the troops might be expected to relax their guard for holiday revelry. He had all the boats on the Delaware River removed and hidden behind Malta Island to escape into Pennsylvania and to prevent General William Howe's (1732–1786) further advance. This was the only time in the war that General Washington commanded naval superiority over the British. His force of 2,400 men under his personal command was to cross the Delaware at McConkey's Ferry, 9 miles upstream from Trenton then proceed in two columns by different routes, converging on the opposite ends of the main street of Trenton early Thursday morning, December 26.

PA-1. Durham boat. General Washington and his men crossed the Delaware River in Durham boats such as the one shown here. The boats were designed to haul heavy cargo down rivers.

A second force of about 1,900 men, mainly militiamen, under Colonel John Cadwalader (1742–1786) was to cross below near Bordentown, New Jersey to attack the Hessian garrison there, as a diversion to prevent the reinforcement of the Trenton garrison. A third column of 1,000 men, also militia, under Brigadier General James Ewing (1736–1805), was to cross directly opposite Trenton at the Trenton Ferry to block the Hessian route of escape across Assunpink Creek.

General Washington's 2,400 men started ferrying across the river about 6 PM Christmas day. Washington expected to have all his men across the river by midnight, but the last men did not cross until about 3 AM, nine hours after the first men crossed. They used specially designed Durham boats that were wide and flat and capable of handling heavy loads. The horses and 18 cannon were ferried across on rafts (see photo PA-2). Colonel John Glover's (1732–1797) Marblehead Regiment ferried the troops across the Delaware, just as they had done in evacuating Long Island.

Christmas night was cold, windy, and snowy, and the Delaware River was filled with blocks of ice. The temperature was well below freezing and snow became mixed with sleet. Elisha Bostwick (1749–1834) recalled the difficulties of crossing and re-crossing the Delaware:

PA-2. Raft for ferrying horses and cannons. The horses and 18 cannon were ferried across the Delaware River on rafts such as this one.

When crossing the Delaware with the prisoners in flat bottom boats the ice continually stuck to the boats, driving them down stream; the boatmen endevering to clear off the ice pounded the boat, and stamping with their feet, beconed to the prisoners to do the same, and they all set to jumping at once with their cues flying up and down, soon shook off the ice from the boats, and the next day re-crossed the Delaware again and returned back to Trenton.[60]

General Washington marched into Trenton from the north intending to take the Hessians by surprise. Neither Colonel Cadwalader nor General Ewing was able to fulfill his part of the plan. Driven on by Washington's indomitable will, the main force did cross as planned and the two columns, commanded respectively by Major General Nathanael Greene (1742–1786) and Major General John Sullivan (1740–1795), converged on Trenton at eight o'clock Thursday morning, December 26. Washington's plan depended on secrecy, darkness, and the enemy's underestimating the capabilities of his army. He took the 1,400 Hessians, commanded by Colonel Johann Gottlieb Rall (1720–1776), completely by surprise.[61]

Whitemarsh (Feb. 19, 1777; Feb. 20, 1777; ca. Nov. 11, 12, 1777; Dec. 5–8, 1777; Feb. 14, 1778; May 20, 1778)
Chestnut Hill (Dec. 6, 1777)
Edge Hill (Dec. 7, 1777)

Whitemarsh was on the Wissahickon Creek in Montgomery County near Nashameny Ferry, about 16 miles northwest of Philadelphia. Chestnut Hill and Edge Hill are now residential communities to the south and east of Whitemarsh. They have no visible remains of the conflicts that occurred there.

After the defeats at the Brandywine and Germantown and before the Valley Forge encampment, General Washington withdrew his army to Whitemarsh about 16

> miles northwest of Philadelphia. His 20,000 troops camped around the estate of William West, a Philadelphia merchant, for a six-week period (November 2 to December 11, 1777). Major John Cochran (1730–1807), General Washington's Surgeon General, lived in the mansion, now known as Hope Lodge (see Photo PA-3) (553 Bethlehem Pike). The soldiers camped around the estate and in what is now Fort Washington State Park (493 acres). Farmar's Mill (now called Mather Mill) (see Photo PA-4) is on Mathers Lane in front of Hope Lodge State Historic Site (553 South Bethlehem Turnpike, Fort Washington) which served as Major General Nathanael Greene's (1742–1786) quarters. Washington made his headquarters at the Emlen house (see Photo PA-5), now a private residence on East Pennsylvania Avenue north of the state park.

A lieutenant of the British artillery was wounded and taken prisoner on Wednesday, February 19, 1777. He was brought to headquarters at Whitemarsh along with one deserter of the 55th Regiment. Four Waldeckers and two British privates were captured the following day.[62]

★ The Crown forces under General Sir William Howe (1732–1786) had captured the Congressional capital of Philadelphia on Friday, September 26, 1777 after a successful landing at Head of Elk, Maryland and an overland march. However, before he could settle in for the winter, he had to maneuver against the Continental forces under General George Washington (1732–1799) in what has been called the Pennsylvania campaign of 1777.

With his army so close to Philadelphia, Washington remained a continuous menace to General Howe. He regularly sent his dragoons south to skirmish with British foragers outside Philadelphia. These encounters were short but violent. In one of these

PA-3. Hope Lodge, Whitemarsh. General Washington's Surgeon General, Major John Cochran, lived in this house. The soldiers camped around the estate and in what is now Fort Washington State Park.

PA-4. Mather Mill. Farmar's Mill (now called Mather Mill) served as Major General Nathanael Greene's quarters.

PA-5. Emlen house. General Washington made his headquarters at the Emlen house during the Whitemarsh encampment.

skirmishes, Captain Leigh, Lieutenant John Craig (d. 1837), and 14 light dragoons attacked a British detachment near Whitemarsh about November 11, 1777 and captured 14 light dragoons and seven foot soldiers.[63]

★ The following day, November 12, 1777, Brigadier General Casimir Pulaski (1747–1779) and his dragoons encountered a British detachment near Whitemarsh. They attacked with swords, killed five and took two British prisoners and wounded several others. They lost one man killed and two captured. Pulaski was captured but later retaken.[64]

★ General Howe decided to try to engage General Washington once more in a battle and defeat him. Howe formed almost his entire army into two columns about midnight on Thursday, December 4, 1777 and headed toward Whitemarsh with no baggage wagons, intending to surprise Washington. They marched along the Manatawny (Ridge Road) and Skippack roads (route PA 73). The advanced corps received a few shots on the march at Beggars' Town (now Mount Airy), near Germantown, and at Chestnut Hill, but they met with no considerable opposition. The light infantry burned a house along the road from which they had been fired upon and suffered five or six slightly wounded.

Captain Allen McLane (1746–1829) spotted the enemy's movements at Three Mile Run on the Skippack Road and reported them to General Washington who immediately began to prepare for the attack. Washington sent McLane, with 100 select dragoons, to observe the enemy's movements, but McLane was not content with observation. He attacked the front division with "brilliant cavalry rushes," forcing it "to change its line of march." He then hovered on the enemy's front and flank, "galling them severely."

The troops arrived at Chestnut Hill about 3 AM on Friday, December 5th and made camp about 3 miles away from the Continental camp. They found Washington's camp extended between 4 and 5 miles, most of it protected by abatis. Fifty-two cannons commanded the road across the plain leading to the camp. Hessian Major Carl Leopold Baurmeister (1734–1803) records that the Continentals had "increased their fires lighting many large ones in straight and deep lines, so that it looked as if fifty thousand men were encamped there. By day we could see this was merely a trick to deceive us."[65]

★ Washington prepared for battle by striking his tents early in the morning on December 6th and sending his heavy baggage to the rear. As he waited for General Howe to begin the assault, he sent Brigadier General James Irvine (1735–1819) and 500 to 600 Pennsylvania militiamen to attack the advance guard (2nd battalion light infantry). They crossed under the cover of the woods and attacked at 11 AM. The British drove them back a mile and a half and wounded and captured General Irvine and a captain. Irvine had several men killed and wounded but the British had only a few wounded.[66]

★ With the loss of their commander, Irvine's troops were driven back, broke ranks, and ran away. The two armies held their positions until December 7th. The Crown forces watched the Continentals on the 6th as they moved their troops from their left to their right where access was more difficult. At 1 AM on the 7th, General Howe's troops marched from Chestnut Hill to Edge Hill, about a mile from Washington's left flank. They formed a curve that threatened both wings of Washington's line. Washington countered by moving Colonel Daniel Morgan's (1736–1802) riflemen, Samuel B. Webb's (1753–1807) Continentals, and Colonel Samuel Potter, Sr.'s (1727–1802) Pennsylvania militia to the right. Archibald Robertson (ca. 1745–1813) recalls:

> The Army mov'd at 1 o'clock in the morning and march'd by German Town, Crossing the Country to Jenkin's Town on the Old York Road with an intention to turn

their left Flank. We reach'd Jenkin's Town after a march of about 12 miles at 8 in the morning where we halted until the Rear Came up, then about 12 moved forwards to Edge hill within a mile of their Camp. Here the 1st Light Infantry were Attacked by a corps of Riffle men, commanded by one Morgan reckon'd a Pick'd Corps, in a very thick Wood but were immediately Drove off with a good deal of Loss. We had 1 Officer Killed and 2 Wounded and about 40 men Killed and Wounded.

Major General Grey with the 3d Brigade Queen's Rangers Jagers and Company of Light Infantry of the Guards were Detach'd from the Column about 2 miles before we reached Jenkin's Town. They march'd to the left and took Post on Edge hill opposite the Centre of the Rebel Camp. They had some Skirmishing but Lost very few men.[67]

★ Also on December 6th, Major General Charles Grey (1729–1807), the Hessian jaegers, Simcoe's Queen's Rangers, the light infantry, and the 3rd brigade headed toward Tyson's Tavern on the Limekiln Road, "where he was to drive in a Post of the Enemy and draw up in view of their camp." "While they presumed an attack impending from that quarter, Sir William Howe with the Elite and main army was to have made the real attack on Washington's left."[68]

Colonel Daniel Morgan's riflemen and Mordecai Gist's (1743–1792) Maryland militia met Grey's troops on the Limekiln Road with a burst of fire from a woody ridge. The jaegers and Simcoe's Queen's Rangers advanced on the right and left, "with great activity and ardor" and outflanked both wings of the Continental forces, compelling them to retreat.

Brigadier General John Cadwalader (1742–1786) and General Joseph Reed (1741–1785) were observers in a wood in Cheltenham Township, on the Continental left, with Potter's Pennsylvania militia and Webb's Continentals. Grey's column attacked them, killing Reed's horse in the first volley and sending Reed to the ground. The Redcoats charged, forcing the Continentals to flee in confusion with the loss of about 50 men. Some of the Redcoats ran to bayonet Reed, but Captain Allen McLane (1746–1829) and his dragoons charged, driving them back and rescuing the injured general.

Christopher Ward notes that "André says one of Simcoe's men was killed and nine chasseurs killed or wounded, while 20 to 30 Americans fell and 15 were taken. Archibald Robertson says a single British officer was killed, two wounded, and about 40 others were killed or wounded. Simcoe claims 'near a hundred' Continental casualties, 'little or none' among the King's troops. John Marshall (1755–1835) admits one officer of Morgan's corps killed and 27 of his men killed or wounded, besides 'a small loss' among the militia."[69]

The main body of the Crown forces occupied the position previously held by Potter and Webb. But Captain John André (1751–1780) noted "the fullest information being procured of the Enemy's position, most people thought an attack upon ground of such difficult access would be an arduous undertaking; nor was it judged that any decisive advantage could be obtained, as the Enemy had reserved the most easy and obvious retreat. Probably for these reasons the Commander in Chief determined to return to Philadelphia."[70]

Both columns headed home; but Grey's column was hampered by the weight of its artillery and an insufficient number of horses. A group of Continental light infantrymen and some horsemen pursued it, "pressed on the rearmost parties and drove them in." The jaegers formed up to oppose the attack, and the Continentals "formed at a fence and deliver[ed] a very brisk fire." The Hessian field pieces drove off the Continentals, ending the Battle of Whitemarsh.

Howe decided that further maneuver was pointless, withdrew his men, and returned to Philadelphia at 1 PM on Monday, December 8th, arriving about 9 PM. Washington eventually moved his army into winter quarters at Valley Forge on Friday, December 19 where the ill clad, tired soldiers spent four days and nights of snow and sleet huddled around campfires unsheltered and in wet clothes waiting for their tents to arrive.[71]

★ A large body of British light infantry, accompanied by a party of light horse, went out into the country in three divisions on Saturday, February 14, 1778. Some went through Germantown where they broke many windows, seized all the leather and stockings and returned to Philadelphia that evening. The others went to the Spring House tavern, near Whitemarsh about 16 miles from Philadelphia, and captured Major Wright of the Pennsylvania militia and several civilians, including magistrates, assessors, constables, etc., whom the Loyalists in that neighborhood pointed out.[72]

Whitemarsh (May 20, 1778) see **Barren Hill** (pp. 68ss).

Chester (Oct. 1, 1777; June 9, 1778; June 14, 1778)
Chester County (Sept. 16, 1777)

> Chester is on the Delaware River, about 13 miles south of Philadelphia.

Mr. William Hughes (b. 1691), a venerable old gentleman from Chester County, was on his way to Newcastle County about Tuesday, September 16, 1777 when he met a party of Hessians who dismounted and stripped him and scourged him. They took his horse and left him for dead.[73]

★ Thomas Levis, a captain of a militia company, and six other militia officers were directed on Wednesday, October 1, 1777, to seize arms, blankets, shoes and stockings, etc., in the district of Chester borough for the use of the Continental army. They targeted the homes of persons believed to be Loyalists.[74]

★ Captain Archibald Dickson's (d.1803) HMS *Greyhound* fired a 3-pounder at troops on shore at Chester on Tuesday, June 9, 1778. He landed the marines who returned at 6 PM.[75]

★ Captain Dickson sent an armed boat from the HMS *Greyhound* to assist a grounded sloop which was under attack at Chester at 4 AM on Sunday, June 14, 1778. When the cutters appeared, they also came under attack. The boats returned at 11 o'clock.[76]

Chadd's Ford
Kennett Square (Sept. 11, 1777)
Battle of the Brandywine (Sept. 11, 1777)

> Brandywine Battlefield Park (website: **http://www.ushistory.org/brandywine/index.htm**) is near Chadd's Ford, along the north side of Route U.S. 1, 1 mile east of Route PA 100.
>   The Battle of the Brandywine covered over 10 square miles, but the state park only encompasses 50 acres. The visitor center contains exhibits about the battle. A reproduction of the farmhouse used by General Washington (see Photo PA-6) as a headquarters is on the grounds, as is the original preserved farmhouse where the Marquis de Lafayette was quartered (see Photo PA-7). A scenic driving tour of the area has a few interpretive signs and memorials.

PA-6. General Washington's headquarters, Brandywine (reconstruction)

PA-7. General Lafayette's headquarters, Brandywine (original)

General William Howe (1732–1786) left New York on Wednesday, July 23, 1777, with an army of 13,000 men on about 260 ships. After maneuvering in New Jersey, he sailed down the coast and up the Chesapeake Bay to Head of Elk (now Elkton, Maryland, a small town at the head of the Elk River), arriving on Monday, August 25.

★ General George Washington (1732–1799) planned a general engagement to defend the city of Philadelphia in 1777. He placed his army at Chadd's Ford on Brandywine Creek on Tuesday, September 9, 1777 in an attempt to block General Howe's probable route from the Chesapeake Bay to Philadelphia. Because he did not have an accurate map of the area, he relied on erroneous information that there was no ford across the creek immediately to the north of his position.

Lieutenant General Wilhelm von Knyphausen (1716–1800) marched the left of the Crown army to New Garden and Kennett Square on the afternoon of September 9, 1777 while General Charles Cornwallis (1738–1805) moved to Hokessen's Meeting House with the right. Both joined the next morning at Kennett Square. They were within 3 miles of the Continental advanced parties.

The entire Crown army advanced in two columns at daybreak on Thursday, the 11th. General Knyphausen now commanded the right which consisted of four Hessian battalions under Major General Sterne, the first and second brigades of British, three battalions of the 71st Regiment, the Queen's American Rangers commanded by Captain James Wemyss (1748–1833) of the 40th Regiment, and one squadron of the 16th dragoons under Major General Grant. They had six medium 12-pounders, four howitzers and the light artillery belonging to the brigades. This column took the direct road to Chadds Ford which is 7 miles from Kennett Square. Brigadier General William Maxwell's (1733–1796) advanced light corps engaged them on the other side of the creek and repulsed them twice and dispersed a body of 300 Hessians. These light troops were engaged with the Hessian advanced parties most of the day. Nevertheless, General Knyphausen's column arrived in front of the enemy at 10 AM.

★ The other column, the main force of 12,500 men, under the command of Lord Cornwallis, Major General Charles Grey (1729–1807), Brigadier Generals Edward Mathew (often misspelled Matthews) (1729–1805) and James Agnew (d. 1777), consisted of the mounted and dismounted chasseurs, two squadrons of the 16th dragoons, two battalions of light infantry, two battalions of British and three of Hessian grenadiers, two battalions of guards, the 3rd and 4th brigades with four light 12-pounders and the artillery of the brigades. They marched about 12 miles to the banks of the Brandywine, crossed at the first breach at Trimble's Ford and the second at Jeffrey's Ford about 2 PM and proceeded 3 miles east, following Great Valley Road (no longer in existence). They then took the road to Dilworth to circle around the Continental right flank at Chadd's Ford in a maneuver similar to the one General Howe used on Long Island to attack Major General John Sullivan (1740–1795) from the rear.[77]

General Washington ordered General Sullivan's, Brigadier General William Alexander's (Earl of Stirling, 1726–1783), and Brigadier General Adam Stevens's (1718–1791) divisions to advance and attack them about 3 PM. These divisions advanced about 3 miles and fell in with the advancing Crown forces. They engaged in a heated contest that lasted about an hour and a half without intermission when the Continentals began to give way because many of them had expended their ammunition.

Lieutenant General Wilhelm von Knyphausen (1716–1800) led 5,000 men to attack the center of the Continental line. His Hessian troops met constant fire from General Washington's sharpshooters opposite the ford. British cannons opened fire at 4 PM. General Cornwallis drove the Continentals back to Dilworth where General Sullivan regrouped his men. General Cornwallis also regrouped his men to keep up his attack, even though four of his battalions had lost their way in the thick woods between Birmingham Meeting House and Dilworth. He forced General Sullivan out of Dilworth, but General Washington brought his reserve under Major General Nathanael Greene (1742–1786) to cover Sullivan's retreat to Chester. Fighting continued until dark.

While this action occurred on the right, the British opened a 7-gun battery on the left, opposite one of an equal number. Brigadier General "Mad Anthony" Wayne (1745–1796) and a division of Pennsylvania troops with Brigadier General William Maxwell's (1733–1796) light corps on the left and Brigadier General Francis Nash's (1742–1777) brigade on the right formed the left wing. The batteries on both sides kept up an incessant cannonade that created so much smoke that the British infantry managed to cross the creek unseen and took possession of a hill opposite General Wayne. Severe action began between the two sides. The British made several attempts to cross the low ground between them and were repulsed each time.

Toward nightfall, General Washington ordered a retreat and retired to Chester for the night. General Knyphausen took advantage of the withdrawal of the Continental troops to cross Chadd's Ford and come to General Cornwallis's assistance. After crossing the ford, Knyphausen's men encountered Cornwallis's four battalions and took them along. The two British columns met after nightfall but were too exhausted to pursue the Continentals any further. They had lost 577 killed and wounded and six missing. Hessian casualties accounted for only 40 of the total.

General Washington suffered a serious defeat but not as bad as at New York where he nearly lost his army. He had lost 11 guns and between 1,200 and 1,300 casualties: 400 as prisoners, 300 dead, and about twice as many wounded, including General Marie Joseph de Motier Marquis de Lafayette (1757–1834). It could have been worse. The casualties could have included General Washington.

Major Patrick Ferguson (1744–1780, of the Royal Welch Fusiliers, scouting ahead of his men, heard the sound of horses' hooves and took cover. He records:

> We had not lain long . . . when a rebel officer, remarkable by a hussar dress, passed towards our army within a hundred yards of my right flank, not perceiving us. He was followed by another dressed in dark green or blue, mounted on a bay horse, with a remarkably large cocked hat.
>
> I ordered three good shots to steal near . . . and fire at them, but the idea disgusted me. I recalled the order. The hussar in returning made a circuit, but the other passed again within a hundred yards of us, upon which I advanced from the woods towards him.
>
> On my calling, he stopped, but after looking at me, proceeded. I again drew his attention and made signs to stop but he slowly continued his way. As I was within that distance at which in the quickest firing I could have lodged half-a-dozen of balls in or about him before he was out of my reach, I had only to determine. But it was not pleasant to fire at the back of an unoffending individual, who was acquitting himself very coolly of his duty, so I let him alone.
>
> The day after, I had been telling this story to some wounded officers who lay in the same room with me, when one of our surgeons, who had been dressing the wounded rebel officers, came in and told us they had been informing him that General Washington was all the morning with the light troops and only attended by a French Officer in a hussar dress, he himself dressed and mounted in every point as above described. I am not sorry that I did not know at the time who it was.

Major Ferguson might have shot Washington and perhaps ended the war at Brandywine. Major Ferguson himself had his right elbow shattered in the battle. Ferguson modified and improved the design of a breech-loading rifle that his company of Royal Welch Fusiliers used in this battle.

General Howe went on to occupy Philadelphia on September 26.[78]

Chestnut Hill (Sept. 12, 1777; Oct. 3, 1777; Dec. 5, 1777; March 6, 1778; June 3, 1778)
Jenkintown (Dec. 7, 1777; April 7, 1778; May 16, 1778)

> Chestnut Hill is north of Philadelphia and west of Germantown. Jenkintown is north of Philadelphia and east of Edge Hill.

After the Battle of Brandywine, the Continental Army marched all night and arrived at Chestnut Hill about daybreak on Tuesday, September 12, 1777. They immediately fell upon the enemy's picket guard with such fury and firmness that they routed them with great slaughter. The whole army then proceeded toward Germantown.[79]

★ General George Washington (1732–1799) was on Skippack Creek, about 20 miles from Philadelphia on Friday, October 3, 1777. The divisions of Major General John Sullivan (1740–1795) and Brigadier General "Mad Anthony" Wayne (1745–1796), flanked by General Thomas Conway's (1733–1800) brigade, were ordered to advance by way of Chestnut Hill, while Brigadier General John Armstrong's (1717–1795), Pennsylvania militia would make a circuit and gain the left and rear of the enemy. The divisions of Major General Nathanael Greene (1742–1786) and General Adam Stephen (ca. 1730–1791), flanked by Brigadier General Alexander McDougall's (1732–1786) brigade (two-thirds of the whole army), were to make a circuitous march and attack the front of the British right wing, while the Maryland and New Jersey militia, under General William Smallwood (1732–1792) and David Forman (1733–1812), would fall upon the rear of that wing. Major General William Alexander (Earl of Stirling, 1726–1783), with the brigades of Brigadier General Francis Nash (1742–1777) and Brigadier General William Maxwell (1733–1796) were to form a reserve.

The Continental Army began their 14-mile march to Germantown during the night of October 3. They tried to reach Chestnut Hill before daylight, but the roughness of the road delayed them. They did not arrive at the hill until it was nearly sunrise. The whole country was then enveloped in thick fog which concealed their advance toward Germantown.[80]

See **Germantown** (p. 40).

★ The British Army began to march out of Philadelphia on Thursday night, December 4, 1777. They got as far as Chestnut Hill where they camped at 3 AM. They "had a fine View of the Rebel Encampment about 3 miles distant on a Ridge of hills lying North of Whitemarsh," at dawn Friday morning. They could see the "smoke and huts being plainly in view." Hessian Major Carl Leopold Baurmeister (1734–1803) noted the Continentals had "increased their fires lighting many large ones in straight and deep lines, so that it looked as if fifty thousand men were encamped there. By day we could see this was merely a trick to deceive us."

General George Washington's (1732–1799) camp was well defended. "Both wings were fortified by strong abatis; the center approaches were completely covered by several batteries; the whole position was strongly fortified by fifty-two heavy pieces." General Washington also took the precaution of striking his tents in the early morning and sending his heavy baggage to the rear.

The pickets of both armies engaged in several skirmishes. General Washington sent Brigadier General James Irvine (1735–1819) and 600 Pennsylvania militiamen to test the enemy's strength at 11 AM. They attacked an advance post held by the 2nd Battalion of British light infantry and supported by British and Hessian grenadiers. Both sides engaged in a heavy fire and had several casualties, including General Irvine who was wounded and captured. His men were driven back, broke ranks, and ran away. The two armies held their respective positions until 1 AM on Sunday December 7 when the Crown forces marched to Edge Hill, less than a mile from the Continental left flank.[81]

December 6, 1777 see **Whitemarsh** (p. 25).

★ A party of Crown troops halted near Jenkin's town (Jenkintown), on the old York Road at 5 AM on Sunday, December 7, 1777 in an apparent attempt to turn the Congressional left. The Continentals then changed their position. When Colonel Daniel Morgan (1736–1802) learned that a large body of Crown troops was advancing in two columns, he ordered his riflemen and the Maryland militia to harass their right flank. They kept up a heavy fire with the British light infantry from about 10 AM until noon. The entire enemy column began to fire at them at 1 PM and continued until 3 PM when it ceased for nearly an hour. Sporadic firing resumed about 4 PM and continued until sunset. About 20 men were killed or wounded in the several skirmishes. The Continentals expected a night attack; but there was nothing more than a little bickering between the pickets.[82]

★ The Crown forces left great fires on their ground and decamped Monday evening, December 8, 1777. It was unsure whether they intended to retreat or were only filing off to prepare for an attack on the Continental right. Brigadier General Casimir Pulaski (1747–1779) followed them with a party of horsemen and a few infantrymen and observed their movements. When he learned their intentions, General Pulaski ordered some light parties to pursue and a larger body to support them. The enemy's march was too rapid to allow them to be overtaken; so General Pulaski's party and a small number of men attacked their rear guard early the following morning after burning a tavern called the Rising Sun near Philadelphia at the junction of the Germantown Road and the Old York Road and stealing a few milk cows and horses.[83]

★ Major Crewe and 200 of the 17th Regiment of Dragoons were detached to Chestnut Hill by way of Germantown about sunset on Friday, March 6, 1778 to surprise some Continental troops. These troops consisted of 260 men whom Brigadier General "Mad Anthony" Wayne (1745–1796) had turned over to Governor William Livingston (1723–1790) before leaving New Jersey on February 24. They crossed the Delaware near Burlington with 25 of Brigadier General Casimir Pulaski's (1747–1779) dragoons on March 4th and proceeded to Fatland Ford on the Schuylkill and then to Norrington where they attempted to recruit militiamen and burn forage and grain. They were advancing to Chestnut Hill when they learned the British dragoons were approaching.

The Continentals assembled on the right bank of Wissahickon Creek, followed the footpaths along this creek to Schuylkill Falls, and crossed the river without the dragoons being able to pursue them. The Crown troops killed five men and captured one officer and 17 soldiers who were too late to cross in safety.[84]

★ Five companies of British light infantry headed toward Jenkintown on Tuesday night, April 7, 1778 to prevent the militia from stopping the people going to market. They fell in with a party of 13, killed 12 and took one badly wounded prisoner. That night, some light dragoons, on their way toward Bristol, fell in with a party of militiamen. They killed seven and took 10 or 12 prisoners.[85]

★ A detachment of 400 British light infantrymen and Major John Graves Simcoe's (1752–1806) Queen's Rangers converged on the market town of Jenkintown at 2 AM on Saturday, May 16, 1778. They were to protect the people bringing their goods to market. The Quartermaster General also needed horses, as the British Army prepared to leave Philadelphia. Major Simcoe escorted the commissaries who were sent to procure them. They proceeded in four divisions and brought a 3-pounder.

They were ambushed on the return trip near the Bristol side of Pennypack Bridge. The first division passed the bridge with the cannon and immediately formed on the opposite bank. Major Simcoe anticipated an attack and secured the route of march for the successive divisions. The British pursued the Congressional troops about 3 miles and killed two or three and captured five prisoners. They lost two dragoons' horses killed and one man wounded.[86]

★ A battalion of British light infantry, all the cavalry, and the 17th, 27th, and 49th Regiments went to Chestnut Hill at 3 AM on Wednesday, June 3, 1778 to cover the market people. They returned minus one light horseman and three infantrymen taken prisoners.[87]

Frazer
Battle of the Clouds (Sept. 16, 1777)
Battle of the Admiral Warren Tavern
Battle of White Horse Tavern

> This engagement is usually known as the battle of "Admiral Warren Tavern" or "White Horse Tavern." It is called the Battle of the Clouds by local residents. The name is derived from the ridge, the highest ground between Philadelphia and Harrisburg.
>
> The Admiral Warren Tavern is near the intersection of Lancaster Road (now Lincoln Highway, Route U.S. 30) and Warren Avenue in Malvern, Pennsylvania. The White Horse Tavern is a private residence on Swedesford Road near the intersection with Boot Road in the village of Planebrook. Contemporary accounts refer to the taverns as being about 3 miles apart.
>
> The battle was fought north of the historical marker in front of Villa Maria Hall, the administration building of Immaculata College, Route PA 352, a little more than a mile south of Route U.S. 30 (3.5 miles west of Paoli).
>
> General Washington's headquarters during the battle were at Malin Hall on a side road off Swedesford Road. Neither Boot Tavern, where General Knyphausen's advance guard routed Washington's right (west) flank, nor the Three Tuns Tavern and Hershey's Mill, where General Cornwallis's vanguard struck the opposite flank are still standing. The Continental line of defense generally followed King Road which was then called Indian King Road. A plaque on the west side of Route PA 352, about 0.2 miles north of Goshenville, identifies the house that Lord Cornwallis used before the battle.

General George Washington (1732–1799) retreated across the Schuylkill River after the Battle of Brandywine). He still wanted to block General William Howe's (1732–1786) march on Philadelphia. He crossed the Schuylkill again and took a position on the Swedesford Road (No. 15023, running into Route PA 401, then U.S. 30 near Malvern). The two armies clashed on Tuesday, September 16, 1777, near the White Horse Tavern, five days after the Battle of Brandywine.

A torrential rainstorm ruined nearly all of the 40,000 musket cartridges issued to the Continental Army. The British had properly designed cartridge boxes that kept their powder dry, so they forced General Washington to retreat again.[88]

Near Valley Forge (Sept. 16, 1777; Sept. 18, 1777; Sept. 23, 1777; Jan. 20, 1778)

> The action of January 20, 1778 probably occurred at the Spread Eagle Tavern 5 miles south of Valley Forge. The Lee Memorial is located off Sugartown Road (Number 15116), about three-quarters of a mile southwest of route U.S. 30 in Berwyn, Chester County.

September 16, 1777 see **Battle of the Clouds** (p. 33).
September 18, 1777 see **Road to Philadelphia** (below).
September 23, 1777 see **Road to Philadelphia** (below).

★ Major Crewe and a party of 200 British dragoons circled around to surprise Captain Elisha Lee's (1740–1815) party of six light horse in their quarters near Valley Forge at dawn on Tuesday morning, January 20, 1778. Lee's dragoons constantly alarmed the British outposts. The rest of Captain Lee's 40 men were quartered in a neighboring house. Captain Lee barely had time to bolt the door. His men fired from the windows and appeared at different places to make it appear that they had more men than they did. The British made several attempts to force their way into the house but were driven off about 25 minutes later, leaving behind two dead and four badly wounded. Captain Lee only had two men slightly wounded. Captain Johann von Ewald (1744–1813) records this event as occurring on February 23, 1778 and says that the British dragoons numbered only 80.[89]

Road to Philadelphia (Sept. 18, 19, 23, 24, 1777)

> Newtown Square is about 11 miles west of Philadelphia.

As General Charles Cornwallis (1738–1805) followed General George Washington (1732–1799) toward Philadelphia in September 1777, their troops engaged in a few conflicts. General Washington's advance was blocked and he retreated to Schuylkill. He sent an express to Brigadier General Alexander McDougall (1732–1786) at Hackensack, New Jersey with orders to march down to Philadelphia to assist him. McDougall sent a captain's picket to the bridge on the road to Philadelphia on Thursday, September 18, 1777. Lieutenant General Wilhelm von Knyphausen's (1716–1800) division of Hessians set out early in the morning and reached White Horse by daylight and continued on toward Swedesford. General Cornwallis's army started marching at 7 AM and joined General Knyphausen's troops. They encamped in two lines on rising grounds in a large valley about 6 or 7 miles from Swedesford, 2 or 3 miles from Valley Forge, and about a mile from the main road. General McDougall's pickets exchanged fire with the Crown forces and took seven prisoners.[90]

★ The following day, Friday, September 19, 1777, British Lieutenant Colonel William Harcourt led a party of dragoons and light infantrymen on the Philadelphia road. They captured 150 horses at Newtown square and took a captain and eight Continentals prisoners.[91]

★ Accounts from Philadelphia reported that Major General John Sullivan's (1740–1795) and Major General William Alexander's (Earl of Stirling, 1726–1783) brigades were almost cut off on Tuesday, September 23, 1777; that they had lost 5,000 killed, wounded and taken; and that they were pursued to the Ford of Schulykill, 5 miles from Philadelphia, where they again made a stand and were defeated on Sunday morning, the 21st. Many of the inhabitants were leaving the city, expecting the British Army to occupy the city that day.[92]

Pennsylvania

The entire British Army crossed Fatland Ford to the north side of the Schuylkill River just after midnight and completed the crossing by 10 AM on Tuesday, September 23, 1777. After proceeding about 1 mile, the army halted to dry themselves and rest. They took the Egypt road to headquarters at Norrington where they arrived by 3 PM. The front of the army extended 0.5 miles along Swedesford Road and 2.5 miles along the Manitawney Road. They received a few scattered shots during the day and captured four light horsemen, some prisoners, wagons and three loads of ammunition and some supplies of liquor. Later that evening, about 9 PM, some British pickets "fired a few shot at some skulking rebels" in the rear.

★ Early the following morning, the 24th, the pickets in the rear fired at some straggling Whigs and, about 9 AM, British foraging parties exchanged four or five shots with the Whigs.[93]

Malvern
Paoli Massacre (Sept. 19, 1777)

> The Paoli Massacre site (see Photo PA-8) is in Malvern Memorial Park, Monument Road, Malvern. Go 0.5 miles west from Warren Avenue on Monument Road. The junction of these streets is 0.4 miles east of King Street and 0.8 miles north of a traffic light on the Paoli Pike.
> Malvern Memorial Park, near the massacre site, contains a mass grave of about 53 of the dead. A polished granite obelisk nearby commemorates the "massacre."

The day after the Battle of Brandywine (Thursday, September 11, 1777), the British headed toward the Schuylkill River, near Philadelphia. General George Washington (1732–1799) sent 1,500 Pennsylvania Continentals under Brigadier General "Mad Anthony" Wayne (1745–1796) against their left flank and rear to delay their advance.

General William Howe (1732–1786) learned of Wayne's encampment from captured messages and Loyalist spies. He ordered Major General Charles Grey (1729–1807) to

PA-8. Paoli massacre site in Malvern Memorial Park. The park also contains a mass grave of about 53 of the dead. A polished granite obelisk nearby commemorates the "massacre."

put an end to this tiresome harassment. General Grey ordered the 5,000 men of the three battalions assigned to him to remove the flints from their muskets so they would not be tempted to open fire and betray their advance. He was later known as "No Flint" Grey for this action. Grey's battalions set out on Friday, September 19, 1777 and caught General Wayne with a sudden surprise attack near an inn known as the Paoli Tavern about 1 o'clock in the morning of September 20.

The British drove off General Wayne's pickets and charged into the camp before the Continentals could defend themselves. They used only bayonets. However, most of the Continentals did not have bayonets, and they had no time to reload in the confusion and close quarters of hand-to-hand combat. Many men were killed as they ran in front of their campfires. Those who tried to hide in the darkness were hunted down and bayoneted. Wayne lost 53 men killed and 100 wounded. The rest fled to the west. The British reported six men killed and 22 wounded.

One of General Grey's officers described what happened:

> The enemy . . . some with arms, others without, [ran] in all directions with the greatest confusion. The light infantry bayoneted every man they came up with. The camp was immediately set on fire, and this, with the cries of the wounded, formed altogether one of the most dreadful scenes I ever beheld. Every man that fired was instantly put to death. Captain Wolfe was killed, and I received a shot in my right hand, soon after we entered the camp. I saw the fellow present at me, and was running up to him when he fired. He was immediately killed. The enemy were pursued for two miles. I kept up till I grew faint from loss of blood and was obliged to sit down. Wayne's brigade was to have marched at one in the morning to attack our battalion while crossing the Schuylkill river, and we surprised them at twelve. Four hundred and sixty of the enemy were counted the next morning, lying dead, and not one shot was fired by us—all done with the bayonet. We had only twenty killed and wounded.

The battle got the epithet of "massacre" from the mangled condition of the bodies and the lopsided casualty figures; but the British were not guilty of any offense—they just enjoyed a one-sided victory. The term "massacre" also fails to account for the 71 prisoners General Grey captured.

The next day, General Grey rejoined General Howe marching to the Schuylkill, plundering farms along the way. General Washington had moved into position to prevent the British crossing the river, so General Howe tricked General Washington by marching upriver to the west. Washington marched parallel to Howe who countermarched at night and crossed the Schuylkill at Fatland Ford near Valley Forge on September 23. This put him between Washington and Philadelphia. The British Army arrived in Germantown on September 25 and entered Philadelphia the next day behind a parade of heavy guns with bands playing triumphant airs and Loyalists cheering.

On the same day as the Paoli Massacre, the Continental Congress fled from Philadelphia to York, Pennsylvania, about 85 miles to the west. Despite heavy casualties at Brandywine and Paoli, General Washington soon replaced his losses, but General Howe could not.[94]

Phoenixville
Gordon's Ford (Sept. 22, 1777)

Gordon's Ford was about 3.5 miles northwest of Valley Forge.

General William Howe (1732–1786) moved most of his soldiers to the Schuylkill River on Saturday, September 20, 1777, just before he discovered Brigadier General "Mad Anthony" Wayne's (1745–1796) location. When he arrived, he found General George Washington (1732–1799) already there, on the opposite shore, with cannons and troops covering the fords. General Howe spent the next two days moving his army upstream from Fatland Ford at Valley Forge up through Bull Tavern to Gordon's Ford. He ordered his engineers to begin constructing a bridge at Gordon's Ford.

Howe hoped that Washington would view this movement as preparation for an assault on his right flank and that he would move his troops upstream to prevent the British from separating his army from its supply depot at Reading. This would allow Howe to cross the Schuylkill at the downstream fords and march on Philadelphia.

Howe's grenadiers (see Photo PA-9) crossed the Schuylkill first at Fatland Ford at 5 AM on Monday, September 22, 1777. They were supported by the light infantry guard. The cold water was three feet deep and 100 yards across at the bend in the river. Once across, the troops lit fires to dry off while they waited for the rest of the soldiers to arrive. About the same time, the Hessian grenadiers feigned a crossing of the Schuylkill at Gordon's Ford. They came under fire of artillery and small arms and turned back after killing two Continentals. Brigadier General Sir William Erskine (1728–1795) patrolled up the Pottsgrove Road which leads to Reading with the mounted

PA-9. *Members of the Brigade of the American Revolution portraying British grenadiers. This photo depicts Scottish Highlanders wearing red regimental coats with black facings, bearskin helmets, and a blue and green kilt. Grenadiers were members of an elite unit selected on the basis of exceptional height and ability.*

and dismounted chasseurs, one squadron of the 16th Dragoons and part of the 2nd Light Infantry at 7 AM. The whole army crossed over on the 23rd and encamped that night with their left on the Schuylkill and their right on the Ridge Road. A battalion dislodged the militiamen at a small redoubt with six field pieces at Swedes' Ford and the British marched toward Philadelphia in two grand divisions on the 25th. One column, under General Charles Cornwallis (1738–1805,) took the Germantown Road; the other, under Lieutenant General Wilhelm von Knyphausen (1716–1800), passed down the Schuylkill toward the falls.

Washington's ill-clad, ill-shod, and ill-fed army lacked the manpower to cover the entire upper Schuylkill. He had to decide to defend either his supply network or Philadelphia. His army could not exist without the gunpowder and provisions at Reading and Lancaster; so he defended those locations.[95]

Norristown
Norrington (Sept. 23–24, 1777)

> Norrington, now called Norristown, is 17 miles northwest of Philadelphia.

The British Army began marching toward Philadelphia at moonrise on Tuesday, September 23, 1777. They went to the right to Fatland Ford where they crossed the Schuylkill in two columns before 8 AM. The jaegers and grenadiers crossed at Scheffs Ford and joined the left wing of the army. Brigadier General James Grant (1720–1806) had remained behind with a brigade of British infantry to cover the baggage, artillery, and provisions train. After General Grant's troops crossed the river and the men had dried themselves, the army continued its march, arriving at Norrington about 3 PM. There, they made camp. Some troops exchanged shots with some Whigs and captured four of their mounted troops.

A battalion of light infantry was posted at Swedes' Ford. The 300 militiamen stationed there abandoned their post as the British Army approached. They left five iron 12-pounders on traveling carriages, some ammunition, and stores. The army remained at Norrington the following day and received a few people from Philadelphia and several deserters from the Continental Army.[96]

Frankford (Sept. 25, 1777; Sept. 27, 1777; Oct. 26, 1777; Feb. 4, 1778; April 8, 1778; May 28, 1778; June 6, 1778)

> Frankford Creek was on the main road from Philadelphia to Bristol Ferry on the Delaware River, about 5 miles north of Philadelphia. The angle at which it flowed into the Delaware was called Point-no-Point. There were many good houses and plantations here. The village of Frankford was on a hill beyond the bridge over the creek. The creek was not fordable at this location but could be easily crossed in many places above it.
>
> Pennypack Creek was 4 miles farther than Frankford. The Red Lion Tavern was 3 miles beyond this, 2 miles south of Bristol, a small town opposite Burlington, New Jersey. Many crossroads intersected the country between these main roads.
>
> Smithfield was probably in northeast Philadelphia in the vicinity of Benjamin Rush State Park.

As the British headed toward Germantown by the Frankford Road on Thursday afternoon, September 25, 1777, their light horsemen captured a colonel, a principal commissary, a captain of a frigate, and a captain of light horsemen and two or three of his men.[97]

★ After the bombardment of Philadelphia [see **Delaware River near Philadelphia** (p. 47)] on Saturday, September 27, 1777, the British collected about 50 boats of all sorts in Philadelphia and procured a Durham boat (see Photo PA-1) from Frankford Creek capable of holding 100 men.[98]

★ The Whigs frequently patrolled as far as Frankford and to a place called the Rocks, about a mile beyond it. They raided the village of Kensington several times, as they could come through the woods and approach very near to the town undiscovered and cross the bridge at Point-no-Point. The inhabitants made a house musket proof to defend this area and took up the bridge. This made it accessible only to cavalry, as infantrymen were liable to be cut off in the angle between the Delaware and the Frankford road.

Pennsylvania 39

The picket occupied a knoll on the left, overlooking the country during the daytime; but corn fields, high enough to conceal the approach of an enemy, reached to the base of the hill.

Continental Brigadier General Sir William Erskine (1728–1795) ordered that the hill not be defended if attacked in force because it projected forward. He also withdrew the sentinels at night. If the enemy approached, the sentinels usually left this post until the corps could get under arms and the light infantry of the guards informed. They would then force the enemy to leave, suffering casualties in their retreat to the woods.

The Queen's Rangers tried to surprise the Congressional post at Frankford. They marched near to the bridge to lay in ambuscade until the Continental cavalry came to the rear of the town. Some dragoons crossed the bridge from Frankford; but the Rangers could not determine whether they were friends or foes in the dim light. When the dragoons turned back, the Queen's Rangers heard a shot and rushed into the town. However, the Continental post had been withdrawn, either by accident or from forewarning.

The Queen's Rangers and 30 dragoons of the 16th Regiment marched at midnight for several days afterward to try to take the same post. They circled around the Jolly Post, a tavern where the guard was kept, and nearly attained the rear of it, when they encountered a patrol on Sunday, October 26, 1777. Cut off from the house, the patrol did not fire but ran toward the wood, pursued by the Queen's Rangers. The infantry crossed the fields behind the house and prepared to attack it. The cavalry circled around to the road in the rear and completely surprised the post, capturing an officer and 20 militiamen, two or three of whom were slightly wounded trying to escape.[99]

★ Some inhabitants near Oxford had informed the Crown forces that a Continental colonel and captain were using considerable force to recruit militiamen in this area. They intended to take the two officers if they could get about 100 men to help them. Lieutenant Colonel John Graves Simcoe (1752–1806) and his legionnaires marched 5 miles beyond Frankford about midnight on Tuesday, February 3, 1778. They captured the colonel and captain and returned by another road the next morning.[100]

★ Captain Richard Hovenden with 40 Philadelphia light dragoons and Captain Evan Thomas (1745–1835) with 50 Bucks County Volunteers set out for Frankford on Tuesday afternoon, April 8, 1778 when they learned that a body of Congressional troops appeared there. They marched toward the advanced picket of 18 privates at a house near Smithfield about midnight. They killed two men and drove the picket back to a party of 50 who were placed half a mile away to support them. This party formed as if to make a stand but when they were attacked vigorously, they soon fled to the main body, consisting of 200 men another half mile away, after concealing 18 men in a stone house along the way.

The dragoons and volunteers pursued, intending to attack the main body; but when they passed the stone house and came under heavy fire, they turned about and stormed the house so vigorously that the occupants could not fire a second time. The Loyalists killed eight and took nine prisoners. They re-formed their ranks and advanced to attack the main body, now consisting of 250 men. They attacked with so much spirit that the Whigs fled into the woods. The Loyalists only had two horses slightly wounded in this action which lasted almost an hour.[101]

★ The 2nd battalion of British light infantry, the 5th, 42nd and 44th Regiments and 140 dragoons went out at 2 AM on Thursday, May 28, 1778 to surprise a body of Congressional troops thought to be at Germantown. The two flank companies of Guards went to Frankford Bridge at the same time. General Henry Clinton (1730–1795) went to Germantown with only 20 dragoons to meet the troops.[102]

★ Captain Allen McLane (1746–1829) and two dragoons were traveling on the Bustletown Road toward Frankford after daybreak on Saturday, June 6, 1778. As they approached the village, they fell into an infantry ambuscade. The Regulars fired on them and forced them into a field on the right toward the Oxford road where they discovered a party of Major John Graves Simcoe's (1752–1806) Queen's Rangers galloping toward them. McLane placed himself between the dragoons and the infantrymen to silence the infantry fire. He approached the dragoons and, when he got within 20 paces of them, wheeled to the right, passing them and gaining the Oxford road.

Major John Graves Simcoe (1752–1806) sent two of his Rangers in pursuit. McLane turned off the road to the left to escape them. He crossed a creek and ascended the bank on the opposite shore when the Rangers came up on his right and left. Believing he had surrendered, they lowered their sabres. McLane had a pistol in his right hand and fired into the right breast of the dragoon on his left. At the same time, the dragoon on his right attempted to draw his sabre. McLane wounded his left hand seizing the tassel of the dragoon's sabre. He gave the man a back-handed blow across the nose with his pistol and repeated the action until he disabled the dragoon and brought him to the pummel of his saddle.[103]

Germantown (Sept. 25, 1777; Oct. 4, 1777; March 6, 1778; April 8, 15, 1778; May 20, 1778; May 28, 1778)

Skippack Road (Feb. 24, 1778)

Mount Airy, near Germantown (May 31, 1778)

> Much of the Battle of Germantown was fought around Cliveden (see Photo PA-10) (website: **www.cliveden.org/**) at 6401 Germantown Avenue in Germantown. Cliveden/Chew Mansion was the summer home of Benjamin Chew (1722–1810) whose daughter Peggy was escorted to the *Mischianza* by Captain John André. Ironically, she later married John Eager Howard in 1787. He commanded the 4th Maryland Regiment at Germantown and later became Governor of Maryland and a U.S. Senator.
>
> Skippack Road coincides almost exactly with the present-day Germantown Avenue/Germantown Pike running west-northwest from Philadelphia. Skippack Creek is about 16 miles from Germantown and the town of Skippack is about 20 miles northwest of Germantown.
>
> Mount Airy, known as Beggar's Town in the 18th century, is about 3 miles west of Germantown and about 1.25 miles south-southeast of Chestnut Hill.

On Monday, September 25, 1777, General William Howe (1732–1786) marched to Germantown where his cavalry captured six stray Continentals. The next day, General Charles Cornwallis (1738–1805) set out for Philadelphia at 8 AM with two English and two Hessian grenadier battalions (von Linsing's and von Lengerke's). They brought six 12-pounders and four howitzers. They arrived at 11 AM and took the city without firing a shot. They posted strong guards in the central part of the city, a battalion of English grenadiers (see photo PA-9) below it on the Delaware River, and above it along the Schuylkill River and divided the artillery between the two posts along the rivers. The rest of the army encamped at and near Germantown until October 19th

PA-10. Cliveden, Chew mansion, where much of the Battle of Germantown was fought

when they moved into the city. The camp at Germantown received a few pop shots which killed two men. The Regulars returned fire and killed a Continental officer and a private.[104]

★ The day the British arrived in Philadelphia, September 26, 1777, General William Howe (1732–1786) dispersed his forces. He stationed 9,000 men north of the city at Germantown, America's first German settlement, 3,000 in New Jersey, and the rest in Philadelphia. The British began constructing fortifications and batteries. They built a 3-gun redoubt, in Philadelphia, at what is now the intersection of Reed and South Columbus Boulevard, another near South Swanson and Christian Streets and another in the upper part of town, on a wharf above Cohocksink Creek. They all had medium 12-pounders and howitzers.[105]

★ General George Washington (1732–1799) took advantage of General Howe's temporarily reduced numbers. He had recently received reinforcements and now had an army totaling about 8,000 Continentals and 3,000 militia, outnumbering the British. His army was encamped 16 miles from Germantown, along the Skippack Road. He decided to make a surprise attack on the main British camp at Germantown just as he had done at Trenton. The plan was much like that used at Trenton but involved far more complicated movements by much larger bodies of troops.

Four columns—two of Continentals under Major General John Sullivan (1740–1795) and Major General Nathanael Greene (1742–1786) and two of militia—moving at night over different roads were to converge on Germantown simultaneously at dawn on Saturday, October 4, 1777. The two columns of Continentals arrived at different times. A thick fog reduced visibility to a few yards, making a difficult plan even more so. Even though the troops wore pieces of white paper in their hats to identify themselves, they sometimes fired on their own men in the fog and smoke. The thick fog also caused the gunpowder smoke to hang in the air, further reducing visibility. The two militia columns never arrived at all.

General Washington's advance troops caught the British pickets by surprise. General Sullivan's and Brigadier General "Mad Anthony" Wayne's (1745–1796) troops attacked the British infantry battalion in front with heavy force. A barrage of grape shot forced them back to their main line in great confusion. General Charles Cornwallis (1738–1805), sleeping soundly in Philadelphia and unaware the enemy was so close, was awakened by the cannonade as was General Howe.

General Howe arrived near the scene of the engagement in time to meet his battalions fleeing. He hurried back to his camp to prepare his troops for action. Lieutenant Colonel Thomas Musgrave (1738–1812) sent part of his 40th Regiment to support the retreating battalions. He and six companies (about 120 British troops) took refuge in and around the stone summer house of Benjamin Chew (1722–1810), former chief justice of Pennsylvania. Most of the fighting took place here as the troops barricaded the doors and lower windows and began firing on the Continentals from the upper windows. They delivered such fearful volleys of musketry upon Brigadier General George Weedon's (1734–1793) brigade that they blocked their advance. The fire of the Continental troops on the building was ineffective and the house still shows evidence of the damage from the musket fire.

Meanwhile, the Continental generals argued whether they could leave a fortress in their rear. Brigadier General Henry Knox (1750–1806) prevailed on General Washington to force the defenders to surrender before allowing the reserve to proceed. They opened fire with artillery, broke the front door, smashed the windows, destroyed the statuary and vases in the yard, but could not penetrate the thick stone walls. Nor were they able to burn it. The Continentals then assaulted the house but suffered heavy casualties from a well-positioned opponent firing at point-blank range.

In the fog and the confusion of fighting, two Continental brigades began to fire at each other. The word spread through the ranks that the British were attacking from behind, and the retreat turned into a rout. The officers could not stop it and had to call off the attack when General Charles Cornwallis (1738–1805) arrived with fresh troops. The battle lasted nearly three hours, and the Continentals retreated about 9 AM, leaving General Howe's troops in command of the field.

Both sides suffered heavy losses. The Crown forces had 537 casualties, the Continentals had 652 and lost 438 more as prisoners. Neither commander had much to show for his efforts. Washington lost his chance to retake Philadelphia; Howe withdrew there for the winter. He found no swarms of Loyalists rallying to the British standards, and he had left Major General John Burgoyne (1722–1792) to lose a whole army in the north.

Even though the Continentals lost the battle, leading statesmen and generals of Europe, particularly the French, were impressed with Washington's boldness and the fighting ability of an army which could recover quickly from a defeat at Brandywine to take the offensive and come so close to a victory. When the French government later learned of Burgoyne's surrender at Saratoga, the ministers remembered Germantown which helped them decide to form an alliance with the Continentals.[106]

★ Captain Richard Hovenden and a part of his Pennsylvania dragoons left Philadelphia with a party of British dragoons at 11 PM Monday, February 23, 1778. They went at least 30 miles up the Skippack Road and took 130 head of fine cattle and captured a number of prisoners. They returned Tuesday afternoon.[107]

★ A party of light horsemen made an excursion to Germanton Friday night, March 6, 1778. They fell in with a Whig captain and 24 men. They killed four and took the rest prisoners.[108]

★ Lord William Schaw Cathcart's (1755–1843) Guard of Light Horse captured one mounted light dragoon at Germantown on Wednesday, April 8, 1778. A week later, they skirmished with some Continentals near Philadelphia during the night of Wednesday, April 15, 1778. They killed one and returned with seven prisoners.[109]

★ General William Howe (1732–1786) received intelligence on Tuesday evening, May 19, 1778 that General George Washington (1732–1799) was marching his army to Germantown. He sent a detachment of British and Hessian troops "to meet and escort them into this city [Philadelphia]." However, General Washington was apprised of their approach and returned to camp.[110]

★ The 2nd Battalion of British light infantry, the 5th, 42nd and 44th Regiments and 140 dragoons went out at 2 AM on Thursday, May 28, 1778 to surprise a body of Congressional troops thought to be at Germantown. The two flank companies of Guards went to Frankford Bridge at the same time. General Henry Clinton (1730–1795) went to Germantown with only 20 dragoons to meet the troops.[111]

★ Captain Allen McLane (1746–1829) and a small detachment fell in with a party of Crown horsemen and infantrymen at Mount Airy, near Germantown, on Sunday, May 31, 1778. They killed one horse and captured the rider and wounded three men, including a cornet, and six horses without losing a man.[112]

Philadelphia (Sept. 26, 1777; Nov. 21, 22, 1777; Dec. 27, 1777; Jan. 5, 1778; June 13, 1778; June 18, 1778)
Battle of the Kegs (Dec. 27, 1777)
Outside Philadelphia (Feb. 14, 1778)
Near Philadelphia (Feb. 20, 1778)

> Philadelphia was the site of the Continental Congresses which met in Carpenters' Hall (320 Chestnut Street) and Independence Hall, originally the Philadelphia State House (Chestnut Street in Independence Square between 5th and 6th Streets). After the signing of the Declaration of Independence, it became the home of Congress until the city was occupied by the British (September 26, 1777 to June 1778) and Congress moved to York.
>
> Independence National Historical Park (**www.nps.gov/inde/index.htm**), in downtown Philadelphia, includes the buildings in Independence Square and others throughout the city that are associated with the Colonial period, the founding of the nation and Philadelphia's early role as the national capital. These buildings include the visitor center (at 3rd and Chestnut Streets) Independence Hall, Congress Hall, the old City Hall, the Liberty Bell Pavilion, the Second Bank of the United States (an 1824 structure that now houses Independence National Historical Park's National Portrait Gallery) and Washington Square (one block southwest of Independence Hall and the site of the Tomb of the Unknown Soldier of the American Revolution (see Photo PA-11).
>
> Other interesting sites include the Declaration (Graff) House (**www.ushistory.org/declaration/graff/**), on the southwest corner of 7th and Market Streets, which is a reconstruction of the dwelling in which Thomas Jefferson drafted the Declaration of Independence in June 1776, the Betsy Ross House (where the colonial seamstress supposedly stitched the first American flag in 1777, Franklin Court (once owned by Benjamin Franklin, who lived in Philadelphia from 1722 until his death in 1790) and

PA-11. Tomb of the Unknown Soldier of the American Revolution. It is located in Washington Square, one block southwest of Independence Hall.

> the Thaddeus Kosciuszko National Memorial (exhibits and audiovisual displays in English and Polish describe Thaddeus Kosciuszko's contributions to the American War for Independence.
>
> Famous churches include St. Peter's Church (erected in 1761, where four signers of the Declaration of Independence worshiped) and Christ Church, the house of worship of 15 signers of the Declaration of Independence. Brass plaques mark the pews once occupied by George Washington, Benjamin Franklin, and Betsy Ross. The church's burial ground contains the graves of Benjamin Franklin and four other signers of the Declaration of Independence. Old St. Joseph's Church was the first Roman Catholic church in Philadelphia. The Marquis de Lafayette and the Comte de Rochambeau worshiped here.
>
> Elfreth's Alley is one of many narrow streets lined with quaint restored houses that have stood since the days of the city's founding.
>
> *The Pennsylvania Ledger* dates the Battle of the Kegs as occurring on January 5, 1778. Other sources date it the following day, January 6. However, Elizabeth Drinker's diary records it already on December 27, 1777.

After General Charles Cornwallis (1738–1805) entered Philadelphia on Thursday, September 26, 1777, a large detachment of Continentals attacked the Queen's Rangers, shot the sentry and another but were repulsed. A lieutenant was found dead on the field after the skirmish. Archibald Robertson (ca. 1745–1813) also reports the death of a private.[113]

★ Fifteen Whig galleys, some gundalows (see photo PA-12) and other vessels began to move from the fleet at Philadelphia about 3 AM on Friday, November 21, 1777. They passed the city between New Jersey and Penrose Island in the moonlight at 4 AM. Meanwhile the troops set fire to all their remaining vessels—a total of 15. When the vessels advanced toward the British guns at the north part of the city, the battery and the HM Armed Ship *Delaware*, anchored off Kensington in the narrow part of the channel,

PA-12. Gundalow or Gondola. An open, flat bottomed vessel about 53 feet long, 15 feet wide, and almost four feet deep in the center. It is equipped with both sails and oars, designed to carry heavy loads, usually armed with one gun at the bow and two mid-ship.

fired on them. The cannonade awoke everybody in Philadelphia at 5 AM and drove an 8-gun armed schooner and an armed sloop on the Jersey shore; but 15 galleys got up the river.
★ Meanwhile, a large party of horsemen and infantrymen attacked the British pickets at the bottom of their lines. The attackers were repulsed with loss.[114]
★ A large party of Continental infantrymen and dragoons attacked the British lines at Philadelphia but were driven off with three wounded. Another attack on British pickets the next day was repulsed with nine Whigs captured.[115]
★ Thirty vessels were taking in forage at Tinicum Island on Saturday, December 27, 1777 when the snow began. Only three of the vessels, which were empty, failed to get back to Philadelphia. They drove up and down the Delaware with the ice for a day or two and went aground on the Jersey shore near Gloucester where the Whigs burned them.[116]
★ The following morning, the HM Armed Schooner *Viper* attempted to go down to assist the army transport brig *Symmetry*. However the ice prevented her and she was captured.[117]
★ David Bushnell (1742–1824) designed some floating mines to be suspended below kegs and tied together with rope. Colonel Joseph Borden's cooperage constructed the kegs to Bushnell's specifications. They were filled with gunpowder and released to float down the Delaware River into the British fleet about sunrise Saturday morning, December 27, 1777, in the hopes of snagging warships and exploding on contact.

The British had hauled their ships into positions that protected them from floating river ice and, consequently, the kegs. Two boys spotted a keg floating in the river, got into a small boat, and tried to take it up; but it exploded, blowing up both boys. However, a few of the mines struck a target. One of the kegs sank a small British barge, killing four sailors and wounding an unknown number. The sudden explosion alerted the British and soldiers mustered on all the wharves with orders to shoot at any piece of wood in the water with cannon and small arms to detonate the mines. The HMS *Roebuck* and other warships fired whole broadsides into the Delaware.

The entire action might have ended by noon, had not an old woman coming down river from the market with her provisions not dropped a small keg of butter overboard. The ebb tide floated it toward the fleet. The gunfire resumed with renewed fury and lasted until evening. The operation did not achieve the desired strategic results, and the British fleet suffered little damage.

Elizabeth Drinker noted in her diary for December 27th:
> A certain something, a piece of Clockwork, a Barrel with Gunpowder &c., was found in our River, which blew up near ye *Roebuck* Man-of-War, and destroyed a boat near it; several others, they say, are found, which are thought to be ye contrivance of some designing, evil minded person or persons, against the shipping.

Francis Hopkinson (1737–1791) parodied the event in a ballad, *The Battle of the Kegs*, which sarcastically praises the "courage" of the British forces and describes the kegs as similar to barrels used to transport "pickled herring." The ballad was meant as a propaganda piece to show that even though the Continental Army had been driven out of Philadelphia and was encamped at Valley Forge under miserable conditions, it did not intend to give up.[118]

Outside Philadelphia (February 14, 1778) see **Spring House Tavern** (p. 67).

Near Philadelphia (February 20, 1778) see **Barren Hill** (pp. 68ss).

★ Crown troops sent on a foraging expedition returned to Philadelphia on Monday, January 5, 1778. They had one man killed and two wounded during the expedition.[119]

★ The Crown forces burned all the vessels on the stocks at Philadelphia on Saturday, June 13, 1778. While the Crown forces were evacuating Philadelphia, Captain Allen McLane's (1746–1829) company of about 50 light horse and 100 infantry came upon a British patrol.

★ They opened fire about daybreak on Thursday, June 18, 1778. Some Continental light infantry pursued the rear guard and skirmishing continued without letup. They captured 32. Many men died because of the intense heat and because of the sandy ground which provided no water during the entire march.[120]

Gray's Ferry Road, below Philadelphia (Sept. 27, 1777)

> Gray's Ferry (or Grays Ferry) is a neighborhood in South Philadelphia bounded by 25th Street on the east, the Schuylkill River on the west, Vare Avenue on the south, and Grays Ferry Avenue on the north. The actual ferry was across from where the Mill Creek empties into the Schuylkill River at about 43rd street. In the 1700s, Gray's Ferry was the southernmost of three ferries that crossed the Schuylkill River to Philadelphia.

Small parties of Continentals continued to harass the British around Philadelphia after they occupied the city. A party of 100 Continentals attacked the Queen's Rangers at Israel Pemberton's plantation on Gray's Ferry road, on Saturday, September 27, 1777. They killed one man and wounded three officers but were driven back with some losses.[121]

See also **Darby, near Gray's Ferry** (p. 52).

Delaware River near Philadelphia (Sept. 27, 1777; Oct. 4, 1777; Oct. 9–11, 1777; Oct. 15, 1777; Oct. 20, 1777; Nov. 5, 1777; March 16–17, 1778; June 13, 1778; June 13, 1778)
Webb's Ferry (Oct. 9, 1777)
Delaware River, near Chester (Oct. 13, 1777)
Delaware River above Wilmington (Jan. 1778)
Gloucester Point, Delaware River near Philadelphia (Dec. 29, 30, 31, 1777)

> Webb's Ferry was on the Delaware River at the mouth of the Schuylkill.

Before the British completed their fortifications and batteries around Philadelphia on Saturday, September 27, 1777, Commodore John Hazlewood (ca. 1726–1800) sent the 24-gun frigate *Delaware*, the 10-gun frigate *Montgomery*, the 8-gun sloop *Fly*, and five row galleys of the Pennsylvania Navy, each with a gun in the bow, to engage them on the Delaware River near Philadelphia early that morning. The *Delaware* anchored within 500 yards of the lower battery and opened fire while the other vessels engaged the other batteries. Both sides exchanged fire with little effect on either side.

The *Delaware* tried to avoid the fire from the shore battery and seemed "inclined to push past our guns" to a position farther upriver when she "receiving some shot and shell which set her on fire, the people were thrown into great disorder, neglected the management of the sails, and she ran aground within 250 yards" of the battery, just off the lower end of Windmill Island. The island, which no longer exists, was an off-shore strip of land about 100 yards wide and about 800 yards long, with long underwater sand bars at each end.

Brigadier General Samuel Cleveland ordered a battery to fire on the *Delaware* (twenty-four 12-pounders, and six 9-pounders) which "returned the fire joined by the other ship and all the galleys...and continued for some time" before the *Delaware* struck her colors. A shot struck her caboose and one of the royal howitzers burst her near her bow. Major James Moncrieff (1744–1793) and the carpenters tried to extinguish the fire by cutting away parts of the *Delaware*'s side. The fire was difficult to extinguish and reignited two or three times.

The battery then turned the guns against the *Montgomery* and the other vessels, forcing all of them except the *Fly*, which was disabled and driven on shore on the New Jersey side of the river, to return to their mooring off Gloucester Point. The high tide re-floated the *Fly* which then returned to her station.

One of the row galleys had her foremast shot away and ran ashore at New Jersey directly opposite the British batteries. The rest of the fleet tried to run past the batteries and sail up the river. As they passed between the Jersey shore and Windmill Island, the Cohocksink battery drove them back in confusion. As she passed the lower batteries, the *Montgomery* had her masts shot away. A schooner, which had also lost her masts, was run ashore and captured. The rest got safe under the guns of the fort on Mud Island.

When the firing ceased, 10 men from the Marine Company of grenadiers boarded the *Delaware*, extinguished the fire, and took possession of her. They found that the crew of 152 men had only one man killed and six wounded. The galley driven ashore had four men killed and six wounded.[122]

★ The masters and pilots of the British squadron removed the chevaux-de-frise (see photo PA-13) from the Delaware River off Billingsport on Saturday morning, October

PA-13. Chevaux-de-frise. These obstacles, consisting of iron-tipped spikes attached to logs, were hidden two or three feet below the water's surface at low tide to block rivers to enemy ships.

4, 1777. About 3 PM that afternoon, several Congressional galleys came down river and fired several guns at the Brig *Dunmore*.[123]

★ A large scow came down the Schuylkill River on Wednesday, October 8, 1777. The Continentals wounded one of the crewmen and secured the scow. They received intelligence that six boats were ready to come down from the lower ferry, known as Gray's Ferry. They learned that evening that a large body was marching down to Webb's Ferry from Philadelphia with 20 pieces of artillery and boats on carriages. Commodore John Hazlewood (ca. 1726–1800) sent nine galleys and gondolas to attack the British battery of two medium 12-pounders at Webb's Ferry on Thursday, October 9, 1777 while the enemy worked along the bank. They were beaten back; but the British lost one grenadier killed and three wounded and a wagoner and two horses killed.[124]

★ The British continued building installations on Carpenter's Island. Commodore John Hazlewood tried to prevent this work on Thursday evening, October 9, 1777. When the tide changed, he sent "a floating Battery . . . between Little Mud Island and Fort Island" supported by two brigs. The battery consisted of a platform for cannon without any other facilities. It began firing at the British batteries under construction at dawn. The British returned fire from a battery "250 yards from the enemy's floating battery, and 500 yards West of the Fort on a dyke in an overflowed meadow."[125]

★ The British completed the batteries on Carpenter's Island on October 10 and began firing at Fort Mifflin, causing much destruction. Lieutenant Colonel Samuel Smith (1752–1839) and Commodore John Hazlewood (ca. 1726–1800) decided to attack Carpenter's Island to destroy the batteries. Commodore Hazlewood sent three galleys to begin a barrage on the British at 9:30 AM on Saturday, October 11, 1777. They did it "so warmly that the Enemy dar'd not to fire one shot." Major Ballard and 100 men then landed to storm the north battery. Almost an hour later, the enemy began coming out to surrender. Ballard said that the surrendering party consisted of a "British captain [who] had his arm broken . . . two young lieutenants and a few men." Ballard immediately paroled the captain so he could get proper medical attention. Major Ballard and his men were loading their prisoners into boats when they saw a detachment of British coming from a house. Some of the prisoners ran off in the confusion.[126]

★ The British completed a new battery to the left, or north, of the two other batteries on Carpenter's Island on October 13th and 14th. Called the left battery, it held two iron 18-pounders. British guard boats gave the alarm at 1:30 AM on Monday, October 13, 1777, that the enemy were sending fire rafts, covered by galleys and gun boats, down the Delaware River to get among the ships. The galleys and gun boats kept a constant fire of grape shot (see photo PA-14) to prevent the British boats from towing the rafts away from the ships. The British returned fire, preventing the galleys and gun boats from advancing nearer. Their boats managed to tow the fire rafts clear of the ships, and grounded them on Little Tinicum Island. The galleys ceased firing at 5 AM.[127]

★ The Congressional forces sent five fire stages chained together under cover of their galleys down the Delaware River toward Billingsport at 2 AM on Tuesday, October 14, 1777. Captain Henry Bellew moved the HMS *Liverpool* a little farther down river and kept up a constant fire on the enemy who sent four more stages at 3 AM. Captain Bellew sent his boats and towed the fire stages on shore. He then sailed up to Billingsport at 6 AM and anchored there.

Some galleys approached the HM Armed Ship *Vigilant*, anchored off Billingsport, at 5 AM. Captain John Henry (1753–1793) fired several shots at them and they retreated after shooting away one palm of the *Vigilant*'s best bower anchor. The Vigilant weighed anchor at 11 AM and approached the chevaux-de-frise to cover the HMS *Liverpool*. The crews of the two ships weighed the chevaux-de-frise and destroyed the platforms of the fort at Billingsport.[128]

★ Shortly after the fog lifted (about 7 AM) on Wednesday morning, October 15, 1777, the four batteries under the command of Major John Montresor (1736–1799) opened fire on Fort Mifflin and the nearby vessels. The vessels weighed anchor and sheered

PA-14. Grape shot. Nine balls such as these were placed between two iron plates and tied together to resemble a cluster of grapes. When fired simultaneously from a cannon, the balls separate into multiple projectiles.

off, except for one floating battery of eighteen 18-pounders which continued firing for about one hour and changed her position to one more distant.

The British batteries consisted of one battery on the north side of Schuylkill Point with two medium 12-pounders, one battery at the Post Houses with two captured iron 18-pounders, the Battery Middle with one 8-inch howitzer and one 8-inch mortar, and the Battery Night with one 8-inch howitzer and one 8-inch mortar.

One of the iron 18-pounders at the Post House Battery burst during the firing, killing one artillery man and wounding three more. The two batteries on the right continued to fire a shell or a howitzer about every half hour during the course of the night but with little effect.[129]

★ Some Congressional galleys fired several shots at the HM Armed Ship *Vigilant* and the Galley *Cornwallis* at 2 PM on Monday, October 20, 1777. The vessels returned fire. They weighed anchor at 4 PM and warped through the chevaux-de-frise to anchor off Billingsport at 5:30.

★ Meanwhile, the HMS *Camilla*, the HM Armed Ship *Vigilant* and the Galley *Cornwallis* anchored off Hog Island at 2 PM. However, Captain John Henry (1753–1793), realizing that he would go aground at low tide, weighed anchor again and proceeded down river as the fort at Mud Island fired at the *Vigilant*. Eight galleys rowed over from Red Bank to assist the fort at 3 PM. The vessels exchanged several shots as the British dropped down river. The *Vigilant*'s only damage was a flat boat that was sunk and some broken oars. She towed the flat boat on shore and repaired her.[130]

★ Congressional forces opened a 2-gun battery a little above Mantua Creek about 9 AM Wednesday, November 5, 1777. They exchanged fire for some time with the HMS *Isis*, HMS *Pearl*, HM Galley *Cornwallis*, and the HMS *Roebuck* in the Delaware River. Some Congressional galleys joined the fight at 11 AM but retreated up river after a few shots. The *Pearl* lost a boy killed and another wounded.

The battery resumed fire about 2 PM along with the 1-gun battery and the galleys drew up in a line. A smart fire ensued. The *Isis* had her spring shot away and received much damage to her and the *Pearl*'s hull and rigging.[131]

See Delaware River in the New Jersey volume.

★ Two brigs and a schooner, part of the fleet that had gone foraging, got caught in the ice and could not return to Philadelphia. They drifted with the tide for two days and ran ashore near Gloucester Point on the New Jersey side of the Delaware River on Monday, December 29, 1777, as did the transport *Adrian*, another foraging vessel. A party of Whigs tried to board the vessels; but Lt. Edward Pakenham had HMS *Viper* fire at them to disperse them and save the vessels.[132]

★ The following day, Captain Pakenham had the *Viper* fire several more shots at the Continentals who attempted to destroy two transports. The Continentals later captured the transports. That same afternoon, the *Viper* fired several guns at some Continentals who boarded the transport *Adrian* and dispersed them. The Continentals boarded the vessels and set them on fire on Wednesday morning, December 31, 1777.[133]

★ HMS *Viper*, Captain Edward Pakenham, exchanged fire with Congressional troops erecting a breastwork on the Pennsylvania shore of the Delaware River on Monday and Tuesday, March 16–17, 1778. Two men deserted from one of the *Viper*'s boats on Saturday morning, June 13, 1778. Captain Pakenham sent an officer with a party of men for the boat at noon. A band of Whigs fired on them and mortally wounded the officer. The party got the boat off at 10 AM the following day and withdrew. Two days later, the *Viper* fired several shots at some Whig boats.[134]

Pennsylvania

Carpenter's Island, near Philadelphia (Oct. 11, 12, 1777)

Carpenter's Island, also known as Province Island, was in the Delaware River within musket range of Fort Mifflin. The battery here was also referred to as the middle battery.

Major John Montresor (1736–1799) usually had his men building batteries at night because the Continentals were so near. As Sunday, October 11, 1777 was a moonlit night, he halted work on the battery but his men made much progress on the following two nights.

A British work party crossed the ferry to get the howitzers and mortars (see Photo PA-15) for the battery on Carpenter's Island about 2:30 AM on Sunday, October 11, 1777. The battery was within 400 or 500 yards of Fort Mifflin on Mud Island and commanded all the shipping in the Delaware River. The workmen carelessly placed an 8-inch howitzer on the barge which sank to the bottom, taking several men and horses. One man and one horse drowned, putting an end to the task for the night. Earlier in the evening, they had taken over two 12-pounders and dragged one of them up to the battery through a mile of mud and water.

Commodore John Hazlewood (ca. 1726–1800) took three galleys and a floating battery to attack a new British battery on Carpenter's Island at high tide, about 6 AM. They maintained a constant fire upon it from all their vessels and batteries until about 4 PM. Some troops landed about 10 AM, marched up to the battery, and attacked the force of less than 200 men. The Redcoats surrendered and the Continentals took possession of it for a little while.

However, a sudden German counterattack prevented Commodore Hazlewood from removing all his prisoners from the island and re-took the battery. Hazlewood managed

PA-15. Mortar used for firing shells (also known as bombs) in a high arc over a short distance, particularly to get behind walls and other high obstacles that cannons cannot reach

to recover 57 prisoners of the grenadiers and 10th Regiment and four artillerymen. He suffered two men killed and five wounded and a shot blew up an ammunition wagon.[135]

★ The Continentals made a second attack on the same battery the following day, the 12th, but found the enemy better prepared this time. The attackers lost two men killed and five wounded while the Crown forces had four killed (two British and two Hessians), and three wounded.[136]

Near Darby (Gray's Ferry) (Oct. 18, 1777; Oct. 20, 1777)
Darby (Nov. 18, 1777; Dec. 22–28, 1777; April 17, 1778)

> The Blue Bell Tavern is at 7303 Woodland Avenue in Darby, the main stagecoach road between Philadelphia and the southern colonies.
> Gray's Ferry (or Grays Ferry) is a neighborhood in South Philadelphia bounded by 25th Street on the east, the Schuylkill River on the west, Vare Avenue on the south, and Grays Ferry Avenue on the north. The actual ferry was across from where the Mill Creek empties into the Schuylkill River at about 43rd Street. In the 1700s, Gray's Ferry was the southernmost of three ferries that crossed the Schuylkill River to Philadelphia and was also known as Lower Ferry.

The British prepared to cross the Schuylkill River over the bridge at Gray's Ferry on Saturday, October 18, 1777. The detachment from Wilmington arrived on the opposite side at 2 PM. The engineer and another man who recovered from his wounds and 500 convalescents arrived with the detachment. However, the high tide overflowed into the meadows and over the platform of the right and middle batteries.[137]

The upper and lower British batteries [the Pest House battery on Province island and the middle and right batteries on Carpenter's Island] fired several times at Fort Mifflin on the 18th, but with little effect. The fort returned fire. The lower British battery fired eight bombs but the enemy fleet moved nearly under Fort Mercer at Red Bank to be out of range.[138]

★ The Crown forces retired from Germantown about 11 PM on Sunday, October 19, 1777. They went as low as Peale Hall on the Falls Road, extending their line from Kensington to the Schuylkill River on their left. They constructed a number of redoubts which they strengthened to enable them to detach in safety. An escort of 1,500 men accompanied 113 wagons which crossed over the Lower Ferry (Gray's Ferry) to go down to the ships for provisions and to forage in the neighborhood. Major General Nathanael Greene (1742–1786) was ordered to cross the Schuylkill to attack them, but a heavy shower came up before he reached the river. He returned as directed in case of rain. A council of war was then held and the majority agreed that it was not yet too late to attack.

Brigadier General Alexander McDougall (1732–1786) was ordered to proceed on the same mission. When he had crossed the river and proceeded about 2 miles, he found that the wagons had returned the preceding evening by way of the Blue Bell. What was supposed to be an escort turned out to be a large detachment that occupied Gray's Ferry and began to fortify it to protect the bridge. Brigadier General James Potter (1729–1789) reinforced General McDougall, bringing his force to about 4,000 men.

General McDougall's troops crossed the river about 10 miles from Philadelphia. Although they had marched all the night before and crossed the river twice, they went back with great spirits, arriving about sunrise. They were greatly surprised to find the post had been evacuated the preceding evening and the bridge broken to pieces. The detachment returned to camp after destroying the remaining huts, works, etc.[139]

★ General Charles Cornwallis (1738–1805) and 2,500 men of the 23rd British Regiment passed the Blue Bell Tavern on Tuesday, November 18, 1777 when some Pennsylvania militiamen fired on them. Cornwallis sent his men into the tavern and bayoneted 33 of them.

★ General William Howe (1732–1786) took 7,000 British soldiers out of Philadelphia on an extensive foraging expedition between Darby and Chester during the week of December 22–28, 1777. Colonel Daniel Morgan (1736–1802) and 700 infantrymen followed and harassed them. They captured 60 British infantrymen, 13 dragoons, and 30 wagons.[140]

★ The entire Hessian jaeger corps had crossed the Schuylkill and advanced 5 miles beyond Darby under the cover of darkness on April 17, 1778 with Captain Carl August von Wreden covering the right. Captain von Wreden's pickets, marching directly in front of him, encountered an infantry patrol of one officer and 18 men. The jaegers fired several shots, revealing their position. They had one man slightly wounded in the exchange of fire and captured one militiaman who revealed the strength of the scouting party but not whether a larger force had followed the patrol.[141]

Fort Mifflin (Mud Fort) (Oct. 19, 1777; Oct. 21, 1777; Oct. 22, 1777; Nov. 3, 1777; Nov. 5, 1777; Nov. 8, 1777; Nov. 11, 1777; Nov. 12, 1777; Nov. 13, 1777; Nov. 14–21, 1777)

Delaware River (Oct. 25, 1777)

> Fort Mifflin (websites: http://www.fortmifflin.us/ and http://www.fortmifflin.com/) is on Fort Mifflin Road at the foot of Island Avenue off I-95 (in Philadelphia). President John Adams ordered the fort rebuilt in 1798. The river side is original, and the reconstruction used much of the 1770s foundation. The bunks are believed to date from 1812. The fort remained in use until 1962. The 13 restored buildings mostly interpret the Civil War era but the tours and demonstrations also cover its Revolutionary origins.

British engineer Captain John Montresor (1736–1799) laid out stone walls on the western shore of the Delaware River, south of Philadelphia, to defend the city in 1771. The fortification, known as Fort Mud or Mud Island, became a Continental stronghold in the fall of 1777, garrisoned by Lieutenant Colonel Samuel Smith (1752–1839) and renamed for Major General Thomas Mifflin (1744–1800).

General George Washington (1732–1799) kept General William Howe (1732–1786) besieged in Philadelphia by controlling the roads in and out of the city and holding two forts that commanded the Delaware River: Fort Mercer, on the New Jersey side at Red Bank, and Fort Mifflin, on Mud Island in the river itself. This broke General Howe's communications and supply routes by sea. General Howe needed to eliminate the forts to allow his supplies to come up the river. He entrusted Captain Montresor with the task of dismantling the fortifications he had once built.

★ Captain John Montresor (1736–1799) began bombarding Fort Mifflin every half hour on October 15, 1777. Red-hot cannonballs set fire to the barracks, but they did not silence the guns at the fort. Reinforcements managed to sneak in at night, and the attackers laid siege to the fort. Heavy rains deterred Montresor's efforts further, as he prepared batteries to assault Fort Mifflin's unprotected land side.

★ The cannon from Fort Mifflin damaged the British right battery on Sunday, October 19, 1777. The British were forced to repair the batteries at night.[142]

★ The HM Armed Schooner *Viper*, the HMS *Roebuck, Augusta, Liverpool* and another ship, the sloop *Merlin* and the galley *Cornwallis* were ordered to sail up the Delaware River at 5 PM on Tuesday, October 21, 1777. The guns of Fort Mifflin and of the Continental galleys began to engage them at 6 PM. The *Augusta* (see Photo PA-16) ran aground and the *Viper* was struck by a shot at 6:30 PM which wounded two men. The *Viper* anchored under the *Augusta*'s stern.[143]

★ Eight flat bottomed boats arrived in the Schuylkill River from the British fleet early Wednesday morning, October 22, 1777. They conveyed 50 hogsheads of rum and received not a single shot from the enemy. The work at the bridgehead at Gray's Ferry was ordered to be stopped at 3 PM. The detachment was ordered back to camp and the bridge to be taken up and carried to Middle Ferry.[144]

★ Captain John Montresor (1736–1799) attacked again on Wednesday, October 22 and was repulsed even though the navy had joined the bombardment. The squadron included the 64-gun *Augusta,* the 44-gun *Roebuck,* the frigates *Pearl* and *Liverpool,* the 18-gun sloop of war *Merlin,* and the galley *Cornwallis.* That night, the *Augusta* and the *Merlin,* ran aground on the mud flats in the river near the second line of chevaux-defrise (see photo PA-13). The next morning, the guns of both Fort Mifflin and Fort Mercer opened upon them setting the *Augusta* afire. Ambrose Serle (1742–1812), secretary to Admiral Richard Howe (1726–1799), claims that the fire started when a flaming wad from a musket fired by a marine struck a hammock. The flames spread almost instantly to the dry, tar-coated rigging and continued to spread quickly throughout the ship. The

PA-16. *Frigate or man-of-war or ship of the line. This photo shows the HMS Victory which was Admiral Keppel's flagship when first commissioned in 1776. It was later re-fitted and became Lord Nelson's flagship at the Battle of Trafalgar.*

crews abandoned the ships, but the *Augusta*'s second lieutenant, chaplain, gunner, and 40 seamen confined to sick bay burned to death. On October 23, the *Augusta* blew up. The explosion caused a soldier at Fort Mifflin to write that it "seemed to shake the earth to its center." Thomas Paine (1737–1809), who was several miles west of Philadelphia, was "stunned with a report as loud as a peal from a hundred cannon at once." The British burned the *Merlin*.

★ Some Congressional galleys and boats came down the Delaware River to plunder the wreck of the HMS *Augusta* at 7 AM on Saturday, October 25, 1777. They fired several shots at the HMS *Pearl, Liverpool* and the galley *Cornwallis* about 10 AM. The British vessels returned fire with many guns and drove them up river. The HMS *Isis* fired some shots at some Congressional boats in the afternoon.[145]

★ The British were busy trying to raise the wreck of the 64-gun HMS *Augusta* during the nights of November 1 and 2. By Monday morning, November 3, 1777, they had almost completed a floating battery of heavy cannon on her hulk which Lieutenant Colonel Samuel Smith (1752–1839) expected the British would open the following day. Some Congressional galleys came down to the vicinity of Billingsport, a mile below Fort Mifflin and fired several shots at the HMS *Pearl* and the HM Sloop *Zebra* about 5 PM. The British returned fire.[146]

★ The British began work on a floating log bridge across the Schuylkill River at Middle Ferry on Wednesday, November 5, 1777. The following day, a floating battery was launched in the Schuylkill but it sank with its guns which were brought from the HMS *Eagle*.[147]

General Washington ordered two Connecticut regiments to Mud Island to help Fort Mifflin. Private Joseph Plumb Martin (1760–1850) recalls the hardships:
> Here, without winter clothing, not a scrap of either shoes or stockings to my legs or feet, I endured hardships sufficient to kill half a dozen horses.

★ There were four row galleys and two floating batteries in the Schuylkill River on Saturday, November 8, 1777 as the British planned to attack Fort Mifflin from the Schuylkill. They also planned a simultaneous attack on Fort Mercer at Red Bank, landing just below Timber Creek. The troops from Billingsport, New Jersey were to move across Mantua Creek and join forces with the troops from Philadelphia in the attack against Fort Mercer.

A large number of men and horses crossed the Schuylkill to Province Island about sunset. The ships below the fort fired their guns as a signal. The Continentals had guard boats between Hog and Carpenter's Islands, the route the enemy boats would take. When the British vessels arrived, they fired on the Continentals and forced them to retreat. Commodore John Hazlewood (ca. 1726–1800) had a chain strung between the islands during the night and placed 14 gun boats in the passage. He and his galleys were positioned on the north end of Mud Island. The floating batteries and xebecs guarded the chevaux-de-frise and were prepared to oppose the British if they tried to advance.

Captain Isaiah Robinson (d. ca. 1781) commanded the Continental brig *Andrew Doria* at the mouth of the Schuylkill while the Continental sloop *Fly* guarded the mouth of Timber Creek. The Continental and militia guards were placed at Timber and Mantua creeks.

★ Two double-deckers, including the HMS *Somerset*, passed through the lower chevaux-de-frise the following day, bringing the total number of vessels at this location to eight; but they were all below the 2-gun battery at Mantua Creek. The British brought six 24-pounders to Carpenter's Island in flat boats from the HMS *Eagle* during the night.[148]

★ Two British brigs and two sloops with provisions passed Fort Mifflin Monday night, November 10, 1777 and went up the Schuylkill River. The fort fired both cannon and small arms at them but did no damage.[149]

★ The Crown forces completed their batteries on nearby Province Island that evening. They consisted of two 32-pounders, six 24-pounders, one 18-pounder, and many lesser guns as well as the guns from ships in the Delaware River. The artillery also launched two floating batteries to bombard Fort Mifflin.

Joseph Plumb Martin reports:

> We had, as I mentioned before, a thirty-two pound cannon in the fort, but had not a single shot for it. The British also had one in their battery upon the Hospital Point, which, as I said before, raked the fort, or rather it was so fixed as to rake the parade in front of the barracks, the only place we could pass up and down the fort. The artillery officers offered a gill [a half pint] of rum for each shot fired from that piece, which the soldiers would procure. I have seen from twenty to fifty men standing on the parade waiting with impatience the coming of the shot, which would often be seized before its motion had fully ceased and conveyed off to our gun to be sent back again to its former owners. When the lucky fellow who had caught it had swallowed his rum, he would return to wait for another, exulting that he had been more lucky or more dexterous than his fellows.[150]

★ The British captured two brigs and one sloop past Mud Island between Carpenter's and Province Islands on November 11, 1777 and were unloading them at Webb's Ferry in the Schuylkill the following day. There was heavy firing at Fort Mifflin from the batteries on the islands; but the fort seldom returned fire.[151]

★ The British batteries continued to fire on Fort Mifflin on Wednesday, November 12, 1777. Their two 8-inch howitzers were still disabled and unrepaired. The HM Galley *Isis* and a sloop fired on the Jersey shore. Fire from the fort remained silent from 1 to 3 PM. The occupants of the fort then opened one gun from their 2-gun battery at 3:30 and one from the shoulder of the Mud Battery. The British had one man killed and another mortally wounded. The officer of artillery was slightly wounded when one of their 8-inch shells burst unexpectedly.[152]

★ The British batteries continued to fire at forts Mifflin and Mercer all day Thursday, November 13, 1777. The Continentals only fired with one gun, an 18-pounder, from the shoulder of Mud Battery and five or six shots from the 2-gun batteries.[153]

★ The Continentals discovered a British floating battery of two 32-pounders about 500 yards from Fort Mifflin at daybreak on Friday, November 14, 1777. They directed all the guns they could against this battery and forced the officer and his men to abandon their post. The British kept up a great fire from their floating battery and from the shore at 7 AM and lost only one man under the heavy fire. At nightfall, some boats went to the battery and towed the floating battery alongside the wharf on the southeastern shore of Province Island at the mouth of Mingo Creek. The crews removed one gun and put it on the platform, leaving the other on the floating battery.[154]

★ The bombardment was increased on November 15 and continued for six days. It was one of the most terrible of the war with cannons firing at the fort at a rate of 50 shots a minute. Seven British ships joined the assault and silenced the Continental guns. The defenders fought valiantly but evacuated Fort Mifflin a week later after one of the most memorable defensive stands ever made on American soil. It took more than a month to capture this poorly manned, undergunned little fort. The Continentals lost an estimated 250–400 men killed while the Crown forces had only 13 dead and 24 wounded in addition to the casualties from the HMS *Augusta*.

★ Fifteen Continental galleys moved at 3 AM on Friday, November 21, 1777. They passed Philadelphia and set fire to all their remaining vessels at 4. As they advanced toward the British guns at the north part of the city, the British fired on them as did the HMS *Delaware*, which drove one 8-gun schooner and one armed sloop to the Jersey shore.[155]

★ A large party of Congressional dragoons and infantrymen attacked some British pickets but were repulsed with some losses.[156]

The loss of Fort Mercer (in New Jersey) and Fort Mifflin meant that General Washington could not starve the British out of Philadelphia. The first British supply ship reached Philadelphia on November 23. The Continentals needed some kind of victory to boost morale. They had a brief skirmish in what is called the Battle of Edge Hill, in early December, before going into winter quarters at a place called Valley Forge, 20 miles northwest of Philadelphia.

General William Howe (1732–1786) had gained his objective but it proved of no lasting value to him. No swarms of loyalists rallied to the British standards. He had left Major General John Burgoyne (1722–1792) to lose a whole army in the north. And, with winter setting in, prolonged campaigning was out of the question. He settled comfortably in Philadelphia. Seven months later, General Henry Clinton (1730–1795) replaced him and evacuated Philadelphia to fortify New York City and Staten Island.[157]

See also National Park, New Jersey (Fort Mercer).

Falls of the Schuylkill (Oct. 20, 1777)
North of Philadelphia (Feb. 24, 1778)
Bristol (April 17, 1778; May 9, 1778)
Flourtown (April 18, 1778)
Crooked Billet (now Hatboro) (May 1, 1778)

> Flourtown is on Bethlehem Pike west of Edge Hill and south of Whitemarsh, about 2 miles south of Route I-276 (Pennsylvania Turnpike). Crooked Billet was near the main road between Philadelphia and New York. A monument to the battle of Crooked Billet is located near the Hatboro Elementary School.

Twelve flat bottomed British boats and a whaleboat arrived at Philadelphia at 4 AM on Monday, October 20, 1777. They received an abundance of grape shot from Fort Mifflin and two galleys. They had no injuries until they arrived near the British battery of two medium 12-pounders at Webb's Ferry, on the north point of the Schuylkill. The garrison was not apprised of their arrival and killed one seaman.

An officer and six mounted jaegers patrolling near the Falls of the Schuylkill encountered a troop of Captain David Plunkett's 4th Continental Dragoons and were forced to flee after having one man killed. Captain Plunkett pursued them too far and fell in with one of the British pickets and was wounded and captured along with another man.[158]

★ The Pennsylvania militia patrolled the area north of Philadelphia between the Delaware and Schuylkill Rivers in early 1778. Its function was to warn about attacks mounted upon Valley Forge, to check enemy foraging raids into the sector, and to prevent farmers from trading with the enemy.

Brigadier General James Potter (1729–1789), commander of the Pennsylvania militia, went home on leave on Wednesday, January 7, 1778. The Supreme Executive Council for the state named Colonel John Lacey (1755–1814) to replace him. The Council also appointed him a brigadier to avoid friction with other Pennsylvania militia colonels. Lacey, 25 years old, was now the youngest general in the Continental Army. When he joined the Bucks County militia in July 1775, the Buckingham (Quaker) Meeting disowned him. He rose from captain to lieutenant colonel and commanded the militia in an area that was subject to constant raids by Loyalist bands and British dragoons.

Captain Thomas commanded a group of Loyalists recruited in Bucks County and Captain Moore Hovenden commanded a company of light dragoons raised in Philadelphia. Both of these units joined forces with the 360 men of the Queen's Rangers under Major John Graves Simcoe (1752–1806). Together, they raided Bensalem, Whitemarsh, Red Lion Tavern, Smithfield, Newtown, and other places in February 1778. They captured soldiers, cloth, wagons, and foodstuffs.

Drovers, with 130 head of cattle gathered by Brigadier General "Mad Anthony" Wayne (1745–1796) in New Jersey for the Continental Army, crossed the Delaware at Coryell's Ferry on Monday, February 23, 1778. They requested Colonel Lacey for an escort; but Lacey denied the request, telling the drovers that they would be safe if they kept the herd north of Philadelphia. When Hovenden's dragoons captured the livestock the next day, General George Washington (1732–1799) became angry at the loss of meat and criticized Lacey who responded that he had only 400 men out of the promised 1,000, that the area was too large to guard, that his troops were inexperienced, and that if he had provided an escort he would have left his force at camp open to an attack.

When Washington urged Lacey to move closer to Philadelphia to discourage the British, Lacey feared leaving his campsite along the Neshaming Creek in upper Bucks County because his force was dwindling rapidly due to the expiration of enlistments. Reinforcements from York and Cumberland counties were ordered to assist Lacey, but these militiamen were delayed for various reasons, such as Native American raids near home, inclement weather conditions, and lost messages.

When six enemy deserters arrived at his camp, Lacey made the mistake of feeding them better than his own men, either to impress them or to earn their trust. This caused some militiamen to complain, but Lacey simply dismissed them. He had more problems with his troops because he was contemptuous of the militiamen due to his service with the Continentals. He also lacked rapport with the men.

In addition to Lacey's problems with his troops, he lost the good will of the farmers when his men pillaged and looted the area. He also ordered civilians to evacuate a 15-mile strip north of Philadelphia and south of his camp when he could not prevent the farmers from taking their produce into enemy lines. This infuriated local inhabitants who sent delegates to the Council of Pennsylvania with complaints, prompting Washington to order Lacey to drop the plan. Tension with the farmers increased when Lacey, following Washington's orders, arrested and imprisoned several farmers who were caught transporting vegetables to Philadelphia and had one of them executed. This did not stop trade with the enemy, and raids continued.

★ A Congressional edict forbade anyone living within 6 miles of Philadelphia to enter the city or to leave the city to go into the country after Wednesday, April 15, 1778. The militiamen were ordered to muster in front of the lines of the Crown forces. They gathered at the following posts:

(1) between Bristol and the Crooked Billet Tavern, 15 miles from Philadelphia;
(2) at Spring House, north of Whitemarsh, 16 miles from Philadelphia; whence a temporary post of 250 men was detached to Germantown;
(3) at Barren Hill near the Schuylkill Falls, 10 miles from Philadelphia.

They also established temporary posts in Darby beyond the Schuylkill, at Reedy Tavern, at the Gulph Mill and placed an observation post at Springfield.

Major Francis Edward Gwin led a detachment of 160 Pennsylvania dragoons (Loyalists) supported by 300 light infantrymen as far as Bristol at 11 PM Thursday night, April 16, 1778. They surprised a much stronger force of Bucks County militiamen, supported by some light infantrymen nearby, the following rainy, windy day. Because the militiamen had neither uniforms nor arms, the dragoons did not recognize them and dispersed with a few casualties. They killed one man, wounded two, and captured 65, including one colonel, one lieutenant colonel, two majors, some captains and subalterns, three captains who had just disembarked from their galleys anchored at Bristol, and several privates. Angry, General George Washington (1732–1799) wrote to Thomas Wharton (1758–1831), president of the Council of Pennsylvania, threatening to have the New Jersey and Maryland militia do the job.[159]

★ A group of Regulars and Loyalists also raided Smithfield and an area north of Germantown on Friday, April 17, 1778.

★ The Crown forces sent out three parties to engage the Congressional troops at some of their posts on April 18th. A party of 50 dragoons had gone to Flourtown by the Germantown Road to engage the Jersey militia from Monmouth County. They killed 16 men, wounded about 20, and took 18 prisoners.

★ Colonel John Lacey's (1755–1814) force had dwindled to only 250 men by mid-April, causing him to fear an attack. That number decreased to 53 by the end of April due to the expiration of terms of service. Lacey led his men on a week-long expedition following a zigzag route to deceive the enemy. He arrived at Crooked Billet Tavern and village in Montgomery County, Pennsylvania, about 17 miles from Philadelphia, on Monday, April 27. Reinforced with 150 militiamen, Lacey sent out a patrol and put one brigade on the alert.

General William Howe (1732–1786) gave Major John Graves Simcoe (1752–1806) permission to attack Crooked Billet to open the supply route to Philadelphia. Simcoe took a circuitous route on a night march to avoid enemy posts or patrols and to get behind the Crooked Billet on Friday, May 1. He attacked from the north with 300 Queen's Rangers while Lieutenant Colonel Robert Abercromby or Abercrombie (1740–1827) and 400 light infantrymen, part of them mounted, and a party of light dragoons took a direct road to attack from the west and south.

Colonel Abercromby could not arrive at his post before daybreak. He sent his cavalry and mounted light-infantry to the place of ambuscade. The Queen's Rangers arrived nearly in Lacey's rear and upon his right flank when a sentinel fired, sounding the alarm. Lacey marched his men toward a nearby wood where they made a stand and exchanged fire with the enemy. Some small parties who were making their escape from the light infantry were killed; but the main body retreated quickly in disorder. However, the Rangers could not overtake them. Overpowered, Lacey abandoned his baggage and barely managed to fight his way out. Simcoe sent 30 dragoons to intercept the baggage-wagons and guard them. Lacey retreated rapidly with the enemy on both his flanks and in his rear. Major Simcoe galloped up to the edge of the wood and summoned Lacey to surrender. His men kept up their fire as best they could for 2 miles before they "made a sudden turn to the left, through a wood, which entirely extricated" them and allowed them to escape north of Warminster.

Lacey reported 30 of his men killed and 17 wounded. He later changed these figures to 26 killed and 8 or 10 severely wounded. Some of the wounded reportedly had 8 or

10 bayonet stabs and were badly cut with broadswords. Some of the wounded were said to have been thrown into a parcel of buckwheat straw which was then set on fire. Other sources say Lacey suffered about 84 casualties while the Crown forces only had nine wounded. The Crown forces returned to Philadelphia. Lacey's baggage was sold and the soldiers each received a dollar. Although this excursion failed in its purpose, it intimidated the militia.

General George Washington (1732–1799) relieved Colonel Lacey of command soon afterward and replaced him with Colonel Samuel Potter, Sr. (1727–1802) on May 13. This engagement is typical of the forage raids in the Middle States. It also shows that a depleted militia force cannot stop enemy raids or prevent trade with the enemy.[160]

★ After raiding Crosswicks and Biles Island, New Jersey, the Regulars marched to Bristol at noon on Saturday, May 9, 1778. They burned two sloops at the ferry and a ship and a brig. The galleys, gunboats and flat boats proceeded down the river to embark the troops at Bristol by 6 PM. The crews of the galley *Philadelphia*, the armed schooners *Viper* and *Pembroke*, and two gunboats burned the remaining vessels consisting of four new ships, one new brig, and an old schooner. The Crown troops arrived at Philadelphia at 6 AM on Sunday morning without losing one man.[161]

See also Biles Island and Crosswicks in the New Jersey volume.

Near Philadelphia (Nov. 8, 1777; Dec. 25, 1777)
Outside Philadelphia (Feb. 4, 1778)

A party of British light horsemen attacked two squadrons of Continental light horsemen near Philadelphia on Saturday, November 8, 1777. The British drove them, capturing a major and a French officer and some horses and a dragoon.[162]

★ A brigade of militia marched down within musket shot of British lines near Philadelphia on Thursday, Christmas day, 1777. They positioned themselves between Third and Fourth streets and fired eight 12-pound balls at the enemy. The British beat to arms and fired their artillery, raking the militia's right and left but doing no damage. The militia captured one prisoner and several horses.[163]

★ The British captured 30 Continental pickets outside Philadelphia on Wednesday, February 4, 1778. They were taken into the city.[164]

Fairhill, John Dickinson's residence (Nov. 22, 1777)

> Stenton was about a mile north of Philadelphia and about a mile south of the Rising Sun tavern.

Skirmishing became such a problem in the area between Germantown and the British redoubts in Northern Liberties (the area north of Vine Street/Interstate 676) that General William Howe (1732–1786) ordered several fine country houses burned on Monday, November 22, 1777. Fairhill, located on the Germantown Road, just below Stenton was one of the first to be burned. This mansion was owned by Isaac Norris, John Dickinson's (1732–1808) father-in-law. John resided there while his own house was being built on Chestnut Street. James Parker noted in his diary:
> Our out centrys on picket have been frequently fired upon for some days past. The Rebels have occupied Mr. Dickinsons house for a lookout post where at Videt was keept, from the top of the house our movements along the front of the line were seen & Signals made by blowing a horn . . . the house with Several others about it were burnt & the Videt taken.[165]

Robert Morton wrote in his diary for November 22:
> This morning about 10 o'clock the British set fire to Fair Hill mansion House, Jon'a Mifflin's and many others amo'tg to 11 besides out houses, Barns, &c. The reason they assign for this destruction of their friends' property is on acco. of the Americans firing from these houses and harassing their Picquets. [166]

While Morton says there were 11 houses burned along with the furniture, other's say the number was 17 or 27 houses. John Dickinson lost part of his library in the blaze.

Black Horse Tavern (also known as Bryn Mawr, Harrington House, or Rebel Hill) (Dec. 11, 1777; March 17, 1778; March 20, 1778)
Gulph Mill (Dec. 11, 1777)

> The Black Horse Tavern was on the Lancaster Road (now Lancaster Avenue), about 5 miles northwest of Philadelphia. The Merion Meeting House (see Photo PA-17) is at the corner of Montgomery Avenue and Meeting House Lane in Narberth, southeast of Haverford.
> The Tunis Ordinary (see Photo PA-18) is the next building on Montgomery Avenue. Opened in 1704, the tavern was known as the William Penn Inn and Streeper's Tavern in addition to the Tunis Ordinary. General George Washington (1732–1799) and Benjamin Franklin (1706–1790) were guests here. After the war, the building was renamed in honor of Brevet Major General "Mad Anthony" Wayne (1745–1796) who lodged here. The building was purchased in 2005 and transformed into a synagogue, Jewish community center and upscale kosher restaurant. One legend says that a Hessian soldier was shot during a skirmish in 1777. Afraid of British reprisals, the local residents hid his body in the cellar of the tavern because the ground was frozen. Another legend says that Edgar Allan Poe worked on "The Raven" there.

PA-17. Merion Meeting House

PA-18. Tunis Ordinary (Anthony Wayne Inn)

> The first mill in the area of Matson's Ford in West Conshohocken was built in 1747 and operated until 1895. It was an important source of flour during the American War for Independence. There are several markers on route PA 23 at Gulph Mills, just west of West Conshohocken, relating to the events here. Major General Marie Jean Paul Joseph du Motier Marquis de Lafayette (1757–1834) used Matson's Ford during his encampment at Barren Hill [see **Barren Hill** (pp. 68ss)].
>
> Washington made his headquarters at Pont Reading, the home of Joshua Humphrey (1751–1838) (see photo PA-19) (2713 Haverford Road, Ardmore) while his men camped in the fields around the Pont Reading House and the Haverford Meeting House. The house was built at various times between 1683 and 1813. Joshua Humphreys, the designer of the frigate *Constitution*, "Old Ironsides," lived here from 1803–1838.

General George Washington (1732–1799) decided to move his camp after the Battle of Whitemarsh. His troops broke camp early Thursday morning, December 11, 1777 and left Whitemarsh toward Valley Forge. Although the distance between the two is not more than 13 miles, Washington's army was on the road to its new camp site for more than a week.

They left Whitemarsh and marched north 3 miles to Gulph Mills and bivouacked. As he prepared for battle at Whitemarsh, Washington had his tents and baggage removed as a precaution. They were now at Trappe, 18 miles to the northwest. He intended to cross to the west side of the Schuylkill River at Matson's Ford by a bridge "consisting of 36 waggons, with a bridge of Rails between each."[167]

The Delaware and Schuylkill rivers protected the city of Philadelphia on three sides, which gave the Crown forces a sense of security. However, the army needed a substantial amount of food, supplies, and other items to sustain life in the city during the almost nine month occupation. The navy could not satisfy the demand using the Delaware

PA-19. Pont Reading. General George Washington made his headquarters at this house while his men camped in the neighboring fields and at the Haverford Meeting House

River, so the supply route had to come overland through Whig territory, and Washington positioned his army across the supply route between the Crown forces and their munitions.

The Continentals could harass the Regulars continually and there were many skirmishes at British outposts using hit-and-run tactics. General William Howe (1732–1786) tried to solve both of these problems by sending General Charles Cornwallis (1738–1805) and 3,500 men on a foraging mission in the countryside west of Philadelphia.

Lord Cornwallis's troops consisted of all the dragoons, most of the light infantry, jaegers, guards, chasseurs, and most of five regular line regiments. They crossed the Schuylkill River at Middle Ferry (today's Market Street) on Thursday, December 11, 1777. On their return that evening with a quantity of forage, cattle, etc., they met a brigade of Continentals who had crossed the Schuylkill after them. The Continentals fired on the foragers as they used the ferry. The British dragoons charged, killing more than 30 and taking nine light horsemen prisoners and forcing the rest to re-cross the river. The British lost only two men killed and Captain Ball, of the 63rd light company, wounded. The column then proceeded west along the Lancaster Road.[168]

The column arrived in the village of Hestonville (where 52nd Street and Lancaster Avenue intersect in West Philadelphia) just before dawn. According to legend, Colonel Edward Heston (1745–1824), a Whig, saw the troops, rushed from his house naked, mounted his horse and rode as quickly as possible to warn General Enoch Poor's (1736–1780) pickets of the Pennsylvania militia at the Black Horse Tavern, about a mile west on the Lancaster Road (where 54th Street crosses City Lane Avenue at St. Joseph's University).

General Washington's orders to the militia were to keep the Crown forces inside Philadelphia and the Pennsylvanians outside to prevent any commerce with the enemy.

Their area of patrol included the rich farmland and many mills in modern West Philadelphia, Delaware County, and Montgomery County south of the Schuylkill River.

Brigadier General James Potter (1729–1789), who had been detached from Brigadier General John Armstrong's (1717–1795) Pennsylvania militia division, commanded between 600 and 1,600 men organized into five militia regiments. They had just returned to this area of Pennsylvania on their way to join the main army at Whitemarsh. Several days before, it appeared that General Howe planned to make a large-scale assault against General Washington; but when General Howe withdrew back into Philadelphia, Colonel Potter went to cover the territory west and south of the Schuylkill River. He made his headquarters at Harrington House, the home of Charles Thomson (1729–1824), secretary of the Continental Congress.

Colonel Heston received warning that General Cornwallis's dragoons were in close pursuit in enough time to chase off the dragoons and await the arrival of Cornwallis's main force. It did not take long for the advancing British infantry to fill the Lancaster Road and the fields bordering it. Both sides exchanged several volleys followed by a sharp skirmish near the Black Horse Tavern. The Redcoats flanked the Continentals and forced them to fall back down the Lancaster Road. The Regulars pursued them to what is today Montgomery Avenue where the first militiamen joined with a second picket at the Merion Meeting House and the Tunis Ordinary (The General Wayne Inn).

Another sustained fight occurred here. The militia veered off the Lancaster Road, were flanked once again, and forced to retreat along the Gulph Road through the Mill Creek Valley. (Mill Creek was Rohens's Mill.) John Roberts (d. 1778), a Quaker miller who had taken refuge in Philadelphia, guided Cornwallis's troops on this expedition. In June 1778, after the British evacuation of Philadelphia, the Continentals captured Roberts, tried him, and executed him for his actions in this affair.

General Potter organized his five militia regiments across the hilly area of what is today called Bryn Mawr (Welsh for Great Hill) to block the British advance. His forward troops fell back on their main body when Lord Cornwallis's troops appeared. The first line of militia fired their weapons and fell back behind the second line which fired in turn. This strategy allowed Potter's militia to hold off a superior force, equipped with superior weapons, and composed of better, professional troops.

Cornwallis's greater numbers and disciplined Regulars eventually forced the militia to retreat. The militiamen held their own as they withdrew slowly and suffered few casualties. After 4 miles, the Regulars pressured the front and flanked the militiamen, forcing them to break ranks and run on the gradual hill along Gulph Road that runs down to Gulph Mills. This is where they suffered most of their casualties as they ran through the Gulph and up onto what is today called Rebel Hill. From here, they had to go down a rugged and steep incline to Matson's Ford (today's Conshohocken) to cross the Schuylkill River to safety.

Major General John Sullivan (1740–1795) happened to be marching the forward units of main part of the Continental Army down to Matson's Ford just as Potter's militia came over the ridge of Rebel Hill above them. Sullivan's division and half of another had already crossed the temporary bridge constructed for the Continental Army when Sullivan saw the Redcoats. He withdrew all his troops back across the Schuylkill and did nothing to help Potter against Cornwallis. Potter's after-action report noted Sullivan's lack of assistance. However, Sullivan felt he could not take the risk. His men were in an awkward position, astride the river with a rickety bridge between the two banks.

Washington recalled Sullivan and the others with him and broke the bridge. The two forces were then aligned in battle formation, face to face, with a river between them which neither dared to cross. But Potter and his militia, who had been operating on the other side, had not been able to get back before the bridge was broken. Cornwallis scattered them and went on with his foraging. Washington returned to Whitemarsh.

Colonel John Lacey (1755–1814), one of Potter's commanders, in the confused retreat through the Gulph, found himself on a relatively slow horse behind his troops. Some British dragoons pursued him and were closing fast. Lacey called upon his men at the rear of the fleeing column to fire on the dragoons to save him. His men fired their weapons without taking the time to either turn or aim, making Lacey realize that he was safer without their help. He ordered them to cease firing, which they did. One of the dragoons stopped at this point, not wanting to come any closer. Another dragoon rode headlong into the column of militiamen at the same time as Lacey when 20 muskets fired at once, killing the rider and horse instantly. Lacey escaped to tell the story.

Washington had no previous intelligence that Cornwallis was out with a large force and could not risk crossing the Schuylkill where he originally intended. He marched his army about 4 miles west to Swede's Ford and crossed the river there (Norristown today) and eventually returned to Gulph Mills long after Cornwallis and his troops had left. He proceeded to Valley Forge where the army went into winter quarters on Friday, December 19.

Cornwallis marched his troops back to Philadelphia, despoiling and pillaging both Whig and Loyalist farms along the way in Lower Merion, Haverford, Radnor, and other areas. He returned to Harrington House, crossed over the Lancaster Road at the Buck Tavern and took the Haverford Road. That night, he made his headquarters in Joshua Humphreys's (1751–1838) home, Pont Reading, while his men camped in the fields around the Pont Reading house and the Haverford Meeting House. Cornwallis returned to Philadelphia on December 13, with the spoils and livestock captured in eastern Chester County (today's Delaware and Montgomery counties).

A letter from East Bradford reported:

> I this day went down to Haverford, and there found the most destructive piece of work I ever saw. – your brother Anthony Morris's house and place is robbed of every thing the merciless wretches (the English) could take away. They have not even left them or the children anything of food, either bed or blanket, or any cloathing except what they had on their backs—Every thing of his, your's, and your father's they could not take off, they took care to destroy; and what is worse, Anthony is wounded, but I hope not mortally: The English light-horse overtook him about a mile from home, with a party of our troop, who were obliged to retreat; they pursued, caught him and wounded him in fifteen different places. All the fingers of one hand are nearly cut off and the rest are so bad that Dr. Morris was obliged to take one off; his upper lip is split, a piece cut out of his nose, both cheeks cut, after which they robbed him of his horse and money. The officer then left the five who had attack'd him, told them to split the damn'd rebel down, and then follow him; after they had given him several wounds on the head, some of which went through his scull, they left him, and he crept down to one Weiss's, where he now lies; his wife is with him, and in great distress, not having any thing to assist him with. I have left them money, but it is of no service, every neighbour being in the same situation as themselves.[169]

General Washington commended to Congress General Potter and his men who "Behaved with bravery and gave the enemy every possible opposition until he was obliged to retreat from their superior numbers." There are no accurate or reliable records of the losses of either side in this engagement. The Continentals suffered less than 100 total casualties while the Crown forces probably suffered fewer than 40.

★ Detachments were usually sent out the evening before a market day to protect the people who risked everything to bring fresh food to the city. Foraging troops were always looking for these people to seize their goods. Often, a farmer would pay the troops for safe conduct which would raise the market price of the food. A detachment of British light infantry surprised some Congressional troops on the Westfield road, on the other side of the Schuylkill, on Tuesday, March 17, 1778. They killed four and took 18 prisoners.[170]

★ A strong Continental outpost was detached from Valley Forge at the Gulph Ferry Mill 15 miles from Philadelphia. A party of 60 men left this post Thursday night, March 19, 1778 and headed close to the Schuylkill opposite the 10th Redoubt. They gathered some cattle and set fires. Captain Karl Friedrich Hieronymus, Freiherr von Münchhausen (1720–1797), the Hessian wing adjutant, and 40 mounted jaegers caught up with this party the following morning near the Black Horse Tavern.

The mounted jaegers kept the Continentals occupied until the foot jaegers arrived and began firing. The mounted jaegers then fell upon them and overthrew the Continental dragoons who tried to withdraw on the broad open road. The Hessians captured one lieutenant and 10 men along with 15 horses and killed or wounded several more. The others managed to escape by hiding behind a swamp. The jaegers had only three horses and five men killed and several wounded.[171]

Smithfield (Feb. 14, 1778; April 8, 1778)
York Road near Branchtown (April 8, 1778)

> Branchtown is now Willow Grove, south of Hatboro (Crooked Billet) and north of Jenkintown.

The Crown forces barricaded the York Road at Dr. George de Benneville's (1703–1793) and Thomas Nedrow's houses near Branchtown. The Pennsylvania militia offered no resistance and seemed to retreat. The first skirmish in Smithfield occurred on Saturday, February 14, 1778 when Loyalist Captain Thomas and a party of foot and horse soldiers advanced up the Newtown Road as far as Smithfield, surprised Brigadier General John Lacey (1755–1814) and the 80 men stationed there to keep a closer watch on the enemy. The Loyalists either killed or captured 40 men—about half of General Lacey's force.[172]

★ A second skirmish in Smithfield occurred on Wednesday, April 8, 1778. Captain Evan Thomas (1745–1835), the Bucks County Volunteer Company, and 40 Pennsylvania dragoons advanced to the Old York crossroad near Branchtown on Tuesday and pursued about 25 Continental troops in the vicinity of Bustleton. The pursuit did not continue farther than Bustleton, so the Continentals thought they were out of danger. They halted at Vanhorn's hotel in Smithfield, to spend the night.

About 2 AM, approximately 300 men, mostly Loyalists, surprised Captain Jacob Humphreys (1751–1826) and his small party. Captain Humphreys narrowly escaped from the house where he was lodging. (Another account reports the attackers as 100 British infantrymen and 20 dragoons.) Humphreys got some of his men out the back of another house just as the enemy entered the front. They left their arms behind and ran to another party of about 12 men a little farther away. Together, they kept up a warm fire until the Loyalists withdrew. One of Humphreys's men fell over a fence, trying to escape, just as a soldier discharged his musket at him and was presumed dead. When the enemy retired, he escaped unharmed. Captain Humphreys lost one officer and 15 soldiers killed, two men wounded, and one officer and nine men captured. The Loyalists' loss is not known, but must have been considerable judging from the blood found on the road the next morning. British Captain John Montresor (1736–1799) also reported on this battle and results of two other patrols by the British 17th dragoons in which the Congressional forces lost 38 killed, 1 wounded, and about 10 captured.[173]

Spring House
Spring House Tavern (Feb. 14, 1778)

> Spring House tavern was on the Bethlehem Road, now Bethlehem Pike, in what is now the Spring House neighborhood of Ambler, about 16 miles north of Philadelphia.

A considerable body of British light infantry, accompanied by a party of light horsemen, made an excursion into the country to a place called the Spring-House tavern, about 16 miles north of Philadelphia on Saturday, February 14, 1778. They captured Major Wright of the Pennsylvania militia and a number of civic leaders, such as magistrates, assessors, constables, etc. who were pointed out by the Loyalists of that neighborhood. They then went out in three divisions, part of them through Germantown, where they broke many windows, seized all the leather, stockings, etc., and returned to Philadelphia the same evening.[174]

Smithfield (Feb. 18, 1778)
Newtown (Feb. 18, 1778)
Jenks's Mill (Feb. 18, 1778)

> Smithfield was probably in northeast Philadelphia in the vicinity of Benjamin Rush State Park. Newtown is about 8 miles north of Smithfield and about 23 miles north of Philadelphia.

Captain Moore Hovenden, with a party of 24 Loyalist dragoons, and Captain Evan Thomas (1745–1835), with 14 foot soldiers, left Philadelphia about 8 PM on Wednesday, February 18, 1778 and headed into Bucks County. They surprised and captured a guard of 30 Continental militiamen at Mr. Jenks's fulling mill (bleachery) in Smithfield. The militiamen were "guarding a considerable quantity of cloth belonging to the poor people of the country." The attackers struck quickly and without firing a gun which would have alarmed another post. They took the whole guard prisoners and proceeded to Newtown, a short distance farther, where they surprised and took the first sentry without alarm.

As the Loyalists approached Major Francis Murray's quarters at Newtown, the sentry at his door fired at them, alarming the guard, a detachment of the 13th Pennsylvania Regiment, about 40 yards away. The 16 guards, under cover of the guardhouse, discharged their weapons on the troops surrounding them. The attackers returned fire and stormed the guardhouse before the guards could reload. They killed five, wounded four, and took the remaining 29 guards prisoners along with a considerable quantity of cloth. They suffered no casualties and returned to Philadelphia about 6 PM the next evening with the wounded and prisoners.[175]

See **near Whitemarsh** (February 14, 1778) (p. 27).

Marcus Hook (mid-March 1778; March 18, 1778)

Marcus Hook is on the Delaware River, about 4 miles south of Chester.

Some small armed vessels were trading off Marcus Hook a few days before March 16, 1778. Captain Enoch Anderson (1745–1820) and a party of 30 infantrymen and horsemen were ordered to observe their movements. The vessels landed more than 30 well-armed men who advanced on Captain Anderson's party which immediately engaged them and routed them, killing four, capturing eight, and wounding several others as they were getting in their boats.[176]

★ Some Crown troops went to Salem, New Jersey to plunder and carry off forage on Wednesday, March 18, 1778. The New Jersey militia captured nine seamen from the small landing party and learned that they intended to destroy the salt works at Egg Harbor, to collect all the forage on both sides of the river, and to destroy Egg Harbor and Marcus Hook on their return. Brigadier General William Smallwood (1732–1792) ordered the "removal of all the Hay that possibly can be carried from the River course" and dispatched a party for that purpose and to burn what could not be moved.[177]

Barren Hill (April 24, 1778; May 20, 1778)

Major General Marie Jean Paul Joseph du Motier Marquis de Lafayette (1757–1834) camped on Barren Hill, now called Lafayette Hill. The site is now occupied by the Masonic Lodge on Ridge Pike. A stone marker on Ridge Pike commemorates Lafayette's encampment. St. Peter's Lutheran Church is on Church Road, off Ridge Pike, just past the Masonic Lodge. A marker on Church Road at Route U.S. 422 identifies the church. In addition to the graves of several soldiers of the Revolutionary War, the cemetery has an enclosed grave site for 6 Oneidas (see Photo PA-20) who died here. Farmar's Mill (now called Mather Mill) (see Photo PA-4) is on Mathers Lane in front of Hope Lodge at the site of the Whitemarsh encampment.

British light infantry skirmished with some Continentals at Barren Hill on Friday, April 24, 1778. They killed one, wounded four, and captured 51.

★ General Henry Clinton (1730–1795) had been appointed to replace General William Howe (1732–1786) who had resigned his command of the Crown forces in North America. The news that the French would support the Congressional cause persuaded Clinton to consider moving his troops to New York City. He feared the French navy would block the mouth of the Delaware River and trap him in Philadelphia.

General George Washington's (1732–1799) army was camped at Valley Forge about 20 miles northwest of Philadelphia. His spies told Washington that the British planned to evacuate Philadelphia, but Washington did not know when they would leave or whether they would travel by land or by sea. He also wondered if the Redcoats would attack Valley Forge before leaving. He needed more intelligence, so he selected 20-year-old Major General Marie Jean Paul Joseph du Motier Marquis de Lafayette (1757–1834) for this mission.

Lafayette was one of the few senior major generals in camp and the most prominent of all Frenchmen serving with the Continental Army at that point. Washington regarded him as a son and selecting him would honor the new French alliance. Washington entrusted him with about 2,200 Continentals, militiamen, and Native Americans—

PA-20. Grave of Oneida warriors in St. Peter's Lutheran Church. The plot is enclosed by an iron rail. The cemetery also contains the graves of several soldiers of the Revolutionary War. (Courtesy of Deborah Mulligan.)

approximately one-third of the strength of his army—and sent them with some horses and five cannons to obtain the needed intelligence.

He instructed Lafayette "to be a security to this camp and a cover to the country between the Delaware and the Schuylkill, to interrupt communications with Philadelphia, to obstruct the incursions of the enemy's parties, and to obtain intelligence of their motions and designs." He also reminded Lafayette: "You will remember, that your detachment is a very valuable one, and that any accident happening to it would be a very severe blow to this army."[178]

★ Lafayette led his troops out of Valley Forge at 10 AM on Monday, May 18, 1778 under overcast but clearing skies. They crossed the Schuylkill River at Swede's Ford, near present-day Norristown, then followed the Ridge Road until they got to Barren Hill, about halfway between Valley Forge and Philadelphia. They made camp on top of Barren Hill, just south of Matson's Ford, where they stayed for two nights.

A network of roads from every direction converged here. The Manatawny or Ridge Road from Philadelphia, via Germantown, passed through Barren Hill on its way north to Swede's Ford. A road from Whitemarsh and Chestnut Hill in the east crossed Ridge Road in the village; and another road from Germantown crossed Ridge Road about a mile north of Barren Hill near Matson's Ford.

The ridge and the river on his right flank gave Lafayette a sense of security. He placed Brigadier General Enoch Poor's (1736–1780) brigade of New York and New Hampshire Continentals in the center on top of the hill on a small elevation south of the church facing south. He placed his five field pieces in front of this line. He positioned the Connecticut Continentals and Brigadier General James Mitchell Varnum's (1748–1789) brigade of Rhode Islanders at St. Peter's Lutheran Church and its burial ground on the left as well as at several stone houses that could be turned easily into miniature fortresses.

The road they followed from Valley Forge, in their rear, could also serve for retreat if necessary. Captain Allen McLane's (1746–1829) dragoons and about 50 Oneida warriors patrolled the Ridge Road about a mile south of the camp as pickets in front of the detachment. Brigadier General James Potter's (1729–1789) 600 Pennsylvania militiamen guarded the road network on the far left, at Whitemarsh, that led to Lafayette's rear. Lafayette himself was in the center of camp, aided and protected by two companies of Washington's personal lifeguard.

Lafayette had all the roads covered as well as the three fords across the Schuylkill in the event of a retreat. He then had McLane send spies into the city to gather intelligence about troop movements in Philadelphia.

The British were celebrating a spectacular event known as the Mischianza to honor their commander, General William Howe (1732–1786), prior to his departure. The wild party began on Monday, May 18 and lasted into the early morning of the 19th. Loyalist informers and scouts informed the general at the party that Lafayette and a force of Continentals had occupied Barren Hill. Howe decided to lead an expedition personally to trap "The Boy" after everyone had recovered from the party.

Even though General Henry Clinton (1730–1795) was technically in command from May 11 on, General Howe retained his leadership role until he departed on May 24. The capture of Lafayette would be a fitting end to his service in North America. He took most of his army out of Philadelphia, leaving General Alexander Leslie (1740–1794) to guard the city with 2,300 men. He divided his troops into four parts. Howe personally led the main body, about 6,000 men, accompanied by Clinton and Admiral Richard Howe (1726–1799). They marched out of Philadelphia at 5:30 AM on Wednesday, May 20, 1778. They proceeded up the Lime-kiln and Old York roads to Germantown where they took the Ridge Road directly toward the center of Lafayette's camp at Barren Hill.

When the dragoons at the head of the column suddenly came upon the Oneidas on picket duty on the Ridge Road, the terrified Oneidas, unaccustomed to mounted troops, sprang up with terrifying whoops and yells that frightened both the horses and the dragoons. The dragoons and the Oneidas fled in opposite directions.

Major General Charles Grey (1729–1807) took a few dragoons and 2,000 grenadiers (see photo PA-9) up past Chestnut Hill to strike Lafayette's left flank. Captain Johann von Ewald (1744–1813) guarded the ford at Levering's Mill near the falls of the Schuylkill with some jaegers and horses. Howe used a maneuver similar to the one he used successfully at Long Island and Brandywine. He sent the main columns in a frontal attack and a flanking column to the rear, trapping the Continentals between the two columns with no escape, to the front or rear.

The flanking column of 5,000 men and 15 guns under Brigadier General James Grant (1720–1806) left first at 10:30 PM on May 19. They took the road for Frankford and New York to deceive enemy spies. These troops comprised the best of the army. The dragoons led the column, followed by the Queen's Rangers, both light infantry battalions, the guards, three line regiments, and 15 cannon. They marched north and circled west along the Old York Road to Church Road. They then took the Skippack Pike to the Broad Axe Inn where they turned left on today's Butler Pike. They marched past the Plymouth Meeting to the junction of the Ridge Road near today's Conshohocken, about 1.5 miles north of Barren Hill. They planned to box in the Continentals on three sides with the river on the fourth, forcing them to surrender in the face of such overwhelming numbers. They would spring the trap the next morning.

Lieutenant Colonel John Graves Simcoe's (1752–1806) Queen's Rangers successfully got behind Lafayette without his knowledge, arriving at their position about daybreak. A Captain Story, of the Pennsylvania militia, who lived along the Wissahickon Creek at Farmar's Mill, north of the junction of the Bethlehem and Skippack roads, heard the troops on the road. He saw the red coats and jumped out his window in his nightclothes and raced to warn Lafayette of the danger. When he reached the camp, Story found the troops asleep. He met Lafayette's surgeon and informed him of the British march. When the surgeon went to Lafayette's tent, the general was interviewing a young lady spy who was going into Philadelphia that day to observe the British. The news did not disturb Lafayette as he had sent some dragoons in red coats to General Potter and his militia. Maybe Story had seen them.

General Grant had already seized the crossroads behind General Lafayette's camp. Lafayette sent couriers to Valley Forge, 11 miles away, requesting Washington for help. They returned with reports that the British had cut off all roads to the rear. Captain McLane and his dragoons, in front of the camp, had also run into the troops coming from Germantown. They captured two grenadiers at Three Mile Run who gave McLane the whole story. McLane immediately sent word to Lafayette who now realized he was caught between two enemy forces who held the roads to the nearest fords, Swede's, Bevin's, and Matson's.

Panic began to spread in the Continental camp as the men thought they were surrounded. Lafayette remained calm in the confusion. His surgeon had returned with information about a secret and hidden path that ran from Barren Hill down to the river and then along it to Matson's Ford 3 miles away. The drop was so sudden, so concealed by the height above, that Lafayette could march his army immediately out of both Grant's and Grey's sight.

If the Continentals could delay General Grant, the rest of the army might be able to retreat. Lafayette sent more men to St. Peter's Church and the burial grounds in an attempt to block the British advance. He also formed columns to march toward the British as if they were going to attack. This action confused Grant who could not decide what to do. He pulled in his pickets, leaving the bluff overlooking Lafayette's escape route totally uncovered. Although Grant's force was closer to Matson's Ford than Lafayette's position, Grant wondered what the attack meant, giving Lafayette an opportunity to evacuate his troops who marched in platoons taking the hidden road to the ford with Poor's division in the lead.

At Matson's Ford, the Schuylkill River ran about three to four feet high with a rapid current. The Continentals linked arms to cross without losing anybody. As the last troops crossed, a brisk skirmish ensued over the two guns, which were the last to cross. The retreat was successful and the guns were saved. The Continentals quickly set up defenses on the heights of the west bank to defend against a British attack which did not come.

The Redcoats on top of the bluff saw the Continentals escaping and begged General Grant for permission to attack. He refused, believing it was a trick to draw him away from the main attack at the church because he saw the enemy columns coming right at him through the woods in front of him.

Realizing that something was wrong, General Washington, in Valley Forge, had three cannons fired as an alarm to alert the entire army to assist Lafayette. Even though some troops got across Sullivan's Bridge, they were not needed. Grant's column alone outnumbered the Continentals two to one; but the Continentals were moving to his rear and preparing to strike him in the front. He now found himself trapped between two

Congressional forces and about to be captured rather than being the captor. He decided to strike out at the attackers to his front.

After most of his troops were safely on their way, Lafayette withdrew his men from the churchyard area. As the rear guard proceeded down the river path with two additional cannons, General Grant mistook them for the van and ordered an immediate advance on St. Peter's and Barren Hill. Grey's troops met Grant's at Barren Hill which was now empty.

General Grant sent Brigadier General William Erskine (1728–1795) down the Ridge Road to meet General Howe who was leading his column toward Barren Hill. When he received Erskine's news of Lafayette's escape, Howe turned his men about and marched back to Philadelphia where they arrived about 2 PM.

General Grant sent his cavalry in pursuit, but they took the Spring Mill Road instead of the more direct route and failed to get to the river bank in time. When they arrived, they clashed with the Continental rear guard. Both sides suffered casualties with the Continentals losing between nine and 40 men killed, wounded, or missing and the Crown forces losing an undetermined number, including seven dragoons killed at Matson's Ford. Grant and his column arrived in Philadelphia in the evening. Some of his officers were so angry with him, they would not speak to him.

Lafayette and his troops proceeded to Gulph Mills and then to Swede's Ford again. The following day, May 21, they crossed the Schuylkill again and returned to their former campground on Barren Hill where they stayed for another three days before rejoining Washington at Valley Forge.[179]

North Wales (April 26, 1778)

A party of Colonel Oliver de Lancey, Jr.'s (1749–1822) light dragoons skirmished with a party of Northhampton County militiamen at the 20 mile stone near North Wales Meeting House on Sunday, April 26, 1778. They killed 12 or 14 and took five prisoners.[180]

Biles Island (May 9, 1778)

> Biles Island is an island in the Delaware River south of Trenton, New Jersey.

After raiding Bordentown, the Crown troops re-embarked, passed over the river and landed. At 5 AM the next morning, Saturday, May 9, 1778, the galleys *Hussar* and *Ferret* and some boats proceeded up to Biles Island, where several vessels were set on fire. The boats went up to Watson's Creek, where they found the Congressional galleys with only their masts above water. The militiamen fired a number of cannon shots at the boats but did no damage. The two galleys ran aground and exchanged some shots with the militiamen from the lower point of the island. The galleys were refloated several hours later.

As the exasperated seamen waited for the tide to rise, they went to Colonel Joseph Kirkbride's (1731–1803) farm where they set fire to the house, all his buildings and the ferry house. General Philemon Dickinson (1739–1809) sent a detachment of militiamen down the river to protect the inhabitants from small raiding parties. They captured an enemy sloop with six men on board and loaded with plunder.

The troops then marched to Bristol where they waited for the vessels. They burned two ships at Bristol and several below Burlington. They destroyed a total of two frigates, two privateers (one of 14, the other of 10 guns), one large ship pierced for 24 guns, nine other ships, and 14 or 15 smaller vessels. The excursion returned on Sunday without losing a man.[181]

2
DELAWARE

The Philadelphia Wagon Road ran through the northern part of Delaware, making it an important transportation crossroads. Delaware contributed a total of 2,762 men to the war effort—376 militia and 2,386 Continental Army (see Photo DE-1). Although it only had a single regiment, that unit fought with distinction in many battles of the war. They earned the nickname the "Blue Hen Chickens" after a particularly fierce breed of fighting gamecock.

> The Historical Society of Delaware (505 Market Street at the intersection of Sixth and Market Streets, Wilmington, DE 19801; phone: 302-655-7161) maintains the Delaware History Museum, a research library, and three historic sites. The state tourism office is at 99 Kings Highway, Dover, DE (phone: 302-739-4271; website: **www.visitdelaware.com**). The Division of Historical and Cultural Affairs and the Delaware State Museum administer the Delaware State Visitors Center at 406 Federal Street, Dover, DE (phone: 302-739-4266; website: **www.destatemuseums.org**).

See the map of Maryland and Delaware.

DE-1. Members of the Brigade of the American Revolution portraying soldiers of the Delaware Regiment

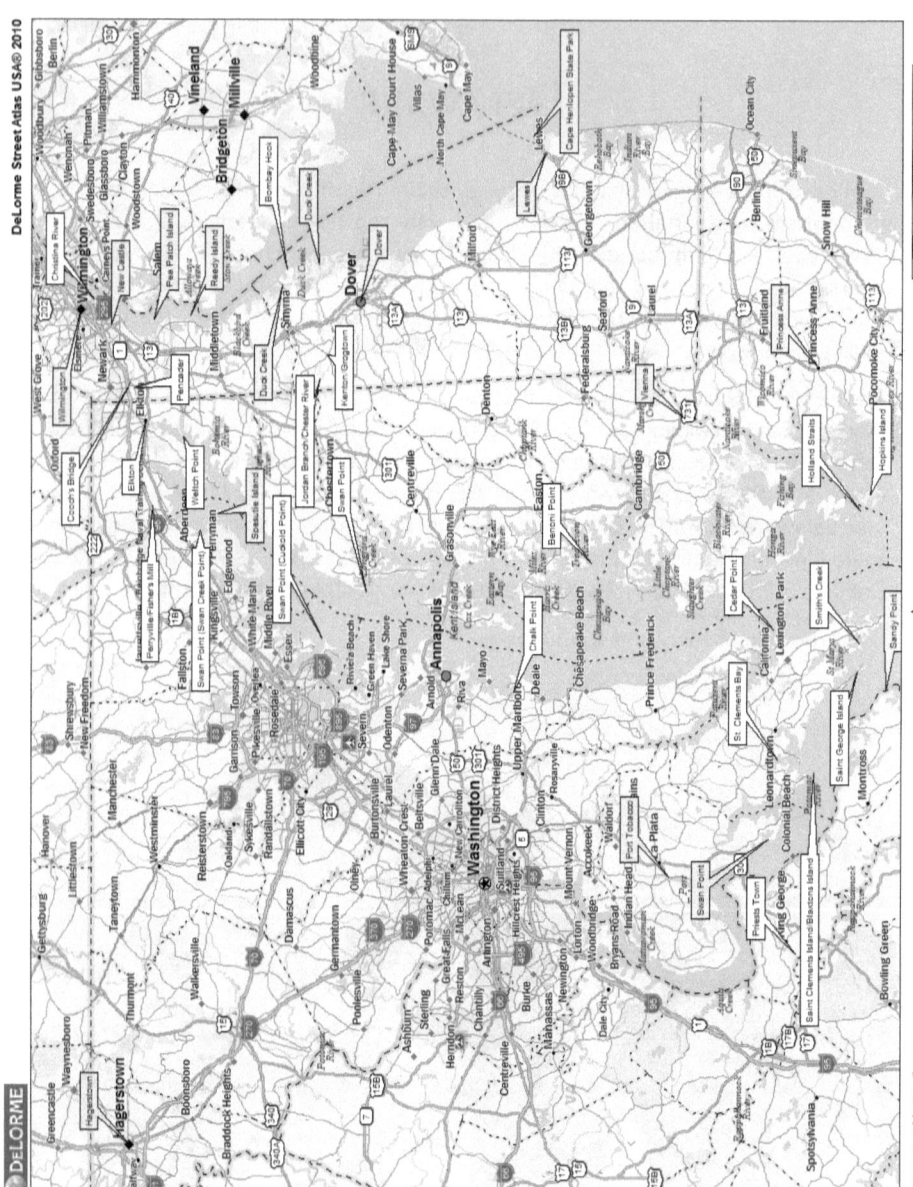

Maryland and Delaware: Map for The Guide to the American Revolutionary War in Pennsylvania, Delaware, Maryland, Virginia, and North Carolina © 2011 DeLorme (www.delorme.com) *Street Atlas USA*®

Lewes (March 28, 1776; May 1776; ca. June 20, 1776; Aug. 6, 1777)

> Lewes is on Delaware Bay south of Dover and opposite Cape May, New Jersey.

Captain Henry Fisher (1735–1792), a pilot from Lewes, notified the Pennsylvania Committee of Safety on Wednesday, March 27, 1776, that British vessels appeared in the Lewes roads. The town began to prepare for resistance. The following morning, the 28th, Captain Andrew Snape Hamond (1738–1828), of HMS *Roebuck* which was headed to Richmond, Virginia, sent the sloop *Plymouth* with Lieutenant George Ball, the *Roebuck*'s third lieutenant, and some sailors to Lewes about 4 AM. The helmsman fell asleep and the boat drifted to shore. The landing party burned the interior of the Cape Henlopen Lighthouse and captured some cattle feeding on the marsh. Colonel John Haslet (1737–1777) divided his two companies of Delaware militiamen and attacked the *Plymouth*, killing two and capturing four, including Lieutenant Ball. The prisoners were put aboard a pilot boat and sent to headquarters.[1]

★ Captain Andrew Snape Hamond (1738–1828), of HMS *Roebuck*, had a few shots fired at the town of Lewes with little effect in early May 1776 when he was joined by the 28-gun sloop of war *Liverpool*. The two vessels sailed northward and cruised between Chester, Pennsylvania and the mouth of the Christina River where they were attacked, in front of Wilmington, by row galleys under Captain Thomas Houston, of Philadelphia, and forced to retreat.

★ On Tuesday, June 11, 1776, the Lewes Committee notified Congress that about 1,000 Loyalists had reportedly assembled about 18 miles from Lewes to cooperate with the British vessels off the coast of Lewes.[2]

★ In June 1776, the Whigs circulated petitions calling for a constitutional convention. The Loyalists circulated a counter-petition and claimed that they had obtained 5,000 signatures while the Whigs only had 300. John Clark of Kent County was on his way to present the Loyalists' petition to Congress when he was seized and the petition destroyed.

Thomas Robinson led a band of 1500 men in insurrection about June 20, 1776. He and his men assembled near Lewes and asked Captain Andrew Snape Hamond, of HMS *Roebuck*, for arms and ammunition. Captain Hamond was forced to refuse the request because of limited supply. Robinson and his men cut off the garrison at Lewes until Colonel Samuel Miles (d. 1805) and 3,000 Pennsylvania militiamen arrived to disperse them. Robinson was forced to post two bonds of £2,500 each. The Assembly later pardoned all the participants.[3]

★ The following year, Captain Daniel Murphy was ordered to go to Cedar Creek with two parties of infantrymen, one on each side of the creek, to seize all the craft there and to prevent the Crown forces from using them to receive supplies. On his way to Cedar Creek on Wednesday, August 6, 1777, he encountered an enemy sloop from New York which prevented him from executing his orders. He seized the sloop then had to defend it against a British attempt to recapture it. He had one man wounded. Colonel Richard Richardson, Sr. (1704–1780) ordered his officers to burn all the vessels in that creek and to disarm the inhabitants before returning to camp.[4]

Near Cape Henlopen (April 7, 1776; April 2, 1777)

> Cape Henlopen is at the tip of Cape Henlopen State Park east of Lewes and at the eastern end of Route U.S. 9.

Boats from HMS *Roebuck*, under Captain Andrew Snape Hamond (1738–1828), chased the schooner *Farmer* ashore near Cape Henlopen on Sunday, April 7, 1776. Captain Charles Pope's (1748–1803) Delaware militia drove off the boats and prevented the capture of the *Farmer*.

★ The HMS *Perseus* spotted the South Carolina Navy brig *Defence* off Cape Henlopen at 10 AM on Wednesday, April 2, 1777. Together with the HMS *Roebuck*, they gave chase at noon. Both frigates fired several volleys of small arms and 9-pounders at the *Defence* and brought her to. Captain Charles Phipps (1753–1786) sent 10 men from the *Perseus* to help the crew of the *Roebuck* take charge of her and to transfer the prisoners to the *Roebuck*. The *Defence* had six 6-pounders and eight 4-pounders and a crew of 87 men. Lieutenant John Orde (1751–1824) went to command the *Defence* with 20 men from the *Roebuck* and 7 from the *Perseus*.[5]

★ During the severe winter of 1779–1780, the HMS *Roebuck* was anchored off Cape Henlopen when a press-gang from her crew was sent ashore to obtain food. They captured 17-year-old Thomas Fisher (1761–1835) at his father's farm near Lewes and brought him and an African American slave aboard the *Roebuck*. Captain Hamond notified the boy's parents that they could ransom their son and the slave only if they delivered 100 bullocks on board the *Roebuck*. The cattle were driven across the solidly frozen bay to the *Roebuck* and the captives were promptly released and returned home unharmed.[6]

Wilmington (May 5–12, 1776; Aug. 31, 1777; Sept. 1, 1777; Sept. 13, 1777; Sept. 25, 1777; Oct. 13, 1777; Dec. 27, 1777; Jan. 14, 1778: June 11, 1778)
Delaware River above Wilmington (Jan. 1778)
Delaware River (Jan. 6, 1778)

> Wilmington is in northeastern Delaware near the junction of Brandywine Creek and the Delaware River. Pea Patch Island is in the Delaware River south of New Castle.

On Sunday, May 5, 1776, General Sir Henry Clinton (1730–1795) issued a proclamation from the sloop of war *Pallas* declaring North Carolina in a state of rebellion. He ordered the dissolution of all congresses and offered pardon to everyone who swore allegiance to the Crown, except the arch-rebels Cornelius Harnett (ca. 1723–1781) and Colonel Robert Howe (1732–1786). The 48-gun HMS *Roebuck,* under Captain Andrew Snape Hamond (1738–1828), and the 28-gun *Liverpool*, together with their tenders, were at anchor in the Delaware River off Wilmington that morning. They had driven a vessel ashore and began to unload her cargo of bread and flour.

The townspeople deployed some militiamen to prevent the sailors from coming ashore for supplies or provisions. They boarded row galleys and launches and engaged the warships about 2 PM. The Royal Navy and the militiamen fired at each other from a distance for two hours, firing between 300 and 400 shots between them. The militia fleet received a single shot which struck the *Camden* but did little damage.

The *Roebuck* and the *Liverpool* forced the militia vessels to enter Wilmington Creek (now known as the Christina River) where they spent the night with the Crown forces anchored abreast of the creek. In the morning of Wednesday, May 8, 1776, a flag of truce went ashore to negotiate the release of Lieutenant George Ball, the *Roebuck*'s third lieutenant captured off Lewes on March 28. About 1 PM, Captain Hammond spotted

Commodore John Hazlewood (ca. 1726–1800) coming down from Philadelphia with a fleet of 13 row galleys, a floating battery of ten 18-pounders, and a sloop fitted as a fire ship. Each row galley had a gun ranging from 18- to 32-pounders.[7]

The HMS *Roebuck* set sail to meet Commodore Hazlewood; but the wind put her at a disadvantage and forced her to keep at a distance. A brisk cannonade ensued between the two forces that lasted for two hours until 4:30 PM. After the men-of-war passed the mouth of Wilmington Creek, Captain Charles Alexander, seeing an opportunity, immediately sailed the *Wasp* out of the creek and captured the brig *Betsey*. The *Roebuck* ran aground on the Jersey shore at Kearney's Point (Carney's Point) a little above Deep Water Point (which is slightly north of where the bridge of I-295 S (U.S. 40) meets the eastern shore of the Delaware River), forcing the *Liverpool* to anchor in order to protect her from the galleys. The *Liverpool* could not get the *Roebuck* off until 4 o'clock the next morning. The militiamen returned to Wilmington Creek. The riflemen and musketmen, who had expended all their cartridges, requested the Pennsylvania Committee of Safety to send more powder and ball.

When the thick fog cleared about 8 AM on May 9th, the galleys were anchored about 3 miles above the British vessels. The wind now blew up the river and the Crown forces set sail to pursue them. The militiamen immediately set sail and used their oars to avoid the British. The chase lasted about two hours, when the wind died, making it impossible to sail against the ebb tide and shallow water, forcing the *Roebuck* to anchor. The galleys anchored on the western shore about 4 miles farther up river.[8]

★ When the people ignored his proclamation, General Henry Clinton (1730–1795) vented his anger upon the property of Colonel Robert Howe (1732–1786) on Sunday, May 12, 1776. General Charles Cornwallis (1738–1805) and a marauding party of 900 men landed at Howe's plantation in Brunswick and ravaged it. They treated some women at his house brutally and burned some mills in the neighborhood. They marched to surprise Major William Davis, who escaped. Cornwallis lost two men killed, one captured, and several wounded before returning to the fleet of 30 ships which then sailed for New York.[9]

★ Sunday morning, August 31, 1777, Lieutenant General Wilhelm von Knyphausen (1716–1800), Brigadier General William Erskine (1728–1795), and Major General Charles Grey (1729–1807) and their troops marched east of Wilmington in search of cattle, wagons and horses which the army needed badly. When a body of Congressional forces appeared, the 23rd Regiment attacked them in a brief skirmish and pushed them back. The Crown forces took three prisoners and two deserters and lost one man killed and five wounded. They took 261 head of horned cattle, 568 sheep and 100 horses. A picket of the 5th Regiment also took 36 head of horned cattle.[10]

★ At daybreak of Monday, September 1, 1777, 200 rangers of Major James Wemyss's (1748–1833) corps attacked an outpost of Congressional forces near Wilmington, capturing the commanding officer, his lieutenant and three prisoners. They killed two and wounded one. The rest of the men—about 100—fled. The attackers reported no casualties. That night, two light horsemen deserted to the Crown forces. In the light rain, two rangers fired at them and both shot the same horse.[11]

★ The Continental Navy frigate *Randolph*, which had recently been refitted at Charleston, South Carolina, captured four vessels near Wilmington a few days before September 19, 1777, probably on Thursday, the 13th. As there were no seamen available there, a number of volunteers and a Mr. John McQueen (1751–1807) with several of his slaves went on board the *Randolph* and proceeded to sea. The *Randolph* took a large three-decked ship of 20 guns and two other vessels of eight guns each bound from Jamaica to New York. Their cargoes consisted of 600 hogsheads of rum, 800 hogsheads of sugar and a chest of johannesses (Portuguese gold currency) believed to belong to the commissary who was also taken aboard the ship. The *Randolph* also retook a French vessel laden with salt.[12]

★ At 4 AM on Thursday, September 25, 1777, at the entrance of Wilmington Creek, a marine lieutenant and 30 privates from the HMS *Liverpool* boarded the HMS *Pearl*. They proceeded down river to Deep Water Point with the HMS *Solebay* and anchored. The *Roebuck* gave the signal at 11 AM for the landing party of marines from the *Pearl* and the *Liverpool* to go ashore to destroy a house where a number of Whigs were lodged.[13]

★ Captain Joseph Stidham (1744–1791), who commanded a company of militiamen, lived in a beautiful home which he called White Hall. It was located near the confluence of Brandywine Creek and the Christina River. When the HMS *Roebuck* and *Liverpool* sailed up Delaware Bay with their tenders to bombard Wilmington, the inhabitants could offer little resistance. Captain Andrew Snape Hamond (1738–1828), of the *Roebuck*, aware that a small body of soldiers was in Wilmington on its way to join General George Washington (1732–1799), sent a company of Hessians ashore in boats to attack the party and disperse them.

The Hessians, supported by the cannon of the men-of-war, overwhelmed the few men who were hidden hastily by their friends. Captain Joseph Stidham was one of them. He fired his weapon at the approaching line of soldiers and fled for his life. He took refuge in the house of Jonas Stidham, Jr. (1744–1811), his cousin, who lived on the outskirts of the village. The *Roebuck*'s gunners saw him enter the house and began to fire upon it. The Hessians attacked it furiously as cannon balls "rained down upon the roof." They broke the doors and windows and rushed into the house searching for Captain Stidham. Stidham did not seek refuge in the many closets and lean-tos of the large, rambling building. Instead, he passed through the house to the barnyard where he slid into the hollow trunk of an oak tree, a favorite boyhood hiding place when he played hide-and-seek. The trunk now had moss and lichen hanging over the opening. The Hessians searched for him in vain, and two of them supposedly sat down on the log while Stidham was in it. The landing party returned to the ship at nightfall, and Stidham escaped to join the Continental Army.[14]

★ The Continentals had constructed earth works both to the land and to the Christina River. The latter had seven cannons. The British 71st Regiment was detached to Wilmington on Monday, October 13, 1777. Major McDonnell took possession of the place without opposition because the works were evacuated. He also took prisoner Mr. John McKinley (1721–1796), the newly appointed president of the Lower Counties on the Delaware.[15]

★ A fleet of 59 British ships, including a 28-gun frigate and a 16-gun sloop came down the Delaware River and anchored at the mouth of Christina Creek Saturday night, December 27, 1777. The wind and tide prevented them from attacking the Continentals at Wilmington.

★ The New Jersey militia captured a prize in the Delaware River north of Wilmington in the first week of January 1778 (probably on Saturday, January 3) and began to unload her. The ice came down the river so thick that the militiamen were obliged to leave her and she drifted to the Delaware shore. The militiamen boarded her and unloaded the following articles: 47 hogsheads of six-year-old Jamaica spirits; 51 pieces of linen; 18 bales of broadcloth; a large quantity of shalloons (a light, twilled woolen fabric used for linings); 17 chests of tea; 60 dozens of stockings, silk, worsted and cotton; 24 dozen of gold and silver laced hats; boxes of glass; 100 dozen of claret and porter, and some pieces of oznaburg. A number of small craft were captured and two topsail vessels were burned by the New Jersey troops. A large ship going down river a few days earlier landed on shore at Reedy Island. The militiamen gathered with a field piece but were unable to capture her. Captain Robert H. Kirkwood (1746–1791) of the Delaware Regiment came down and attempted to capture her.[16]

★ About Tuesday, January 6, 1778, a large schooner drove on shore upon the Pea Patch in the Delaware River due to the ice. She had on board 101 hogsheads of rum and spirits, a large quantity of fine and coarse cloth, India silk, bohea tea, etc. The ice cut through the vessel and the crew surrendered to the Salem County militia. Most of the cargo was saved and stored in a safe place.[17]

★ Captain Brown's sloop *Charming Polly* and Captain Moore's armed brig *Kitty* arrived in Philadelphia on Wednesday, January 14, 1778 from New York. The *Charming Polly* had a cargo of merchandise and sailed from New York on the 6th. As she was anchored off Wilmington on Tuesday the 13th, the Whigs sent a 1-gun sloop and three boats, one with a prow gun (see Photo DE-2), full of armed men from Christina Creek to capture them. As they appeared, the *Kitty* weighed anchor and dropped down with the tide to meet them. The Whig sloop fired at her and the *Kitty* returned fire. The boats hesitated to pursue. The *Charming Polly* fired four or five shots and rowed into the creek.[18]

★ Captain John Collins took some Loyalists aboard the HMS *Camilla* for protection on Thursday, June 11, 1778 and brought them to Philadelphia. He fired a 9-pounder and three rounds of shot from a gunboat at some Congressional forces at Wilmington.[19]

DE-2. Reproduction of a whaleboat with a 1½-pound swivel gun

Dover (June 10, 1776)

> Dover is south of Wilmington.

Captain Richard Bassett (1745–1815) was preparing his Loyalist light horsemen to attack Dover from the north on Friday, June 9, 1776. He planned to deal harshly with the Whigs who favored a new government for the colony and to burn the town. One of Bassett's dragoons revealed the plot to militia Captain Charles Pope (1748–1803) at Duck Creek Crossroads. Pope sent an express to Thomas Rodney (1744–1811) and William Killen, a young lawyer. The messenger arrived in Dover at midnight. Rodney and Killen expected that the Loyalists would try to burn Colonel John Haslett's (1737–1777) house; so they instructed Captain Pope to guard it. Captain Pope sent a party to capture Bassett. They took him in bed early Saturday morning and placed him under parole. They captured other "suspected persons," who were placed under guard, and confiscated ammunition.

When the Loyalists gathered at Puncheon Run, about a quarter of a mile from Dover, to undertake the attack, they learned of the Whig actions. They sent a messenger to request a parley. The request was refused twice. However, two clergymen intervened and negotiated peace.[20]

Newark
Cooch's Bridge (Sept. 3, 1777)
Iron Hill
Pencadder (Sept. 3, 1777)

> The Battle of Cooch's Bridge is also known as the Battle of Iron Hill. Cooch's Bridge Battlefield (website: http://www.dessar.org/History/Coocgift.htm) is on Old Baltimore Pike, off Route DE 896. The only display commemorating the battle is a small memorial of four small cannons (see Photo DE-3) and a descriptive plaque is on Old Baltimore Pike at Old Coochs Bridge Road about half a mile east of Route DE 896 (South College Avenue).
>
> Iron Hill is about a mile west of the Cooch's Bridge Battlefield monument, north of Old Baltimore Pike, and about 2 miles east of the Maryland line. A park occupies the site.
>
> Pencadder is a little less than a mile south-southwest of Cooch's Bridge and near Iron Hill in Newark.

The Crown forces planned to move their main forces from New Jersey to Delaware in the summer of 1777 in preparation for an assault on the colonial capital of Philadelphia, Pennsylvania. They went by sea around the Delmarva Peninsula and disembarked at Head of Elk, now Elkton, Maryland, on the west side of the Elk River, on August 28, 1777. Generals George Washington (1732–1799), Nathanael Greene (1742–1786) and Marie Jean Paul Joseph du Motier Marquis de Lafayette (1757–1834) went to Iron Hill on August 26, 1777, hoping to view the British Army landing along the Elk River. They could only see a few tents. As a severe thunderstorm was approaching, they spent the night at a nearby farm house. After 33 days, the Crown forces were only 20 miles closer to Philadelphia than they were at Perth Amboy, New Jersey, earlier in the summer.

DE-3. Monument commemorating the Battle of Cooch's Bridge. This small memorial of four small 19th-century cannons and a descriptive plaque is the only display commemorating the battle.

They divided into two columns. General Charles Cornwallis (1738–1805) commanded the first column at the Head of Elk and Lieutenant General Wilhelm von Knyphausen (1716–1800) commanded the second at Cecil Courthouse. Major General James Grant (1720–1806) remained at the Head of Elk on Wednesday, September 3, 1777 to preserve communication with the fleet while the two columns joined at Pencadder, about 4 miles east of Elk on the road to Christina Bridge.

The Hessians and the Anspach chasseurs and the second battalion of light infantry, who were at the head of Lord Cornwallis's column, fell in with a chosen corps of 1000 men of the Continental Army who were posted in an advantageous position in the woods near Pencadder. The British defeated the enemy with a loss of only two officers wounded, three men killed and 19 wounded. The Continentals lost no less than 50 killed and many more wounded, according to General William Howe's (1732–1786) report.[21]

★ After harassing the Crown forces for a week, Brigadier General William Maxwell (1733–1796) positioned his 800 light infantrymen (composed of Continentals from New Jersey, North Carolina and Virginia as well as militiamen from New Castle and Chester Counties) near Cooch's Bridge to block General William Howe's (1732–1786) advance on Philadelphia. Maxwell's Corps covered the crucial main road to Philadelphia (today's Old Baltimore Pike).

Lieutenant Colonel Friedrich Wilhelm von Wumb led Howe's advance column, consisting of about 2,000 British light infantrymen and Hessian and Anspach jaegers, on Wednesday morning, September 3, 1777. The advanced guard marched north along the Glasgow to Newark Road into a well-prepared ambush. Some of Maxwell's men fired on the jaegers from concealed positions along the road. The light infantrymen were to engage the enemy and delay their advance.

When they recovered from the surprise, the jaegers overran the first Congressional position, enveloped Maxwell's forces and followed with a bayonet charge. The battle continued for about 2 miles along the road. Maxwell's light infantry performed a series of delaying actions until General Howe reinforced the jaegers with two battalions of British light infantry. These troops tried to outflank Maxwell's position. The area to the right led to an area known as Purgatory Swamp. The approach in this direction effectively removed one battalion from the action.

The drive to the left, on Iron Hill, was more successful in outflanking Maxwell's position. The Continentals held a position at Cooch's Bridge until the Hessians broke their line and forced them across Christina Creek. The infantry fought a series of small delaying actions and risked facing the rest of the Crown forces; so they fled eastward to General Washington's main line north of Cooch's Bridge.

There is great discrepancy in the casualty reports. The militia lost approximately 30 killed and an undetermined number of wounded while the Crown forces suffered between 20 and 30 total casualties. British pioneers buried at least 24 Americans on the field in unmarked graves. The British Army occupied the area from Iron Hill to Aikens Tavern (Glasgow). General Cornwallis made his headquarters at the Cooch house. The Crown forces encamped in the area until September 8 when they marched north through Newark. Both armies clashed again three days later at the Battle of Brandywine (September 11).

The Battle of Cooch's Bridge accomplished little more than delaying the British advance on Philadelphia. The newly formed Congressional light infantry saw its first action here. Legend has it that the "Betsy Ross flag" flew for the first time at Cooch's Bridge. However, the flag may have been the more common one in 1777 of stars in alternating rows of 3, 2, 3, 2, 3 rather than in a circle.[22]

New Castle (Oct. 15, 1777; Dec. 30, 1777)

> New Castle is on the Delaware River 6 miles south of Wilmington, at the junction of Route U.S. 13 (U.S. 40, South Dupont Highway) and Route U.S. 202 (DE 141, West Basin Road).

A party of 60 Delaware militiamen seized three or four British sailors ashore at New Castle on Wednesday, October 15, 1777.

★ On Monday, December 29, 1777, Brigadier General William Smallwood (1732–1792) sent Captain Thomas Erskine (1727–1807) and a party of about 100 Congressional troops to reconnoiter the area around New Castle. At the wharf, they took a sloop loaded with flour, pork, poultry and supplies destined for Philadelphia. Captain Erskine tried to run the sloop up into Christina Creek; but the wind was against him, preventing him from turning up the creek. Captain Erskine ran the sloop on shore in a cove and took the skipper and crew of 68 soldiers and a dozen seamen prisoners, leaving an officer and four men to guard her.

General Smallwood had ordered a party to get her cargo on shore; but ice detained their crossing. A band of Loyalists in an armed shallop appeared within an hour and drove the guard away and retook the sloop. As it was impossible to get the sloop off shore, the Loyalists had an opportunity to gut her.

A short while later, General Smallwood learned that the large armed transport brig *Symmetry* with six 4-pounders and some swivels (see Photo DE-2), bound from New York to Philadelphia, was blown ashore about 5 miles below Wilmington with some soldiers on board. He immediately detached a strong party and two field pieces. Captain Monkman, of the *Symmetry*, thinking they only had muskets, refused to surrender and prepared for battle. After the Congressional forces fired two shots, the *Symmetry* surrendered.

Captain Carmichael, of the 10th Regiment, and 67 soldiers, the master mate and 12 or 15 seamen, and about 40 women, some officers' wives, were taken prisoners. They also took the cargo which was thought to consist of the officers' baggage of four regiments, the camp equipage, some soldiers' clothing and arms, four or five puncheons of rum, some sugar and tea, and possibly the clothing for four regiments and 1,000 or 1,500 stand of arms, pork, butter, and some ammunition. The mud and ice made it difficult for the party of 300 men to unload her. They had to make a bridge almost 100 yards long on the mud and had only one longboat (see Photo DE-4) and a small yawl to remove the cargo. General Smallwood used all the wagons he could muster to bring the goods to town. Three other vessels were also supposedly driven ashore on the Jersey side and their cargoes seized.[23]

DE-4. Longboat of HMS Victory. Longboats were used to ferry troops to and from shore.

Bombay Hook (Jan. 2, 1778; March 7, 1778)
Lower Delaware River (March 9, 1778)

> Bombay Hook is on the Delaware River about 12 miles north of Dover. The March 9, 1778 event occurred between Reedy Island and Christina Creek. Reedy Island is 1 mile east of Port Penn in the Delaware River. Christina Creek is now called the Christina River. It is located in the southern part of Wilmington.

Lieutenant Silas Snow (1760–1793) and about 30 Delaware militiamen attempted to capture an enemy ship caught in the ice at Bombay Hook on Friday, January 2, 1778.[24]

★ Seven half-manned Continental Navy boats attacked and captured two British transport ships near Bombay Hook on Saturday, March 7, 1778. One of the transports was the *Mermaid*, J. Youart, master, with six 4-pounders. The other was the *Kitty*, Joseph Mallet, master, with two swivels (see Photo DE-2). Each had a crew of 14. The boats also captured the armed schooner *Alert*, Daniel Moore, master, belonging to the Engineers Department of the British Army.[25]

★ Seven British transports loaded with hay were on their way from Rhode Island on Monday, March 9, 1778. Commander Christopher Mason's HM Sloop *Dispatch* headed up the Delaware River between Port Penn and Reedy Island that afternoon. As she approached, Captain John Barry (1745–1803) with five armed boats consisting of two barges from the Continental Navy frigate *Effingham*, commanded by Barry and Lieutenant Luke Matthewman (b. 1754), together with a Pennsylvania Navy schooner and two gun boats went out the opposite end of the passage. They set fire to the transport *Mermaid* and fired several shots at the *Dispatch* from a battery.

The *Dispatch*, returned several broadsides as she passed and gave chase to the schooner and gun boats. The gun boats rowed to the shoals, but the *Dispatch* caught the schooner after exchanging several shots and drove her ashore 7 miles below New Castle. With the arrival of the *Experiment,* the *Dispatch* sent her boats to get the schooner off. She proved to be Daniel Moore's armed schooner *Alert* with eight double fortified 4-pounders and twelve 4-pound howitzers. The *Alert*, which had been put under the command of Captain John Montresor (1736–1799) of the Engineers, was carrying much baggage from New York for Captain Montresor and other English officers when she was captured by Captain Barry.[26]

Kenton
Grogtown (April 14, 1778)

> Kenton (Grogtown) is 8 miles northwest of Dover. The area known as the site of "Cheney Clow's Rebellion" is now part of a farm and was selected in 1975 as one of Delaware's first listings in the National Register of Historic Places.
> Cheney (or China) Clow (1734–1788), a Loyalist, built a small fort in western Kent County at two prongs in the Gravelly Branch, a few hundred yards north of what is now Everett's Corner, just east of the Delaware/Maryland border. No visible evidence of the fort remains today. In the early 1990s, a bulldozer leveling the site, unearthed a 15-by-15 foot area of scorched ground along with a 6-by-2 foot area which might have been the site of Clow's unmarked grave. The lack of available records and some of the myths that have grown up around Clow over the years make it difficult to verify the story of the events.

Cheney (or China) Clow (1734–1788), an ardent Loyalist who had been an officer in the British Army during the Seven Years War (French and Indian War), built his fort on land owned by two staunch supporters of the Revolution. He kept his officer's commission during the American War for Independence and, together with his supporters, conducted raids on nearby farms. The farmers of the area appealed to the government in Dover for military protection. Delaware president Caesar Rodney (1728–1784) ordered Lieutenant Colonel Charles Pope (1748–1803) and 140 militiamen to march to western Kent County to put a stop to Clow's raids in April 1778. Pope and his troops camped at Grogtown (now known as Kenton).

Pope reported to Rodney that, on Tuesday, April 14, he and his men got "within a gunshot of their works" and that Clow's 150 men fired on them, forcing them to retreat with the loss of one man killed. Pope requested that Rodney send additional rifle cartridges, whiskey, provisions and a small artillery piece. While Pope was assembling a larger expedition, the Loyalists fled. When Pope's militia returned, they burned the "fort" and a stolen supply of bacon and two barrels of flour. Had Clow not been stopped, he might have marched against Dover where the legislature was in session. Rodney reported to the General Assembly, on April 18, that Pope had, "routed Mr. Clow & his army, and burnt the fort." Clow escaped, probably into Maryland, but about 50 of his men were captured later.[27]

Clow was back in Delaware by 1782. As his home was so close to the Maryland border, he may have considered himself a Marylander. When Clow refused to take an oath of allegiance, authorities issued an arrest warrant, charging him with treason. The Kent County sheriff sent a large posse to capture Clow. Joseph Moore (d. 1782), one of the sheriff's men, was killed in a furious gun battle that occurred at the Clow homestead. The sheriff's forces battered down the door to find only Clow and his wounded wife. They let Clow change into his British army uniform before taking him to jail in Dover.

Clow was tried for treason in December 1782 but was acquitted, claiming his status as a British officer. He was later charged with the murder of Joseph Moore, convicted and sentenced to death, despite his plea of not guilty and evidence that Moore might have been accidentally shot by his own men. He languished in jail for more than five years when he was hanged in 1788 and buried in an unmarked grave.[28]

Jordan's Island, Chester River (April 17, 1778)

Jordan's Island may have been in the Jordan Branch of the Chester River, about 10 to 12 miles northwest of Dover.

Brigadier General William Smallwood (1732–1792) stationed at Wilmington in April 1778, sent Lieutenant Colonel Charles Pope (1748–1803) to suppress an insurrection of Loyalists at Jordan's Island on Friday, April 17, 1778.[29]

Duck Creek, Kent County (May 8, 1778; Feb. 19, 1783; March 17, 1783)

Duck Creek runs on the west side of Bombay Hook and empties into the outlet called the "Thoroughfare." The main branch of Duck Creek originally followed the course of old Duck Creek to the west of Bombay Hook and Little Bombay Hook, and entered the bay at the mouth of Simon's or Dona Creek. Little Duck Creek, then known as the southwest branch, emptied into the main branch at the point near where it now enters the bay—the canal between Bombay Hook and Little Bombay Hook.[30] Cedar Swamp is north of the "Thoroughfare."

Mr. Joseph Judson was court martialed before May 17, 1778 for trading with the British and for heading a party in the neighborhood of Port Penn and capturing Lieutenant John Vance Hyatt (1755–1806) of the Delaware Regiment on Sunday, April 26, 1778. Lieutenant Hyatt went to his father's house to recover from a wound he received. Mr. Judson also stole a good deal of property at the same time. His plundering was mainly concentrated in the area of Duck Creek and Bombay Hook. He was captured in the "Thoroughfare "of Duck Creek on May 12 after a smart engagement with Captain Peter Jaquett (1755–1834) who had been detached to Cantwells Bridge with 50 men to guard and escort the removal of the stores. Judson was in a barge carrying a 2-pounder in her bow, two swivels and two howitzers along with a Captain Cook and 16 men armed with muskets. The barge was loaded with goods and wheat which he had just traded for.

Judson was on board his schooner of 10 carriage guns. He had used the schooner for trading all winter, loading her twice a week at Duck Creek until Captain Peter Jaquett attacked him with 30 men, took the barge, and killed, wounded and captured 14, including Captain Cook and his mate on Friday, May 8, 1778.[31]

★ During the night of Wednesday, February 19, 1783, some men landed at Thoroughfare Point, at Duck Creek and burned the houses at the landing and about 20 cords of wood. They threatened to burn the farms and stores while the inhabitants watched their activities on the shore.[32]

★ On Monday, March 17, 1783, Captain Allen McLane (1746–1829) and five militiamen attacked Loyalist Captain Brooks, took his boats, and scattered his crew in Cedar Swamp.

Off the Delaware Capes (Aug. 6, 1781; Aug. 8, 1781)

The HMS *General Monk* captured the schooner *Liberty* and the 10-gun privateer sloop *Mercury* from New London on Monday night, August 6, 1781. The crew of the *General Monk* manned the *Mercury* and also brought in a brig with flour.

★ The *Trumbull* was captured off the Delaware Capes after a running battle of more than an hour on Wednesday, August 8, 1781. She set sail the day before under Captain James Nicholson (1737–1804) and a crew of 170 men, mostly Europeans forced into service. She sailed for Cape Francois in convoy with 15 other vessels all loaded with flour. However, the *Trumbull* got separated from the convoy in a gale of wind which destroyed her fore topmast. Three of the convoy returned to port and several frigates and some privateers went in search of the others.[33]

3
MARYLAND

Maryland's governor Robert Eden (1741–1784) acted as if nothing extraordinary was happening as Maryland joined the other colonies in opposing the Coercive Acts and selecting delegates to the First Continental Congress in the summer of 1774 and joined the Continental Association in October 1774. He essentially paid little attention to both the British ministry and the revolutionaries. Marylanders burned the brigantine *Peggy Stewart* and her cargo of tea in Annapolis on October 19, 1774. The colony contributed 3,919 men to the militia and 13,912 to the Continental Army—a total of 17,831 men. These troops fought in almost every major engagement.

> The Maryland Office of Tourism (217 East Redwood Street, Baltimore, MD 21202; phone: 888-639-3526; website: **www.visitmaryland.org**) and the Maryland Historical Society (201 West Monument Street, Baltimore, MD 21201; phone: 410-685-3750; website: **www.mdhs.org**) are sources for tourism and historical information.

See the map of Maryland and Delaware.

Near Hagerstown (Nov. 23, 1775)

> Hagerstown is about 60 miles northwest of Baltimore.

Lord John Murray, 4th Earl of Dunmore (1732–1809) became governor of Virginia in 1771. When he found the people of his colony supported the cause of freedom in 1775, he tried to get the Native Americans to support the British on the Virginia frontier. He commissioned Dr. John Connelly, a Loyalist physician and native of Pennsylvania who lived at Fort Pitt (Pittsburgh), to lead a movement to sustain the claims of Virginia in the district of Pennsylvania west of the Allegheny Mountains in 1774. Dr. Connelly may have even suggested the plan of recruiting the Native Americans in the west against the colonists.

In November 1775, Lord Dunmore formed a regiment he called the Queen's Royal Rangers, which was to be composed of Loyalists and Native Americans recruited "in the back parts and Canada." He appointed Dr. Connelly, a nephew of a British Indian agent, a lieutenant colonel and made him commander of the new regiment.

Immediately after his return to Williamsburg from a visit to General Thomas Gage (1721–1787), at Boston, early in the autumn of 1775, Dr. Connelly departed for the Ohio country with two companions (John Ferdinand Dalzial Smyth or Smith (1745-1814), a storekeeper and physician who owned property in North Carolina, Virginia and Maryland, and Allen or Alan or Allan Cameron (1750–1828), an alleged Indian agent). These three men were stopped as suspicious persons and captured near Hagerstown on Thursday, November 23, 1775 a few days after creation of the Queen's Royal Rangers.

They were sent back to Frederick where an examination of Connelly found he was carrying papers with the plans for the Ohio Valley takeover. He also carried Lord Dunmore's commission of colonel in the Queen's Royal Rangers and instructions to raise a regiment in the western country and Canada. The new regiment would rendezvous at Detroit, where hostilities against the white people might be more easily fomented among the Native Americans. They would then march to Virginia in the spring and meet Lord Dunmore's military and naval force at Alexandria on the Potomac.

The arrest foiled the plan. Dr. Connelly was put in jail and his papers were sent to the Continental Congress. He was kept a prisoner until close to the end of the war. Smyth escaped the log jail for traitors at Frederick but was caught again and imprisoned in Philadelphia. He stayed there for six months and then was transferred to the jail in Baltimore in December 1776. He escaped from the Baltimore jail and crossed the Chesapeake Bay and came up the Nanticoke River into Somerset County to help plan a Loyalist revolt.[1]

Swan Point, Chesapeake Bay (April 16–17, 1776)

> There are three Swan Points in relatively close proximity to each other around Baltimore. One is at the mouth of the Back River, east of Edgemere. It is now called Sparrows Point and was also called Cuckold Point. Another is about 9 miles southeast, across the Chesapeake Bay, near the mouth of Swan Creek. The third, and most likely location, is in Havre de Grace, north of Aberdeen Proving Ground. The site was also called Swan Creek Point. Another Swan Creek empties into the branch of the Chesapeake Bay that lies to the west of this site. Jack Parker points out that modern navigational charts show the water in this vicinity as being too shallow to accommodate a vessel with a draft of 10.5 to 11 feet (that commonly given for a brig). However, John A. Robertson found an 1857 chart of the same area that showed water depths generally double what they currently are. Another Swan Point is located at the end of a peninsula in the Potomac River in the town of Issue. However, this may be a more modern designation that may not have existed in the 18th century.
>
> Howard Henry Peckham lists two raids at Swan Point on the same date, a year apart. They may have been the same event.

A 16-gun brig appeared off Swan Point on Wednesday, April 16, 1777. A smaller boat came ashore to destroy a vessel that was in the stocks near the point. Captain Robert Harris (1741–1809) and a unit of the Charles County militia seized the boat and the crew.[2]

★ The next day before 11 AM, the rest of the vessels that had been up the Potomac passed Cedar Point and apparently anchored off of Blackstone Island which was due north of Hollis Marsh on the Virginia shore between Stratford and Nomini Bay. Richard Henry Lee (1732–1794) and his Westmoreland County militia were on guard here.

A small ship in the fleet returned to Boyd's Hole a few days later where it reportedly destroyed some houses but not the tobacco warehouses.

Brigadier General George Weedon (1734–1793) arrived from Williamsburg on an inspection mission about this time and later provided Governor Thomas Jefferson (1743–1826) with a sketchy account of the various raids. He also speculated that because there were no regular troops on the privateers, the raids' principal motivation was to divert attention from British action elsewhere and from the task of mobilizing recruits for Major General Nathanael Greene's (1742–1786) army. Oliver Towles (1736–1825), lieutenant in the Spottsylvania County militia, had reported two other opinions about enemy objectives: "to maraud and plunder near the Water" and to attack Hunter's Works and Frederickburg. Nobody apparently realized the primary purpose of the raids and Jefferson could only offer 200 muskets which were at that time in Maryland.[3]

Sandy Point (April 18, 1776; July 23, 1776)
Saint George Island raid (July 16, 23, 25, 27, 1776)
Off Smith's Creek (July 20, 1776)
Potomac River (Dec. 12, 1777)

> Saint George Island is in southeastern Maryland near the mouth of the Potomac River which separates Maryland from Virginia. Sandy Point is on the Virginia shore opposite Saint George Island and should not be confused with Sandy Point in Sandy Point State Park in Annapolis. Smith's Creek is an inlet of the Potomac River east of St. George Island.

Congressional forces prevented the crew of two British tenders from capturing a grounded vessel at Sandy Point on Thursday, April 18, 1776. They killed three Redcoats and lost only one man killed.

★ John Matthews and William Stoddert joined three companies of the 26th battalion of the Maryland militia under the command of Colonel William Harrison (1747–1789) at Sandy Point on Tuesday morning, July 23, 1776. About nine o'clock, they saw the ships begin to man their tenders and small boats. A few minutes later, Colonel Harrison ordered Captain Francis Martin's company of about 45 men to take a position at the head of a valley which led down to the river nearly opposite the HMS *Roebuck*. They had orders to march down and post themselves behind the beach if the enemy tried to land there.

A little while later, Captain Robert Conway (1749–1790/91), his lieutenant, and two men arrived and informed Colonel Harrison that they had come up the river on their way to Alexandria. They had landed a little below in two small boats. By this time ten rowboats, two tenders and one gondola (see Photo PA-12) were filled with men alongside the *Roebuck*, about 400 yards from the Maryland shore. The militia expected an attack at any moment.

The boats, tenders and gondola left the *Roebuck* about 10 o'clock and went over to Virginia, where they landed and set fire to Mr. Brent's house. Before the troops returned from Virginia, Captain Martin's company was reinforced with about 120 men under Colonel Samuel Hanson (d. 1781).

The small tender and the gondola left the *Roebuck* about 5 or 6 PM and headed toward the bay where Captain Conway's boats had landed. Colonel Harrison, thinking they intended to take Captain Conway's boats, ordered Captain Martin to take about 20 of his best armed men to observe the motions of the tender and gondola. They quickly proceeded toward the bay and met Captain Conway and some of his men near the head of a valley. The combined forces went down the valley where Captain Conway showed them where his boats were hidden. The tender arrived in the bay before the militiamen reached their post. As soon as they halted, the tender, about 150 yards off, fired one of her carriage guns which was immediately followed by a discharge of grape shot (see Photo PA-14) from the gondola.

When Captain Conway thought the gondola, now 70 or 80 yards away, was preparing to rake the valley, he advised Colonel Harrison to order a retreat which he did. Meanwhile, the *Roebuck* had come downstream and began to fire on them along with the tender. They then retreated back to the main body.[4]

★ After his defeat at the Battle of Gwynn's Island (July 8–10, 1776) (see p. 120), deposed Royal Governor Lord John Murray, 4th Earl of Dunmore (1732–1809) fled from Virginia to New York City. He and his band of Loyalists raided Saint George Island along the way on Sunday, July 16, 1776. On the way to Saint George Island, the fleet, consisting of the HMS *Roebuck*, the HMS *Fowey*, with Governor Sir Robert Eden (1741–1784) on board, the HM Sloop *Otter*, the HM Armed Brig *Dunmore*, and a number of tenders, encountered a gale that drove several small vessels ashore, damaging sails and rigging. Most of the ships lost their anchors and boats. Many vessels were condemned to be destroyed as a result.

Colonel Richard Barnes (ca. 1745–1804) commanded the lower battalion of the militia at St. Mary's County. They numbered 200–300 men. Barnes requested Colonel Jeremiah Johnson to supply another 100 to 200 men from the upper battalion.

> I recd information on Friday the 12th July that there was a considerable number of Ships and Small Vessels between Smiths Point & Point Lookout, on which I ordered five Companys of Militia to repare there as fast as possible, and Imediately set out to the Point myself in order to git further information, on my arrival there I found about forty Sail of Vessels, they were then about twenty five miles off the Point in the Bay, where they continued till in the Night, in the Morning about fifty eight Sail were discovered opposite Smiths Creek in Potomack, & eight in the Bay, on which I gave orders to call the Companys of my Battalion immediately to march to Potomack in order to prevent their landing in the District of the 21st Battn. We have had two small Vessells drove on shore from the Fleet, on board of one of them was three Whites & two Negroes, three of which now have the small Pox on them, on[e] of the White Men informed us the Fleet was Dunmores, and that Govr Eden was on board the Fo[w]ey, & that he heard it surmised that they intended to take possession of St Georges Island, since which the Fo[w]ey and her Tender have come to in St Marys River, and I don't doubt but the greatest part if not all of the Fleet will be there in the morning, we have between two and three hundred of our Militia stationed in different places, and I have just sent off an express to Colo [Jeremiah] Jordan to supply me with one or two hundred Men of his Battalion if Possible, from the above affair I think it would be proper Captn [Reazin] Bealls company from Drum Point should be ordered here and their place there supplied with the Militia of the Co[un]ty. I should be glad of your advice and assistance. I should have wrote you more particularly but have been marching from place to place from the morning till now, which is twelve Oclock in the Night, and am much Tired.[5]

Jeremiah Jordan (1753–1840) wrote to the Maryland Council of Safety on July 15:

> Gentlemen This serves to inform you that there is now lying off the Mouth of St. Mary's River, between Seventy and eighty Sail of Vessels – I am now at Leonard Town in my way down, with part of the 6th Battalion under my Command, when I received an Express from Colo Barnes (who is now at St Inagoes Neck with the Lower Battalion) informing me that this Morning Ten Boats full of men Landed on St Georges Island and had returned for more – I expect to be opposite the Island some time this Night, and shall endeavour to get the best intelligence I can of their Numbers, and give the earliest notice. . . .[6]

Two days later, he reported:

> I arrived down here on the 15th Instant with about One hundred of the Militia, where I found Capt Beall with part of his Company and one Company of Colo Barnes's Battalion – about day Break yesterday we were Visited by a Row Galley or Row Gondola Carrying 5 Swivels (see Photo DE-2) on each Side and a Six pounder in her head and another in her Stern, they Rowed Close along side our Centinels and not a Man to be seen & instantly began a very heavy fireing which lasted about One hour but without doing any execution, althoug their shot raked the ground

on every part where the Men were stationed – In the even[i]ng she returned again and engaged us again for upwards of two hours, and at the same time the Troops landed from the Ships on Saint George's Island to the amount of about 300 hundred pushed down to the point opposite to us with Swivels & Musquet[r]y and kept up a very heavy fire, from which Capt Beall was dangerously wounded in the Shoulder with a Ball (as he says) from a Riffle, which has rendered him incap[able] of Duty.[7]

The Congressional forces had only one man wounded [Captain Reazin Beal (1723–1809)] while the Crown forces had several killed and many more wounded. Many dead bodies of those who died of diseases floated on shore. They included those of many African Americans, of whom more than 1,000 died of smallpox during the previous six months. Lord Dunmore and his force then sailed up the Potomac River into Occoquan Creek where they destroyed a mill on Tuesday, July 23 before being driven away by the local militia.

Purdie's *Virginia Gazette* printed the following item about Dunmore's departure on Friday, August 9, 1776:

By advices from Hampton, we learn that last Wednesday morning [August 7, 1776] the Right Hon. the Earl of Dunmore, Viscount Fincastle, and Baron Murray of Blair, Mouilli, and Tillimet, after dividing his fleet, and burning ten or a dozen vessels, took leave of the Capes of Virginia, where he has, for more than a twelve-month past, perpetrated crimes that would even have disgraced the noted pirate BLACKBEARD.[8]

See also the **Battle of the Barges** under the Virginia Chesapeake Bay section (pp. 153–154).

★ There was a brisk and severe cannonade from two or three tenders and a row galley off Smith's Creek about 6 AM on Saturday, July 20, 1776.[9]

★ Captain George Montagu (1750–1829), of HMS *Fowey,* discovered some Rebels on St. George Island at 7 AM on Thursday, July 25, 1776. He had four 9-pounders fired at them which forced them to retreat to the mainland.[10]

★ That same day, Major Thomas Price (1732–1795) led a band of Maryland militiamen in an attack on a British watering party. They killed about 10 Redcoats.[11]

★ Two days later, on July 27, 1776, Major Thomas Price's (1732–1795) Maryland militia fired on Captain Andrew Snape Hamond's (1738–1828) HMS *Roebuck* and Captain George Montagu's HMS *Fowey,* about 5 miles off Saint George Island as they returned down the Potomac River.

Major Price received word at 2 AM on Sunday, the 28th, that Captain James Nicholson (1737–1804) intended to attack the fleet at daybreak. He immediately dispatched an officer with orders to speak to Captain Nicholson, if possible, to let him know that the ships had returned down the river and were within 9 or 10 miles of the fleet and that he did not think it prudent to attack them.

Major Price ordered his troops under arms and dispatched Captain John Allen Thomas (d. 1797) with about 40 men on the island to alarm the enemy in that quarter. Major James Eden (1752–1814) took the same number of men to the Point with a 4-pounder, while Major Price took the remaining 25 on board two boats and canoes. They went down the Saint George River as close to the enemy as they could safely get.

Meanwhile, the men in the lower camp had been at work all night. At dawn, they mounted the two largest cannon about an hour after spotting the South Carolina Navy brig *Defence* heading toward the fleet. The *Fowey,* about a mile from the battery, either did not see her or seemed to take no notice of her for more than an hour. Major Price ordered the cannon fired at her. They fired four times from the 9-pounders and twice from the 4-pounders. One of the shots, probably from the 9-pounder, hulled the *Defence,* and another shot struck a boat laying at her stern.[12]

★ The British ships of war *Phoenix* and *Emerald* with two tenders, appeared off Sandy Point, in the Potomac River on Tuesday, November 25, 1777, They were headed up that river in search of provisions which they needed badly. A boat from HMS *Emerald* landed with three men and was captured by sentries on Friday, December 12, 1777.[13]

Hopkins Island (June 25, 1776)

> Hopkins Island, also known as Jones Island, Two Brothers, or Seven Brothers, is now part of the Martin National Wildlife Refuge in Princess Anne County.

According to an intelligence report received on Saturday, June 25, 1776, five tenders, then in Hoopers Straights, landed on Hopkins Island and took more than 60 head of cattle together with two young men and everything else of value on the island. They had committed considerable depredation on the Somerset shore and terrorized the region. Consequently, Thomas Ennals ordered Colonel John Ennals and Major Robert Harrison (d. 1780) to go there to get further information and to take any necessary steps demanded by the situation. When they arrived, they found the situation was as described.

The tenders had gone down the Chesapeake Bay with their plunder a few hours before Ennals and Harrison arrived. The Maryland militia was still on duty but many of the men were tired and anxious to go home. They were all discharged except for about 40 who remained to keep a lookout.

When a large ship and seven other vessels, believed to be tenders, appeared in Nanticoke Sound that evening, the inhabitants became very uneasy. They ordered as many militiamen as they could muster to assemble to prevent the enemy from committing any further damage.[14]

Cedar Point, Chesapeake Bay (July 21, 1776; Jan. 22, 1781)
Chesapeake Bay (before Aug. 29, 1780; Aug. 31, 1780)
Off Cedar Point (April 5–7, 1781)

> Cedar Point is at the mouth of the Patuxent River on the Chesapeake Bay east of Lexington Park.

The HMS *Roebuck* fired several 18-pounders at a Maryland house on Cedar Point where several Rebels were supposed to have assembled on Sunday, July 21, 1776.[15]

★ Small Loyalist privateers cruising between the Capes and the mouth of the Patuxent River captured several valuable bay craft in the days before Tuesday, August 29, 1780. Some of these vessels were richly loaded. One of them, commanded by Baltimore Captain Joseph White (1752–1835), had effects on board worth more than 100,000 pounds.

★ Captain Frederick Folger's *Felicity* went down the Chesapeake Bay a few days before Tuesday, August 29, 1780. He engaged and captured an armed barge from New York with 25 men commanded by Jemmy Anderson, formerly of Fell's Point (Baltimore).[16]

★ Some Maryland militia under Colonel William Webb Haddaway, Jr. (1736–1810) seized two Loyalists in a boat on Thursday, August 31, 1780. They were part of a raiding party in the Chesapeake Bay.[17]

★ A British frigate drove three Maryland state chartered vessels ashore at Cedar Point, near the mouth of the Patuxent River on Monday, January 22, 1781. Two of the vessels were destroyed. The Crown forces also conducted raids on plantations at Point Lookout and Smith Creek on the Potomac River as well as in St. Mary's County. They also seized a schooner several days later on the St. Mary's River and burned it.

★ Sometime on Thursday, April 5, 1781, the British fleet split up off Cedar Point. Three large schooners and several smaller vessels went back up the Potomac River. A few vessels apparently remained in the St. George Island area, from where they engaged in occasional raids. The main fleet sailed to a point between Cedar Point on the Maryland side and Hoe's Ferry in King George County on the Virginia side (south of Port Tobacco, Maryland).

Pirates landed at Mr. Hoe's on the 5th and "plundered his House and what they could not carry away they utterly distroyed. The also took off 4 of his Negroes and set fire to his House which the Captain of the gang permited the Overseer to extinguish."

The vessels also went a few miles more up the river to Robert Washington's (1730–1798) plantation on Choptank Creek, "where the same horrid scene was again renewd with every agrevating circumstance that can be conceiv'd. They carried off 4 of his Negros and distroyd almost every article of furniture that Gentleman was possessed of; they then returnd on board."

Other raiders focused on the Maryland side of the river that same evening. The most complete and reliable report of the action was filed by Daniel of St. Thomas Jenifer (1723–1790) of Port Tobacco:

> On thursday evening [April 5th] two arm'd Schooners with a Cutter and some Barges came above Cedar point. Landed some of their Men at Mrs. Youngs Ferry, and plundered her of her most valuable Effects; at 2 o'Clock friday morning this town was alarm'd with an Acc't of two barges being at the Ware house, possibly they being apprized of an Alarm being given was the means of preventing any damage being done either to the Warehouse or town[.] [F]rom thence they proceeded to Walter Hanson Esq. pillaged himself and family of every kind of wearing apparel and other valuable Effects & carried off his son Sam'l a Lieutenant of the State Regiment and exceedingly insulted the whole Family. They then moved to the Rev'd Mr. Matthew's and committed the same Devastages, and then moved farther down and shewed an intention of Landing at G. B. Causin Esq'r which was prevented by the appearance of some Militia who had marched from this place; from thence they proceeded to the Elegant Seat of Geo. Dent Esq'r and after having plundered him retired; But being strongly Reenforced with three additional Barges; they again Landed and reduced to Ashes all the houses in the place save the Corn house which happended to stand at a considerable distance. The Evening of the same day some Barges were sent into Nanjem[o]y Creek where they took out a Vessel Loaded with Indian corn and returned to their Vessels without doing farther damage.

Mr. Stone (probably Thomas Stone (1743–1787)), another Charles County observer, reported that the pirates seized everything that they could carry away from Rev. Matthew's; among the items destroyed there was "Church furniture." Stone also passed on the information that the enemy vessels carried a total of 300 men.

The action resumed on the 7th according to Jenifer's account:

> Yesterday . . . upon observing some people busied in removing tobacco from Cedar point Warehouse, they immediately fell down and secured it; by lying three Vessels in such a manner as to Subject any person opposing 'em to a Cross fire from the

Vessels: However some few of the Militia march'd down and attacked their Centries by which one of their Men was killed. The situation of these few [Militia] Men being too dangerous they retired. Many [of the enemy] were busied all night in getting the tobacco on Board their Vessels, which they perfectly Effected, having only 2 Hh'ds [left] in the Ware house and a bulk of unprized tobacco belonging to the State.

Stone indicated that the barges then moved around Cedar Point and proceeded to Swan Point.[18]

Holland Straits (late July 1776)

> Holland Straights is in the Chesapeake Bay east of Holland Island and west of Deal Island.

Major Daniel Fallen (1735–1800) sent a party of 30 men to capture a small Loyalist schooner in a little creek heading out of Holland Straights in late July 1776. The detachment captured the schooner and her cargo of a hogshead and a half of rum; 30 bushels of salt; the sails and rigging of a sloop; a large quantity of old iron; and a few guns, swords and cartridge boxes. The crew of four men, three of whom had just survived smallpox, were sent to Daniel of St. Thomas Jenifer (1723–1790) for sentencing.[19]

Spesutie Island, Chesapeake Bay (Aug. 22, 1777)

> Spesutie Island, opposite Elk Neck State Park, is now part of the Aberdeen Proving Grounds.

The British landed 200 men on Spesutie Island on Friday, August 22, 1777 to take stock. The following day, Colonel Aquila Hall (1727–1779) ordered the militia to assemble at Swan Town, about a mile north. Captain Francis Holland took a small party and crossed over to the island, intending to drive off what stock they could. But before they returned with some of the cattle, a sloop and a schooner, both armed, anchored about a quarter of a mile opposite a sand bar where Captain Holland had to drive the cattle. As soon as Captain Holland appeared on the beach, the British sent a boat with men to head him off. At the same time, they began to fire on him and his men with cannon balls and grape shot (see Photo PA-14) which drove the cattle back. Captain Holland was forced to retreat down the island where Colonel Aquila Hall (1727—1779) had sent canoes to take them off.[20]

Off Weltch Point, Elk River (Aug. 27, 1777)

> Weltch Point is west of Chesapeake City at the point where Back Creek joins the Elk River.

The HM Sloop *Haerlem*, moored in the Elk River off Weltch Point, sent a boat with a petty officer and five armed men to capture a Whig flat boat on Wednesday morning, August 27, 1777. The Whigs surrounded the boat and took it. The *Haerlem* sent another party of armed men in the afternoon and took the boat.[21]

Elkton (Aug. 24, 1777; Aug. 28, 1777)

> Elkton is in northeastern Maryland, near the Delaware state line. Elkton Landing is at 590 Landing Lane. Zebulon Hollingsworth acquired two parcels of land at the

> head of the Elk River in the early 1700s and created Elk Landing. The landing was a key part of the nation's earliest north-south transportation corridor.
>
> Grey's Hill (now Red Hill) is about one third of the way from Elkton to Iron Hill. It was directly on General William Howe's (1732–1786) route. General George Washington (1732–1799) and Captain John Montresor (1736–1799) both identify Grey's Hill as the location of the skirmish on August 28, 1777.²²

★ General William Howe (1732–1786) landed at Oldfields Point with 15,000 to 18,000 troops in August 1777. The troops rowed to Elk Landing, marched across Zebulon Hollingsworth, Jr.'s property (see Photo MD-1) and then to head of Elk where they camped before marching to the Battle of the Brandywine and Philadelphia. Some Crown forces who had landed at Elkton on Sunday, August 24, 1777 exchanged shots with Colonel Samuel Patterson's troops and captured three of them.

★ While Lieutenant General Wilhelm von Knyphausen (1716–1800) and the main army crossed the Elk River to Cecil Court House (on North Street, slightly north of the junction with East Main Street and West Main Street in Elkton) to forage, General William Howe (1732–1786) took all the light troops, two brigades of artillery, the 1st and 2nd British infantry brigades, the Guards, the 71st Regiment, and half of the 16th Regiment of dragoons, dismounted, and marched to Elkton early Thursday morning, August 28, 1777. They took a position between Elk Town and Iron Hill, with the 71st Regiment posted by battalions at strategic places between the two encampments to maintain communications.

General Howe's troops scattered about 600 Congressional troops whom they encountered on Iron Hill and captured about 16 boats in the Elk River. He distributed

MD-1. Elk's Landing, Elkton. Zebulon Hollingsworth acquired two parcels of land at the head of the Elk River in the early 1700s and created Elk Landing which was a key part of the nation's earliest north-south transportation corridor.

most of the cargoes of tobacco, Indian corn, coffee, sugar, and flour among the army. However, the flour and corn were sent to the English commissariat.[23]

See also **Newark, Cooch's Bridge** (pp. 80–82).

Perryville
Fisher's Mill (Aug. 31, 1777)

> Fisher's Mill was located about four hours march (about 12 miles) west of Elkton. It was probably on Mill Creek in Perryville, near exit 93 off I-95 or near where Route U.S. 40 (Pulaski Highway) crosses Mill Creek in Perryville across the Susquehanna River from Havre de Grace.

On Sunday, August 31, 1777, Quartermaster Brigadier General William Erskine (1728–1795) took about 1,000 men of the 23rd and 49th British regiments to Fisher's Mill. The Crown forces captured the mill, occupied by 300 Congressional troops, and secured a considerable flour storehouse. They captured a colonel, several officers, and 50 men. Some of the prisoners told them that Brigadier General William Maxwell (1733–1796) had occupied Iron Hill with 3000 men, and that the main army under General George Washington (1732–1799) was stationed behind Brandywine Creek.[24]

Princess Anne County (before Sept. 5, 1777)

> Princess Anne is the county seat of Princess Anne County.

Colonel William Harrison (1747–1789), of the artillery, heard that some of the HMS *Solebay*'s crew were on shore in Princess Anne County trying to capture a vessel that they had run on shore before Friday, September 5, 1777. He sent a party of men who fell in with the sailors and captured a lieutenant, three midshipmen and 10 seamen. He might have taken four boat loads of prisoners had he received the information in proper time.[25]

Priests Town (Dec. 18, 1777)

> Priests Town may have been Powhatan on the Rappahannock River in King George County, Virginia. Powhatan is sometimes translated as priest's town.
> Blaxtons Island (also known as Blackstones Island or St. Clement's Island and now Blakiston Island) is at the mouth of Clements Bay (present day St. Clements Bay).

The HMS *Phoenix* and *Emerald* anchored off the south end of Blaxtons Island late Thursday afternoon, December 18, 1777. The *Phoenix* sent the *Mosquito* to shore to prevent some of the militiamen there from crossing a small creek that divides the island from the mainland. A party of marines landed and took possession of the island and took the stock that was there. That night, the sailors tried to land at Priests Town in a boat but the militiamen fired on them and prevented them from doing so.[26]

Benoni Point, Choptank River (Nov. 8, 1780)

> Benoni Point is located at the end of Ferry Neck Road, Ferry Neck, west of Oxford. The Point separates Tred Avon from the Choptank River southwest of Easton on the Eastern shore.

On Tuesday, November 7, 1780, the Loyalist schooner *Spitfire*, with a 4-pound cannon and a crew of about 40 men, entered Third Haven Creek (now Tred Avon River) and anchored off Benoni Point which separates Tred Avon from the Choptank River. A landing party intended to pillage the farm house there; but the Talbot militia, under Major Jeremiah Banning drove them off. The landing party probably lost one man in the raid and captured three men who lived there but one escaped as they were being taken back to the ship.

The *Spitfire*'s captain hoped the prisoners would guide him to nearby Oxford but they refused. The *Spitfire* then sailed up the Choptank River and seized the schooner *Mayflower* at the home of Captain Ned Noel.

The *Spitfire* returned to Benoni Point on the 9th to release the two prisoners. However, the militiamen, unaware of their intentions, fired on the *Spitfire* which released the prisoners in neck-deep water and sailed away.[27]

Vienna (March 10, 1781)

Vienna is on the Nanticoke River about 15 miles east-southeast of Cambridge. Some sources identify this engagement as occurring in Worcester County. Vienna is now in Dorchester County.

Plundering and foraging raids continued on both the eastern and western shores of the Chesapeake Bay in the spring of 1781. Joseph Wheland, a Loyalist released from jail on bond, seemed to be a principal force behind the raids. Colonel Joseph Dashiell (1736–1787) of Worcester County was particularly upset over his release as well as over the Loyalist presence on the islands in Tangier Sound. He volunteered to help remove the people and stock from the islands. Dashiell repeatedly blamed British cruisers and the picaroons from the larger islands in the sound for the raids.

On Saturday morning, March 10, 1781, a joint privateer-picaroon expedition attacked the town of Vienna. The raiders came up the Nanticoke River in a brig and two sloops, one of them newly built and armed with fourteen 18-pounders. After a heavy bombardment of the town with both round and grape shot (see photo PA-14), a few militiamen commanded by Colonel John Dickinson (1732–1808) and Captain William Barton Smoot (1750–1794), gathered along the riverbank. When an enemy barge loaded with men rowed toward the shore, the militiamen opened fire on them.

The raiders attempted to land three times and were beaten back each time. The intense fire from the ships eventually drove the militiamen back, allowing the barge to reach the shore. The raiders lost three wounded and one killed, while the defenders suffered one killed.

Shortly after the raiders came ashore, they sent a flag of truce to the militiamen. They said they only wanted the grain stored in the town and promised to pay the market price for it. If the militiamen would let them have it, they would not plunder the town and leave a part of it for the inhabitants. However, if the defenders refused to agree to the deal and resumed hostilities, the raiders would burn the town to the ground and destroy everything in it. Colonel Henry Hooper (1718/1720–1790), who had arrived just before the landing, realized that, as his force "could defend nothing, the Town and Grain lying under the command of their Vessels we agreed to their Terms."

The raiders loaded between 900 and 1,000 bushels of Indian corn on their vessels while a privateer brig guarded the mouth of the river, preventing possible relief or rescue by water. Colonel Henry Hooper spoke with several of the raiders and learned that they were foraging for General Benedict Arnold's (1741–1801) forces in Virginia and were disappointed that they did not find more grain stored in the town. They hinted that they might also try the Choptank or Wicomico rivers for additional grain supplies. The raiders were also looking for planks to complete the construction of about 40 flat-bottomed boats being built at Portsmouth and had already captured two or three lumber boats during their short visit to the Nanticoke. The raiders kept their word and departed on Monday morning.

The Crown forces continued raids in the bay, blockading the port of Annapolis with warships, threatening the Elk River area, and landing on Poole's Island and in Harford County. Loyalist barges ran a schooner ashore, homes were looted and burned, and waterborne commerce devastated.[28]

Annapolis
Chalk Point, near Annapolis (March 31, 1781)

Chalk Point is a peninsula in the West River, south of Annapolis.

On Saturday, March 31, 1781, a raiding party of about 100 men from the HMS *Monk* and HMS *Hope* proceeded up the West River in three barges to destroy the property of Mr. Stephen Steward (1758–1796), about a mile from Chalk Point, where they landed. They were probably guided by one of Mr. Steward's escaped slaves. A battery of six men and a 6-pound cannon located at Chalk Point expected any approach would be from the front unless the attackers knew the position of the cannon. They received the alarm too late to make use of their cannon as the raiders were already a few yards from the shore and well behind the guards. When they were challenged, the raiders answered, "Friends to Congress from Annapolis." The guards fired at them but only two of the muskets fired. The others misfired and some of the guards, frightened at being severely outnumbered, ran off, taking all the ammunition with them.

As it was now impracticable to resist further, the landing party proceeded to Mr. Steward's by land. As only six or seven men could be mustered to defend the property, the defenders retreated to Captain Garrison's and there made whatever resistance they could with the help of any neighbors who joined them.

The raiding party totally destroyed Mr. Steward's property and burned the dwelling house with most of the furniture; two or three store-houses filled with provisions, tools, timber and shipbuilding tools and equipment; and a ship of 20 guns that would have been launched in a few days. The shipyard was defended by a cannon; but the well-informed raiders approached from a different direction. The raiders were only interested in destroying Mr. Steward's property. After completing their work, they retreated, passing Mr. Harrison's house without damaging it. Nor did they molest any other properties they passed on their way up and returning.[29]

Port Tobacco (ca. April 15, 1781)

Port Tobacco is on the Port Tobacco River which runs off the Potomac River south of Washington, D.C.

Some vessels of the British fleet were on the eastern bank of the Potomac River on Saturday morning, April 14, 1781. They went ashore at Lyles's fishing landing and killed some hogs in the vicinity. Two vessels returned in the evening. This time, a body of militiamen under the command of Lieutenants Osborn Williams (1762–1819) and Henry Lyles intercepted the eleven-man landing party and, in the face of covering fire from boats on the water, took them prisoner.[30]

★ Colonel Harris and nine Maryland militiamen repulsed a landing party of Crown forces at Port Tobacco around April 15, 1781.[31]

4
VIRGINIA

Virginia was the largest colony in North America in the 18th-century. As the growing population took up all the land along the tidal rivers and creeks, pioneers moved westward into the Piedmont, the Great Valley and the mountains. This westward expansion conflicted with French interests in the area and led to the Seven Years War (French and Indian War) (1756–1763).

When the Treaty of Paris, which ended the Seven Years War in 1763, failed to halt the westward expansion, Native Americans frequently raided the frontier settlements (now mostly in West Virginia) in the early 1770s. Lord John Murray, 4th Earl of Dunmore (1732–1809) and governor of Virginia, led a campaign, known as Lord Dunmore's War, to quell these attacks in 1774.

Virginians took a leading role in protesting British policies during the Stamp Act crisis in 1765 and against the Townshend duties in 1768 to 1771. When Parliament closed the port of Boston, Massachusetts, in 1774, until the people paid for the tea destroyed in the Boston Tea Party, some Virginians viewed it as an invasion. The House of Burgesses made the day of the port closing (June 1, 1774) a day of "fasting, humiliation, and prayer" to show their support for Boston. Lord Dunmore, angered at this action, dissolved the House of Burgesses. Its members decided to meet in Williamsburg without permission on August 1, 1774. They called themselves the First Virginia Convention and elected delegates to the First Continental Congress. Peyton Randolph (ca. 1721–1775) was elected president of the First Continental Congress.

The Second Virginia Convention met at St. John's Church in Richmond (see Photo VA-1) on Thursday, March 23, 1775. Here, Patrick Henry (1736–1799) gave his famous "Give me liberty or give me death!" speech and called on Virginia to prepare for its own military defense. Governor Dunmore, fearing an armed rebellion, ordered a detachment of Royal Marines to remove the gunpowder from the powder magazine at Williamsburg early in Friday morning, April 21, 1775, two days after armed conflict erupted in Lexington and Concord, Massachusetts.

When the militia learned of the seizure of the gunpowder, they mustered at the capitol to demand its return. Lord Dunmore refused to return the gunpowder to them but eventually paid them for it. He fled to the safety of a British warship and declared martial law in the province. He called on all Loyalists to rise and support him and proclaimed that all the slaves of Rebel masters who would run away to join him would be freed. These slaves became his Ethiopian Regiment (see **Great Bridge,** pp. 115–117). Dunmore's Loyalists and freed slaves raided plantations at several places along the Chesapeake Bay in the spring of 1776.

The Second Continental Congress appointed George Washington (1732–1799), a Virginian, as commander-in-chief of the Continental Army on Wednesday, June 14, 1775, three days before the Battle of Bunker Hill. Washington assumed command of the army in Cambridge, Massachusetts on Monday, July 3, 1775. Virginia contributed more than 30,678 men to the war effort—more than 4,000 militia and 26,678 in the Continental Army. A larger proportion of the people of Virginia opposed the Crown than in any other southern colony and many officers of the Continental Army came from Virginia.

VA-1. St. John's Episcopal Church on Church Hill in Richmond. The Second Virginia Convention met here on Thursday, March 23, 1775. Patrick Henry delivered his famous "Give me liberty or give me death!" speech here and called on Virginia to prepare for its own military defense. A historic marker in front of the church explains the church's significance and another marker, across the street, explains Brigadier General Benedict Arnold's invasion of Richmond.

Unable to regain any territory in raids in the spring of 1776, Lord Dunmore sailed for New York in July.

> The Department of Historic Resources (formerly the Historic Landmarks Commission) provides an impressive list of books dealing with the state's history. It includes *A Guidebook to Virginia's Historical Markers* (1994) and *The Virginia Landmarks Register* (2000). They are all available from the department's website (**www.dhr.virginia.gov**) or by calling the University of Virginia Press at 800-831-3406. The website also offers a wealth of information on historic preservation and state landmarks. The Virginia Historical Society (428 North Boulevard, Richmond, VA 23221; **www.vahistorical.org**; phone 804-358-4901) operates a museum (phone 804-342-9671) and a library.
>
> The Virginia State Tourism Corporation (901 East Byrd Street, Richmond, VA 23219; **www.virginia.org**; phone 800-847-4882) distributes an assortment of travel guides and maps, some of which cover the state's colonial landmarks. However, as with most states in the south, there's more focus on the Civil War than on the Revolutionary War.

See the map of Virginia east.

Hampton (Sept. 2, 1775; Oct. 24, 1775; before Feb. 7, 1776)
Point Comfort (Oct. 31, 1775; Dec. 12, 1775; ca. Jan. 10, 1776; before Jan. 27, 1776; June 11, 1776; Oct. 23, 1780)
Leslie's Expedition (Oct. 20–Nov. 22, 1780)

> Hampton is about 13 miles north of Norfolk. Nothing remains of the original 18th-century Hampton, Virginia waterfront. Commercial fishing companies now occupy the waterfront area on the Hampton River at the foot of King Street. The wharf on which Captain Mathew Squire's men hoped to land has long since been replaced by a terminal for fishing boats. The brick homes and willow trees that sheltered the town's defenders have been replaced by more recent and less attractive structures.
>
> Point Comfort is at the mouth of the James River. It is located at the end of Route U.S. 258 (Ingalls Road) southeast of Hampton. The Crown forces built several batteries here in 1781 at the time of the siege of Yorktown. Formerly the site of Fort George and now Fort Monroe, the site is marked by a lighthouse. The present fortress, which was first garrisoned in 1823, has a hexagon-shape and is surrounded by a moat.

The first armed confrontations between Crown forces and Rebels in Virginia occurred in Hampton when the weather forced Captain Mathew Squire, in command of the British sloop *Otter,* to seek shelter in the James River near the town on Saturday, September 2, 1775. Some local Whigs saw an opportunity to capture the vessel's guns and burn one of her small boats while a local Whig entertained Squire at his home.

★ Captain Squire returned to Hampton on Tuesday, October 24, 1775, under orders from Lord John Murray, 4th Earl of Dunmore (1732–1809), the Royal Governor of Virginia. The residents, expecting his return, had sunk five sloops across the entrance to Hampton Creek, now called Hampton River, and had sent a message to Williamsburg requesting reinforcements.

Virginia

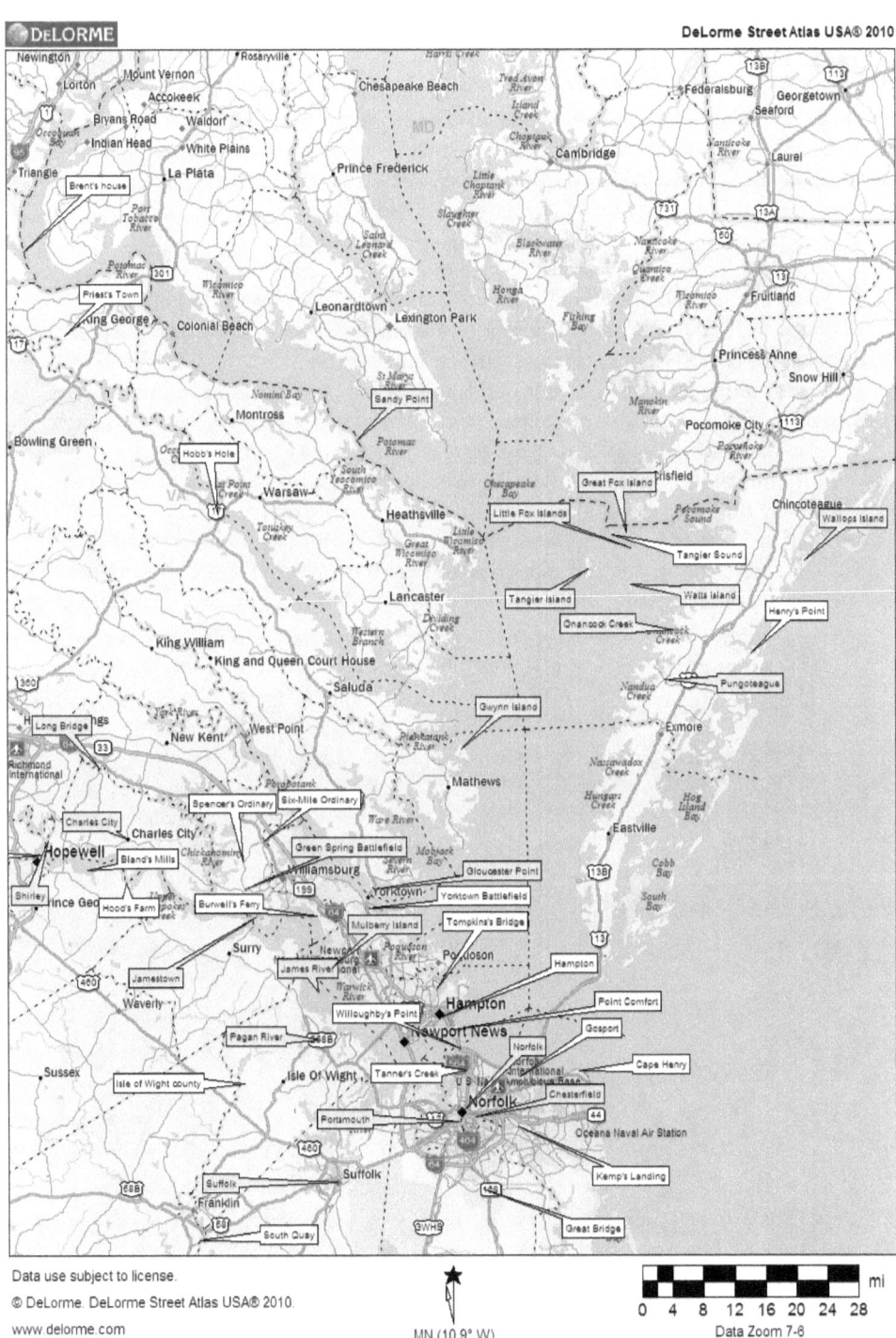

Virginia east: Map for The Guide to the American Revolutionary War in Pennsylvania, Delaware, Maryland, Virginia, and North Carolina © *2011 DeLorme (www.delorme .com) Street Atlas USA®*

Unable to sail the *Otter* into Hampton Creek, Captain Squire sailed six tenders into it and began firing on the town. He also sent a landing party to burn the town; but they never reached the shore, as the residents were waiting for them, sheltered behind the brick homes and willow trees that then lined the waterfront.

Unable to get his men ashore, Captain Squire moved his vessels into positions from which he could enfilade the town. He waited through the night as 100 militiamen rode from Williamsburg. They arrived by daybreak when Squire resumed the bombardment (see Photo VA-2). The musket fire from the shore was so effective that Squire ordered his fleet to withdraw. The attackers inflicted minimal damage to the town, burning only St. John's Church and one other building. Captain Squire lost two men killed and two wounded while the Virginians reported no casualties. Captain Squire made repeated demands for the return of his supplies but was unsuccessful.

Reports of the incident arrived in Williamsburg about 9 PM and a company of riflemen under the command of the colonel of the 2nd Virginia regiment left immediately to assist Hampton. They arrived about eight o'clock the next morning; but the raiders had cut through the sunken boats during the night and made a passage for their vessels, which were drawn up close to the town. They began to fire on the town soon after the arrival of the party from Williamsburg but left hastily, leaving behind a small tender with five white men, one woman and two slaves, six swivels (see Photo DE-2), seven muskets, some small arms, a sword, pistol, and several papers belonging to a Lieutenant Wright,

VA-2. Shell, also called a bomb, is hollow metal ball filled with gunpowder. It has a large touch-hole for a slow-burning fuse which is held in place by pieces of wood and fastened with a cement made of quicklime, ashes, brick dust, and steel filings worked together with glutinous water. A bomb is shot from a mortar (see Photo PA-15) mounted on a carriage. It is fired in a high arc over fortifications and often detonates in the air, raining metal fragments with high velocity on the fort's occupants

who escaped by jumping overboard and swimming away. The vessel also contained two men mortally wounded. Reporters also say that nine bodies were thrown overboard from another vessel.[1]

★ HM Sloop *Kingsfisher* anchored off Point Comfort at 2 PM on Tuesday, October 31, 1775. Captain James Montagu (1752–1794) sent his boats on shore, manned and armed, to destroy several pieces of cannon.[2]

★ Nine African Americans, including two women, tried to get to Norfolk in a boat on Tuesday, December 12, 1775. When they got ashore at Point Comfort, some people who pursued them fired at them, captured them, and brought them to Williamsburg on Thursday. Two of the men were wounded. The others were expected to be "made examples of."[3]

★ A British tender landed a party near Hampton, probably at Point Comfort, about January 10, 1776. A guard at a lighthouse drove them off, killing six and capturing one.[4]

★ A tender chased an old man named Wootten as far as Sewell's Point a few days before Saturday, January 27, 1776. Wootten left Hampton in a canoe, hauled his canoe on shore at Sewell's Point, and ran into the woods, pursued by some men from the tender. A guard stationed at Sewell's Point, soon discovered them and fired at them, killing three of them on the spot.[5]

★ HM Sloop *Kingsfisher,* under Captain James Montagu (1752–1794), fired three guns at a band of Rebels on shore at Point Comfort Wednesday morning, February 7, 1776. The Rebels fired on the *Kingfisher* in the afternoon and the ship returned fire with six guns.[6]

★ HM Sloop *Otter,* under Captain Matthew Squire, weighed anchor and sailed into Hampton Road at 5 PM on Tuesday, June 11, 1776. As she passed the Old Fort, a party of Rebels fired on the tender *Augusta*. The *Otter* fired two 6-pounders to disperse them. The following day, at 3 PM, the *Otter* fired two shots at a boat passing Sewells Point.[7]

★ Commodore George Gayton (1723–1797) commanded a small British fleet from New York that consisted of three ships (the 44-gun *Romulus*, the 32-gun *Blonde*, and the 16-gun *Delight*), as well as some privateers and several smaller craft. They had several prominent Loyalists from the Norfolk area on board as well as Brigadier General Alexander Leslie (1740–1794) and his force of over 2,200 men. They headed up the Chesapeake Bay on Friday, October 20, 1780. They landed 800 men near Portsmouth and more on the bay side of Princess Anne County on Sunday, October 22, 1780. They landed 1,000 infantrymen and 100 dragoons at Newport News the following morning. These men immediately took possession of Hampton. The cavalry went to capture Kemp's Landing and Great Bridge and then moved northwest of Newport News.

General Leslie's orders were to provide "a diversion in favor of Lieutenant General Earl Cornwallis" who was planning an invasion of the Carolinas. With a base at Portsmouth, General Leslie could raid the major Congressional supply depots at Richmond and Petersburg. He might even be able to move inland as far as Taylor's Ferry on the Roanoke River to prevent reinforcements and stores from crossing to Major General Horatio Gates (1728–1806) in North Carolina and also be able to join forces with General Charles Cornwallis (1738–1805).

The Virginians expected the attack. Governor Thomas Jefferson (1743–1826) instructed William Eaton (1723–1787), the state commissary, to seize any supplies that might be of use to the enemy in and around Portsmouth. General Gates sent his chief engineer, Colonel John Christian Senf, to coordinate the town's defenses. Part of the militia gathered at Pagan Creek under Brigadier General John Peter Gabriel Muhlenberg

(1746–1807) and Brigadier General George Weedon (1734–1793). Another part mustered on the lower peninsula under General Thomas Nelson, Jr. (1738–1789).

About a week after landing, Leslie withdrew his troops from the Newport News–Hampton side of the James River and moved to the southwest where he captured Suffolk. The British controlled all the vital creeks and swamp passes. They impressed as many horses and wagons as they could find, apparently preparing for a land battle, when a packet ship from Charleston, South Carolina brought new orders that reversed British plans. General Cornwallis ordered Leslie to move directly to Charleston, after the British defeat at Kings Mountain, and to forget a joint invasion of North Carolina.

The British abandoned Portsmouth during the night of November 15–16; but Leslie remained at the mouth of the James River for another week thinking about executing another raid up the river. He finally put out to sea Friday evening, November 22, 1780, leaving several hundred African Americans, who fled to the British lines, stranded because there was no room for them aboard the vessels. He did not destroy the fortifications he had begun around the city as he hoped to use them later. Nor did he destroy the vessels on the shipyard stocks.⁸

Poquoson, near Hampton
Tompkins's (Tomkin's) Bridge (March 8, 1781)

> Tompkins's Bridge may have been where Route VA-134 (North Armistead Avenue) crosses what is now called Newmarket Creek a few hundred yards north of exit 265A of I-64 W (VA-168).
> The Halfway House was probably in the vicinity of the intersection of Yorktown Road and route VA-171 (Victory Boulevard) about 4 miles northwest of Langley Air Force Base.

Lieutenant Colonel Thomas Dundas (1750–1794) and 300 of General Benedict Arnold's (1741–1801) troops landed at Robert Shield's farm on the north side of Back River, at what is now Poquoson, about 2 AM on Friday, March 8, 1781. They marched by detachments and attacked several stables by surprise. They stole about 30 mares and colts. A party of Lieutenant Colonel John Graves Simcoe's (1752–1806) legion then proceeded to the Halfway House between York and Hampton, intending to bayonet all the Congressional forces they encountered.

Colonel Simcoe stopped at the Halfway House, killed a cow or two, and issued his men several days' back rations. Colonel Francis (1741–1781) and about 40 militiamen in the area began to skirmish with the rangers who headed toward Newport News, about 5 miles southwest of Hampton. The militiamen harassed their flanks and recaptured some plunder. The militiamen, although outnumbered almost ten to one, took possession of Tompkins's Bridge and annoyed the enemy for some time.

Colonel Francis Mallory (1741–1781) and six privates fell in the skirmish and Colonel Curle and four others were taken prisoner and tortured. Colonel Dundas had his horse shot under him and lost Captain James Stewart (1746–1781) killed and Lieutenant Salisbury (d. 1781) and two other officers wounded and seven captured. Major William Overton Callis (1756–1814) and a small party of volunteer horsemen arrived and attacked the flanks of the Crown forces, driving them through the swamps. They had to march several miles in knee-deep water before they reached their vessels, which they boarded about 8 PM, and sailed for Portsmouth.⁹

Norfolk (Oct. 15, 17, 19, 20, 21, 1775; ca. Nov. 29, 1775; Dec. 17, 1775; Dec. 29, 1775; Jan. 1, 1776; Jan. 4, 1776; before Jan. 13, 1776; Jan. 17, 1776; Jan. 21, 1776; Jan. 22, 1776; Feb. 1, 1776; Feb. 7, 1776; April 5, 19, 1776; May 20, 1776; May 9, 1779; Oct. 20–Nov. 22, 1780)

> Norfolk is in southeastern Virginia on the eastern bank of the Elizabeth River. It had a population of about 6,000 in 1775.
> Blue "Norfolk Tour" signs lead visitors to points of interest in the city. An information center on route VA-192 features an orientation film.
> The only structure to survive the destruction of early 1776 is St. Paul's Church (St. Paul's Boulevard and City Hall Avenue), built in 1739 on the site of a chapel that had been there almost a century. The south wall still has a cannonball embedded in it. A stone tablet says it was fired by Lord Dunmore on January 1, 1776.

Some time during the week of October 8–14, 1775, Royal Governor Lord John Murray, 4th Earl of Dunmore (1732–1809), learned that 19 cannon were assembled and would soon be placed on the wharves in Norfolk to annoy the war ships. A number of men were expected to arrive from Williamsburg any day to fire them from behind hogsheads filled with sand. Lord Dunmore consequently sent a party of soldiers on horse under the command of two officers. They proceeded through Norfolk on a series of five raids on October 15, 17, 19, 20, 21. Captain Samuel Leslie began the series of raids with a sortie on Saturday, October 12. Lord Dunmore's forces located and captured or destroyed either 17 or more than 70 cannon, depending on the account.[10]

★ The Virginia Committee of Safety ordered troops to Norfolk under the command of Colonel William Woodford (1734–1780) on Tuesday, October 24, 1775. Chairman Edmund Pendleton had been informed on October 15 that Royal Governor Lord John Murray, 4th Earl of Dunmore (1732–1809) had only 160 men entrenched in that suburb of Portsmouth. The committee could raise a larger force but gunpowder was in short supply at Williamsburg, the capitol. The governor's superior naval power more than compensated for his inferiority on land. His ships could easily fire on the cities of Hampton Roads; and the many rivers and streams gave him much greater mobility.

Colonel Woodford and his own men left Williamsburg with five companies of minutemen from Culpeper County. They would later be joined by two companies of minutemen at Smithfield and one at Kemp's Landing.[11]

★ Colonel William Woodford (1734–1780) and his militia encountered a party of 12 or 13 of Lord John Murray, 4th Earl of Dunmore's troops near Norfolk around Tuesday, November 29, 1775 and captured them. Colonel Woodford and his troops entered Norfolk without opposition on December 14. Governor Dunmore had withdrawn his fleet of ships and gone 10 miles down river.[12]

★ A party of Rebels fired at a boat going up the Elizabeth River at 10 AM on Sunday, December 17, 1775. The HM Sloop *Otter* fired two 6-pounders which made them cease firing.[13]

★ Rebels fired on the HM Sloop *Otter* from a wharf on the Elizabeth River on Friday, December 29, 1775. The *Otter* responded by firing several 6-pounders at them. Two days later, the Rebels fired on a boat rowing guard on Sunday afternoon. The boat returned fire and the *Otter* fired two 6-pounders at them to cover the boat.[14]

★ Lord John Murray, 4th Earl of Dunmore (1732–1809), the royal governor of Virginia, fled Williamsburg in 1775 and established a base at Norfolk, which shortly became the only city in Virginia remaining under British control. He threatened to free the slaves and reduce Williamsburg to ashes in April 1775 if the colonists rebelled against British authority.

After skirmishing at Great Bridge in December 1775, Dunmore realized that he would not be able to hold Norfolk. He, the Loyalists, and his small army of Regulars, militia, and slaves boarded Royal Navy ships anchored offshore. Whig Colonel William Woodford (1734–1780) occupied the city on Wednesday, December 13. The Rebels refused to supply Dunmore's fleet and fired on the ships with rifles. Negotiations with Rebel leaders to allow foraging in Norfolk proved fruitless.

Dunmore retaliated at 4 AM on Monday, January 1, 1776 by bombarding the city. He also sent landing parties to burn waterfront warehouses. The militia responded by torching the homes of prominent Loyalists. The conflict soon got out of control, and the militiamen destroyed the entire town to prevent its use by the Crown forces.

Dunmore moved back to Norfolk and had temporary barracks built. He departed soon afterward and the Rebels reoccupied the city in February. They completed the destruction of the town, rendering it practically useless as a base of operations. It would not revive until after the war.

There are no records of casualties, but several noncombatants were killed or wounded. The battle is significant because it ended British rule in Virginia early in the war.[15]

★ The HM Sloop *Otter* anchored in the Elizabeth River to guard the watering place on Thursday, January 4, 1776. She fired several times at parties of Rebels and Rebel sentries at the Mills on the Norfolk side during the afternoon.

A party of armed men from the Continental Army, stationed in Norfolk, went to Gosport about sunset that night. They broke open all the warehouses and plundered them and set fire to all the buildings there belonging to Andrew Sprowle (1714–1776) and burned them to the ground. Besides the valuable warehouses and dwelling houses, his store contained many heavy and bulky goods of considerable value. The loss was estimated at more than £1,000. In addition, Mr. Sprowle had two houses burned in Norfolk.[16]

★ Before Saturday, January 13, 1776, Crown forces fired on Norfolk to cover a landing. Congressional forces lost three killed and wounded several of the landing party.[17]

★ The longboat (see Photo DE-4) of the HMS *Liverpool* went ashore for water on Wednesday, January 17, 1776. A party of Rebels attacked the crew and captured them along with a petty officer. Captain Henry Bellew sent his cutter ashore two days later to retrieve the longboat.[18]

★ Nearly 100 Crown troops from the men-of-war (see Photo PA-16) landed at Norfolk under heavy cannon fire on Sunday morning, January 21, 1776. They set three houses on fire but were soon forced to retire with unknown losses. The company of minutemen lost three men killed by cannon shot.[19]

★ Rebels fired on a party of Volunteers who were bringing from shore tobacco belonging to the British merchants at Norfolk on Monday, January 22, 1776. The HMS *Liverpool* fired several shots and dispersed them.[20]

★ A party from the British men-of-war went on shore at Norfolk, under cover of their cannon, on Thursday, February 1, 1776. They took 5 hogsheads of tobacco out of the warehouses, despite constant fire from the riflemen. Colonel Robert Howe (1732–1786) ordered his men to burn the houses that night. The ships gave them a heavy discharge of cannon fire.[21]

See also **Elizabeth River** (pp. 118-119).

Virginia

★ The provincials abandoned Norfolk and went to Great Bridge on Tuesday, February 6, 1776 after sending away the remaining inhabitants, burning whatever houses remained to prevent the enemy from taking shelter in them, and demolishing Lord John Murray, 4th Earl of Dunmore's (1732–1809) entrenchments. Dunmore's troops were quartered at Kempsville, Great Bridge, and Suffolk which were more accessible than Norfolk and easier to supply.[22]

★ Maryland militiamen under Captains James Kent and William Henry (1734–1784) drove Captain Mathew Squire's HM Sloop *Otter* and two tenders away from Whig schooners on Wednesday, February 7, 1776.

★ Captain Matthew Squire's HM Sloop *Otter* fired on a party of Rebels who were firing on a canoe from Portsmouth in Norfolk Road at 6:30 AM on Friday, April 5, 1776. The *Otter* carried out a warp to the *Hinchinbrook*, and fired four 6-pounders at them.[23]

★ Captain Matthew Squire had the HM Sloop *Otter* fire at Rebels on shore at Norfolk on Friday, April 19, 1776. He repeated the action three days later.

★ Major General Charles Lee (1731–1782) arrived at Williamsburg on Friday, March 29, 1776, to take command of all the Continental and local forces in Virginia. He immediately began to organize his troops and attempted to raise a company of cavalry. When he felt his troops were sufficiently ready, he marched to Norfolk where he fought a skirmish from the shore with the ships on Monday, May 20, 1776.

★ Vice Admiral Sir George Collier (1738–1795) sailed from Sandy Hook, New Jersey on Wednesday, May 5, 1779 with 22 transports and a strong convoy of warships. Aboard was Major General Edward Mathew (1729–1805) in command of 1,800 troops consisting of the grenadiers (see Photo PA-9) and light infantry of the Guards, the 42nd Regiment, the Hessian Regiment Prince Charles, the Tory Royal Volunteers of Ireland, and a detachment of artillery.

They landed at Portsmouth, Virginia five days later, on May 10, and occupied the town without opposition. General Mathew sent detachments to capture Suffolk, Gosport, and other small towns. The detachments encountered no opposition except in Gosport where the 100-man garrison of Fort Nelson resisted for a short while before abandoning the redoubt. The defenders burned a nearly completed war vessel and two French ships loaded with tobacco and other merchandise to prevent their capture. The Crown forces sacked the shipyard, ropewalks (see Photo VA-3), and a rather considerable store of ship timbers and naval stores at Gosport and burned the town. They also looted the neighboring plantations, destroyed or carried off 130 vessels

VA-3. Ropewalk is a long narrow building for making rope. This photo shows a winding machine that twists smaller ropes into larger ones.

and 3,000 hogsheads of tobacco. They damaged an estimated £2,000,000 of property before sailing away with all sorts of plunder, without losing a single man.[24]

October 20–November 22, 1780 see **Hampton, Leslie's Expedition** (October 20–November 22, 1780) (p. 102).

Norfolk
Andrew Sprowle's Plantation (Jan. 20, 1776; Jan. 21, 1776)

> Tanner's Creek, now known as the Lafayette River, is north of downtown Norfolk. Andrew Sprowle was the proprietor of the Gosport navy yard which eventually became the Norfolk Naval Shipyard in Portsmouth, west of the Chesapeake Bay Bridge. The executor of his estate reported:

> > The place named Gosport, in Virginia, of which Mr. Sprowle was sole Proprietor, is situated on the south branch of Elizabeth River, in the County of Norfolk, and separated from the town of Portsmouth by a small creek [Crab Creek], from which it extends, in front, along the river, about half a mile, in all which space the river, near the shore, is deep. . . .[25]

Colonel William Woodford's (1734–1780) militiamen were stationed at Tanner's Creek in mid-January, 1776. A landing party from a tender's boat tried to land at Andrew Sprowle's (1714–1776) plantation about 8 PM on Saturday, January 20, 1776. The militiamen forced them to retire, killing one man.

★ About 4 PM on Sunday, January 21, 1776, a party of Rebels fired on a merchantman's boats transporting tobacco from Norfolk. The men-of-war *HMS Liverpool* and HM Sloop *Otter* began a heavy cannonade to cover the lieutenant of the *Liverpool* who went ashore with a party of armed men from that ship and from the *Otter*. The cannonade lasted until 8 PM. They burned some buildings that remained in ruins near Town Point wharf after Lord John Murray, 4th Earl of Dunmore's (1732–1809) cannonade of the city on January 1, 1776. Colonel Woodford sent strong reinforcements to aid the water guards. They fired on the sailors in a sharp skirmish. Both sides lost several killed and wounded. Woodford lost three men killed by cannon shot and one wounded. He reported finding one sailor and two African Americans dead and supposed the Crown forces lost many others killed and wounded who were carried off in their boats.[26]

Norfolk
Chesterfield Courthouse (April 27, 1781)

> Chesterfield Courthouse no longer exists. There is a neighborhood in southeast Norfolk known as Chesterfield. Chesterfield Courthouse may have been located around Kimball Terrace east of Forbes Street about 0.5 miles east of the Campostella Bridge in Norfolk.

Major General William Phillips (1731–1781) continued his raids along the Virginia coast in April, 1781. He marched to Chesterfield Courthouse on Friday, April 27 with the light infantry and detachments of jaegers and of the Queen's Rangers. There, he burned a range of barracks for 2,000 men, 300 barrels of flour, and other stores without opposition. Meanwhile, General Benedict Arnold (1741–1801) proceeded to Osborne's.[27]

Kempsville
Kemp's Landing (Oct. 17, 1775; Nov. 14, 1775; Oct. 20–Nov. 22, 1780)

> Kemp's Landing was a village on the headwaters of the East Branch of the Elizabeth River, a few miles southeast of Norfolk. It is now Kempsville in Virginia Beach. The village was at the intersection of several roads which made it a place of some strategic importance in an area with few roads and many swamps. A historical marker on route VA-165 (Princess Anne Road) just west of the intersection with route VA-190 (Kempsville Road) commemorates the skirmish which occurred at a strategically important bridge about 0.25 miles west.

Lord John Murray, 4th Earl of Dunmore (1732–1809) and 140 men boarded Captain James Montagu's (1752–1794) HM Sloop *Kingfisher* and several other vessels about 2 PM on Tuesday, October 17, 1775. They landed at Newtown and marched to Kemp's Landing where they broke open a blacksmith's shop and destroyed about 50 muskets which were being repaired. They also took or destroyed musket locks, a little powder and ball, two drums and a quantity of buck shot. They also pillaged several houses and captured Captain Thomas Matthews (1742–1812) of the Virginia militia and William Robinson, a delegate from Princess Anne County to the Virginia Convention and four privates. Their main objective was to seize the gunpowder which had recently been imported; but the powder had been taken away and hidden some time before. The troops marched back at 11 PM and returned safely about 2 AM the following morning.[28]

★ A week after he signed his proclamation offering freedom to all African-Americans who joined His Majesty's Troops, Royal Governor Lord John Murray, 4th Earl of Dunmore (1732–1809) left Norfolk on Tuesday, November 14, 1775, with about 150 grenadiers and 50 or more Loyalists and African Americans. They marched to Great Bridge on the South Branch of the Elizabeth River, 12 miles due south of Norfolk to prevent a party of North Carolina militiamen from reinforcing the Virginia militia. When he learned that the Carolinians had not reached Great Bridge, Dunmore turned east along the edge of a large forest to Kempsville where about 300 militiamen had gathered in the woods along the highway and were prepared for resistance.

Captain Samuel Leslie landed "about day light four or five miles below the Great-Bridge with an intention to dislodge a number of men in arms from North Carolina, who had taken possession of that pass. . . ." As Leslie approached, the militiamen retired and dispersed. Captain Leslie's force proceeded 9 or 10 miles farther to Kemp's Landing where Colonel Anthony Lawson (1736–1785) and 300 to 400 Rebels awaited them. Lawson's men, concealed in thick woods, fired twice on Leslie's advance guard as they arrived at Kemp's Landing but without effect. The guards returned fire, rushed the snipers and routed them, driving them into the nearby river. The militia lost five killed and many wounded. Two drowned trying to escape across the river. The guards captured Colonel Joseph Hutchings and seven others in the field and Colonel Lawson and eight others a day or two later. Some Englishmen told of finding an American colonel (Hutchings) lying flat on his back on the battlefield crying, "We'll die in the bed of honor." They said he was already dead—"dead drunk." Leslie had only one grenadier wounded in the knee. Dunmore occupied the village the next day and "erected the Kings Standered." He also declared martial law, ordering all loyal men to rally around the standard under the penalty of being considered traitors and proclaiming freedom to the slaves and indented servants of Rebels. Dunmore declared that about 3,000 citizens signed an oath of allegiance.[29]

Captain Leslie took possession of the town on Saturday, November 23 and began entrenching to protect his troops against Colonel William Woodford's (1734–1780) force of 800 to 900 men who had left Williamsburg about October 24 and were now 8 or 9 miles away. Lord Dunmore waited a few days after the victory at Kemp's Landing before occupying Norfolk.[30]

October 20–November 22, 1780 see **Hampton, Leslie's Expedition** (October 20–November 22, 1780) (p. 102).

Jamestown (Nov. 1, 1775; Nov. 14, 1775; Nov. 16, 1775)

> Jamestown is on the James River, 6 miles southwest of Williamsburg.

On Wednesday afternoon, November 1, 1775, two British tenders fired from the James River for a considerable time on Jamestown and at the sentinels placed there. They did little damage except for two or three small cannon balls fired through the ferry house.[31]

★ During the night of Monday, November 13, 1775, Captain James Montagu's (1752–1794) HM Sloop *Kingfisher* proceeded to Jamestown but kept out of rifle range and made no attempt to land any men. The following day, a tender arrived with reinforcements from Norfolk; but Captain John Green (d. 1793) was ready to receive them with some of his riflemen and part of a minute company. That night, a boat full of men attempted to land about half a mile below the place where Captain Green stationed two sentinels with rifles on the Jamestown beach. The sentinels immediately challenged them. When they received no answer, they fired at the boat, about 50 yards away. One of the sentinels ran off to Captain Green to bring him to the place. The boat returned fire. The other sentinel reloaded and fired as the boat still approached. He soon heard a terrible shrieking on board and saw the boat tack about and escape before Captain Green could arrive.

Meanwhile, Royal Governor Lord John Murray, 4th Earl of Dunmore (1732–1809) learned that about 200 Princess Anne militiamen were marching to join the forces protecting the lower parts of the country. Dunmore left Norfolk about 1 PM on the 14th with about 350 men consisting of regular soldiers, sailors, run away slaves, and Loyalists. They intercepted the militiamen by surprise. Outnumbered and hemmed in by a fence, the militiamen fought for a considerable time before being forced to retreat and losing seven men taken prisoner.

★ On November 16, Sergeant Kelly (Alexander (1755–1838) or James (1737–1802)), the first man to board the tender taken at Hampton, headed to Princess Anne with news of the recent skirmish. He crossed a little above where the man-of-war and tenders lay. The sailors fired several shots at him but he managed to escape with his dispatches. The man-of-war also fired a few shots at Colonel Champion Travis's (1747–1810) houses at Jamestown. One shot went through the kitchen chimney.[32]

Burwell's Ferry (Nov. 9, 1775; April 17–20, 1781)

> Burwell's Ferry was on the James River, about 7 miles below Williamsburg, near Carter's Grove. Long Bridge was on route VA-106 (VA-609|Roxbury Road) where it crosses the Chickahominy River north of Charles City. A marker on route U.S. 60, 4.9 miles southeast of Bottoms Bridge, notes that Long Bridge is 1 mile south over the Chickahominy River. Benedict Arnold sent Colonel John Graves Simcoe

> here during his raid on Richmond. There are two other markers on route U.S. 60 at Bottoms Bridge. One notes that New Kent Road was the main road to Williamsburg and that General Cornwallis used it in June 1781 as he withdrew eastward. The other says that the Marquis de Lafayette camped near here on May 4, 1781 and that General Cornwallis camped here on May 28, 1781 in pursuit of Lafayette. He camped here again on June 21, 1781 pursued by Lafayette and General Anthony Wayne.

Captain James Montagu's (1752–1794) sloop of war *Kingfisher* and three tenders arrived at Burwell's ferry about one o'clock on Thursday, November 9, 1775. Captain Montagu sent a boat to board a small vessel lying near shore; but the rifle guard stationed there fired on the boat's crew. The boat immediately tacked about and returned to the *Kingfisher* which began a heavy cannonading along with the tenders. One 6-pounder went through the storehouse at the water side and many of the shot hit the ferry house in which lodged a large family. Fortunately, nobody was hurt. They began a second cannonade about three hours later, firing three or four broadsides.[33]

★ Lieutenant Colonel John Graves Simcoe (1752–1806) and his Queen's Rangers arrived at Burwell's landing on Tuesday, April 17, 1781. The landing had been secured with entrenchments that appeared to be fully manned. He anchored about 2 miles from the shore and the crew aboard his vessel assembled the boats. He planned to land about a mile below the ferry where a small creek ran a little way into the land from the James River. As Captain Johann von Ewald (1744–1813) had been disabled a month earlier, his jaegers were divided between the Queen's Rangers and the light infantry and Captain Althause's company of riflemen was placed under the command of Lieutenant Colonel Simcoe.

A gun boat preceded the boats moving directly toward Burwell's ferry. When the signal was given, the gun boat continued its course while the others, under Major Armstrong, turned and rowed rapidly toward the landing site, assisted by the wind and tide. Major Armstrong kept the boats out of musket range and fired his 6-pounder at the entrenchments and at a gully on the left which the defenders would have to pass to oppose any landing.

The troops disembarked as planned. Captain John McKay (d. 1822) and a detachment of Queen's Rangers and jaegers landed below the inlet to eliminate any attempts at an ambuscade there and to protect the right flank. Lieutenant Colonel Simcoe encountered no opposition in his march to Burwell's ferry which the Congressional forces quickly abandoned immediately after Major General William Phillips (1731–1781) landed there with the army.

Major General Phillips ordered Lieutenant Colonel Simcoe to proceed to Yorktown where there were only a few militiamen and the artillerymen at the battery. He marched with 40 dragoons while the infantry of the Queen's Rangers proceeded with the army to Williamsburg. Lieutenant Colonel Simcoe halted at a farm house for the night which was unusually dark and stormy. The next morning, he galloped into Yorktown and surprised and secured a few of the artillerymen while the others escaped in a boat. The guns of the batteries, already loaded, were fired as a signal to the sloop *Bonetta* which sailed up and anchored off the town. Simcoe burned the barracks.

Hearing cannon at Williamsburg, Simcoe headed there only to find that a skirmish occurred at the outpost of that town, where the troops had arrived the preceding evening without molestation. The hussars of the Queen's Rangers had charged and dispersed the only patrol, a party of volunteers under the command of Major Armistead, stationed near the College of William and Mary. The hussars drove the pickets into their barracks, killing one and wounding two. They lost seven men, including an officer.[34]

The light infantry, part of the 76th and 80th regiments, Queen's Rangers, jaegers and American Legion embarked at Portsmouth on April 18, 1781. They went down to Hampton Road and proceeded up the James River to Burwell's Ferry the next day.

★ Lieutenant Colonel Robert Abercromby or Abercrombie (1740–1827) went up the Chickahominy River in boats on the 20th and Lieutenant Colonel John Graves Simcoe (1752–1806) went to York with his detachment. Lieutenant Colonel Thomas Dundas (1750–1794) landed at the mouth of the Chickahominy with his detachment. They intended to destroy the vessels there and at Burwell's ferry.

Meanwhile Major General William Phillips (1731–1781) and Brigadier General Benedict Arnold (1741–1801) landed with part of the army at Williamsburg where 500 militiamen were posted. The militiamen retired as the British approached. The militiamen at York crossed the river before Colonel Simcoe arrived. Simcoe captured a few prisoners, spiked and destroyed some cannon and returned to Williamsburg the next day.

Lieutenant Colonel Robert Abercromby's troops marched to Chickahominy on the 22nd. Lieutenant Colonel Dundas and his detachment met them on the road, about 5 miles from the mouth of the river. They destroyed the shipyard on the Chickahominy, including a number of naval craft and the warehouses. Colonel James Inness (Innis) sent 200 militiamen to skirmish with the larger enemy force and drove them off. The troops, cavalry, artillery, etc., were re-embarked that evening.

The fleet weighed anchor at 10 AM and proceeded up the James River to City Point where the troops were all landed by 6 PM on the evening of the 24th. They marched for Petersburgh on the 25th where they arrived at 5 PM that evening. Brigadier General John Peter Gabriel Muhlenberg (1746–1807) and a body of about 1,000 to 1,200 militiamen opposed them about a mile from the town. They put up a stiff opposition but; outnumbered, they were soon forced to retreat over the bridge, having lost between 40 and 100 men killed and wounded. The British lost only one man killed and 10 wounded. The militiamen took up the bridge to prevent the British from pursuing them. The Crown forces then proceeded to destroy all the tobacco (4,000 hogsheads) and public stores they could find in Blandford and Petersburg as well as one ship, and a number of small vessels on the stocks and in the river on the 26th.[35]

James River (Nov. 16, 1775; Nov. 18, 1775; Nov. 19, 1775; March 15–18, 1776) On Thursday morning, November 16, 1775, Captain James Montagu's (1752–1794) HM Sloop *Kingfisher* fired eight guns at the Rebels on shore. The following Saturday (18th), she fired three guns and small arms in the morning and 14 guns and small arms in the afternoon. She repeated fire again on Sunday with 14 guns and small arms in the morning and three guns and small arms in the afternoon.[36]

★ When he learned that several vessels were going up the James River on Friday, March 15, 1776 and that there was a quantity of provisions and stock on a farm that were intended for the Continental Army, Captain Andrew Snape Hamond (1738–1828) sent a party of men on board one of his captured vessels. They joined another party sent by the HMS *Liverpool* which also dispatched the 14th Regiment. They ran aground just under one of the Rebel guard houses in the foggy night. As the tide was ebbing, only one of the schooners managed to get off under a hot fire from the enemy. They took out all the guns and ammunition and set fire to the vessel when they found they could not get her off. They then proceeded up the river, took a considerable number of cattle, a sloop loaded with different sorts of merchandise and two schooners. They returned to the fleet on Monday, March 18, 1776.[37]

Great Bridge (Nov. 22, 1775; Nov. 29, 1775; Dec. 1, 1775; Dec. 3, 1775; Dec. 4, 1775; Dec. 6, 1775; Dec. 9, 1775; Oct. 20–Nov. 22, 1780; March 11, 1781)
Near Great Bridge (Feb. 5, 1781)

> Great Bridge was built over what is called the southern branch of the Elizabeth River, 12 miles south of Norfolk at the intersection of routes VA-165 (Mt. Pleasant Road) and VA-168 Business (Battlefield Boulevard). Nothing remains of the site.
> The land on each side was marshy, except for two pieces of firm land at the two extremities of the bridge. These small islands, surrounded by water and marsh, were joined to the mainland by causeways. Royal Governor Lord John Murray, 4th Earl of Dunmore (1732–1809) erected his fort on the little piece of firm ground on the farther, or Norfolk, side of the bridge in such a manner that his cannon commanded the causeway on his own side and the bridge between him and the Rebels. The causeway on the Rebel side was about 160 yards long. The island on this side of the river (the nearest to the bridge) contained six or seven houses.

Lord Dunmore issued a proclamation on board the HMS *William* off Norfolk on Tuesday, November 7, 1775. The proclamation placed the colony under martial law and offered freedom to all African Americans who joined "His Majesty's Troops . . . for the more speedily reducing the Colony to a proper sense of their duty, to His Majesty's crown and dignity." Lord Dunmore needed men badly as he had fewer than 300 British troops in Virginia when the hostilities began. Most of the Regular troops had been sent to the North to keep the peace. He began recruiting a Loyalist army on November 17, 1775.

Dunmore saw recruitment of African Americans as a quick way to build his army. Five hundred African Americans offered their services within a week. Dunmore formed them into the Ethiopia Regiment, giving them guns as fast as they arrived and outfitting them in uniforms that had the words "Liberty to Slaves" inscribed across their breasts. This action raised the army Dunmore needed but lost the support of almost every plantation owner.

Dunmore also knew that his proclamation attacked his enemies' economic system. Without slaves, many southern plantation owners could not run their plantations successfully. Plantation owners saw Dunmore's Ethiopia Regiment as a nightmare come true: Their own slaves were now given guns and turned against them. The *Virginia Gazette* published frantic appeals that the slaves remain loyal to their masters and ignore Dunmore's offers: "be not then, ye negroes, tempted by this proclamation to ruin your selves" ran one article, implying that awful punishments awaited any slave who was caught trying to join the Crown forces. Patrick Henry (1736–1799) wrote that Dunmore's action was "fatal to the publick safety" and called for "early and unremitting Attention to the Government of the Slaves."

Colonel William Woodford (1734–1780) took immediate steps to prevent the enaction of Dunmore's proclamation. The governor, informed of Colonel Woodford's plans, detached a party to occupy and build entrenchments at "the Great Bridge" on the south branch of the Elizabeth River, the only route by which Colonel Woodford could approach Norfolk.

★ Colonel Woodford reached Great Bridge about Friday, December 1 and occupied the south side of the river. Lord Dunmore's artillery opened fire; and Woodford's riflemen returned fire. Woodford lost one man killed. Lord Dunmore's losses are unknown but probably greater. Skirmishing continued for several days as both parties attempted to seize and hold all the boats on their side.

The Loyalists built their earthworks on the eastern end of the bridge and furnished them with two 4-pounders and several swivels (see Photo DE-2) and wall-pieces (see Photo VA-4) which commanded the causeways, the bridge, and the surrounding marshes. The Rebels built a breastwork at the western end and posted a guard. The main body of troops occupied the meeting house, which stood at the head of the street about 400 yards away.

The Crown garrison in the fort at Great Bridge resisted attacks by Rebels under Lieutenant Colonel Charles Scott (ca. 1739–1813) between November 22 and 29, 1775. They killed two Rebels and wounded one.[38]

★ The Crown forces burned some of the houses in Great Bridge during the night of Sunday, December 3, 1775, when some slaves crossed the river and set fire to them. Colonel William Woodford (1734–1780) retaliated the following night by sending a scouting party across the river. Woodford posted a guard every night in the other houses but withdrew them before daybreak so they would not be exposed to enemy gunfire in re-crossing the causeway.[39]

★ About midnight on December 4, 1775, Colonel Edward Stevens (d. 1820) and a guard of about 30 men, mostly African Americans, advanced on the British garrison at Great Bridge. They reached the sentinels undiscovered. The sentinels challenged them and received no answer. Then Colonel Stevens fired. The rest of his men began to fire immediately, without orders. The fire continued for almost 15 minutes, killing one.

VA-4. Wall gun. The bottom weapon is a wall gun. It is an oversize musket or rifle (compare with the rifles above it). It is usually mounted on fort walls or fortifications. Because of its weight, it is usually supported in a device such as the one at the bottom of the photo to facilitate aiming.

Another was burned in the house. Stevens's men defeated the guard and captured two African American prisoners with four very fine muskets.[40]

★ Colonel William Woodford (1734–1780) sent another detachment across the river on Wednesday, December 6 to attack the enemy's boat guards downstream. The riflemen surprised a mixed force of whites and blacks and routed them with a loss of five killed and several wounded and taken prisoners. Lord Dunmore sent his Regulars from Norfolk to attack Woodford's militia.[41]

★ Colonel William Woodford's (1734–1780) force of about 900, made up of 400 Virginia Continentals, local militiamen, and North Carolinians, camped at the west end of the bridge, rather than risk a costly assault across the narrow causeway and bridge. Woodford had his own redoubt constructed on the west end of the bridge and defended it with 90 men. He supposedly used an African-American servant of John Marshall's (1755–1835) father who pretended to be a deserter to trick Lord Dunmore into thinking he had weak defenses.

The Ethiopia Regiment (a core of regular soldiers, some 60 Loyalists, a band of mariners, and more than 200 African-American troops) made two assaults against Colonel William Woodford's 2nd Virginia Regiment shortly after daybreak on Saturday, December 9, 1775. The Rebels defeated the first assault. Dunmore's troops advanced across the causeway a second time with the support of two cannon. The Virginians held their fire until the attackers rushed forward, thinking the redoubt had been abandoned. They ran right into a volley that drove them back again. The Rebels attacked Dunmore's flank, forced them back to their redoubt, and captured both guns and a number of prisoners. In less than a half-hour of fighting, Dunmore's 62 casualties included 13 deaths while the Rebels numbered only one wounded. This victory over a better-trained enemy cleared the way for the colonials to move into Norfolk as Lord Dunmore and his small armed force took refuge on board warships in Norfolk harbor.

October 20–November 22, 1780 see **Hampton, Leslie's Expedition** (October 20–November 22, 1780) (p. 102).

★ Lieutenant Colonel Thomas Dundas (1750–1794) commanding some Queen's Rangers had a skirmish with some Virginia militiamen near Great Bridge on Monday, February 5, 1781 and captured one of them.

★ Captain McCrea and a band of 200 Queen's Rangers attacked a party of militiamen under Captain Weeks at Great Bridge on Sunday morning, March 11, 1781. The Rangers lay in ambush for a good hour past the posts along the roads to Edmunds Bridge and to Suffolk. About 10 or 11 AM, a patrol of two dragoons and four riflemen appeared. They stopped, looked around for a while and returned quietly.

That afternoon a party of about 40 horse and 100 foot soldiers appeared and approached the ambuscade. The rangers advanced but the Continental forces retired toward Edmunds Bridge. The rangers killed one man and captured two others before marching back to Portsmouth that evening.[42]

Cobham (before Nov. 24, 1775; Jan. 12, 1781)

Cobham was across the James River from Jamestown.

Colonel William Woodford (1734–1780) embarked his men at Sandy Point to cross over to join the first detachment at Cobham before Friday, November 24, 1775. He was determined to attack a large sloop tender which had been sent up to prevent his passage. However, as soon as he boarded the boats and pulled away from shore, the tender tacked about and headed to Jamestown. The HM Sloop *Kingfisher* and tenders fired at Colonel Woodford's men with great fury for some time.

The next day, they all fell down the river to reinforce former governor Lord John Murray, 4th Earl of Dunmore (1732–1809) at Gosport. As the tender came up the river, she came within about 400 yards of the shore. Captain John Green (d. 1793) and 10 of his men fired a salute which so disconcerted the crew that they headed away and ran aground on the opposite shore where they remained stuck for some time. Colonel Charles Scott (ca. 1739–1813), who was at Cobham, opposite Jamestown, saw a flat loaded with oysters trying to go to the *Kingfisher*. He sent a boat or two to prevent her from doing so.

The *Kingfisher* fired at the boats but Colonel Scott's men forced the flat to pass by, driving her so near the Jamestown shore that Captain Green and his men got her within range of their rifles and captured her. They ate the oysters and skimmed the shells on the water to show their contempt for the *Kingfisher* and her tenders.[43]

★ Brigadier General George Rogers Clark (1752–1818) embarked his men and moved down river to Cobham where they plundered the warehouses and carried off about 60 hogsheads of tobacco on Friday, January 12, 1781. They were heading to Newport News on the 16th.[44]

Mulberry Island (Nov. 28, 1775)

Mulberry Island is located about 13 miles south of Williamsburg, between the James and Warwick rivers. It is now occupied by Fort Eustis.

A party of about 12 of Lord John Murray, 4th Earl of Dunmore's (1732–1809) men, mostly African American, landed at Mulberry Island early Wednesday morning, November 28, 1775. They went to the house of Mr. Benjamin Wells (1722–1794). They threatened and beat him and robbed him of all his valuables and took two of his female slaves.[45]

Elizabeth River (Jan. 6, 1776; Jan. 8, 1776; Feb. 1, 1776; Feb. 3, 1776)

The Elizabeth River flows along the western perimeter of Norfolk. For some reason, Peckham dates the February event on the 3rd despite the ship's log entries for the 1st.

A band of Rebels attempted to set fire to the mills at the Point in the Elizabeth River on Saturday, January 6, 1776 or Monday the 8th. Captain Matthew Squire saw the mills on fire. He ordered the HM Sloop *Otter*, in the Elizabeth River, to fire several 6-pounders to disperse the Rebels.[46]

★ A detachment of Rebel troops under Major Francis Eppes (d. 1776) attacked a number of black and white people from the HMS *Liverpool* and the HM Sloop *Otter*, anchored in the Elizabeth River, on Thursday, February 1, 1776. The men had landed to steal tobacco. Major Eppes drove them back, killing four black and two white men when the *Liverpool* and the *Otter* began to fire at 9 AM. At the same time, some of the Rebels on shore fired on the *Friendship,* a merchant ship loaded with tobacco destined for Great Britain. The ship returned fire and dispersed them. A party of marines and seamen was then sent ashore to forage. The raiders seized nine bullocks and some pigs. They also fired several shots at a party of Rebels who fired at some Volunteers removing some tobacco belonging to local merchants.[47]

★ With the support of Captain Andrew Snape Hamond (1738–1828), Lord John Murray, 4th Earl of Dunmore (1732–1809) occupied Tucker's Point, a small promontory jutting into the Elizabeth River from the Portsmouth side, in early February 1776. Although some of the buildings had been damaged during the burning of Norfolk, the windmill remained intact. Lord Dunmore proceeded to add ovens and wells there to relieve the shortage of food and water on board his ships. He had barracks constructed to relieve the overcrowding on board ship. They also provided a place where the sick could be housed when smallpox broke out.[48]

Isle of Wight County (Jan. 21–27, 1776)

Isle of Wight County is west of Hampton, Portsmouth, Norfolk, and Virginia Beach and south of the James River.

Six white men and four African Americans landed in Isle of Wight County during the week of January 21–27, 1776. They intended to steal some sheep they knew were on Mr. Narsworthy's plantation and to capture Mr. Narsworthy and hold him for ransom, expecting to collect a large quantity of stock. A slave who happened to be in the yard saw one of the African Americans dressed in the uniform of the 14th Regiment. He immediately went to inform his master that some of the governor's men had landed. Mr. Narsworthy sent his slave to a guard stationed a small distance away. The guards pursued the raiders, captured the uniformed African American and drove the others back to their boat without any stock.[49]

Hobb's Hole (Tappahannock) (April 23, 1776)

Hobb's Hole is a body of open water branching off the Rappahannock River south of Tappahannock.

A tender came up the Rappahannock on Sunday, April 21, 1776 and chased an outward bound New England schooner into Hobb's Hole and captured her. On the way down river, the schooner ran aground on an oyster bank where she remained until the following Tuesday. The neighborhood militia assembled four sailing vessels and set out to retake the prize and to board the tender if possible. The tender had on board a large quantity of sail canvas and other stores. When the tender's crew saw the boats approaching them, they set fire to the schooner and abandoned her. Some small boats departed from the shore and arrived in time to extinguish the fire which only burned one or two of the sails.

The commanders of two of the vessels, Mr. Hugh Walker (1740–1800) and Mr. Richard Bank, quickly caught up with the tender and engaged her at close quarters for at least 15 or 20 minutes with small arms. The pilot of Mr. Walker's vessel, a valuable African American, was shot through the head trying to board the tender. When a breeze sprung up, the tender's captain left his prize behind and took the advantage to run off as three or four of her crew were seen to fall.[50]

Wallops Island (May 17, 1776)

Wallop's Island is on Virginia's eastern shore southwest of Chincoteague.

Captain Andrew Snape Hamond (1738–1828), aboard the 44-gun HMS *Roebuck*, sent his tender *Pembroke* and schooner *Ranger* for provisions on Friday morning, May

17, 1776. Accompanied by Master Edward James's pilot boat *Dolphin*, the vessels entered Chincoteague Inlet and anchored off Wallop's Island where they landed about 40 armed men. These men forced the tenants on the island to corral their cattle. They said that they were in great need of fresh provisions and were willing to pay the owners for it and intended no violence, unless the inhabitants resisted. As the islanders moved slowly, the British feared possible militia attacks. They killed and butchered the first six cattle and tied up two others which were carried off alive. The British did not compensate the islanders. As they sailed away, they exchanged fire with the islanders; but neither side had any casualties. The vessels returned to the *Roebuck* which headed to the Elizabeth River.[51]

Gwynn's Island, Chesapeake Bay (May 27, 1776; July 8 to 10, 1776)

Gwynn's Island lies in the lower Chesapeake Bay off the Piankatank River. There is no evidence—not even a marker—of the earthworks Brigadier General Andrew Lewis (1720–1781) had constructed on Cricket Hill to protect his guns. The Coast Guard station and private homes have covered any evidence of them. Cricket Hill State Park on the mainland less than half a mile south of the bridge on route VA-223 (Cricket Hill Road) offers camping and picnic facilities as does the island.

Lord John Murray, 4th Earl of Dunmore (1732–1809), has the dubious honor of being colonial Virginia's last royal governor. In June 1775, afraid of growing resentment and mounting resistance to British rule, he fled from his capital at Williamsburg, to the HMS *Fowey*, a Royal Navy warship anchored in the York River. He quickly sought revenge against his former subjects by collecting a mixed force of soldiers, sailors, Loyalists, and slaves to strike back. With his small army, he unsuccessfully attempted to destroy the port of Hampton, raised the King's standard at Norfolk, and proclaimed martial law throughout Virginia, with the promise of freedom for all slaves who served Britain's cause. From Norfolk harbor, Dunmore's small fleet raided and destroyed Rebel property along the Elizabeth and James rivers. Instead of crushing the resistance to his authority through these acts, he managed to arouse most of lower Virginia against him.

In May 1776, three British ships seized Gwynn's Island, about 2,000 acres located in the Chesapeake Bay near the mouth of the Piankatank River. Lord Dunmore removed his entire command here and began building a fort. He hoped this island would serve as a rallying point for the Loyalists in the surrounding areas. The sudden move to Gwynn's Island caught Virginia by surprise. General Andrew Lewis (1720–1781), who commanded many of the Congressional troops in the area, supposedly stated: "I never heard of such a place before the enemy reached it." His men fired on the builders of the fort.[52]

★ Patrick Henry (1736–1799), the new governor of Virginia, considered the move as a threat that could not be ignored. Concerned that Lord Dunmore could become another military front and occupy valuable troops vitally needed elsewhere, General George Washington (1732–1799) and the Continental Congress exerted heavy pressure on Virginia's authorities to take immediate steps to attack Dunmore. Purdie's *Virginia Gazette* reported on Friday July 5, 1776:

> Lord Dunmore sent a flag of truce some few days ago to Gwyn's Island, with a letter for General [Andrew] Lewis, wherein he proposes an exchange of prisoners, and tells the general, that if he has not a sufficient number of our people, that he shall give him credit for the overplus, and pay him as soon as he can. General Lewis, we hear answered his lordship's very *witty* and *ingenious* proposal as it deserved.[53]

Brigadier General Andrew Lewis and 10 companies of veterans arrived off the coast of Gwynn's Island Monday morning, July 8, to reinforce the troops already stationed there and to search for cattle, wood and water. However, many of the springs had dried up. About 8 AM the following morning, Lewis began a furious attack upon the enemy's ships, camp, and fortifications, from two batteries at the narrowest point of the channel separating the two forces. One of the batteries mounted five 6- and 9-pounders, the other had two 18-pounders. They fired at the enemy forces encamped on a point of the island nearly opposite to the five gun battery. They found cover behind a long breastwork with a battery with four embrasures (see Photo VA-5). Other troops were stationed farther away to prevent General Lewis from landing. They were protected by a stockade fort and two other batteries. Three tenders were in the harbor: the sloop *Lady Charlotte* mounted six carriage guns; a schooner had two carriage guns, six swivels (see Photo DE-2), and a cohorn, while the pilot boat was poorly armed. Captain Andrew Snape Hamond (1738–1828) of the HMS *Roebuck* ordered the tenders to prevent the Rebel boats from landing on the island and to annoy them by every possible means.

General Lewis fired the first shot from an 18-pounder which passed through the hull of the nearest ship, the HMS *Dunmore*, about 400 or 500 yards away, causing considerable damage. The *Dunmore* returned fire but her small guns had no effect on either of the batteries. The 5-gun battery then fired on the fleet, the enemy camp, and earthworks. The fire soon became so intense that the *Dunmore* received 10 shots, some of which raked her fore and aft, forcing her to cut her cables and withdraw out of range. The HM Sloop *Otter*, anchored next to the *Dunmore*, immediately slipped her cable and fled, without firing a gun. The rest of the fleet also began to slip their cables in great confusion. General Lewis's 18-pounders on the upper battery raked the whole fleet, causing much damage and forcing them to run ashore on the island where they were set on fire. One of the tenders was completely destroyed; but some of General

VA-5. *Embrasures for four guns with earthen façade. This is part of the Grand French Battery at Yorktown.*

Lewis's men boarded some armed boats and the other tender. They extinguished the fire and captured the tender with her two remaining cannons which the crew had not thrown overboard.[54]

Captain Samuel Denny, in command of the other battery, soon silenced the enemy, knocking down several tents and throwing the camp into great confusion. The firing ceased at 9:30 and resumed again at noon with renewed energy from both batteries. Had General Lewis had a sufficient number of vessels, he could have landed on the island during the cannonade. He lost only one officer, a Captain Dohickey Arundel (d. 1776), killed in the explosion of a defective mortar (see Photo PA-15). Dunmore lost one man killed and one wounded in the incident. Dunmore, who was himself wounded when a 9-pounder shattered a large timber whose splinters struck him in the legs, decided to evacuate the island.

He withdrew and sailed into the Chesapeake Bay toward the Potomac River under the cover of darkness, leaving behind some 30 African American soldiers who were too ill to move, one double fortified 9-pounder which was spiked, a large quantity of baggage with several tents and marquees, horses, cattle, and furniture. Lord Dunmore tried to land on St. George Island in Maryland; but the militia prevented him from doing so. He plundered and burned several plantation houses along the Potomac and on St. George Island. He eventually dismissed most of his fleet with its Loyalist passengers who went to Bermuda, the West Indies, and St. Augustine. Dunmore himself sailed to New York City and returned to Great Britain in late 1776.[55]

See also **St. George's Island** (pp. 89–92).

★ Early Wednesday morning, July 10, 1776, General Andrew Lewis (1720–1781) ordered Colonel Alexander McClanahan (1734–1797) and 200 men to cross the channel and assault the British positions while two brass field pieces on lower Windmill Point fired on the British tenders. The troops attacked the island only to discover that Lord John Murray, 4th Earl of Dunmore (1732–1809) had already departed the scene of death and destruction. Fire had destroyed the barracks. Graves "(or rather holes, loosely covered over with earth) close together, many of them large enough to hold a corporal's guard" covered the landscape. There were at least 130 graves for about 500 people who died of smallpox and other diseases in the previous months. The landing party also found a "number of dead bodies, in a state of putrefaction, strewed all the way from their battery to Cherry point, about two miles in length, without a shovelful of earth upon them; others gasping for life; and some had crawled to the water's edge."[56]

Cherokee Campaign of 1776 (July 1, 1776–May 20, 1777) see Tennessee chapter in the volume on the Deep South and the Frontier.

Eastern Shore (July 13 or 14, 1776)

A squall of wind drove a British tender mounting two carriage and 12 swivel guns ashore on the Eastern Shore on Sunday or Monday July 13 or 14, 1776. She had 18 men on board, including Mr. James Parker (1729–1815), a merchant formerly from Norfolk. They immediately surrendered themselves to a party of Congressional troops and begged for quarters. A boat from another tender, her consort, attempted to cut her out from the creek where she was secured. However, the Whigs, realizing their intent, lay in ambush for them. When the crewmen came close enough, the Whigs rushed into the water and fired on them, killing five. Three were seen to fall overboard and two others fell in the boat. The British then tacked about and rowed to their tender faster than they came.[57]

Brent's House, Potomac River (July 23, 1776)
Potomac River (April 29, 1781)

> Brent's house or plantation was on the Virginia Shore of the Potomac River about 11.5 miles southeast of Dumfries and about 8 miles south of the U.S. Marine Corps Training Base at Quantico probably near the end of route VA-658 (Brent Point Road). The Dumfries area was strategically important during the Revolutionary War. The Tayloe family operated the Neabsco Mills Ironworks just north of Dumfries on a 5,000-acre iron plantation between 1737 and 1828. The complex was an important supplier of iron for weaponry during both the Revolutionary War and the War of 1812. It also supplied pig iron and shot to the Virginia navy which was based at what is now the U.S. Marine Corps Training Base at Quantico. A marker for the Neabsco Mills Ironworks is located at the rest area on I-95 at Woodbridge. Another marker, on U.S. 1 (Jefferson Davis Highway and known as the King's Highway in the 18th century), north of Dumfries marks the site of "Leesylvania," the home of Henry Lee II and mentions the Neabsco Mills Ironworks. Other markers on U.S. 1 (Jefferson Davis Highway), a little south of this one, give a brief history of Dumfries and the Revolutionary War Campaign of 1781. A marker off U.S. 1 (Jefferson Davis Highway) at the entrance to the U.S. Marine Corps Training Base at Quantico gives a brief history of the area and the development of the military base.

★ On Monday, July 22, 1776, the HMS *Roebuck* and *Fowey,* the sloop *Otter* and an armed ship came up the Potomac River and anchored 2 miles below Dumfries where the water is fresh. About 6 AM the following morning, when he saw a number of armed men near Colonel William Brent's house on the Virginia shore of the river, Captain Andrew Snape Hamond (1738–1828), of HMS *Roebuck,* sent a landing party of marines and a detachment of the 14th Regiment. Captain Joseph James (1743–1804) and about 60 militiamen were sleeping at the house, without any cover, after a night of drinking when the sailors landed. They were soon reinforced with about 120 men under Colonel Samuel Hanson (d. 1781). A gondola (see Photo PA-12) fired a 9-pounder and grape shot (see Photo PA-14), forcing the militiamen to retreat.

About 180 men landed at this time under cover of two small tenders and a small row galley and burned Mr. Brent's out-houses. They intended to burn his mill and other houses; but the *Roebuck* hoisted a white flag when the crew observed the Prince William militia approaching. The landing party retreated immediately without doing any further damage, returning to the *Roebuck* about noon. The attackers killed three men and had four or five wounded, including Lieutenant Wallis of the 14th and a drummer. About 4 PM that afternoon, another group of armed Maryland militiamen gathered near a boat in a creek. Captain Hamond dispatched a galley which captured the boat.[58]

★ The fleet, re-supplied with fresh water, proceeded down the river the next day. They found three white men and four African Americans dead on shore. Two of the whites, sewn up in hammocks, were probably officers, as they wore fine Holland shirts and were shot through the breast. A gold-laced hat was also found with a bullet hole through both sides of the crown. There were probably several more killed, as the riflemen had a clear shot at them.[59]

★ Some British ships went up the Potomac River on Sunday, April 29, 1781, alarming the residents along the shore. The militia from the neighboring counties, particularly the militia from Caroline County, mustered and marched to Fredericksburg to protect James Hunter's (1746–1788) iron works near the falls of the Rappahannock River.⁶⁰

Tangier Island, Chesapeake Bay (Sept. 10, 1777; after April 4, 1779; July 16, 1780)

At 4 PM on Wednesday, September 10, 1777, Captain George Keith Elphinstone, viscount Keith (1746–1823) ordered the HMS *Perseus* to fire four 9-pounders charged with round and grape shot at a number of armed Congressional troops "lurcking near some tents" on shore at Tangier Island.⁶¹

★ Captain William Barton Smoot's (1750–1794) Maryland militia routed out some Loyalists in the Lower Tangier Islands after Sunday, April 4, 1779.⁶²

★ Captain William Thompson and a Loyalist crew boarded a Delaware ship at Tangier Island on Sunday, July 16, 1780. Captain Allen McLane's (1746–1829) militia repulsed them, killing two, wounding four and capturing four others.⁶³

Off Willoughby's Point (Dec. 10, 1777; Feb. 17–23, 1782)

> Willoughby's Point is at the mouth of the James River near the Norfolk Naval Base opposite Fort Monroe. It is at the southern end of the Hampton Roads Bridge Tunnel.

Captain Richard Onslow saw the 6-gun brig *Arc en Ciel* from Nantes heading into the Chesapeake Bay on Wednesday, December 10, 1777. He ordered the HMS *St. Albans* to fire several guns at her. The *Arc en Ciel* ran to shore on Hampton Bar. Captain Onslow manned and armed all his boats and sent them after the *Arc en Ciel*. However, when they saw two Whig galleys coming to the brig's assistance, the boats returned to the *St. Albans* which fired swivel guns at the brig. The *Arc en Ciel* got off at 5 AM and tried to pass the *St. Albans* at 7. The *St. Albans* fired at her and sank her on Willoughby's Point. Captain Onslow manned his boats to take possession of her. She was loaded with salt, sugar and woolens for the Continental Army. All the boats were busy bringing on board a variety of goods. The British tried to lighten her by unrigging; but they found that she was bilged on December 14; so they cut away her masts. Captain Onslow sent his pinnace (see Photo VA-6) to tow her masts to the *St. Albans* but that proved impossible. They broke up the *Arc en Ciel* for firewood between December 18 and 22.⁶⁴

★ Two vessels came up the James River as high as Willoughby's Point during the week of February 17–23, 1782. They captured two vessels loaded with corn.⁶⁵

Off Cape Henry (Oct. 1778; March 9, 1779; March 16, 1781)

> Cape Henry is on the Chesapeake Bay, north of Virginia Beach. It is about 6 miles due east of where the Chesapeake Bay Bridge (U.S. 13) meets U.S. 60 (Shore Drive). It is along Atlantic Avenue just west of Cape Henry Road.

A tender belonging to Captain Daniel McNeal's *Bellona* became separated from the *Bellona* in a gale in October 1778. She headed for Hampton Road where she remained until the weather improved. She then headed out to sea. The militia learned of the tender's situation and sent two privateers with 40 men each. They approached the *Bellona* off Cape Henry. Captain McNeal's small crew of 16 men resisted obstinately until every man was either killed or wounded. McNeal did not strike his colors until boarded and resisted. He was put in irons and sent to Williamsburg as a prisoner.⁶⁶

VA-6. Pinnace (left) of the HMS Victory. A pinnace was a 28-foot boat used to convey the captain or officers ashore or to other ships. It was generally rowed by eight oarsmen but could be rowed by four.

★ The HMS *Delaware, Sphynx,* and *Richmond* spotted a sloop off Cape Henry on Tuesday morning, March 9, 1779. They set sail to chase her at 10:30 and ran her on shore at 11. Congressional forces on land fired at the ships after they anchored. Captain Gudoin had the HMS *Richmond* return fire with thirty-five 12-pound rounds to disperse the troops. He also sent his boats to destroy the sloop, but the surf was too great and the boats returned.[67]

★ On Friday, March 16, 1781, the British and French fleets encountered each other off Cape Henry. The west wind prevented both fleets from sailing directly into the bay. Admiral Marriot Arbuthnot (1711–1794), in the lead, came about and formed his ships into line of battle off Cape Henry and prepared to engage Admiral Charles René Dominique Sochet Destouches (1727–1792). It took both fleets a while to tack to get into position. Destouches tried to position his ships on the leeward side of the British line.

Both fleets were about equal in strength. The *Robust* fired on the ships in the French van, beginning the battle. The ensuing exchange of fire inflicted much damage on both vans and broke the French line. Instead of taking advantage of the wind which had now "settled down to the northeast" and was favorable to enter the bay, Destouches led the rest of his squadron out to sea, firing broadsides at the British ships along the way. Arbuthnot pursued in the *Royal Oak,* but soon lost sight of the French ships which disappeared in the haze. Destouches's departure left Major General Marie Jean Paul Joseph du Motier Marquis de Lafayette (1757–1834) without the naval support he hoped for.

Admiral Arbuthnot abandoned the chase and entered the Chesapeake Bay because the *Robust, Prudent, Europe* and *London* were disabled by the heavy enemy fire. The squadron anchored in Lynnhaven Bay. Although they suffered the most damage in the engagement, the British succeeded in getting control of the entrance to the Chesapeake Bay, allowing Major General William Phillips (1731–1781) to sail to Portsmouth with reinforcements for General Benedict Arnold (1741–1801).[68]

Portsmouth (May 10, 1779; May 23, 1779)
Collier–Mathew Expedition (May 8–24, 1779)
Leslie's Expedition (Oct. 20–Nov. 22, 1780)

> Portsmouth is south of Norfolk, across the Eastern branch of the Elizabeth River. Highway markers explain the events that took place here. A monument on the grounds of the U.S. Naval Hospital (established in 1827), on the peninsula at the north end of Green Street, marks the site of Fort Nelson. In front of the entrance to the Portsmouth Shipyard Museum on Crawford Parkway, there's a little park at the edge of the U.S. Naval Shipyard. General Charles Cornwallis (1738–1805) embarked his troops for Yorktown from this point.

Portsmouth was a strategic military objective in early conflicts. Commodore Sir George Collier (1738–1795) and a flotilla of 28 British ships, led by the 64-gun *Raisonable* and the 44-gun *Rainbow*, entered the Virginia Capes late on Saturday, May 8, 1779 and anchored off Willoughby's Point near Norfolk. Commodore Collier and Major General Edward Mathew (often misspelled Matthews) (1729–1805) launched a "desultory expedition" in the south to distract the Congressional forces. They planned to hurry back to surprise the main Continental Army at King's Ferry and West Point in New York.

Because the *Raisonable*'s greater draft might put her aground in the tidal waters, Collier left her to blockade Hampton while he entered the Elizabeth River on board the *Rainbow*. Major General Mathew landed his force of 1,800 men on Monday afternoon, May 10, 1779. He sent some troops to Gosport where they encountered Major Thomas Mathews's (1742–1812) force of 100 militiamen at a redoubt called Fort Nelson which guarded Portsmouth. The fort had 14-foot parapets and 48 gun embrasures (see Photo VA-5). The militiamen offered some resistance; but, as they were greatly outnumbered, they abandoned the fort the next day after burning the 28-gun *Virginia*, which was almost ready to be launched, and two merchantmen, one of them loaded with more than 1,000 hogsheads of tobacco. The British seized supplies and weapons and captured or destroyed about 130 vessels without any casualties.

Collier and Mathew, in six or seven small vessels, pursued the Virginians up the South Branch of the Elizabeth River and burned or captured 22 Virginia craft. Major Mathews had to destroy the powder he brought with him from the fort and retreated into North Carolina.

Meanwhile, a detachment of Royal Highlanders raided Kemp's Landing and captured or destroyed a cache of arms and stores. Another detachment went to Suffolk which had become a major supply center. The British caused great damage and burned most of the town, destroying several thousand barrels of tobacco, salt provisions and naval stores. Loyalists suffered some of the severest losses because the state had expropriated many of their warehouses that were burned in this expedition. The British planned to go to Smithfield but returned to Portsmouth when they learned a large force of militiamen was heading toward them. The British had only two men wounded. After seven British vessels bombarded (see Photo VA-2) and set fire to the city and the surrounding tidewater areas, they set up their headquarters and their line of defense at Fort Nelson (which is now called Hospital Point).[69]

The Collier–Mathew expedition terrorized Virginia. Governor Patrick Henry (1736–1799) called up the militia. More than 1000 mustered in the Yorktown–Williamsburg area and a similar number turned out at Hampton and Smithfield. However, because of the delay in getting intelligence from Portsmouth, they did not mobilize until May 14.

★ Commodore Sir George Collier (1738–1795) based enough ships in the Chesapeake Bay in May 1779 to execute destructive raids intended to break the rebellion. His fleet consisted of the 64-gun *Raisonable*, the 40-gun *Rainbow*, the 14-gun *Otter*, and several other armed and unarmed vessels and about 1800 infantrymen commanded by Brigadier General Edward Mathew (often misspelled Matthews) (1729–1805). On one of these raids, he sent seamen from his flagship, HMS *Rainbow*, to set fire to 130 vessels on the stocks in the Portsmouth shipyard on Sunday, May 23, 1779. The men burned houses, plundered "a considerable quantity of tobacco, lumber, and merchandize of all sorts" and kidnapped slaves. They departed for Hampton on Tuesday with 17 prize ships loaded with as much captured supplies as the ships could hold. They also brought 90 Loyalists, including 44 women and children, and 518 blacks who sought British protection. The stores that could not be moved were burned, including "five thousand loads of fine seasoned oak knees for shipbuilding; an infinite quantity of plank, masts, cordage at the shipyard at Gosport.[70]

The expedition captured or destroyed a total of 137 vessels and stores valued at £2,000,000. When the expedition returned to New York, three privateers remained behind and destroyed the tobacco warehouses at Wicomico. Governor Patrick Henry (1736–1799) issued a proclamation demanding the cessation of Loyalist attacks. When they continued, Congress sent two frigates to chase the privateers. The British responded by sending the *Rainbow* and the *Solebay* to the Chesapeake Bay. They interfered with traffic and commerce throughout the summer.

Leslie's Expedition (October 20–November 22, 1780) see **Hampton, Leslie's Expedition** (October 20–November 22, 1780) (p. 102).

Portsmouth–Great Bridge Road (Jan. 25, 1781)
Near Portsmouth (March 19, 1781)

> The road from Portsmouth to Great Bridge probably corresponds with today's route VA-168 Business (Battlefield Boulevard).

Crown forces artillery units had done some foraging along the road from Portsmouth to Great Bridge on Thursday, January 25, 1781. On the way back to Portsmouth, they fell into an ambuscade at Pallet's Mill near Kemp's Landing east of Portsmouth. A light infantry corps commanded by a Major Weeks caught their rear by surprise and killed one artillery officer and captured several artillerymen.

Lieutenant Colonel John Graves Simcoe (1752–1806) and the jaegers and rangers marched to Great Bridge on Sunday the 28th to protect the workers who were constructing a redoubt for 100 men and two guns. About 300 African Americans were brought there by water about the same time. They completed the work in three days and then removed a part of the Great Bridge and laid a footbridge for communication by land. The redoubt was garrisoned by one captain and 100 men of the 80th Regiment.[71]

★ The Crown forces landed at Burwell's ferry on Sunday, March 18, 1781, as planned. They proceeded by way of Smithfield and Sleepy Hole to Portsmouth which they controlled by 11 o'clock without so much as a single shot having been fired.[72]

★ Captain Johann von Ewald's (1744–1813) detachment of Hessians attacked Brigadier General John Peter Gabriel Muhlenberg's (1746–1807) brigade of 500 to 700 on Monday, March 19, 1781. General Muhlenberg advanced against the Crown forces, scattered and partially captured a picket of chasseurs. He then approached Captain Ewald's position defended by a non-commissioned officer and 16 men. The captain and 19 more men hastened to assist them.

General Muhlenberg's forces had to advance shoulder-to-shoulder over a narrow dike about 60 feet long. Every shot cut into their ranks, leaving 29 killed or wounded. The chasseurs lost only two men killed, three wounded, and five captured. Captain Ewald, who was wounded in the knee in this skirmish, wrote: "On these occasions, we must screw the heels of our shoes firmly to the ground and not think of moving off, and we shall seldom find an adversary who will run over us in such a position." Muhlenberg withdrew his force.

As Captain Ewald was being taken behind the lines to safety, he met General Benedict Arnold (1741–1801) at the end of the wood. Arnold expressed his sorrow and asked Ewald if the enemy would possibly take the post. Ewald, who had received no reinforcements (because Arnold thought the position would be lost) and was angry, responded "No! As long as one jager lives, no damned American will come across the causeway!" Arnold's report made no mention of the jaegers' gallant behavior which displeased Ewald. When Arnold sent his adjutant, Lieutenant Isaiah Robinson (d. ca. 1781) (a Native American), to inquire about Ewald's condition a short while later, Ewald thanked the general very much for his kindness, but let him know of his dissatisfaction that Arnold did not acknowledge the excellent conduct of the jaegers. The general himself went to Ewald to appease him and to assure him that he would make a commendation that evening. Ewald reported losing five men killed and four wounded in his corps and another six killed or wounded in another corps.[73]

Suffolk (May 12, 1779)

> Suffolk is about 20 miles southwest of Norfolk.

Colonel Edward Riddick (1735–1783) sent a party of militiamen to spy on a British advance at Suffolk on Wednesday, May 12, 1779. The enemy discovered the party and attacked them, killing one and capturing three.[74]

Henry's Point (ca. Jan. 1, 1780)

> Henry's Point (see Photo VA-7) is on the south side of Folly Creek which is on the seaside, to the east of Accomac, east of route U.S. 13. The creek leads to Cedar Island, a seaside marsh, and through an inlet to the ocean. To get to Henry's Point, take route VA-605 (Drummondtown Rd.) from Accomac, bear left onto route VA-648 (Custis Neck Rd.) and bear right on Henrys Point Lane. The area is private property.

Small units of the British fleet under the command of Commodore John Kidd were in the Atlantic Ocean off Accomack County in late December 1779. Commodore Kidd sent the *Victory*, a large schooner-rigged barge, and her crew of 65 men toward Virginia's

Virginia

VA-7. Henry's Point is on the south side of Folly Creek which is on the seaside, to the east of Accomac. The creek leads to Cedar Island, a seaside marsh, and through an inlet to the ocean.

Eastern shore. The vessel sailed through Metompkin Inlet at the mouth of Folly Creek in darkness and headed up Folly Creek toward Bowman's Folly plantation on a plundering expedition for booty and food. The raiders had moved well into the inlet before being discovered. They dropped anchor east of Bowman's Folly and landed 50 troops who fanned out over the countryside. Some headed toward Bowman's Folly, unaware that 24-year-old Colonel John Cropper (1755–1821), at home there, was warned and had already sent out messengers to alert militiamen in the neighborhood before they landed.

Cropper led the small number of armed men who had gathered and proceeded toward the mouth of Folly Creek in an attempt to cut off the Crown forces. The raiders would have to retreat past Henry's Point which juts well out into the south side of Folly Creek near Bowman's Folly. So a group of militiamen dragged some small cannons, with great difficulty, to some solid ground on the creek's edge at the point commanding the outlet to Folly Creek and effectively trapped the barge. Cropper and a few others crawled through the marsh on their bellies and began to fire their muskets at the barge.

The raiders were soon recalled; and the *Victory* sailed up Folly Creek past Henry's Point where Colonel Cropper and his men waited in the marshes. The militiamen threatened to capture or sink the barge which returned a heavy fire. Trapped, the Crown forces jumped into the water and waded toward the militiamen. They soon discovered they outnumbered the militiamen, many of whom ran away, leaving 200-pound Cropper literally stuck in the mud in the marsh where he had sunk above the knees. The harder he tried to get out, the deeper he went; and the enemy now ran toward him with fixed bayonets.

George Latchom, one of Colonel Cropper's servants, extracted Cropper from the muck and brought him to firmer ground, just ahead of the charging troops who then waded back to the *Victory* which set sail past Henry's Point and toward Metompkin Inlet. As the barge sailed through the inlet, a cannon shot struck the *Victory*, scattering her crew and shattering the vessel's wooden frame. The hull filled rapidly with water as she headed to the Atlantic where she sank to the bottom just past the inlet.[75]

Newport News (October 22, 1780) see **Hampton** (pp. 105–106).

Charles City Courthouse (Jan. 8, 1781)

> Charles City is about 20 miles west-northwest of Williamsburg. A historical marker for the Charles City Courthouse on route VA-5 E (John Tyler Memorial Hwy.) at Courthouse Road commemorates Colonel John Graves Simcoe's attack. Nothing remains of the courthouse.

General Benedict Arnold (1741–1801) marched back to Westover after his raid on Richmond. He arrived there on Sunday, January 7, 1781, after marching in the pouring rain. Virginia militiamen were gathering to oppose the Crown troops. Colonel John Graves Simcoe (1752–1806) decided to attack General Thomas Nelson, Jr.'s (1738–1789) 150 militiamen under the command of Colonel Guilford Dudley (1756–1833) at Charles City Courthouse. The main body of Simcoe's party of 40 men advanced on the left while the buglers approached on the right, sounding a charge. In a loud voice, Simcoe ordered the light infantry, which he did not have, to charge. The militiamen, thinking they were about to be caught in a pincers attack, panicked, gave a confused and scattering fire, and started to disperse. Simcoe's dragoons then pursued the bewildered militiamen, killing 20 and capturing eight, according to Lieutenant Colonel Banastre Tarleton's (1744–1833) account. Other accounts say he killed or wounded four. Simcoe lost one man killed and three wounded. He then returned to Westover where he joined Benedict Arnold.[76]

Bland's Mills (Jan. 10, 1781)

> Bland's Mills were on Powell's Creek (see Photo VA-8) at Flowerdew Hundred (Fleur de Hundred, Flour de Hundred—corruptions of Flowerdew Hundred), 9 miles northwest of Hood's. A historic marker at route VA-156 (Jordan Point Road) and Jordan Parkway marks the site of the house of Richard Bland (1710–1776). The area is now a housing development. Another marker about 5 miles southeast on route VA-10 (James River Drive) near the intersection with route VA-639 (Flowerdew Hundred Road) commemorates Bland's Mills.

General Benedict Arnold (1741–1801) embarked his troops on Tuesday, January 9, 1781, and headed down river the following day to Flowerdew Hundred where he intended to surprise a force of 600 to 800 Congressional troops at Bland's mills. He landed 120 rangers, 170 Loyal Americans, 50 jaegers and 30 artillery at 7 PM; and the boats returned for the 80th Regiment. He ordered Colonel John Graves Simcoe (1752–1806) and 300 men to march about 2 miles to the crossroads where the Congressional forces were posted and to attack them.

Captain Christopher Hatch commanded the Loyal Americans (Loyalists) in the vanguard that attacked a picket and drove them to their main body under the command of General Friedrich Wilhelm Ludolf Gerhard Augustin Baron von Steuben (1730–1794). The Congressional forces kept up a heavy fire that killed three men, wounded Captain Hatch, Ensign Sword, and about 20 privates of the Loyal American Regiment.

VA-8. Powell Creek, which was the site of Bland's Mills

Outnumbered, the Virginians withdrew and the attackers charged and pursued the fleeing enemy for about 2 miles until the darkness of the night, the poor roads, and a heavy rain shower prevented them from going further. They captured two or three heavy guns and sank the rest.[77]

Near Smithfield
Pagan Creek (Jan. 15, 1781)

> Pagan Creek is near Smithfield on the south side of the James River about 10 miles due west of Newport News.

Lieutenant Colonel John Graves Simcoe (1752–1806) and his Queen's Rangers went up Pagan Creek in boats and landed at Smithfield, on the south side of the James River on Monday, January 15, 1781. General Friedrich Wilhelm Ludolf Gerhard Augustin Baron von Steuben (1730–1794) was at Cabin Point, about 30 miles north of Smithfield. General Thomas Nelson, Jr. (1738–1789) was at Williamsburg and Brigadier General George Weedon (1734–1793) at Fredericksburg. Brigadier General John Peter Gabriel Muhlenberg (1746–1807) and a company of riflemen went to reinforce von Steuben and Nelson. Simcoe's Rangers surprised two parties of Virginia militiamen and captured 25.[78]

Chesapeake Bay Shore (ca. March 31, 1781)

Captain Allen McLane (1746–1829) and his detachment proceeded up Chesapeake Bay around March 31, 1781 when they encountered a prize schooner with three noted Loyalist plunderers aboard. McLane and his men boarded the vessel whose crew surrendered without resistance when McLane ordered his men to fix bayonets. McLane brought his prisoners to Rappahannock and delivered them to the victims of their plundering. He returned the vessel and her cargo of tobacco to the original owners.[79]

Williamsburg (April 21, 1781) see **Burwell's Ferry** (pp. 112–114).

Chickahominy River (April 21, 1781) see **Burwell's Ferry** (pp. 112–114).

Bermuda Hundred (May 2, 1781)

> Bermuda Hundred is located north of Hopewell, across the James River, west of Shirley.

After the raid at Osborne's Landing, The British moved to Bermuda Hundred to get fresh provisions on Wednesday, May 2, 1781. They then embarked and proceeded down the James River, destroying, along the way, whatever horses and cattle they could not use. The plantation owners lost many slaves who "flocked to the Enemy from all quarters even from very remote parts."[80]

Shirley (May 13, 1781)

> Shirley Plantation (see Photo VA-9) is on the James River in Charles City, across the river from Hopewell. It is west of the intersection of route VA-5 (VA-156|John Tyler Memorial Highway) and route VA-106 (VA-156|Roxbury Road) with access roads from either route. The Queen Anne style mansion oversees Virginia's oldest plantation which is owned by the 11th generation of the Carter family. It is probably the nation's oldest family-run business.

A British boat with six men arrived at Shirley on Sunday, May 13, 1781 to plunder the home of Charles Carter, Esq. (ca. 1750–1806). A party of militiamen stationed there fired upon them and killed them all. The next day the militiamen captured a gun boat with 16 men after a small resistance.[81]

VA-9. Shirley Plantation

Spencer's Ordinary (tavern) (June 28, 1781)

> Spencer's Ordinary was about 6 miles west of Williamsburg around the intersection of Route VA-611 (Jolly Pond Road and Route VA-614 (Centerville Road). In 1781, Route VA-611 was the Chickahominy Road which Lieutenant Colonel John Graves Simcoe used. Route VA-614 was part of Jamestown Road, the main road between Williamsburg and Jamestown. Most of the fighting occurred along the Chickahominy Road on the high ground behind the church.

The engagement at Spencer's Ordinary is the first encounter of Major General Marie Jean Paul Joseph du Motier Marquis de Lafayette's (1757–1834) army with General Charles Cornwallis's (1738–1805) army in the Virginia campaign of 1781. Cornwallis, now in command in the south, had ended his raids by the middle of June 1781 and now marched east through Richmond and toward the former capital at Williamsburg. Here, he hoped to receive additional instructions from General Henry Clinton (1730–1795), commander of the Crown forces in North America. Clinton and Cornwallis did not get along. Clinton's communications to Cornwallis were often confusing and contradictory; but Cornwallis hoped the new orders would be clearer.

Lafayette and his force of about 4,500 men followed Cornwallis, keeping about 20 miles behind. He did his best to give the impression that his force was larger and more powerful than it was, hoping to lure Cornwallis into battle on favorable terms; but Cornwallis ignored him. Lieutenant Colonel Banastre Tarleton (1744–1833) and his legionnaires guarded Cornwallis's rear.

Cornwallis had sent Lieutenant Colonel John Graves Simcoe (1752–1806) and a large detachment on a foraging mission to the Chickahominy River area on Saturday, June 23, 1781. They had gathered a large number of cattle that they were driving to Williamsburg, burning tobacco and other crops along the way. Simcoe's force arrived at Spencer's Ordinary (tavern), about 6 miles from Williamsburg, in the early morning of June 26, a peaceful but hot summer morning.

Captain Johann von Ewald (1744–1813) ordered his jaegers to stop and rest their horses and to eat breakfast along the road in front of Spencer's while Simcoe guarded the rear and eventually joined Ewald's men at Spencer's.

Meanwhile, Lafayette's army moved to Bird's Tavern, 10 miles from Williamsburg. Lafayette made his headquarters at Tyre's plantation, halfway between Spencer's Ordinary and Bird's Tavern. When his scouts alerted him to Simcoe's movements, Lafayette sent a large force to trap Simcoe and destroy him. Tarleton's troops, north of Simcoe's men, guarding the rear, never detected Colonel Richard Butler's (1743–1791) detachment that caught the Crown forces by surprise while Ewald was asleep. They had marched all night, arriving about an hour away from the Crown forces about dawn. When the Crown forces stopped for breakfast, Butler's men caught up.

While Lafayette's original plan was to cut the road between Cornwallis and Simcoe and attack Simcoe's flank and rear, Butler saw an advantage in surprise and took it without waiting for Brigadier General "Mad Anthony" Wayne's (1745–1796) reinforcements. He attacked too hastily. Major William McPherson (d. 1813), with 50 dragoons and 50 mounted light infantrymen, had ridden hard and charged Simcoe's outposts suddenly without waiting for Colonel Butler to get his troops into position. The outposts rode into camp and gave the alarm. When Butler's force charged down the Jamestown Road, they failed to notice the unmounted British dragoons resting in a field to the right of the road.

When the dragoons saw the pickets retreating and spreading the alarm, they saddled up and charged Butler's men unexpectedly and with such force that Major McPherson was knocked from his horse. Vicious saber-to-saber fighting ensued and McPherson managed to escape unharmed.

Simcoe rallied his men and forced the Congressional horsemen to retreat. He also sent a rider to Cornwallis in Williamsburg for assistance. Ewald, awakened by the gunfire and shouting, formed the rangers, the light infantry, the grenadiers (see Photo PA-9), and his jaegers in line in the fields along the road. They moved north toward the Ordinary's orchard where they ran into Majors William Call (1735–1815) and William Willis (1761–1852) approaching quickly with the Virginia riflemen and 150 mounted troopers under Major William McPherson.

Ewald noticed that his line overlapped the enemy's left. He ordered the jaegers to flank the Continentals and strike their rear. He then ordered the British light infantry and grenadiers to execute a bayonet charge. Despite being flanked on the left and attacked in the front with the bayonet, the riflemen waited until the Crown forces were about 40 yards away when they fired a volley into their line, bringing down about half the grenadiers. The Crown troops kept advancing, forcing the riflemen, without bayonets, to retreat to the woods, closely pursued by Ewald's force.

Ewald attacked before the riflemen could rally, throwing them into confusion. However, in the limited visibility caused by the smoke of the musketry hanging low in the woods, the flanking force of jaegers became dispersed in the woods and lost their cohesion and firepower. The hot fight drove the riflemen and cavalry back in hand-to-hand combat. They soon encountered Colonel Butler's Continental light infantry line advancing to support them.

Ewald, realizing that he was now outnumbered by fresh troops, recalled his men and requested Simcoe to order a retreat. The Crown forces withdrew 2 miles along the Williamsburg Road when they met Cornwallis coming from Williamsburg to support them. Without reliable intelligence on the enemy's location, Cornwallis could not afford to lose men when Clinton was expecting them in New York.

Butler did not pursue the retreating Crown forces because Cornwallis outnumbered him. Nor did Butler want to bring on a general engagement at this point. The Congressional forces claimed a victory and returned to Tyre's plantation and Bird's Tavern. The Crown forces also claimed winning a sizable victory, despite retreating and leaving dead and wounded behind. They later removed the dead and wounded while Cornwallis shielded the area. Real casualty figures are difficult to determine. Simcoe reported 10 killed and 23 wounded. However, Lafayette claimed he inflicted 60 killed and over 100 wounded. The Congressional forces reported nine killed, 14 wounded, and 14 missing; but the British claimed they captured three officers and 28 privates.

Cornwallis returned to Williamsburg where he received orders to send some of his best troops to New York City to reinforce Clinton who felt himself surrounded by the French and American armies and the French fleet. Lafayette moved his camp almost daily to avoid being caught by surprise.[82]

Green Spring (July 6, 1781)

The Green Spring Battlefield is between Williamsburg and Jamestown, near the junction of County Road 614 (Greensprings Road) and Derby Lane, north of 4-H Club Road. There are no markers to interpret the action that occurred here.

As British General William Howe (1732–1786) and Major General John Burgoyne (1722–1792) went their separate ways in 1777, seemingly determined to satisfy only their personal ambitions, so General Henry Clinton (1730–1795) and General Charles Cornwallis (1738–1805) paved the road to Yorktown in 1781 by their disagreements and lack of coordination. Clinton was Cornwallis's superior in this case, but the latter enjoyed the confidence of Colonial Secretary Sir George Germain (1716–1785) to an extent that Clinton did not. Clinton, believing that the British could not operate far from coastal bases without large reinforcements, had opposed Cornwallis's ventures in the interior of the Carolinas; and, when Cornwallis came to Virginia, he did so without even informing his superior of his intention.

Since 1779, Clinton had sought to paralyze the state of Virginia by conducting raids up its great rivers, arousing the Loyalists, and establishing a base in the Chesapeake Bay region. He thought this base might eventually be used as a starting point for one arm of a pincers movement against Pennsylvania for which his own idle force in New York would provide the other. A raid conducted in the Hampton Roads area in 1779 was highly successful, but when Clinton sought to follow it up in 1780, the force sent for the purpose had to be diverted to Charleston, South Carolina to bail Cornwallis out after Kings Mountain. Finally, in 1781, he got an expedition into Virginia, a contingent of 1,600 men under the Continental traitor, Benedict Arnold (1741–1801). Arnold conducted a destructive raid up the James River all the way to Richmond in January 1781. His presence soon proved to be a magnet, drawing forces of both sides to Virginia.

Then, on Sunday, May 20, 1781, Cornwallis arrived from Wilmington, North Carolina and took over command from Major General William Phillips (1731–1781). With additional reinforcements sent by Clinton, he was able to field a force of about 7,000 men, approximately a quarter of the British strength in America.

Cornwallis and Clinton were soon working at cross-purposes. Cornwallis proposed to carry out major operations in the interior of Virginia, but Clinton saw as little practical value in this tactic as Cornwallis did in Clinton's plan to establish a base in Virginia for a pincers movement against Pennsylvania. Cornwallis at first turned to the interior and engaged in a fruitless pursuit of General Marie Joseph de Motier Marquis de Lafayette (1757–1834) north of Richmond. Then, on receiving Clinton's positive order to return to the coast, establish a base, and return part of his force to New York, Cornwallis moved back down the Virginia peninsula to take a position at Yorktown, a small tobacco port on the York River just off the Chesapeake Bay. In the face of Cornwallis's insistence that he must keep all his troops with him, Clinton vacillated, reversing his own orders several times and, in the end, granting Cornwallis's request.

Cornwallis was also confused by Clinton's letters. Not only did they use convoluted and ambiguous wording but they did not arrive in the order in which they had been written. Cornwallis received one letter on July 8 followed four days later by three other letters, all written before it. Another letter arrived on July 20 countermanding previous instructions and advising contradictory measures.

Major General Lafayette followed General Charles Cornwallis as he traveled down the peninsula to Williamsburg, intending to cross the James and establish a base near Portsmouth. Lafayette was looking for an opportunity to catch the Crown forces in a vulnerable position crossing the river. Brigadier General "Mad Anthony" Wayne (1745–1796), leading an advance guard of about 500 men, later reinforced to 900, thought he was attacking Cornwallis's rear guard near Green Spring. He soon found himself engaged with Cornwallis's main force of 7,000. Lafayette could not get to Wayne in time to provide much support.

Cornwallis hoped to draw Lafayette's main force into battle and deliver a decisive blow by extending his line in both directions beyond Wayne's flanks. Wayne charged, catching Cornwallis by surprise. He attacked through grape shot and musket fire to within 70 yards and stopped the British advance for 15 minutes. Lafayette arrived in time to support the Pennsylvanians' withdrawal. He had two horses shot from under him in the action. Cornwallis reported to General Henry Clinton (1730–1795) that he waited until "near sunset" to attack. With only about an hour of daylight for the entire action, he was unable to pursue the retreating enemy who attained the reserve line at the Green Spring plantation. They remained there for a few hours and withdrew to Chickahominy Church during the night. Of the 900 troops engaged, Wayne lost 28 killed, 99 wounded, and 12 missing. He also lost two guns. Cornwallis had 75 killed and wounded.[83]

South Quay (July 16, 1781)

> There were two South Quays in southeastern Virginia in the 18th century. One was a community in Nansemond County on the east bank of the Blackwater River. The other was Old South Quay in Southampton County on the west bank. They were only a mile or so from each other. The Blackwater port of South Quay on the west bank became an important supply center for the Southern armies while the British occupied the Chesapeake Bay during the American War for Independence because it opened into Albemarle Sound. The British eventually attacked it and destroyed it.[84]

Lieutenant Colonel Josiah Parker (1751–1810) of Wight County, commanded all the militia in southeast Virginia. Major General Friedrich Wilhelm Ludolf Gerhard Augustin Baron von Steuben (1730–1794), then at Petersburg, ordered him to give particular attention to the safety of all the artillery and ammunition stored at South Quay.

Mary Fisher (d. 1795) realized that the British intended to destroy the port and feared for her own and her teenage daughter's safety. She sent her daughter, Tembte, who was engaged to be married, to live with friends in nearby Southampton County where she might be married in safety. However the bride did not reside in the county and no member of her family was there to give consent to her marriage so she could not get a license. Redmond Hackett, the prospective groom, hastened to Mrs. Fisher who wrote a letter describing the circumstances and giving her consent to the marriage as her guardian on March 13, 1781. Tembte was married but died shortly after her marriage.

Lieutenant Colonel Banastre Tarleton (1744–1833) came from Portsmouth to South Quay with 700 men on July 16, 1781. They burned anything they considered useful. Outnumbered, Parker's forces retreated with some losses.[85]

Pungoteague (July 27, 1781)

> Pungoteague is a hamlet of about a dozen houses nestled in farm fields. It is at the intersection of routes VA-180 (Pungoteague Road) and VA-718 (Bobtown Road) 3 miles west of U.S. 13 (Lankford Highway). A marker on U.S. 13 (Lankford Hwy) at Melfa describes a battle that occurred here on May 30, 1814 but makes no mention of the skirmish of July 27, 1781.

The Loyalists began to rob remote plantations and tried to enlist slaves to support them in the summer of 1781. A planter was shot dead when he accidentally surprised some Loyalists trying to recruit some African Americans. Neighboring farmers, outraged by this, armed themselves, forced a confession from a slave, and hanged three Loyalists.[86] The Crown forces avenged the lynching by sending four barges manned by 100 men, mostly African Americans commanded by Captain Isaiah Robinson (d. ca. 1781), to Pungoteague.

A few local militiamen mustered to prevent the raiders from landing. A brief skirmish ensued in which one man was killed. The Crown forces withdrew to their barges. The militiamen pursued the raiders up Chesapeake Bay for four days and nights but failed to overtake them. When the militiamen returned, John Lyon, rector of St. George Parish, Accomac, was court-martialed and tried for helping the enemy and discouraging the militiamen from taking arms against Robinson's raiders.

Rev. Lyon, a known Loyalist had gone on board Robinson's barge at night, probably unwillingly. He received a fair trial and was sentenced to five years in prison. Some of his parishioners petitioned the governor to change the pastor's sentence to exile. Colonel John Cropper (1755–1821), the county lieutenant, said that Lyon deserved a halter[87] and sent Lyon as a prisoner to Richmond along with John Curtis, William Garrison, and five others, the worst offenders in the Accomac outbreak. He also recommended leniency. Lyon's sentence was changed to residence in the country 20 miles from Richmond, eventually allowing him to return to Accomac.[88]

Six Mile Ordinary, near Williamsburg (Aug. 22, 1781)

According to Lieutenant Colonel John Graves Simcoe, the Six Mile Ordinary was along the Chickahominy Road, modern Route VA-611 (Jolly Pond Road), up behind the church where the road curves around to the right before turning left to go down to the river. A marker on route U.S. 60 (Richmond Road) in Lightfoot notes that militiamen under Colonel James Inness (Innis) camped here on Friday, April 20, 1781 and that Lieutenant Colonel Banastre Tarleton attacked Colonel Thomas Mathews and his militia on August 22, 1781. Nothing remains of the site. Other markers at this location note the action at Spencer's Ordinary 4 miles south but give the date of June 24, 1781. Another marker notes that Green Spring, the home of Governor Sir William Berkeley is 5 miles south and that the Marquis de Lafayette attacked General Charles Cornwallis there on July 6, 1781.

A marker on route U.S. 60, 3 miles northwest of Toano, notes that Cornwallis camped about a mile north on June 24, 1781 and that part of Lafayette's army camped at the same place three days later. Another marker on route U.S. 60, 7.25 miles east of Providence Forge near Diascund Creek Reservoir, notes that Cornwallis obtained supplies at Cooper's Mill half a mile north up Diascund Creek on June 23–24, 1781.

Markers on route U.S. 60 in Toano, 4.3 miles north, note that Cornwallis passed a colonial tavern there on his way to Williamsburg on June 25, 1781. After its destruction by fire, it was known as "Burnt Ordinary." The Chickahominy Church, now destroyed, was 2 miles south and served as the site of Lafayette's camp, July 6–8, 1781, and as a hospital after the battle of Green Spring, July 6, 1781. General Phillips burned the state shipyard 5 miles west on April 21–22, 1781.

Crown forces under Lieutenant Colonel Banastre Tarleton (1744–1833) surprised a picket guard of Lieutenant Colonel Thomas Mathews's (1742–1812) militia on Wednesday, August 22, 1781. They killed about five and wounded about 10 militiamen.[89]

Yorktown (April 21, 1781; Sept. 30, 1781; Oct. 10, 1781; Oct. 16, 1781)
Siege of Yorktown (Sept. 28–Oct. 19, 1781)
Chesapeake Bay (Sept. 5, 1781)
Gloucester, Near (Oct. 3, 1781)

Yorktown is one part of Colonial National Historical Park (http://www.nps.gov/york/planyourvisit/visitorcenters.htm) which is on the peninsula between the York and James rivers. The park covers 9,000 acres and includes Yorktown Battlefield; Jamestown, the Original Site; the Colonial Parkway; and the Cape Henry Memorial at Cape Henry. Park headquarters is in the Yorktown Visitor Center.

The Yorktown Visitor Center/Yorktown Battlefield is 0.75 miles south of Yorktown, on the edge of town, at the east end of the Colonial Parkway. The center includes parts of General Washington's campaign tents, an observation deck, a reconstructed section of a gun deck and a British frigate captain's cabin. A 16-minute film relates the events of the siege. Automobile tours begin at this point as do self-guiding and taped tours of the battlefield. Tour leaflets and tape rentals are available in the center.

The Yorktown Victory Center (http://www.historyisfun.org/yorktown-victory-center.htm), off I-64 exit 247 on Old VA-238 near the Colonial Parkway and route U.S. 17, is a museum of the War for American Independence. "Road to Revolution," an open-air walkway, chronicles the events that led to the colonies declaring independence from Great Britain. "Witnesses to Revolution," the first in a series of themed indoor galleries, presents the stories of a representative group of 10 people whose lives were affected by the Revolution.

The "Converging on Yorktown" gallery has exhibits that tell how Yorktown became the setting for the decisive battle of the War for American Independence and describe the multinational nature of forces that converged there in 1781. "Yorktown's Sunken Fleet" reveals the story of the *Betsy* and other British ships scuttled or lost in the York River during the siege of Yorktown. Other exhibits relate the experiences of ordinary soldiers and describe the final step in America's journey to nationhood—the development of the Constitution and Bill of Rights.

Daily life during and just after the Revolution is re-created outdoors in a Continental Army encampment and an 18th-century farm where costumed interpreters demonstrate firing muskets and a cannon, discuss 18th-century medical practices, prepare meals, plant and cultivate crops and process fiber into cloth.

Yorktown Monument, between the battlefield and the entrance into town, commemorates the victory in 1781.

Nelson house (see Photo VA-10) is at the southwest corner of Main and Nelson streets. The Georgian style house built about 1711 was the home of General Thomas Nelson Jr., a signer of the Declaration of Independence, who commanded the Virginia militia during the battle. General Cornwallis used it as his headquarters during the siege; and General Nelson is reported to have told General Washington to fire on the house. A cannonball is still embedded in a wall on the third floor.

VA-10. Nelson House, Yorktown. During the siege of Yorktown, General Cornwallis used the home of Thomas Nelson, Governor of Virginia, as his headquarters. This photo shows a cannonball lodged in the wall of the third floor (between the two windows).

> Grace Episcopal Church was built of native marl (mixture of clay and limestone) about 1697. The British used it as a magazine during the siege of Yorktown. It was partially burned in 1814 but rebuilt later. General Thomas Nelson Jr. is buried in the churchyard.
>
> The Moore house (see Photo VA-11) is accessible from the battlefield tour route. The commissioners from the combined American and French armies met in the house with British representatives on October 18, 1781, and drafted the terms of General Charles Cornwallis's surrender.
>
> Surrender Field (see Photo VA-12) is south of the battlefield on route U.S. 17. A split rail fence marks the route the Crown forces followed to lay down their arms in the formal surrender ceremony. Interpretive markers tell the story; and there's a display of some of the artillery surrendered at that time.
>
> Gloucester is on the north bank of the York River, opposite Yorktown.

April 21, 1781 see **Burwell's Ferry** (pp. 112-114).

★ General George Washington (1732–1799) had been trying to persuade the French to co-operate in a combined land and naval assault on New York in the summer of 1781. General Jean Baptiste Donatien de Vimeur Comte de Rochambeau (1725–1807), commander of the French army in America, brought his 4,000 troops from Newport, Rhode Island in April and placed them under Washington's command. The prospects were still bleak since the combined Franco-American force numbered only 10,000 against General Henry Clinton's (1730–1795) 17,000 in well-fortified positions.

Then, on Tuesday, August 14, Washington learned that the French fleet of 29 ships and over 3,000 troops in the West Indies, commanded by Admiral François Joseph Paul Comte de Grasse (1722–1788), would not come to New York but would arrive in the Chesapeake later in the month and remain there until Monday, October 15. He saw immediately that if he could achieve a superior concentration of force on the land side

VA-11. Moore House, Yorktown, where the surrender documents were signed

Virginia 141

VA-12. Surrender field, Yorktown. The split rail fence marks the route that the defeated British Army supposedly took to lay down their arms. The soldiers then assembled in the open field.

while de Grasse still held the bay he could destroy the British Army at Yorktown before Clinton had a chance to relieve it.

Even without unified command of army and navy forces, Franco-American cooperation this time was excellent. Admiral Louis, Comte de Barras (d. ca. 1800), immediately put out to sea from Newport to join de Grasse. Washington sent orders to General Marie Joseph de Motier Marquis de Lafayette (1757–1834) to contain General Charles Cornwallis (1738–1805) at Yorktown. He then made a feint in the direction of New York to deceive Clinton. On August 21, Washington started the major portion of the Allied Army on a rapid secret movement to Virginia, via the Chesapeake Bay, leaving only 2,000 Continentals behind to watch Clinton. Washington kept his plans secret from the entire army so Clinton would not learn of his plans from deserters or prisoners. He arrived in Philadelphia, Pennsylvania on September 2; at Head of Elk, Maryland on September 6; and in Williamsburg, Virginia on the 14th with Lafayette.

Chesapeake Bay (Sept. 5, 1781)
Battle of the Chesapeake

On Thursday, August 30, 1781, while General George Washington (1732–1799) was on the move southward, Admiral François Joseph Paul Comte de Grasse (1722–1788) arrived in the Chesapeake with his entire fleet of 24 ships of the line and debarked 3,000 French troops a few days later to join General Marie Joseph de Motier Marquis de Lafayette (1757–1834).

General Charles Cornwallis (1738–1805) wrote a coded message to General Henry Clinton (1730–1795) on August 31, 1781, telling him that he could clearly see the sails of about 40 enemy vessels between Cape Charles and Cape Henry off the Virginia coast, "mostly ships of war and some of them very large." Clinton responded that he would try to help Cornwallis, either by sending reinforcements or by mounting a diversion. Clinton decided he could not send reinforcements until the Royal Navy could transport them or protect them on the long march overland. He decided to mount a diversion instead. He sent Benedict Arnold (1741–1801) on a raid on Fort Trumbull in New London, Connecticut and on Fort Griswold in Groton, Connecticut, hoping this would convince General Washington to keep troops in New England rather than move them south.

Admiral Thomas Graves (1725–1802), the British naval commander in New York, meanwhile had put out to sea in late August with 19 ships of the line, hoping either to intercept Admiral Louis, Comte de Barras's (d. ca. 1800), squadron or to block de Grasse's entry into the Chesapeake. He failed to find de Barras, and, when he arrived off Hampton Roads on September 5, he found de Grasse already in the bay.

When Graves saw the French ships coming out past Cape Henry, he ordered his fleet to reverse their order in the battle line. Admiral Samuel 1st Viscount Hood (1724–1816), who preceded the fleet, now occupied the rear. He assumed that Graves would attack the French who had not yet formed for battle. Graves delayed for an hour, giving de Grasse time to finish drawing up his battle line. Around mid-afternoon, Graves ordered the attack.

De Grasse knew that Admiral de Barras was on his way from Newport, Rhode Island to the Chesapeake with General Jean Baptiste Donatien de Vimeur Comte de Rochambeau's (1725–1807) siege artillery. He could not let the British fleet intercept him, but he had to wait for the tide to turn. When the tide turned, around noon, de Grasse ordered his ships to prepare for battle.

The French, who had more ships and greater firing power, sallied forth to meet Graves. Both fleets were badly damaged in the inconclusive engagement off the Virginia capes that lasted two and a half hours. The British suffered more damage because the French had greater gun power. The British lost the only vessel sunk in the battle—the 74-gun *Thunderer* which sank two days later.

For all practical purposes the victory lay with the French. While the fleets maneuvered at sea for five days following the battle, de Barras's squadron slipped into the Chesapeake and the French and Continental troops got past the British fleet into the James River. Then, de Grasse returned to the Chesapeake on Monday, September 10 where he joined with de Barras's squadron, with several heavy cannon and tons of salt beef aboard his ships. The combined French fleet now numbered 35 ships of the line.

Graves thought the enemy now had "so great a naval force in the Chesapeake that they [were] absolute masters of its navigation." He turned to Admiral Hood, his second-in-command, for advice. Hood replied, "Sir Samuel would be very glad to send an opinion, but he really knows not what to say in the truly lamentable state we have brought ourselves." Graves decided his only alternative was to bring his "shattered fleet" to New York to refit. The Battle of the Chesapeake confirmed French command of the Chesapeake and sealed the fate of Cornwallis's army.[90]

Siege of Yorktown (September 28–October 19, 1781)

★ When General Charles Cornwallis (1738–1805) set off for Yorktown, he planned to obtain a good seaport and harbor, never thinking that he would have to defend it against a siege from the land. Yorktown had some natural advantages as a naval station. Gloucester lay less than a mile to the north, on the northern bank of the York River opposite Yorktown, and swamps were on the east and west. He intended to fortify Yorktown and

Gloucester. Both places were on low ground and would require building exceptionally strong fortifications to make them safe as naval stations. A strong British squadron was expected to sail by October 5, 1781, to take a position between the two towns. A Congressional force coming by sea would have to come from the south.

Cornwallis thought that his men's time and energy could be better employed in other ways. Even using as many African Americans as he could muster, he would have to put the whole army to work either building the fortifications with the few entrenching tools with which his army was supplied or in guarding the working parties. He used the home of Thomas Nelson, Jr. (1738–1789), Governor of Virginia, as his headquarters during the siege and began constructing an outer line of redoubts and an inner line of earthworks, redoubts, and batteries around the town. Two redoubts, Numbers 9 (see Photo VA-13) and 10, strengthened the east end of the line. Two ravines in the rear of the town, Yorktown Creek and Wormley Creek, offered a little protection against an attack. Cornwallis also constructed a series of outworks on both sides of Wormley Creek northwest of Yorktown near the river. This star-shaped redoubt became known as the Fusiliers' Redoubt (see Photo VA-14) because some of the Royal Welch Fusiliers manned it.

When General George Washington's (1732–1799) army arrived at Yorktown on Wednesday, September 26, 1781, the French fleet was in firm control of the Chesapeake Bay, blocking General Cornwallis's sea route of escape. A decisive concentration had been achieved. Counting 3,000 Virginia militiamen, Washington had a force of about 8,850 Continental and 7,800 French troops—a far greater number than Cornwallis had expected. Cornwallis had an army of only about 7,400 men, including about 2,000 German troops, to defend Yorktown and Gloucester. He concentrated on Yorktown from the beginning.

VA-13. Redoubt Number 9, Yorktown. This photo shows the exterior of reconstructed Redoubt Number 9 with openings for gun emplacements.

VA-14. Fusiliers' Redoubt, Yorktown. The Fusiliers' Redoubt was named for the Royal Welch Fusiliers who manned it.

Preparations

The Continentals and French prepared for the siege of Yorktown that proceeded in the best military traditions of Sebastien Le Prestre de Vauban (1633–1707) under the direction of French engineers. Cornwallis soon realized that he could not hold Yorktown without reinforcements. Even though Clinton promised to send help, Cornwallis knew he could not count on him.

Major Generals Marie Joseph de Motier Marquis de Lafayette (1757–1834), Benjamin Lincoln (1733–1810) (who had been exchanged after his capture at Charleston, South Carolina), and Friedrich Wilhelm von Steuben (1730–1794) each commanded two brigades of Continental troops. General Thomas Nelson (1738–1789), Governor of Virginia and a native of Yorktown commanded the militia. General Jean Baptiste Donatien de Vimeur Comte de Rochambeau (1725–1807) commanded the French wing (see Photo VA-5), on the left, which consisted of seven regiments organized into three brigades. Both armies also had their own complements of engineers, cavalry, and artillery. Brigadier General Henry Knox (1750–1806) commanded the Continental artillery brigade.

On September 27, Washington ordered his troops to encircle Yorktown within a mile of the British fortifications. The troops encountered no opposition until midday when they came close to Yorktown where they met a few enemy pickets.

★ The Crown forces, trapped in Yorktown and under siege by Continental and French forces, lacked forage and slaughtered 600 to 700 horses. Their carcasses floated down the river almost continually during the siege of Yorktown. When the Crown forces realized that the Congressional troops constructed two redoubts during the night of Saturday, September 29, 1781, they began a furious cannonade. The troops continued their work despite heavy cannon and mortar (see Photo PA-15) fire. One shot killed three men and mortally wounded another. Rev. Evans, the chaplain, was standing near General George Washington (1732–1799) when a shot struck the ground nearby covering his hat with sand. Rev. Evans, much agitated, showed it to the commander-in-chief who replied with his usual composure: "Mr. Evans, you had better carry that home and show it to your wife and children."

The Continental wing on the right, or east side, of the line tightened the circle by moving farther to the right and nearer the enemy. The allied (Continental and French) army established permanent camps that formed a six-mile-long curve extending from the York River, northwest of the town, around to the south through woods and fields, then east to Wormley Creek. The swamps and marshes of Beaverdam Creek separated the Continental wing on the right and the French wing on the left.

★ Colonel Alexander Scammel (1747–1781), commanding a regiment of light-infantrymen, mistook a few of the enemy's light horsemen for Colonel Stephen Moylan's (1734–1811) brigade while reconnoitering some outworks the Crown forces had just evacuated. He thought he knew the officer in the front and was therefore not alarmed. However, two enemy soldiers came up to him on Sunday, September 30, 1781. One seized the bridle of Scammel's horse while the other pointed a pistol at him. As Scammel inquired who they were, a third man rode up and shot him in the back at point-blank range, burning his coat with the powder. At the same time, another soldier thrust his sword at the colonel, who, weakened with his wound, fell to the ground when his horse started at the sound of the pistol firing. The soldiers then plundered the colonel and took him to York as a prisoner. General George Washington (1732–1799) requested General Charles Cornwallis (1738–1805) to allow him to be taken to Williamsburg, where he died of his wounds on Wednesday, October 3.[91]

Cornwallis abandoned his forward position during the night of Sunday, September 30, except for the Fusiliers' Redoubt (see Photo VA-14) northwest of Yorktown and Redoubts 9 (see Photo VA-13) and 10 close to the river on the east side of the town. The day before, he received information from Clinton that a large fleet and 5,000 men would sail to reinforce him within a few days. He decided that he only needed to hold out for a few days and that he could do so more easily by occupying the inner defense line. As delays inevitably occur in war, Clinton's fleet waited for a favorable wind and tide and actually sailed from New York on the day of Cornwallis's surrender.

The Continentals and French immediately occupied the abandoned fortifications and began additional construction, including a new redoubt. The French advanced against the Fusiliers' Redoubt on the left and drove in the pickets, but the position was too strongly defended. British guns in the main fortifications maintained a heavy and sustained fire on the allies, but they continued to work on new construction, completing it in about four days.

The allies completed preparations for the siege during the first days of October. Advanced detachments, including general officers and engineers, reconnoitered the British lines on Monday and Tuesday, October 1 and 2, 1781 and soon determined that they would make the main attack on the left or west. They brought up the heavy guns which had been landed at the James River, 6 miles to the southwest, and fired a few cannon shots from the embrasures (see Photo- VA-5) overlooking the works the Crown forces were finishing on the gorge.

Gloucester Point (Oct. 3, 1781)

★ Gloucester was defended by a line of entrenchments across the Point and by about 700 British infantrymen commanded by Lieutenant Colonel Thomas Dundas (1750–1794). Lieutenant Colonel Banastre Tarleton (1744–1833) and his cavalry joined him, raising his strength to 1,000. They faced 1,500 Virginia militiamen under Brigadier General George Weedon (1734–1793) who were stationed there to check foraging expeditions and to close a possible escape route for the British Army. The Continentals were joined later by 600 French dragoons and 800 French marines.

Another force of Continental and French troops formed an arc across the interior of the point. (A French map of the Yorktown campaign shows the British fort on Gloucester Point as a semicircular structure with its broad, open end on the southeast shore of the point and extending across most of the point. A National Park Service booklet on the siege says the fortifications enclosed the village of Gloucester Point and consisted of a single line of entrenchments with four redoubts and three batteries. Nothing appears to remain of the structures, and route U.S. 17 cuts right through the area it encompassed. Most of the French troops were probably placed east of U.S. 17, extending several miles to the northwest.)

On Tuesday evening, October 2, 1781, Lieutenant Colonel Banastre Tarleton's (1744–1833) Legion of 250 cavalrymen and mounted infantrymen crossed the York River to Gloucester since there was no forage or room for the horses at York and they were useless there. The following morning, Lieutenant Colonel Dundas, who commanded the post at Gloucester, led detachments from all the corps to forage the country. The wagons and the pack horses were loaded with Indian corn about 3 miles from Gloucester and began to return at 10 AM with the infantry of the covering party. The dragoons in the rear guard formed an ambuscade for some militia horsemen who came by. If the enemy attempted to capture the forage, Colonel Dundas would rush out with the legion and capture them.

The wagons and infantry had nearly reached the York River when the cavalry began to retreat. When they reached the wood in front of Gloucester, Lieutenant Cameron, who had been sent to the rear with a patrol, reported that the enemy were advancing in force. They soon saw a column of dust and then some French hussars (see Photo VA-15). Lieutenant Colonel Tarleton ordered part of the legion, the 17th Regiment, and Simcoe's dragoons to face about in the wood while he and Lieutenant Cameron's party reconnoitered the enemy.

Armand Louis de Gontaut-Biron, Duc de Lauzun's (1747–1793) 300 hussars and Lieutenant Colonel John Francis Mercer's (1759–1821) infantrymen attacked Tarleton's Legion while Lieutenant General Claude Gabriel Marquis de Choisy (1723–1799), at the head of a great part of the corps sent to blockade Gloucester, marched down the road with a corps of cavalrymen and infantrymen to support them. The British rear guard was forming at the edge of a wood more than a mile away, in sight of the skirmish, when one of the hussars struck the horse of one of Tarleton's legionnaires. The horse plunged and overthrew Lieutenant Colonel Tarleton and his horse near the French line.

The entire British cavalry, concerned for the safety of their commanding officer, set out at full speed and arrived in such disorder that the charge failed to have any effect on the Duc de Lauzun's hussars who had already formed on the plain. Meanwhile, Tarleton escaped, obtained another horse and ordered a retreat to reorganize his men.

Tarleton dismounted 40 infantrymen who had just arrived under Captain Champagne. He placed them in a thicket on his right, about 300 yards from the French

VA-15. French hussars usually wore furred bonnets adorned with a cock's feather, a doublet with a pair of breeches, to which their stockings are fastened, and boots. They were armed with a saber, carbines, and pistols. This reenactor portrays a hussar from Lauzun's Legion.

squadrons. Their fire held off the Duc de Lauzun's hussars; and the Crown forces soon rallied. They immediately prepared to charge the front of the hussars with 150 dragoons while a detachment wheeled upon their flank.

The French hussars retired behind their infantry and a large body of militiamen who had arrived at the edge of the plain. They fired on Tarleton's Legion who had gathered behind a rail. Tarleton again ordered a retreat and made many unsuccessful attempts to detach the French hussars from their infantry. Tarleton reported one officer and 11 men killed and wounded and two officers and 14 French hussars killed and wounded. Captain Johann von Ewald (1744–1813), of the jaegers, reported losing one officer and four men killed and nine men wounded by the lances of the French hussars.

The next day, General de Choisy, reinforced by a detachment of marines, proceeded to cut off all land communications between the country and Gloucester.[92]

Afterward, the allies established their camps closer to the British camp and contained them until the end of the siege. Closing the siege lines around the Gloucester Point fort, the Continentals forced Tarleton to surrender. The Crown forces were paroled in 1782. Tarleton returned to England and never returned to America.

★ The French made a diversionary attack against the Fusiliers' Redoubt (see Photo VA-14) early Saturday evening, October 6 as 4,300 men began digging the first parallel trench between the lines. This trench extended about 2,000 yards and ran approximately parallel to the British inner defense line. The average distance of the line from the British defenses was only 800 yards except opposite Redoubts 9 (see Photo VA-13) and 10. The officers put 1,500 men to work digging, while 2,800 men guarded them. By morning, the trenches were deep enough to protect the sappers digging the next day.

The allies placed artillery along the trench and began an immense cannonade on October 9. The French constructed a small defense opposite the Fusiliers' Redoubt from which they could fire their guns against the British ships anchored in the harbor.

★ All the batteries of the Congressional forces opened fire with a terrible roar early Thursday morning, October 10, 1781. General George Washington (1732–1799) fired the first shot. The batteries fired 60 cannons and mortars until 10 o'clock, silencing the enemy guns. About 3 PM that afternoon, the batteries on both wings opened fire, driving back to Gloucester Point the frigate *Guadeloupe* and the sloop *Formidable*, which covered the advanced redoubt from the right on the York River.

Captain Johann von Ewald (1744–1813) was seated at table when the first cannon shot was fired. Commissary Perkins was killed at table and Lieutenant Robertson, of the 76th Regiment, lost his left leg. Commissary Perkins's wife was seated between the two men.

The batteries resumed heavy fire at three British ships in the York River in the evening. The French and Continental artillery nearly silenced the British guns. The forty cannon and 16 mortars (see Photo PA-15) fired 3,600 shots on the first day. Red-hot shot from the French battery struck the frigate *Charon*, a 44-gun ship situated to greatly annoy the troops in the battery above the town. The *Charon* caught fire and burned to the water. One transport was also lost. The batteries continued to fire the following day, burning another ship.[93]

Food supplies, even of putrid meat and worm-holed biscuits, were running so low that the British drove African Americans out of the town. The numbers of sick and dead increased daily. A German soldier noted the bodies lying unburied in the town, some of them with "heads, arms and legs shot off." Stephen Popp in the British lines remembered:

> We could find no refuge in or out of the town. The people fled to the waterside and hid in hastily contrived shelters on the banks, but many of them were killed by bursting bombs. More than eighty were thus lost, besides many wounded, and their houses utterly destroyed. Our ships suffered, too, under the heavy fire, for the enemy fired in one day thirty-six hundred shot from their heavy guns and batteries. Soldiers and sailors deserted in great numbers. The Hessian Regiment von Bose lost heavily, although it was in our rear in the second line, but in full range of the enemy's fire. Our two regiments lost very heavily too. The Light Infantry posted at an angle had the worst position and the heaviest loss. Sailors and marines all served in defending our lines on shore.[94]

Colonel Philip van Cortlandt, of the 2nd New York Regiment later recalled:

> The first gun which was fired I could distinctly hear pass through the town. . . . I could hear the ball strike from house to house, and I was afterwards informed that it went through the one where many of the officers were at dinner, and over the tables, discomposing the dishes, and either killed or wounded the one at the head of the table. And I also heard that the gun was fired by the Commander-in-Chief, who was designedly present in the battery for the express purpose of putting the first match.[95]

General Charles Cornwallis (1738–1805) was forced to conclude that "against so powerful an attack, [he could] not hope to make a very long resistance." He had about 3,250 men fit for duty and faced an allied army he estimated at about 16,000 men.

The sappers finished digging a zigzag communicating trench (see Photo VA-16) 200 yards forward by October 11. About dusk, they began work on a second parallel, completing about 750 yards that night. They continued working for the next three days, but they could not complete the line to the York River on the right because of the two British redoubts, Numbers 9 (see Photo VA-13) and 10.

VA-16. Remains of the communicating trench linking the second siege line to Redoubt Number 9. The zigzag pattern provides added protection to the attackers.

The allies decided to capture the two redoubts on Sunday night, October 14. The French were to attack Redoubt Number 9, the stronger of the two forts with 120 British and Hessians, and the Continentals would take Redoubt Number 10, defended by 70 men. Each force consisted of 400 men. Lieutenant Colonel Guillaume Comte de Forbach Comte de Deux Ponts (1754–1813) led the French, and Lieutenant Colonel Alexander Hamilton (1755–1804) commanded the Continentals.

Both columns began their assault at 8 PM. A "forlorn hope" preceded each column to cut through the abatis. The Continentals advanced with unloaded muskets and fixed bayonets and took Redoubt Number 10 in about 10 minutes. They did not wait for the sappers to chop through the abatis and lost fewer men. The French encountered some difficulties but captured their objective in less than half an hour. Sergeant Joseph Plumb Martin (1760–1850) recorded his observations of the assault on Redoubt Number 10:

> We arrived at the trenches a little before sunset. I saw several officers fixing bayonets on long staves. I then concluded we were about to make a general assault upon the enemy's works, but before dark I was informed of the whole plan. . . .
>
> The sappers and miners were furnished with axes and were to proceed in front and cut a passage for the troops through the abatis. . . . At dark the detachment . . . advanced beyond the trenches and lay down on the ground to await the signal for . . . the attack, which was to be three shells from a certain battery. . . . All the batteries in our line were silent, and we lay anxiously waiting for the signal. . . . Our watchword was, 'Rochambeau'. . . . Being pronounced, 'Ro-sham-bow,' it sounded when pronounced quick like, 'Rush on boys.'
>
> We had not lain here long before the . . . signal was given for us and the French . . . the three shells with their fiery trains mounting the air in quick succession. The word, 'up up' was then reiterated through the detachment. We . . . moved toward the redoubt we were to attack with unloaded muskets.[96]

The French had 15 men killed and 77 wounded taking Redoubt Number 9. The Continentals lost 9 killed and 25 wounded. The sappers continued digging the trenches immediately after the capture of the two redoubts, incorporating both into the second parallel by morning.

★ About 4 AM on Tuesday, October 16, 1781, Lieutenant Colonel Robert Abercromby or Abercrombie (1740–1827) and eight companies of light troops (about 350 to 400 men) made a sortie near the center of the line against two unfinished redoubts occupied by the French. They spiked seven or eight pieces of cannon and killed 20 French and one Continental before being repulsed with a loss of 8 killed and 12 captured. The disabled guns were repaired and soon resumed firing on Yorktown. General Charles Cornwallis (1738–1805) was in a hopeless situation. He hoped to get some of his troops across the river, break through the Gloucester lines, and escape to New York. He embarked some of his men in small boats and landed them on the opposite shore before midnight of October 16. A storm scattered the boats and prevented a second trip across.[97]

Surrender (Oct. 19, 1781)

★ The following day, the defenses of the allied troops were completed. They mounted more than 100 pieces of heavy ordnance that had been in continual operation during the previous 24 hours. The incessant cannonade caused the whole peninsula to tremble and silenced the enemy guns. At 10 AM on the fourth anniversary of Major General John Burgoyne's (1722–1792) surrender at Saratoga, New York and the very day that Admiral Thomas Graves (1725–1802) set sail from New York with a reinforced fleet and 7,000 troops for the relief of Yorktown, a drummer began to beat a "parley." The guns ceased fire; a British officer appeared, was blindfolded and taken into the American lines.

General Charles Cornwallis (1738–1805) proposed a cessation of arms for 24 hours so commissioners could prepare and adjust the terms of capitulation. General George Washington (1732–1799) consented to a cessation of hostilities for only two hours. Two or three flags of truce passed in the course of the day. Cornwallis surrendered two days later. Admiral Graves arrived five days too late.

Cornwallis requested that the Loyalist civilians and Continental Army deserters at Yorktown and Gloucester not be punished for supporting the British. He also asked permission for his troops to return to Europe as Major General Horatio Gates (1728–1806) had done with General Burgoyne's army at Saratoga. General George Washington (1732–1799) would not comply with these requests. Because Brigadier General Charles O'Hara (1740–1802) did not allow Major General Benjamin Lincoln (1733–1810) to march out with drums beating and flags flying at the surrender at Charleston, South Carolina, the British Army would endure the same humiliation at Yorktown.

Cornwallis protested that he was not responsible for O'Hara's harshness at Charleston. One of the Continental negotiators replied, "It is not the individual that is here considered. It is the nation." Washington later agreed to let the British parade to music, provided it was not a parody of any Continental tunes which the British bands enjoyed playing. During the negotiations, soldiers on both sides rested in the sun, and bands entertained each other with music.

The defeated British army marched out from Yorktown (see Photo VA-17) at 2 PM on Friday, October 19, 1781, dressed in new uniforms so they would not have to surrender them to the Continentals. The allies formed two lines with the French on one side and the Continentals on the other. The French wore white uniforms with black gaiters and

VA-17. Surrender at Yorktown, commemoration

their white standards with gold fleurs-de-lis flew above their heads. The Continentals wore darker, drabber clothes; the British turned their gaze away from them. The British Army marched between these two lines to a tune called "When the King Shall Enjoy His Own Again." Someone later switched the name of the piece to "The World Turned Upside Down" to make a political statement.

Cornwallis pleaded illness and did not attend. He sent Brigadier General Charles O'Hara (1740–1802) of the British Guards, his second-in-command and the only other general officer on the British side, in his place. General O'Hara tried first to give Cornwallis's sword to General Jean Baptiste Donatien de Vimeur Comte de Rochambeau (1725–1807), acknowledging that the British were surrendering to the French rather than to the Continentals. Rochambeau motioned him toward Washington who indicated that he should hand the sword to General Lincoln who had surrendered to the British under similar circumstances at Charleston the year before. General Lincoln accepted the sword and then returned it. The troops then marched to the surrender field where they laid down their arms (see Photo VA-12). Mathieu Dumas (1753–1837), who met the troops and directed them, recalls:

> I placed myself at General O'Hara's left hand. . . . He asked me where General Rochambeau was. "On our left," I said, "at the head of the French line." The English general urged his horse forward to present his sword to the French general. Guessing his intention, I galloped on to place myself between him and M. de Rochambeau, who at that moment made me a sign, pointing to General Washington who was opposite to him.
>
> "You are mistaken," said I to General O'Hara. "The commander-in-chief of our army is on the right." I accompanied him, and the moment that he presented his sword, General Washington, anticipating him said, "Never from such a good hand."

The British soldiers passed between the two lines of allied troops and laid down their arms. Some of them threw their weapons down angrily, as though they wanted to smash them on the ground until General O'Hara prevented them from doing so. As they marched away, some appeared drunk and many were close to tears, biting their lips or weeping.

Lieutenant Colonel Banastre Tarleton (1744–1833) surrendered the troops in the Gloucester lines across the river. Before doing so, he told Lieutenant General Claude Gabriel Marquis de Choisy (1723–1799), the allied commander, that, because of his evil reputation, he feared for his life if left in the hands of the militia. De Choisy excluded some of the militia from the surrender ceremony and everything proceeded smoothly.

The British surrendered 7,247 officers and soldiers and 840 seamen at Yorktown and Gloucester. They also gave up 264 cannon, 6,658 muskets, 457 horses and over £2,000 (approximately $288,200) in cash. Ironically, there were still 30,000 British and Loyalist troops fit for duty in America. Casualties during the siege were fewer than expected. Total Crown forces casualties were 596 killed and wounded and 8081 captured. The French suffered 60 killed and 192 wounded during the siege. The Continentals had a total of 24 killed and 65 wounded.[98]

Despite General Cornwallis's surrender, the Crown forces still held New York City and the main port cities of the South. They continued to raid the lower Chesapeake in 1782 and fighting continued in South Carolina and Georgia and on the Ohio frontier. Both General Nathanael Greene (1742–1786) and General Washington maintained their armies in position near New York and Charleston for nearly two more years. King George III (1738–1820) wanted to continue the war, but the British people were overwhelmingly opposed. The ministry fell and a new cabinet that decided the war in America was lost was appointed. General Sir Guy Carleton (1724–1808) succeeded General Henry Clinton (1730–1795) in the spring of 1782. Shortly after assuming command in New York, he wrote Washington to ask for a cessation of hostilities. With some success, Britain devoted its energies to trying to salvage what it could in the West Indies and in India.

Peace negotiations began in 1781 and dragged on until 1783. The British finally declared an end to hostilities in February 1783. Congress did the same in April. The treaty of peace, The Peace Treaty of Paris, acknowledging the independence of the United States of America was formally signed on Wednesday, September 3, 1783 and ratified by Congress in January 1784. The treaty also defined the boundaries of the new nation, settled fishing rights, and made arrangements for the payment of debts, the treatment of Loyalists, and the evacuation of Crown forces.[99]

Cherokee Campaign of 1782 see Tennessee chapter in the volume on the Deep South and the Frontier.

Little Fox and Great Fox Islands
Battle of Cager's (Cagey's) Strait (Battle of the Barges) (Nov. 30, 1782)

> Erosion has divided Cager's [Kedges, Kedgers, Kaigers] Strait into Little Fox and Great Fox Islands. A marker on route U.S. 13 (Lankford Highway) 2 miles south of Accomac and 2 miles east of Onancock notes that Onancock housed militia barracks during the Revolution and that Colonel John Cropper went from Onancock to aid Commodore Whaley in the last naval action of the Revolutionary War.

Even though General Charles Cornwallis (1738–1805) had surrendered over a year before the Battle of the Barges, raids continued on the lower Chesapeake in 1782. One of the raiders was a Virginia Loyalist named John Kidd who commanded a flotilla of six large barges. The crews of Loyalists and escaped slaves plundered property along the Chesapeake, not only in Virginia but also Maryland and North Carolina.

One of these raids occurred about 1 PM on Wednesday, November 27, 1782. The barges came out of Onancock Creek and spotted a fleet of seven vessels heading toward Tangier Sound. Captain Daniel Bryan of the *Flying Fish*, having the advantage of the wind, went to reconnoiter. He returned to confirm a previous report that a galley had joined the fleet. The barges anchored at Watts Island for the night only 5 miles from Onancock bar and about 3 miles from Tangier Island.

Early the following morning, several vessels were anchored off lower Tangier Island. Whig Commodore Zedekiah Walley (Whaley) (d. 1782) assumed they were the same ones he saw the previous afternoon. However, he could not reconnoiter to verify his assumption because the wind shifted to the northwest, almost directly to windward. He sent an express to Colonel John Cropper (1755–1821) requesting reinforcements. Before the express returned, Commodore Walley brought his fleet to Onancock where he arrived a little before dark.

When Walley reached Onancock harbor, he was informed that a sufficient number of volunteers had mustered to crew the *Victory* and the *Langodoc*. The *Victory* was a barge captured by the British which was lying idle at Onancock. The *Langodoc* was a small barge with a crew of eight men captured from the enemy earlier. They were placed under the command of Lieutenant Samuel Handy (1741–1828) of *Protector*.[100]

On the morning of Friday, November 29, Commodore Walley ordered Captain William Frazier (1752–1817) and 40 men selected from the fleet to take the barge *Defence* to Tangier Island as quickly as possible to reconnoiter the enemy. When he arrived at Tangier Island, Captain Frazier could not see any vessels. He landed at Crockett's place under British colors and inquired about the Congressional forces. Crockett told him that he saw five of them the day before on the leeward side of Watts Island and that Kidd's squadron of five barges and a prize had spent two nights there. Kidd's squadron had left early that morning in the direction of Fox Island, further up Tangier Sound. They intended to stop at Cager's Strait that night.

Captain Frazier then returned to Onancock where he joined the commodore and the other barges between Watts Island and Onancock. He reported his findings to Commodore Walley who was determined to pursue the enemy. Walley ordered *Victory* to return home with the minimum crew required to take the barge back because she could not keep up with the fleet. The rest of her crew was assigned to the other barges. Colonel Cropper was appointed second in command of *Protector* which also had Major Smith Snead, Captain William Snead, Captain George Christian (d. 1782), and Mr. John Revell (1740–1806) assigned. Captain Thomas Parker (1757–1819) boarded another barge.

The fleet headed to Fox Island where it anchored between 9 and 10 PM. Commodore Walley ordered Captain Levin Handy (1754–1799), captain of the marines aboard *Protector*, to join Lieutenant Samuel Handy on the *Langodoc*. They were to go ashore to obtain intelligence of the enemy. They learned that the British barges left there at 2 PM and headed toward Cager's Strait.[101]

Commodore Walley's fleet set sail at 4 AM on Thursday, November 30 and headed up Tangier Sound. They anchored off the northern end of Janes Island, southeast of Cager's

Strait. The captain of a small schooner, anchored above Janes Island, assured the commodore that the British barges were at anchor in Cager's Strait as he saw their lights at daybreak as the barges drew rations from the *Flying Fish*.

The little fleet set sail with *Protector* in the lead. The crews prepared for battle with a larger force. Captain Kidd's force headed westward through Cager's Strait. The swifter *Protector* had outdistanced the rest of the fleet between 8 and 9 AM. Cropper and Christian both advised the commodore to wait for his other ships; but Walley continued the pursuit, afraid of losing his prey.

Meanwhile Captain Kidd reversed course and prepared for battle. As he approached the enemy, Captain Kidd saw an opportunity. He formed his vessels into a line abreast and rowed to the attack. Colonel Joseph Dashiell (1736–1787), Captain Frazier, and Spedden also tried to form a line abreast with *Protector*, *Fearnaught*, and *Defence* arranged from left to right.

When Kidd closed to approximately 200 yards of *Protector* at about 9:30, he opened fire. *Defence* was the first to return fire, followed by Walley's *Protector* and *Fearnaught*. Dashiell's *Terrible* dropped to the rear of the line, probably to protect the trailing schooner. The Crown forces had the advantage with two to one. Kidd ordered his men to concentrate their fire on the Marylanders' flagship. Both squadrons suffered considerable casualties in the close range fighting.

Shortly after firing began, powder was spilled on *Protector*'s deck in the heat of battle. A spark ignited it and fire followed the powder trail to the ammunition chest in the stern which blew up. A second chest amidships exploded a short while afterward, killing several men and wounding many others. Some jumped overboard to extinguish the fire on their clothes. *Protector* drifted helplessly. *Defence* and *Fearnaught* withdrew to join the *Terrible* after the two explosions.

Captain Kidd took advantage of the confusion aboard the *Protector*. He signaled another barge to join his *Kidnapper* to go alongside *Protector* to board her. Meanwhile, four Crown barges took position to prevent any reinforcements from the other Maryland barges from coming to the *Protector*'s aid.

Vicious hand-to-hand combat ensued aboard the *Protector*. Commodore Walley was hit by a musket ball about this time. He refused to strike his colors and ordered his men to repel the enemy who had already started to board the *Protector*. Colonel Cropper assumed command. The futile battle continued for about half an hour. The captains of three of the remaining barges realized the battle was lost and turned about and headed up the Bay with the enemy barges in pursuit. *Langodoc* and *Flying Fish* went to the Annamessex River.

When the engagement ended, Commodore Walley, Captain Christian, and 25 crewmen were dead. Colonel Cropper and 29 others were wounded. Captain Allen (d. 1782) aboard one of the Crown forces barges was killed. Captain Kidd was wounded and 18 of his men were killed or wounded. The *Protector*'s survivors were put aboard the *Kidnapper* and taken to Onancock. Colonel Cropper arranged for the care of the Crown forces' wounded, provided that Captain Kidd would parole the prisoners. Kidd agreed, provided that all the prisoners captured aboard his barge *Jolly Tar* on November 15 be released and sent to his base on Hog Island.[102]

See the map of Virginia west.

Virginia 155

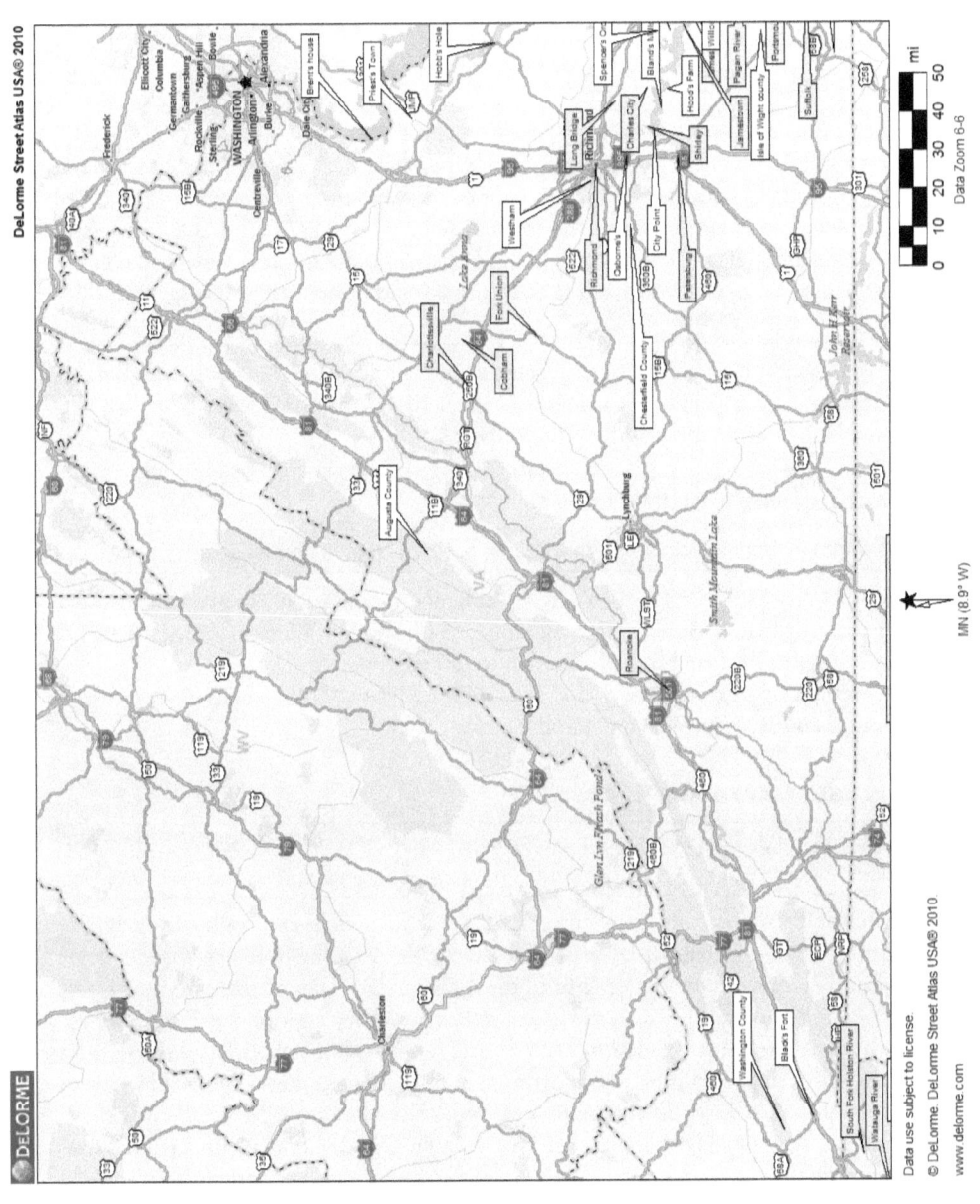

Virginia west: Map for *The Guide to the American Revolutionary War in Pennsylvania, Delaware, Maryland, Virginia, and North Carolina* © 2011 DeLorme (*www.delorme.com*) *Street Atlas USA*®

Abingdon
Black's Fort (July 24, 1776)

> Black's Fort was established in 1774 by Joseph Black (1747–1825) to protect settlers in the region from attacks by Native Americans during Lord Dunmore's War. The community became the county seat of newly formed Washington County in 1776 and was incorporated as the town of Abingdon in 1778. The site of the fort may have been along Town Creek in the vicinity of Blacks Fort Lane, three blocks east of the intersection of routes U.S. 11 (East Main Street|Lee Highway) and U.S. 58A (Cummings Street).

A group of militiamen ambushed some hostile Native Americans at Black's Fort on Wednesday, July 24, 1776 and killed 11 of them. The Native Americans retaliated, killing one militiaman and wounding three others.[103]

Washington County (April 10, 1777)

> Washington County is in western Virginia, north of Bristol, Tennessee.

Captain James Robertson (1742–1814) and nine Virginia militiamen pursued a band of marauding Native Americans in Washington County on Thursday, April 10, 1777. They killed one of them but had two men wounded in the skirmish.[104]

Westmoreland County (Sept. 2, 1777) see Pennsylvania, **Conemaugh River between Torrance and Bolivar, Westmoreland County** (p. 5).

Augusta County (Dec. 15, 1777)

> Augusta County is in western Virginia, west of Staunton and Charlottesville. Most of Augusta County in 1777 was in what is now West Virginia.

About 20 Native Americans entered the settlement in Tygart Valley in early December 1777. Snow fell as they waited to attack. Not wanting to return without some trophy, they concealed themselves until the snow melted. They advanced on the house of Darby Connoly (d. 1777) at the upper end of the Valley on Monday, December 15. The Native Americans killed him, his wife, and several of their children and took three others prisoners. They proceeded to the next house where they killed John Stewart (ca. 1719–1777), his wife and child and took Miss Hamilton, Mrs. Stewart's sister, prisoners. They quickly changed their direction and headed home with their captives and plunder.

John Hadden (1760–1819) passed by Connoly's house that evening and saw an elk, which the family raised, lying dead in the yard. Suspecting that all was not right, he entered the house, and saw the dead bodies. He hurried to alert the neighborhood and sent an express to Captain Benjamin Wilson, Jr. (1759–1839), who lived about 20 miles down the Valley. Captain Wilson quickly went through the settlement, mustering as many volunteers as he could to pursue the murderers. The following morning, he and his band of 30 men set out in pursuit. They tracked the raiders for five cold and wet days, often wading and swimming streams and then traveling many miles before the icicles could be thawed off. With no sign of the enemy after several days, the men refused to go any farther and returned home.[105]

City Point (Jan. 4, 1781; before Jan. 20, 1781; May 27–30 1781)

City Point (see Photo VA-18) is in Hopewell overlooking the junction of the James and Appomattox rivers. It was an important colonial port. Peter Francisco (ca.1760–1831) was put ashore here on the city docks in 1765. General Ulysses S. Grant made his headquarters here for the siege of Petersburg in 1864.

VA-18. City Point was an important colonial port. Peter Francisco was put ashore here on the city docks in 1765. General Ulysses S. Grant made his headquarters here for the siege of Petersburg in 1864.

The Royal Navy shelled (see Photo VA-2) and captured City Point on January 4, 1781 and returned in April and May with 2,500 troops.

★ Major General William Smallwood (1732–1792) led a party of 200 to 300 militiamen armed only with muskets. They forced some armed vessels to retire from a prize they had taken at Broadways before January 20, 1781. General Smallwood renewed his attack the following day with one or two 4-pounders, forcing some of the vessels to retreat from City Point to the main fleet at Westover. He had four men wounded.[106]

★ General Benedict Arnold (1741–1801) was returning from his raid at Chesterfield County between May 27 and 30, 1781. As he proceeded down the James River, his troops came under fire and destroyed a bridge at City Point.

Hood's Farm (Jan. 5, 1781; Jan. 10, 1781)
Richmond (Jan. 5, 1781)
Westham raid (Jan. 5, 1781)

Hood's Farm or Fort was on the James River, 50 miles south of Richmond, at the first narrow channel upriver from Norfolk. It was on the south side of the river opposite Point Weyanoke and between "Flower de Hundred" Creek and Ward's Creek and about 4 miles east of Powell's Creek in Hopewell. From route VA-10 (James River Drive), turn left onto VA-614 (Nobles Road) and go to the end. The fort was located about 2 miles northeast of the intersection with VA-614 (Wards Creek Road). The property is now privately owned. The battery was intended to protect Petersburg and Richmond from an attack from the river.

During the American War for Independence, Richmond was a town of less than 6,000 people, mostly slaves. Most of the town north of the downtown area is built on what was then known as Richmond Hill. St. John's Episcopal Church (see Photo VA-1) is on Church Hill on route U.S. 60 (East Broad Street) at North 24th Street. Patrick Henry gave his famous "Liberty or Death" speech here on Thursday, March 23, 1775. It is still an active parish. There's a historic marker in front of the church that explains the church's significance. Another marker, across the street, explains Brigadier General Benedict Arnold's (1741–1801) invasion of Richmond. Shockoe Hill is farther east at North 29th Street and Libby Terrace.

Westham is currently part of Richmond. The neighborhood of Westham is located in the northwest quadrant of the city, south of route VA-6 (Patterson Avenue) and west of route VA-356 (Three Chopt Road) around Woodberry Road and Sweetbriar Road. However, the arsenal may have been closer to the James River west of Charmian Road and the river opposite Williams Island.

After the raids of the Crown forces on Portsmouth on Sunday, May 23, 1779, and the burning of the nearby town of Suffolk, the Virginia General Assembly decided to move the capital from Williamsburg to a more secure location. They selected the small town of Richmond late in 1779, as it seemed more centrally located than any other town on navigable water.

About a year later, General Benedict Arnold's (1741–1801) fleet anchored in Hampton Roads with a force of 1,600 soldiers on Saturday, December 30, 1780. He took a small but powerful amphibious force up the James River to Richmond. The party departed the following day in small vessels accompanied by the warships *Hope*, *Swift*, and *Bonetta*. They planned to destroy supplies that General Friedrich Wilhelm Ludolf Gerhard Augustin Baron von Steuben (1730–1794) had gathered to support Major General Nathanael Greene's (1742–1786) army in the South and to prevent troops from joining Greene's forces. The raiders arrived at the estate of William Byrd III at Westover, about half a mile from Hood's fort, Wednesday night, January 3, 1781 and anchored.

The small battery of about 50 militiamen under Major James Cocke and the state artillery regiment under Captain John Allen fired on Arnold's vessels as they approached. They began about 10 PM on January 3 and fired twice every half hour. One schooner, not seeing the signal to anchor, proceeded upriver. The battery's 18-pounder fired on her, sending the captain and crew for cover below deck; but the ship passed the battery.[107]

Arnold sent Lieutenant Colonel John Graves Simcoe (1752–1806) with 130 of the Queen's Rangers and the light infantry and grenadiers (see Photo PA-9) of the 80th (Edinburgh) Regiment and a detachment of New York Loyalists under Captain Althause to spike the guns at Hood's while Captain Graves had the HMS *Swift* cover their landing. General Arnold's report to General Henry Clinton (1730–1795) stated that the fort "kept up a brisk fire upon us from a Battery of 3 eighteen, one 24 pounders, Iron and one Brass 8 inch howitz which killed one man."[108]

When 20 to 30 boats landed about 600 yards away, Major Cocke saw he was outnumbered five to one and gave orders to evacuate the fort. The rangers spiked the guns and took the howitzer. One of the wounded, Sergeant Adams (d. 1781) of the Queen's Rangers, died on January 9 and was buried with military honors and supposedly wrapped in the colors captured at Hood's battery.[109]

Arnold's troops and artillery disembarked in a heavy rain at Westover plantation, about 25 miles south of Richmond, the following day and immediately set out for Richmond by the Darbytown Road. They halted at Fourmile Creek, 12 miles from Richmond and camped for the night. They arrived in Richmond, 33 miles away, without opposition on the morning of Friday, January 5.

Arnold entered Richmond about 1 PM and sent a deputation to Governor Thomas Jefferson (1743–1826), a few miles upriver at Britton's (the location of the ferry at Westham). Arnold offered to buy supplies (tobacco, West India goods, wine, sailcloth, etc.) at half their value if the merchants would load them aboard his ships. Jefferson rejected the offer. So Arnold began to seize or destroy the goods, reporting to Clinton:

> . . . I found myself under the disagreeable necessity of ordering a large Quantity of Rum to be stove, several warehouses of Salt to be destroyed, several public storehouses and Smiths' shops with their contents were consumed by the flames—a very fine Rope [walk] full of material, private property, was burnt without my orders. . . . [The officer thought it was public property.][110]

The wind spread the fire to several houses and one of the town's two printing presses and types which "were also purified by the Flames." They spared the old warehouse which served as the capitol, probably because it was the property of the British-owned William Cuninghame and Company. They did not damage the wine or other private property. They also spared more than 30 vessels loaded with tobacco that lay in the river between Westover and Richmond because they were already in British hands.[111]

Meanwhile, several hundred Virginia militiamen from Henrico and Chesterfield counties were gathering in Manchester across the James River, south of Richmond. Only about 100 had crossed the James River to Richmond. Many of the troops had no weapons because they had been taken to Manchester to prevent their capture. General Friedrich Wilhelm Ludolf Gerhard Augustin Baron von Steuben (1730–1794) ordered Major Alexander Dick (1758–ca. 1785) who commanded the militia in Richmond to march to oppose Arnold's force. They were to fire one volley, then retreat back to Richmond.

The militia left Richmond late in the evening of the 4th. Major Dick was unfamiliar with the terrain and had received poor intelligence. His troops stumbled through woods and swamps for 24 hours, always in retreat, and never fired a shot at the enemy. They retreated all the way to Richmond Hill (now Church Hill), which Major Dick thought would be too steep for Colonel Simcoe's cavalry.

The 200 to 300 militiamen under Colonel John Nicholas (1757–1836) on the hill, near St. John's Church, spotted the first redcoats coming down the road shortly after noon on Friday, January 5. Arnold had his troops strung out to give the impression of larger numbers. He gave Colonel Simcoe permission to attack the hill, even though Arnold thought the militia would not fight.

Simcoe had his cavalry dismount and lead their horses up the hill. The militia fired a single volley and fled several miles into the woods. Meanwhile, Lieutenant Colonel Thomas Dundas (1750–1794) led the main force into the lower town. A small party of Congressional forces on horseback retreated across Shockoe Creek and up Shockoe Hill (four blocks from St. John's Episcopal Church) to join the others. Simcoe planned to descend to their rear but many "militia, [and] spectators, some with and some without arms" were on horseback on top of Shockoe Hill; so Simcoe's rangers galloped up the hill, causing them to flee in every direction through the woods. Simcoe's Rangers pursued them 4 or 5 miles but only captured about six of them.

Arnold then dispatched Simcoe and 400 men, consisting of his rangers and the "flank companies of the 80th" under Major Andrew Gordon, to destroy the munitions and foundry at Westham, 7 miles upriver (west). They set out in mid-afternoon and arrived at the foundry just before dusk on January 7, as about 300 militiamen "had arrived at Westham on their way down, and arms were actually re-crossing for them, but hearing of the Enemy's approach and being without Arms, they dispersed."

Simcoe destroyed a large quantity of small arms and military stores and broke the trunnions (see Photo VA-19) off some iron field pieces. Instead of blowing up the magazine as he planned—a move that he later considered too dangerous—he had the five or six tons of powder carried down the cliffs and poured into the river. He then burned the ordnance repair shop, John Ballendine's house, and one or two warehouses as well as the papers of the auditor's office and the books and papers of the council office brought to Westham for safekeeping. He captured 26 cannons, five brass field-pieces, 150 stand of arms, 120 sides of leather, the tools in the workshops, three wagons and a large magazine of oats and various stores.

His men also set fire to the state cannon foundry which had eight furnaces, a mill to bore cannon, a powder magazine, and buildings to house the 60 man labor force. However, only the roof burned, leaving the furnaces, chimneys and walls intact. The foundry, which could cast and bore four small cannon per week, operated from 1778 until its destruction in 1781. The raiders returned to Richmond that same evening without the loss of a man. They left the city about noon on Saturday, January 6, arrived at Westover

VA-19. Trunnions are two pieces of metal sticking out of the sides of an artillery piece. They serve to hold the artillery piece on the carriage and allow it to be raised or lowered. The trunnions are generally as long as the diameter of the cannonball and have the same diameter.

the next day, and later returned to Portsmouth where they entrenched and camped for the winter.[112]

Colonel George Rogers Clark (1752–1818) and 230 men prepared an ambuscade near Hood's farm Wednesday night, January 10, 1781. They fired on the enemy, killing 17 on the spot and wounding 30. The Crown forces returned the fire in confusion, wounding four. As Colonel Clarke's force was much smaller than the enemy's, they retired.[113]

Petersburg (April 25, 1781; May 10, 1781)

> There are two historical markers and a granite marker, on South Crater Road at the Blandford Cemetery in Petersburg, marking the site of the battle (see Photo VA-20). The village was called Blandford in 1781. Another marker at the intersection of North Adams and Bollingbrook streets identifies the site of Bollingbrook where Generals Phillips, Arnold, and later Cornwallis stayed. The house, no longer standing, was in the line of fire when Major General Marie Jean Paul Joseph du Motier Marquis de Lafayette (1757–1834) bombarded (see Photo VA-2) the Crown forces in Petersburg on May 10, 1781. General Phillips became ill shortly after taking Petersburg and died at Bollingbrook. Tradition says he was buried in Blandford Cemetery in an unmarked grave. Another marker at Old Street and Market Street identifies the site of the Golden Ball Tavern where Cornwallis's officers were supposedly quartered. The building was demolished in 1944.

VA-20. Markers at the Blandford Cemetery, site of the Battle of Petersburg. There are two historical markers and a granite marker, on South Crater Road at the Blandford Cemetery marking the site of the battle.

General Benedict Arnold (1741–1801), now in command of Crown troops, disembarked his whole force at City Point on the south bank of the Appomattox River, to the east of Petersburg, on Tuesday, April 24, 1781 and marched toward the city. Brigadier General John Peter Gabriel Muhlenberg (1746–1807) and about 1,200 militiamen guarded the town and the great supplies of tobacco and military stores. However, the town was unfortified and only small bodies of pickets guarded the approaches. Muhlenberg posted his fifth militia battalion inside Petersburg at the foot of Pocahontas Bridge. He placed his small band of cavalry and two brass 6-pounders on an elevation east of Blandford, a village about a mile east of Petersburg to cover the eventual retreat. They could then retire without having to cross the bridge along with the infantry. It would be difficult enough for the infantry to withdraw from Petersburg in an orderly fashion. If they panicked it could be catastrophic if they had to share the bridge with horses and guns.

Arnold divided his force into two columns and sent Lieutenant Colonel Robert Abercromby or Abercrombie (1740–1827) and the main body directly toward the enemy while Major General William Phillips (1731–1781), commanding the bulk of his force, consisting of some light infantrymen and the 76th and 80th Regiments of Foot, pressed steadily onward with fixed bayonets toward Muhlenberg's first line. Colonel John Graves Simcoe's (1752–1806) Queen's Rangers moved quietly around the British rear and arced south around the Muhlenberg right flank in an attempt to envelop the militia's flank and push them toward the river.

Abercromby's infantry had to advance over a broad stretch of swampy low ground, cross Poor's Creek and move uphill toward Blandford to get at the first line, the British first. Muhlenberg's militiamen were carefully placed in such a way that they could rely on firepower instead of the bayonet. Phillips's force greatly outnumbered Muhlenberg's. The militiamen held their ground, pouring volley after volley into the Crown troops advancing slowly through Poor's Creek. Just as the British were about to overtake the militia's right flank, Muhlenberg ordered the first line to withdraw to the second line. They retreated without panic or disorder.

The British now had to advance across low, marshy ground and cross yet another creek, Lieutenant's Run, which separated Petersburg from Blandford. They faced four battalions of Virginia militiamen all of whom fired devastating volleys of musketry. The militia beat back two assaults in nearly two hours and were beginning to run low on ammunition. Both sides now resorted to their artillery.

Muhlenberg's artillery fired grape shot (see Photo PA-14) at Abercromby's column and held it off for a considerable length of time. When Abercromby brought up four or five field pieces and placed them on a hill to Muhlenberg's right, he battered Muhlenberg's position so badly that Muhlenberg decided to withdraw across the Appomattox River by a bridge near the current Pocahontas Bridge before Simcoe's Rangers could attack his flank and rear.

The four militia battalions retreated through the streets of Petersburg, firing as they marched toward the bridge. The British pursued them closely as there were no real obstacles to slow their advance. They caught up to the militia's rear guard and began to close in for hand-to-hand fighting in the narrow lanes and alleys of Petersburg. The militiamen did not panic, fighting back with fists and clubbed muskets and a few bayonets while the rest of the troops crossed the bridge to safety on the north bank. When the rear guard broke off the action and crossed the bridge, they took up the bridge's planking to safeguard their retreat to Chesterfield Courthouse, leaving Petersburg to the enemy.

After capturing Petersburg, the Crown forces burned 4,000 hogsheads of tobacco and several small vessels but spared the buildings. Generals Arnold and Phillips, who assumed overall command at the end of March, raided the countryside between Petersburg and Richmond and then tried to retake Richmond. Arnold returned to New York and Phillips returned to Petersburg via Jamestown. However, Phillips discovered that Major General Marie Jean Paul Joseph du Motier Marquis de Lafayette (1757–1834) had arrived at Osborn's on May 8 and was preparing to cross the Appomattox River to Petersburg when General Phillips caught him by surprise. The British captured two majors, one aide de camp to Baron Steuben, the other to General William Smallwood (1732–1792); one captain and three lieutenants of dragoons; two lieutenants of foot, a commissary and a surgeon. Some of the prisoners had arrived only two hours before with the intention of collecting boats for the marquis to cross his army. The British also captured a considerable magazine of flour and bread near Petersburg.[114]

General Phillips occupied Petersburg on May 9. His right flank was covered by the James River and his front by the Appomattox River, on which the bridges had been destroyed. His left flank was only attackable by a long circuit through fords that were rather uncertain at this time of year. There, Phillips waited for General Charles Cornwallis (1738–1805) who was marching north from North Carolina.

Lafayette set up his artillery on May 10. Colonel Jean-Joseph Sourbader de Gimat's (b. 1743/4) battalion and four field pieces cannonaded their position from across the river. One of the cannonballs supposedly hit Bollingbrook, General Phillips's headquarters.[115]

General Cornwallis arrived at Petersburg on Sunday, May 20 with a brigade of the Guards, the 22nd, 33rd, and 71st Regiments, the light infantry of the 82nd, the Hessian Regiment von Bose, Tarleton's Legion, and Hamilton's Loyalists. A few days later, two more British regiments and two battalions of Anspachers, sent by General Henry Clinton (1730–1795), arrived, bringing Cornwallis's army up to 7,200 troops. They moved north across the James River and then west toward Charlottesville. Lafayette had withdrawn before him and kept his men out of Cornwallis's reach. He too had received reinforcements to his original force of 2,000 Virginia militiamen and 40 dragoons, the relics of Brigadier General Charles Armand's (Charles-Armand Tuffin, Marquis de la Rouerie) (d. 1793) Legion. He had now about 3,000 men—less than half Cornwallis's force.

Lafayette wrote to Washington on May 24:

> Were I to fight a battle, I should be cut to pieces, the militia dispersed and the arms lost. Were I to decline fighting, the country would think itself given up. I am therefore determined to skirmish, but not to engage too far, and particularly to take care against their immense and excellent body of horse, whom the militia fear as they would so many wild beasts. . . . Were I anyways equal to the enemy, I should be extremely happy in my present command, but I am not strong enough even to get beaten."[116]

Osborne's (Osburn's) (April 27, 1781)

Osborne's Landing (see Photo VA-21) is on the James River about 7.5 miles south of the Richmond city limits along Osborne Turnpike.

After capturing Petersburg, General Benedict Arnold (1741–1801) learned that Governor Thomas Jefferson (1743–1826) had assembled a flotilla of impressed merchantmen and privateers and two state warships to attack Arnold at Portsmouth. The vessels

VA-21. Osborne's Landing as it appeared in 2006

were anchored in the James River below Richmond because there were not enough men to crew them. The vessels gathered at Turkey Island, then sailed upriver and anchored off Osborne's Wharf. The flotilla, on Thursday, April 26, 1781, consisted of six ships, eight brigs, five sloops, two schooners, and a number of smaller craft:

Vessel and Number of Pounders	Normal Full Complement	Present Complement	Status
Tempest 16 6-pdrs.	120 men	6 men	Va. State Navy
Jefferson 14 4-pdrs.	70	23	Va. State Navy
Renown 16 6-pdrs.	120	23	Impressed privateer or merchantman
Apollo 18 6-pdrs.	120	5	Impressed privateer or merchantman
Willing Lass 12 4-pdrs.	60	13	Impressed privateer or merchantman
Wilkes 12 4- and 6-pdrs.	60	5	Impressed privateer or merchantman
Mars 8 4-pdrs.	40	3	
96 guns	590 men	78 men	

There were also two large unmanned vessels, *American Fabius* and *Morning Star*, and several other merchantmen. The fleet had been anchored in a semicircle at Osborne's for a month, inviting capture.[117]

When Arnold arrived at Osborne's about noon on Friday, April 27, 1781, with the 76th and 80th British Regiments, the American Legion, and some of the jaegers and the Queen's Rangers, he offered the Congressional forces half of their cargoes if they surrendered. Lieutenant Colonel John Graves Simcoe (1752–1806) reported that the enemy "were determined and ready to defend their ships, and would sink in them rather than surrender."

On the river bank opposite Arnold's force, 200 to 300 militiamen had mustered to oppose the Crown forces; but they were out of effective musket range and did not intend to get closer. Arnold set up his batteries of two brass 6-pounders and two brass 3-pounders both at the river's edge, nearly level with the water and on one of the small hills overlooking the anchorage. Several of his cannon were less than 100 yards from the *Tempest*. As the batteries fired at some of the vessels, parties in small boats boarded several unmanned merchantmen. One shot cut the *Tempest*'s cable and she swung around, exposing herself to a raking fire from Arnold's artillery. Her crew panicked and escaped under musket fire from the jaegers. The frigate *State*, anchored near the *Tempest*, was struck by the artillery. The explosion set fire to her topgallant and fore staysail which set ablaze. Her captors cut her cable to avoid danger and she drifted to shore and was taken by the Highlanders who extinguished the flames and secured her. Some of the crews scuttled or set fire to their vessels before fleeing ashore. Every single vessel was destroyed or captured in the two-hour attack. Arnold reported:

> Two ships, three brigantines, five sloops and two schooners loaded with tobacco, cordage, flour, etc. fell into our hands. Four ships, five brigantines, and a number of small vessels were sunk and burnt—we had not a man killed or wounded.[118]

The lack of boats and the hard wind prevented the British from capturing many of the seamen who took to their boats and escaped after scuttling and setting fire to some of their vessels which could not be saved.

Major General Phillips and General Arnold joined forces after their raids on Chesterfield Courthouse and Osborne's. They then marched to Manchester where they captured and burned 1,200 hogsheads of tobacco. They destroyed 500 barrels of flour, the flouring mills, and several warehouses there and more tobacco and five vessels at Warwick.

A few days after the action at Osborne's, Major General Marie Jean Paul Joseph du Motier Marquis de Lafayette (1757–1834) marched into Richmond with a small army of Continentals. When Arnold arrived at Manchester and was informed of that, he retired to his boats and proceeded down the river to Sandy Point. He then went to Petersburg to await the arrival of Lord Cornwallis from the south.[119]

Chesterfield County
Warwick, Cary's Mills (May 23, 1781; May 30, 1781)
Manchester (May 30, 1781)

> Chesterfield County is southwest of Richmond.

Lieutenant Colonel Banastre Tarleton (1744–1833) and his Legion were sent to protect a large body of Loyalists residing between the Haw and Deep rivers on Wednesday, May 23, 1781, as they mustered at Cary's Mills in Chesterfield County. A detachment of Congressional light troops had crossed the same day and, by accident, encountered about 200 Loyalists under Colonel John Pyle (1723–1804), on their way to Hillsborough to join General Charles Cornwallis (1738–1805). The Loyalists mistook the Whigs for Lieutenant Colonel Tarleton's corps and allowed themselves to be surrounded. They were captured without resistance. When Tarleton caught up with them, a skirmish ensued in which six Congressional troops were killed and 40 captured.[120]

Tarleton's troops remained in this vicinity until the 29th, when they proceeded toward Manchester. The bridge at Robert's mills, which had been destroyed, was repaired; and the army encamped near Cary's house. The next morning, they marched to Manchester where they destroyed about 1,200 hogsheads of tobacco. Major General Marie Jean Paul Joseph du Motier Marquis de Lafayette (1757–1834) arrived at Richmond, opposite Manchester, the day before. His army, encamped on the heights of Richmond, was joined by the militiamen who had been driven from Petersburg and Williamsburg. They observed the conflagration but did nothing to prevent it.

The British returned to Warwick that evening as Lieutenant Colonel John Graves Simcoe (1752–1806), with the rear guard, had orders to destroy a large quantity of flour (500 barrels) in Cary's mills. They also burned several warehouses with 150 hogsheads of tobacco, a large ship and a brigantine afloat, and three vessels on the stocks, a large range of public ropewalks (see Photo VA-3) and storehouses, some tan and bark houses full of hides and bark.

When Simcoe reported to Major General William Phillips (1731–1781) that he could not finish his task in the allotted time, General Phillips directed him to burn the mills and the flour which was destined for the Spaniards, but probably would have been used as supplies for Lafayette's army.

The next day, the troops proceeded by Osborne's to the Bermuda Hundreds where the Queen's Rangers had collected a number of cattle for them. A detachment of the Queen's Rangers conveyed the captured ships down the river. The militia commanded by Lieutenant Colonel Isaac Allen (1741–1806) ran along the shore and fired at the ships which only suffered minor damage.[121]

Point of Fork
Fork Union (June 1, 1781)

> Point of Fork is located in what is now Fork Union where the Fluvanna and Rivanna rivers join to form the James. Point of Fork was the site of an important arsenal and a major military supply depot in Virginia during the American War for Independence. David Ross (1755–1800), quartermaster in the Virginia militia, owned the land on which it stood. There are two historical markers on the left side of the road 0.8 miles west of the little town of Columbia. One relates to the arsenal and Lieutenant Colonel John Graves Simcoe's raid which was located on the high ground behind the marker.

After occupying Petersburg in May 1781, General Charles Cornwallis (1738–1805) sent Lieutenant Colonel John Graves Simcoe (1752–1806) and Lieutenant Colonel Banastre Tarleton (1744–1833) went on raids. Simcoe and 500 men from the Queen's Rangers and the 2nd battalion of the 71st Regiment went to Point of Fork on Friday, June 1, 1781. Tarleton went to Charlottesville on June 4.

General Friedrich Wilhelm Ludolf Gerhard Augustin Baron von Steuben (1730–1794) was at Point of Fork with 500 or 600 Continental recruits he was training for Major General Nathanael Greene's (1742–1786) army and guarding the main depot of military stores. Alerted to Colonel Simcoe's advance, Von Steuben had withdrawn the supplies across the Fluvanna and was moving his whole force there when Simcoe captured a lingering group of 30 of his men. Simcoe entered the arsenal and destroyed the buildings. He wrote in his journal that he captured "two thousand five hundred stand of arms, a large quantity of gunpowder case shot, etc., several casks of saltpeter, sulphur and brimstone, and upwards of sixty hogsheads of rum and brandy, several chests of carpenter's tools and upwards of four hundred intrenching tools...."[122]

He could not pursue von Steuben's main body because he did not have enough boats; so he displayed his small force widely along the river bank. They lit many campfires to give the appearance of great numbers, hoping that von Steuben would think they were the advance of the whole British Army. Von Steuben abandoned the supplies and retreated rapidly southward to Cole's Ferry whereupon Simcoe sent some men across the river in canoes to destroy the stores.[123]

Another account at the Virginia State Library in Richmond says that von Steuben removed most of the arsenal's supplies and concealed the gunpowder in local tobacco barns. Simcoe threw much of what he found into the Fluvanna and burned the rest; but, after his departure, David Ross (1755–1800) retrieved most of what Simcoe's men threw into the river. He also found 200 horses Simcoe left behind, sold them, and charged the state for the forage. Local residents found where von Steuben had hidden the gunpowder but kept it for themselves, instead of returning it to the state and the militia.[124]

Raid on Charlottesville (June 4, 1781)

Charlottesville is located at the junction of routes U.S. 29 (Seminole Trail) and U.S. 250 Business (Ivy Road).

The Virginia legislature was in session in Charlottesville on Monday, June 4, 1781 when General Charles Cornwallis (1738–1805) dispatched Lieutenant Colonel Banastre Tarleton (1744–1833) with 180 of the American Legion's dragoons and 70 mounted infantrymen against the town. Along the way, Tarleton captured and burned a train of 12 wagons bringing much-needed clothing to Major General Nathanael Greene's (1742–1786) army. The legislature was notified of Tarleton's advance and had adjourned. Even so, Tarleton captured several legislators; but Governor Thomas Jefferson (1743–1826) made a narrow escape and fled to the mountains about 10 minutes before their arrival.

Tarleton took and destroyed a quantity of powder and tobacco and 1,000 muskets. He and Lieutenant Colonel John Graves Simcoe (1752–1806) (coming from Point of Fork) then re-joined Cornwallis at Westover. Cornwallis was preparing to order Tarleton out on another raid to the west when he learned that Brigadier General "Mad Anthony" Wayne (1745–1796) had joined forces with Major General Marie Jean Paul Joseph du Motier Marquis de Lafayette (1757–1834) and that both were advancing on Elk Hill. Cornwallis decided to return to Richmond.

Jefferson complained in a letter about the damage the Crown forces had wrought at Elk Hill. They destroyed the barns and took all the corn and livestock and every horse that could be ridden or hitched to a wagon. They killed the young colts, turned out the servants, and marched the slaves off with the livestock.[125]

New London and Bedford
Tarleton's Raid (July 9–24, 1781)

New London is about 11 miles southwest of Lynchburg and Bedford is about 22 miles west-southwest of Lynchburg.

General Charles Cornwallis (1738–1805), at his new base at Suffolk on the south side of the James River, ordered Lieutenant Colonel Banastre Tarleton (1744–1833) to ride through Prince Edward Courthouse to New London, Virginia, more than 150 miles west, to destroy the public and private stores of the Continental Army. Tarleton left Cobham on Monday, July 9, 1781. He rode through Petersburg, Amelia Courthouse, Prince Edward Courthouse, Charlotte, New London, and Bedford. He camped in the rich grasslands at the foot of the Blue Ridge Mountains at Bedford for two days and collected some fine horses.

Major General Marie Jean Paul Joseph du Motier Marquis de Lafayette (1757–1834) sent Brigadier General "Mad Anthony" Wayne (1745–1796) into Amelia County to try to intercept Colonel Tarleton on his return. Meanwhile, Brigadier General Daniel Morgan (1736–1802) was assembling a strong force at Goode's Bridge, near Petersburg for the same purpose.

Tarleton, informed of the danger, burned his three light wagons and returned by a more southerly route through Lunenburg County. The intense July heat limited his movement to the early morning and late afternoon, but he still managed to cover 30 or 40 miles a day. He moved so fast that he was never in danger, as intelligence reports could not keep up with his location. He returned to Suffolk on Tuesday, July 24, 1781. He covered 400 miles in 15 days and reported:

> The stores destroyed, either of a public or private nature, were not in quantity or value equivalent to the damage sustained in the skirmishes on the route, and the loss of men and horses by the excessive heat of the climate.[126]

5
NORTH CAROLINA

The Stamp Act debate aroused tensions in North Carolina over the colony's relationship with Great Britain. The Sons of Liberty led a mob to prevent the stamps from being unloaded in Wilmington in 1765. The imposition of additional taxes incited further clashes between the governor and his Assembly, particularly over the funding of the colonial court system. The courts ceased functioning by 1772.

North Carolina sent delegates to the First Continental Congress in Philadelphia, Pennsylvania in the fall of 1774, even though governor Josiah Martin (1737–1786) tried to prevent their appointment. Fifty-one women of the town signed a resolution supporting the actions and resolutions of that congress and mailed it to England. One of the resolutions banned the import and consumption of British tea. A London cartoonist satirized the event by depicting the ladies as matrons gathered at a tea party to sign the document. The provincials pretended that the event actually happened and invented a site, the home of Mrs. Elizabeth King. They marked it with a bronze teapot on a post. While the "Edenton Tea Party" probably never occurred, the story shows the political activism of the women during the American War for Independence.

When news of the fighting at Lexington and Concord, Massachusetts arrived in Charlotte in May 1775, a group of citizens meeting there supposedly adopted the Mecklenburg Declaration which called for the colony to break its relationship with Great Britain. Militiamen all over North Carolina began drilling, and members of the Assembly began to discuss joining in the rebellion. Loyalties were sharply divided. Governor Martin fled to an English warship and called on Loyalists to rise up and crush the rebellion. North Carolina contributed 11,238 men to the war—3,975 militia and 7,263 in the Continental Army.

North Carolina Loyalists were slow to become organized and oppose the Whigs. They were badly defeated at Moores Creek Bridge on February 27, 1776. General Thomas Gage (1719–1837), Commander-in-Chief of British forces in America, was convinced that there was strong support in the South, so he organized a strong expeditionary force under General Charles Cornwallis (1738–1805), General Henry Clinton (1730–1795), and Admiral Sir Peter Parker (1721–1811) to go to Brunswick Town.

Clinton sailed from Boston on January 20, 1776, planning to meet Cornwallis's force arriving from Ireland. Clinton arrived at Cape Fear, near Wilmington, in March 1776. However, Clinton was forced to wait until the end of May before all of Cornwallis's troops arrived due to a terrible storm in the North Atlantic.

Gage planned for the Loyalists to join the British forces near Cape Fear. By February 18, 1776, approximately 1,500 Loyalists, consisting mostly of recently immigrated Highland Scots and about 130 ex-Regulators gathered to march toward the coast. Colonel James Moore (1729–1777), commanding 650 men of the 1st North Carolina Regiment, left Wilmington to oppose them. Three groups of Whig militia joined them, bringing the force to 1,100 men.

> The State Department of Archives and History (4622 Mail Service Center, Raleigh, NC 27699-4622; phone: 919-733-7442) publishes the *Guide to North Carolina Historical Highway Markers* that includes almost 1,400 markers, giving text descriptions

and locations. It also has photographs of sites, a map and an index. As the guide was published in 1990, information about any markers erected since then can be found at the department's web site (**www.hpo.dcr.state.nc.us**). The State Historic Preservation Office (phone: 919-733-4763), a division of The State Department of Archives and History, is another important source of information.

The Department of Conservation and Development, Travel and Promotion Division (phone: 919-733-8372; website: **www.visitnc.com**) offers general tourist literature, some of which covers the state's colonial history. Another department within the division (phone: 919-733-8302; website: **www.NCCommerce.com**) publishes the *Official North Carolina Travel Guide* and several other useful publications.

The Historic Preservation Foundation of North Carolina, Inc. (phone: 919-832-3652; website: **www.presnc.org**), known as the North Carolina Society for the Preservation of Antiquities until 1974, is a private non-profit that sells books and other publications. Some of them provide considerable information about the state's Revolutionary War landmarks. Another helpful source is Daniel W. Barefoot's *Touring North Carolina's Revolutionary War Sites* (Winston-Salem: John F. Blair, 1998).

See the map of North Carolina east.

Brunswick, Cape Fear and vicinity

Fort Johnston, Cape Fear (Nov. 14, 1775; Nov. 16, 1775; Nov. 17, 1775; Nov. 19, 1775; Nov. 20, 1775; Jan. 27, 28, 1776; March 8–12, 1776; March 23, 1776; April 7, 9, 12, 13, 14, 16, 17, 18, 1776; May 1–3, 1776; May 20, 1776; May 22, 23, 24, 27, 1776)

Brunswick (April 6–27, 1776; ca. May 10, 1776; May 16, 17, 1776)

Wilmington River, Cape Fear River (April 21, 22, 26, 1776; May 2, 16, 24, 27, 1776; July 1776)

Orton Mill and Kendal Plantation (May 11, 1776)

Newtown Ferry House (May 16, 17, 20, 1776)

Fort George, Bald Head Island (Sept. 6–7, 1776)

The Cape Fear River is southwest of Wilmington between Wilmington and Brunswick. Brunswick is on the Cape Fear River about 12 miles north of its mouth. Fort Johnston was at Bay St. in Southport.

In 1745, the North Carolina Assembly authorized the construction of a fort in Southport to protect the Cape Fear River from the Spanish. Erected in the 1740s, the fort is today the smallest working military installation in the world, used by the Sunny Point U.S. Military Ocean Terminal. Wilson Angley's *A History of Fort Johnston on the Lower Cape Fear* (Southport, NC: Southport Historical Society, 1996) chronicles the history of the fort, named for Gabriel Johnston (1699–1752), the royal governor.

A marker on East Bay Street east of South Davis Street in Southport bears the inscription: "This tablet was erected May, 1911 by the North Carolina Society of Colonial Dames of America to mark the site of Fort Johnston, the first fort in the Province of North Carolina, built under Act of Assembly of 1745 and completed 1764, and named in honour of Governor Gabriel Johnston. The Patriots of the Cape Fear

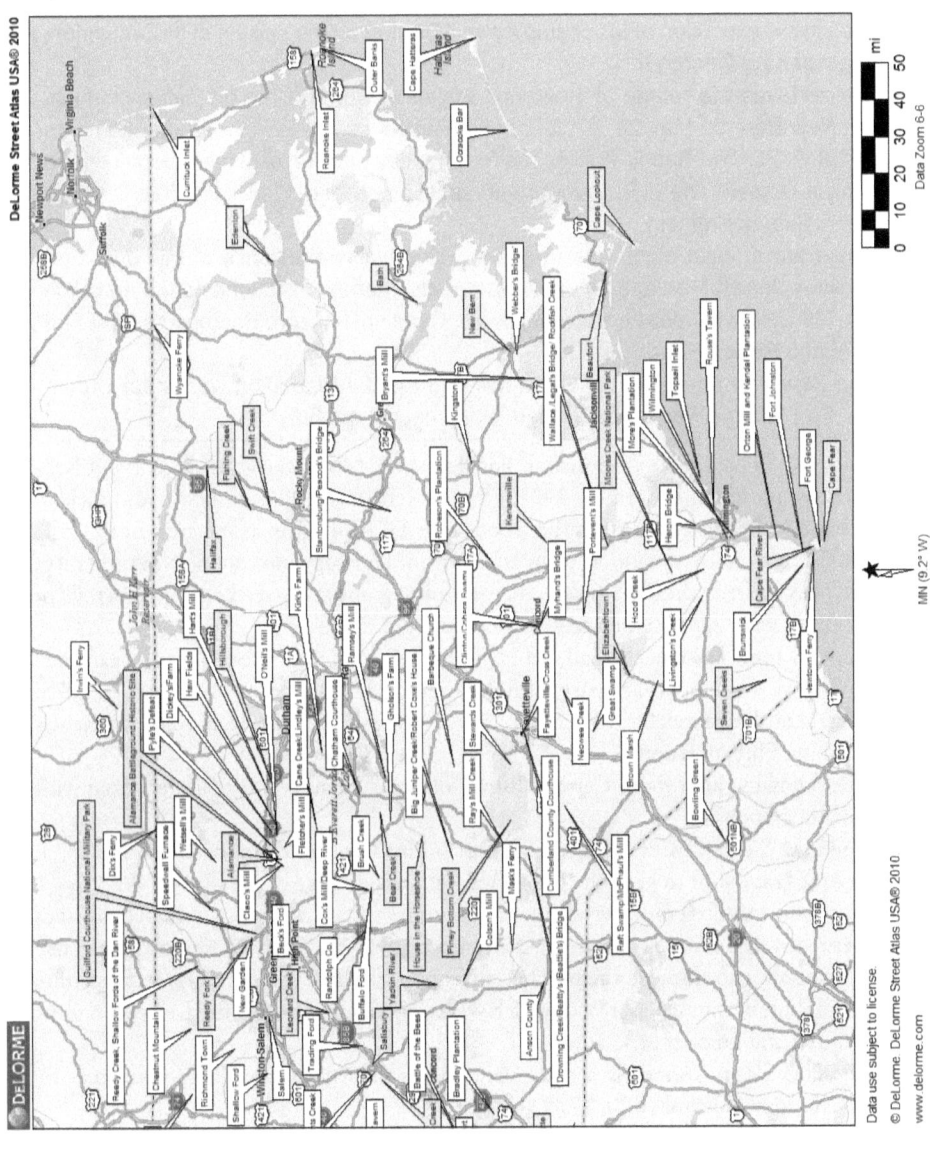

North Carolina east: Map for The Guide to the American Revolutionary War in Pennsylvania, Delaware, Maryland, Virginia, and North Carolina © 2011 DeLorme (www.delorme.com) Street Atlas USA®

resisting the execution of the Stamp Act in 1766 forced the spiking of its 24 cannon, the gift of King George II."

The fort was the refuge of Governor Josiah Martin (1737–1786) after his flight from New Bern on May 24, 1775 until the Rebels compelled him to abandon it on July 18, 1775. The Rebels burned the fort that day and Royal Government in North Carolina ceased. The U.S. government rebuilt it between 1794 and 1809. Only the officers quarters remain.

There are at least eight other markers within walking distance of this one: Fort Johnston, Josiah Martin, a different marker also named Fort Johnston, Map of the First 100 Lots, Mrs. Jessie Stevens Taylor, Catalino Tingzon, Southport's First Fire Alarm and Robert Ruark.

The Newtown Ferry House, Orton Mill and Kendal Plantation were near Brunswick. Fort George was on Bald Head Island near Cape Fear.

The HM Sloop *Cruizer*, moored off Fort Johnston, fired some guns at a party of Rebels Tuesday afternoon, November 14, 1775. The Rebels withdrew to the woods quickly.[1]

★ A band of Rebels appeared in the woods near Fort Johnston as the crew of the HM Sloop *Cruizer* removed cannon from the fort on Thursday afternoon, November 16, 1775. They retired when the *Cruizer* began to fire grape shot (see Photo PA-14). Captain Francis Parry sent 40 men to keep possession of the fort.[2]

★ Captain John Tollemache had the HM Sloop *Scorpion*, moored in Cape Fear Harbour, fire two 6-pounders at a party of Rebels Thursday afternoon, November 16, 1775. He then sent the lieutenant master and 15 men with the marines to prevent the Rebels from taking Fort Johnston.

★ The following afternoon, Captain John Tollemache had two 6-pounders fired with round and grape shot.[3]

★ The HM Sloop *Cruizer*, moored off Fort Johnston on Friday November 17, 1775, fired some grape shot to keep the Rebels out of musket range of the fort.[4]

★ Fort Johnston fired four swivel guns and several muskets at a party of Rebels advancing near the fort on Sunday morning, November 19, 1775. The HM Sloop *Cruizer* also fired grape shot to disperse them. That afternoon, the HM Sloop *Scorpion* fired nine 6-pound shots at the Rebels, five of which were grape shot. The fort fired 12 swivel guns with round and grape shot.[5]

★ The HM Sloop *Cruizer* fired five guns to scour the woods near Fort Johnston at 11 PM on Monday November 20, 1775.[6]

★ A body of Rebels was seen in and about Fort Johnston at 8 AM on Saturday, January 27, 1776. A party of waterers hailed the HM Sloop *Scorpion* at 9 AM and Captain John Tollemache sent his boats to bring them off. He then fired 15 round and 11 grape shots at the Rebels in Fort Johnston at 11 AM. The HM Sloop *Cruizer* also fired her great guns and small arms until the Rebels appeared from behind the walls. The Rebels returned fire with some small arms. They also burned or took six hogsheads and four barrels of powder.[7]

★ Captain Francis Parry saw a number of Rebels at work in Fort Johnston at 1 AM Sunday, January 28, 1776. He ordered the HM Sloop *Cruizer* to fire some grape shot at them. The Rebels returned fire with small arms and dispersed.[8]

★ Captain Francis Parry's *Cruizer* was stationed off the coast near Fort Johnston on the Cape Fear River in early March 1776. Whenever the occupants of the fort appeared, the *Cruizer* would fire round and grape shot at them. Captain Parry sent an officer and eleven men to destroy the fort on Sunday, March 10, 1776 but they were driven back by the militia without any losses.

★ Captain Parry received reinforcements from General Henry Clinton's (1730–1795) fleet on March 12, 1776. Captain John Tollemache's *Scorpion* fired on Fort Johnston again in March and Captain Tollemache sent his boat to reduce the breastworks.[9]

★ Congress appointed James Moore (1729–1777) a brigadier general in command of all the forces in North Carolina after his victory at Moores Creek Bridge (Tuesday, February 27, 1776). He marched 120 men of the 2nd North Carolina Regiment and 449 men of the 1st North Carolina Regiment to Wilmington when he learned that the British fleet arrived off Cape Fear on Tuesday, March 12, 1776. Moore's force of 1,847 men, including the local militia, erected two batteries on the Brunswick shore to oppose the 700 British Regulars in the fleet. The batteries were armed with 6- and 9-pounders and the hulks of ships were sunk in the Cape Fear River to block the channel below Wilmington.

The British landed some foraging parties along the shore and captured one officer and five men in one skirmish. The Royal Navy remained in the Cape Fear area, firing artillery at any Rebels who appeared on the shore. General Henry Clinton (1730–1795) issued a proclamation calling for the citizens of the Carolinas to reaffirm their allegiance to the King and promised to pardon anybody who did so, except Robert Howe (1732–1786) and Cornelius Harnett (ca. 1723–1781) who organized the first militias used against the King and were named as outlaws by the parliament.[10]

★ On Saturday, March 23, 1776, the 24-gun *Scorpion*, with Governor Josiah Martin (1737–1786) on board, the 18-gun *Raven,* the 10-gun sloop *Cruiser,* three or four small armed vessels and a few transports with about 400 land forces and some captured vessels anchored in the Cape Fear River off Fort Johnston and Brunswick. The flotilla of some 20 vessels awaited the arrival of General Henry Clinton's (1730–1795) fleet which had been scattered by stormy weather. General Charles Cornwallis's (1738–1805) fleet from Ireland had not yet arrived. General Clinton learned of the defeat at Moores Creek Bridge and decided not to risk landing his troops on the mainland.

The ships of war (see Photo PA-16) and transports had a vast quantity of military supplies and apparatus on board. Captain John Abraham Collett, formerly commander of Fort Johnston, was a passenger aboard the armed vessel *General Gage.* He was "well known to be a pert audacious little scoundrel" who set fire to the elegant house of Colonel William Dry (1720–1781), a former Royal Councilman and collector of the customs for the port of Brunswick. The fire destroyed "all the valuable furniture, liquors &c." Dry also burned the house of William Hooper, Esq. (1742–1790), one of the continental delegates and a signer of the Declaration of Independence, about 3 miles below Wilmington, and two deserted pilot houses near Fort Johnston where the Crown troops landed frequently in small parties to pillage and carry off some slaves.

In one of their excursions, they lost eight men. Many of the residents left Wilmington to seek refuge in the country. Provincial troops occupied the area and began making preparations to defend it by constructing entrenchments along the river, both in and below the town. Troops came from everywhere to join them and they soon expected to have at least 5,000 men there.[11]

★ Lieutenant John Graves's HM Schooner *St. Lawrence* exchanged shots with Rebels who fired from the shore near Fort Johnston on Sunday morning, April 7, 1776 as she headed up the river with the watering sloop. The *St. Lawrence* fired seven 4-pounders, 12 swivels (see Photo DE-2) and small arms before anchoring at 1 PM. Firing was repeated at 4 AM on Tuesday the 9th when four Refugees who had escaped from the Rebels boarded the *St. Lawrence*. She weighed anchor at 9 and kept firing at the Rebels who continued their fire.[12]

★ The HM Sloop *Scorpion* fired three 6-pounders at some Rebels on shore near Fort Johnston on Friday, April 12, 1776. The following day, she fired one 6-pounder with round and one with grape and canister shot at a party of Rebels trying to impede the ship. The obstruction work continued on Sunday, the 14th, so she fired several volleys of small arms at the Rebels in the morning and a 6-pounder, a swivel and several muskets in the afternoon.[13]

★ The HM Sloop *Scorpion* fired a 6-pounder and several muskets at the Rebels again on Tuesday, April 16, 1776. The action continued for the next 2 days, with two 6-pounders on the 17th and one 6-pounder on the 18th.[14]

★ The crew of Captain John Tollemache's sloop *Scorpion* fired several muskets and three 6-pounders with grape and canister shot at a band of Rebels along the Cape Fear River on Sunday morning, April 21, 1776. The following day, some Rebels fired at the *Scorpion* and Lieutenant John Graves's schooner *St. Lawrence* which returned fire with muskets while the *Scorpion* fired muskets and six 6-pounders. The Rebels resumed fire on the *St. Lawrence* on Tuesday. The *St. Lawrence* responded with six 4-pounders and six swivels (see Photo DE-2). The *Scorpion* exchanged fire again on the 26th.[15]

★ General Henry Clinton (1730–1795) destroyed Fort Johnston on Wednesday, May 1, 1776 because riflemen had used it to shoot at the British fleet for several days. The sniping did not stop, however. Even though the Royal Navy had moved 200 yards from the shore, the marksmen still fired at them. Five shots struck the armed transport *Sovereign*. Some of the shots struck men on the transport *Glasgow Packet* behind her, killing two men and wounding two others. The *Cruizer* and the *Sovereign* returned fire with their artillery and drove the snipers away.

The vessels withdrew and anchored 400 yards from shore. "Between fifty and sixty of the Rebels well armed, and draped in caps and hunting frocks" continued firing but to little effect due to the distance. The schooner *St. Lawrence* returned fire with 4-pounders and swivel guns but to no effect.

General Clinton landed 10 companies near Fort Johnston to try to eliminate the snipers the following day. The soldiers only found tracks from the riflemen's horses. They searched inland for 4 miles but found nothing.[16]

★ Lieutenant John Graves's *St. Lawrence* fired four 4-pounders and six swivels at a band of Rebels on shore at 4 PM on Thursday, May 2, 1776. He then sent his cutter after a small schooner boat with three Refugees on board.[17]

★ The snipers returned Friday morning, the 3rd. The *Cruizer* fired her guns at them and quieted them for the day.

★ The 15th and 28th British regiments landed on a peninsula at the mouth of the Cape Fear River on Sunday, May 7, 1776. They reconnoitered the country, found no Rebels and re-embarked. A few days later, the 27th and 33rd regiments went 15 miles up the river and captured a Rebel post at Brunswick. They took a few prisoners and had one man killed. They then returned to their ships with 20 bullocks.[18]

★ General Henry Clinton (1730–1795) and General Charles Cornwallis (1738–1805) led about 1000 Regulars on a night raid on the bridge at Orton Mill early Sunday morning, May 11, 1776. They rowed 15 miles upstream with muffled oars. When they reached Kendal Plantation between 2 and 3 AM, they pulled into shore. Kendal Plantation was Brigadier General Robert Howe's (1732–1786) home. He had formed the first North Carolina militia units early in 1775 and General Clinton wanted to pay him a special visit. However, the British soldiers made so much noise that the sentries heard them, alerted the guard of about 200 foot and 20 light horse, and gathered their horses and opened the gates of the cattle pens. They fired at the Regulars as they marched up the causeway from the river, killing Private George McIntosh (d. 1776) of the 44th Regiment Light Infantry.

General Clinton ordered his men to fix bayonets and surround the house. They did not find any soldiers. They shot an old woman in the hip, stabbed another with a bayonet, and beat out the front teeth of a third. The raid cost the British two killed, one captain wounded, and two taken prisoners, including a sergeant of the 33rd Regiment.

The Regulars then headed to Orton Mill intending to surprise Major William Davis (1724–1780) who commanded a detachment of 90 North Carolina Regulars. Davis received the guard's alarm and withdrew with his baggage and two swivel guns (see Photo DE-2). The British burned the mill and then plundered homes along the way back to their vessels at the fort. All they got from this raid was three horses and three cows.[19]

The 15th, 28th, 33rd, 37th, and 54th regiments landed and encamped near Fort Johnston on Wednesday, May 15th. The 57th regiment camped on the opposite shore and the 46th remained on board. Some Rebels were only 2 or 3 miles away; but their strongest post was at Wilmington, about 20 miles away.[20]

★ Carolina snipers along the shore of the Cape Fear River continued to fire upon British vessels throughout the month of May 1776. They attacked at night and sniped from cover during the day. They fired at Captain John Linzee's sloop *Falcon* and Lieutenant John Graves's *St. Lawrence* on Thursday, May 16, 1776. The *Falcon* returned fire with round and grape shot but with little effect. The HM Schooner *St. Lawrence*, in the Wilmington River (Cape Fear River), near Cape Fear, fired six 4-pounders.

★ The following day, the 17th, General Charles Cornwallis (1738–1805) led a secret mission to burn Brunswick, a Rebel base. He and 900 Regulars left in the night and rowed up the Cape Fear River. They surprised the guards on the outskirts of town and captured Brunswick with the loss of only one man killed. The town had been abandoned for some time with only a small garrison left to protect it, so the British could only find 20 bullocks and six horses to take with them.[21]

★ Lieutenant John Graves sent the master and nine men from the *St. Lawrence* to assist Captain John Linzee in dislodging a party of Rebels from the Newtown Ferry House at 11 PM on Friday, May 17, 1776.[22]

★ The Rebels sent a fire raft down the Cape Fear River three days later, on Monday night, May 20, 1776, hoping to burn the HM Schooner *St. Lawrence* and the British transport *Glasgow Packet*. However, Lieutenant Graves sent a boat to intercept the raft and tow it to the edge of Marsh Island where the crew set it on fire.[23]

★ General Henry Clinton (1730–1795) occupied Fort Johnston in late May and moved all of his troops there. His men there were living off of rice and "cabbage trees" (palmetto trees). They would set fire to pine trees at night to illuminate their camps and to watch for snipers. A party of Rebel horsemen approached Fort Johnston during the night of Wednesday, May 22, 1776. A company of the British light infantry surprised them and drove them off. Neither side suffered any injuries.

The following night, during a violent thunderstorm that Doctor Forster of the British hospital described as

> a Thunder Storm by much the most dreadful one I ever saw in my Life, it terminated in a most violent storm of Rain and Wind, several Tents were thrown down and others blown some distance from the spot where they were pitched and many of the highest Trees shiver'd to threads by Lightning and others torn up by the Roots by the violence of the Wind, it was a most shocking night to pass in Camp.

Three Rebels crept up to the British camp and fired at Private James Wilcox, the sentry, wounding him in the hand. He returned fire, killing one of the attackers and sounding the alarm. The other two Carolinians fled, leaving their dead comrade.

★ The schooner *St. Lawrence* exchanged fire with the Rebels on the shore on Friday, May 24th and again on the 27th. General Henry Clinton (1730–1795) had been considering whether to invade the Chesapeake or to move to Charleston, South Carolina. When Major James Moncrieff (1744–1793) gave him erroneous information that the Charleston harbor lacked strong defenses, General Clinton sailed south to invade South Carolina on May 30th.[24]

★ A British officer reported that the Rebels wounded one of his sentinels at Cape Fear in July 1776.[25]

★ After the British fleet sailed south to Charleston, South Carolina, General Henry Clinton (1730–1795) kept a fort on Bald Head Island. He called it Fort George, in honor of the King, and garrisoned it with 30 sailors from different British warships. Unfortunately they only had 12 muskets. Captain John Linzee sent 20 men and two officers on shore to work on Fort George on Friday morning, September 6, 1776.

Colonel Thomas Polk (1732–1794) commanded the 4th North Carolina Regiment at Fort Johnston on the Cape Fear River to observe the British in the area. When he learned of Fort George's weak defenses, Colonel Polk decided to capture it. He sailed with 150 of his men on Friday night, September 6, 1776 and landed on Bald Head Island.

Five sailors of the HM Sloop *Cruizer* discovered the soldiers as they plodded through the woods. The militiamen captured five men belonging to the *Cruizer* who were straggling in the woods before they came to the fort. The remaining 25 or 30 sailors, from different ships of war, were alerted and took refuge in Fort George where they fired at the North Carolinians with their 12 muskets for about 10 minutes. The firing from the fort signaled the HM Sloop *Falcon* and the HM Sloop *Scorpion* to send all their boats manned and armed to support the fort.

Lieutenant Dickerson's sloop *Defiance* came into Bald Head at 10 AM the following morning. Captain Francis Parry put four of the *Cruizer*'s 3-pounders on board to block Colonel Polk's escape and to prevent his men from getting near Bald Head. Colonel Polk decided to withdraw before the relief force arrived. His men burned a British cutter to prevent it from being used to pursue them. The *Defiance* sailed around the island with five other boats. Lieutenant Dickerson discovered two of Polk's landing boats at Buzzard's Bay near the mainland at 1 PM. The *Defiance* and the *Falcon* fired their 6-pounders, swivels and muskets into the woods at Buzzard's Bay to cover a landing party, knowing the soldiers were there. The Carolinians returned fire with a 3-pounder. The British sloops kept their distance and their crews were unable to destroy the boats. The cannonade killed one soldier and wounded another. The British had no casualties and withdrew before dawn.[26]

Fayetteville and vicinity
Cross Creek, Guilford County (Cochrane's Mill) (early Feb. 1776; March 29, 1776)
Neowee Creek (Oct. 28, 1776)
Cumberland County Courthouse (Aug. 14, 1781)

> Cross Creek is now Fayetteville which is in the center of Cumberland County. The Cumberland County Courthouse was located at 300 Maiden Lane where the Cumberland County Library is today. Campbellton was near Fayetteville. The March 29, 1776 event is also known as Cochrane's Mill. Neowee Creek was a creek in the vicinity of Fayetteville since renamed. It may have been what is now Turnbull Creek about 16 miles southeast of Fayetteville.

Captain William Dent and a band of North Carolina militiamen tried to stop some Loyalists heading for Cross Creek (Fayetteville) in Guilford County in early February 1776. They lost one man killed in the skirmish.

★ Unaware of the Rebel victory at Moores Creek Bridge on Tuesday, February 27, 1776, Captain Thomas Reid (1758–post-1833) gathered 100 Loyalist militiamen and marched to join Brigadier General Donald McDonald's (b. 1712) army at Cross Creek. When they received the news as they approached the town, Captain Reid, Captain Walter Cunningham (1740–1807) and 14 men decided to proceed and to offer any assistance they could. When they entered Cross Creek, they learned that Colonel William Graham (1742–1835) and a superior force of his Tryon County militia, returning home from their victory at Moores Creek Bridge, had occupied Cochrane's Mill. They were exhausted and did not expect any Loyalists in the area, so they posted no guards.

Captain Reid arrived at the mill door, made Colonel Graham believe he had a larger force and demanded his surrender. Colonel Graham surrendered his militia without any resistance. Captain Reid disarmed them and released them. He and his men then proceeded toward Fort Johnston where they boarded a British sloop of war.[27]

★ A party of Native Americans fired on five men of Colonel Thomas Neel's regiment about 2 miles from the camp at Neowee Creek on Monday morning, October 28, 1776. Two of the men returned to camp and reported the attack. Colonel Andrew Williamson (ca. 1730–1836) sent out a party, but they could not find the attackers. Williamson then continued his campaign of destruction through the Middle, Lower, and Valley Cherokee towns.[28]

★ After the Battle of Guilford Courthouse (March 15, 1781), General Charles Cornwallis (1738–1805) stopped at Cross Creek on his way to Wilmington. When he arrived, he had nearly 600 sick and wounded soldiers and a third of his troops had no shoes. He soon found there was not one ration for the 1,500 men in his army. Major James Henry Craig (1742–1812) had not sent the shoes and other supplies up the Cape Fear River from Wilmington.

Craig explained in a letter to Cornwallis that the distance, narrowness of the river and the hostile inhabitants rendered the resupply mission impracticable. Brigadier General John Alexander Lillington's (ca. 1725–1786) militia would riddle anything that moved down that river.

Cornwallis wanted to leave quickly from Cross Creek, but Lillington had destroyed or removed all the boats in the area. When the British marched from Cross Creek to

Wilmington, they left a trail of roadside graves, from the wounded from Guilford Courthouse. By the time they reached Wilmington there were over 100 casualties. There were no ambulances in the Revolutionary War, so the wounded had to be carried in wagons, or on a litter swung between two horses. Among the dead buried along the road from Guilford to Wilmington was Lieutenant Colonel James Webster (ca. 1743–1781) of the 33rd Regiment, Captain William Schutz (d. 1781) of the Guards, and Captain Wilmonski (d. 1781) of the Regiment von Bose.[29]

★ When Colonel David Fanning (1755–1825) learned that Whig Colonel Thomas Wade (1722–1786) retaliated for the Piney Bottom massacre, he and his men seized weapons and horses and headed toward Campbellton. Before they arrived, Colonel John Slingsby (d. 1781) and his band of Loyalists raided the Cumberland Courthouse across the river from Campbellton. With Slingsby were Colonel Archibald McDougal or McDugald, Colonel Duncan Ray and Colonel Hector McNeil (1756–1830) who had joined him. The Loyalists captured the courthouse early Tuesday morning, August 14, 1781. They captured several town leaders and took possession of Cross Creek across the river which they used as a base to raid the countryside.[30]

Currie
Moores Creek (Feb. 27, 1776)

> Moores Creek National Battlefield (website: www.nps.gov/mocr/index.htm) lies near the town of Currie at 200 Moores Creek Road about 20 miles northwest of Wilmington and 4 miles west of route U.S. 421, off route NC 210.
>
> Moores Creek National Military Park, established in 1926, contains 50 acres of land. A visitor center near the park entrance offers explanatory exhibits, displays, and an audiovisual program that depict the battle. It is also the starting point of two self-guiding trails with interpretive exhibits. The Rebel earthworks and the bridge have been reconstructed. A plaque shows the earthworks were in the shape of a horseshoe with a two-foot high parapet and a ditch three feet below.
>
> The park is a comparatively small, self-contained area that is excellent for walking and reconstructing the events. There are two guns placed approximately where the Rebel guns pointed at the creek. They represent the two guns the Rebels called "Old Mother Covington and her daughter." Old Mother Covington was a 2½-pound cast-iron British cannon, dated 1750, mounted on a galloper carriage. The daughter was a small brass swivel gun (see Photo NC-1) which fired a ½-pound ball 750 to 900 yards. Swivel guns were usually mounted on tree stumps and were easy to move and set up.
>
> The park includes several monuments. The Heroic Women Monument was erected in memory of Mary Slocum (1760–1836) and other women of the Cape Fear region. Mary, the wife of a militiaman, rode 65 miles to help the wounded. The James Moore Monument honors the commander of the 1st North Carolina Regiment. The Grady Monument marks the grave of private John Grady, the only Rebel to die in the battle. A picnic area is available.

When the Whigs along the coast learned, in early February 1776, that the Loyalists were gathering in substantial numbers on the upper Cape Fear River, their militia units started preparing to oppose them. The New Bern Committee of Safety selected Colonel Richard Caswell (1729–1789) to head its militia. The Whigs in Wilmington gave command to Colonel John Alexander Lillington (ca. 1725–1786). Colonel James

NC-1. *Old Mother Covington and her daughter. Old Mother Covington was a 2½-pound cast-iron British cannon mounted on a galloper carriage (rear). The Daughter was a small brass swivel gun. (Courtesy of Robert Dunkerly)*

Moore (1729–1777) commanded another force that would become a regiment of the Continental Line and would eventually muster about 1,100 men. They marched from Wilmington and headed northwest along the southern bank of the Cape Fear River. They set up defenses beside Rockfish Creek, just 7 miles southeast of the Loyalist stronghold of Cross Creek on Thursday, February 15.

Moore commanded the Whig troops, including those serving under Caswell and Lillington. He assumed that Donald McDonald's (b. 1712) Loyalists would remain on the south side of the river and try to move directly across Rockfish Creek to strike the Whig defenses. If they succeeded, they would probably take the most direct route to Brunswick.

The Loyalists advanced to within 4 miles of Moore's encampment on Sunday night, February 18, 1776 and stopped. Moore's militiamen anticipated a frontal assault and prepared to defend themselves. Some of MacDonald's younger Loyalist officers wanted to storm the enemy's defenses, but he refused to follow their advice. Instead, he ordered his militiamen to retreat a short distance to Campbell Town where they crossed the Cape Fear River with no opposition on February 20. Moore thought the Loyalists remained along his front until February 21, when he learned that MacDonald and his men crossed to the north shore of the Cape Fear the day before.

A large body of armed Loyalists now headed toward the sea unopposed. Colonel Moore knew that MacDonald's men had to cross two tributaries of the Cape Fear, the South River and the Black River. So he ordered Caswell's militia to go to Corbett's Ferry on the Black River. Caswell had two light artillery pieces, nicknamed Old Mother Covington and Her Daughter (see Photo NC-1) that gave him an advantage. Moore then sent Alexander Lillington and his soldiers to reinforce Caswell. If they could not rendezvous with Caswell, they were to proceed to the bridge across Moores Creek and defend it. Moores Creek is a murky stream a few miles south of Corbett's Ferry and about 17 miles north of Wilmington.

The Loyalists advanced, completely unaware of Moore's efforts to block them. MacDonald ordered Donald McLeod to organize a cavalry force of 100 Highland Scots to precede the main body of Loyalist militiamen. They were ordered to reconnoiter the countryside and to locate and take control of key bridges. McLeod sent a messenger to MacDonald on February 23 to alert him that Caswell was encamped at Corbett's Ferry, only 4 miles in front of the Loyalist vanguard.

As the Loyalists had already burned the boats they had used to cross the Cape Fear to prevent easy pursuit, they had no choice but to prepare for an attack, as a contingent of Moore's militiamen now occupied Cross Creek.

Captain John Campbell (d. 1806) commanded a volunteer force of 100 men armed with claymores (cumbersome 35-inch, singled-bladed broadswords with basket hilt and fishtail grip). They were placed at the center of the Loyalist army to lead the attack. They were to swarm forward to the beat of drums and the drone of bagpipes to create panic and dismay among Caswell's untested militiamen.

Shortly before MacDonald was to give the signal to charge, a body of Loyalist cavalrymen arrived with information gathered from a local African American. They reported that the soldiers could cross the Black River a few miles north of Corbett's Ferry by using a flat-bottomed boat that was submerged just below the surface and that could easily be raised. As MacDonald's objective was not to engage the enemy in combat but to get his men safely to the coast, he decided to avoid a direct assault.

Instead, he sent a small force to demonstrate on Caswell's front. He ordered them to play bagpipes, beat drums, fire muskets, and make a lot of noise. Meanwhile, MacDonald took the main army to the alternate crossing site. MacDonald sent McLeod's cavalry across the Black River to continue scouting while he had a bridge constructed for his troops and supply wagons. The last of MacDonald's troops had crossed the Black shortly after daybreak on February 26 and were again marching toward the sea unopposed but they still had another crossing at Moores Creek Bridge.

Colonel Moore was encamped at Elizabethtown on the Cape Fear River when he learned that the Loyalists had bypassed Corbett's Ferry. He ordered Caswell to reinforce Lillington at Moores Creek Bridge while he and his troops sailed down the Cape Fear. He then marched overland in an attempt to rendezvous with Lillington before the Loyalists arrived.

Caswell arrived at Moores Creek Bridge on Friday afternoon, February 26 ahead of the Loyalists but Moore did not get there in time. Lillington's force of 150 militiamen were now reinforced by Caswell's force of 800 men and two artillery pieces. They selected a good location to defend. Moores Creek was an imposing barrier. This tributary of the Black River is a slow-moving, ink-black stream that meanders through a dense swamp in a series of severe, twisting loops. At the location of Moores Creek Bridge, it is five feet deep and approximately 50 feet wide.

The bridge probably consisted of two logs across the creek with planks nailed across them. The Whigs erected earthworks on the east side of the bridge and defended the bridge with 150 men on February 25. They also placed two guns there to cover the bridge. The remaining force guarded the western bank but later withdrew to the eastern bank. The Whigs also removed many of the planks of the bridge and greased the bridge stringers to discourage any attempt at crossing.

MacDonald's troops could not flank Caswell and Lillington. When they approached from the northwest, they would have to come straight at the defenders who strengthened their defenses during the afternoon and evening of February 26 in preparation for the Battle of Moores Creek Bridge which ensued the next day.[31]

The Loyalists camped on the bridge's upper side until evening when they left to join another group of Loyalists. When they returned about dawn on Tuesday, February 27, 1776, they expected to catch the enemy by surprise, but they found them entrenched on the other side of the bridge. The Loyalists decided to take it.

About an hour before dawn, a party of 75 Highlanders charged out of the woods with their broadswords raised and bagpipes playing. They found their way over the bridge in the fog and met a withering volley of musket and cannon fire at a range of 30 yards before they reached the earthworks on the opposite bank. The volley, combined with the grease, left many of the attackers struggling in the creek where many drowned. The others turned and fled. Some Whigs rushed forward, replaced the planks, and crossed the creek in a counterattack that confused and demoralized the Loyalists and sealed the victory. The fight lasted only three minutes.

The Whigs lost one man killed and one man wounded; the Loyalists lost 30 killed and 40 wounded and 850 prisoners. The Whigs also captured the Loyalists' baggage which included 350 guns and shot bags, 1,500 muskets, 150 swords and dirks, two medicine chests, 13 wagons and their horses, and $75,000 in gold.[32]

The Battle of Moores Creek Bridge demonstrated the surprising Whig strength in North Carolina and eliminated any chances of Loyalist militiamen joining the British in North Carolina. The British departed the area and sailed to Charleston, South Carolina, where they were defeated at the Battle of Sullivan's Island several months later. They would not return to North Carolina until 1780 during the pursuit of the Continental Army after the Battle of Cowpens. In retaliation for the Loyalist defeat, General Henry Clinton (1730–1795) burned the town of Brunswick and Kendal Plantation the home of Colonel Robert Howe (1732–1786). Brunswick was not rebuilt and remains in ruins to this day.

Ocracoke Bar (March 5, 1776)
Ocracoke Inlet (April 14, 1776; April 17, 1776; April 4, 1778; Sept. 1780; Nov. 1780)
Topsail Inlet (May 12, 1778)

Ocracoke is off the coast of North Carolina, northeast of Beaufort.

The HMS *Syren* captured a Congressional vessel off the North Carolina coast. Mr. Robert Atchison, midshipman of the *Syren*, and three sailors were conducting the prize to Boston when they were driven over Ocracoke Bar in distress on Tuesday, March 5, 1776. Two of them were captured and taken to New Bern. Mr. Atchison and one of the sailors were sent to Halifax as prisoners. The other two sailors were released.[33]

★ The Virginia Committee of Safety sent Captain John Goodrich, Sr. (b. 1756) to procure gunpowder from the West Indies early in the war. Goodrich, a Virginia ship owner and merchant, delegated the task to his son William. When William returned with 1400 pounds of powder, Lord John Murray, 4th Earl of Dunmore (1732–1809) was informed, had William Goodrich confined in irons and confiscated his ship. Dunmore then had John Goodrich, Sr. and his other son, John, Jr. report to his ship on the 10th of every month. Governor Dunmore eventually convinced Goodrich to swear loyalty to the King.

★ Silas Henry (1754–1832) sailed the merchant schooner *Polly*, owned by James Buchanan, Mr. Henry, and Archibald Campbell of Edenton, through the Outer Banks on Sunday, April 14, 1776. The *Polly* was bound from Edenton to the island of Madeira with a cargo of Indian corn, staves and heading when Captain John Goodrich, Jr., on the armed sloop *Lilly*, a tender which Lord Dunmore had fitted to capture vessels at the Ocracoke Bar, hailed her as she proceeded to the Swash, near Ocracoke Island about 4 PM the same day. He ordered Mr. Henry to come on board the *Lilly* and to bring his papers. Mr. Henry and James Buchanan, half owner of the *Polly* and her cargo, delivered their papers to Captain Goodrich who examined them and told Mr. Buchanan that he was taking the *Polly* as a prize. He also kept the papers.

Lieutenant John Wright, master of the Royal Navy armed sloop *Fincastle*, came over the Ocracoke Bar about 8 PM that evening and sent a boat with armed men to board the *Polly*, disarm the crew and plunder all the livestock. He left a prize master and four armed men on board. They remained on board for 58 or 59 hours.

"A brave young man, Benjamin Bonner of Pamplico River," led a party of 23 Ocracoke pilots on Wednesday, April 17th. They set out in five whaleboats full of armed men, boarded the *Lilly*, took her and recaptured the *Polly*. When they captured the *Lilly*, they also took John Goodrich, seven of his "Negro crew," Captain George Blair of the Ethiopian Regiment, and a soldier of the 14th Regiment prisoners. Goodrich was imprisoned in Charlottesville for at least 18 months. The vessels were sent to New Bern and used as tenders for the North Carolina Navy brigantines, *King Tammany* and *Pennsylvania Farmer*.

Two armed independent companies were raised a few days later to protect the shipping around Ocracoke. Captain James Anderson (1746–1813) commanded one of the companies posted at Ocracoke Island. Captain Enoch Ward (1743–1785) commanded the other company posted at Core Sound.[34]

★ The frigate HMS *Ariel* was the only British warship stationed off the coast of North Carolina in the Spring of 1778. She patrolled between Cape Hatteras and Cape Lookout and captured six vessels in two months. The crews of two other vessels burned them to avoid capture. Despite the *Ariel*'s raids along the coast, the pilots of Ocracoke were not alarmed when a sloop came into the Ocracoke Bar and anchored. They recognized the vessel, as she had recently sailed from that port. When they boarded the ship, the pilots discovered that it was a British privateer from St. Augustine, Florida. Her captain demanded that the pilots help carry the ship over the bar to attack a French merchant ship and a brig or be put to death. They complied.

The privateers boarded the French ship and seized 100 hogsheads of tobacco and captured a sloop from Bermuda with a load of salt on Saturday, April 4, 1778. This attack persuaded North Carolina to purchase a large row galley named the *Caswell*. After several months, she was outfitted and manned with 145 men to protect the ships passing near Ocracoke. North Carolina also had batteries placed at Ocracoke Inlet and Cape Lookout Bay. The *Caswell* remained in service for about a year, became worm-eaten and sank. The *Ariel* left the North Carolina coast in June. There were no other British warships in that area until 1780.[35]

★ Privateers plagued the coast of North Carolina in 1778. Captain John Goodrich, Jr. had been captured by men from Ocracoke in 1777, but he returned to sea in 1778. He was now one of the most notorious privateers attacking the Outer Banks. Congress ordered the Continental frigate *Raleigh* and the brigantine *Resistance* to operate between Cape Henlopen, Delaware and Ocracoke to stop him.

Goodrich and two other privateers, Captains McFarling and Henry Neale (1736–1788), took several vessels near Ocracoke in May 1778. They decoyed the pilots at Topsail Inlet on Tuesday, May 12, 1778 and came into the inlet where they burned a brig that the *Raleigh* had just captured and sent into Topsail. The burning brig had 1,200 bushels of salt on board.[36]

★ Captain Daniel Deshon's (1754–1826) 20-gun North Carolina privateer brig *General Nash* captured two brigs at Ocracoke Inlet in September 1780. One brig was from *St. Christopher* with a cargo of rum and sugar and the other from Scotland. They were both taken into the port at Cape Fear.[37]

★ The North Carolina privateer *General Nash* captured the brigs *Aggie, Prince of Wales* and *Kattie* near the Ocracoke Inlet in November 1780.[38]

Outer Banks (March 15, 1776)
Bath
Outer Banks, near Bath Town (June 29, 1779)

Captain Tobias Furneaux (1735–1781) saw a brig to the east at daybreak on Friday, March 15, 1776. The HMS *Syren* gave chase and fired a shot at 7 AM that brought her to at 10. She was a brig from Philadelphia bound for Charleston, South Carolina with a company of artillery. Captain Francis Proctor, Jr. (1756–1814) and his 78 artillerymen were taken prisoner on board. Captain Furneaux sent some crewmen on board the prize at 1 PM. The prisoners were transferred to the HMS *Mercury* on Tuesday, March 26, 1776.[39]

★ The *General Green* captured the Loyalist privateer *Impertinent* in early June 1779. The *Impertinent* was quickly re-fitted and sent to harass British shipping around North Carolina's Outer Banks. She spotted the Royal sloop *Harlem* on Tuesday, June 29 and gave chase. The *Harlem* threw her guns overboard in a futile attempt to gain speed. Her captain and crew then tried to escape in a small boat which was overturned because it was "carrying too much sail." The captain and crew all drowned. Lieutenant Rogers, left on board the *Harlem*, surrendered the sloop which was sent to Bath.[40]

Cherokee Campaign of 1776 (July 1, 1776–May 20, 1777) see Tennessee in *The Guide to the American Revolutionary War in the Deep South and on the Frontier.*

Watauga (July 1776) see Cherokee Campaign of 1776 in the Tennessee chapter of *The Guide to the American Revolutionary War in the Deep South and on the Frontier.*

Roanoke Inlet (ca. Aug. 15, 1776)

> Roanoke Inlet was a breach in the Outer Banks about 4.5 miles south of Nags Head and about 0.5 miles south of route U.S. 64 (U.S. 264|Virginia Dare Trail). The waterway no longer exists and the area is now developed land.

About 25 men landed from some vessel of war near Roanoke inlet about Thursday, August 15, 1776, apparently to capture a few of the cattle they had seen grazing along the shore. Captain Dennis Dauge (b. 1740), commanding an independent company between Currituck and Roanoke, attacked them, killing some and taking the rest prisoners.[41]

Cape Lookout, Ocracoke Inlet (Nov. 1, 1776)
Cape Lookout Bay (Oct. 1777)

> Cape Lookout is southeast of Beaufort.

The British brig *Aurora*, bound for New York with 18 other vessels that were transporting supplies to the Royal Navy, foundered near Ocracoke Inlet on Friday, November 1, 1776. The Independent Company of Carteret County, stationed near Cape Lookout, sailed to the *Aurora*, seized her captain, crew, and cargo.[42]

★ The privateer *Liverpool* was on her way from Providence to New York in October 1777. She sailed into Cape Lookout Bay as a "pretended friend" to determine which vessels would be leaving the port soon. A British ship discovered her. Captain Enoch Ward (1743–1785) and his Independent Company stationed at Core Sound captured the ship.[43]

North Carolina coast (Feb. 6–8, 1777; Sept. 26, 1777; July 14, 15, 17, 22, 1778; Sept. 1778)

The frigate HMS *Solebay* cruised off the Cape Fear shoals from Thursday, February 6, 1777 through the 8th. She captured the sloop *Speedwell*, bound from Charleston, South Carolina to Philadelphia, Pennsylvania with a cargo of rice and indigo, in the early afternoon of the 6th. Captain Thomas Symonds (d. 1793) sent an officer and some men on board to sail the prize to Jamaica. The following morning, the *Solebay* captured the schooner *Hope* bound from St. Croix to St. Pierre. The *Solebay* pursued the brig *Fortune* at 5:30 AM on the 8th and captured her. She then gave chase to the schooner *Little Dick* at 7:30 and captured her about 10 AM. The prizes were sent to Jamaica and St. Augustine where they arrived safely, except for the *Little Dick* which was lost on the Nassau Bar.[44]

★ Captain Robert Cochran's (1735–1824) South Carolina brigantine, *Notre Dame*, was sent to France for supplies. A large portion of her crew consisted of French sailors taken on at Nantes. As the *Notre Dame* approached her destination, Charleston, South Carolina, on Friday, February 7, 1777, after a passage of seven weeks, Captain Cochran spotted the Royal Navy victualler *Mackerel*, bound for New York from Cork. The *Notre Dame* captured the *Mackerel* easily. Captain Cochran placed a prize crew on her to sail her to Charleston.

The frigate HMS *Camilla* spotted the *Mackerel*'s sails at 7 AM the following morning and gave chase. By 9 PM, the *Camilla* lit a signal fire and fired a 9-pounder to alert the frigate HMS *Perseus* nearby. Both frigates pursued the *Mackerel*, closing in on her by 10 PM. They recaptured her and Captain George Keith Elphinstone, viscount Keith (1746–1823), of the *Perseus* put a petty officer and seven men on board as a prize crew, noting that all but one of the *Mackerel*'s crew were French.[45]

★ The New Bern privateer *Nancy* captured a British prize ship and a ship from Guinea with 100 slaves, ivory and other valuables on Friday, September 26, 1777. The ships were sent to Georgia.[46]

★ Captain David Squires's *Enterprize* captured a French snow bound from Bordeaux to North Carolina, laden with salt and dry goods on Tuesday, July 14, 1778. Squires sent the snow to St. Augustine, Florida and captured a sloop out of Bogue inlet laden with naval stores the next day. Squires took the snow *David* carrying salt and dry goods on the 17th and the sloop *Betsey* on the 22nd. The *Betsey* had a cargo of rum, gin, sugar, salt and dry goods when she was captured near Ocracoke Island. The *Enterprize* then headed to New York.[47]

★ The *Bellona* sailed to North Carolina as part of a convoy coming from St. Eustatius under the protection of the French frigate *Dilligente* in August 1778. She was outfitted as a privateer with 12 cannon in September. The merchants of New Bern further outfitted her with 16 to 18 guns for action against the British. They also outfitted the 18-gun privateer *Chatham*.

The *Bellona* sailed from New Bern in September and captured the St. Augustine brig *Elizabeth* with a cargo of indigo and lumber. She also captured the New York schooner *Actason*, a sloop and the New York privateer *Harlecan* which had been outfitted with six carriage guns, four brass cabrons and eight swivel guns (see Photo DE-2), but surrendered without a fight.[48]

Cape Hatteras (May 22, 1777; May 1778; June 27, 1779; June 7, 1780)

Cape Hatteras is at the eastern tip of Hatteras Island.

Thomas Tucker, a ship pilot, owned five schooners and served as commissioner to equip schooners for the defense of Charleston, South Carolina in 1775. He had commanded a gun battery on Wadmalaw Island in 1776. He was captain of the brig *Fanny*, bound from Charleston to Virginia, in May 1777.

Captain St. John Chinnery's (1727–1787) frigate HMS *Daphne* was bound from New York to St. Augustine, Florida in company with Captain Sir James Wallace's (1731–1803) *Union*. The *Daphne* carried six chests of money to pay the British troops in Florida and the *Union* had a load of clothing and ordnance stores. Captain Chinnery encountered the *Fanny* off Cape Hatteras on Thursday, May 22, 1777 and quickly captured her. He released the *Fanny*'s crew when he arrived at St. Augustine.[49]

Cape Hatteras (May 1778) see **Topsail Inlet** (pp. 181–183).

★ Several privateers were harassing the ships around the coast of North Carolina in June 1779. A tender chased an Edenton vessel over the Ocracoke Bar on Saturday, June 26, 1779 and followed her for several miles until darkness set in and made it impossible to follow.

Colonel Thomas Bonner (1720–1787), of the Beaufort Militia, anticipated a raid by the privateers and took a boat to Matamuskeet. The men there did not wait for his militia and prepared an ambush in the hills north of Cape Hatteras, near present-day Kitty Hawk. They set a herd of cattle grazing on the hills to entice the privateers on shore. Their fleet consisted of two brigs, one schooner and one sloop. When they spotted the cattle, the privateers sent three boats ashore. As the raiders approached the cattle, the men rushed down from their hiding place in the hills and killed five raiders. The ships fired upon the ambushers while the rest of the landing party escaped to their boats. The militiamen took the weapons off the dead and sold their belongings for $900.[50]

★ The Whig merchant ship *Adventure*, bound from St. Croix, had been at sea for 17 days with a cargo of rum, sugar and fruit when she was spotted by the brig *Hammond* and the sloop *Randall*, two privateers from Bermuda on Wednesday, June 7, 1780. The ships maneuvered around each other for three hours, 40 leagues east of Cape Hatteras, most of the time within "pistol shot." The *Adventure* put up a strong fight. The *Hammond* suffered severe damage and struck her colors. As the *Adventure*'s sails and rigging had been disabled in the fight, she could not take possession of the brig which escaped by having the *Randall* tow her off. The *Adventure* suffered no casualties in the engagement. As the *Adventure* headed to the James River, she was joined by the brig *General Wayne* and the schooner *Grand Tyger*. They spotted 11 privateers in the distance but left them alone.[51]

Currituck Inlet (Nov. 15, 1778)

> Currituck Inlet was a breach in the Outer Banks about 0.5 miles south of the Virginia border. The waterway connected to Currituck Sound. The area has changed considerably since 1776. Knotts Island Bay does not appear on Mouzon's 1776 map and what was once Currituck Inlet is now developed land.

Congress ordered the Continental frigate *Raleigh* and the brigantine *Resistance* to operate between Cape Henlopen, Delaware and Ocracoke to stop privateer Captain John Goodrich, Jr. who threatened the North Carolina coast. The two Continental ships sailed from Boston, Massachusetts on Friday, September 25, 1778. They encountered a larger Royal Navy force which captured the *Raleigh*. This allowed Captain Goodrich to raid the coast with no opposition. He frequently went into the Currituck Inlet to capture and burn any vessels he could find.

Captain Goodrich sailed into the Currituck Inlet on Sunday, November 15th and burned two vessels that were trying to leave the inlet, along with the cargo and cattle on board. Goodrich sailed out into the ocean before the local militia could sail out to assist the two vessels.[52]

Wilmington and vicinity

Wilmington (Dec. 30 or 31, 1778; Feb. 1, 1781; April 1781; July 4–10, 1781; July 23, 1781; Nov. 15, 1781; Nov. 16–18, 1781)
Heron Bridge (Jan. 30, 1781)
Rouse's Tavern (March 1781)
Portevent's Mill (May 16, 1781)
Hood Creek (Sept. 1781)
More's Plantation (Nov. 14, 1781)

> The only site connected with the British occupation of Wilmington is the Burgwin-Wright House at the intersection of Market and Third streets. It was built in 1771 and served as General Cornwallis's headquarters. The house has a Georgian façade and an imposing flight of steps leading to the front door. The interior is furnished in period but has no furnishings of the first owners or anything connected with Lord Cornwallis. The basement served as a prison and there's an 18th-century formal garden, also open to the public.
>
> There were fortifications built around the town before and during the occupation, but there is no longer any trace of them. Point Peter was once called Negro Head Point because the head of "a famous Negro outlaw" was put on a stake at this point as a warning to evildoers in the early years of the settlement. Point Peter was formed by the confluence of the northwest and northeast branches of the Cape Fear River about 400 or 500 yards northwest of the Market Street dock.
>
> Heron Bridge was 10 miles north of Wilmington, probably where I-40 crosses the Northeast Cape Fear River. Rouse's Tavern was 9 miles northeast of Wilmington on what is now route U.S. 17 about 1.25 miles south of its junction with route I-140.
>
> Portevent's Mill, a mill probably belonging to Samuel Portevints of New Hanover County, was at the confluence of the Black River and the junction of the Tarkill Branch and Six Runs Creek north of Wilmington. The first part of this action is also

> known as Mynheer's Ambush because one of the men, a German named Mynheer, had a son who resisted the Loyalists and was shot and had his body burned. The second part is also called Six Runs and probably occurred about 4.5 miles east, near Union High School (1189 Kader Merritt Road) in Clinton. Elizabethtown Road is near route U.S. 701 South.
>
> Hood Creek is about 10 miles north of Wilmington and empties into the Cape Fear River. More's Plantation was a mile south of the ferry at Wilmington.

A body of Continental troops, commanded by Brigadier General William Smallwood (1732–1792), stationed at Wilmington on the Delaware River captured a large brig on Wednesday or Thursday, December 30 or 31, 1778. The brig, bound from New York to Philadelphia, was blown ashore about 5 miles below Wilmington. A detachment with two field pieces was sent down to fire on her. She struck her colors after a few shots. The men captured her crew of one captain, three subalterns, and 60 privates, and about 40 officers' ladies and the brig's cargo which consisted of 250 chests of arms, with 25 stand in each, clothing for four regiments, and a quantity of wine and spirits.[53]

★ Before General Charles Cornwallis (1738–1805) entered North Carolina, he sent Major James Henry Craig (1742–1812) and a detachment of the 82nd Regiment to occupy Wilmington, a town of about 200 houses and a population of almost 1,000. Major Craig sailed from Charleston, South Carolina on Sunday, January 21, 1781 with a frigate, two sloops of war, and 18 transports carrying 300 to 450 troops. A contingent of British marines landed 12 miles from Wilmington and marched overland, while the fleet sailed up the Cape Fear River which was navigable as far inland as Cross Creek (now Fayetteville). Wilmington would provide the Crown forces with a port to receive supplies and to support the invasion of North Carolina. Major Craig made it a strong Loyalist center and supported the Loyalists in the Cape Fear area. He vigorously suppressed the Whigs and caused Whig-Loyalist violence to escalate. He also began putting up fortifications around the town.

Brigadier General Alexander Lillington's (ca. 1725–1786) North Carolina militiamen (some accounts say they numbered 50 men; others say they totaled 400 to 500) arrived too late to prevent Craig's landing, but they prevented him from opening up communications with Cross Creek. The militiamen spiked the seventeen 9- and 12-pounders in the two batteries protecting Wilmington when the British fleet anchored in the Cape Fear River near the town on Sunday, January 28, 1781. They sent large amounts of military supplies out of the town to prevent their capture and then went to negotiate their terms of surrender. Major Craig occupied the town on Thursday, February 1st and ignored the town's terms of surrender. He then began to upgrade the town's fortifications.[54]

★ Colonel Henry Young rendezvoused with Brigadier General John Alexander Lillington's (ca. 1725–1786) militia in January 1781 and the combined forces fortified a position at Heron Bridge, 10 miles northeast of Wilmington. The position consisted of a bridge with a narrow causeway on one end. A deep marsh a quarter mile wide was located beside the hill that the militia had camped on.

Major James Henry Craig (1742–1812) learned of Young's position and decided to make a surprise attack. He marched from Wilmington with 250 men of the 82nd Regiment, the marines, and two 3-pounders at 4 PM on Wednesday, January 30, 1781. Major Daniel Manson and the Royal North Carolina Regiment remained behind to guard Wilmington.

One of Craig's light infantrymen captured a mounted militiaman after sundown and learned the exact location of Young's camp. Major Craig moved to a position near Heron Bridge and had his men rest. He planned to attack the militia camp at 4 AM the next day but a mounted patrol discovered them. Craig's Redcoats opened fire and charged the patrol, driving them across the bridge. Young's militiamen fled, leaving the camp and equipment. Captain Colebrook Nesbitt, of the 82nd Regiment and Captain Thomas Pitcairn, of the 82nd, pursued the fleeing militiamen. A running battle ensued in which Nesbitt was shot twice in the leg.

The British captured several militia weapons and canteens in the camp, along with an iron 3-pound cannon which they disassembled and threw in the river. Craig waited at the bridge for a possible counterattack, but had his men burn the bridge and march back to Wilmington when he determined that his men had totally dispersed the militiamen.

After his return, Craig took a detachment of the 82nd Regiment up the Cape Fear River in two gunboats and a galley under the command of Lieutenant Robert Winters. They captured all but two of the boats fleeing from Wilmington. The two vessels that escaped were a schooner and the North Carolina State Navy brigantine *Pennsylvania Farmer* which was loaded with arms and ammunition. Both vessels ran aground and were burned by their crews.

Craig marched 5 miles down the river the next day, burning Whig plantations and destroying stores that could be of use to the militia. General Lillington's 500 militiamen prevented Craig from securing the Cape Fear. General Lillington did not want to attack Craig's fortifications at Wilmington, so a stalemate ensued.[55]

★ Major James Henry Craig (1742–1812) sent a detachment to gather cattle from the farms around Wilmington to feed General Charles Cornwallis's (1738–1805) approaching army in March 1781. When the advance guard learned that a detachment of light horsemen, sent by Brigadier General Alexander Lillington (ca. 1725–1786) to drive off the cattle, were at Rouse's Tavern, they disobeyed orders and went to the tavern for a drink.[56]

Captain James Love (1704/5-1781) and William Jones (1753-1822) were both in the tavern and were both wanted by the British as they would often ride into Wilmington

> mounted on swift horses [and shoot] down the sentinels and such of the military as came within the reach of their rifle barrelled carbines; and instead of flying directly to the woods, would wait patiently in the suburbs for the British dragoons: keeping far enough ahead to be out of reach of their pistols, and as they decoyed one or two of their numbers in advance of the rest, turned suddenly upon them, giving the contents of their carbines, or cutting them down with their broad swords manufactured in the blacksmith shops of the country.

Major Craig also wanted to kill Love and Jones because, after he had taken Wilmington, Craig developed a habit of riding out on the New Bern road every evening, accompanied by Captain John Gordon (d. 1781) and escorted by 12 or 15 dragoons. When Love recognized a pattern, he mustered "25 or 30 men picked promiscuously from the sound & neighborhood & laid in ambush in a thick swamp" about a mile from Wilmington. When Major Craig's party prepared to cross a bridge in a single file, Love's men could pick them off easily.

When the militiamen in the tavern saw the dragoons approach, they panicked and fled, leaving Love and Jones alone. Love aimed his rifle, but Jones told him that it would be suicide to fire it. They both left without firing a shot.

The dragoons caroused at the tavern, intending to return to camp before midnight. They forgot about the time and lay down to rest on the floor about 12:30 AM, using their saddles for pillows.

Craig sent a detachment of infantrymen from the 82nd Regiment to Rouse's Tavern with orders to give the men there no quarter. About 60 or 70 men, mostly dragoons but some equipped as foot soldiers with muskets and bayonets, surrounded the tavern. The captain ordered his men to pry open the tavern door with a crowbar which had been brought for that purpose.

When James Love heard the dragoons approach, he kicked the door open, and grabbed his saddle to use as a shield. Deciding to make the British pay dearly for his life, Love cut his way out of the tavern, slashing his way for 30 yards toward a mulberry tree. A desperate fight ensued, but Love, outnumbered, was bayoneted several times and killed. When he fell, he lifted up his hand "which contained the broken stump of a sword as if to give a parting blow to his foes."

The dragoons began to systematically kill every man inside the tavern. Many were bayoneted in their sleep, never waking up. One of the militiamen, named Wilson, was found hiding in the back and was told that he would be spared if he would disclose the position of other Whigs. After giving the soldiers information about some other militiamen staying at a house a few miles away, Wilson was immediately put to death. The dragoons killed 11 Whigs at Rouse's Tavern. Only one escaped, most likely Lieutenant David Jones who was on recruiting duty from the 4th North Carolina Regiment. Craig wrote that "sixteen Rebels in the house fell to the bayonet." Lillington wrote that "the British bayoneted eight and wounded two more."

Craig's dragoons proceeded to widow Collier's house, 5 miles from Rouse's Tavern, most likely on Mr. Wilson's information. There, they attacked and captured Captain George Reed and five militiamen.

When Captain Thomas Bludworth (or Bloodworth) (1755–1836), a friend of James Love, heard the firing of the muskets, he gathered his militiamen to investigate. When they arrived at Rouse's Tavern, they found James Love's body near the mulberry tree. The tavern floor was "covered with dead bodies & almost swimming in blood, & battered brains smoking on the walls." An old woman and some children huddled in fear near the fireplace. Captain Bludworth and his men followed the trail of blood from several wounded soldiers. He swore revenge and planned to kill as many enemy soldiers as possible.[57]

★ General Charles Cornwallis (1738–1805) marched to Wilmington to recuperate after the battle of Guilford Courthouse (March 15, 1781). Brigadier General Alexander Lillington (ca. 1725–1786) and the Bladen militia attacked the rear of Cornwallis's army in early April 1781, as he was retreating to Wilmington. They killed 13 men and took between 15 and 20 prisoners.[58]

Cornwallis arrived in Wilmington on Saturday, April 7, 1781 and left for Virginia 18 days later. After the surrender at Yorktown, Cornwallis's troops returned to Wilmington to be evacuated in November 1781.[59]

★ Colonel James Kenan (1740–1810) did not know where the Loyalists went after the skirmish at Myhand's Bridge or what happened to the infantrymen who went to Boykin's Plantation without orders. Kenan's men rode down the Elizabethtown Road, along the Little Coharie River, in search of the infantry the first week in May 1781. They traveled slowly, taking two days to reach Boykin's Plantation. They slept on the road that ran between the Coharie River and a mosquito infested swamp that night. As they approached the plantation one of the mounted men was almost killed by friendly fire as he galloped across a field trying to escape the swarms of biting flies and mosquitoes. Many of the militiamen were drunk and wanted to go home.

Some Loyalist told Kenan that Middleton Mobley (b. ca. 1740) had received reinforcements of 150 men. However, some of the hungry men went to forage for food. Some got lost, others went home. The stragglers sometimes surrendered to the militiamen; but, more often, they would fire at them and disappear into the swamps, making the militiamen jumpy, unsure of whether the Loyalists would surrender or shoot. Many militiamen shot first and asked questions later. An approaching messenger was wounded by his own brother.

Kenan took his men back through Clinton's Crossroads to Boykin's Plantation. The infantrymen mounted the horses behind the horsemen and proceeded down both sides of the Coharie River. When they found the flats and dugouts Mobley's men used to escape down the Coharie until a fallen tree blocked the river, they found two bodies tangled in the tree limbs.

The militiamen came upon a camp of tired and hungry Loyalists, killed 12 of them and left them lying in the swamp. The militiamen and horsemen met each other at the river when they heard the sound of the shooting. They both suspected an ambush and began firing at each other but nobody was injured.

Kenan sent scouts to locate the Loyalist camp while he headed to the most likely location: the confluence of the Big Coharie and Six Runs to form the Black River. However, the Loyalists were actually 10 miles closer, at Portevent's Mill where the Black River and the Tarkill Branch come together.

A scout found the Loyalists grinding corn at the mill and informed Kenan who sent a detachment of infantrymen up the Tarkill Branch while the rest of his men doubled up with the cavalry. Some of his dragoons opened fire on the Loyalists across the river as they rode. The others rode down the road from Moore's Bridge, firing their pistols and slashing the Loyalists with swords "made from saws." The Loyalists returned fire from the millhouse. Obstacles in the millhouse yard slowed the cavalry charge.

One of the Loyalists, trying to rally his men, was wounded when his horse fell on him, pinned him to a tree and crushed his rifle. The Loyalists slowly pushed the militiamen back until the cavalry charged and scattered them. Some fled to the stream where they either drowned or swam away. Others ran in every direction, leaving their dead and wounded. A group of Loyalists running up the stream in a panic overwhelmed some infantrymen on the Tarkill Branch who fired a well-timed volley at them. The Loyalists returned a ragged volley, wounding several men and sending the infantry into the creek. Some accounts report that Owen Kenan (1743–1781), Colonel Kenan's brother, was killed here instead of at Cohera Swamp on Friday, May 11, 1781.

Casualties were surprisingly light. The militia had three killed and several wounded, including Kenan's slave, three horses killed and two wounded. The Loyalists had four men wounded and several drowned in the river. They lost all their baggage and baggage horses.

★ The militiamen reorganized and pursued the Loyalists up the Six Runs River where they fought a chaotic skirmish. The cavalry dismounted and set up a hasty ambush which Biggars Mobley discovered. Mobley and his men attacked the militia's flank while another group attacked their front. Some of the militiamen rushed the Loyalists, using their musket butts, swords and "long knives" in fierce hand-to-hand combat on a hot Wednesday afternoon, May 16, 1781.

The Loyalists fled back into the swamp, leaving a few of their men behind as prisoners. A few deserted and joined their pursuers. Biggars Mobley and his men headed to Wilmington while Middleton Mobley (b. ca. 1740) stayed in Duplin County and continued his attacks. Kenan had three men killed and several more wounded while the Loyalists lost 12 men killed, four wounded, and 12 captured.⁶⁰

★ Captain Thomas Bludworth (or Bloodworth) (1755–1836) wanted to avenge the death of Captain James Love (1704/5–1781) at Rouse's Tavern in March 1781. Since he did not have enough troops to attack the Crown forces stationed in Wilmington, he had to find a way of getting his revenge from a distance. One morning, while hunting a fox, he saw the fox go inside a tall cypress tree on Negro Head Point (now Point Peter), across the Cape Fear River from Wilmington. Bludworth found the cypress to be hollow. It was seven feet in diameter at the base and 70 feet to the first limb.

Bludworth, a gunsmith, made a rifle [probably an 0.83 caliber smoothbore wall gun (see Photo VA-4)] that could fire a two-ounce ball from the cypress tree at Negro Head Point to the British formation area on Market Dock about 400 to 500 yards away. Captain Bludworth took his son Tim and his servant to Negro Head Point in early July 1781 on the pretense of hunting fox or raccoon. He told the boys to bring enough food for a long hunt. They canoed down the river until they arrived at the cypress tree when Captain Bludworth told the boys his plan and that he expected they would live in the tree for two weeks or more.

They built a scaffold inside the tree, made an opening and bore other holes for light and air. Bludworth cleared away enough leaves and branches to give him a clear shot at the wharf. He expected the wind to carry the smoke down the river. He saw a group of five soldiers waiting in front of a liquor store on Wednesday morning, July 4, 1781. He aimed and fired, knocking down one of the men. The other four quickly carried him into the store. A second shot brought another man down which started a panic.

When a column of soldiers marched to the wharf, Captain Bludworth's slave asked if he could try his hand at shooting. The captain consented. The shot broke the formation and sent the soldiers running for cover. They sent boats across the river to look for the sniper, but nobody approached the tree, thinking it was out of range for any shots.

The soldiers would usually line up at the liquor store at grog time, but there was nobody on the wharf the next morning. The soldiers gathered in the store at 11 AM, afraid the sniper might strike again. When there was no shooting that morning, they became more confident and waited near the shop door. Bludworth fired another shot at noon, saw a soldier fall and dragged into the shop. A dragoon rode up to the dock to scrutinize the opposite shore. Another shot knocked him from the saddle and into the water.

The sniping continued for a week when a Loyalist reported that he had seen Bludworth and two others go to Negro Head Point with a large weapon. He said that Bludworth was probably hidden at Negro Head Point and they should cut down all the trees and underbrush that might conceal them. When Bludworth saw boats crossing the river, he closed the gun hole. The landing party of 20 men began to cut away the undergrowth with axes. They arrived at the sniper's hiding place late in the evening and decided to wait until morning to cut down the huge tree.

They left 10 men and three sentinels on the Point. Bludworth thought of tomahawking the guard by his concealed canoe, but the sentinel discovered the slave and challenged him. The slave made the sounds of a wild hog. The guard relaxed and soon fell asleep. The captain then approached the guard from behind, wedged a stick in his mouth and bound him hand and foot. The snipers then escaped safely.⁶¹

★ About 100 Crown light horsemen and about 470 infantrymen left Wilmington and proceeded to the Long Bridge to rebuild it. They intended to arrive at Duplin Court on Monday July 23, 1781 to confiscate the property of anybody who would not swear allegiance to the King and sell it. Colonel James Kenan (1740–1810) had no ammunition and pleaded with Governor Thomas Burke (ca.1747–1783) for help.[62]

★ Major James Henry Craig (1742–1812) was determined to break up the encampment that Colonel Leonard and 30 militiamen set up a few miles above Wilmington to cut off supplies to the Loyalist camp and to prevent slaves from going there. Major Craig sent a detachment to create an ambush at a bridge on Hood's Creek in September 1781 while the main force marched to the rear of Colonel Leonard's camp to cut off his retreat. When the guide heard the orders given to the Loyalists that they were to show no quarter and put to death every Whig found with arms in their hands, he decided not to take the Loyalists to Leonard's camp right away because many of the men there were his friends and neighbors. The guide took Major Craig's troops through the woods from swamp to swamp, until he thought Colonel Leonard would have learned of the Loyalists' movements.

Meanwhile, the detachment at Hood's Creek Bridge became impatient waiting for the main force. They sounded the bugle to let Major Craig know they were ready. The militiamen in the camp heard the signal and first thought it was a boatman. When the sound continued, they sent two men to the bridge to reconnoiter. When they saw the troops, they turned about under a volley of musket fire. One man had his hat shot off. The other was badly wounded and fell off his horse. The Loyalists rushed forward and bayoneted him to death. Meanwhile, the militiamen withdrew to safety.[63]

★ After the battle at Raft Swamp, General Griffith Rutherford (ca. 1731–1800) headed down the south side of the Cape Fear River toward Wilmington on Wednesday, November 14, 1781. He divided his troops and sent Colonel Robert Smith down the north side of the river while he proceeded down the south side. Colonel Smith detached Major Joseph Graham (1759–1836) and sent him toward Wilmington.

Major Graham surprised a party of 100 Loyalists at More's plantation, a mile south of the ferry at Wilmington. He raced into the plantation and killed 12 Loyalists, wounded 30 and scattered the rest without any serious loss of his own.[64]

★ General Griffith Rutherford's (ca. 1731–1800) 1,050-man army proceeded down the Cape Fear River toward Wilmington on Thursday, November 15, 1781. They arrived at a British post located in a brick house opposite Wilmington. The fort consisted of the house, an abatis and 50 soldiers. While most of the officers did not want to attack, the militiamen did. The troops advanced on the fort and Captain John Kennedy demanded the surrender which was declined. A brief skirmish ensued in which the attackers lost one man killed and several wounded before Rutherford ordered a retreat.[65]

The Crown forces evacuated Wilmington between November 16 and 18, 1781.

Halifax (June 1780; May 7–11, 1781)

| Halifax is northeast of Rocky Mount and east of route U.S. 301 near the Virginia border. |

Many Continental soldiers were held prisoner aboard prison ships in Charleston Harbor after the surrender of Charleston, South Carolina on Friday, May 12, 1780. Lieutenant Edward Barnwell (1757–1808), captured at St. John's Island, was imprisoned aboard the *Packhorse*. He and 35 men took over the vessel and ran it aground at Halifax, North Carolina as it headed north in June 1780. Lieutenant Barnwell was promoted to Lieutenant Colonel and given command of the Beaufort Regiment upon his return.[66]

★ When Lieutenant Colonel Banastre Tarleton (1744–1833) learned that a fairly large contingent of North Carolina militia was assembling at Halifax, he managed to surprise them on Monday, May 7, 1781 by traveling across country and approaching the town from an unexpected direction. A cavalry charge routed the disorganized militiamen after a brief fight in which Tarleton lost three men and several horses. Some of the militiamen began constructing earthworks on the far side of the Roanoke River where Colonel Engineer Thaddeus Kosciusko (1746–1817) had constructed a redoubt when he suspected that the Crown forces might attack Halifax.

Brigadier General Richard Caswell (1729–1789) commanded the redoubt before the battle of Guilford Courthouse. From here, his men fired a hail of musket balls whenever the enemy snipers approached the stream. The militiamen were such a nuisance that Tarleton sent a small force across the river to drive them out. Tarleton records:

> The British took the shortest road to Halifax, to prevent the militia receiving reinforcements, and recovering from the consternation probably diffused throughout that place by the fugitives from the creeks. The event answered the expectation: The Americans were charged and defeated in detached parties, in the environs and in the town, before they had settled any regular plan of operation: The ground about half a mile in front of Halifax afforded a strong position, of which they did not avail themselves; but they were surprised whilst assembling on the wrong side of the bridge over a deep ravine, and were routed with confusion and loss: The only useful expedient which they had adopted was the securing a number of the boats belonging to the inhabitants of the place on the other side of the river, where a party began to intrench themselves, and from whence they fired upon the British when they approached the bank: This circumstance, however, could only be a temporary inconvenience to the King's troops, because the Americans would be obliged to abandon that post on the arrival of the cannon, the eminence on the side of Halifax so perfectly commanded the opposite shore.[67]

Tarleton realized that higher ground on the Halifax side overlooked the redoubt. He requested General Charles Cornwallis (1738–1805) to send a cannon. The cannon did not drive the militia away. They continued to fire on the Crown troops, even as Cornwallis occupied the town on Friday, May 11, 1781. Cornwallis sent a detachment across the river to drive them off.

After General Cornwallis's troops occupied the town, the citizens of Halifax suffered many indignities. The soldiers and camp followers insulted the people and plundered their homes of valuables. No Whig dared sleep in his house for fear of capture. Many were seized and taken to Wilmington, where some were imprisoned and tortured. Loyalist Charles Stedman (1753–1812) said, "Some enormities were committed that were a disgrace to the name of man." The situation got so bad that a sergeant and a dragoon were courtmartialled for outrages for which they had been responsible. They were found guilty and executed. After a short rest in Halifax, Cornwallis marched to Petersburg, where he arrived on May 20.[68]

Colson's Mill (July 21, 1780)

> Colson's Mill was near the Rocky River near the junction of the Rocky and Pee Dee Rivers just east of the intersection of routes NC 24 (NC 27 W) and NC 73 W about 6.5 miles northeast of Norwood. The battle site is now inaccessible.

The junction of the Rocky and Pee Dee Rivers was a strategically important location in the 18th century. It was the site of a mill (Colson's Mill), an ordinary (a tavern), stagecoach relays, and a ferry crossing.

★ Colonel William Lee Davidson (1746–1781), a Continental officer, learned that Colonel Samuel Bryan (1756–1813) and a band of 500 to 600 Loyalists used a farm near Colson's Mill as their headquarters. Davidson advanced on the farm on Saturday, July 21, 1780 and divided his army of about 160 light-horsemen, intending to surround the Loyalists. As he deployed his men in front of and behind Bryan's troops, the Loyalists opened fire. Davidson quickly formed his men into line and led the attack.

Enemy fire brought him down as a musket ball struck him in the stomach and exited near his kidneys, nearly killing him. Lieutenant Joseph Graham (1759–1836) recalled that Davidson "had inspired a confidence nothing could shake." Davidson's militia continued fighting and quickly routed the Loyalists who left behind three or four dead, five wounded and 40 captives. Graham said the Loyalists were lucky: "Being in their own neighborhood and where they knew the country, most of them escaped. Their number exceeded that of their assailants, which was about two hundred and fifty. On the Whigs no person was injured save Col. Davidson and one other."[70]

Anson County (ca. Sept. 9, 1780)

> Wadesboro is at the center of Anson County.

Colonel Abel Kolb (1750–1781) led 80 to 100 South Carolina militiamen against Loyalists in two locations in Anson County, North Carolina on Saturday, September 9, 1780. The militiamen killed three Loyalists and wounded five. They had two men wounded.[71]

Mask's Ferry (also known as William Mast's Ferry) (Sept. 10, 1780)

> Mask's Ferry was on the Pee Dee River in the town of Lilesville.

Captain Herrick and his light horse militia attacked a party of Loyalists near Mask's Ferry on the Pee Dee River on Sunday, September 10, 1780. They killed some Loyalists and took 11 prisoners.[72]

Yadkin River (Sept. 1780)
Forks of the Yadkin (March 1782)

> The Yadkin River is about 7.5 miles northeast of Albemarle.

Colonel John Paisley's (1745–1811) North Carolina militia marched to Salisbury to join General William Lee Davidson's (1746–1781) brigade in September 1780. When they reached McCalpine's Creek in Mecklenburg County, they spotted a British patrol and retreated to the north side of the Yadkin River. They were overtaken and had a skirmish in which several men were killed.[73]

★ The British captured Captain Johnson (d. 1782) in February 1781 and then paroled him. He returned to his home near the Forks of the Yadkin and honored his parole. Loyalist Colonel John Elrod (d. 1782) was returning from the Wilmington area with two men named Still (d. 1782) and Robbins in March 1782 when they met Captain Johnson carrying a rifle. Captain Johnson was hunting with his friend, Robert Tucker.

Aware that Captain Johnson was on parole, Colonel Elrod told him that he should not be carrying a rifle and struck him on the head with the flat of his sword, breaking it in two. Still fired a rifle ball into Johnson's head. Robbins was going to shoot Tucker, but Tucker grabbed Robbins's weapon and the shot passed over his head. Tucker ran to the nearest Whig house and sounded the alarm. Robbins knew that he would be pursued, so he left the group and was never heard from again.

Colonel Thomas Dugan or Dougan (1748–1822) raised a troop of mounted men to pursue the Loyalists. As he knew that Elrod had murdered Captain Johnson, Colonel Dugan and his militiamen rode to Elrod's house. He sent a scout to look in the house. The scout reported that Elrod and Still were both sleeping in the house. Captain John Clarke and a man named Jack Veach were going to break open the door and capture the men. However, before they reached the house, Veach refused to go any farther and both men returned to the militia. Clarke then headed toward the house with a man named Henry Grogan (1748–1827), who, like Veach, also refused to go any farther. Clarke called out for any of the men to follow him. He grabbed a fence rail and charged for the door. He hit it so hard, he knocked it off its hinges. Clarke grabbed Mr. Still in the bed and pulled him to the fireplace saying, "I have got hold of you Mr. Still!" Still denied that was his name, but Clarke hit Still's head on the fireplace until he admitted it.

The militiamen sentenced both Colonel Elrod and Mr. Still to death. They marched both prisoners a half mile from the house the following morning and tied them to trees to shoot them. Still tried to escape and complained until a bullet silenced him. Elrod remained calm and was executed after leaving messages for some of his friends.[74]

Richmond Town (Oct. 3, 1780; Oct. 8, 1780)

> Old Richmond was about 10 miles north of Winston-Salem.

North Carolina militiamen, joined by the Over the Mountain men from Virginia and Tennessee, gathered at Quaker Meadows on Monday, September 25, 1780 to oppose Major Patrick Ferguson's (1744–1780) expedition into the western region of South Carolina near Morgantown. Colonels Gideon Wright (d. 1782) and Hezekiah Wright (1728–1780) raised a large band of Loyalists in Surry County to support Major Ferguson. Colonel Gideon Wright attacked the Surry Courthouse in Richmond Town on Tuesday, October 3rd, killed the sheriff, and captured several prisoners. His men also raided the home of Captain William Shepherd (1737–1807) who marched with the militia to fight Ferguson.[75]

★ Colonels Gideon and Hezekiah Wright's Loyalist militia in Surry County had increased to 300 men. As there were insufficient Whig militiamen to oppose them, the Wright brothers took advantage of the situation and attacked Richmond again on Sunday, October 8, 1780. They wounded Captain John Crause as he stood guard. The remaining Whig militiamen in town fled into the countryside and Colonel Wright moved his army to Bethabara after the raid.[76]

Shallow Ford (Oct. 14, 1780; Feb. 6, 1781)
Shallow Fords of the Yadkin River (Feb. 7, 1781)
Graham's Patrol
Reedy Creek, Shallow Fords of the Dan River (Feb. 8, 1781)

> The engagement at Shallow Ford occurred about a mile west of the Shallow Ford crossing in what are now Huntsville and Yadkinville. From route NC 1716 (Farmington Road), turn right onto route NC 1001 (Courtney Huntsville Road) in Huntsville

> and drive 1.1 miles to the Yadkin River. Courtney Huntsville Road becomes Shallowford Road where it crosses the river. Turn right just before the bridge. The road leads to the Bob Pate Memorial Access Area overlooking the river. Shallow Ford is to the south in Forsyth County.
>
> Reedy Creek (now Reed Creek) is about 19 miles north-northwest of Guilford Courthouse National Military Park.

Five hundred Loyalists (some reports say they numbered as many as 900) arrived in Bethabara on Saturday, October 13, 1780, plundering Whig homes along the way. They then marched south to join the British Army in Charlotte the next day. When Andrew Carson (1756–1840), who lived about 15 miles west of the Shallow Ford, heard the first reports of a Loyalist uprising, he rode to General William Lee Davidson's (1746–1781) headquarters. Davidson had assumed command of the militia in western North Carolina near Charlotte when General Griffith Rutherford (ca. 1731–1800) was captured at Camden. Davidson gave Carson 52 men and sent them out to meet the Loyalists under Colonels Gideon Wright (d. 1782) and Hezekiah Wright (1728–1780).

Captain Pray became ill after a skirmish on the north side of the Yadkin River and Richard Vernon (1756–1840) assumed command of the company. Colonel John Paisley (1745–1811) (or Peasley) was also dispatched with 750 militiamen to find and "to disperse a body of about 380 Tories collected on the shallow ford of the Yadkin, in Surry County." Major General Jethro Sumner (1735–1785) also sent two companies of 30 men each under Captains Jacob Nichols (b. 1726) and Miller with the same orders. Major Joseph Cloyd (1742–1833) and four companies (about 160 men) from Montgomery County, Virginia also went to meet Major Patrick Ferguson (1744–1780). When they learned of Ferguson's defeat at Kings Mountain, South Carolina (October 7, 1780), they headed to Surry County where they joined the North Carolina militiamen who had not pursued Ferguson.

The 350 Congressional troops were on the west side of a small stream (now called the Battle Branch) near the Shallow Ford crossing of the Yadkin River about 9:30 Saturday morning, October 14, 1780 when they saw the Loyalists who had threatened the county for the past weeks. The Loyalists were on the other side of the Yadkin River, moving westward on Mulberry Fields Road. Both sides hurried to form ranks and fire across the river.

Loyalist Captain James Bryan (1725–1780) fell first with five balls through him and his horse. Captain Isaac Campbell (ca. 1755–1784), of the Virginia militia, fled under the intense fire, leaving his men to fend for themselves. As the Congressional troops advanced toward the ford, the Loyalists fell back and re-formed. Virginia militia Captain Henry Francis (1725–1780) was shot through the head and died a few steps from his son Henry. Despite being outnumbered, the Congressional troops soon brought down 13 other Loyalists and gained the advantage. They exchanged several shots, and the Loyalists withdrew across the Yadkin River.

The militiamen clubbed the wounded Loyalists to death after their comrades had fled. An African American Loyalist named Ball Turner (d. 1780) continued to fire at the militiamen until they charged his location and riddled his body with bullets. Colonel John Paisley's 300 militiamen arrived at the end of the battle along with Colonel Joseph Williams (1748–1827), of Surry County, who heard the musket fire from his nearby house. General William Smallwood (1732–1792) arrived in Salem about noon the next day with about 150 horsemen, 30 infantrymen, and three wagons. He left Guilford

Courthouse the day before and found the Loyalists fleeing from their defeat at Kings Mountain, so he ordered his men to pursue them.

Richard Vernon (1756–1840) wrote, "We killed several and took 30 or 40 prisoner. Among the killed was Captain Jas. Bryant. Col. Pasely took charge of the prisoners and we conducted them to Moravian town and left them under guard." General Smallwood noted that he found 15 Loyalists dead and four wounded scattered in the woods and that the Whigs lost one captain killed and four privates wounded in the battle which lasted about 45 minutes. Captain Francis was buried on the battlefield. The dead Loyalists were buried in a separate common grave. The four wounded Whigs and one wounded Loyalist were cared for by a Moravian physician and his assistant, first in the area of the battle, and then in Bethania, where they were taken to recover from their wounds. Over the next several days, the Whigs, cold and wet from the rains that began late on the 14th, went to the Moravian towns (Winston–Salem).

The victory at Shallow Ford dispersed the Surry County Loyalists. They never mustered as many men again. When Hezekiah Wright was later shot and wounded in his own house, his brother Gideon fled to Charleston, South Carolina where he would die on August 9, 1782.[77]

★ It rained all day and night on Thursday, February 1, 1781 and most of the 2nd. Major General Nathanael Greene (1742–1786) had joined with Colonel Daniel Morgan (1736–1802) and they proceeded to cross the Yadkin River at Trading Ford. Thanks to Greene's pre-planning, Colonel Thaddeus Kosciusko (1746–1817) had already gathered several boats at Trading Ford and others were hauled there by wagon. Greene's forces were already camped on the eastern side by nightfall on the 3rd.

General Charles Cornwallis's (1738–1805) main army moved slowly toward Shallow Ford. His troops engaged in considerable plundering and burned several houses along the way. Knowing the rain would have caused the Yadkin to rise, he wanted to catch up with Morgan and Greene before they had a chance to cross. He expected to trap them against the river, not knowing that they had boats.

The rain had made the road muddy and some of Cornwallis's wagons sank to their hubs. As he burned more baggage so he could double his teams to get the few remaining wagons out of the mud, he sent his and Brigadier General Charles O'Hara's (1740–1802) mounted infantrymen to catch Greene before he crossed the Yadkin. They arrived at Trading Ford around midnight on February 3rd to find some of the militiamen still on the west bank of the Yadkin guarding a few baggage wagons. They exchanged musket fire and the guards dispersed. General O'Hara only captured the wagons. General Greene was on the other side with all the boats and O'Hara could not cross.

Cornwallis succeeded in extricating his wagons from the mud and reached Salisbury by 3 pm on February 3rd—only 7 miles from Trading Ford and Greene's army. O'Hara had sent his cavalry back to Salisbury but placed his infantry on high ground overlooking the river. When he received some field pieces Cornwallis sent him, O'Hara tried to bombard Greene's camp across the river. Greene's only artillery, two little "grasshoppers" (3-pounders) (see Photo NC-2) captured at Cowpens, had been sent away with his prisoners. Greene could not return fire, but his camp was behind a high, rocky ridge parallel to the stream. The only damage the bombardment did was to knock the roof off a cabin in which he was busy writing his letters. Dr. William Read (1754–1845) noted that "his pen never rested, but when a new visitor arrived . . . answer was given with calmness and precision, and the pen immediately resumed."[78]

NC-2. Grasshopper, a 3-pound cannon. The linstock holds a slow match to ignite the powder charge.

The river began to fall on the evening of February 4th, but it was still too deep even for horses. Greene broke camp and went north before Cornwallis could pursue. He stopped at Abbott's Creek, a few miles from the Moravian settlement at Salem. Here, he obtained definite information about Cornwallis's course. Morgan then turned east and marched the army to Guilford Courthouse where he arrived on the 6th. He covered 47 miles in 48 hours—excellent progress considering the continuously rainy weather, the state of the roads, the shortage of food, and the condition of the men. Greene stayed at Abbott's Creek until Tuesday morning, February 8, when he was sure Cornwallis had taken his bait.

Cornwallis's army proceeded to Shallow Ford, 10 miles upriver, on February 6th. The route involved a wide swing to the west from Greene, but the ford was always passable, unlike the lower fords on the Dan which were impassable at this time of the year. A short time later, Lieutenant Colonel Banastre Tarleton (1744–1833) and his men encountered Colonel Francis Locke's (1732–1796) militia at a bridge over Grants Creek. Locke's men put up such a fierce opposition that it delayed the army's advance by some three hours. They destroyed the bridge which Cornwallis's troops had to rebuild before proceeding. They camped at Rencher's Ford on the South Fork of the Yadkin River that night.

Instead of trying to catch Greene and Morgan before they could join with General Isaac Huger (1743–1797), Cornwallis decided to intercept their combined forces before they could reach the upper fords. He stayed at Salisbury four days, collecting food, and crossed the Yadkin at Shallow Ford on the 8th and camped at Lindsay's Plantation.

★ Captain Joseph Graham's (1759–1836) company of about 20 militiamen followed the British Army after Lieutenant Colonel Banastre Tarleton's (1744–1833) legionnaires ambushed them at Trading Ford and crossed the Yadkin. As they marched from

Shallow Ford, on the Yadkin, to Salem, they pursued the British for about 3 miles when two soldiers, who were about 100 yards ahead, signaled they saw the enemy. When Captain Graham came up, he saw about 50 dragoons marching slowly in close order. He followed them unnoticed for 2 miles. They kept the same order and Captain Graham thought it imprudent to proceed as they were in country favorable to the British.

Graham's cavalry turned back about a mile to look for other targets. On Wednesday, February 7, 1781, they found three men in red coats who fled but surrendered when they were overtaken. A little further, they encountered a Hessian and a Briton who also fled. When they were overtaken, the Briton surrendered, but the Hessian would not give up and held his weapon to charge. He was cut down and killed. Graham's troops captured two armed Loyalists who were following them before reaching the ford. Graham's men re-crossed the ford with their six prisoners.[79]

★ Major General Nathanael Greene (1742–1786) sent word to Lieutenant Colonel Henry "Light-Horse Harry" Lee (1756–1818) to abandon his raids on the British outposts in the South Carolina low country. Lee was to join Greene's army, while Brigadier General Francis Marion (1732–1795) was to remain and continue his guerilla warfare on the lower Santee and keep Greene informed of any enemy movements. General Greene also asked North Carolina Governor Abner Nash (1740–1786) for men and supplies, especially muskets to equip the unarmed militiamen who arrived in his camp.

General Greene organized a light corps to cover his retreat. He offered the command to Brigadier General Daniel Morgan (1736–1802) who declined because of ill health. He was granted permission to leave the army until he recovered. Colonel Otho Holland Williams (1749–1794) assumed command of the light troops who consisted of the most trusted and effective officers and the most experienced soldiers: the Maryland and Delaware Continentals (see Photo DE-1), Lee's and Lieutenant Colonel William Washington's (1752–1810) cavalry, and Lieutenant-Colonel Richard Campbell's (d. 1781) Virginia riflemen.

General Greene positioned the light corps between General Cornwallis and the prisoners taken at Cowpens. His army stripped the ground clean of any food and forage, leaving nothing for the Crown forces to glean. They also destroyed any boats along their route to keep General Cornwallis from crossing over the rivers. Nevertheless, General Cornwallis tried to intercept General Greene and his prisoners.

Colonel Williams was ordered to move his men to the Shallow Fords of the Dan River to act as a decoy. General Greene would move the main army, supplies, and prisoners toward Irwin's and Beatty's Fords, 25 miles downstream. He would notify Colonel Williams to cross and rejoin him after the army crossed the Yadkin River.

General Cornwallis's army advanced on Colonel Williams's troops at Reedy Creek on Thursday, February 8, 1781; but Colonel Williams had his men move on before they could become engaged. They also destroyed the bridge across Reedy Creek to slow down the pursuers by several hours. Sergeant Major Seymour wrote that Lee and his cavalry met "their vanguard, consisting of an officer and twenty men, which they killed, wounded and made prisoners, all but one man."[80]

Colonel Williams had his men travel on a road between the armies of General Cornwallis and General Greene. This allowed them to intercept any enemy movement toward General Greene and slowed General Cornwallis's rate of march to avoid being ambushed. The Continentals were not allowed to make camp until 9 PM so as to keep ahead of the Crown forces. They did not use any tents to save time in the morning.

Only half of the men were allowed to sleep while the other half patrolled the perimeter and did picket duty. One man stayed awake by the campfire to keep it burning. The troops were on the move every morning by 3 AM. Some men were sent forward to find a location for breakfast. They started fires for breakfast, their single daily meal. The others marched there from the previous night's camp. The men who had been on night patrol were the first to eat.[81]

Great Swamp, Bladen County (Nov. 3, 1780)
Bladen County Courthouse (Sept. 1782)

> Great Swamp is about 7 miles east of route I-95 in St. Paul's on the western edge of Bladen County and about 0.75 miles west of route NC 1300 (Chicken Foot Road) 2 miles south of its intersection with route NC 20.
> Some accounts date the Bladen County Courthouse event as November 1782.

Engineer Colonel John Senf and 90 Camden militiamen attacked some Loyalists at Great Swamp in Bladen County on Friday, November 3, 1780. They killed two and wounded several others while having only one man wounded.[82]

★ Captain Robert Raiford (1754–1793) and 30 men from the 8th Continental Regiment entered the Bladen County Courthouse in September 1782. They claimed the Loyalists were being favored in land disputes and feared that the troops would not be treated fairly. Captain Raiford attacked Archibald MacLaine (1722–1804) with his sword for defending a Loyalist who was on trial. Captain Raiford and his men beat the court clerk and then went out into the street and marched around the County apprehending Loyalists without any orders. The court issued a warrant for Raiford's arrest but he had already returned to Major General Nathanael Greene's (1742–1786) army where he commanded the light infantry. He was brought to trial a year later and was acquitted.[83]

Hillsborough and vicinity
Hart's Mill (Jan. 1781; Feb. 17, 1781)
Cane Creek (also known as the Battle of Lindley's Mill or Sutphin Mill) (Sept. 12, 1781; Sept. 13, 1781)
Bear Creek (Oct. 7, 1781)
Near Lindley's Mill

> Hart's Mill, also known as Hartford Plantation, was on the upper Eno River near the mouth of McGowan's Creek near Hillsborough. It was approximately 1.5 miles west-northwest of Hillsborough, the county seat of Orange County, about where route U.S. 70 now crosses the river. Nothing remains of the mill complex. A good portion of Hartford Plantation is now the Hillsborough Division of Duke Forest. Accounts vary in dating the February event. Some place it on February 17 others on the 20th and still others on the 23rd or 24th.
> The Nash–Hooper House (118 Tryon Street, off route NC 86, Churton Street in Hillsborough), a two-story frame house set back from the street out of line with the other houses on the block, is the only remaining home of a signer of the Declaration of Independence in North Carolina. General Francis Nash built it in 1772 and sold

it to William Hooper (1742–1790), a signer of the Declaration of Independence, in 1781. Many of the houses in Hillsborough were built in the 18th century and have placards indicating the year they were built.

Although the Colonial Inn (153 King Street, Hillsborough), a large house with a long veranda in front is not a colonial building, it occupies the site where an inn has stood since earliest colonial times. According to tradition, General Cornwallis's soldiers laid down the flat flagstones in front of it and paved the entire street for 150 yards in all directions from the intersection of King and Churton streets.

General Cornwallis and his men camped in the vicinity of route NC 1002 (St. Mary's Road) and Cameron Street near the Cameron Park Elementary School in Hillsborough in 1781. Montrose, a house built in 1898, now occupies the site. Cornwallis supposedly stayed at William Courtney's Yellow House (141 King Street just opposite Court Street) and at Faddis Tavern next door. He moved back and forth from one to the other for security reasons.

Cornwallis stayed at the W. A. Graham house but soon moved to the home of John L. Bailey which eventually became known as Morris's Hillsborough House on King Street.

Lindley's Mill was on Cane Creek in southern Alamance County (Orange County in 1781). Cane Creek is about 20 miles southwest of Hillsborough in the town of Graham, near Sutphin. A bridge crosses over Cane Creek at Lindley's Mill on route NC 1003 (Lindley's Mill Road) 1 mile south of the intersection with route NC 1005 (East Greensboro Chapel Hill Road). A state historical marker at the junction of routes NC 1005 and NC 87, about 2.5 miles east of the intersection of routes NC 1003 and NC 1005, commemorates the Battle of Lindley's Mill, the last significant Revolutionary War battle in North Carolina. On the ridge where Brigadier General John Butler's (1728–1796) men made their stand, a crude, homemade stone marker reads, "For Justice, here was fought the Battle of Lindley's Mill Sept. 14, 1781." These are the only commemorations for the more than 300 casualties in the four-hour battle. A modern Lindley Mills, Inc. (est. 1755) structure now occupies the site.

A historical marker on route NC 2351 (Bethel South Fork Road), a few hundred yards south of route NC 1005 (East Greensboro Chapel Hill Road) in Snow Camp, notes that General Charles Cornwallis camped in this area after the battle of Guilford Courthouse.

Bear Creek is on the south side of Deep River about 19 miles south of Lindley's Mill and about 8 miles southwest of Pittsboro.

Brigadier General Andrew Pickens (1739–1817) and his militia harassed General Charles Cornwallis (1738–1805) as he pursued Major General Nathanael Greene (1742–1786) across North Carolina after the Battle of Cowpens (January 17, 1781). Pickens sent two militia companies in a surprise attack on a British post at Hart's Mill near Hillsboro. They inflicted eight casualties and captured 25 prisoners.

★ Colonel Thomas Hart (1730–1808) was the wealthiest man in Orange County with an assessed worth of £70,431.2 in 1779. General Charles Cornwallis (1738–1805) established his headquarters at Hartford Plantation in February 1781. Captain Joseph Graham (1759–1836) with about 20 North Carolina dragoons and Captain Richard Simmons with about 20 North Carolina mounted riflemen set out at dark on Friday, February 16, 1781. After traveling less than 3 miles, they met two men coming from Hillsborough who gave them information about the British Army in the area. They learned its position and headquarters and that a guard of 28 men (a British lieutenant, a sergeant, 24 privates and two Loyalists) was at Hart's Mill, on the Eno River, which was grinding for the army.

The night was dark, with occasional rain showers which became heavy before daybreak. The party moved slowly, stopping during hard showers to try to keep their arms dry. They approached Hart's Mill from the west and halted about half a mile from the mill until dawn. They proceeded when the riflemen could see the sights on their guns. A sentinel, at a fork in the road, halted their advance and fired. The militiamen filed to the right in a thicket between the roads. The riflemen dismounted and tied their horses. The British sergeant-of-the-guard came to the support of the sentinel with a file of men. The British fired into the thicket as they could not see the attackers. The musket balls passed through the tree tops above their heads.

Captain Graham and a few cavalrymen made a dash at the enemy while their weapons were empty, hoping to get a view of the ground and the position of their main force. When he arrived at the great road, Captain Graham saw the sergeant and his party running. The British guard was drawn up in the open yard in front of the dwelling house to the right of the road. There were two small buildings, perhaps a stable and a smith shop, on the same side of the road, about 50 or 60 yards from the house and the ground descended behind them.

Captain Graham's party returned, and Captain Graham gave Captain Simmons directions to go behind the swell in the ground until he got the buildings between him and the guard, and then to advance. The cavalry created a diversion on the left while Simmons got his men in position. As Captain Simmons led his men across the great road, the cavalry turned to the left and entered, in open order, an old field more than 200 yards from the British. They sustained no damage from enemy fire due to the great distance. As soon as the riflemen got into their concealed position, they fired and the dragoons then galloped across the field at right angles to the British lines. The British wheeled about and fired at the cavalrymen.

When Simmons's party began firing from the corners of both small buildings at the same time, the Redcoats fled. The dragoons attacked at full charge. The lieutenant ran into the house and shut the door. He peeped out occasionally until he saw Captain Simmons, whom he recognized as an officer. He then opened the door and stepped out to present his sword in a polite manner and request protection. When the British guard had fled eastward about 100 yards beyond the Eno River, the dragoons overtook their front and killed or wounded one sergeant and eight privates and captured the rest of the party (one lieutenant, 16 British privates and two Loyalists).

The dead were later buried where they fell. The mills were stripped bare of every usable thing and the dwelling house was plundered of all valuables, the furniture destroyed and the house greatly damaged by attempts to set it on fire in different places. However, as General Graham and his men departed so quickly, the looting and damage were probably done by neighborhood partisans or looters before the owners returned.

The cavalrymen had barely brought the prisoners back to the riflemen, when Captain Graham heard a noise "like distant thunder" coming from the direction of Hillsborough. He immediately recognized it as the sound of horses' hooves. Captain Graham and six troopers who had the best horses took a position where the road leads off to Stoney Creek to draw the enemy's attention in that direction. They could then disperse if pressed.

The enemy came into view at a slow gallop, just as the party with the prisoners had passed out of sight. Graham's party remained in position until the enemy's front had crossed the river. They then retreated up the Stoney Creek road. They arrived at Brigadier General Andrew Pickens's (1739–1817) camp only 10 or 12 minutes before Captain Simmons arrived by another road with the prisoners. When the pickets saw red coats in Captain Simmons's party, they began to fire upon him. Captain Simmons rode forward to explain and they allowed him to pass. However, the firing alarmed the whole army which was immediately formed for action.[84]

General Charles Cornwallis (1738–1805) arrived in Hillsborough on Tuesday, February 20, 1781, looking for food and rest for his tired men after chasing Major General Nathanael Greene (1742–1786) to the Dan River. He issued a proclamation on February 22, inviting the local population to escape "the cruel tyranny" of the Rebels by joining him. He also offered 10 days' food rations to anyone who rallied to the cause. He seems to have had few takers. He put his men to work repaving the town streets to keep them from getting bored and to ease transporting the cannons. The pavement extended 150 yards in four directions.

Brigadier General Charles O'Hara (1740–1802) noted:
> The novelty of a camp in the backwoods of America more than any other cause brought several people to stare at us. Their curiosity once satisfied, they returned to their homes. I am certain that in our march of near a thousand miles, almost in as many directions, thro' every part of North Carolina, tho every means possible was taken to persuade our friends as they are called and indeed as they called themselves to join us, we never had with us at any one time one hundred men in arms. Without the experiment had been made, it would have been impossible to conceive that government could in so important a matter have been so grossly deceived. Fatal infatuation! When will government see these people thro' the proper medium? I am persuaded never.[85]

Cornwallis left Hillsborough on February 26, three days after Greene crossed the Dan River back into North Carolina on his way to Guilford Courthouse. He headed toward the Haw River.

★ Colonel David Fanning (1755–1825) operated off and on from a base near Cox's Mill during the American War for Independence. His activity increased during late 1780 and early 1781 with the arrival of General Charles Cornwallis's (1738–1805) army. After the Battle of Raft Swamp (September 1, 1781), many Loyalists joined him. He mustered 950 militiamen in September 1781—the largest force of his career—but only 435 were equipped and armed. Colonel Hector McNeil, Sr. (d. 1781) arrived with 70 men and Colonel Archibald McDougal or McDugald with 200 Highlanders from Cumberland County on Sunday, September 9th.

Fanning's army of more than 600 Loyalists set out on Tuesday, September 11, 1781 and marched all day and night. They arrived early on a foggy Wednesday morning for a surprise attack on Hillsborough, the seat of government. They formed three divisions, surrounded the town and attacked at 7 AM. Their only resistance came from some snipers who fired from the windows of houses. The snipers were quickly silenced.

The Loyalists found more resistance at the governor's house where Fanning lost one man wounded and left 35 defenders dead and wounded in a brief skirmish. Fanning overwhelmed the weak defenses and captured the entire Whig government of North Carolina: Governor Thomas Burke (ca.1747–1783), the state council, several legislators, and more than 70 Continentals (some sources say as many as 200 Continentals) and took them to Wilmington into captivity.

Burke, a native of Hillsborough, had been elected governor by the general assembly in June 1781 and went to New Bern, the capital. He returned to Hillsborough with his wife on Sunday, September 9th to organize a campaign aimed at suppressing Loyalist activities in the Pee Dee and Cape Fear River areas. He appointed Brigadier General John Butler (1728–1796) to raise a large army to undertake this mission. Butler mustered militiamen from Caswell, Randolph, Chatham, Wake and Orange Counties at Ramsey's Mills in the forks of the Deep and Haw Rivers.

Fanning also encountered a little resistance from a group of North Carolina Continentals, mostly new recruits headed to join Major General Nathanael Greene's (1742–1786) army in South Carolina. They had barricaded themselves inside the town church and soon surrendered. The Loyalists had completed their task by 9 AM and broke into the town jail to release 30 Loyalist prisoners who were to be hanged that day. They also took two swivel guns (see Photo NC-1) from the jail and plundered some homes.[86]

★ Colonel Fanning was heading back to his base at Cox's Mill with his prisoners by noon on Thursday, September 13, 1781. Brigadier General John Butler (1728–1796), camped on the south bank of the Haw River at Ramsey's mill, was notified by a resident who escaped from Hillsborough and alerted the countryside. Knowing that Fanning would head to Wilmington with his prisoners, Butler hurried to Thomas Lindley's (1706–1781) Mill on Cane Creek, an obvious fording place. He set up an ambush on the high ground overlooking the route to the creek.

Fanning crossed Woody's Ford on the Haw River without opposition but when he got to Lindley's Mill on Cane Creek, General Butler and 400 Continentals were waiting for him at a 60-acre plateau near Lindley's Mill where the Hillsborough and Alamance Roads met. Colonel Fanning rode forward to Stafford's Branch on Cane Creek to determine why Colonel Hector McNeil, Sr. (d. 1781) had not placed any scouts out in front of the column.

Butler's marksmen were placed on the brow of a hill on the southern side of Cane Creek several hundred yards downstream from the mill. They fired a volley as McNeil and Colonel Archibald McDougal or McDugald advanced along the road with several hundred Scots. They were coming from the ford, through a narrow piece of low ground, in the early afternoon of September 13th. The Scots led the advance while Fanning's Loyalists were in the rear with the prisoners. Several Scots fell and the rest took shelter under the creek bank. They tried unsuccessfully to dislodge Butler's men.

McNeil ordered his men to fall back beyond the range of the enemy weapons. Colonel Archibald McDougal, outraged by the order to retreat, questioned McNeil's courage. McNeil changed his mind and charged the militia on top of the hill. McNeil was struck by eight musket balls and fell from his horse which had also been shot five times. The Loyalists retreated up the road to where McNeil had previously wanted to go.

The gunfire alerted Fanning who secured Governor Burke and the other prisoners before crossing the stream higher up. When the bulk of Fanning's army arrived, they outnumbered Butler's forces two to one. They launched a vicious counterattack on Butler's militia pursuing the rear of Fanning's column. Fanning's attack threw Butler's men into momentary confusion but they soon rallied. Nearly every Whig killed in the action fell during this period of confusion. Meanwhile, the prisoners were secured in the Spring Friends Meetinghouse, thereby allowing some of the guards to go fight.

Anticipating that Butler would try to free the prisoners, Fanning ordered all his men to withdraw to the meetinghouse. Colonel McDougal threatened to kill all the prisoners if the militia flanked the church; so Butler withdrew his men to their position on the hill beside Stafford Branch which McDougal was ordered to attack while Fanning crossed the creek and circled behind Butler.

The two armies engaged in a bitter fight that lasted for four hours. On the verge of victory, the militiamen began to run out of ammunition and Butler ordered a retreat, leaving his dead and wounded. Colonel Robert Mebane (ca. 1748–1781), unwilling to leave the field, ignored the order to withdraw and rallied his men to continue fighting a delaying action. His men were running low on ammunition, so Colonel Mebane carried powder and musket balls in his hat, distributing it as needed.

Just as it appeared Mebane's force would be overwhelmed, Fanning was shot in the arm. The bullet shattered the bone and severed an artery. Some of his men took him from his horse and hid him in the forest. Captain John Rains (1759–1835) assumed command, but the loss of their leader broke the spirit of the Loyalists. Both sides withdrew—the militia to Alamance Creek and the Loyalists to Wilmington with their prisoners.

Colonel Fanning won, but he and several of his men were badly wounded. He lost 27 killed, 60 so badly wounded that they could not be moved, and 30 other wounded who remained with the main body. Colonel Hector McNeil, Sr. fell dead on the field. Butler lost 125 men killed and 20 wounded. Nearly one fifth of the participants were killed or wounded and 34 soldiers were buried in a mass grave near the battlefield. Doctor John Pyle (1723–1804), who had commanded the Loyalists in the Haw River massacre, was one of the first people to reach the battlefield after the skirmish. He ministered to both Whigs and Loyalists and received a pardon for his past "transgressions." Governor Burke remained in captivity. He and the other prisoners then endured a difficult march during which they suffered very much.[87]

Fanning's victory, his major accomplishment, had little practical impact as it occurred only a month before General Charles Cornwallis's (1738–1805) surrender at Yorktown.

Thomas Lindley (1706–1781) who owned the mill where the battle was fought was a devout Quaker who sided with the Regulators and even hosted one of their meetings on May 11, 1768. When he was forced to choose between the Regulator movement and the church, he chose the church. He died on the day of the battle at his mill at the age of 75. Local tradition says that he died from the shock of seeing all the bloodshed at his mill, but the true cause of his death remains unknown.

★ Colonel David Fanning (1755–1825) wanted to kill James Harding, a staunch Whig supporter, who lived on Bear Creek on the south side of Deep River. Some Loyalists captured Harding on a scouting mission and took him to Fanning's camp where Harding approached Fanning and shook his hand. Harding told Fanning that he was glad that he now had a chance to join his force and that he had been trying to get away from the Whigs for some time. Fanning believed Harding was sincere and let him stay in the camp. He befriended many of the Loyalists and told Fanning about Captain Charles Gholson's company of Chatham County militia on the other side of Deep River.

Harding convinced Fanning that he could lead Gholson's militia into an ambush. Fanning agreed to the plan. Harding went to meet Gholson and made a different arrangement with him. Gholson's men would wait in ambush on Sunday night, October 7, 1781, while Harding led Fanning to the ambush site. When they reached the site, Harding gave the signal for Gholson's men to fire a volley into Fanning's column as he dashed forward. The volley killed or wounded several Loyalists; but Fanning managed to escape.[88]

Danbury
Chestnut Mountain (Feb. 1781)

> Tory House is now known as Tory's Den. It is located near Hanging Rock State Park, about 4 miles northwest of Danbury, in Stokes County, beside Tory's Falls.

Captain Stanly and a party of Loyalists went to the house of a farmer named Blackburne in February 1781. They robbed him of all his possessions, including his clothes. Blackburne went to Town Fork and reported the robbery. Colonel Joseph Winston (1746–1815) gave him a pair of pants and sent a runner to call out his militia. He mustered about 15 militiamen and set out in pursuit of the Loyalists a few hours later. They hanged a boy who had been carrying bread to the Loyalists and cut him down before he died. The boy told Winston that Captain Stanly and his men were on Chestnut Mountain, in a natural cave known as Tory House, in the Sauratown Mountains, on the Virginia border.

Winston's militiamen caught up with Captain Stanly's Loyalists, attacked and scattered them. They then hunted down and killed the fugitives. Only Captain Stanly and a man named Horton (d. 1781) escaped. Jack Martin, one of Winston's men, pursued Horton who fired at Martin when he was close. Martin stopped his horse and threw himself on the ground. The ball hit the horse in the eye. Martin returned fire, hitting Horton in the back. He got away but died three days later. Captain Stanly was taken as a prisoner of war and exchanged later.[89]

Winston–Salem
Near Salem (Feb. 10, 1781)

> Salem is located 25 miles west of Guilford Courthouse and is now known as Winston–Salem.

General Charles Cornwallis (1738–1805) arrived at Salem on Friday, February 9, 1781. He was now in a good position to cut off Major General Nathanael Greene (1742–1786) from the Dan River. Greene held a council of war with his chief officers, General Isaac Huger (1743–1797), Brigadier General Daniel Morgan (1736–1802), and Colonel Otho Holland Williams (1749–1794), to decide whether the army should give battle. Their army consisted of 1,426 infantrymen and 600 militiamen who needed arms and supplies badly. They decided to continue retreating as rapidly as possible across the Dan into the friendly districts of Virginia to gather more forces.

The Dan was 70 miles away, Greene reluctantly decided to cross it and leave North Carolina. He divided the army, putting Colonel Otho Williams in command of the cavalry of the 1st and 3rd Regiments and the Legion amounting to 240 men. He also commanded a detachment of 280 infantrymen under Lieutenant Colonel John Eager Howard (1752–1827), the infantry of Lieutenant Colonel Henry "Light–Horse Harry" Lee's (1756–1818) Legion and 60 Virginia riflemen. This force totaled 700 men which would be joined with the militia to harass the enemy advance, check their progress and, if possible, give General Greene an opportunity to retire without general action. They were to march north to screen the retreat of the main body while General Greene marched the main army northeast.

General Cornwallis assumed that General Greene would head west to cross the Dan at the shallower part of the river, unaware that Greene had pre-positioned boats at the lower end of the river in the opposite direction. General Cornwallis followed Colonel Williams on an extremely arduous march as Lieutenant Colonel Lee's (1756–1818) dragoons fought minor skirmishes on his rear.

Cornwallis realized, on February 13th, that Greene planned to cross at the lower ford. He had followed Williams 20 miles to the east and his troops were exhausted as Lee's cavalry continued to skirmish, along the way, into the night.

Both sides stopped briefly to rest until 2 PM on February 14th, when part of Greene's troops began cross the Dan. By 5:30, Greene wrote to Williams, saying: "All our troops are over.... I am ready to receive you with a hearty welcome." Williams crossed at sunset while Lee's cavalry held off the British. They crossed between 8 and 9 PM and General Cornwallis arrived too late to do anything. He retreated to Hillsborough on Saturday, February 17th.[90]

Chatham County

Cox's Mill (Feb. 1781; May 11, 12, 1781; June 8, 1781; July 29, 30, 1781; Dec. 10, 1781; April 24, 1782)
Buffalo Ford (May 11–12, 1781)
Gholson's Farm (Jan. 7, 1782)
Deep River (May 9, 1781; Feb. 1782)
Randolph County (March 12, 1782)

> Chatham Courthouse was located on the south side of Robertson's Creek in Pittsboro. Horton Middle School [79 Horton Street, east of route U.S 15 (U.S. 501/NC 87/Sanford Road) about 0.4 miles south of the intersection with route U.S. 64 (East Street)] now occupies the site. Pittsboro is the center of Chatham County.
>
> Gholson's Farm was about 11 miles southwest of Pittsboro in Goldston. To get to the site, take route U.S. 421, which runs south from Greensboro, to St. Lukes Church Road. Follow St. Lukes Church Road about a mile to Horton Road. Turn on Horton Road and the site of Gholson's Farm is about 100 yards on the left.
>
> Cox's Mill (see Photo NC-3), built by William Cox (d. 1767), was located near the junction of Mill Greek and the west side of Deep River in Randolph County a few miles south of the town of Ramseur.[91]
>
> A marker at the junction of Liberty Street, Main Street and route NC 22 (Coleridge Road) in Ramseur notes that Colonel David Fanning's headquarters was 4.5 miles south. Cox's Mill is on the northeast side of a viaduct on route NC 2657 (Mill Creek Road) crossing Mill Creek. To get there, take route NC 2656 (Hinshaw Town Road) off route NC 22 south of Ramseur. Proceed west for 0.6 mile to route NC 2607 (Buffalo Ford Road). Go another 0.6 mile and turn right (north) onto route NC 2657 (Mill Creek Road). The mill is about three quarters of a mile ahead on the right. There is still plenty of open field around the mill which has been neglected.
>
> Buffalo Ford is on the Deep River about 1 mile south of Cox's Mill.

When Colonel David Fanning (1755–1825) learned of the approach of General Charles Cornwallis's (1738–1805) army in February 1781, he immediately published an advertisement offering inducements to those who would join Lieutenant Colonel John Hamilton's (d. 1817) Royal North Carolina Regiment. He promised that the recruits would only serve in the Carolinas or Georgia and would each receive an enlistment

NC- 3. Cox's Mill

bonus of three guineas and a land grant at the end of the war. Fanning's offer recruited several men.

Fanning also proposed to hunt down Charles Sherring, a noted horse thief in the area, who had been sentenced to death in 1779 but was pardoned by a special act of the legislature. Sherring continued his thefts in 1781, targeting Loyalists. He lived near Fanning's base at Cox's Mill and slept in a corncrib beside his house where he assumed nobody would look for him and exact revenge.

Fanning went to Sherring's cabin alone one night in February 1781 and searched it. Sherring's family claimed they could not give Fanning any information because they did not know where he went each night. When Fanning saw the corncrib, he looked into it and poked his rifle between the log walls and fired. The ball passed through Sherring's neck bone and windpipe but did not kill him. As Sherring did not move after being shot, Fanning thought he must have fired at a piece of wood and returned home. Sherring then traveled 8 miles to Cornelius Tyson's (1720–1789) house where he was treated. He eventually recovered.[92]

★ When Captain John Henry Hinds (1745–1811) learned that Colonel David Fanning (1755–1825) was camped at a friend's house on Deep River in early May 1781, he and 11 militiamen rode hard to raid the Loyalist camp. Hinds surprised Fanning on Wednesday, May 9, 1781. As the militiamen approached the house, the Loyalists ran out firing. They killed one man as they rushed past the militiamen into the woods. They took three horses and some weapons. Captain Hinds captured two of Fanning's men in their dash to the woods. One was shot; the other hanged on the spot where the Loyalists had killed a man a few days earlier.[93]

★ Colonel David Fanning (1755–1825) was determined to get revenge for the deaths of his two men. He mustered 17 well-armed men in a few days and prepared an ambush at Buffalo Ford on Deep River, intending to capture Colonel John Collier (1732–1792) and Lieutenant Colonel Andrew Balfour (1735–1783) of the Randolph County Militia, Captain Hinds's superior officers. Fanning sent out spies on Friday, May 11, 1781. One of them returned within two hours and reported that the militiamen had stopped to plunder a house 3 miles away and would be delayed in reaching the river. Fanning and his men rode to the house to attack the militiamen. They attacked the plunderers in a field near the house and kept up a smart fire for half an hour. The Loyalists killed the militia captain and a private, wounded three and took two prisoners, eight well appointed horses and several swords.[94]

★ The same day, Colonel David Fanning (1755–1825) and his men pursued another party of militiamen and caught up with them. They attacked the militiamen the following morning, killed four of them on the spot, seriously wounded three, and took one of the wounded prisoner with all seven horses and accoutrements. About an hour later, they killed one of their prisoners and captured two more in the pursuit.[95]

★ Colonel David Fanning (1755–1825) learned, on Friday, June 8, 1781, that Colonel John Collier (1732–1792) had mustered 160 Randolph County militiamen 10 miles away to attack Cox's Mill. Fanning set out with 49 men that night to attack Collier's camp. His guide was captured as they approached the camp. When the Loyalists came within 30 steps of them, the sentries fired. The militiamen sought shelter in the houses and outbuildings of a nearby farm while a gunfight ensued in the dark for the next four hours. The Loyalists withdrew at dawn after losing two men killed, six wounded, and six captured. Colonel Collier executed Fanning's guide in the morning. The Loyalists retreated to Deep River, leaving their wounded with friends along the way. Fanning disbanded his militia, deciding it was too dangerous to continue any military actions, and headed for the Uwharrie Mountains.[96]

★ While Colonel David Fanning (1755–1825) was attacking Colonel Philip Alston's (1740–1788) house, known as the House in the Horseshoe (see Photo NC-4), on Sunday morning, July 29, 1781, some Whig militiamen unsuccessfully attacked his base at Cox's Mill. They left when they learned Fanning was returning. Meanwhile, Fanning learned that a wagonload of salt destined for the Continental Army had passed by Deep River early that morning. He took eight men and rode hard for 16 miles. When they caught up with the wagon, they captured it and returned to Cox's Mill with the salt the next morning.[97]

When he arrived at the mill, Fanning gathered his militia to pursue the men who dared to attack him. The Whig militia sent a flag of truce asking Fanning to surrender but he refused. The Whigs withdrew with Fanning in hot pursuit. Along the way, Fanning learned that the Whig militiamen joined forces with Colonel John Paisley (1745–1811) at Brown's Plantation. They now numbered 400. Although greatly outnumbered, Fanning rode forward with about 150 men and sent word to Paisley that he was ready to fight. When the Loyalists arrived at Brown's Plantation, they found it deserted. The Whigs had withdrawn to Salisbury, expecting only a larger force would attack.[98]

★ Colonel Elijah Isaacs (1730–1790) and 300 men took over Colonel David Fanning's (1755–1825) base of operations at Cox's Mill on Monday, December 10, 1781, intending to stop Loyalist attacks. They burned several Loyalist houses. Captain John Stinson hanged David Jackson (d. 1781), who had been captured with Colonel John Pyle (1723–1804) at Moores Creek Bridge and then escaped from the jail in Halifax, for his activities in 1776.

NC-4. Alston house or House in the Horseshoe. Bullet holes around the door remain as reminders of the battle.

Colonel Isaacs offered protection to all Loyalists who would meet with him; and Acting Governor Alexander Martin (1740–1807) issued a proclamation pardoning all Loyalists except those guilty of murder, robbery, and housebreaking. When the Loyalists gathered, Isaacs took them prisoners and brought them to the Salisbury jail. One of them was shot while trying to escape.

Fanning did not try to take on Isaacs's larger army, but instead moved southeast, away from territory under the control of the Whigs. After the evacuation of Wilmington, Fanning was unable to get the supplies and ammunition he needed to maintain larger operations. Due to this he was no longer able to assemble large forces of Loyalist partisans.[99]

★ Colonel Elijah Isaacs (1730–1790) had sacked Loyalist Colonel David Fanning's (1755–1825) base camp at Cox's Mill in December 1781. He then proceeded westward while Colonel Fanning captured any stragglers. Colonel Isaacs placed covering forces behind to ambush Fanning's pursuing Loyalists but Colonel Fanning was not fooled. Rather, he hunted the rear guard, killing two and wounding many others. He later killed two more of Colonel Isaacs's men.

★ Captain Charles Gholson was one of the men Colonel Fanning (1755–1825) pursued because he was the commander of the Chatham County regiment of militia. Colonel Fanning found Captain Gholson's company plundering the property of a Loyalist in January 1782. Captain Gholson fled, but one of his men was captured and hanged. Captain Fanning continued pursuing Captain Gholson but never managed to catch him, so he rode to Captain Gholson's home and burned the farm in retaliation on Monday, January 7, 1782. His men burned two more houses near Gholson's farm and executed "a man who had been very anxious" to have some of Fanning's Loyalists executed.

Colonel Fanning captured John Thompson (1749–1811), a "Rebel magistrate," during his return to his base camp at Cox's Mill in Randolph County. He forced Thompson to take a message to acting Governor Alexander Martin (1740–1807), saying that he would retaliate in kind with more executions if the Whigs did not cease harassing the Loyalists.

John Thompson informed Colonel Fanning that some of the other Loyalist leaders, Colonel Archibald McDougal or McDugald and Colonel Hector McNeil (1756–1830), had taken refuge in South Carolina. Fanning offered the authorities his terms for peace in North Carolina. He demanded that all Loyalists be allowed to return to their homes unmolested. He also wanted the Loyalists to be under no restrictions to do anything against the Royal government and to not have to pay any taxes to support the war against the King.

Several Whig leaders, tired of the constant fighting, supported the prospect for peace and took the terms to Brigadier General John Butler (1728–1796) of the Hillsborough District Brigade of Militia. However, the killing continued during the negotiations. Meanwhile, one of Fanning's men, Captain William Lindley (1742–1784), quit the Loyalist militia and went to the Blue Ridge Mountains. Three former comrades followed him and hacked him to death. When Colonel Fanning was informed, he had two of the killers, William White (d. 1782) and John Magaherty (d. 1782), hanged. The third man escaped into the wilderness.

Colonel Fanning was supposed to meet with a group of Whigs at Baalam Thompson's (1745–1798) home near the Wilcox Iron Works on Friday, January 11, 1782 . He came to discuss his terms for peace under a flag of truce. John Thompson warned Fanning that Captain Charles Gholson and Captain Robert Scobey were waiting to ambush him as he rode by. Colonel Fanning no longer trusted the Whigs and ceased to consider peace as an option.[100]

★ Captain Stephen Walker, one of Colonel David Fanning's (1755–1825) officers, surprised and captured a company of Whig militiamen at a muster field at Deep River in February 1782. He later dismissed them on their paroles. Lieutenant Colonel Andrew Balfour (1735–1783), of the Randolph County militia, was raising a body of men to go after Fanning about this time. He forced those men whom Walker had paroled to join him, telling them that a parole to a Loyalist was not binding.

Balfour marched against Fanning but could not catch up with him. He then returned home and dismissed his party, reserving only two officers and six privates as a safe guard. Their horses were scarcely let loose when Fanning, who had always been hovering about them, came suddenly up to Balfour's house and captured him and his men. The privates were sent away on parole, but the officers, including Balfour, were taken 80 miles away to a place called the Cross Roads in Guilford County. Here, where David Jackson (d. 1781), one of Fanning's captains, had been hanged a short time earlier, Fanning executed his three prisoners.

Another party of Whigs was now searching for Fanning. When they learned of the executions, they headed toward Guilford. While they were looking for Fanning at Deep River, Fanning attacked the guard at Guilford and killed seven of them. He released six or seven Loyalists confined there, burned the courthouse, jail and other buildings, and then retreated to Deep River, slipping by a body of Whigs marching against him, believing that he was still at Guilford.[101]

The Loyalists remained at Deep River until June 8 when Colonel John Collier (1732–1792), and Lieutenant Colonel Balfour and 160 militiamen came to attack him. Colonel Fanning marched 10 miles to their camp during the night with 49 men. The Whigs captured one of his guides which alerted them to Fanning's approach. Fanning, being unacquainted with the ground, advanced with great caution. The sentry discovered them, fired, and retreated. The Whigs secured themselves under cover of the houses and fences and began to fire.

Both sides exchanged fire for four hours in the cloudy and dark night. Fanning lost one man killed and six wounded and the guide taken prisoner who was killed the next morning. Fanning retreated at dawn and returned to Deep River, leaving his wounded men at a friend's house. The militia then kept so many scouting parties on constant watch that Fanning had to lay low for some time.[102]

★ A party of Loyalists under Colonel David Fanning (1755–1825) killed Lieutenant Colonel Andrew Balfour (1735–1782) in his own house in Randolph County on Tuesday, March 12, 1782.[103]

★ Colonel David Fanning (1755–1825) was engaged to marry 16-year-old Sarah Carr (1766–1833), the sister of Captain William Carr, one of his officers. Captain William Carr and Captain William Hooker (d. 1782) also planned to marry on the same day as their commanding officer. Colonel Fanning designed a uniform for the occasion that was "Linen frocks died Black, with Red Cuffs do Ellbows and shoulder cape also, and Belted with Scarlet, which was a total Disguise to the Rebels which the red was all fringed with Large white fringe."

As captains Carr and Hooker rode to get their fiancées on Wednesday, April 24, 1782, a patrol of Congressional militiamen attacked them killing Captain Hooker on the spot. Captain Carr managed to escape. Colonel Fanning learned about the attack as he rode to the location of his wedding in Chatham County. He also learned of the militiamen's location and rode there with five men. They surrounded William Dowdy's (d. 1782) house and Fanning yelled for the militiamen to come out. They all came out except for William Dowdy (1759–1782) who ran from the house into the nearby woods.

The Loyalists fired and wounded Dowdy in the shoulder. Colonel Fanning rode up to him and fired both of his pistols into his chest, killing him instantly. He paroled the rest of the militiamen and proceeded to his wedding. Colonel Fanning and Captain Carr were both married that day and "Kept two Days merriment" before going back into hiding.[104]

Summerfield
Reedy Fork (Feb. 12, 1781)
Bruce's Cross Roads, Gillies's Death (Feb. 12, 1781)
Near Dix's Ferry (Feb. 13, 1781)

> The event at Reedy Fork is also called Bruce's Crossroads, Gillies's Death, Oak Ridge, and Reedy Fork and is also dated as February 11 and 13. Reedy Fork is on route U.S. 220 (Battleground Avenue) near Strawberry Road at the Greensboro city limits, about 9.5 miles northeast of Guilford Courthouse. Bruce's Crossroads, also known as Oak Ridge, and now Summerfield, is less than a mile north of Reedy Fork. About 0.6 miles north of the intersection of route U.S. 220 (Battleground Avenue) and Strawberry Road, bear left on Summerfield Road and proceed about 300 yards to the Summerfield Elementary School before the junction with Centerfield Road. A monument in front of the school notes that Charles Bruce and James Gillies (or Gillis) are buried here. However, the Bruce family cemetery is across the street near a highway marker. The graves themselves are unmarked (see Photo NC-5). A granite monument to Gillies stands near the Visitors Center at Guilford Courthouse.

NC-5. Bruce family cemetery. Charles Bruce's grave. Charles Bruce and James Gillies (or Gillis) are buried in the Bruce family cemetery but the actual graves are unmarked.

> Dix's (or Dixon's) Ferry crossed the Dan River at the North Carolina–Virginia line in Rockingham County, northeast of Providence, about 40 miles northeast of Guilford Courthouse. Irwin's (also Irvine's) Ferry was 35 miles east of Dix's Ferry and about 2 miles west of where the Hyco River pours into the Dan. Boyd's Ferry was 3 to 4 miles east of Irwin's. Irwin's Ferry was closer to Halifax, Virginia, where General Greene headed after the crossing.

The British were 25 miles from Guilford Courthouse and 20 miles below Dix's Ferry in early February 1781. Brigadier General Charles O'Hara (1740–1802) commanded the advance guard of light infantry and traveled about 30 miles per day despite the weather and difficult ground. They had brief clashes with Lieutenant Colonel Henry "Light-Horse Harry" Lee's (1756–1818) and Lieutenant Colonel William Washington's (1752–1810) dragoons.

Meanwhile Colonel Otho Holland Williams (1749–1794) was drawing the Redcoats toward Dix's Ferry, away from Major General Nathanael Greene's (1742–1786) main army. Earlier that morning, Williams had received orders to proceed to Irwin's Ferry, about 6 miles upstream from Dix's Ferry, which Greene's army was approaching. Williams immediately forwarded the message to Lee who was guarding his rear.

★ Colonel Otho Holland Williams's (1749–1794) men were eating breakfast at the home of Charles Bruce (1733–1832) on Monday morning, February 12, 1781, when Isaac Wright, one of Bruce's neighbors, told them that General Charles Cornwallis's (1738–1805) army was about 4 miles behind. Colonel Williams sent Captain James Armstrong and a group of dragoons from Lieutenant Colonel Henry "Light-Horse Harry" Lee's Legion to investigate.

Colonel Williams then sent Lieutenant Colonel Lee to reinforce Captain Armstrong who had advanced about a mile. Lee proceeded 2 miles further but saw no enemy and returned for breakfast at a nearby farm. Shots from his pickets announced the approach of the van of the British Army under Brigadier General O'Hara. Lee quickly mustered his dragoons and set out after them.

Captain Armstrong and three dragoons and their guide proceeded to where Wright had seen the Redcoats an hour earlier. The dragoons were selected because they had the swiftest horses. James Gillies (1767–1781), a 14-year-old bugler, loaned his horse to Wright so he could lead the dragoons to the British. Gillies then headed back to camp with the farmer's tired horse.

The scouts located the British and withdrew with some of Lieutenant Colonel Banastre Tarleton's (1744–1833) legionnaires in pursuit. A party of legionnaires knocked the 14-year-old bugler from his horse and hacked him to death by the road. Lieutenant Colonel Lee had pulled his men off the road and concealed them in the woods along the road. As Tarleton's Legion advanced on the same road, Lee's dragoons attacked them from the rear after they had passed. Seeing his dying bugler, Lee attacked in a rage, killing seven legionnaires.

Captain Thomas Miller, commanding the lead element of Tarleton's Legion, ordered his men into the fight and lost 13 more men "severely cut in the face, neck, and shoulders." Lieutenant Stephen Lewis (1757–1792) caught Captain Miller trying to escape. Furious at Gillies's death, Lee ordered Lewis to show no quarter. He reprimanded Lewis on the spot for disobeying orders when he brought back Captain Miller and two other prisoners.

Lee held Miller responsible for his bugler's death and gave Miller a pencil and paper to write his last words to his friends. The forward troops of Cornwallis's army appeared just as Lee was about to hang Miller, forcing him to rejoin Colonel Williams. Captain Miller was sent to General Greene as a prisoner of war. Lee lost only one man in the skirmish. The main body of the British Army arrived the next day and buried their dead alongside the road and camped at Bruce's plantation that night.[105]

Lee resumed his position as Williams's rear guard. He secured a bridge to get the infantry across the nearby stream before the British arrived. The cavalry covered the retreat as the British pursued them all day on the 13th, often in clear sight. Even though the two armies came within musket range several times, they did not engage in combat. Lee managed to escape and moved along the road to Dix's and then to Boyd's Ferry.

When Lee and Williams saw campfires burning ahead of them, they wondered if they were from Greene's army or from the Redcoats. It turned out they were tended by Continentals after Greene's army departed two days earlier. Williams and Lee continued toward Irwin's Ferry and stopped to sleep for a few hours only when they learned that the Redcoats stopped to rest.

Greene crossed the Dan River at Irwin's Ferry with the main army, using boats collected by Lieutenant Colonel Edward Carrington (1749–1810) and a survey of the river made by Captain John Smith (1747–1832) of the Maryland line.

Williams and Lee resumed their march on the 14th and arrived at the ferry about dusk. Williams crossed before sunset, followed by Lee's troops. The last troops crossed the Dan after 9 PM after re-capturing some horses that fled at being forced to swim the river—less than an hour before O'Hara arrived to find them on the other side of the Dan. General Cornwallis's army reached Irwin's Ferry six hours later.[106]

Speedwell Furnace or Iron Works (Feb. 12, 1781)

> Troublesome Iron Works on Troublesome Creek is 1.5 miles north of Monroeton and about 7 miles southwest of Reidville in Rockingham County. It is sometimes referred to as Speedwell Iron Works or Speedwell Furnace because of the neighboring village.[107]
>
> A highway marker on route U.S. 158 just north of the intersection with Monroeton Road and across from the Monroeton Golf Club notes that the site is 1.5 miles north. General Nathanael Greene's army camped there after the battle of Guilford Courthouse and President George Washington visited the site in 1791.
>
> The site is on Monroeton Road about 400 yards before its intersection with Iron Works Lane. The only identification of the site is a millstone on the east side of Monroeton Road. The ruins of the furnace's foundations are visible on both sides of the road just north of the bridge over Troublesome Creek. Visitors with a discriminating eye will identify the earthworks overgrown with vegetation on the high ground north of the creek. The hard use of the ironworks during the war and the vandalism by the armies probably left the furnace in ruins by the end of the war. The site was placed on the National Register of Historic Places in 1972.

Colonel Otho Holland Williams (1749–1794) occupied a good piece of ground near the Speedwell Iron Works to delay the British advance as much as possible on Monday, February 12, 1781. Thomas Archer (1729–1797), an Irishman from Guilford County who "hardly ever missed his aim at any distance within two hundred yards" was in Williams's light infantry. When the Royal Artillery brought up a field piece, Archer demanded that they remove it from the road or he would have to shoot them.

When they failed to remove the cannon, Archer steadied his rifle against a tree and fired, hitting gunner number two holding the linstock (see Photo NC-2). Colonel Williams's dragoons mounted their horses and rode away before the artillerists recovered and were ready to fire. The Congressional troops delayed General Cornwallis's army for two hours.

Lieutenant Colonel Lee crossed at the Irwin Ferry later that day and stopped so his men could eat and rest. Brigadier General Charles O'Hara (1740–1802) and the British vanguard arrived just as Lee's men began to eat. They fired on Lee's pickets. Lee formed his men quickly and hurried away. General O'Hara's troops, surprised by the sudden engagement, stopped and awaited orders.

Lee took advantage of the delay to withdraw his infantry; but the British soon pursued them closely, covering 30 miles that day into the cold night. Lee's infantry had to almost run to keep up. Colonel Williams saw campfires in the road ahead. Thinking it might be Major General Nathanael Greene's (1742–1786) army, he sent a messenger ahead to warn them that the British were coming. His messenger returned to report that it was indeed Greene's campsite but from two days before. Greene left the campfires burning to guide the light troops.

Both armies stopped for the night, but Colonel Williams awakened his men about midnight. General Cornwallis was pursuing him again. It was difficult to march on the deeply rutted road covered with a heavy frost. Cornwallis thought that he had Greene pinned against the Dan River, so swollen by a recent rainfall that he needed boats to cross. However, General Greene had the foresight to have boats waiting for him when he reached the Dan.

Colonel Williams received word on Wednesday afternoon, February 14th, that Greene had crossed the Dan River and was safely in Virginia. Williams marched his men to Irwin's Ferry where they were ferried into Virginia by sunset. When the Crown forces arrived after sundown, they found that the Continentals had already crossed the river which was too swollen to attempt fording it. They had marched 40 miles in 16 hours and won the race to the Dan.[108]

★ The Continental Army retreated to Speedwell Iron Works after the battle of Guilford Courthouse to rest and reorganize. They spent five days at the site and prepared for an attack which never came.

Burlington vicinity
O'Neil's Mill (before Sept. 10, 1775)
Haw River
Haw Fields (March 1779)
Pyle's Defeat (Feb. 25, 1781)
Dickey's Farm (Feb. 26, 1781)

> O'Neil's Mill was near the Haw River south of Burlington.
> To get to the site of Pyle's defeat, take route I-85/40 exit for route NC 49 South (Maple Ave.) and go south on route NC 49 for 0.2 miles to a state historical marker at the intersection with Anthony Road. The marker notes the defeat occurred on February 23, 1781. Another marker is located at the site of the battle which occurred 0.75 miles to the southwest between Anthony Road and Industry Drive.
> Haw Fields is in Mebane a little more than half a mile south-southeast of exit 152 of route I-40|I-85 at the intersection of routes NC 2126 (Old Hillsborough Road) and NC 119. Dickey's Farm was on the west bank of the Haw River southeast of Burlington and probably about 6 miles east of the site of Pyle's defeat.

A party of Loyalists were gathering at O'Neil's Mill before Sunday, September 10, 1775 when 100 militiamen were sent to disperse them. They were joined by John Drayton (1766–1822) and 125 men, consisting of 84 Georgia volunteers and 141 Carolina militiamen, including officers. Along the way, they learned that Colonel Thomas Fletchall (1725–1789) and a large body of men joined the Loyalists about 2 AM, intending to attack the Ninety Six Courthouse.

Major James Mayson (1739–1799), Major Andrew Williamson (ca. 1730–1786) and Captain John Hammond (1722–1820) held a council of war to consider whether they should retreat toward the ridge where Colonel William Thompson (1727–1796) and his Rangers were located, to defend Ninety Six, or to march and ambush the enemy. They decided to set up an ambuscade, hoping to surprise the Loyalists during a night march, and throw them into confusion and probably a general rout. They placed four swivel guns (see Photo NC-1) in the four windows of the jail to command every access point. They also posted a number of men with ammunition and a supply of water. They considered the jail impregnable, except for a fire on the shingle roof.

A party of 100 of Major Mayson's men prepared an ambush about midway between the Ninety Six Courthouse and the Island ford, 6 miles from the courthouse. The Loyalists had to pass the ford on their way to the courthouse. The ambuscade was completed by 10 PM that night. When Mr. Drayton and Major Williamson arrived at the Island ford to inspect Major Mayson's troops, they placed the men in such a way as to deliver a diagonal fire upon Fletchall's Loyalists as they crossed the Saluda River.

They then waited until 2:30 AM when Mr. Drayton received a false alarm. Major Mayson and his men held the post until daylight, while Mr. Drayton and Major Williamson returned to Ninety Six with the rest of the troops between 3 and 4 AM.[109]

★ North Carolina Loyalists began gathering at a place called the Haw Fields early in March 1779, intending to join the British in Georgia. Colonel William Lytle (1755–1829) and Captain Henry Connelly (1741–1840) and their militiamen dispersed them.[110]

★ Major General Nathanael Greene (1742–1786) sent Major General Henry "Light-Horse Harry" Lee (1756–1818) from Virginia to North Carolina on Sunday, February 18, 1781 with orders to harass the Crown forces. Lee crossed the Dan River with his Legion and Brigadier General Andrew Pickens's (1739–1817) South Carolina militia. He tried to surprise Lieutenant Colonel Banastre Tarleton (1744–1833) on the morning of February 25. However, Tarleton had already broken camp.

As Lee pursued Tarleton, the front of Lee's Legion encountered two mounted Loyalists who mistook them for Tarleton's Legion, probably because they wore green coats similar to those worn by Tarleton's men. The Loyalists were taken to Lee who took advantage of their mistake by posing as Tarleton. He learned that Colonel John Pyle (1723–1804) had recruited about 400 Loyalists and that they were on their way to join Tarleton. Lee sent one of the men back to Pyle to congratulate him on raising his force, directing him to ask Pyle if "he would be so good as to draw out on the margin of the road, so as to give convenient room for his much fatigued troops to pass without delay to their night position."

Lee then ordered riflemen into the woods to cover his left flank while the messenger brought the dispatch to Pyle and returned. Lee took the lead of his column and soon saw Pyle's men lined up on the right side of the road. He rode toward Pyle, speaking occasionally to the Loyalists, complimenting them on their "good looks and commendable conduct." The South Carolina militiamen exposed themselves prematurely and shooting broke out as Lee was shaking hands with Pyle, intending to identify himself and to offer the Loyalists safety if they would go home or join his men.

Lee's Legion immediately wheeled to their right and charged the Loyalists with drawn sabres. Lee recorded "The conflict was quickly decided, and bloody on one side only." Many of the Loyalists, thinking a mistake had been made, shouted "You are killing your own men!" or "I am a friend to his Majesty!" or "Hurrah for King George!" At least 90 Loyalists were killed in the brief skirmish and most of the rest wounded, including Pyle who was left for dead.

The action is called a "defeat," but it resembles British victories by Tarleton at the Waxhaws and Major General Charles "No Flint" Grey (1729–1807) at Paoli, which were called "massacres." The importance of this skirmish is that it destroyed any hopes General Charles Cornwallis (1738–1805) had of getting help from the Loyalists of North Carolina at a time when he needed all the help he could get.[111]

★ Brigadier General Andrew Pickens (1739–1817), aware that Lieutenant Colonel Banastre Tarleton (1744–1833) was looking for him, placed Major Micajah Lewis (d. 1781), of the North Carolina Line, and his men as part of a rearguard at the ford of a branch near Dickey's house. Lewis heard a body of troops approaching in the dark on Monday, February 26, 1781. He mounted his horse and went to meet them, not knowing they were Loyalists. They told him that Major General Nathanael Greene (1742–1786) sent them to join General Pickens.

Lewis ordered the officer to meet him halfway and dismounted from his horse. As Lewis reached the halfway point, the soldiers fired a volley, hitting Lewis and his horse several times. A musket ball struck Lewis in the thigh. His men brought Lewis to Dickey's house where he died the next day. General Pickens, unaware of the number of enemies in the area, moved his men 3 miles away.[112]

Alamance River (March 5, 7, 1781; March 15, 1781)
Clapp's Mill (March 1, 2, and 4, 1781)

The Alamance Battleground State Historic Site (**http://www.nchistoricsites.org/alamance/**) (see Photo NC-6) is located near Burlington, exit 143 off route I-85, then 6 miles southwest on route NC 62. The park commemorates the 1771 battle between Loyalist governor William Tryon's (1729–1788) militia and an inexperienced army of colonial reformers known as the "Regulators." The John Allen III (1749–1826) house, a log home typical of 1780s North Carolina, is on the battlefield near the visitor center which offers a 25-minute audiovisual presentation about the battle.

The Clapp's Mill incident is also known as Alamance River. It is documented as having occurred on March 1, 2, and 4. The mill was on Beaver Creek 200 feet from its confluence with Big Alamance Creek in Burlington. To get there, take exit 141 (route NC 1158 (Huffman Mill Road)) off route I-85 and proceed southwest about 2 miles to the entrance to Lake Mackintosh Park and Marina. A short distance past the entrance, take a right on Clubhouse Drive and go to the parking lot at the end. The clubhouse, on the right of the parking area, is near the site of Clapp's Mill which was about 0.8 miles south-southeast of MacIntosh Park where Lake Mackintosh inundated Pond Road. The site of the battle was probably closer to the Alamance Battleground Historic Site.

Across the parking area, there's a pile of stones (see Photo NC-7) which includes several stones from the Clapp's Mill dam and the mill's cornerstone. To the left of these stones, there's a commemorative area with upright stones around a millstone (see Photo NC-8). These stones bear plaques that give a brief history of the area,

NC-6. Alamance battleground. The monument marks the site of the Battle of the Alamance. The flags denote the relative positions of both sides.

NC-7. Clapp's Mill monument. The monument includes several stones from the Clapp's Mill dam and the mill's cornerstone.

NC-8. Millstone, Clapp's Mill. Commemorative area around a millstone used at Clapp's Mill. The upright stones around the millstone bear plaques that give a brief history of the area, describe the action and commemorate the troops.

> describe the action and commemorate the troops involved. A historical marker on route NC 62 at the intersection of route NC 1135 (Porter Sharpe Road) southwest of the Alamance Battleground also commemorates the event.

Colonel Otho Holland Williams (1749–1794) sent a company of 30 riflemen under Captain Robert H. Kirkwood (1746–1791) to Clapp's Mill on Alamance Creek on the night of March 1, 1781 to obtain intelligence of enemy movements and to harass General Charles Cornwallis's (1738–1805) advance guard led by Lieutenant Colonel Banastre Tarleton (1744–1833). They killed two pickets and captured two prisoners. The clash only induced Tarleton to leave his camp quickly early the next morning, leaving behind a considerable quantity of supplies.

Colonel Williams sent Lieutenant Colonel Henry "Light-Horse Harry" Lee's (1756–1818) Legion, Captain Joseph Graham's (1759–1836) company of mounted riflemen, Thomas Rowland's (1744–1814) Botetourt rifle battalion, and a company of Catawbas south across Alamance Creek early Friday morning, March 2, 1781. This force was about one-third of Colonel Williams's troops (705 of 2039). Colonel William Preston's (1729–1783) Virginia militia riflemen and Brigadier General Andrew Pickens's (1739–1817) militia followed in reserve and were positioned in thick woods about 9 AM. Lee moved forward "with great circumspection" as the Crown forces headed toward the Alamance River, hoping to trap Colonel Williams's force and bring Major General Nathanael Greene (1742–1786) to their aid.

Captain Richard Hovenden spotted some Continental dragoons near John Clapp's mill as he covered a forage party. The site had a double barn with a thick coppice of woods to the right and center and an open field to the left. He reported this to Lieutenant Colonel Tarleton who set out with his dragoons, a small body of mounted infantry, Lieutenant Colonel Thomas Dundas's (1750–1794) Light Company, and 150 men of the 23rd Regiment of Foot.

Lieutenant Colonel Lee's scouts reported on Tarleton's movements. Lee placed his men behind a rail fence to ambush the British while his cavalry protected their flanks. As at Cowpens, the riflemen were to fire two shots and retreat behind the line of the concealed Continentals. As the British entered the ambush, about noon, one of the Catawbas snorted like a deer and his comrades ran forward and fired. The riflemen fired a volley that sent the British running for cover.

The advancing columns of Congressional troops under Major Henry Dickson (1740–1782) and Colonel William Preston (1729–1783) dismounted, tied their horses to a fence and advanced in line. Major John Rudolph formed Lee's dragoons behind the double barn. When both sides began heavy fire, the Catawbas turned and ran. The saplings and bushes were so thick that the heavy fire fractured the bark and twigs, causing them to fly and hit the men on their cheeks and shoulders. As the men dodged the splinters, they could not load and fire as fast as they might have done. After a few rounds, the whole line panicked and retreated without orders.

Tarleton ordered Dundas's infantry to advance and explore the thick woods. As the British approached the plantations where they were to obtain forage, they came under heavy fire from the thickets on each side of the road. The main part of the British cavalry was passing in the lane behind Rudolph who retreated. Another party of about 50 British advanced through the field until they came to the middle fence where Lieutenant Joseph Graham's (1759–1836) party was positioned. The British hesitated until they discovered their main force was passing where the middle fence joined the lane. They advanced and Lieutenant Graham retreated.

Captain Kirkwood's Delaware troops (see Photo DE-1) and Captain Edward Oldham's (1756–1798) Maryland light infantry were on a rise, about 80 yards ahead, to provide covering fire for the retreating troops. They began a heavy fire on the British cavalry, over the heads of the retreating troops. The dragoons withdrew a short distance until their infantry arrived. Lee's and Preston's militiamen formed on both sides of the road.

The 15-minute engagement left about eight killed and two to four wounded, mostly riflemen. The British lost one officer wounded and 17 men killed and three wounded, mostly from the Brigade of Guards. Many militiamen thought that they had been sacrificed by the Continentals at the battle of Clapp's mill and there was deep resentment in their ranks. Desertions became common and many did not renew their enlistments. Pickens's brigade, which once numbered 1,050 men, was reduced to 453 men by March 4.[113]

★ Lieutenant Colonel Henry "Light-Horse Harry" Lee (1756–1818) sent Captain Joseph Graham (1759–1836) and 25 dragoons to see if the British were still at the battlefield the following day. They had buried their dead and left, so Graham proceeded until he came within half a mile of the British lines. He sent a sergeant and six men, at dusk, to report their location to Lee. Graham then headed through the woods to capture two sentries he had seen earlier. The sentries fired at them which brought out a squad. When the British approached, Graham's men fired at them at point blank range and drove them back. After Graham captured their officer, the jumpy sentries fired at shadows for most of the night.[114]

★ A patrol of Lieutenant Colonel William Washington's (1752–1810) dragoons killed 23 Loyalist drovers driving cattle to General Charles Cornwallis's (1738–1805) camp along the Alamance River on Monday, March 5, 1781. This action, combined with the slaughter of Colonel John Pyle's (1723–1804) men at the Haw River, made many of the Loyalist militiamen on the way to join Cornwallis slip home to see to the defense of their homes.[115]

★ Colonel Otho Holland Williams (1749–1794) decided to try to surprise Lieutenant Colonel Banastre Tarleton's (1744–1833) camp after the skirmish at Wetzell's Mill. He sent Captain Robert H. Kirkwood (1746–1791) and his Delaware Continentals with 40 riflemen. They reconnoitered the camp and attacked at 1 AM on Wednesday, March 7, 1781. The sentries challenged Kirkwood's men, fired their weapons when they received no answer, and ran into the guardhouse. The raiders captured one sentry who guided them to the guard post where the raiders "fired very briskly at them." Tarleton formed his men and moved his camp closer to the main army 2 miles away.

Along the way, Tarleton's dragoons encountered a large group of Loyalists heading to the main army camp to join General Charles Cornwallis (1738–1805). Mistaking them for Rebels, the dragoons began to cut them down. The Loyalists fought back. Sergeant Major Seymour wrote, "There commenced a smart skirmish in which great numbers of the Tories were sent to the lower regions." After this incident and Pyle's massacre on Sunday, February 25, 1781, few Loyalists came to fight. Kirkwood's men "marched all night through deep swamps, morasses, and thickets, which rendered our marching unpleasant and tiresome, twenty-six miles." They arrived at their camp at daybreak.[116]

★ Captain Jacob Duckworth (1755–1842) surprised Colonel David Fanning (1755–1825) in his camp at the Alamance and attacked on Thursday, March 15, 1781. Both sides lost one man killed before Fanning fled with his recruits, leaving their horses and weapons. Later, Fanning took three men and pursued Duckworth. They managed to re-take 14 horses.[117]

Fletcher's Mill (March 2, 1781)

> The site of Fletcher's Mill is not known. It may have been on Big Alamance Creek, about 3 miles east of Alamance.

When he learned that Major General Nathanael Greene's (1742–1786) light infantrymen were near his post on Deep River, General Charles Cornwallis (1738–1805) sent Lieutenant Colonel Banastre Tarleton (1744–1833) to determine their location. Tarleton soon encountered Lieutenant Colonel Henry "Light-Horse Harry" Lee's (1756–1818) Legion supported by Colonel William Preston's (1729–1783) Virginia riflemen at Fletcher's Mill on Friday, March 2, 1781. Tarleton attacked. The Continentals withdrew, but Tarleton did not pursue them, as he did not know if they were a minor patrol or the vanguard of all of General Greene's army.[118]

Wetsell's (Wetzell's, Weitzell's, Whitsell's or Whitsall's) Mill (March 6, 1781)
Near Wetsell's Mill (March 5, 1781)
Reedy Fork Creek (March 7, 1781)

> Wetsell's Mill was located on Reedy Fork Creek in present-day Gibsonville, east of Guilford Courthouse. It was near Deermont Road, about 200 yards above the point where route NC 61 crosses Reedy Fork Creek northeast of Greensboro about 1.3 miles north of route NC 2770. A state historical marker is located 6 miles west on the left side of route U.S. 29, 0.5 miles south of route NC 2565 (Hicone–Skylark Road). The mill was located 10 miles north of Clapp's Mill (see Burlington). All that remains of the mill are a few scattered stones.
> Reedy Fork is about 9.5 miles northeast of Guilford.

General Charles Cornwallis (1738–1805) camped between the Haw and Deep rivers at the junction of the roads from Salisbury, Guilford and Hillsborough. Consequently, he controlled the direct road to Wilmington where his clothing and supplies were stored. Late Monday night, March 5, 1781, Colonel Otho Holland Williams (1749–1794) sent a small party to capture a small party of Redcoats at a mill about a mile from his camp. When they arrived there, they learned that Cornwallis had already left at 5:30 AM in thick fog.

Colonel Williams posted several observation parties behind his column after the skirmish at Wetsell's Mill. Sergeant Major John Perry and Quartermaster Sergeant William Lunsford, of the 3rd Continental Dragoons, led two of these parties, each with four dragoons. When they spotted 16 to 18 British recruits ride to a farmhouse and a few dismounted, the two sergeants joined forces and charged, killing every recruit in plain view of the British Legion on the other side of the farmhouse fence. They then rode away without a scratch.[119]

By the time Colonel Williams received the news that General Cornwallis was on the march, 1,000 of Cornwallis's light infantrymen under Lieutenant Colonel James Webster (ca. 1743–1781) and Lieutenant Colonel Banastre Tarleton's (1744–1833) British Legion were within 2 miles of his left flank. Williams sent Lieutenant Colonel Henry

"Light-Horse Harry" Lee (1756–1818) and Lieutenant Colonel William Washington (1752–1810) to support Colonel William Campbell's (1745–1781) Virginia militia. The remaining troops retreated toward the ford across Reedy Fork at Wetzell's Mills. Tarleton's cavalry and Colonel Webster's light infantry proceeded to the ford at the mills as fast as they could along parallel roads. Williams arrived first, just as Tarleton and Webster appeared on rising ground in his rear. Williams ordered Colonel William Preston (1729–1783) to establish a covering party of riflemen from his Virginia militia to protect the crossing.

Lee, Washington, and Campbell delayed the Crown forces and crossed shortly after Williams, with the British van in hot pursuit. As several nearby fords above and below Reedy Fork exposed him to a flank attack, Williams ordered Lee, Washington, and Campbell to hold the pass as long as possible, without hazarding serious injury. He then withdrew the rest of his men.

Lee posted a company of Preston's Virginians at the ford by the mill. The rest of the infantry formed a line along the stream. The cavalry was placed in the rear. Lee concealed Campbell's riflemen and the rest of Preston's riflemen in the woods on the right with 25 expert marksmen in a little log schoolhouse on the right. These veterans of Kings Mountain, South Carolina had orders to concentrate their fire on the officers.

When Cornwallis arrived at the stream, he ordered Webster's men to form a line and attack while the rest of his army remained in column. Webster's brigade consisted of the Royal Welch Fusiliers, the 33rd Regiment, and Fraser's Highlanders, with a light company of the Coldstream Guards and the Hessian jaegers. Webster sent a detachment to the ford with the Coldstream Guards in the lead. He ordered the Guards to cross and attack, but a heavy and well directed fire began as they entered the water. They fell back in disorder. Webster rode up, plunged into the stream and led his men to the opposite shore, which lay under a high bank. Every one of the marksmen in the schoolhouse aimed at Webster as he crossed. They fired and missed. The men "discharged their rifles at him, one by one, each man sure of knocking him over . . . eight or nine of them emptied their guns a second time. Strange to tell . . . himself and horse were untouched."

At this point, Lee withdrew his flanks and reformed them behind the cavalry in the rear. The center of the line kept firing on Webster's men as they advanced from the water's edge. Lee could not stop them and retreated under heavy fire. Webster continued a rear-guard action for about 5 miles. When Webster ceased the pursuit, Williams made camp and Cornwallis returned to his former camp on the Alamance River. Greene withdrew from Reedy Fork and camped at the ironworks on Troublesome Creek. Each side lost about 20 men. Tarleton records:

> On the 5th information was conveyed to head quarters of the principal part of General Greene's army being situated near Guildford court house, and that the light troops and militia extended down Reedy fork towards the Haw river, to protect the country, and guard the communications with Virginia, and the upper parts of North Carolina. Several reports confirming the validity of this intelligence, Earl Cornwallis determined to move the next day to disturb the enemy's communications, and derange their projects. Early in the morning he passed the Allamance: The light troops led the column, supported by Colonel Webster's brigade: The regiment of Bose was followed by the brigade of guards; and Hamilton's corps, with the wagons, brought up the rear. The British dragoons soon pushed Colonel Lee's cavalry from their advanced situation: They retired to Wetzell's mill on the Reedy fork: Lieutenant-colonel Tarleton discovered the enemy to be in force at that place, and reported the circumstance to Earl Cornwallis, who directed Colonel Webster to form his brigade

into line with the light company of the guards and the yagers. This disposition being made, the front line advanced, the rest of the King's troops remaining in column. The enemy did not oppose the right wing of the British so steadily as the left: The 23d and 71st moved forwards to the creek without any great impediment; and the ardent bravery of the 33d and the light company of the guards soon dislodged them from their strong position. The infantry mounted the hill above the creek, and dispersed the Americans so effectually, that the cavalry could only collect a few stragglers from the woods in front. The militia who guarded this pass had upwards of one hundred men killed, wounded, and taken. The killed and wounded of the British amounted to about thirty.[120]

★ Sergeant Major William Seymour, of the Delaware Regiment, gives the only account of the action at Reedy Fork on Wednesday, March 7, 1781. General Charles Cornwallis (1738–1805) came within a mile of Colonel Otho Holland Williams's (1749–1794) troops before being discovered on Wednesday, March 7, 1781. The Continentals "crossed Reedy Fork and drew up in order of battle, leaving some riflemen on the other side, when the enemy advanced and attacked the militia who retreated off with great precipitation, but, the British not advancing over the river, our troops marched and crossed the Haw River."[121]

Greensboro
New Garden Meetinghouse (March 15, 1781)
Guilford Courthouse (March 15, 1781)

The village of New Garden has been completely changed by urban development. Guilford College now occupies the site of the New Garden Meetinghouse. The original Quaker meetinghouse has been replaced by a newer one. The neighboring cemetery contains the graves of several soldiers. However, as the community is still an active Quaker congregation, they discourage visitors.

The engagement here was the first phase of the Battle of Guilford Courthouse. The site of the first engagement of Lee's and Tarleton's dragoons was probably near the entrance to the Jefferson Standard Country Club. The Cross Roads was an intersection of three roads (Salisbury road, Ballinger Road, and the road to Oak Ridge) leading to New Garden Meetinghouse 0.7 miles away.

Guilford Courthouse National Military Park (website: **www.nps.gov/guco/index.htm**) covers 220 acres in northwest Greensboro, off route U.S. 220 (Battleground Avenue) 6 miles north of the city. The park includes wayside exhibits throughout the battlefield and a visitor center with displays, films, and brochures. A 2.5-mile auto tour leads to many of the monuments, including the graves of John Penn (1740–1788) and William Hooper (1742–1790), signers of the Declaration of Independence.

The Cavalry Monument honors all American cavalry, including Virginian Peter Francisco, known as "The Goliath of the Revolution." At the Battle of Guilford Courthouse, Francisco—who weighed 260 pounds and stood six feet six inches tall—supposedly used a five-foot sword to kill 11 men. It was given to "the strongest man in Virginia" by George Washington.

The Stuart Monument (see Photo NC-9) honors Colonel James Stuart of the Queen's Guard. It marks the spot where Stuart fell in hand-to-hand combat and where his sword was found in 1866.

NC-9. Stuart monument. The monument honors Colonel James Stuart of the Queen's Guard. It marks the spot where Stuart fell in hand-to-hand combat and where his sword was found in 1866.

> The Turner monument (see Photo NC-10) honors Kerenhappuck Norman Turner (1716–1781). When she learned that her son was badly wounded in the battle at Guilford Courthouse, she rode 300 miles on horseback to nurse him and the other soldiers. Her son had a fever, so she made holes in a tub, suspended it from the rafters, and filled it with water. The cool water dripping slowly on her son's wounds and body acted like a modern ice pack and lessened the fever.

NC-10. Turner monument. The monument honors Kerenhappuck Norman Turner who nursed her badly wounded son and the other soldiers after the battle at Guilford Courthouse.

> Tannenbaum Park is 0.25 miles west on route U.S. 220 at 103 Green Acres Lane. The park contains picnic areas, two log cabins, and a former British military hospital built in 1778. The Hoskins/Wyrick House (see Photo NC-11) served as British headquarters during the battle of Guilford Courthouse. It also served as a field hospital for both sides.

The war reached a stalemate in the North in 1778. The British shifted their attention to the South, conquering South Carolina and Georgia by 1780.

NC-11. Hoskins/Wyrick House. The house served as British headquarters during the battle of Guilford Courthouse and as a field hospital for both sides afterward.

General Nathanael Greene (1742–1786) was appointed to replace Major General Horatio Gates (1728–1806) after the defeat at Camden, South Carolina on Wednesday, August 16, 1780. When Greene arrived at Charlotte, North Carolina, on Saturday, December 2, 1780, he found a command that consisted of 1,500 men fit for duty, only 949 of them Continentals. The army lacked clothing and provisions and had little systematic means of procuring them. Greene decided that he must not engage General Charles Cornwallis's (1738–1805) army in battle until he had built up his strength and that he must instead pursue delaying tactics to wear down his stronger opponent.

The first thing he did was to take the unorthodox step of dividing his army in the face of a superior force, moving part under his personal command to Cheraw Hill and sending the rest under Brigadier General Daniel Morgan (1736–1802) west across the Catawba River over 100 miles away. Greene wrote:

> I am well satisfied with the movement. . . . It makes the most of my inferior force, for it compels my adversary to divide his, and holds him in doubt as to his own line of conduct. He cannot leave Morgan behind him to come at me, or his posts at Ninety Six and Augusta would be exposed. And he cannot chase Morgan far, or prosecute his views upon Virginia while I am here with the whole country open before me. I am as near to Charleston as he and as near Hillsborough as I was at Charlotte; so that I am in no danger of being cut off from my reinforcements.

Divided forces could live off the land much easier than one large force and constitute two rallying points for local militia instead of one. Greene was, in effect, sacrificing mass to enhance maneuver.

General Cornwallis, an aggressive commander, had determined to gamble everything on a renewed invasion of North Carolina. Ignoring General Henry Clinton's (1730–1795) warnings, he depleted his base in Charleston, South Carolina by bringing almost all his supplies forward. In the face of Greene's dispositions, Cornwallis divided his army into not two but three parts. He sent a holding force to Camden, South Carolina to contain Greene, directed Lieutenant Colonel Banastre Tarleton (1744–1833) to find and crush Morgan with a fast-moving contingent of 1,100 infantrymen and cavalrymen, and, with the remainder of his army moved cautiously up into North Carolina to cut off any of Morgan's force that escaped Tarleton.

General Greene's strategy was to defend North Carolina and harass General Cornwallis as he moved northward. General Cornwallis still had two armies left which were larger than Greene's and Brigadier General Daniel Morgan's, and he was uniting them and placing them between the Continental forces.

Lieutenant Colonel Tarleton moved with his Legion to find and crush Morgan, but, as it turned out, it was Morgan who defeated Tarleton at Cowpens, South Carolina on January 17, 1781. When Cornwallis learned of the defeat at Cowpens, he himself set out after Morgan, determined to crush the Continentals and release their 525 prisoners. Morgan had to move fast to escape Cornwallis. Although he was encumbered with both his own wounded and those of the Crown forces plus all his prisoners, Morgan covered 100 miles and crossed two rivers in five days. He stayed a day's march ahead of Cornwallis and eventually rejoined Greene at Guilford Courthouse on Thursday, February 8, 1781. Greene continued to retreat northward through North Carolina up to the Dan River, just over the Virginia border, then back into North Carolina again, keeping just far enough in front of his adversary to avoid battle with Cornwallis's superior force.

Cornwallis was too heavily committed to the campaign in North Carolina by now to withdraw. Hoping to match the swift movement of the Continentals, he destroyed all his superfluous supplies, baggage, and wagons but lost time in doing so. He set forth in pursuit of Greene's army but could get nothing from the countryside. He lacked food and boats to follow the Continentals across the river, so he returned to Hillsborough, hoping to enlist Loyalists in the area. He found only a few. One group that responded to his call mistook a party of Continental cavalry for Tarleton's British Legion [see **Pyle's defeat** (pp. 216–217)]. They were soon surrounded and slaughtered. This discouraged other Loyalists from joining Cornwallis.

Finally on March 15, 1781, at Guilford Courthouse, on ground he himself had chosen (Greene surveyed it weeks before during the retreat), Greene halted and gave battle. By this time he had collected 1,500 Continentals and 3,000 militiamen to the 1,900 tired, ill-clothed, and hungry Regulars the British could muster.

★ The Battle of Guilford Courthouse, the largest battle in North Carolina, began in a community of pacifists. Twenty-five-year-old Lieutenant Colonel Henry "Light-Horse Harry" Lee (1756–1818) and his 617 dragoons met 26-year-old Lieutenant Colonel Banastre Tarleton (1744–1833) and his 842 legionnaires early Thursday morning, March 15, 1781. The engagement included three separate encounters that lasted most of the morning in contrast to the Battle of Guilford Courthouse, which began about 1 PM and lasted only two hours.

Major General Greene deployed his army on carefully selected ground west of Guilford Courthouse along both sides of New Garden Road. General Cornwallis began his 12-mile march from the Deep River Friends Meetinghouse to Guilford Courthouse at 5:30 AM. General Greene ordered Lieutenant Colonel Lee and his Legion to move onto New Garden Road to delay the Crown forces headed by Lieutenant Colonel Tarleton and a strong advance guard.

The Crown forces had marched 7 miles when the pickets noticed Lieutenant Charles Heard's (1734–1792) troop at a sharp bend on the Salisbury road, at the New Garden Meetinghouse. Both sides fired a volley and Heard retreated. Tarleton's dragoons followed him into an ambush. Lee had placed his men behind high rail fences on both sides of New Garden Road. This limited Tarleton's movements to striking only a few Continentals in the front ranks. Tarleton's Legion attacked twice with little effect. Lieutenant Colonel Lee ordered a counter-charge that unhorsed some of the dragoons who were killed or captured. Tarleton ordered a retreat, leaving behind several of his dragoons. Not a single Continental soldier or horse was injured.

Colonel Tarleton traveled down a road branching southeast from New Garden Road, probably across what is now the campus of Guilford College. He proceeded approximately half a mile to the road from Buffalo Creek and turned right toward the New Garden Meetinghouse and the Salisbury Road along which the main Crown army was advancing. Lee rode hard to occupy the crossroads at the New Garden Meetinghouse to cut off Tarleton from the main army. However, he ran into the Guards' light infantry which fired a volley at close range. Lee wrote in his memoirs, "The sun had just risen above the trees, and shining bright [about 7:15], the refulgence from the British muskets, as the soldiers presented, frightened Lee's horse, so as to compel him to throw himself off." Lee's horse kept running until it came to a farm. The farmer retrieved the horse and sold it to Tarleton the next day.

Lee ordered a retreat when Tarleton's Legion arrived at the fight. He countermanded the order when his own Legion infantry deployed and began firing, followed by the riflemen who used the meetinghouse for cover, firing from behind, through windows or through holes made in the chinking between the logs. Both sides were pretty evenly matched and maintained a sharp action for about 30 to 40 minutes, with many charges and counter-charges. As more Crown troops arrived and began to outnumber the Continentals, Lee ordered a retreat, leaving the dead and wounded behind. The Hessians attacked him continuously during the retreat.

Lee's cavalry covered the retreat to the Cross Roads, 3 miles away, where General Greene took advantage of the delaying action to deploy his army in the woods there. The 16-year-old son of the Hunt family, living in a large log house near the southeast of a spring, hid in some bushes, near a small field in front of the woods where the Continentals had taken their position, to observe the action.

When the British light horse came into the field, the captain intended a flank movement. The bugle sounded a charge when the Hunt boy fired his musket. Captain Goodrick (d. 1781) of the Guards fell dead. The dragoons thought the fence was lined with sharpshooters. They turned and fled. The Delaware Continentals (see Photo DE-1) reinforced Lee who continued to fight until 11 AM before withdrawing to join the main army at Guilford Courthouse. Colonel Tarleton noted that "between twenty and thirty of the guards, dragoons, and yagers were killed and wounded" in the encounter at the Cross Roads. The two engagements at New Garden Meetinghouse and the Cross Roads lasted four hours. The Crown forces still had to fight the main Continental Army waiting for them at Guilford Courthouse.[122]

Both sides suffered numerous casualties in the 40-minute skirmish. Lieutenant Colonel Banastre Tarleton was one of them. A musket ball ripped away the first and middle fingers of his right hand, leaving him incapable of using a weapon at the Battle of Guilford Courthouse.

The Battle of New Garden was a strategic victory for the Congressional forces. Lee delayed General Cornwallis's advance toward Guilford Courthouse for four hours, giving General Greene enough time to make the final preparations for the battle.

★ Major General Nathanael Greene (1742–1786) hid his troops in the woods on either side of the road and kept a reserve immediately in front of the Guilford courthouse. He used Brigadier General Daniel Morgan's (1736–1802) tactic and placed the inexperienced North Carolina militia in the front line behind a rail fence with the woods at their back. Here, they could fire at the Crown forces crossing the open fields. He then placed the Virginia militia a quarter mile further east in heavy woods which would break up the tight enemy formations at the same time they protected the militia. Greene then placed his 1,400 Continentals about 500 yards away on a slight rise and behind another cleared field.

Cornwallis placed his men on either side of the road, just as Greene had done. He left three guns in the road and held a corps of German jaegers, the light infantry and the cavalry of the British Legion, all under the command of Lieutenant Colonel Banastre Tarleton (1744–1833), in reserve.

The Crown forces, tired from a 12-mile march that morning to reach the battlefield, began the attack at about 1 PM after a brief artillery duel. They met heavy and continuous fire, but they came on steadily. The North Carolina militia fired two rounds and retreated into the woods. The sharpshooters on either side of them also withdrew from tree to tree, while the cavalry under Lieutenant Colonel William Washington (1752–1810) and Lieutenant Colonel Henry "Light-Horse Harry" Lee (1756–1818) moved slowly back with them. Lee's Legion and supporting troops on the Continental left, or south flank, were forced up a hill so far from the army that they were engaged in a separate battle until the main action was almost over.

The north flank, on the right, fell back to the second line, 350 yards to the rear in the woods, and formed on their right flank. When the North Carolina militia broke and fled, "throwing away arms, knapsacks, and even canteens [as] they rushed like a torrent headlong through the woods," the Crown forces encountered the Virginia militia in the second line. The Virginians allowed the British light infantry, with the 23rd Foot and the jaegers under Colonel James Webster (ca. 1743–1781), to get within a few yards and then charged with the bayonet, driving the Crown forces back in confusion. The Redcoats rallied and eventually forced the second line to give way and seek cover behind the Continental troops or in the woods.

The Crown forces came out of the woods, after fighting two battles, to find another open field with 1,400 Continental regulars on the other side. The third line included Greene's best infantry: Brigadier General Isaac Huger's (1743–1797) two regiments of Virginia militia on the right and Colonel Otho Holland Williams's (1749–1794) two Maryland regiments on the left. This line was drawn up on the hill in front of and northwest of Guilford Courthouse about 350 yards behind the second line. They saw the Crown forces break through the right half of the second line, but they held their fire until the enemy came within 100 feet (about 100 yards past the Visitor's Center building).

The 1st Maryland fired a volley and charged the Crown forces with bayonets across a ravine and up an adjacent slope where they eventually rallied. Colonel Washington saw this and drove his dragoons forward into the midst of the enemy and scattered them. Peter Francisco (ca. 1760–1831), a six-foot six-inch giant, swinging a five-foot sword given to him by George Washington, killed 11 men before falling wounded.

General Cornwallis sent his three guns to the edge of the woods where they soon opened fire. Brigadier General Charles O'Hara's (1740–1802) grenadiers (see Photo PA-9) and battalion of Guards charged. The 2nd Maryland Regiment broke under the pressure. Colonel Washington's cavalry struck the Guards in the rear while the 1st Maryland Regiment turned to attack their flank in savage fighting.

Cornwallis's three field guns, firing grape shot (see Photo PA-14), halted the massacre but killed as many British guardsmen as Continental dragoons. General Greene ordered a retreat, and the Continentals left the field, abandoning their guns and marching northward.

Greene might have been able to destroy Cornwallis's army before these troops rallied; but, if a counterattack failed, he might lose the army, the last organized force in the south. So he relented. The Americans lost 79 killed and 185 wounded. Cornwallis lost over 500 killed and wounded—between a third and a quarter of the force engaged. His army, already outnumbered by more than two to one before the battle, could hardly afford such heavy losses. The Guards alone had 11 of its 19 officers fall as casualties and more than 200 of the 462 men. The survivors, who had eaten nothing since their four ounces of flour and four ounces of dry beef the previous afternoon, lay down in the steady rain without food or shelter.

The British held the field after a hard-fought battle; but, like Bunker Hill, it was a Pyrrhic victory. When Colonial Secretary Sir George Germain (1716–1785) announced the victory to Parliament, Charles James Fox (1749–1806) remarked: "Another such victory would ruin the British army." His ranks depleted and his supplies exhausted, Cornwallis withdrew to Wilmington on the coast, and then decided to move northward to join the British forces General Henry Clinton (1730–1795) had sent to Virginia.

After the Battle of Guilford Courthouse, General Greene recorded his observations in a letter:

> The battle was fought at or near Guilford Court-House, the very place from whence we began our retreat after the Light Infantry joined the army from the Pedee. The battle was long, obstinate and bloody. We were obliged to give up the ground and lost our artillery, but the enemy have been so soundly beaten that they dare not move towards us since the action, notwithstanding we lay within ten miles of him for two days. Except the ground and the artillery, they have gained no advantage. On the contrary, they are little short of being ruined. The enemy's loss in killed and wounded cannot be less than between six and seven hundred, perhaps more.
>
> Victory was long doubtful, and had the North Carolina militia done their duty, it was certain. They had the most advantageous position I ever saw, and left it without making scarcely the shadow of opposition. Their general and field officers exerted themselves, but the men would not stand. Many threw away their arms and fled with the utmost precipitation, even before a gun was fired at them. The Virginia militia behaved nobly and annoyed the enemy greatly. The horse, at different times in the course of the day, performed wonders. Indeed, the horse is our great safeguard, and without them the militia could not keep the field in this country . . . Never did an army labour under so many disadvantages as this; but the fortitude and patience of the officers and soldiery rise superior to all difficulties. We have little to eat, less to drink, and lodge in the woods in the midst of smoke. Indeed, our fatigue is excessive. I was so much overcome night before last that I fainted.
>
> Our army is in good spirits, but the militia are leaving us in great numbers to return home to kiss their wives and sweethearts.
>
> I have never felt an easy moment since the enemy crossed the Catawba until since the defeat of the 15th, but now I am perfectly easy, being persuaded it is out of the enemy's power to do us any great injury. Indeed, I think they will retire as soon as they can get off their wounded.

After the Battle of Guilford Courthouse, Cornwallis spent two miserable, rain-soaked days on the field tending to the wounded of both sides and burying his dead. He realized he could not afford to risk another battle in an unfriendly country with his small force. He was so short of supplies and had so little transportation that he had to leave several of his wounded in Greene's care when he left the field. He found few committed Loyalists and many determined rebels in the south. Many rivers obstructed the army, and he found it virtually impossible to find adequate provisions and forage in that inhospitable land. So, he decided to abandon the Carolinas and go to Virginia.

Cornwallis left Lord Francis Rawdon (1754–1826) in command in the Carolinas and headed to Wilmington, North Carolina where his army could get supplies by sea. Greene pursued for a short distance until April 8, then turned south into South Carolina. Without consulting General Clinton, Cornwallis left Wilmington for Virginia on Wednesday morning, April 25 with no more than 1,435 men fit for duty. Although defeated in battle, Greene won his objective and Cornwallis moved to Virginia, where he finally surrendered his army at Yorktown on October 19, 1781.

Greene, a Quaker himself, asked the Quakers at New Garden to minister to 250 of his most severely wounded soldiers which he could not take with him:

> *To the Members of the New Garden Monthly Meeting near Guilford Court House:*
>
> *Friends and Countrymen*: I address myself to your humanity for the relief of the suffering wounded at Guilford Court House. As a people I am persuaded you disclaim any connection with measures calculated to promote military operations; but I know of no order of men more remarkable for the exercise of humanity and benevolence; and perhaps no instance ever had a higher claim upon your neighborhood.
>
> I was born and educated in the professions and principles of your Society; and am perfectly acquainted with your religious sentiments and general good conduct as citizens. I am also sensible from the prejudices of many belonging to other religious societies, and the misconduct of a few of your own, that you are generally considered as enemies to the independence of America. I entertain other sentiments, both of your principles and wishes. I respect you as a people, and shall always be ready to protect you from every violence and oppression which the confusion of the times afford but too many instances of. Do not be deceived. This is no religious dispute. The contest is for political liberty, without which cannot be enjoyed the free exercise of your religion.
>
> The British are flattering you with conquest and exciting your apprehensions respecting religious liberty. They deceive you in both. They can neither conquer this country, nor will you be molested in the exercise of your sentiments. It is true, they may spread desolation and distress over many parts of the country, but when the inhabitants exert their force, the enemy must flee before them. There is but one way to put a speedy end to the extremities of war, which is, for the people to be united. It is the interest of your enemy to create divisions among you, and while they prevail your distress will continue. Look at the horrid misorders which are among the Whigs and Tories. Have the enemy any friends to suffer or feel for? They have not, neither do they care how great your calamities if it but contributes to the gratification of their pride and ambition. You would neither have liberty nor property could the enemy succeed in their measures. How have they deceived you in their proclamations? and how have they violated their faith with your friends in South Carolina? They are now fleeing before us, and must soon be expelled from our border if the people will continue to aid the operations of the army.
>
> Having given you this information, I have only to remark that I shall be exceedingly obliged to you to contribute all in your power to relieve the unfortunates at Guilford, and Dr. Wallace is directed to point out the things most wanted, and to

receive and apply donations, and from the liberality of your order upon the occasion I shall be able to judge of your feelings as men . . . and principles as a Society.

Given at Headquarters, North Carolina, March 26, 1781, and the fifth year of American Independence.

Nathanael Greene,

Major General Continental Army.

The response was as follows:

To Major General Nathaniel Greene:

Friend Greene: We received thine, being dated March 26, 1781. Agreeable to thy request we shall do all that lies in our power, although this may inform that from our present situation we are ill able to assist as much as we would be glad to do, as the Americans have lain much upon us, and of late the British have plundered and entirely broken up many among us, which renders it hard, and there is at our meetinghouse in New Garden upward of one hundred now living, that have no means of provision, except what hospitality the neighborhood affords them, which we look upon as a hardship upon us, if not an imposition; but notwithstanding all this, we are determined, by the assistance of Providence, while we have anything among us, that the distressed both at the Court House and here shall have part of it with us. As we have as yet made no distinction as to party and their cause—and as we have none to commit our cause to but God alone, but hold it the duty of true Christians, at all times to assist the distressed.

Guilford Court House, N. C. Third mo. 30, 1781.[123]

Moncure
Ramsey's Mill (March 19, 1781)

> The engagement at Ramsey's Mill occurred near where route U.S. 1 crosses Deep River west of present day Moncure.

General Charles Cornwallis (1738–1805) stopped at Ramsey's Mill on Deep River to procure provisions and rest as one third of his army was ill and wounded from the battle at Guilford Courthouse on Thursday, March 15, 1781. He ordered his men to build a bridge across the river but Thomas Riddle (1739–1809) and his riflemen occupied a house across the river and fired at the work parties, inflicting numerous casualties.

Lieutenant Colonel Henry "Light-Horse Harry" Lee (1756–1818) was ordered to cross the Deep River 10 miles upstream, make a night march, and attack Cornwallis from the rear at Ramsey's Mill on Monday, March 19, 1781. Lee cancelled the attack, thinking that he could not execute it successfully. When Cornwallis learned of Lee's plan, he had his men destroy the bridge and broke camp so quickly that he left, unburied, several men who had died of their wounds. The Continentals remained at Ramsey's Mill for several days to replenish their supplies.[124]

Stewards (Stewart's, Stuart's) Creek, southeastern North Carolina (March 25, 1781; July 26 1781)

> Stewards (Stewart's, Stuart's) Creek, also known as Stuart's Ford, is located at Fort Bragg, northeast of Fayetteville.

Captain John Taylor (1747–1826) and his mounted Granville County Militia encountered eight British dragoons near Stewards Ford on Sunday, March 25, 1781. They killed one of the dragoons and captured three others. When the British began to cross the 700 yard wide ford on Stewards River, Taylor's men began firing at them from the far side. Brigadier General Charles O'Hara (1740–1802), unable to walk from a wound he received at Guilford Courthouse 10 days earlier, had a grenadier (see Photo PA-9) of the 23rd Regiment carry him across. Armed with a "double barrelled fusee" he fired several shots at the militiamen while being carried across, hitting three men probably with a load of buck and ball. The rest of the militiamen fled before they were surrounded.[125]

★ Colonel Peter Robison and 300 Bladen County militiamen stopped at Stewards Creek on the Big Rock Fish to make breakfast on Thursday, July 26, 1781. They butchered some of Steward's cattle and were preparing to execute two Loyalist prisoners when Colonel Hector McNeil (1756–1830) discovered them and approached with his band of Loyalists as the firing squad was taking aim. One of the men in the firing squad pulled his trigger but his weapon flashed in the pan. The others fled as the Loyalists charged. McNeil lost three men killed in a brief fight.[126]

★ Colonel Archibald Murphy (1742–1817) and some Pee Dee, Cumberland and Bladen County militiamen skirmished with Colonel Hector McNeil (1756–1830) near Stewards Creek on Thursday afternoon, July 26, 1781. McNeil retreated and continued firing until night. Both sides suffered considerable losses. McNeil retreated to Wilmington where he was re-supplied with arms and ammunition. He was reinforced with 60 Loyalists and headed to Cross Creek (Fayetteville) the next day.[127]

Sanford
Barbeque Church (April 29, 1781)

> The modern Barbeque Presbyterian Church located at 124 Barbeque Church Road in Sanford, Harnett County, replaces the Barbeque Church named after Barbeque Creek. A historical marker at the corner of routes NC 27 and NC 1209 (Barbeque Church Road) gives a brief history of the church but does not mention the skirmish. The recorded date of this event is April 29; but it may have occurred a few weeks earlier, possibly on March 29th, as General Cornwallis's army was closer to Wilmington at this time.

Major General Nathanael Greene (1742–1786) ordered Brigadier General Alexander Lillington's (ca. 1725–1786) militia to remove the British stores at Cross Creek (Fayetteville) and annoy General Charles Cornwallis's (1738–1805) troops as much as possible. They harassed him constantly on his march to Wilmington as he withdrew from Guilford Courthouse.

The Crown forces set up camp at the home of William Buie. The next day, Lieutenant Colonel Banastre Tarleton (1744–1833) and his legionnaires found Captain Daniel Buie (d. 1823) and his Cumberland County militiamen waiting for them at the Barbeque Church. They engaged in a brief but bloody skirmish in which Duncan Buie's head was split open by a sword. He was left for dead but recovered and lived for many more years. Most of the militiamen were captured and confined in a bull pen. A few managed to escape during the night, but the rest were taken to Wilmington. Some were later exchanged, but Daniel Buie died aboard a prison ship anchored at Wilmington.[128]

Stantonsburg
Peacock's Bridge (May 6, 1781)

Peacock's Bridge was on Contentnea Creek about 1.5 miles south of Stantonsburg where route NC 58 crosses Contentnea Creek 100 yards south of Peacock Bridge Road.

General Charles Cornwallis (1738–1805) reached Peacock's Bridge on the Contentnea Creek near Stantonsburg, on Sunday, May 6, 1781. Colonel James Gorham (1745–1804) held the bridge with 400 militiamen from Pitt County until Lieutenant Colonel Banastre Tarleton (1744–1833) and his Legion drove them off by a cavalry charge. This was the only opposition Cornwallis encountered here. Cornwallis then sent Tarleton across the Tar River to scout for any Whigs who might cause trouble and to disperse them. Tarleton found some small detachments at Swift Creek and Fishing Creek and dispersed them easily.[129]

Swift Creek and Fishing Creek (May 7, 1781)

Swift Creek is about 50 miles northeast of Raleigh near exit 145 of route I-95. Fishing Creek is about 6 miles farther north. Route I-95 crosses Fishing Creek near mile marker 151. The event here may have occurred about a mile west of route I-95, near Culpeppers Bridge on route NC 4 (NC 48).

Another militia unit tried to stop General Charles Cornwallis (1738–1805) at Swift Creek on Monday, May 7, 1781, the day after the skirmish at Peacock's Bridge. Lieutenant Colonel Banastre Tarleton (1744–1833) and his dragoons dispersed them. The same militia attempted to stop Cornwallis's army again at Fishing Creek 6 miles from Swift Creek later the same day. Tarleton scattered them again.[130]

Clinton
Cohera Swamp (May 11, 1781)

The site of the Cohera Swamp is in present-day Clinton. The community around Captain Richard Clinton's (d. 1794) plantation was known as Clinton's Crossroads in 1775. The skirmish occurred near the 12th green of the Coharie Country Club.

Some Loyalists camped in the Cohera Swamp in early May 1781 and declared their allegiance to King George III (1738–1820) there. However, they had not chosen a leader and had no organization. They had captured some young Whigs and forced them to take paroles.

When Colonel James Kenan (1740–1810) of the Duplin County Militia learned of the Loyalist camp, he mustered 12 to 15 men and went to search the swamp for them, planning to disperse them before they became too powerful. His scouts were surprised by a hidden picket guard. Both sides fired. Owen Kenan (1743–1781), Colonel Kenan's brother was shot and killed. Both sides retreated, unsure of the other's strength.

The Loyalists claimed the victory because they did not have any casualties. When other Loyalists heard that they defeated Colonel Kenan's force, 120 of them joined the

Loyalist camp. The Loyalists chose Middleton Mobley (b. ca. 1740) and his brother, Biggars, as their leaders. Biggars Mobley brought in 50 men and the Loyalists moved their camp to the west side of the swamp near the bridge on Cross Creek road (now Highway 24).

Colonel Kenan continued to observe the Loyalists while he waited for reinforcements. When Captain James C. Williams's light horsemen arrived, they were short of horses. One section of about 30 men was mounted; the second section doubled up with the first section on the few horses they had. The third section was on foot. Colonel Kenan then moved his camp to Captain Richard Clinton's (d. 1794) Plantation, about 3 miles from the Loyalist camp.

Middleton Mobley learned that Kenan was nearby and retreated toward the Black River Friday night, May 11, 1781. The Whigs followed the Loyalists for several days, not wanting to lose track of them as Colonel Kenan wanted revenge for the death of his brother.[131]

Wallace
Legat's Bridge (May 13, 1781)
Rockfish Creek (Aug. 2, 1781)

> Legat's Bridge is also known as Rockfish. It was located on Rockfish Creek where route U.S. 117 (NC 11) crosses the creek just south of the where the two routes meet about 1.5 miles south of present-day Wallace. A state historical marker and a chipped marble monument are the only reminders of the spirited battle that occurred on the banks of this tributary of the Northeast Cape Fear River on August 2, 1781.

Colonel David Fanning (1755–1825) learned on Saturday evening, May 12, 1781, that Captain Fletcher (d. 1781) was gathering a party of Whigs at Legat's Bridge about 30 miles away and prepared to attack them. Thinking it best to surprise them where they were gathering, he and 17 men marched all night. They attacked Captain Fletcher's camp at 10 AM on Sunday morning. The 25 Cumberland County militiamen returned fire for about 10 minutes. They then retreated, taking three wounded men with them and leaving four dead, a prisoner and 18 horses behind. Fanning only had one man wounded mortally.

Two of his prisoners (who were then paroled) informed Colonel Fanning that Lieutenant Colonel Guilford Dudley (1756–1833) was coming from Major General Nathanael Greene's (1742–1786) camp at Camden. He and his men were returning home with their baggage wagons and an escort of light cavalry. Fanning and his men rode off to search for them. They hid by the side of the road in ambush; but, when Colonel Dudley did not come by at the expected time, Colonel Fanning grew impatient and took one of his men to go search for Colonel Dudley.

They found Colonel Dudley and his baggage 1.5 miles away. When they got about 100 yards from him, the Loyalists turned around and returned to the ambuscade with Dudley and his dragoons close behind them, trying to fire their pistols several times. The Loyalists fired from their hiding places and killed five of Dudley's dragoons. The rest fled with Fanning and his men in pursuit. They caught up with them 2.5 miles down the road and captured three prisoners, nine horses and all the baggage, valued at £1,000. The baggage was divided among the men before returning to Cox's Mill.[132]

★ Strong bands of Loyalists continued to menace the Whigs of North Carolina in 1781, five years after the Declaration of Independence. General Charles Cornwallis (1738–1805) and his army had left the area long before but Major James Henry Craig (1748–1812) operated out of Wilmington.

Colonel James Kenan (1740–1810) and about 250 Duplin County militiamen at Rockfish Bridge on the Wilmington Road tried to prevent any Crown troops from foraging in the county at the end of July 1781. Brigadier General Richard Caswell (1729–1789) joined him with approximately another 180 men when Major Craig passed through Duplin on his way to New Bern. Forewarned, Colonel Kenan began construction of a slight breastwork along Rockfish Creek in preparation to defend the area. Major Craig arrived on the southern side of Rockfish Creek with 600 Loyalists on Thursday, August 2, 1781, intending to plunder the counties of eastern North Carolina. Colonel Kenan placed his 250 militiamen and Richard Caswell's 180 reinforcements behind breastworks along the creek banks to oppose the crossing.

Major Craig attacked the breastwork with his cannon while Captain John Gordon (d. 1781) attacked in the rear with about 60 dragoons and two companies of infantry. They took a circuitous route through the woods and were close to the rear before being discovered. The militia broke in confusion before half of them had discharged their weapons, despite the efforts of Colonel Kenan and some of his officers to rally the men.

The Loyalists wounded 8 or 10 men and captured about 30 along with their ammunition, baggage, and provisions. Colonel Kenan had nobody killed, but the Loyalists had one man killed.[133]

Major Craig remained in Duplin County for 10 days and burned the homes of anyone who did not take the oath of allegiance. One of the destroyed houses belonged to Brigadier General John Alexander Lillington (ca. 1725–1786). During this time, 300 Loyalists joined his army. Small mounted militia parties struck his column whenever possible on their way to New Bern. They arrived in New Bern about 2 PM on Sunday, August 19, 1781.[134]

Kenansville
Myhand's Bridge (Oct. 1780; May 13, 1781)

> Kenansville is in the center of Duplin County. There is no definite date for the first engagement. It is listed as having occurred either in the fall of 1779 or 1780. The date of October 1780 would put it around the time of General Cornwallis's expedition into North Carolina.
> Myhand's Bridge probably crossed Great Coharie Creek where route NC 24 (Roseboro Highway) now crosses it about midway between Clinton and Concord.

The North Carolina Loyalists began to assemble and organize when General Charles Cornwallis (1738–1805) moved into North Carolina. Captain John C. Williams and his men patrolled in Duplin County to put down any Loyalist activities. Middleton Mobley (b. ca. 1740), one of the Loyalist leaders, mustered some of his men and laid an ambush at Myhand's Bridge to disrupt any traffic going through the county. After capturing some wagons, Mobley spotted Williams and his mounted militiamen and fired at them, killing one and wounding several others and creating confusion among them. Williams and his men pursued Mobley's men who escaped into the swamps and down the Cross Creek Road, sniping at Williams's men.

Williams demanded that a wagon driver, the last man standing, surrender a load of meal and cloth that he thought had been stolen by a raiding party. When the wagoner refused and threatened Williams and two men with a musket and a sword, Williams shot him in the face with his pistol.[135]

★ Colonel James Kenan (1740–1810) waited for 12 men and a swivel gun (see Photo NC-1) to come from the "old Ferry" at Helltown Ford before attacking Middleton Mobley's (b. ca. 1740) Loyalists. When it appeared that Mobley would get reinforcements and outnumber his two cavalry troops before the swivel gun would arrive, Kenan and his men rode near Myhand's Bridge on Sunday morning, May 13, 1781 to draw the Loyalists out of their fortified camp, unaware that Mobley's 120 Loyalists already outnumbered his 75.

The Loyalists crossed a narrow causeway leading to two bridges over the swamp. They had already stripped the first bridge of its planks to build their defenses. As they came over the causeway, the militiamen opened fire on the Loyalists' flank and came behind them, causing them to panic. Under fire from every side, the Loyalists pushed through the militia's left and fled down the Little Coharie, leaving three dead, two seriously wounded, and about 10 men captured. Kenan's men pursued, but the Loyalists, in a tangled, irregular and deep swamp with only a small, horse-wide path leading down the side of the Little Coharie Creek, had the advantage.

Kenan's militia had several men wounded. One of the mounted men died when a "serpent which attacked from a Tree" frightened his horse and bit him in the face and shoulders. The militiamen withdrew, plundered the Loyalist camp, and drank a large quantity of rum. They then pursued the Loyalists to Boykin's Plantation, using canoes, dugouts or small boats to cross the creek. When the militiamen arrived at the plantation and found themselves badly outnumbered, they withdrew while the Loyalists plundered the house.

The Loyalists destroyed the blacksmith shop, threw a large anvil into the Coharie River, took two cows and slaughtered them in the front yard. They stole the boats from the plantation and headed downstream toward Wilmington by nightfall to join Major James Henry Craig (1748–1812). The militiamen then took up positions around the Boykin house and helped to repair some of the damage.[136]

Edenton (June 1781; Feb. 25, 1782)

Edenton is on Albemarle Sound about 33 miles south of the Virginia border.

Captain Michael Quinn (d. 1781), who had been in the 10th North Carolina Regiment in 1776 and had retired in June 1778, was recalled for duty in 1779. He later joined the Crown forces and was made commander of the row galley *General Arnold* in June 1781. When the *General Arnold* entered Edenton harbor after burning ships up the Chowan River, she ran aground. Local militiamen captured the row galley when Captain Quinn was not able to free her. Captain Quinn was taken prisoner and murdered by a guard who was pardoned by the governor and not punished.[137]

★ A schooner from Charleston, South Carolina arrived at Edenton under a flag of truce on February 25, 1782. She had several merchants on board who formerly resided in North Carolina and who expected to be received as citizens. They brought a cargo of goods amounting to £8,000. She was not in port long when the privateer *Grand Turk* captured her.[138]

Southern Pines
Drays Mill Creek
Ray's Mill Creek (July 28, 1781)
Deep River, Cumberland County
House in the Horseshoe (July 29, 1781)

> Ray's Mill Creek is about 2 miles southwest of Southern Pines and is now called Drays Mill Creek. It runs west from Powell's Pond to Aberdeen Creek which it joins in Aberdeen, south of Pages Lake.
> The Alston House (see Photo NC-4) is in the northeast corner of Moore County at 288 Alston House Road, Sanford, NC 27330 phone: 910-947-2051. It is called the House in the Horseshoe because it is in a large horseshoe bend of Deep River. A historical marker is located on route NC 24 (SR 27|Monroe Street) at the intersection with route NC 1006 (Glendon Carthage Road) about 10 miles south. The outside of the house is riddled with bullet holes around both the front and back doors.
> The traditional date of this event has been August 5, 1781. However, Colonel Philip Alston's parole (see below) is dated a week earlier—July 29—and must be the correct date.

Colonel Philip Alston (1740–1788), a noted enemy of Loyalists, shot Thomas Taylor at his house on Ray's Mill Creek on July 28, 1781.

★ Colonel David Fanning (1755–1825) was delivering some Whig prisoners to Wilmington in July 1781. He stopped at the house of his friend, Kenneth Black (ca. 1730–1781), to spend the night. The next morning, Black accompanied him for several miles along the way as a guide. Before the two friends parted company, Black switched his fresh horse for Fanning's tired one. On his return trip, Black encountered a party of Whigs commanded by Colonel Philip Alston (1740–1788) who immediately gave chase. Black turned to flee, but Alston's men soon overtook him and shot him. Black proceeded about 200 feet and fell off the horse. He begged for his life but Alston's men smashed his head with the butt of his own musket. He lived to tell Fanning who his attackers were.

When Alston returned to his house at Deep River he stopped at the home of Colonel Hector McNeil (not the Loyalist officer) and accused him of stealing one of his slaves. Alston put a pistol to the old man's head and squeezed the trigger a few times, threatening to hang him if he did not return the slave. Mrs. McNeil sent her own slave to search for Alston's missing one. He found the slave and returned him to Alston.

Fanning stopped at the Black house on his way back and learned about his friend's murder. He set out immediately to avenge him. A party of Whigs were camped at Colonel Alston's house, known as the House in the Horseshoe, on Sunday morning, July 29, 1781 when Colonel Fanning and a slightly larger (about two dozen) band of Loyalists attacked. The Loyalists captured two guards asleep at the gate. The other two woke, fired, and ran to the porch where most of the other militiamen were sleeping. They all ran into the house and barricaded it in preparation for a fight. Alston protected his children by standing them up on a small table inside the brick fireplace. His wife, Temperance, lay in her bed on the second floor as bullets passed through the boards over her head.

After two hours of fighting, a Lieutenant McKay grew impatient with the situation and rushed the house and broke the doors under an intense covering fire. Alston's men fired a volley, hitting McKay in the head and wounding most of the men who followed him. (Some accounts say McKay was shot in the heart as soon as he jumped over the fence to attack the house.) Fanning then bribed "a free Negro" to set fire to the house. A shot from a window wounded him severely as he started to light the fire.

Fanning's men found an oxcart in the barn, filled it with hay and set it on fire, intending to roll it against the house to burn it. Alston decided to surrender but would not show himself because he knew he would be shot. Temperance Alston raised a white flag and stepped onto the porch. She offered to surrender, on condition that nobody would be injured. Fanning had many men wounded and realized an assault would be almost suicidal. Moreover, if he burned down a house with women and children in it, he would lose any support from area Loyalists. He agreed to the terms and kept his word. Both sides had several casualties in the skirmish. Colonel Alston lost four men killed, seven wounded, and 14 captured and his house was riddled with bullet holes. All of Alston's men immediately surrendered and then were paroled. Alston signed the following parole:

> I do hereby acknowledge myself a prisoner of War, upon my Parole to his Excellency Sir Henry Clinton, and that I am hereby engaged till I shall be exchanged or otherwise Released therefrom to Proceed Emediately to my plantation on Dunnams Creek Cumberland County or elsewhere North Carolina there to Remain or within five miles thereof and that I shall not in the mean time do or Cause any thing to be done prejuditial to the success of his Majesties arms or have Intercourse or hold Correspondence with the enemies of his Majesty, and that upon a Summons from his Excellency or other Persons having authority thereto that I will surrender myself up to him or them at such time & place as shall hereafter be required---
>
> Cumberland County Deep River July 29th 1781
> Philip Alston Col'n
> Witness
> David Fanning, Col'n Com'd Loyal Militia[139]

New Bern (ca. July 8, 1781; Aug. 1781)
Webber's Bridge, Trent River (Aug. 17, 1781)
Bryant's Mill, near New Bern (Aug. 21, 1781)

New Bern is at the confluence of the Neuse and Trent Rivers. Webber's Bridge was on the Trent River near New Bern. Bryant's Mill was near New Bern.

The re-created (1952–1959) Tryon Palace and Gardens (website: **www.tryonpalace.org**; phone: 252-514-4900), destroyed by fire in 1798, is on Pollack and George Streets. To get there, take the Trent Road/Pembroke Exit off Highway 70 and turn left at the light. Turn right on Broad Street, then right on George Street, and right again on Pollock Street.

The palace was the residence of Governor William Tryon (1729–1788) who received a commission in the British Army in 1751. He was appointed lieutenant governor of North Carolina in 1764 and became governor the following year. He built the palace in 1767 to 1770 at a cost of £15,000 at a time when the provincials already objected to taxes levied by royal officials.

The late-Georgian structure consisted of a two-story central block with a full basement and attic and two connecting wings. The east wing contained the secretary's office and the kitchen while the west wing had the stables. The governor resided and held meetings of the assembly in the central portion.

> Bryant's Mill may have been on the West Prong, about 10 miles west-southwest of New Bern.

The Crown forces had about 250 infantrymen and 40 light horsemen at Rutherford's Mill on Friday, July 6, 1781 intent on taking stock from Duplin and Onslow Counties. Brigadier General John Alexander Lillington (ca. 1725–1786) called for all the men of the county to join him to oppose the Crown forces. He mustered only about 150 and kept about 50 light horsemen near enemy lines to observe their movements.

Brigadier General Richard Caswell (1729–1789) ordered his militiamen to oppose any Crown raiding parties from Wilmington. They engaged a forage party at New Bern on Sunday, July 8, 1781 but retreated quickly after killing one and wounding several.[140]

★ Major James Henry Craig (1742–1812) encouraged and helped Colonel David Fanning (1755–1825) and personally led punitive expeditions into the interior and north along the coast. He burned plantations near New Bern in August 1781 and occupied that town for two days. As he was about to proceed even further, he learned that Brigadier General "Mad Anthony" Wayne (1745–1796) was on his way from Virginia to join Major General Nathanael Greene (1742–1786) in North Carolina. As Wayne was already in North Carolina, Craig hurried back to Wilmington, leaving the Loyalists in the Cape Fear region with no protection. Craig's absence allowed the Whigs to launch fresh attacks against the Loyalists.

★ As Major James Henry Craig (1742–1812) and his Loyalists marched toward New Bern on Friday, August 17, 1781, Brigadier General John Alexander Lillington (ca. 1725–1786) and his militia delayed them at Webber's Bridge, killing three and wounding five. The militia did not pursue the Loyalists as Governor Thomas Burke (ca.1747–1783) had ordered General Lillington not to risk a major battle with Major Craig.[141]

★ Major James Henry Craig (1742–1812) continued his 75-mile raid from Wilmington to New Bern after Brigadier General John Alexander Lillington's (ca. 1725–1786) militia delayed them at Webber's Bridge. Major Craig entered New Bern on Sunday, August 19, 1781 under sporadic musket fire. One of the shots killed Captain John Gordon (d. 1781), after which there was no more opposition.

The Loyalists occupied New Bern for two days and burned Whig plantations and General Alexander Lillington's house. They also destroyed the rigging of all the ships in port and their cargo, including 3,000 barrels of salt. Doctor Alexander Gaston (1753?–1781) tried to escape by rowing across the Trent River but was shot dead by an officer right before his wife's eyes. The raiders left New Bern and marched toward Kingston on Tuesday.[142]

★ After Major James Henry Craig (1742–1812) left New Bern with 32 Regulars of the 82nd Regiment and 78 North Carolina Independent Dragoons on Tuesday, August 21, 1781, he headed toward Kingston. He skirmished briefly with Colonel James Gorham's (1745–1804) 150 militiamen at Bryant's Mill. Captain Robert Gillies assumed command of the North Carolina Independent Dragoons after Captain John Gordon's death. The dragoons had found some liquor and left their flank open and were soon driven off.

Major Craig camped at Bryant's Mill that night and burned four houses, including that of Brigadier General William Bryan (1730–1810). He might have burned more had he not received information that Brigadier General "Mad Anthony" Wayne (1745–1796) was coming from Virginia with 500 men to join Major General Nathanael Greene (1742–1786) in South Carolina. Major Craig quickly returned to Wilmington. He lost 30 men killed, wounded or captured during his week-long raid.[143]

Wyanoke Ferry (July 1781)

> Wyanoke Ferry was on the Chowan River at the Virginia border about 10 miles north of Winton.

As General Charles Cornwallis (1738–1805) headed north to Yorktown, Virginia, a Loyalist raiding party burned the settlement at Wyanoke Ferry.[144]

Pittsboro
Chatham Courthouse (July 17, 1781)
Chatham County (Nov. 1781)

> Chatham Courthouse was located on the south side of Robertson's Creek in Pittsboro. Horton Middle School (79 Horton Road, Pittsboro) now occupies the site. Pittsboro is the center of Chatham County.

Colonel David Fanning (1755–1825) came out of seclusion in the Uwharrie Mountains after Major General Nathanael Greene (1742–1786) moved into South Carolina. Nobody had filled his place as overall commander of the Loyalists in his absence. Captain William Elrod (1735–1822) started spreading rumors about Fanning to undermine his authority; so Fanning asked all the field officers in the area to vote their choice for commander. They selected Fanning to lead the Loyal Militia of Randolph and Chatham Counties.

Fanning returned to Cox's Mill and called a general muster on Thursday, July 12, 1781. One hundred and fifty men reported for duty, but only one-third of them were armed. He kept the 53 armed Loyalists and sent the others home to report for duty when needed.

When Fanning learned that nine Loyalist militia leaders were tried and sentenced to hang at Chatham Courthouse on Monday, July 16, 1781, he and his men rode all night and arrived at 7 AM the following morning. They surrounded the courthouse and waited for the members of the court martial to arrive about eight o'clock. Fanning also posted men on all the roads leading to the courthouse. They captured 53 prisoners within two hours, including General Herndon Ramsey, Colonel Ambrose Ramsey, all the local militia officers, and three delegates of the Assembly. Fanning paroled all but 14 of his prisoners. He took those 14 to Wilmington and handed them over to Major James Henry Craig (1742–1812) on July 24th.[145]

★ When the Congressional militia units disbanded after the victory at Yorktown, Virginia, they headed home in small groups. Colonel David Fanning (1755–1825) and 30 of his Loyalists waited for them along their route home. Captain Thomas Kennedy, of Burke County, stopped in Chatham County to loot some Loyalist homes in the last week of November 1781. He took "a number of horses and a quantity of household furniture." When Fanning learned about this, he pursued Kennedy and his nine men for 5 miles before he overtook them and captured them along with all their plunder.

Fanning locked Kennedy and his men in a house with two guards. He and his men then went to ambush Captain John Lopp's men. They hid along the road and waited for Lopp's men to come by. When Lopp and his men came down the road, the Loyalists fired three volleys into their ranks. Lopp's men fled through the woods where the Loyalists could not pursue them in the darkness. When Fanning returned, he paroled Captain Kennedy and all his men because they remained quiet throughout the ambush.[146]

Drowning Creek
Piney Bottom Creek
Piney Bottom Massacre (Aug. 3, 1781)
Beatty's (Beattie's) Bridge (Aug. 4, 1781)
Richmond and Cumberland County (Aug. 9–12, 1781; Sept. 4, 1781; Oct. 1781)

> Drowning Creek is between Montgomery and Moore Counties. It runs along the eastern edge of Richmond County. Longstreet Church is located on Longstreet Road in Fort Bragg. Beatty's (Beattie's) Bridge probably crossed Drowning Creek where Ashemont Road now crosses it. Cumberland County is farther east with Fayetteville in the center and includes part of Fort Bragg.

Colonel Thomas Wade (1722–1786) and Captain Culp (d. 1781) dismissed the North Carolina militia after Major General Nathanael Greene (1742–1786) took command of the Continental Army into South Carolina. When the militiamen crossed McNeill's Ferry, some of them stole a piece of coarse cloth from a servant girl named Marren McDaniel. John "Cunning John" McNeill, the ferry owner, learned where the militiamen camped for the night and sent runners to alert the Loyalist militia. They mustered at the Longstreet Church the following day and marched toward the militia camp at Piney Bottom Creek, a branch of Rockfish Creek, where they arrived about an hour before dawn on Friday, August 3, 1781.

All militiamen were asleep except one sentinel who challenged the advancing Loyalists. They did not answer, so he challenged them a second time. When he did not receive an answer the second time, the sentinel fired. The Loyalists returned fire and a ball broke the sentry's arm. The Loyalists then charged the camp and shot six militiamen. The others ran away, leaving everything behind, including a boy in a wagon. The boy pleaded for his life and tried to run away, but one of the attackers split his skull with his broadsword.

The Loyalists plundered the wagons. The officers took all the money. The men took everything they could carry and burned the wagons. Marren McDaniel's piece of cloth was found on a corpse and returned to her.

Colonel Thomas Wade (1722–1786) called out his militiamen after the massacre at Piney Bottom to avenge the death of the boy who was hacked to death there. The Montgomery and Richmond County militias also joined Wade because Colonel Hector McNeil's (1756–1830) and Colonel Duncan Ray's men had driven off the cattle of the Cumberland County Whigs and tried to force the Whigs to give up their arms.

Wade and 100 men rode out to find the Loyalists and caught up with them at Beatty's Bridge over Drowning Creek on Saturday night, August 4, 1781. They fired at each other until after midnight when the Loyalists decided to withdraw. Wade had four men wounded. Colonel McNeil had 12 men killed and 15 wounded.

The *Royal Georgia Gazette* account is almost diametrically opposite. It says the skirmish began at 11 AM and lasted a considerable time when "the Rebels retreated in disorder" and were pursued until 2 PM, leaving "about 20 killed and wounded in the pursuit." It goes on to say that the Loyalists lost nobody killed and only three or four wounded, that they "took 52 prisoners and 100 horses, besides arms and ammunition; 28 of the prisoners were sent to this town [Wilmington], the rest were paroled."

★ British Major James Henry Craig (1748–1812) encamped at Colonel Thomas Rutledge's (1729–1801) house on Saturday, August 4, 1781 and remained for about three days. He gathered some cattle, destroyed some corn, burned the houses of Captain Daniel Gillespie (1743–1829) and Lieutenant Henry Houston (1746–1736) and destroyed whatever property they could not carry away. They then marched toward New Bern, plundering and enticing slaves to desert their masters and to accompany them. Some militiamen from Duplin, Onslow and Dobbs Counties followed and harassed the Loyalists. Captain John Gordon (d. 1781), of the British dragoons, was killed by some of the Onslow men in the first week in August 1781.[147]

★ As Colonel Thomas Wade's (1722–1786) militiamen searched for the Loyalists involved in the Piney Bottom massacre, they camped at the home of Daniel Patterson (1731–1809), who lived on Drowning Creek, between Thursday, August 9, 1781 and Sunday, the 12th. They beat the old man until he revealed the names of all the participants. The next day, some of the militiamen crossed the creek and went to Kenneth Clarke's house where they caught six men, including a British deserter wearing a red coat, in a potato field, but only two of them had been at Piney Bottom.

That evening, Captain Patrick Bogan and his company of light horsemen were all drunk when they crossed the creek. Bogan ordered the prisoners to be put to death with a sword, just as the boy was murdered at Piney Bottom. When the drunken militiamen began slashing at them from horseback, the Loyalists ducked and ran away. The militiamen shot one of them with three musket balls and killed him on the spot. Another was shot and managed to get inside his house where he died. A third man was shot and killed trying to climb over a fence. Another man came into the house begging for his life. His arm was broken by a musket ball and he had been hit in three other places.

Bogan's men shot him in the chest. One man tried to hide behind his wife as she held a child in her arms. A militiaman pulled the man's wife away and tied his hands, but the man ran out a door into some nearby woods. He was caught a quarter mile away and shot several times before his head was cleft to the nose with a sword. Mr. Clarke was told to bury the bodies before the next evening or he would also be killed. The militiamen took the British deserter and killed him sometime during the night.

Colonel Wade and his men went to David Buchan's (b. ca. 1760) house the next day, Sunday, and set it on fire when he was not there. They then went to Kenneth Black's (ca. 1730–1781) house where Captain Culp (d. 1781) brought Black and his son after finding them hiding. They beat the old man, slapped him with their swords, and screwed his thumb in a gunlock but he revealed nothing. The militiamen rode their horses inside Black's house until the entire family squeezed themselves up the chimney. While searching for some "light wood" to burn the house, the militiamen found two large chests which some British army officers entrusted to Black while they were away. The raiders smashed all the chinaware that filled one chest. The other chest was full of books, which were cut apart and thrown on the floor.

When two daughters of a neighbor, who lived 4 miles away, came to see their friends, they were surprised to find men on horseback in the house. The militiamen took the girls' jewelry and pointed a sword at their breasts, cutting their dresses. They then had the two girls stripped. Mrs. Black noticed a man sitting peaceably on his horse, not taking part in the plundering. She asked him why he did not take anything. He responded that she did not have anything he wanted. He was the father of the boy killed at Piney Bottom.

The Black family had just gotten over the smallpox and Mrs. Black told the militiamen that all of the items they were taking were infested with the pox. They threw the stolen items down and took Kenneth Black (ca. 1730–1781) to guide them to Mr. Duncan Ray's house. Some of the militiamen wanted to kill Black, but Captain Culp did not let them.

The raiders split into two groups. One party went to Alexander Graham's (1739–1794) to find that he had smallpox. When they heard musket fire coming from Alexander Black's (1761–1812) house, where the other group went, the first group rushed over there to find Mr. Black dying of gunshot wounds. The raiders then went to the house of Peter Blue where they shot him and Archibald McBride (d. 1781). Blue was wounded but McBride was killed for staying in the house of a man who had been at the Piney Bottom massacre.

After avenging themselves for the Piney Bottom massacre, the militiamen disbanded; but a mulatto man named Turner and some Loyalists followed Captain Culp home. They demanded that Culp come out of the house or they would burn the house. After the house was set on fire, Culp came out carrying his sons who begged for their father's life. The mulatto told the boys to leave or they would also be killed. When the boys moved away, the Loyalists shot Culp in his own yard and burned his house.[148]

★ Colonel Thomas Wade (1722–1786) and more than 400 militiamen marched to attack Colonel Hector McNeil (1756–1830) near Drowning Creek on Tuesday, September 4, 1781. McNeil was reinforced by Colonel David Fanning's (1755–1825) Loyalists who defeated Wade's detachment, killing 23 and capturing 50.

Kingston (Aug. 16, 1781; Aug. 21, 1781)

> Kingston or Kingstown is now Kinston, northwest of New Bern.

Major James Henry Craig (1742–1812) and his 82nd Regiment used Wilmington as a base to raid the countryside in 1781. As they headed up the coast toward New Bern on Thursday, August 16, 1781, they encountered Brigadier General Richard Caswell's (1729–1789) militiamen who tried to stop them near Kingston. The Loyalists retreated when Captain John Gordon's (d. 1781) North Carolina Independent Dragoons charged. There is no record of casualties.[149]

August 21, 1781 see **Bryant's Mill** (pp. 240–241).

Robeson's Plantation, Cape Fear River (Aug. 17, 1781)

> Robeson's Plantation was near White Oak south of Mount Olive.

When Colonel David Fanning's (1755–1825) forces crossed the Neuse River at Campbellton and marched down the Cape Fear River toward Wilmington, they passed the home of Captain Peter Robeson (1746–1794) which they burned on Friday, August 17, 1781. Colonel Fanning sent a detachment across the river to burn the plantation of Colonel Thomas Robeson, Jr. (1740–1785), Peter's brother. They took several men prisoners and paroled all but 20 of them. The Loyalists continued raiding for a week, after which they delivered their prisoners to Captain John Leggett, Major James Henry Craig's (1748–1812) second in command, on August 24th.[150]

Fanning's Mill (Aug. 28, 1781)

> Richard Fanning's Mill was on Little River in Montgomery County. The Little River runs from the northeast corner of Montgomery County to the center of the southern border of the county. The exact site of the mill is unknown.

After the capture of the Cumberland County Courthouse on Tuesday, August 14, 1781, the Loyalists tried to prevent any disruption of British operations in North or South Carolina. When Colonel Hector McNeil (1756–1830) learned that some of Colonel Thomas Wade's (1722–1786) militiamen were at Richard Fanning's Mill, he rode there with 70 Loyalists. He surprised Wade's men on Tuesday, August 28, 1781, capturing several of them. Wade learned of the raid and pursued McNeil with 400 mounted militiamen.[151]

Elizabethtown (Aug. 29, 1781)

> Two small markers near the Bladen County Courthouse (route NC 87|Broad Street) commemorate the battle that took place near here in August 1781. One of them honors Sallie Salter (1742–1800), a member of a distinguished local family who volunteered to go to the Loyalist camp under the pretext of selling eggs. Having gathered her information, she returned to Colonel Thomas Robeson, Jr. (1740–1785) and gave him a detailed account of the camp and helped him plan his strategy.
>
> A state historical marker commemorating the battle is one block west on Broad Street near a covered walkway known as "Tory Hole Alley." Proceeding on Broad Street, route NC 87 intersects with route U.S. 701. Tory Hole Park is located on U.S. 701 0.2 miles north of the intersection. The park along the banks of the Cape Fear River is named for the nearby gully into which the fleeing Loyalists plunged in 1781. It offers picnic facilities, hiking trails, and a boat landing in a picturesque, forested setting.

Elizabethtown was in the middle of an area under Loyalist control in the summer of 1781. The notorious Loyalist leader Colonel David Fanning (1755–1825) operated to the west. Cross Creek (Fayetteville) to the north was also dominated by Loyalists. Crown troops occupied Wilmington to the southeast, and Colonel John Slingsby (d. 1781), a native of England, was encamped in Elizabethtown with 400 Loyalist soldiers and used it as his base for raiding the surrounding countryside and ravaging the plantations of local Whigs.

On August 11, 1781, Colonel David Fanning, Colonel John Slingsby, Colonel Hector McNeil (1756–1830), and Colonel Duncan Ray all met with their respective forces at Cross Creek and together they scoured the country on either side of the Cape Fear River, taking prisoners, ravaging plantations and desolating the Whig settlements.

The local Whig militia under the immediate command of Colonel Thomas Robeson, Jr. (1740–1785) had dwindled to 70 men headquartered in Duplin County. They gathered some 150 Bladen men who vowed to drive the Loyalists from the town or die in the attempt. Armed with long rifles and equipped with worn-out horses, the small band marched toward Elizabethtown on Wednesday night, August 29, 1781. They left their horses with an attendant, undressed, tied their clothing and ammunition on their heads, and crossed the Cape Fear River one mile south of the town. They all reached the opposite shore safely, dressed, prepared their weapons for action, ascended the high hills, crossed King's Road leading through the town, and took position in its rear. They formed and began a furious attack on Slingsby's garrison of 400 just before daybreak and one hour after the crossing.

Outnumbered almost three to one, Robeson divided his men into three companies which would approach the enemy from different directions. At a given signal, the militia charged forward yelling, "Washington!" The first musket volley surprised the Loyalists and spread panic throughout the camp. The attack drove in the sentries and guards. The attackers kept up a brisk fire as they advanced rapidly. From the center of the line, Robeson shouted out orders to phantom companies in a loud, clear voice: "On the right! Colonel Dodd's Company! Advance! On the left! Colonel Gillespie's Company!"

The Loyalist officers tried to form their men into line, but many were shot down. Without their leaders, the Loyalists fled. There were many Whig prisoners in the camp which probably contributed to the early flight of the garrison. Colonel Slingsby fell mortally wounded along with 15 of his men. The others retreated, some taking refuge in houses. Many of the fleeing Loyalists fell into a deep ravine (now filled) in the dim light. The ravine has since been known as "Tories' Hole."

The Whigs released a number of prisoners, collected the arms and stores in the camp and retreated across the river with their booty, knowing they did not have the strength to engage the Loyalists in an open battle. The supply of arms and ammunition equipped the Whigs for larger operations. The action disheartened the Loyalists of Bladen County and ended their power along the Cape Fear.

Archibald Maclaine (1722–1804), from Sampson Hall, wrote about three weeks later: "In this action, we had only one man wounded; killed, wounded and taken of the enemy, nineteen. Slingsby since dead of his wounds." Colonel Godden (d. 1781) and most of the other officers of the garrison were also killed.[152]

Raft Swamp (McPhaul's or McFall's Mill, Burnt Swamp)
(Sept. 1, 1781; Sept. 13, 1781; Oct. 15, 1781)

> Raft Swamp is a wilderness area that extends from Southern Hoke County into central Robeson County. The area was the center of local Loyalist activity during the American War for Independence. A state historical marker at Antioch calls attention to the Battle of McPhaul's Mill, one of several fights in the swamp. The battle site is about 23 miles west-southwest of Fayetteville, off route NC 1124, 1.7 miles west of route NC 211. A large stone with an engraved tablet marks the site of McPhaul's mill built before the war. A historical marker for the site of the Battle of Raft Swamp is on route NC 211, 2.5 miles south of the intersection of routes NC 211 and NC 71 in Red Springs.

Governor Thomas Burke (ca.1747–1783) had ordered General John Butler's (1728–1796) militia to patrol the country between the Cape Fear and the Neuse Rivers to curb the activities of Colonel David Fanning (1755–1825) and other Loyalists. A few days after the battle at Elizabethtown, Fanning gathered a force of Loyalists from Cumberland and Bladen counties and marched toward Butler, who was then camped at Cox's Mill on Deep River, near the Chatham line.

The Loyalists retaliated quickly for the attack at Elizabethtown. Colonel Fanning hurried to assist Colonel John Slingsby (d. 1781) with a fresh supply of ammunition but he arrived too late. He continued to McPhaul's Mill, about 60 miles away, where he learned that Colonel Thomas Wade (1722–1786) and his men were encamped on Drowning Creek, on the eastern side of the Lumber River about a mile from the bridge with a narrow causeway between Wade and the bridge. Wade was headed to attack Colonel Hector McNeil's (1756–1830) forces in the Raft Swamp. Fanning marched toward Wade and joined McNeil and his men. Together, they surprised Wade in a narrow section of Raft Swamp on Saturday, September 1, 1781.

Fanning directed McNeill to move down the swamp to cut off Wade's retreat route. He then launched an attack on Wade's position just before noon. The first volley was directed at the charging horsemen and killed 18. The Loyalists dismounted and attacked with a vengeance, firing as they advanced. When the Loyalists came within 25 yards of them, Wade's militiamen broke and ran away in confusion along the causeway and across the bridge.

McNeill was not in position as directed by Fanning, so he lost the opportunity of capturing or destroying Wade's entire force. Fanning's men quickly remounted and pursued the fleeing enemy for 7 miles. They captured 54 prisoners and 250 horses and killed 19 of Wade's men. Fanning stated his own loss at only one killed and a few wounded. He distributed the horses to his troops who were not mounted in the action and paroled the prisoners, except for 30 who were sent to Wilmington. Fanning then returned to McPhaul's mill. Their victory in Raft Swamp avenged the Loyalist rout at Elizabethtown.

★ Colonel Archibald McDougal or McDugald commanded the remnants of Colonel David Fanning's (1755–1825) army after the battle of Lindley's Mill on Thursday, September 13, 1781. He and his men moved slowly, since they brought their wounded and prisoners with them, and many of the mounted militiamen had no horses. Instead of going to Cox's Mill, McDougal went to the Sandhills by way of McPhaul's Mill. They stopped at Hickory Mountain in Chatham County on the night of September 13th.

The Loyalists broke camp early the following morning and continued their march. When they reached the ford on Rocky River, between 12 and 20 Whigs fired at them. The large column of Loyalists soon chased them away. Colonel Duncan Ray and his Anson County Militia met McDougal at McPhaul's Mill. Ray's fresh troops took McDougal's to Wilmington.[153]

★ On Sunday, October 15, 1781, just four days before General Charles Cornwallis (1738–1805) surrendered at Yorktown, Virginia, General Griffith Rutherford's (ca. 1731–1800) cavalry had a slight engagement with a detachment of Loyalists. They obtained information from prisoners that a force of between 300 and 600 Loyalists under Colonels John Elrod (d. 1782), Duncan Ray, Hector McNeil (1756–1830), and Archibald McDougal or McDugald were camped at Raft Swamp. Colonel David Fanning (1755–1825) was still hiding on Brush Creek, in the Deep River area, recovering from his wounds. He had regained enough strength that he was preparing to take the field again. He sent messengers to Wilmington for a supply of ammunition, which Major James Henry Craig (1742–1812) sent him on October 13th. The Loyalists at Raft Swamp had been with Fanning when he captured Governor Thomas Burke (ca.1747–1783).

General Griffith Rutherford's (ca. 1731–1800) force of 1,400 men came upon the Loyalists in the swampy wilderness of Raft Swamp. He arranged his men in a single line, five steps apart, under the leadership of Colonel Thomas Owen (1742–1825) and Major Joseph Graham (1759–1836) and beat through the swamp. Some accounts say the Whigs routed the Loyalists, killing 16 and wounding 50. Others say that the action was unsuccessful and that the Loyalists made good their escape.[154]

The Loyalists made a stand on a hill near Raft Swamp overlooking a causeway. They removed the planks of the bridge on the causeway leading across the swamp to slow down any cavalry. Major Graham's dragoons surprised them while they were preparing their defenses. The dragoons rode right into the swamp without even slowing down or bothering to use the bridge. Graham wrote:

The enemy broke and fled as fast as they could, but the stout horses and expert riders of the west soon overtook them; and when they came in contact with the sand-hill ponies, went through, trod down, and turned over horses and riders. After their first fire, the enemy thought of no further resistance, but endeavored to make their escape, and aimed for a branch of Raft Swamp to their front, over which there was a causeway two hundred yards wide. Our troops entered the causeway with them, using sabre against all they could reach. As soon as it was felt, the Tories would throw themselves off each side into the ditch, quitting their horses and making off in the swamp; the dragoons near the front fired their pistols at them in their retreat. By the time the Whigs got half way through, the causeway was crowded with dismounted ponies for twenty steps before them, so that it was impossible to pass. Two or three stout men dismounted, and commenced pushing them over into the ditch, out of the way. When it was a little cleared, the dragoons rushed over.[155]

About 35 Loyalists tried to defend the causeway, but Graham's dragoons cut through their ranks and chased them. Many Loyalists were shot or drowned in the swamp. Graham noted, "As the enemy were much scattered and completely beaten, it was thought inexpedient to pursue the victory further. The men were collected by the sound of the trumpet, at the west side of the swamp, and marched back to where General Rutherford had encamped, near McFall's Mill, where they arrived about 10 o'clock at night."

The Loyalists went home. Others fled the county to South Carolina. Rutherford's militiamen searched the swamp for any survivors the next day but found none. They then marched to Brown Marsh where they camped for several days.[156]

Livingston's Creek (Sept. 23, 1781)

Livingston's Creek is in Bladen County.

Colonel Archibald McDougal or McDugald and Colonel Duncan Ray skirmished with some horsemen pursuing them two days after joining forces at McPhaul's Mill. McDougal's men set up a defensive position at Hammond's Creek Bridge outside of Elizabethtown and fought a delaying action that allowed McDougal to bring his prisoners to Major James Henry Craig (1742–1812) in Wilmington. Major Craig anticipated them and took a detachment of the 82nd Regiment toward Cross Creek to meet the Loyalists on Sunday, September 23, 1781.

Major Craig found McDougal at Livingston's Creek, in Bladen County, still avoiding the horsemen pursuing him. About 50 horsemen appeared four hours after Ray and McDougal arrived at Livingston's Creek. Craig ordered his dragoons and 60 infantrymen to disperse the attackers. They chased the mounted militiamen 3 miles up the road where they found 200 militiamen in their defenses on the road. The Crown troops attacked and the militiamen retreated to Elizabethtown but the dragoons returned to Major Craig, not knowing what awaited them further down the road. They then returned to Wilmington.[157]

Clarkton
Brown Marsh (Sept. 1781)

Brown Marsh is near present day Clarkton. It is also known as Baldwin's Old Field.

Brigadier General John Butler (1728–1796) planned to retaliate on the men who raided Hillsborough and captured Governor Thomas Burke (ca.1747–1783). He gathered his men near Brown Marsh in Bladen County. When Major James Henry Craig

(1748–1812) learned of this, he sent Major Daniel Manson (b. ca. 1733) and 180 Provincials to Brown Marsh with Colonel Duncan Ray. He divided his forces in three and placed guides with each division. The Royal North Carolina Regiment, Duncan Ray's Anson County Militia, and Colonel David Fanning's (1755–1825) Regiment were to strike Butler's camp from different angles in September 1781.

The guides became lost in Brown Swamp and the plan soon fell apart. Fanning's Regiment got out of the swamp and into position, but Ray's militiamen were lost. General Butler's men could hear them breaking brush and getting tangled in the vines and bushes as they trudged through the swamp. They set up their defenses facing the swamp. Manson, unaware of the situation of his other two divisions, ordered the attack to begin early in the morning before dawn.

Butler's defenses faced the swamp and his men did not expect an attack on their flanks. Manson's division fired the first volley. Butler assumed that they had field pieces and ordered a retreat. Colonel Robert Mebane (ca. 1748–1781) disobeyed Butler's order and continued to fight as he had done at Cane Creek. Colonel Thomas Owen's (1725–1803) Bladen County militiamen joined Mebane and fought until they were overpowered and forced to retreat.

The Loyalists captured the camp in less than an hour, having lost two killed and five wounded. General Butler lost three killed and two wounded, but Manson wrote to Craig that

> The Rebels were completely dispers'd, leaving twenty dead & five & twenty prisoners. They had also a number of wounded who in the darkness of the night got off. We took between 30 & 40 horses but the militia the next day got upwards of a hundred more who were running loose in the woods.[158]

Beck's Ford (Sept. 1781)

Beck's Ford was on the Deep River, probably where Interstate 85 crosses it between Greensboro and High Point, about 25 miles north of David Fanning's headquarters at Cox's Mill.

Captain Robert Roper and a small party of Whigs marched up Deep River to attack Colonel David Fanning (1755–1825) at Beck's Ford in September 1781. Fanning saw some of Roper's men on the other side of the river and tried to cross with another Loyalist. The militiamen shot at the two men as soon as they entered the water. Fanning's companion was wounded and they quickly withdrew.

Fanning ordered his men to mount up and rode to a ford a few miles down the river. They were too late. Roper had withdrawn from the area. The Loyalists pursued the Whigs throughout the night and into the next day, finally giving up the chase. Fanning captured two men on the return route. He wanted to hang them, but his men stopped him.[159]

Kirk's Farm (Sept. 12, 1781)

Kirk's Farm, known as Kirk's Old Field, was owned by "Old Kirk," an English hatter, frequently suspected of aiding the Whigs. Some authorities place Kirk's Farm along the New Hope River, southeast of Chapel Hill, probably where the New Hope empties into B. Everett Jordan Lake. Others place it on the road from Hillsborough to Lindley's Mill at Cane Creek about 12 miles west of Chapel Hill near where it empties into the Haw River.

As Colonel David Fanning (1755–1825) rode to attack Hillsborough, he learned that a small force of 25 men (part of Colonel James Hinton's (1750–1794) militia from Wake County) was camped at Kirk's Farm on the New Hope River between Fanning and Brigadier General John Butler's (1728–1796) 400 man army at Ramsey's Mill. He dispatched a company of men under Captain Richard Edwards to silence them and to divert or confuse General Butler's army.

Colonel Hinton and his men crossed the Cape Fear River toward the end of August 1781 in search of Loyalists but had only found a few after 10 days. They stopped to rest at Kirk's Farm, assuming that there were no Loyalists in the area. Captain Richard Edwards (1750s–1781) arrived at the farm at sunrise on Wednesday, September 12, 1781 and began to surround the farm when a sentinel discovered them and fired his weapon. He was killed after his shot alarmed the rest of the militiamen who reacted so slowly that the attackers had time to hide in a thicket.

The Loyalists fired at some men who rushed out of the house. The others put up a fierce defense, killing Edwards and 10 of his men. Captain Edwards's brother, Edward (1740s–1781) assumed command and defeated the militiamen. Nearly one third of all the men engaged in the skirmish were killed or wounded. In addition to the eleven Loyalists killed in the skirmish, several others died of their wounds within a few days. The defenders lost at least two men wounded, one mortally. Captain Edward Edwards then returned to Fanning's army headed to Hillsborough.[160]

Brush Creek (Oct. 1781)

> Brush Creek runs parallel to Deep River southwest of Siler City and south of Cox's Mill, David Fanning's headquarters.

General Griffith Rutherford (ca. 1731–1800), in command of the militia in the western part of North Carolina in 1781, had set up camp at Monroe's Bridge on Drowning Creek by Monday, October 15, 1781. The remnants of Brigadier General John Butler's (1728–1796) army met him there, bringing his force to almost 1,500 men. Colonel David Fanning (1755–1825) gathered 140 Loyalist militiamen and captured a large amount of leather destined for the Continental Army in South Carolina.

When the Whigs learned of the leather raid, 170 mounted militiamen rode to Brush Creek. Told that 600 men were coming against them, many of the Loyalists fled. Fanning organized the remaining men in two lines to receive the Whigs. They repulsed the first assault after an hour's fighting that left three Loyalists killed and three wounded. The attackers lost one killed and several wounded. They retreated about a mile and regrouped. When the Whigs made a second assault, Fanning thought they had been reinforced and he told his men to break up into small parties and withdraw. They withdrew to the Uwharrie Mountains where they hid until the middle of October.[161]

Cumberland County (Oct. 1781)

Colonel Robert Mebane (ca. 1748–1781) departed for the northern part of North Carolina in October 1781, taking only his servant with him. He encountered the "noted Tory and horse thief Henry Hightower" along the way. Mebane charged after Hightower. When Mebane got close enough to strike Hightower with his sword, Hightower wheeled and fired his musket, killing Mebane. Hightower was later captured and hanged in Williams Township for the murder.[162]

Leonard Creek (Nov. 2, 1781)

Leonard Creek is east of Lexington.

Two neighbors along Leonard's Creek, Valentin Leonhardt (d. 1781) and Wooldrich Fritz (d. 1781), fought with the Continental Army in the battle of Guilford Courthouse. Leonhardt enlisted at the age of 55 and all his sons served in the army. When the men returned home, many of their German Loyalist neighbors wanted revenge. They shot Leonhardt and Fritz in their homes on Leonard Creek on Friday, November 2, 1781, two weeks after the British surrendered at Yorktown. Fritz died immediately. Leonhardt survived for 11 days. Both men were buried together in the cemetery of what is now the Pilgrim United Church of Christ.[163]

Seven Creeks (Nov. 15, 1781)

Seven Creeks is about 42 miles southwest of Wilmington, and about 8 miles from the South Carolina border near route NC 905 (Seven Creeks Road).

General Griffith Rutherford (ca. 1731–1800) ordered Captain Joseph Graham (1759–1836) to reconnoiter the defenses around Wilmington on Thursday, November 15, 1781. They were patrolling near Brunswick Town, at a place called Seven Creeks, near the South Carolina border, around midnight when Colonel Micajah Ganey or Gainey discovered Graham and his dragoons and ambushed them. Graham charged into the ambush and killed one of Ganey's men and wounded two others. He lost his lieutenant killed and several horses. Lieutenant Colonel Henry "Light-Horse Harry" Lee (1756–1818) arrived the next morning with news that General Cornwallis surrendered at Yorktown, Virginia.[164]

When General Rutherford announced the surrender to his troops, the camp erupted into celebration, firing their weapons in the air. Rutherford learned that the Crown forces were planning to evacuate Wilmington. He ordered his men to cross the Cape Fear River and march toward the town. They camped within 4 miles of town that night. They got no opposition from the troops preparing to leave, but some of the militiamen wanted revenge for the destruction of their homes and for the murders of their friends at Rouse's Tavern.

The Crown troops formed columns and marched down to the transport ships after sunrise on Sunday, November 18, 1781, leaving their horses behind. At this time, some Whig light horsemen thundered down the street at full speed. One of them, Thomas Tyer (1720–1790), left the ranks, drew his hanger, and rushed upon a Loyalist who stood in the road, holding out his hand "as if to salute the troop. Tyer, whose father had been hanged with a grapevine by the man, gave him a vertical blow that cleft his head, "the divided parts falling on each other."

One column of troops had not boarded the boats when the cavalry attacked. The broken column fired at them, slightly wounding two or three of the horsemen. The vessels fired upon the town, but the cavalry had already ridden away.

General Rutherford marched his men into the town as the transport ships were just leaving the Cape Fear. One of his officers, shocked at the violence directed at the Loyalists, placed a dragoon at the door of each Loyalist family. While this action diminished the hostility, it did not stop it. The militiamen rounded up all the men they could and put them in a pen made of rails "near the Episcopal church, where they were exhibited to the public gaze, and received the scoffing taunts of boys."[165]

Carthage
Big Juniper Creek (Dec. 1781)

> Big Juniper Creek is also known as McLendon's Creek. Robert Coxe's house was in the forks of Big Juniper Creek and McLendon's Creek about 5 miles west of the present town of Carthage. Nothing remains of the house and there are no markers.

Colonel David Fanning (1755–1825) rode to Captain John Coxe's house in December 1781. Coxe was staying in Chatham County with a friend when Fanning arrived and destroyed his house. Fanning and his men then rode to the house of Robert Coxe, John's father, in the forks of Big Juniper Creek and McLendon's Creek. They arrived around midnight and rushed the house. The occupants heard them approach and ran for their horses. Some of them ran by the place where Fanning had hid his horses and took the Loyalists' horses. Fanning found nobody home and burned the house down.

The three occupants [Robert Coxe, Robert Lowe (d. 1781), and William Jackson (d. 1781)] returned to observe Fanning. The sentries posted around the house spotted them and Loyalists pursued them. The three men split up. Fanning and one of his men pursued one man who turned and fired, hitting the man with Fanning. Fanning returned fire and killed him.

Another man was captured and brought back to the burning house. When Fanning recognized him as one of his militiamen who had changed sides, he ordered the man shot. He was still alive despite being shot several times, so Fanning drew his own pistol and killed him. Robert Coxe escaped when his pursuer's horse fell in a creek.[166]

Cherokee Campaign of 1782 see Tennessee chapter in the volume on the Deep South and the Frontier.

Beaufort (April 4, 1782)

> Beaufort was a port town and a haven for privateers who preyed on ships bringing supplies for the British Army from the West Indies. The Old Town Restoration on Turner Street is a complex of restored houses, shops, and public buildings that give visitors a flavor of Beaufort in colonial and Revolutionary War times.

Several warships of the Royal Navy sailed into Beaufort on April 4, 1782, almost six months after General Charles Cornwallis (1738–1805) surrendered at Yorktown, Virginia. After the ships dropped anchor, several local citizens sailed out to meet them under a flag of truce but they were arrested as soon as they came aboard. British landing parties raided and pillaged the town over the course of the next 10 days.

Colonel John Easton mustered a group of defenders and engaged the raiding parties when they came into town. Both sides suffered casualties and captured prisoners. The townspeople also set several boats and rafts on fire and sent them toward the fleet at anchor in the harbor, but the wind shifted direction and the fiery flotilla never reached its destination. The ships sailed away two weeks later, on April 17, one day short of the seventh anniversary of the first battle of the American War for Independence.[167]

In May 1782, Major General Nathanael Greene (1742–1786), apparently not convinced the war was over, sent an alarming report to Governor Thomas Burke (ca.1747–1783), who had returned from captivity. The report stated that the British were planning an attack on Beaufort. Governor Burke ordered out two brigades of 500 men each under brigadiers William Caswell (1754–1786) and Allen Jones (1739–1798). The attack never occurred. The British no longer had the desire or the forces to continue fighting. They evacuated Savannah, Georgia on Thursday, July 11, 1782.[168]

See the map of North Carolina west.

Morganton
Quaker Meadows (early July 1776)
McDowell's Station (July 3–12, 1776)

> Quaker Meadows is the area east and northeast of Morganton in Burke County. McDowell's Station was located at Quaker Meadows along the upper Catawba River in Rowan County. A marker on route NC 181 near the junction with route NC 126 commemorates the event.

A band of Cherokees attacked the North Carolina frontier in late June and early July 1776, killing 37 settlers on the Catawba River and forcing the rest to take refuge in the forts and stockades. The raid was planned to synchronize with Sir Peter Parker's (1721–1811) attack on Charleston, South Carolina. The settlements loyal to the King were instructed to erect "Passover poles" to identify themselves so they would be spared. Major Joseph McJunkin (1755–1846) wrote:

> In the early of 1776 a combination was entered into by the Tories and Indians for a general massacre of the Whigs residing along the frontiers from North Carolina to Georgia. The Tories set up peeled poles at their houses, around which white cloth was wrapped. These were called passovers. On June 20, in accordance with previous arrangements, the Indians commenced the work of death among the Whigs, but the Tories sat under their passovers in safety. To this, however, there was one exception. Capt. James Ford, who resided on the Enoree River at a place called the Canebrake, was killed while sitting under his passover. His wife was also killed and his two daughters taken captives.

★ After killing 37 settlers on the Catawba River, the Cherokees attacked and laid siege to Colonel Charles McDowell's (1743–1815) Station. The 10 men and 120 women and children in the surrounding area took refuge in the fort.

General Griffith Rutherford (ca. 1731–1800) mounted an expedition to relieve the fort even though he expected to find the settlers massacred. However, the settlers managed to hold out. The arrival of Rutherford's militia broke the siege, but the Cherokees continued to harass them until the rest of the 2,400 backwoods militiamen arrived. Rutherford then invaded the Cherokee territory and destroyed 32 middle settlement towns and villages, temporarily breaking Cherokee power in North Carolina.[169]

★ Captain Matthias Barringer (1747–1776) was on a scouting expedition in the Quaker Meadows of Burke County with seven of his Catawba County militiamen in early July 1776. A "Cherokee war party armed with British rifles" attacked them and massacred them. The attacks brought devastating retaliation. More than 4,000 militiamen from Virginia and the Carolinas, along with some Loyalist settlers who joined the backwoods militiamen to punish the Cherokees, destroyed their villages.[170]

North Carolina

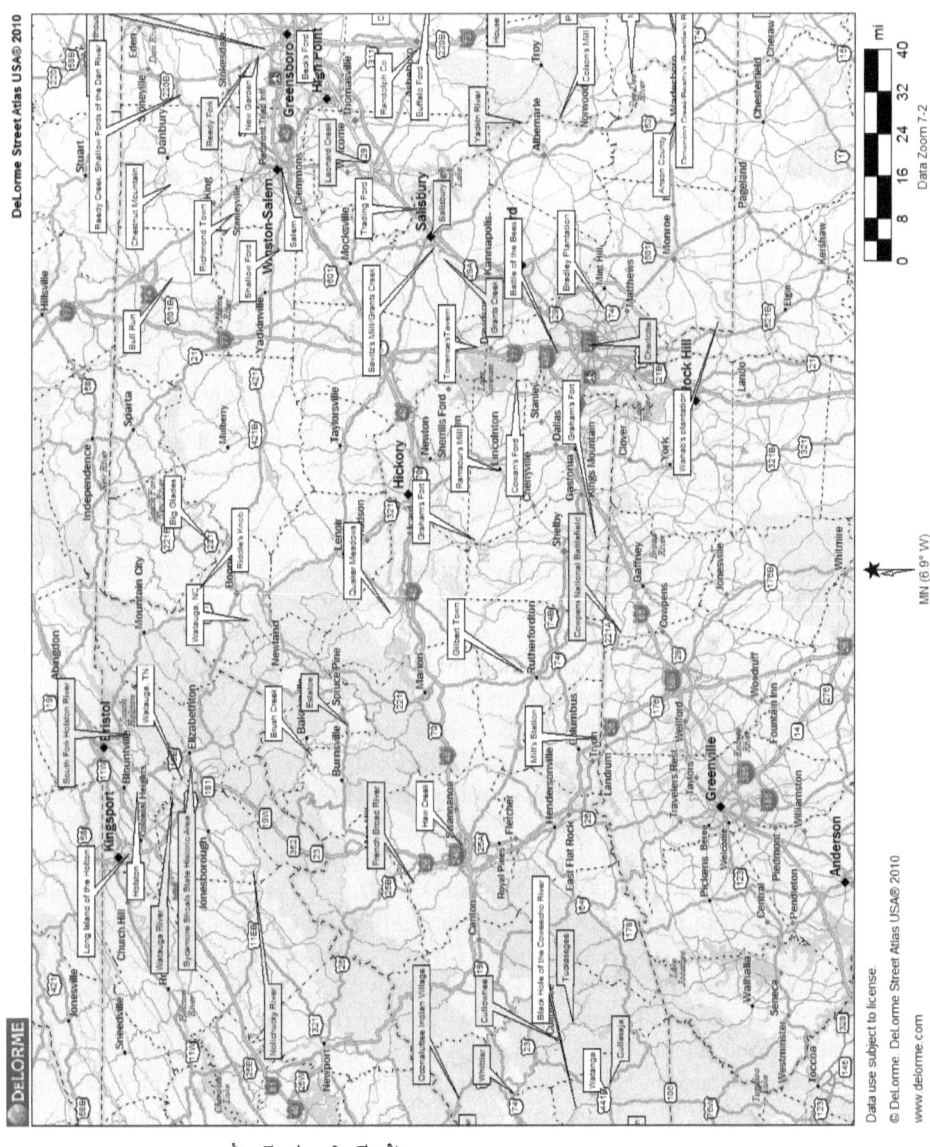

North Carolina west: Map for The Guide to the American Revolutionary War in Pennsylvania, Delaware, Maryland, Virginia, and North Carolina © 2011 DeLorme (www.delorme.com) Street Atlas USA®

Franklin
Wayah
Black Hole of the Coweecho River (Sept. 19, 1776)

> Black Hole was 5.7 miles north of the present town of Franklin at what is now Cowee. There are historical markers commemorating General Griffith Rutherford's (ca. 1731–1800) expedition against the Cherokees at routes:
> U.S. 19/23/74 at Hominy Creek east of Canton
> U.S. 276 at Pigeon Gap east of Waynesville
> NC 1243 (Old U.S. 19 Alternate/23) at Balsam Gap southwest of Waynesville
> U.S. 23/441 at NC 116 southwest of Webster
> U.S. 23/441 southwest of Dillsboro at the Jackson/Macon County line.[171]

★ The governments of Virginia, North Carolina, South Carolina, and Georgia cooperated to mount a campaign against the Cherokees in retaliation for their raids in July and August 1776. General Griffith Rutherford's (ca. 1731–1800) North Carolinians were to rendezvous with Colonel Andrew Williamson's (ca. 1730–1836) South Carolinians to attack the lower and middle Cherokee settlements. Colonel William Christian's (ca. 1743–1786) Virginians were to strike the Over-Hill Cherokees in the west. The Georgians were to head north to attack the settlements in northern Georgia.

General Rutherford's expedition against the Cherokees proceeded as far as their middle towns (present-day Chattanooga) and drove the Cherokees from their villages on the Little Tennessee River, destroyed their houses and crops, and drove away their cattle. The route of his march was long known as Rutherford's Trace. It passed along Hominy Creek east of Canton, through Pigeon Gap and Balsam Gap, along Savannah Creek, and through Cowee Gap.

See also Tamassee in *The Guide to the American Revolutionary War in South Carolina*.

Colonel Williamson left 300 men to guard Fort Rutledge at Esseneca while he took 2,000 militiamen to rendezvous with General Rutherford. Catawba scouts guided his party through Rabun Gap to the Tennessee River. They reached the town of Coweechee on Tuesday, September 17, 1776 but Rutherford was not there. The South Carolinians followed the Coweecho River through narrow trails up the mountains. They fell into an ambush at Wayah, a mountain cove known as the Black Hole (about 9 miles west of the present town of Franklin, North Carolina) on Thursday, the 19th. Lieutenant Edward Hampton's (1740–1781) advance party was attacked by 300 Cherokees and Loyalist militiamen. Major McJunkin recorded the event:

> In an instant in front, in rear, on the right and the left, the warwhoop sounded.
>
> The warwhoop was answered by a shout of defiance, and the rifles of the Indians answered by an aim equally deadly. The whites were pressed into a circle by their foes and hence the battle was called the Ring Fight. As soon as the firing was heard the main army pressed to the rescue. Before their arrival the advance had to contend with fearful odds. It was not only a woodsman's fight from tree to tree, but often from hand to hand. Among these, Major Ross of York District had a hard scuffle with an Indian.[172]

See also Tamassee (Tomassy), Ring Fight in *The Guide to the American Revolutionary War in South Carolina.*.

Captain Edward Hampton's (1746–1781) men held off the Cherokees until Colonel Thomas Neal's (1730–1799) regiment and the militia arrived from Ninety Six, South Carolina. The Cherokees mistook the Catawbas, fighting with the militia, as allies, and did not fire at them. They soon realized their mistake. Noticing the Catawbas wore a buck tail in their hair to distinguish them from the Cherokees, the Cherokees began firing at anybody wearing a buck tail.

The only way to counterattack in the gorge was to charge straight at the Cherokees, which the South Carolinians did with fixed bayonets. The Cherokees were low on powder and withdrew. McJunkin noted that "a large quantity of parched corn, dressed deerskins and moccasins were left on the ground."

The South Carolinians lost 10 militiamen and one Catawba killed and 22 militiamen and two Catawbas wounded in the two-hour battle. The two wounded Catawbas died that night. The Cherokees lost four dead. Had the South Carolinians not mistaken the Cherokees for the Catawbas and held their fire several times during the battle, their loss would have been much greater. Williamson joined forces with Rutherford at Hiwassee, Tennessee on Friday, September 26th. Their combined force now numbered 4,000 men.[173]

Western North Carolina (Sept. 1776; Sept. 1–18, 1776; late Oct. 1776)

Most of what is described here happened in Tennessee, which was part of North Carolina at the time.

Colonel Andrew Williamson (ca. 1730–1836) reported an ambush and other Cherokee attacks during his Cherokee campaign in Western North Carolina in September 1776. Williamson lost 15 men killed and 21 wounded. His men killed at least 35 Cherokees.

★ General Griffith Rutherford (ca. 1731–1800) and about 2,500 North Carolina militiamen set out on Sunday, September 1, 1776. They marched west to attack the middle Cherokee villages along the Little Tennessee River. When he did not find Colonel Andrew Williamson (ca. 1730–1836), General Rutherford split his force. He left 800 men at Muquassee (now Franklin) and marched further west with the rest of his men. They attacked the valley towns and eventually rendezvoused with Williamson at Hiwassee (now Murphy), Tennessee. Rutherford burned all the villages along his route and returned home.

Colonel William Christian (ca. 1743–1786) and 2,000 Virginia and North Carolina militiamen proceeded down the Holston River from the north and burned the Overhill Cherokee villages. Realizing that they would get little assistance from the British, the dispirited Cherokees sued for peace. They ceded all their lands east of the Blue Ridge mountains and dropped their claims to land north of the Nolachucky River in the treaties of Dewitt's Corner, South Carolina (May 20, 1777) and the Long Island of the Holston (present-day Tennessee) (July 20, 1777).[174]

★ Captain Patrick Moore reported to General Griffith Rutherford (ca. 1731–1800) that he had killed two Cherokees in their deserted town in Western North Carolina in late October 1776.[174a]

French Broad River (Oct. 1776)

The French Broad River runs north and south of Asheville.

Colonel William Christian's (ca. 1743–1786) army of 2,000 Virginians and "over-the-mountain" men from Watauga, Tennessee crossed the Holston River on Tuesday, October 1, 1776 and proceeded to destroy the villages of the Overhill Cherokees from the valley of the Holston southwest into what is now East Tennessee. They paused for several days to gather additional troops, then followed a path that brought them to the

French Broad River two days ahead of the projected arrival date, October 15. The troops rested at "Six Mile Camp" at Chimney Top Mountain. Colonel John Sevier (1745–1815) and Colonel James Robertson (1742–1814) joined them here.

The combined forces headed toward the Tennessee River. They found that the Cherokees had withdrawn into the mountains, leaving behind their horses, cattle, pigs, 50,000 bushels of corn and 15,000 bushels of potatoes which they destroyed.[175]

Salisbury and vicinity
Salisbury (July 1778; Jan. 1782; March 13, 1782)
Savitz's (Savis's) Mill (ca. Feb. 2, 1781)
Trading Ford (Feb. 3–5, 1781)
Grants Creek (Feb. 4, 1781)

> Salisbury was a small frontier town which served as the military headquarters for western North Carolina during the Revolutionary War. Major General Nathanael Greene (1742–1786) was appalled to find "1700 stand of Continental Arms in one Store, kept for the use of the Militia, in the most miserable order you [can] imagine."
>
> The Savitz Mill was probably near where route NC 150 crosses Grants Creek west of Salisbury. General Charles Cornwallis and his army camped at Salisbury in 1780. A marker near the town well on South Church Street, near the northeast corner of the South Rowan library (201 W. Fisher Street), commemorates the camp.
>
> Trading Ford was also known as Island Ford. The site is flooded by High Rock Lake and is occupied by the Duke Power Company's Buck Steam Plant a few hundred yards downstream from where route I-85 crosses the Yadkin just northeast of Salisbury. The ford was on the old Trading Path which ran from Petersburg, Virginia to the Waxhaws. It was a critical location in the "Race to the Dan."
>
> The most direct route to the Dan River for General Daniel Morgan and his 1,800 men was east along the old Beattie's Ford Road to its junction with the Trading Path, called the Great Road at this time. From there, the road followed the route north, roughly parallel to Highway 29. According to Lieutenant Thomas Anderson's journal[176], the march was difficult, "every step up to our Knees in Mud it raining On us all the Way." Greene followed the same route a day later. Historians are less sure of the route taken by the 2,500 to 3,000 Crown troops.
>
> The citizens of Davidson County and the North Carolina Historical Commission dedicated a monument on October 19, 1929 to commemorate General Greene's crossing at Trading Ford. The monument was situated on a 1.1 acre lot which included the road over which Greene's forces passed. The bronze plaque reads: "Trading Ford General Nathanael Greene in his masterly retreat from the British Army under Lord Cornwallis, crossed the Yadkin at Trading Ford, 0.5 miles southeast of this spot, February 2–3, 1781. A sudden rise in the river prevented the passage of the British and permitted the Continental army to escape and prepare for the Battle of Guilford Court House"[177]
>
> Grants Creek is not far from what is now Greensboro in Rowan County. It is a little west of Salisbury.

David Fanning (1755–1825) escaped from jail at Ninety Six, South Carolina on June 1, 1778, after two days of imprisonment. He stole a horse and went to his cabin on Raeburn's Creek. The horse must have been very valuable because his pursuers offered

Fanning four horses in exchange for it. Fanning agreed to the deal and was allowed to return to Ninety Six. His captors broke their word and took him prisoner again, putting Fanning in an unknown jail near the Tyger River. They also took his clothes to prevent another escape. Fanning appeared before the local magistrate the next morning and was released on bail. When he went back to get his clothes and his horse, he was arrested again and taken before another magistrate who ordered him to jail.[178]

Fanning and another prisoner were tied together on the way to jail. Fanning managed to get a knife and cut the rope when the guards stopped for lunch. He jumped out a window and escaped without his traveling companion who had fallen asleep. Fanning arrived in North Carolina and joined Colonel Ambrose Mills (1722–1786) and his North Carolina Loyalist Militia who were preparing to go to St. Augustine, Florida. One of the recruits, a spy for the Whigs, informed Captain Henry Connelly (1741–1840) of the Loyalist militia's location. Governor Thomas Burke (ca.1747–1783) had given Connelly a commission to track down Fanning; so Connelly set out immediately with his North Carolina cavalry. They captured Colonel Mills and 16 of his men.

Fanning soon learned of Colonel Mills's capture and organized a party of 14 men to pursue Captain Connelly all the way to Gilbert Town. Connelly received reinforcements and went after Fanning again. He and his men pursued Fanning all night and were ambushed the following morning. They skirmished for an hour before the Loyalists withdrew. Neither side had any casualties.

Fanning was captured again a short time later and sent back to jail at Ninety Six. He escaped again by cutting through the bars with "two files and a knife." He would be captured several more times in 1778, but he managed to escape each time.[179]

★ Captain William Armstrong (1737–1783) and nine mounted militiamen encountered "42 footmen and 15 dragoons" on a foraging raid at Savitz's Mill in Rowan County about Friday, February 2, 1781. They exchanged fire and the foraging party withdrew.[180]

★ The Race for the Dan River began after the Continental and Crown armies crossed Cowan's Ford on Thursday, February 1, 1781. It is called a race because both armies tried to reach the Dan River, the North Carolina and Virginia border, as quickly as possible. If Major General Nathanael Greene (1742–1786) crossed into Virginia first, General Charles Cornwallis (1738–1805) would remain in North Carolina, cut off from his supplies. If Cornwallis crossed the Dan first, he could destroy Greene's army.

General Cornwallis reached Salisbury on Saturday, February 3rd and learned that Brigadier General Daniel Morgan (1736–1802) was at the Trading Ford preparing to cross the Yadkin River. He sent Brigadier General Charles O'Hara (1740–1802) and the Guards to prevent Morgan from crossing the river and pin him against the Yadkin which was overflowing its banks after several days of rain. However, Morgan and his men had already crossed the river in flat boats.

General O'Hara approached the river at midnight and found some militia wagons stuck in the mud. Major David Campbell (1750–1812) and 100 Virginia riflemen and 50 of Captain Joseph Graham's (1759–1836) North Carolina militia cavalry were waiting in ambush nearby in a branch of the south side of the river, and under the darkness of the trees. Graham says that

> the militia were drawn up near a half mile from the ford, where a branch crosses which was covered with small timber and bushes, and there was an old field along the road in their front. . . . The American position was low along the branch, under shade of the timber; that of the advancing foe was open and on higher ground, and between them and the sky, was quite visible. When they came within sixty steps, the

Americans commenced firing, the enemy returned it and began to form in line. As their rear came up, they extended their line to the right, and were turning the left flank of the militia by crossing the branch above. This being discovered, a retreat was ordered after having fired, some two, some three rounds.[181]

Major David Campbell (1750–1812) ordered his Virginia riflemen to fire two shots, then leave the ford. The moonlight silhouetted the Crown troops marching along the higher ground. The riflemen fired their two shots, killing or wounding about 10 or 12 Redcoats. The Crown troops charged with the bayonet, killed two militiamen and captured 10 riflemen. The remaining riflemen and militiamen withdrew quickly to the Yadkin. They boarded canoes that were hidden there and crossed the river. General O'Hara learned that the riflemen were guarding some baggage wagons. His men captured the wagons which carried the baggage of the defeated militia from Cowan's Ford.

General O'Hara returned to Salisbury that night, despite the poor roads. His men had marched 34 miles that day and part of the night. They remained in Salisbury to rest on the 4th.

General Cornwallis reached Trading Ford the morning of the 4th and positioned some artillery on the "Heights of Gowerie", and began firing into General Greene's camp across the river. They fired round shot which only hit a cabin where General Greene had set up his headquarters. The balls splintered the walls and shingles, but General Greene remained inside the cabin writing orders, according to Dr. William Read's (1754–1845) eyewitness account.[182]

★ Brigadier General Daniel Morgan's (1736–1802) army at Trading Ford prevented General Charles Cornwallis (1738–1805) from crossing the Yadkin; so General Cornwallis sent Lieutenant Colonel Banastre Tarleton (1744–1833) to reconnoiter other crossing sites on Sunday, February 4, 1781. Colonel Francis Locke's (1732–1796) 100 North Carolina militiamen, engaged in destroying the bridge at Grants Creek, kept Tarleton's dragoons from crossing for three hours. Tarleton's legionnaires crossed the river upstream near the mouth of the creek and circled around to the militia's rear. The militiamen fled with the dragoons in pursuit. They had only one man wounded while retreating. The legionnaires then continued reconnoitering without any opposition.

Major General Nathanael Greene (1742–1786) marched toward Guilford later in the evening while General Cornwallis returned to Salisbury on the morning of the 5th and remained there until the 6th when they set out for the Shallow Ford, 40 miles to the north. General Cornwallis crossed the Yadkin river during the night and was on the opposite bank by the 7th. He went to Salem, a small Moravian town. The camp followers looted the village, and a band of Whig guerrillas came behind the camp followers and stripped the town clean of what was left, including the inhabitants' clothes.[183]

★ Colonel David Fanning (1755–1825) rode to the Randolph County Courthouse early Wednesday morning, March 13, 1782. He hoped to capture all the Whig leaders as elections were scheduled for this day. However, the leaders were warned that he was coming, so they did not show up and the election did not occur. Colonel Fanning torched the property of known Whig officers within 40 miles.

The Loyalists rode to Major Thomas Dugan's or Dougan (1748–1822) plantation on Deep River. Dugan was not at home, but his property was destroyed. After leaving Dugan's plantation, Fanning's men caught Lieutenant Colonel Archibald Murphy (d. 1782) of the Caswell County Regiment of Militia with several Loyalists in a wagon. They were being taken to Salisbury to be hanged. After asking the condemned men what should be done with Lieutenant Colonel Murphy, Colonel Fanning immediately took him to a tree and hanged him.

Captain Joseph Clark (1756–before 1793) and a force of about 300 North Carolina militiamen rode toward the Loyalists less than 15 minutes later. The Loyalists fled. As the Loyalists had better horses, Captain Clark's men could not catch them. However, Captain Clark did catch John Dugan, one of Fanning's men who stayed behind to plunder Lieutenant Colonel Murphy's corpse. Major Dugan was wounded and convinced Captain Clark that he was dying. The Whigs left him for dead and, as soon as they left, Dugan got up and ran away.

Governor Thomas Burke (ca.1747–1783) asked Colonel Fanning to remain neutral while his demands were being considered in April. However, Governor Burke was not being totally honest. He simply wanted a cease fire while the General Assembly met in Hillsborough. A temporary truce went into effect and when the General Assembly adjourned, Governor Burke notified Colonel Fanning that the legislature had turned down his proposal. The governor also ordered Major Thomas Hogg and the North Carolina State Legion to take an expedition into the Deep River settlements to keep Colonel Fanning occupied. However, this expedition did not happen due to an argument between Major Hogg and Major Bennett Crafton over who would be in charge.[184]

The residents of the Salisbury district complained that the militia
> Committed and perpetrated Numberless barbarities, Assassinations, Murders, and Robberies throughout the whole district…and whenever they apprehended a person or more either in his own house the Woods or Highways if he was not immediately hanged, shot, or otherwise put to Death, he would be ordered under a Guard, and under pretense of sending such supposed Offender to Salisbury Jail, and then on the way thither were oftentimes murdered in Cool blood, others again have been hanged up two or three times until almost dead, and then shot by way of diversion, thus put to Death in the most torturing manner; many have been the cruel and barbarous methods…Numbers of persons such as Women and Children have been tortured, hung up and strangled, cut down, and hung up again, sometimes branded with brands or other hot irons in order to extort Confessions from them…and after torturing them, and practicing every kind of Cruelty the most Savage heart could suggest, then would go off triumphantly, after first having plundered and rob'd the poor man's house of every Article they could lay their hands on, and sometimes set the house on fire.[185]

Lincolnton
Ramsour's (Ramsaur's or Ramseur's) Mill (June 20, 1780)
Near Ramsour's Mill (July 1780)

Ramsour's mill was about 0.5 miles north of the present village of Lincolnton and 34 miles northwest of Charlotte. The town and the county are named for Major General Benjamin Lincoln (1733–1810), who commanded the Southern Department of the Continental Army. At the intersection of route NC 27 W (West Main Street) and North Aspen Street, go north on North Aspen Street for about half a mile to the Lincolnton High School where a historical marker commemorates the Battle of Ramsour's Mill.

Ramsour's Mill was located along Clark Creek about 400 yards west of Battleground Road, just before it becomes Jeb Seagle Drive. The millpond has been filled in and there is nothing to identify the location of the mill. To get to the battlefield, turn onto Paul H. Lawing Drive (Skip Lawing Drive) just south of the marker and go west for 0.3 miles to Jeb Seagle Drive. Follow Jeb Seagle Drive around Battleground

Stadium on the left and Lincolnton Middle School on the right. Turn right into the school's parking lot. (Jeb Seagle Drive also runs west off North Aspen Street north of the historical marker.)

The construction of the three public schools has changed the battlefield's historical integrity, but there is still much to see here. A grove of trees on a hill between Lincolnton Middle School and Battleground Elementary School has an audio station (which was not functioning at the time of our visit) which gives a brief synopsis of the battle. A small marker near the audio station marks the spot where the Loyalists made their final stand in a long trench. It also marks a mass grave where some 70 bodies were buried the day after the battle (see Photo NC-12). As the men did not wear uniforms, it was impossible to distinguish between Whigs and Loyalists, so the dead from both sides were respectfully buried together in a deep trench on the west side of the hill. As men continued to die from their wounds in subsequent days, other graves had to be opened. There are four known burial sites in the area around the schools. John Martin Shuford's (1744–1780) grave is on Jeb Seagle Drive at Tuckaseegee Road, across from the schools.

The Warlick Monument (see Photo NC-13), at the summit of the hill near the playground behind (south of) the Battleground Elementary School, commemorates Captain Johann Nicholas Warlick (1736–1780), a Loyalist officer who died in an attack on horseback. His brother, Philip (1748–1780), and Israel Sain (d. 1780), another Loyalist are also buried here. Any surface evidence of the grave was obliterated by the grading that accompanied the building of the school and the neighboring development. A small park on the east side of the bus parking lot at the rear

NC-12. Site of the battle of Ramsour's Mill. The small marker identifies the spot where the Loyalists made their final stand in a long trench. The square area is a mass grave where some 70 bodies of the dead from both sides were buried the day after the battle.

NC-13. Warlick Monument. The monument commemorates Captain Johann Nicholas Warlick, a Loyalist officer who died in the attack on horseback, his brother Philip and Israel Sain, another Loyalist.

of Lincolnton Middle School contains millstones from Ramsour's Mill (see Photo NC-14).

General Charles Cornwallis (1738–1805) and 2,500 soldiers camped here, a few hundred yards from the mill, on January 24, 1781, just seven months after the battle. They were in pursuit of Brigadier General Daniel Morgan (1736–1802) who was moving to join forces with Major General Greene. Here, he burned his baggage to hasten his pursuit.

Go to the southern end of Lincolnton Middle School and go around the corner of the building. In the trees south of the athletic field, look to the left down the hill. A large brick tomb (see Photo NC-15) between the field and Jeb Seagle Drive is the

NC-14. Millstones from Ramsour's Mill

NC-15. Tomb of six Whig captains who died in the battle at Ramsour's Mill, including John Dobson, John Bowman and Galbraith Falls who led the initial charge on horseback and was the first man killed in the battle.

final resting place of six Whig captains who died in the battle, including John Dobson (d. 1780), John Bowman (d. 1780) and Galbraith Falls (1730–1780). Captain Falls led the initial charge on horseback and was the first soldier killed in the battle.

The lobby of the James W. Warren Citizens Center (115 West Main Street), across the street from the Lincoln County Courthouse on Court Square, has a wall-size mural depicting Ramsour's Mill just before the start of the battle. A granite rock near the end of the northern lawn of the courthouse grounds was moved here from the Ramsour's Mill battleground. It is known as "Tarleton's Tea Table." Legend has it that Lieutenant Colonel Banastre Tarleton (1744–1833) enjoyed tea upon the rock while he camped in Lincolnton in 1781 (see Photo NC-16).

Partisan warfare began in North Carolina on Tuesday, June 20, 1780 at Jacob Ramsour's Mill. Loyalist Colonel John Moore (1758–1836) returned to his home near Ramsour's Mill in Lincoln County in early June 1780 after serving with General Charles Cornwallis (1738–1805) in South Carolina. He convened a meeting at his father's house, about 6 miles west of Ramsour's Mill, on Saturday, June 10. Moore told the 40 or so men who attended that General Cornwallis planned to invade North Carolina in early September now that South Carolina and Georgia were well under control. He wanted Loyalists to rally to the King's standards at Ramsour's Mill on June 13. Loyalists saw an opportunity to avenge their defeat at the Battle of Moores Creek and to settle old grudges. Moore proclaimed himself as lieutenant colonel of Lieutenant Colonel John Hamilton's (d. 1817) North Carolina Loyalist regiment. About 200 Loyalists gathered on the east bank of Clark's Creek opposite Ramsour's Mill on Tuesday, June 13th and more continued to arrive over the following days. By June 20, 1,100 to 1,300 men had

NC-16. Tarleton's Tea Table. According to legend, Lieutenant Colonel Banastre Tarleton enjoyed tea on this rock while he camped in Lincolnton in 1781.

come. About one-quarter (300) of them were unarmed. Others were either too young or too old to fight.

The Whigs only had militiamen to resist the Loyalists until a new Continental Army arrived. General Griffith Rutherford (ca. 1731–1800) mustered about 800 men at a plantation near Charlotte (35 miles away) and organized them in three divisions: Major William Richardson Davie (1756–1820) commanded a body of 65 dragoons, Colonel William Lee Davidson (1746–1781) led a battalion of 300 light infantrymen and General Rutherford commanded the remaining infantrymen. Colonel Francis Locke (1732–1796) mustered additional militiamen at Mountain Creek, 16 miles northeast of Ramsour's Mill. Major Joseph McDowell (1756–1801) assembled another group of 270 which brought Locke's total to 400 men. Locke, who was closer than Rutherford, set out to attack Moore's Loyalists on June 19 with three small companies of mounted men leading an unorganized crowd of inexperienced, undisciplined, armed civilians. Rutherford remained in place so as not to leave Charlotte undefended. The Whigs wore white papers in their hats to distinguish themselves from the Loyalists who wore twigs of pine.

Moore's forces apparently held a fairly secure position along the crest of a long ridge about 300 yards from the mill, just north of the present town of Lincolnton. The long, clear slope in front of them gave them a good field of fire for more than 200 yards. They outnumbered the militiamen almost three to one, but they were equally irregular in organization and discipline. Moore stationed a picket guard of 12 men about 600 yards in front of the encampment.

Locke's dragoons approached about daybreak in thick fog that limited visibility to about 50 feet. They surprised the pickets who fired a few volleys and fled to the camp, throwing it into confusion. The cavalry galloped up the hill after them. Some of the Loyalists fled without firing a single shot. Others, seeing only the few dragoons rallied, opened fire and drove the dragoons back down the hill. When the Continental infantry appeared, they formed a line at the foot of the slope (see Photo NC-15) and opened fire.

The Loyalists responded and retreated over the top of the hill and came forward again. A small group of Whigs flanked them on the right and another group flanked them on the left, causing them to retreat to the hilltop. This event was purely accidental, as there was no central command of the units and each captain led his men as he deemed proper at the moment.

Nonetheless, Locke's forces got to the rear of the Loyalists and engaged them at close quarters. Nobody had any bayonets, so they fought with clubbed muskets. Some used rocks or fists. Some had been hit so hard that impressions of the gunlocks were embedded in their heads. The papers and twigs quickly fell off the hats in the heat of combat, causing great confusion, as neither side could distinguish friend from foe.

When Loyalist Captain Johann Nicholas Warlick (1736–1780) was shot, his men fled down the far side of the hill and across a creek where they halted. Warlick had been particularly effective as a commander in the conflict. His death caused Loyalists' efforts to collapse.

Locke tried to re-form his men on the top of the hill, expecting the Loyalists to resume the fight. However, he could muster only 110 of his original 400 men. He sent a messenger to Rutherford, who was already on the march and only about 7 miles away, "to hasten with all possible speed," but Moore requested a truce to collect the wounded and bury the dead (see Photo NC-13). Locke refused the request and gave the Loyalists

10 minutes to surrender. During this time, Moore told his men to scatter; so, when the flag of truce returned, only 50 men remained and they left almost immediately. Moore and 30 men joined Lord Francis Rawdon (1754–1826) at Camden. Moore was threatened with a court-martial, which was considered politically unwise, for leading the Loyalists into battle before Cornwallis had instructed him.

The two-hour action at Ramsour's Mill was more a clash of armed mobs than a real battle. Only about 250 of Locke's 400 men were in the fight, but more than 150 were killed or wounded. The Loyalists had about 700 engaged and had about an equal number of losses, including about 50 prisoners, most of whom were quickly paroled.

The Loyalists had waited four years for the British troops to come to North Carolina. They were discouraged again, disheartened, and weary of fighting. When Major Patrick Ferguson (1744–1780) arrived in the area later that year, they were not eager to join him. The battle at Ramsour's Mill may have deprived Ferguson of 1,000 troops who might have changed the outcome of the battle at Kings Mountain.

Colonel Daniel Morgan (1736–1802) passed by Ramsour's Mill after the Battle of Cowpens, and Cornwallis stopped there soon afterward to burn his baggage to lighten his load for his pursuit of Morgan and Major General Nathanael Greene (1742–1786). Brigadier General Charles O'Hara (1740–1802) questioned his commander's judgment:

> In the situation, without baggage, necessaries, or provisions of any sort for officer or soldier, in the most barren, inhospitable, unhealthy part of North America, opposed to the most savage, inveterate, perfidious, cruel enemy, with zeal and bayonets only, it was resolved to follow Greene's army to the end of the world.[186]

★ Brigadier General Thomas Sumter (1734–1832) missed the battle at Ramsour's Mill as he waited for much needed supplies. When he arrived, he set up camp and a small party of Georgia militiamen joined him. One of those militiamen was Patrick Carr, commonly known as Paddy Carr. After he arrived in camp in July 1780, Carr and another militiaman went to the home of a Loyalist near Ramsour's Mill. Carr asked the man if he had joined Colonel John Moore's (1758–1836) Loyalists at the battle. He responded that he had and was captured and later pardoned by General Griffith Rutherford (ca. 1731–1800). As it was getting dark, Carr asked the man if he knew the way to Sumter's camp. The Loyalist told him to take the path and turn at the fork. Carr asked the man to show him the way. The man agreed. When they arrived at the fork, the man indicated the direction to take and Carr shot him dead.

After returning to camp, Carr told Colonel Richard Winn (1750–1818) about the incident. Winn brought Carr to the local magistrate for committing murder. The magistrate released Carr the next day without a trial.[187]

Laurel Hill, Lincoln County
Graham's Fort (Sept. 1780)

> Graham's Fort was on route U.S. 226 about 400 yards north of Buffalo Creek in Cleveland County.

The Loyalists wanted to capture Colonel William Graham (1742–1835), a delegate to the Fifth Provincial Congress, a framer of North Carolina's first state constitution, and a participant in the conflicts at Moores Creek Bridge and Ramsour's Mill. Graham had constructed a large log cabin on Buffalo Creek. It became known as Graham's Fort because it was the strongest house in the area. Many people would gather here to protect themselves from the Loyalists.

A band of Loyalists approached the fort in September 1780 and demanded to enter the fort which was occupied by Graham, two other men, and many young, old and infirmed settlers. Colonel Graham refused to let the Loyalists in. They attacked, firing at the house and demanding Graham to surrender after each volley. Since the Loyalists caused little damage, Graham refused. John Burke (d. 1780), one of the Loyalists, ran to the cabin and put the barrel of his musket through a crack, pointed at 19-year-old William Twitty (1761–1816). Before Burke fired, Susan Twitty (1763–1825), William's 17-year-old sister, pulled him to safety and the musket ball hit the wall. As Burke reloaded, William fired through the crack, hitting Burke in the head. Susan ran out of the fort, grabbed Burke's musket and ammunition and returned inside, firing at the Loyalists as fast as she could load.

The Loyalists withdrew after losing Burke and having four others wounded. Graham sent his pregnant wife and the others in the fort to a safer location before moving his men to another site. The Loyalists then returned to plunder the fort and capture six slaves.[188]

Gilbert Town (June 1778; Sept. 12, 1780; Oct. 1780)

Gilbert Town was located about 3 miles north of present-day Rutherfordton about 1.5 miles east of route US 221 N and 1 mile west of route US 64. It was on the high ground between Cathey's Creek to the north and Holland's (Shepherd's) Creek to the south, about 3 miles east of Rutherfordton. Ferguson's Hill overlooked it all on the west. (Ferguson's Hill is now generally called Ferguson's Ridge.) Roads entered from Cane Creek, Fort McGauhey, and Brittain Church to the east; Quaker Meadows and Camp Creek to the north; Montford's Cove and Mountain Creek to the west; and the Broad River and Cleghorn's Creek to the south. Marlin's Knob in the South Mountains on the east side of Cane Creek was easily visible from Ferguson's Hill and the other high points. Loyalist Lieutenant Anthony Allaire, in his diary,[189] describes Gilbert Town as consisting of "one dwelling house, one barn, a blacksmith's shop, and some out-houses." The site is now private property.

★ Loyalist Lieutenant Colonel Samuel Smith (1752–1839) and his men joined Colonel David Fanning (1755–1825), but they were soon captured by Captain John Gowen (1740–1810) near Gilbert Town in June 1778 and sent to the jail at Ninety Six in South Carolina. Fanning escaped two days after his arrival in July.

★ Major Patrick Ferguson (1744–1780) arrived at Gilbert Town on Friday, September 1, 1780 and set up camp there. He used William Gilbert's (ca. 1732–1790) home while his troops camped on the high hill behind the Gilbert house, ever since known as "Ferguson's Hill." Ferguson led his men to the head of Cane Creek to surprise Colonel Charles McDowell (1743–1815) and the Burke County militia.

McDowell learned that Ferguson was camped at White Oak Spring, 2 miles east of Brindletown, on the road from Morganton to Gilbert Town. Too weak to meet Ferguson on equal terms, McDowell took his men to Bedford's Hill to ambush Ferguson as he marched south. This spot is located about 15 miles from Gilbert Town, in a narrow valley of Cane Creek. It is near a crossing called Cowan's Ford (not to be confused with the Cowan's Ford northwest of Charlotte where Colonel William Lee Davidson (1746–1781) was killed after the battle of Cowpens).

McDowell surprised Ferguson and defeated him on Tuesday, September 12, 1780. Major James Dunlap (1740–1781) was wounded and Ferguson retired to Gilbert Town.

Ferguson and his men took poultry, stock, cattle, and anything else of use to them. Ferguson assigned 20 men to protect Major Dunlap during his recuperation. They stayed 11 days. Meanwhile Ferguson used Gilbert Town as his base for foraging raids. Major Ferguson and his men left Gilbert Town on September 27 as the Overmountain Men pursued him to Kings Mountain.

★ Captain James Dunlap (d. 1781), wounded at Cane Creek in September 1780, was recovering at Mrs. Gilbert's house in Gilbert Town in October. Captain Daniel Gillespie (1743–1829) and two or three men rode up from Spartanburg, South Carolina to find Captain Dunlap as General Charles Cornwallis (1738–1805) retreated from North Carolina. When they arrived at the Gilbert house, Mrs. Gilbert mistook them for Loyalists who had some important communication for Dunlap and let them in. Gillespie told her that he and his men were there to kill Dunlap because he had killed some of their friends and abducted Captain Gillespie's fiancée, Mary McRea.

Dunlap had kept Mary McRea hoping she would accede to his desires, but she supposedly died of a broken heart instead. Gillespie climbed the stairs to Dunlap's bed demanding where Mary McRae was. Dunlap replied she was in heaven, whereupon Gillespie shot him and left him for dead. Dunlap did not die; but his friends hid him and took him to Ninety Six, South Carolina.[190]

Charlotte and vicinity
Wahab's (Wahub's) Plantation (Sept. 21, 1780)
Charlotte (Sept. 26, 1780; Oct. 7, 1780)
The Battle of the Bees (Oct. 3, 1780)
Polk's Mill (Oct. 9, 1780)
Evacuation of Charlotte Town (Oct. 13, 1780)
Bradley's Plantation (Nov. 14, 1780)

> The plantation owned by Captain James Wahab (or Wauchope) (1724–1798), one of Colonel William Richardson Davie's (1756–1820) officers, was located about 25 miles south of Charlotte, near Waxhaw Creek in Waxhaw. The plantation was probably north of the intersection of Walkup (also known as Wauchope) Road and Jaars Road.[191]
>
> The McIntyre Farm was at the intersection of McIntyre Avenue and route NC 2074 (Beatties Ford Road), about a mile west of route I-77 S (U.S. 21|Shoreway Drive) and 6 miles north of Charlotte. The site contains the foundation of the log house which John McIntyre built soon after he purchased the property in 1769 and which was destroyed in the early 1940s. A pathway with signs interpret the history of the site and its historical context.[192]
>
> Francis Bradley's (1743–1780) plantation was 8 miles southeast of Charlotte.

General Charles Cornwallis (1738–1805) commanded the King's army in the South in September 1780. He decided to move northward from South Carolina toward Virginia, but Whig militiamen kept attacking his outposts and detached units. One of these skirmishes occurred at Wahab's Plantation. Cornwallis led the main column up the left (east) side of the Wateree River toward the Waxhaws. The column comprised the 7th, 23rd, 33rd, and 71st regiments of infantry, the Volunteers of Ireland, Lieutenant Colonel John Hamilton's (d. 1817) and Colonel Samuel Bryan's (1756–1813) North

Carolina Tory regiments, a detachment of horse and four guns. They marched on Friday, September 8, 1780.

Lieutenant Colonel Banastre Tarleton (1744–1833) led the second column up the right side of the river parallel with Cornwallis. His column consisted of the British Legion cavalry and infantry and an additional detachment of light infantry with one small field piece. Tarleton was ill and temporarily turned over command of his Legion to Major George Hanger (ca. 1751–1824). Hanger and his men camped at Wahab's plantation some distance away from Cornwallis on Wednesday, September 20, 1780.

Colonel William Richardson Davie (1756–1820), in command of 80 mounted North Carolina militiamen and 70 riflemen under Major George Davidson (1735–1811), surprised Hanger and a band of about 60 legionnaires at Wahab's Plantation the following morning. Davie, acting on information from a local spy, positioned his men to trap the Loyalists. The legionnaires had pulled in their sentries and were resting near a cornfield. Most of Davidson's riflemen crept through the corn while Davie's mounted troops and the remaining riflemen went to the other end of a lane that ran through the plantation.

The riflemen took possession of one of the plantation buildings in the rear and began to fire on the legionnaires. At the first shots, Hanger and his men charged, sending the Loyalists fleeing in confusion. As they fled, they came under a sharp fire from Davidson's riflemen which killed 15 or 20 and wounded 40 more. Davie had only one man wounded—from friendly fire. His men captured 96 fully equipped horses and 120 stand of arms. Davie quickly retired to his camp at Providence before Cornwallis's troops arrived. The Loyalists later burned the plantation house in retaliation.[193]

★ General Charles Cornwallis (1738–1805) and his army advanced to Charlotte, thinking that large numbers of North Carolina Loyalists would join his army. Captain Joseph Graham's (1759–1836) pickets discovered the British advance guard moving toward the town on Tuesday morning, September 26, 1780. Colonel William Richardson Davie (1756–1820) had placed Captain John Brandon's militia at the courthouse where they had the protection of a chest-high stone wall. Major Joseph Dickson (1745–1825) and his men were posted in front of Graham, in houses to the left and right of the courthouse.

Lieutenant Colonel Banastre Tarleton (1744–1833) arrived with his American Legion, but, as he was ill from yellow fever, he soon turned over command to Major George Hanger (ca. 1751–1824). Graham's pickets sniped at the British as they formed into line 300 yards in front of the courthouse. The British dragoons deployed in subdivisions and the infantry in platoons with their columns about 100 yards apart.

Hanger's dragoons charged Davie's militia. When they got within 60 yards of the courthouse, the militiamen rose from behind a wall and fired a volley which broke the charge. The Legion withdrew and the British light infantry advanced to flank the militia. The dragoons reformed and charged the center. Another militia volley sent them back in confusion. The Legion infantry and the light infantry turned Davie's flank. His companies withdrew and formed a single line at the end of the street, 100 yards from the courthouse. The dragoons tried to break Davie's line, but they retired behind the houses after receiving an intense volley.

By this time, General Cornwallis had ridden to the front and encouraged Hanger's men to advance, dispersing the militia through the woods. The militia withdrew to the Salisbury road and out of the town to gather at Kennedy Creek to wait for another British attack. When a platoon of infantry appeared, they fired. The British returned fire, but the musket balls had little effect in the trees, so they withdrew.

Graham and Brandon's men held a hill at Sugar Creek Church and began to fire on the British light infantry about 250 yards away. The light infantry took positions behind trees and fences. Both sides exchanged fire for nearly half an hour at long range with little effect.

Hanger arrived with his dragoons and charged into the militia, wounding Graham badly with three bullet wounds in the thigh, a saber thrust in the side, a gash on the neck, and four cuts to the forehead. He later wrote of his head wound that, "some of my brains exuded." Lieutenant George Locke (1752–1780), the son of General Matthew Locke (1730–1801), was cut to pieces by the Legion sabers as he tried to shield himself with his rifle barrel. Graham's men fled into the woods.

As the British withdrew to Charlotte, they found Graham badly wounded and left him to die. He managed to crawl to a spring near a church where Susan Wilson discovered him at sunset. She rushed to get her mother and they brought Graham back to their home and nursed his wounds. Five months later, Graham was at Cowan's Ford, trying to stop Cornwallis again. Davie's men inflicted 22 casualties but lost about eight men killed, 10 wounded, and 12 captured. General Cornwallis occupied the town that day and remained until October 14th.

★ General William Lee Davidson (1746–1781) came to support Colonel William Richardson Davie (1756–1820) with the Rowan and Mecklenburg militia on Saturday, September 30, 1780. They detached parties of riflemen to snipe at the enemy's pickets and surprise their foraging parties. General Charles Cornwallis (1738–1805) sent out foraging parties to replenish his supplies a week after arriving in Charlotte. He sent Captain John Doyle (ca. 1750–1834) and a large foraging party of 450 Provincials, probably the Volunteers of Ireland, out on Beattie's Ford Road with 60 wagons on Tuesday, October 3, 1780 (some sources date this event as occurring on October 5).

A boy alerted the McIntyre family that the Loyalists were coming and then rode to inform local militia Captain James Thompson. Thompson mustered Captain James Knox (1752–1794) and 13 Scotch-Irish farmers to harass Doyle's troops. They hid some riflemen in two sections at the McIntyre farm. The foragers tied their horses to the farm wagons and plundered the barns and livestock pens. They loaded bags of corn and oats onto the baggage wagons when they arrived.

Someone accidentally knocked over some beehives during the pillaging and the Loyalists were soon attacked by the bees. An officer stood in the doorway laughing at the men swatting at the bees. As the Loyalists ran from the bees, Thompson and his men approached them. Thompson yelled to his men to pick a target and fire. The raiders formed a line to defend themselves while Thompson and his men reloaded and fired a second volley.

The raiders released some dogs that pursued a group of Thompson's men. "The dogs came on the trail of these retreating men, and the leading one sprung upon the heels of a man who had just discharged his rifle. A pistol-shot laid him dead; and the other dogs, coming up to him, paused, gave a howl, and returned." Believing he was attacked by a much larger force, Doyle ordered the retreat back to Charlotte. They rode so hard that "many of their horses fell dead in the streets." Farmers concealed along the retreat route fired at the foragers. The raiders lost eight men and two horses killed in the attack and twelve others wounded.[194]

★ Captains Edward Rutledge (1749–1800) and Joseph Dickson (1745–1825) and a detachment of militiamen attacked some Loyalists around Charlotte on Saturday, October 7, 1780. They lost one man killed and another wounded.

★ General Charles Cornwallis (1738–1805) established a post for foraging at Thomas Polk's (1732–1794) grist mill after he occupied Charlotte Town. When he returned from Kings Mountain, Captain Joseph Dickson (1745–1825) and a detachment of 120 mounted riflemen attacked Lieutenant Stephen Guyon's 20 Royal Welch Fusiliers and a detachment of Loyalist militia at Polk's mill on Monday, October 9, 1780. They captured the sentry of the Fusiliers and eight militiamen. Lieutenant Guyon defended the blockhouse and drove off the attackers, killing one and wounding another. A party of 50 riflemen stole 50 horses from Polk's plantation later that night.[195]

★ When General Charles Cornwallis (1738–1805) learned of the defeat at Kings Mountain, he decided to leave Charlotte Town and withdraw to Winnsboro, as his flank was now open. The British marched out of Charlotte on Thursday, October 12, 1780 guided by William McCafferty, a Charlotte merchant. They heard that General William Lee Davidson (1746–1781) was pursuing them with 5,000 soldiers and left Charlotte in a panic. General Davidson actually only had about 300 men. The roads turned to mud in the rain and the British abandoned 30 wagons 5 miles from Charlotte so they could move faster.

McCafferty, fearing reprisals from the Whigs, deserted as soon as it was dark, leaving the British to wander through the night. They became extremely disorganized and could not reunite until noon the following day. McCafferty rode all night to reach Major William Richardson Davie's (1756–1820) camp on Sugar Creek to inform him of the British retreat. Davie sent a large detachment to harass General Cornwallis's troops. They had a skirmish but the results are not known. Davie's men recovered the abandoned wagons which contained a printing press, supplies for the army, and the knapsacks of the light infantry and the British Legion. This left the Redcoats without provisions. They survived only on corn gathered from the fields they passed by for the next five days. They had no tents and had to sleep on the open ground with only their blankets. Many of the men, including Cornwallis, had yellow fever.

Charles Stedman (1753–1812) wrote that the Loyalist "militia were maltreated by abusive language, and even beaten by some of the officers in the Quarter-Master General's department. In consequence of this ill usage, several of them left the army the next morning forever, choosing to run the risk of meeting the resentment of their enemies, rather than submit to the derision and abuse of those to whom they looked up as friends."[196]

Davie's troops hounded the British for 15 days before they finally arrived in Winnsboro.[197]

★ Francis Bradley (1743–1780) who had participated in the "Battle of the Bees" terrorized the Loyalists in Mecklenburg County by harassing their scouts and foraging parties. He killed a number of British sentries at long range with his rifle during General Cornwallis's stay in Charlotte. Fed up, four Loyalists ambushed and killed Bradley at his plantation, 8 miles from Charlotte, on Tuesday, November 14, 1780.[198]

Cornelius
Cowan's Ford (Feb. 1, 1781)

> Cowan's Ford, also called McCowan's Ford, was near the Lincoln and Mecklenberg County border. The Battle at Cowan's Ford occurred between the bridge and the dam, near route NC 73 where it crosses the Catawba River south of Lake Norman,

> 8 miles west of the town of Cornelius. A marker on route NC 73 along the east shore of the reservoir commemorates the event.
>
> A monument to General William Lee Davidson is at Hicks Crossroads near the intersection of routes NC 73 and SR 2128 (Beatties Ford Road) about 2 miles east of where route NC 73 crosses the Catawba River near Cowan's Ford.

After the Continentals defeated the Crown forces at the Battle of Cowpens (in South Carolina) on Wednesday, January 17, 1781, Lord General Charles Cornwallis (1738–1805) wanted to defeat the forces commanded by Major General Nathanael Greene (1742–1786) and Brigadier General Daniel Morgan (1736–1802). When Cornwallis reached the Catawba River at Cowan's Ford, he had the option of taking a straight route suitable for wagons or a shallower one, for horses, that turned and crossed a small island before reaching the east bank some distance south of the other ford.

General William Lee Davidson (1746–1781) and his force of about 300 militiamen defended the shorter but harder horse route which Cornwallis took across the river. Dick Beale, Cornwallis's Loyalist guide, deserted without warning him about the two fords. Many British deserted and fled under enemy fire as they crossed the 500-yard-wide ford on Thursday, February 1, 1781. They inadvertently took the wagon route that made it tougher to cross the water but led to the more lightly defended route. Cornwallis's troops scrambled up the lightly defended banks and defeated Davidson before he could move reinforcements from the horse ford. As 34-year-old Davidson was forming his men along the high bank to delay Cornwallis as long as possible, a Loyalist fired from the middle of the stream and killed him. His men withdrew, leaving Cornwallis securely established on Greene's side of the Catawba. Cornwallis and Colonel James Webster (ca. 1743–1781), who crossed at Beatty's Ford 6 miles above Cowan's, joined forces at Givens's plantation, 2 miles from Beatty's Ford and 1 mile south of the Salisbury Road, in the afternoon after the crossing. Lieutenant Colonel Banastre Tarleton (1744–1833) joined them before night.

Robert Henry (1765–1863?), a local schoolboy posted at the wagon ford, thinks Davidson's militia inflicted many more casualties in the river crossing than they have been given credit for. He says that the swift current carried away most of the wounded who fell into the stream and drowned when they were hit. Tarleton gives the losses as 40 militiamen killed and wounded and the British losses as three killed and 26 wounded.[199]

Torrence's (Tarrant's or Torrance's) Tavern (Feb. 1, 1781)

> A state historical marker on route NC 115 near the intersection with route NC 1102 (Langtree Road), 0.3 miles south of Mount Mourne, commemorates the skirmish at Torrence's Tavern. The marker had been near the intersection with route NC 1108 but a road crew who probably mistook one intersection for another moved it here. The tavern was at neither intersection but probably between the two along route NC 115. The Whigs chose this location as their rendezvous on February 1, 1781 because of its proximity to Cowan's Ford and its importance for the defense of the Catawba. The Daughters of the American Revolution erected a marker nearby to mark the spot of the tavern and to honor the Revolutionary War soldiers from Centre Presbyterian.

After the Battle of Cowpens (January 17, 1781), General Charles Cornwallis (1738–1805), pursued Major General Nathanael Greene (1742–1786) across North Carolina hoping to catch and defeat him. He led his troops across the Catawba River at Cowan's Ford on Thursday, February 1, 1781 and scattered the rearguard of Greene's militia under Colonel William Lee Davidson (1746–1781).

Later the same day, Lieutenant Colonel Banastre Tarleton (1744–1833), on a reconnaissance mission with his cavalry, reinforced by the 23rd Regiment of Foot, attacked Davidson's militiamen as they tried to regroup at Torrence's Tavern, about 10 miles from the river. Tarleton claims to have attacked a force of nearly 500 with a much smaller detachment of his British Legion and the 23rd Regiment of Foot. He ordered them forward shouting, "Remember the Cowpens." The militiamen fired hastily and ran to their horses. Tarleton claims to have scattered and routed more than 500 militiamen, killing 50 and wounding many while only losing seven men and 20 horses. General Henry Clinton (1730–1795) gives the number of North Carolina militiamen dispersed by Tarleton as 300. Other sources say the militiamen only numbered between 100 and 300 and they lost only 10 dead. Several of these dead seem to have been unarmed old men who had come to the tavern when the alarm went out. Major Joseph Graham (1759–1836) mentions that the tavern itself was burned down after the attack.[200]

Greene waited for the militia at the rendezvous point (David Carr's house was 6 miles from Torrence's Tavern) until midnight when a messenger notified him that Davidson was dead and the militia dispersed, and that Cornwallis crossed the river. Greene rode on alone to Steele's Tavern in Salisbury, almost getting captured along the way. When he told his friend, Mr. Steele, that he was "alone, tired, hungry and penniless," Mrs. Steele overheard him. After she prepared the general's breakfast, she brought two little bags of hard money and gave them to him, saying, "You need them more than I do." Those two little bags contained the entire military treasury of the Grand Army of the Southern Department of the United States of America.

According to tradition, a portrait of George III hung over the fireplace when General Greene received this gift. He turned its face to the wall and wrote on the back of it, "Hide thy face, George, and blush."[201]

Greene wrote to Colonel Isaac Huger (1743–1797) (pronounced *Eugee*) instructing him to change direction and proceed toward the northwest to join Colonel Daniel Morgan (1736–1802) at Guilford Courthouse. While he was here, he also learned that the 1,700 muskets promised by the North Carolina government had arrived. However, due to poor storage, they had rusted and were useless. Greene then proceeded to join with Morgan.[202]

After defeating the militia at Cowan's Ford and Torrence's Tavern, General Cornwallis's troops could move through the area without any further resistance. These engagements hampered the recruitment of militia in the region for several weeks.[203]

Webster

Tuckasegee (March 1781)

> Tuckasegee was near present Webster.

Colonel John Sevier (1745–1815) and about 150 militia horsemen rode through the mountains in March 1781 to surprise the Cherokees at Tuckasegee near the head waters of the Little Tennessee River. They suspected the Cherokees of conspiring against the white settlers. Sevier lost only one man killed and one wounded but killed 30 Cherokees and took many more prisoners. He burned six towns and captured many horses and supplies before returning home.[204]

Mount Airy
Bull Run or Bull Creek (March 13, 1781)

> Bull Run or Bull Creek is about 7 miles south of Mount Airy near the junction of routes NC 2019 (Ararat Road) and NC 1003 (Siloam Road). The site was called Edwards Cross Roads in the 19th century.

Major General Nathanael Greene's (1742–1786) light infantry monitored General Charles Cornwallis's (1738–1805) movements toward the Deep River Quaker Meetinghouse on Tuesday, March 13, 1781. Lieutenant Colonel Henry "Light-Horse Harry" Lee (1756–1818) and his dragoons waited until the rear of the British column came to cross a branch of the Deep River before striking. They killed and wounded a great many and took 30 prisoners.

Lieutenant Colonel Banastre Tarleton (1744–1833) wrote that "The legion dragoons repulsed the enemy's detachment with some loss, and the royal army encamped on the 13th at the Quaker's meeting-house." Captain Edward Edwards (1740s–1781), who was with his father and a neighbor that day, noted the next day that he "counted twenty-six horses lying dead on the ground, nine of which were within a space of twenty steps. . . . One of Col Lee's men was so badly wounded that he died within a few days at a house in the neighborhood."[205]

Boone, Ashe County
Riddle's Knob
Big Glades (July 1780; April 15, 16, 1781)

> This incident is also known as Wolf's Den or Riddle's (Rittle's) Knob. The site is in Ashe County, about 7.5 miles north of Boone.

Robert Love (1762–1853) commanded a party of Whigs against a party of about 150 Loyalists in July 1780. The Whigs routed the Loyalists up New River at the Big Glades as they were on the way to join General Charles Cornwallis (1738–1805). Robert Love captured one of the Loyalists and hanged him at the Big Glades.[206]

★ When Loyalist Captain William Riddle learned that Colonel Benjamin Cleveland (1738–1806) arrived at his cattle farm, known as the "Old Fields," on the southern fork of the New River, on Saturday, April 14, 1781, he decided to rid the area of the "fat colonel." Riddle stole Cleveland's horse which formerly belonged to Major Patrick Ferguson (1744–1780) who was killed at the Battle of Kings Mountain on Saturday, October 7, 1780. Riddle then laid an ambush for him.

When Colonel Cleveland and Captain Richard Calloway (1719–1780) went to search for the horse, Riddle opened fire. Calloway was unarmed and was seriously wounded in the thigh. Cleveland had two pistols and grabbed Abigail Walters to use as a shield until Riddle promised that he would not kill him.

Cleveland and Calloway were captured and taken to the Wolf's Den, a cavern in Riddle's Knob that William Riddle used as a hideout. Riddle intended to take him to Ninety Six, South Carolina to receive a reward. Along the way, Cleveland broke overhanging twigs to mark the route. When Joseph Calloway (1754–1821) learned that the two men had been captured, he rode to Robert Cleveland's (1744–1812) cabin, Benjamin's younger brother. Robert mustered his brother's troops and set out in search of Colonel Cleveland and Captain Richard Calloway.

The next day, as the Loyalists prepared breakfast, a sentinel held Colonel Cleveland under heavy guard. Riddle ordered him to write passes certifying that each of the Loyalists was a good Whig, but Cleveland delayed as much as he could, expecting Riddle to kill him after he finished. As he got to the last pass, Cleveland's brother arrived and attacked. Cleveland rolled behind the tree he had been sitting against and used it for shelter. Riddle and his Loyalists escaped, except for one man wounded, but they were captured later. Cleveland presided over the court-martial of Riddle and two of his men who were found guilty and hanged from the "Tory Oak." Two other Loyalists were hanged for stealing horses.[207]

Mill's Station (Nov. 1781)

> Mill's Station was probably in southwestern North Carolina in the vicinity of Gowen's Fort.

William ("Bloody") Bates sent a part of his force to attack a small fort called Mill's Station in early November 1781 (probably Thursday, the 1st) when he decided to attack Gowen's Fort and the settlements in South Carolina. The Loyalists and Chickamaugas attacked several families and their houses on the way to Mill's Fort. The small fort was caught by surprise and surrendered with no resistance. Nevertheless, the attackers massacred the fort's inhabitants. Major John Gowen's (1740–1810) servant spread the alarm after Bates left Gowen's Fort. Captain Major Parsons's militia pursued the Loyalists and overtook and defeated them at the headwaters of the Tyger River.[208]

See also Gowen's Fort in *The Guide to the American Revolutionary War in South Carolina.*

NOTES

ABBREVIATION

NDAR: United States. Naval History Division. *Naval Documents of the American Revolution*. William Bell Clark, editor; with a foreword by President John F. Kennedy and an introd. by Ernest McNeill Eller. Washington: Naval History. Division, Dept. of the Navy: For sale by the Supt. of Docs., U.S. G.P.O., 1964–.

Preface

1. Desmarais, Norman. *Battlegrounds of Freedom: A Historical Guide to the Battlefields of the War of American Independence.* Ithaca, N.Y.: Busca, 2005.

2. Heitman, Francis B. *Historical Register of Officers of the Continental Army during the War of the Revolution, April 1775 to December 1783.* Washington, D.C.: The Rare Book Shop Publishing Company, 1914; Baltimore: Genealogical Publishing Company, 1967.

3. Peckham, Howard Henry. *The Toll of Independence: Engagements & Battle Casualties of the American Revolution.* Chicago: University of Chicago Press, 1974.

4. Boatner, Mark Mayo. *Encyclopedia of the American Revolution.* 3d ed., New York: McKay, 1980.

5. Boatner, Mark Mayo. *Landmarks of the American Revolution: A Guide to Locating and Knowing What Happened at the Sites of Independence.* Stackpole Books: Harrisburg, Pa., 1973; 2nd ed.—Library of Military History. Detroit: Charles Scribner's Sons, 2007.

6. Selesky Harold E., editor in chief. *Encyclopedia of the American Revolution*, 2nd ed. Detroit: Charles Scribner's Sons, 2007.

7. Fremont-Barnes, Gregory, Richard Alan Ryerson, eds. *The Encyclopedia of the American Revolutionary War: A Political, Social, and Military History.* Santa Barbara, Calif.: ABC-CLIO, 2006.

8. Anderson, Fred. *A People's Army: Massachusetts Soldiers and Society in the Seven Years' War.* Chapel Hill, N.C., 1984. pp. 84–85, 129.

9. Waller, George M. *The American Revolution in the West.* Chicago: Nelson Hall, 1976. pp. 30–31.

10. Adams, Charles F., ed. *The Works of John Adams.* Boston: Charles C. Little and James Brown, 1850. vol. 10 p. 110.

11. Ibid., pp. 192–93.

12. Raphael, Ray. *A People's History of the American Revolution: How Common People Shaped the Fight for Independence.* New York: New Press, 2001. pp. 145, 342.

Pennsylvania

1. Bausman, Joseph Henderson; John Samuel Duss. *History of Beaver County, Pennsylvania and Its Centennial Celebration.* Knickerbocker Press, 1904. p. 1320.

2. Bausman, Joseph Henderson; John Samuel Duss. *History of Beaver County, Pennsylvania and Its Centennial Celebration.* Knickerbocker Press, 1904. p. 149. Letter from Col. John Gibson to Gen. Edward Hand. Wisconsin Historical Society. Draper Manuscript 1 U70 in Thwaites, Reuben Gold; Kellogg, Louise Phelps. *Frontier Defense on the Upper Ohio, 1777–1778.* Draper Series, Volume III. Madison: Wisconsin Historical Society, 1912. pp. 33–36. Peckham, Howard Henry. *Toll of Independence: Engagements & Battle Casualties of the American Revolution.* Edited by Howard H. Peckham. Chicago: University of Chicago Press, 1974. p. 21.

3. Peckham, Howard Henry. *Toll of Independence: Engagements & Battle Casualties of the American Revolution.* Edited by Howard H. Peckham. Chicago: University of Chicago Press, 1974. p. 61. Letter from Col. Brodhead to Gen. Washington, dated at Fort Pitt, July 31st, 1779, postscript in *Report of the Commission to Locate the Site of the Frontier Forts of Pennsylvania.* [s.l.]: Clarence M. Busch, 1896. vol. 2 p. 491. *Pennsylvania Archives.* Hazard, Samuel; Linn, John Blair, and others. [s.l.: s.n.], 1852–? 12: 146.

4. Calendar of letters and documents. Wisconsin Historical Society. Draper Manuscript 1U56, 58, 59; 3NN46, June 19–30 in Thwaites, Reuben Gold; Kellogg, Louise Phelps. *Frontier Defense on the Upper Ohio, 1777–1778.* Draper Series, Volume III. Madison: Wisconsin Historical Society, 1912. Peckham, Howard Henry. *Toll of Independence: Engagements & Battle Casualties of the American Revolution.* Edited by Howard H. Peckham. Chicago: University of Chicago Press, 1974. p. 35.

5. Col. Thomas Gaddis to Lieut.-Col. Thomas Brown, August 26, 1777 in *Frontier Defense on the Upper Ohio, 1777–1778*: compiled from the Draper manuscripts in the library of the Wisconsin Historical Society and pub. at the charge of the Wisconsin Society of the Sons of the American Revolution. Edited by Reuben Gold Thwaites and Louise Phelps Kellogg. Madison: Wisconsin Historical Society, 1912. pp. 51–53.

6. Calendar of letters. Wisconsin Historical Society. Draper Manuscript 1U74–79, 81, 82; 4ZZ10; 3NN146. Stember, Sol. *The Bicentennial Guide to the American Revolution.* Saturday Review Press: New York, [distributed by] Dutton, 1794; [s.l.]: New York Times and Arno Press, 1969. 3: 76–78. Darlington's *Fort Pitt*, p. 226, Aug. 2–13 in

Thwaites, Reuben Gold; Kellogg, Louise Phelps. *Frontier Defense on the Upper Ohio, 1777–1778.* Draper Series, Volume III. Madison: Wisconsin Historical Society, 1912. pp. 36–37. Agnew, Daniel. *"Logstown," on the Ohio: A Historical Sketch.* Pittsburgh: Myers, Shinkle & Co., 1894. digital.library.pitt.edu/cgi-bin/t/text/text-idx?idno=00afs4564m;view=toc ;c=pitttext.

7. Archibald Steel to Gen. Edward Hand Octr. 21, 1777. Wisconsin Historical Society. Draper Manuscript IU125 in Thwaites, Reuben Gold; Kellogg, Louise Phelps. *Frontier Defense on the Upper Ohio, 1777–1778.* Draper Series, Volume III. Madison: Wisconsin Historical Society, 1912. p. 138.

8. Smith, Robert Walter. *History of Armstrong County, Pennsylvania.* Apollo, Pa.: Closson Press, 1995, 1883, p. 106. *Report of the Commission to Locate the Site of the Frontier Forts of Pennsylvania.* [s.l.]: Clarence M. Busch, 1896. 2: 476.

9. Letter of Captain Samuel Moorhead to Gen. Edward Hand in Thwaites, Reuben Gold; Kellogg, Louise Phelps. *Frontier Defense on the Upper Ohio, 1777–1778.* Draper Series, Volume III. Madison: Wisconsin Historical Society, 1912. p. 46. Peckham, Howard Henry. *Toll of Independence: Engagements & Battle Casualties of the American Revolution.* Edited by Howard H. Peckham. Chicago: University of Chicago Press, 1974. p. 38.

10. www.accessible.com/amcnty/PA/Westmoreland/Westmoreland18.htm.

11. Albert, George Dallas, ed. *History of the County of Westmoreland, Pennsylvania, with biographical sketches of many of its pioneers and prominent men.* Philadelphia, L. H. Everts & Co., 1882. pp. 63–66. www.pa-roots.com/~westmoreland/historyproject/vol1/chap3.html. www.accessible.com/amcnty/PA/Westmoreland/Westmoreland13.htm.

12. From the London Gazette Extraordinary. Published by Authority. Tuesday, December, 2, 1777. *The Pennsylvania Ledger: or the Philadelphia Market-Day Advertiser* (March 4, 1778) CXXXII p. 1. Extracts from a Journal Kept by a Gentleman Present at All the Movements of the Royal Army since Their Landing in Chesapeake Bay. *The Pennsylvania Ledger: or the Philadelphia Market-Day Advertiser* (December 6, 1778) CVII p. 1. From the Antigua Gazette, New-York, Nov, 6 Extracts from a Journal Kept by a Gentleman Present. *Maryland Journal* (February 24, 1778) V: 225 p. 1. Copy of a letter from General Sir William Howe to Lord George Germain, dated head-quarters, Germantown, October 4, 1777. *The London Gazette, Extraordinary. The Massachusetts Spy: Or, American Oracle of Liberty* (March 12,1778) VIII: 358 p. 13.

13. Meginness, John Franklin. *Otzinachson, or, A History of the West Branch Valley of the Susquehanna Embracing a Full Account of its Settlement, Trials and Privations Endured by the Early Pioneers, Full Accounts of the Indian Wars, Predatory Incursions, Abductions, and Massacres, &c., Together with an Account of the Fair Play System; and the Trying Scenes of the Big Runaway; Interspersed with Biographical Sketches of Some of the Leading Settlers, Families, etc., Together with Pertinent Anecdotes, Statistics, and Much Valuable Matter Entirely New.* Philadelphia: H. B. Ashmead, 1857. pp. 488, 489.

14. Letter from Col. Lochry to President Wharton, dated May 13th, 1778. *Pennsylvania Archives.* Hazard, Samuel; Linn, John Blair, and others. [s.l.: s.n.], 1852–?6: 469; 495. www.rootsweb.com/~usgenweb/pa/1pa/1picts/frontierforts/ff30.html.

16. Engagement at Susquehannah. *The Massachusetts Spy: Or, American Oracle of Liberty* (July 23, 1778) VIII: 377 p. 3. *Encyclopedia of the American Revolution.* Harold E. Selesky, editor in chief. 2nd ed. Detroit: Charles Scribner's Sons, 2007. II: 1286–1288. *The Encyclopedia of the American Revolutionary War: A Political, Social, and Military History.* Gregory Fremont-Barnes, Richard Alan Ryerson, editors. Santa Barbara, Calif.: ABC-CLIO, 2006. IV: 1376–1378. Calloway, Colin G. *The American Revolution in Indian Country: Crisis and Diversity in Native American Communities.* Cambridge: Cambridge University Press, 1995. Commager, Henry Steele. *The Spirit of Seventy Six: The Story of the American Revolution as Told by Participants.* New York, Harper & Row [1967]. Mancall, Peter C. *Valley of Opportunity: Economic Culture along the Susquehanna, 1700–1800.* Ithaca, N.Y.: Cornell University Press, 1991. Smith, Page. *A New Age Now Begins.* New York: McGraw-Hill, 1976. Swiggett, Howard. *War Out of Niagara: Walter Butler and the Tory Rangers.* New York: Columbia University Press, 1933.

17. Extract of a letter from Thomas Scott to T. Matlack dated August 1st, 1778. *Pennsylvania Archives.* Hazard, Samuel; Linn, John Blair, and others. [s.l.: s.n.], 1852–? 6: 673. A deposition made by Hon. William Jack, a Justice of the Peace, dates the event on July 13, 1778. Westmoreland County Biographical Sketches of its Pioneers & Prominent Men. genforum.genealogy.com/pa/messages/31188.html. Hassler Edgar W. Old Westmoreland. Part I. www.geocities.com/lydick_1999/History/o1w.html.

18. www.geocities.com/massyharbisonforthanddar/the storyofforthand.

19. *The Pennsylvania Gazette* (July 14, 1779).

20. Peckham, Howard Henry. *Toll of Independence: Engagements & Battle Casualties of the American Revolution.* Edited by Howard H. Peckham. Chicago: University of Chicago Press, 1974. p. 59.

21. Hackenburg, Randy W. *Montour County and the American Revolution.* Boiling Springs, Pa.: Privately Published, 2009. pp. 24–26. Carl Carmer. *The Susquehanna.* New York: David McKay Company, Inc., 1955. pp. 136–146. Godcharles, Frederic Antes. *Pennsylvania, Political, Governmental, Military and Civil.* New York : American Historical Society, 1933. pp. 249, 251. *Northumberland County in the American Revolution.* [Sunbury, Pa.]: Northumberland County Historical Society, 1976. pp. 120–124. *The Pennsylvania Packet or the General Advertiser* (October 17, 1778) p. 1. *The Independent Ledger, and the American Advertiser* (November 2, 1778) I: 21 p. 2. *The New–York Gazette; and The Weekly Mercury* 1411 (November 2, 1778) p. 1. Bradsby, H. C., ed. *History of Luzerne County, Pennsylvania, with Biographical Selections.* Chicago: S. B. Nelson & Co., Publishers, 1893. pp. 123–124.

22. Hackenburg, Randy W. *Montour County and the American Revolution.* Boiling Springs, Pa.: Privately Published, 2009. pp. 26–27. Meginness, John Franklin. *Otzinachson, or, A History of the West Branch Valley of the Susquehanna Embracing a Full Account of its Settlement, Trials and Privations Endured by the Early Pioneers, Full Accounts of the Indian Wars, Predatory Incursions, Abductions, and Massacres, &c., Together with an Account of the Fair Play System; and the Trying Scenes of the Big Runaway; Interspersed with Biographical Sketches of Some of the Leading Settlers, Families, etc., Together with Pertinent Anecdotes, Statistics, and Much Valuable Matter Entirely New.* Philadelphia: H. B. Ashmead, 1857, p. 228. Meginness, John

Franklin. *Otzinachson: A History of the West Branch Valley of the Susquehanna: its First Settlement, Privations Endured by the Early Pioneers, Indian Wars, Predatory Incursions, Abductions and Massacres, Together with an Account of the Fair Play System; and the Trying Scenes of the Big Run-away. Biographical Sketches of the Leading Settlers*. Rev. ed. Williamsport, Pa. Gazette and Bulletin Printing House, 1889. pp. 550–551, 555. Rupp, I. Daniel. *History and Topography of Northumberland, Huntingdon, Mifflin, Centre, Union, Columbia, Juniata and Clinton Counties, Pa.: embracing local and general events, leading incidents, description of the principal boroughs, towns, villages, etc., etc.; with a copious appendix: embellished by engravings*. Lancaster, Pa.: Published by G. Hills, 1847. *Northumberland County in the American Revolution*. [Sunbury, Pa.]: Northumberland County Historical Society, 1976. p. 369. Godcharles, Frederic Antes. *Daily Stories of Pennsylvania: prepared for publication in the leading daily newspapers of the state*. Milton, Pa.: [s.n.], 1924. pp. 296–297.

23. Letter of Colonel Hunter to Col. Matthew Smith July 23, 1779. *Pennsylvania Archives*. Selected And Arranged From Original Documents In The Office of the Secretary of the Commonwealth, Conformably to Acts of the General Assembly, February 18, 1851, & March 1, 1852. By Samuel Hazard. Commencing 1778. Volume VII. Philadelphia: Printed by Joseph Severns & Co., 1853. pp. 589–593. *Connecticut Courant* (August 24, 1779) 761: 2. *History of that part of the Susquehanna and Juniata Valleys, Embraced in the Counties of Mifflin, Juniata, Perry, Union and Snyder In The Commonwealth of Pennsylvania*. In Two Volumes. Philadelphia: Everts, Peck & Richards, 1886. 1: 97–99.

24. Extract of a letter from Fort Augusta, April 17, 1779. *The Independent Ledger, and the American Advertiser* I: 51 (May 31, 1779) p. 2.

25. Hackenburg, Randy W. *Montour County and the American Revolution*. Boiling Springs, Pa.: Privately Published, 2009. p. 27. *Northumberland County in the American Revolution*. [Sunbury, Pa.]: Northumberland County Historical Society (Pa.), 1976. p. 371. Godcharles, Frederic Antes. *Daily Stories of Pennsylvania: prepared for publication in the leading daily newspapers of the state*. Milton, Pa.: [s.n.], 1924. pp. 295–297. Linn, John Blair. *Annals of Buffalo Valley, Pennsylvania*. Harrisburg, Pa.: Lane S. Brut, Printer And Binder, 1877. pp. 170–171. Meginness, John Franklin. *Otzinachson, or, A History of the West Branch Valley of the Susquehanna Embracing a Full Account of its Settlement, Trials and Privations Endured by the Early Pioneers, Full Accounts of the Indian Wars, Predatory Incursions, Abductions, and Massacres, &c., Together with an Account of the Fair Play System; and the Trying Scenes of the Big Runaway; Interspersed with Biographical Sketches of Some of the Leading Settlers, Families, etc., Together with Pertinent Anecdotes, Statistics, and Much Valuable Matter Entirely New*. Philadelphia: H. B. Ashmead, 1857. pp. 241–242. Meginness, John Franklin. *Otzinachson: A History of the West Branch Valley of the Susquehanna: its First Settlement, Privations Endured by the Early Pioneers, Indian Wars, Predatory Incursions, Abductions and Massacres, Together with an Account of the Fair Play System; and the Trying Scenes of the Big Run-away. Biographical Sketches of the Leading Settlers*. Rev. ed. Williamsport, Pa. Gazette and Bulletin Printing House, 1889. p. 586. Bell, Herbert C. *History of Northumberland County, Pennsylvania*. Chicago: Brown, Runk and Co., 1891. pp. 125–126.

26. Letter of Colonel Hunter to Col. Matthew Smith July 23, 1779. *Pennsylvania Archives*. Selected And Arranged From Original Documents In The Office of the Secretary of the Commonwealth, Conformably To Acts of the General Assembly, February 18, 1851, & March 1, 1852. by Samuel Hazard. Commencing 1778. Volume VII. Philadelphia: Printed by Joseph Severns & Co., 1853. pp. 589–593. *Connecticut Courant* 761 (August 24, 1779) p. 2. *History of That Part of the Susquehanna and Juniata Valleys, Embraced in the Counties of Mifflin, Juniata, Perry, Union and Snyder in the Commonwealth of Pennsylvania*. In Two Volumes, Philadelphia: Everts, Peck & Richards 1886. 1: 97–99.

27. Hackenburg, Randy W. *Montour County and the American Revolution*. Boiling Springs, Pa.: Privately Published, 2009. p. 27. *Northumberland County in the American Revolution*. [Sunbury, Pa.]: Northumberland County Historical Society (Pa.), 1976. pp. 372–373. Meginness, John Franklin. *Otzinachson, or, A History of the West Branch Valley of the Susquehanna Embracing a Full Account of its Settlement, Trials and Privations Endured by the Early Pioneers, Full Accounts of the Indian Wars, Predatory Incursions, Abductions, and Massacres, &c., Together with an Account of the Fair Play System; and the Trying Scenes of the Big Runaway; Interspersed with Biographical Sketches of Some of the Leading Settlers, Families, etc., Together with Pertinent Anecdotes, Statistics, and Much Valuable Matter Entirely New*. Philadelphia: H. B. Ashmead, 1857. pp. 245–246.

28. *Connecticut Courant* 761 (August 24, 1779) p. 2. Letter of Colonel Hunter to Col. Matthew Smith July 23, 1779. *Pennsylvania Archives. Selected And Arranged from Original Documents in the Office of the Secretary of the Commonwealth, Conformably to Acts of the General Assembly, February 18, 1851, & March 1, 1852*. By Samuel Hazard. Commencing 1778. Volume VII. Philadelphia: Printed by Joseph Severns & Co., 1853. pp. 589–593. www.usgennet.org/usa/pa/county/lycoming/History/Chapter–10.html. *History of that Part of the Susquehanna and Juniata Valleys, Embraced in the Counties of Mifflin, Juniata, Perry, Union and Snyder In the Commonwealth of Pennsylvania*. In Two Volumes. Philadelphia: Everts, Peck & Richards 1886. 1: 97–99. Hackenburg, Randy W. *Montour County and the American Revolution*. Boiling Springs, Pa.: Privately Published, 2009. pp. 27–29. Loudon, Archibald. *Loudon's Indian Narratives*. Lewisburg, Pa.: Wennawoods Pub., 1996, 1888. Meginness, J. F. *Otzinachson: A History of the West Branch of the Susquehanna*. Baltimore, Md.: Gateway Press, 1991 (reprint of 1889 edition). Sipe, C. Hale. *The Indian Wars of Pennsylvania: An Account of the Indian Events, in Pennsylvania, of the French and Indian War, Pontiac's War, Lord Dunmore's War, the Revolutionary War and the Indian Uprising from 1779–1785*. Lewisburg, Pa.: Wennawoods Publishing, 1995 (reprint of the 1931 edition). Sipe, C. Hale. *The Indian Chiefs of Pennsylvania or a Story of the Part Played by American Indians in the History of Pennsylvania, Based Primarily on the Pennsylvania Archives and Colonial Records, and Built Around the Outstanding Chiefs*. Lewisburg, Pa.: Wennawoods Publishing, 1994 (reprint of the 1927 edition). Swartz, Roger G. *Fields of Honor, The Battle of Fort Freeland, July 28, 1779*. Turbotville, Pa.: Warrior Run; Fort Freeland Heritage Society, 1996. Godcharles, Frederic Antes. *Pennsylvania, Political, Governmental, Military and Civil*. New York : American Historical Society, 1933. pp. 256–258. Godcharles, Frederic Antes. *Daily Stories of Pennsylvania: prepared for publication in the leading daily newspapers of the state*. Milton, Pa.: [s.n.], 1924. pp. 515–516. Linn, John Blair. *Annals of Buffalo Valley, Pennsylvania*. Harrisburg, PA.: Lane S. Brut, Printer and Binder, 1877. pp. 175–179. Meginness, John Franklin. *Otzinachson, or, A History of the West Branch Valley of the Susquehanna Embracing a Full Account of its Settlement, Trials and Privations Endured by the Early Pioneers, Full Accounts of the Indian Wars, Predatory Incursions, Abductions, and Massacres, &c., Together with an Account of the Fair Play System; and the Trying Scenes of the Big Runaway; Interspersed with Biographical Sketches of Some of the Leading Settlers, Families, etc., Together with Pertinent Anecdotes, Statistics, and Much Valuable Matter Entirely New*. Philadelphia: H. B. Ashmead, 1857. pp. 248–258. Meginness, John

Franklin. *Otzinachson: A History of the West Branch Valley of the Susquehanna: its First Settlement, Privations Endured by the Early Pioneers, Indian Wars, Predatory Incursions, Abductions and Massacres, Together with an Account of the Fair Play System; and the Trying Scenes of the Big Run-away. Biographical Sketches of the Leading Settlers*. Rev. ed. Williamsport, Pa. Gazette and Bulletin Printing House, 1889, pp. 594–614. *Northumberland County in the American Revolution*. [Sunbury, Pa.]: Northumberland County Historical Society, 1976. pp. 131–173, 373. For roster of Ft. Freeland garrison Bell, Herbert C. *History of Northumberland County, Pennsylvania*. Chicago: Brown, Runk and Co., 1891. pp. 129–131, 133.

29. Sullivan, John. *Letters and Papers of Major-General John Sullivan, Continental Army*. Edited by Otis G. Hammond. Concord, N.H.: New Hampshire Historical Society, 1930–39. III: 97.

30. *The New-Hampshire Gazette, and Historical Chronicle*. II: 83 (September 21, 1779). p. 2.

31. *Journals of Dr. Jabez Campfield; Lieut. Col. Adam Hubley; Lieut. William McKendry. Capt. Charles Nukerck. Journals of the Military Expedition of Major General John Sullivan Against the Six Nations of Indians in 1779 with Records of Centennial Celebrations*. by Frederick Cook. Auburn, N Y.: Knapp, Peck, & Thomson, 1887. pp. 50, 166, 208, 219.

32. Hackenburg, Randy W. *Montour County and the American Revolution*. Boiling Springs, Pa.: Privately Published, 2009. p. 26. Meginness, John Franklin. *Otzinachson, or, A History of the West Branch Valley of the Susquehanna Embracing a Full Account of its Settlement, Trials and Privations Endured by the Early Pioneers, Full Accounts of the Indian Wars, Predatory Incursions, Abductions, and Massacres, &c., Together with an Account of the Fair Play System; and the Trying Scenes of the Big Runaway; Interspersed with Biographical Sketches of Some of the Leading Settlers, Families, etc., Together with Pertinent Anecdotes, Statistics, and Much Valuable Matter Entirely New*. Philadelphia: H. B. Ashmead, 1857. p. 237. *Northumberland County in the American Revolution*. [Sunbury, Pa.]: Northumberland County Historical Society, 1976. pp. 125, 370.

33. Hackenburg, Randy W. *Montour County and the American Revolution*. Boiling Springs, Pa.: Privately Published, 2009. p. 33. Meginness, John Franklin. *Otzinachson, or, A History of the West Branch Valley of the Susquehanna Embracing a Full Account of its Settlement, Trials and Privations Endured by the Early Pioneers, Full Accounts of the Indian Wars, Predatory Incursions, Abductions, and Massacres, &c., Together with an Account of the Fair Play System; and the Trying Scenes of the Big Runaway; Interspersed with Biographical Sketches of Some of the Leading Settlers, Families, etc., Together with Pertinent Anecdotes, Statistics, and Much Valuable Matter Entirely New*. Philadelphia: H. B. Ashmead, 1857. p. 271. Meginness, John Franklin. *Otzinachson: A History of the West Branch Valley of the Susquehanna: its First Settlement, Privations Endured by the Early Pioneers, Indian Wars, Predatory Incursions, Abductions and Massacres, Together with an Account of the Fair Play System; and the Trying Scenes of the Big Run-away. Biographical Sketches of the Leading Settlers*. Rev. ed. Williamsport, Pa. Gazette and Bulletin Printing House, 1889. pp. 638–639. *Historical and Biographical Annals of Columbia and Montour Counties, Pennsylvania, containing a concise history of the two counties and a genealogical and biographical record of representative families...* Chicago: J. H. Beers & Co., 1915. p. 583. Godcharles, Frederic Antes. *Daily stories of Pennsylvania: prepared for publication in the leading daily newspapers of the state*. Milton, Pa.: [s.n.], 1924. p. 137.

34. Extract of a letter from Fort Augusta, April 17, 1779. *The Independent Ledger, and the American Advertiser* I: 51 (May 31, 1779) p. 2.

35. Extract of a letter from the Camp at Wyoming, July 2. *The Royal Gazette* No. 294, July 24, 1779. *Documents Relating to the Revolutionary History, State of New Jersey*. Edited by William S. Stryker. Trenton: The John L. Murphy Publishing Co., 1901. Series 2. III: 514–515.

36. Moore, Frank. *Diary of the American Revolution: from Newspapers and Original Documents*. New York: Charles Scribner; London: Sampson Low, Son & Co., 1890. 2: 216–219. Brodhead, Daniel. Brodhead's Expedition. Colonel Brodhead's Report of his Expedition, see *Journals of the Military Expedition of Major General John Sullivan Against the Six Nations of Indians in 1779 with Records of Centennial Celebration*s. by Frederick Cook. Auburn, N Y.: Knapp, Peck, & Thomson, 1887. pp. 306–309. *Pennsylvania Archives*, 12: 138, 154, 155. *Pennsylvania Packet*, September 11, 1779. *Pennsylvania Packet or the General Advertiser*. Philadelphia, Tuesday, October 19, 1779. *Magazine of American History*. 3 (1879): 672–676.

37. Boatner, Mark Mayo. *Landmarks of the American Revolution*. 2nd ed.—Library of Military History. Detroit: Charles Scribner's Sons, 2007. p. 303. *Encyclopedia of the American Revolution*. Harold E. Selesky, editor in chief. 2nd ed. Detroit: Charles Scribner's Sons, 2007. 1: 111. Brady, William Young. "Brodhead's Trail up the Allegheny, 1779." *Western Pennsylvania Historical Magazine* 37 (March 1954): 19–31. Commager, Henry Steele. *The Spirit of Seventy Six*. New York, Harper & Row [1967] pp. 1023–1024.

38. Hackenburg, Randy W. *Montour County and the American Revolution*. Boiling Springs, Pa.: Privately Published, 2009. p. 30. Wagner's "Van Campen," *Daniel Van Campen Declaration*, p. 3. Niles, Hubbard, 8. J. *Sketches of Border Adventures in the Life and Times of Major Moses Van Campen*. Belmont, N.Y.: Allegany County Historical Society, 1982 (reprint of 1893 publication). pp. 148–163.

39. www.motherbedford.com/Frankstown.htm.

40. Extract of a letter from Shippensburg, in Pennsylvania, dated the 22nd instant. *The New-York Gazette, and Weekly Mercury* 1495 (June 12, 1780) p. 2.

41. Letter of Lt. George Ashman to President Reed, May 19, 1781, in Samuel Hazard, *Pennsylvania Archives*. Philadelphia: Joseph Stevens & Co., 1854. p. 152.

42. Extract of a Letter from the Lieutenant of Bedford County, Dated June 2, 1781. *The New-York Gazette, and Weekly Mercury* 1548 (June 18, 1781) p. 2. Letter of Arthur Buchanan to Captain Postlethwaite dated June 5, 1781, in Samuel Hazard, *Pennsylvania Archives*. Philadelphia: Joseph Stevens & Co., 1854. IX: 192.

43. Letter of Lt. George Ashman to President Reed, June 12, 1781, in Samuel Hazard, *Pennsylvania Archives*. Philadelphia: Joseph Stevens & Co., 1854. IX: 192.

44. Extract of a letter from a gentleman in Sussex county, New Jersey, dated May 16. *Documents Relating to the Revolutionary History, State of New Jersey*. Edited by William S. Stryker. Trenton: The John L. Murphy Publishing Co., 1901. Series 2. IV: 406.

45. www.kykinfolk.com/pendleton/French_Jacob.pdf.

46. Hackenburg, Rand y W. *Montour County and the American Revolution*. Boiling Springs, Pa.: Privately Published, 2009. p. 30. *Northumberland County in the American Revolution*. [Sunbury, Pa.]: Northumberland County Historical Society (Pa.), 1976. pp. 373–375.

47. Hackenburg, Rand y W. *Montour County and the American Revolution*. Boiling Springs, Pa.: Privately Published, 2009. p. 31. Meginness, John Franklin. *Otzinachson, or, A History of the West Branch Valley of the Susquehanna Embracing a Full Account of its Settlement, Trials and Privations Endured by the Early Pioneers, Full Accounts of the Indian Wars, Predatory Incursions, Abductions, and Massacres, &c., Together with an Account of the Fair Play System; and the Trying Scenes of the Big Runaway; Interspersed with Biographical Sketches of Some of the Leading Settlers, Families, etc., Together with Pertinent Anecdotes, Statistics, and Much Valuable Matter Entirely New*. Philadelphia: H. B. Ashmead, 1857. p. 260. *Historical and Biographical Annals of Columbia and Montour Counties, Pennsylvania, containing a concise history of the two counties and a genealogical and biographical record of representative families...* Chicago, J. H. Beers & Co., 1915. Vol. 2, p. 1161. Godcharles, Frederic Antes. *Daily stories of Pennsylvania: prepared for publication in the leading daily newspapers of the state*. Milton, Pa.: [s.n.], 1924. pp. 1128–1129.

48. Echoes from the Back Woods of Pennsylvania. *American Monthly Magazine* XI (July–Dec.) 1897. pp. 475–477. Hackenburg, Rand y W. *Montour County and the American Revolution*. Boiling Springs, Pa.: Privately Published, 2009. p. 30. Simington memoir (a more complete account is given in Chapter 3 under Robert Curry). Battle, Montour County section, pp. 133–134.

49. Moore, Rogan Hart. *The Bloodstained Field: A History of the Sugarloaf Massacre, September 11, 1780*. Bowie, Md.: Heritage Books, 2000. Bradsby, H. C., ed. *History of Luzerne County, Pennsylvania, with Biographical Selections*. Chicago: S. B. Nelson & Co., Publishers, 1893. pp. 199–209. *Pennsylvania Archives*. Hazard, Samuel. Linn, John Blair and others. [S.l.: s.n.], 1852–?.

50. Hackenburg, Rand y W. *Montour County and the American Revolution*. Boiling Springs, Pa.: Privately Published, 2009. p. 31.

60. Bostwick, Elisha. A Connecticut Soldier Under Washington: Elisha Bostwick's Memoirs of the First Years of the Revolution. William S. Powell, ed. *The William and Mary Quarterly*, 3rd Ser. 6: 1 (Jan. 1949) p. 103.

61. Fast, Howard. *The Crossing*. New York: Ibooks, 1971, 1999. Fischer, David Hackett. *Washington's Crossing*. Oxford: Oxford University Press, 2004.

62. *Connecticut Journal* (March 19, 1777) 492 p. 2.

63. Washington, George. *The Writings of George Washington*. Ed. John C. Fitzpatrick. Washington, D.C., 1963 X: 20–21. Samuel Hay letter to William Irvine Nov. 14, 1777 as cited in Hocker, Edward W. Day by Day Record of the American Army's Encampment at Whitemash Pennsylvania. Whitemarsh, Pa., 1996 in Williams, James A. "The Whitemarsh Encampment." *Bulletin of the Historical Society of Montgomery County*. 21 (Spring 1979) p. 310.

64. Washington, George. *The Writings of George Washington*. Ed. John C. Fitzpatrick. Washington, D.C., 1963 X: 20–21. Williams, James A. "The Whitemarsh Encampment." *Bulletin of the Historical Society of Montgomery County*, 21 (Spring 1979) p. 310.

65. Baurmeister, Carl Leopold. *Letters from Major Baurmeister to Colonel von Jungkenn*. Bernhard A. Uhlendorf and Edna Vosper, editors. Philadelphia: The Historical Society of Pennsylvania 1937. p. 36.

66. Robertson, Archibald. *Archibald Robertson, Lieutenant-General Royal Engineers: his diaries and sketches in America, 1762–1780*. Edited with an introduction by Harry Miller Lydenberg. New York: The New York Public Library, 1930; The New York Public Library and The New York Times & Arno Press, 1971. pp. 159–160.

67. Robertson, Archibald. *Archibald Robertson, Lieutenant-General Royal Engineers: his diaries and sketches in America, 1762–1780*. Edited with an introduction by Harry Miller Lydenberg. New York: The New York Public Library, 1930; The New York Public Library and The New York Times & Arno Press, 1971. p. 160.

68. André, John. *Major André's Journal: Operations of the British Army under Lieutenant Generals Sir William Howe and Sir Henry Clinton June 1777 to November 1778*. Tarrytown, N.Y.: William Abbatt, 1930; New York Times & Arno Press, 1968. p. 68.

69. Ward, Christopher. *The War of the Revolution*. New York: Macmillan, 1952. p. 471 note 44.

70. André, John. *Major André's Journal: Operations of the British Army under Lieutenant Generals Sir William Howe and Sir Henry Clinton June 1777 to November 1778*. Tarrytown, N.Y.: William Abbatt, 1930; New York Times & Arno Press, 1968. p. 70.

71. *The New-Jersey Gazette* I: 4 (December 24, 1777) p. 3.

72. *Connecticut Courant* 686 (March 17, 1778) p. 1. Head-Quarters Valley Forge, February 18, 1778. *The New-London Gazette* (March 13, 1778) XV: 748 p. 3.

73. Extract of a Letter from Chester County. *The Virginia Gazette* (October 3, 1777) 140: 1.

74. History of Delaware County Pennsylvania - Chapter 25 Henry Graham Ashmead, 1884. http://www.pa-roots .com/index.php/delaware-county/204-History-of-delaware-county-pennsylvania/783- Historyofdelawarecountychapter25.

75. Journal of HMS *Greyhound*. British National Archives, Admiralty 51/420 – Cpt Log 420 Part 5 (1778) p. 208. Peckham, Howard Henry. *Toll of Independence: Engagements & Battle Casualties of the American Revolution*. Edited by Howard H. Peckham. Chicago: University of Chicago Press, 1974. p. 51.

76. Journal of HMS *Greyhound*. British National Archives, Admiralty 51/420 – Cpt Log 420 Part 5 (1778) p. 209. Peckham, Howard Henry. *Toll of Independence: Engagements & Battle Casualties of the American Revolution*. Edited by Howard H. Peckham. Chicago: University of Chicago Press, 1974. p. 52.

77. *Continental Journal* LXXI (October 2, 1777) p. 4. Copy of a letter from General Sir William Howe to Lord George Germain, dated head-quarters, Germantown, October 4, 1777. *The London Gazette, Extraordinary*. *The Massachusetts Spy: Or, American Oracle of Liberty* (March 12,1778) VIII: 358 p. 13.

78. *Encyclopedia of the American Revolution*. Harold E. Selesky, editor in chief. 2nd ed. Detroit: Charles Scribner's Sons, 2007. I: 101–106. *The Encyclopedia of the American Revolutionary War: A Political, Social, and Military History*. Gregory Fremont-Barnes, Richard Alan Ryerson, editors. Santa Barbara, Calif.: ABC-CLIO, 2006. I: 129–133. André, John. *Major André's Journal: Operations of the British Army under Lieutenant Generals Sir William Howe and Sir Henry Clinton June 1777 to November 1778*. Tarrytown, N.Y.: William Abbatt, 1930; New York Times & Arno Press, 1968. Black, Jeremy. *War for America: the Fight for Independence*. Stroud, UK: Alan Sutton, 1991. Canby, Henry S. *The Brandywine*. New York: Farrar and Rinehart, 1941. Carrington, Henry B. *Battles of the American Revolution 1775–1781, Including Battle Maps and Charts of the American Revolution*. New York: Promontory Press (1974), originally published in 1877 and 1881. Conway, Stephen. *The War of American Independence, 1775–1783*. London: Arnold, 1995. Ewald, Johann. *Diary of the American War: A Hessian Journal*, Captain Johann Ewald; Translated and edited by Joseph P. Tustin. New Haven and London: Yale University Press, 1979. Greene, Francis V. *The Revolutionary War and the Military Policy of the United States*. New York: Scribner, 1911. Higginbotham, Don. *The War of American Independence: Military Attitudes, Policies, and Practice, 1763–1789*. New York: Macmillan, 1971. Lengel, Edward G. *General George Washington, A Military Life*. New York: Random House, 2005. Mackesy, Piers. *The War for America, 1775–1783*. Lincoln: University of Nebraska Press, 1993. Reed, John F. *Campaign to Valley Forge: July 1, 1777–December 19, 1777*. Philadelphia: University of Pennsylvania Press, 1965. Smith, Samuel Stelle, *The Battle of Brandywine*. Monmouth Beach, N.J.: Philip Freneau Press, 1976. Taafe, Stephen. *The Philadelphia Campaign, 1777–1778*. Lawrence, KS: University Press of Kansas, 2003. Townshend, Joseph. *The Battle of Brandywine*. 1846; New York: New York Times, 1969. Ward, Christopher. *The War of the Revolution*. New York: Macmillan, 1952. pp. 341–354. *Continental Journal* LXXI (October 2, 1777) p. 4. Copy of a letter from General Sir William Howe to Lord George Germain, dated head-quarters, Germantown, October 4, 1777. *The London Gazette, Extraordinary*. *The Massachusetts Spy: Or, American Oracle of Liberty* (March 12,1778) VIII: 358 p. 13.

79. *The Virginia Gazette* (October 17, 1777) 142: 2.

80. McGuire, Thomas J. *The Philadelphia Campaign*. Mechanicsburg, Pa.: Stackpole Books, 2006–2007. 2: 59. Hill, Baylor. *A Gentleman of Fortune: the Diary of Baylor Hill, First Continental Light Dragoons, 1777–1781*. Baylor Hill, John T. Hayes. Fort Lauderdale, Fla.: Saddlebag Press, 1995. 1: 77–78.

81. Ward, Christopher. *The War of the Revolution*. New York: Macmillan, 1952. p. 380.

82. *The Boston Gazette, and Country Journal* 1217 (December 29, 1777) p 2. Extract of a Letter from an Officer at the Camp, Dated December 10. *The Pennsylvania Packet or the General Advertiser* (December 17, 1777) p. 2.

83. *The Virginia Gazette* (October 17, 1777) 142: 2. *The Maryland Journal and Baltimore Advertiser* V: 215 (December 16, 1777) p. 3. Baltimore, December 16. Extract of a Letter from an Officer at Camp, Dated Dec. 10. *Virginia Gazette* 1395 (December 26, 1777) p. 1.

84. *Revolution in America: Confidential Letters and Journals 1776–1784 of Adjutant General Major Baurmeister of the Hessian Forces*. Translated and annotated by Bernhard A. Uhlendorf. New Brunswick, N.J.: Rutgers University Press, 1957. pp. 154–155.

85. Robertson, Archibald. *Archibald Robertson, Lieutenant-General Royal Engineers: his Diaries and Sketches in America, 1762–1780*. Edited with an introduction by Harry Miller Lydenberg. New York: The New York Public Library, 1930; The New York Public Library and the New York Times & Arno Press, 1971. p. 171.

86. Simcoe, John Graves. *Simcoe's Military Journal. A History of the Operations of a Partisan Corps, Called the Queen's Rangers, Commanded by Lieut. Col. J. G. Simcoe*. New-York: Bartlett & Welford, 1844, pp. 61–62. Scull, G. D. (Gideon Delaplaine). *The Montresor Journals*. Ed. and annotated by G. D. Scull: [New York, Printed for the Society, 1882]; July 1, 1777, to July 1, 1778. p. 492.

87. Scull, G. D. (Gideon Delaplaine). *The Montresor Journals. Ed.* and annotated by G. D. Scull: [New York, Printed for the Society, 1882]; July 1, 1777, to July 1, 1778: [New York: the New York Historical Society, 1882] pp. 474, 495–496. Peckham, Howard Henry. *Toll of Independence: Engagements & Battle Casualties of the American Revolution*. Edited by Howard H. Peckham. Chicago: University of Chicago Press, 1974. p. 51.

88. *Encyclopedia of the American Revolution*. Harold E. Selesky, editor in chief. 2nd ed. Detroit: Charles Scribner's Sons, 2007. II: 1267. *The Encyclopedia of the American Revolutionary War: A Political, Social, and Military History*. Gregory Fremont-Barnes, Richard Alan Ryerson, editors. Santa Barbara, Calif.: ABC-CLIO, 2006. IV: 1352–1353. McGuire, Thomas J. *The Battle of Paoli*. Harrisburg, Pa.: Stackpole Books, 2000. Reed, John F. *Campaign to Valley Forge: July 1, 1777–December 19, 1777*. Philadelphia: University of Pennsylvania Press, 1965.

89. *The Massachusetts Spy: Or, American Oracle of Liberty*. VIII: 357 (March 5, 1778) p 3. Extract of a Letter from a Gentleman at Camp, at the Valley Forge, Dated January 21, 1778. *The New-Jersey Gazette* (January 28, 1778) I: 9 p. 2. Ewald, Johann. *Diary of the American War: A Hessian Journal. Captain Johann Ewald*. Translated and edited by Joseph P. Tustin. New Haven and London: Yale University Press, 1979. pp. 121–122. Boatner, Mark Mayo. *Landmarks of the American Revolution*. 2nd ed. Library of Military History. Detroit: Charles Scribner's Sons, 2007.

90. *The Independent Chronicle and the Universal Advertiser* X: 478 (October 16, 1777) p. 2. Peebles, John. *John Peebles' American War: the Diary of a Scottish Grenadier, 1776–1782*. Edited by Ira D. Gruber. Mechanicsburg, Pa.: Stackpole Books, 1998. p. 135. Robertson, Archibald. *Archibald Robertson, Lieutenant-General Royal Engineers: his Diaries and Sketches in America, 1762–1780*. Edited with an introduction by Harry Miller Lydenberg. New York: The New York Public Library, 1930; The New York Public Library and the New York Times & Arno Press, 1971. p. 148.

91. The Scull, G. D. (Gideon Delaplaine). *The Montresor Journals*. Ed. and annotated by G. D. Scull: [New York, Printed for the Society, 1882]; July 1, 1777, to July 1, 1778. Edited and annotated by G. D. Scull. Collections of the New York Historical Society, 1881. New York: the Society, 1882. p. 455. Robertson, Archibald. *Archibald Robertson:*

His Diaries and Sketches In America 1762–1780. Edited with an Introduction by Harry Miller Lydenberg. New York: The New York Public Library, 1930. p. 148.

92. *The Independent Chronicle and the Universal Advertiser* X: 478 (October 16, 1777) p. 2.

93. The Scull, G. D. (Gideon Delaplaine). *The Montresor Journals,* ed. and annotated by G. D. Scull: [New York, Printed for the Society, 1882]; July 1, 1777, to July 1, 1778. Edited and annotated by G. D. Scull. Collections of the New York Historical Society, 1881. New York: the Society, 1882. p. 457.

94. *Encyclopedia of the American Revolution.* Harold E. Selesky, editor in chief. 2nd ed. Detroit: Charles Scribner's Sons, 2007. I: 870–871. *The Encyclopedia of the American Revolutionary War: A Political, Social, and Military History.* Gregory Fremont-Barnes, Richard Alan Ryerson, editors. Santa Barbara, Calif.: ABC-CLIO, 2006. III: 947–949. McGuire, Thomas J. *The Battle of Paoli.* Harisburg, Pa.: Stackpole Books, 2000. Reed, John F. *Campaign to Valley Forge: July 1, 1777–December 19, 1777.* Philadelphia: University of Pennsylvania Press, 1965. Nelson, Paul David. *Anthony Wayne: Soldier of the Early Republic.* Bloomington: Indiana University Press, 1985. Nelson, Paul David. *Sir Charles Grey, First Earl Grey: Royal Soldier, Family Patriarch.* Madison, N.J.: Fairleigh Dickinson University Press, 1996. Stillé, Charles J. *Major-General Anthony Wayne and the Pennsylvania Line in the Continental Army.* Philadelphia: Lippincott, 1893. Ward, Christopher. *The War of the Revolution.* New York: Macmillan, 1952.

95. Scull, G. D. (Gideon Delaplaine). *The Montresor Journals.* Ed. and annotated by G. D. Scull: [New York, Printed for the Society, 1882]; July 1, 1777, to July 1, 1778.; ed. and annotated by G. D. Scull: [New York: the New York Historical Society, 1882]. pp. 456–457, 474. Scharf, J. Thomas and Westcott, Thompson. *History of Philadelphia 1609–1884.* Philadelphia: L. H. Everts & Co. 1884. I: 349. Taaffe, Stephen R. *The Philadelphia Campaign, 1777–1778.* Lawrence, KS: University Press of Kansas, 2003. pp. 87–88.

96. *Revolution in America: Confidential Letters and Journals 1776–1784 of Adjutant General Major Baurmeister of the Hessian Forces.* Translated and annotated by Bernhard A. Uhlendorf. New Brunswick, N.J.: Rutgers University Press, 1957. pp. 116–117. Andre, Major John. *Major Andre's Journal: Operations of the British Army under Lieutenant Generals Sir William Howe, and Sir Henry Clinton, June 1777, to November 1778,* edited by Henry Cabot Lodge, Boston, 1902; Tarrytown, N.Y.: William Abbatt, 1930. p. 52.

97. Scull, G. D. (Gideon Delaplaine). *The Montresor Journals.* Ed. and annotated by G. D. Scull: [New York, Printed for the Society, 1882]; July 1, 1777, to July 1, 1778. p. 458.

98. Scull, G. D. (Gideon Delaplaine). *The Montresor Journals.* Ed. and annotated by G. D. Scull: [New York, Printed for the Society, 1882]; July 1, 1777, to July 1, 1778. p. 459.

99. Simcoe, John Graves. *Simcoe's Military Journal. A History of the Operations of a Partisan Corps, Called the Queen's Rangers, Commanded by Lieut. Col. J. G. Simcoe* New-York: Bartlett & Welford, 1844. pp. 23–29.

100. Muenchhausen, Friedrich von. *At General Howe's Side 1776–1778: The Diary of General William Howe's Aide de Camp, Captain Friedrich von Muenchhausen.* Translated by Ernst Kipping and annotated by Samuel Smith. Monmouth Beach, N.J.: Philip Freneau Press, 1974. p. 47.

101. *The Pennsylvania Evening Post* (April 10, 1778) IV: 478 p. 156. *The Pennsylvania Ledger: or the Philadelphia Market-Day Advertiser* (April 11, 1778) CXLIII p. 3.

102. Scull, G. D. (Gideon Delaplaine). *The Montresor Journals.* Ed. and annotated by G. D. Scull: [New York, Printed for the Society, 1882]; July 1, 1777, to July 1, 1778. 494.

103. Wilkinson, James. *Memoirs of My Own Times.* Philadelphia: Printed by Abraham Small, 1816. I: 835–836.

104. Robertson, Archibald. *Archibald Robertson, Lieutenant-General Royal Engineers: his Diaries and Sketches in America, 1762–1780.* Edited with an introduction by Harry Miller Lydenberg. New York: The New York Public Library, 1930; The New York Public Library and the New York Times & Arno Press, 1971. p. 150.

105. Scharf, J. Thomas and Westcott, Thompson. *History of Philadelphia 1609–1884.* Philadelphia: L. H. Everts & Co. 1884. I: 349.

106. *Encyclopedia of the American Revolution.* Harold E. Selesky, editor in chief. 2nd ed. Detroit: Charles Scribner's Sons, 2007. I: 425–432. *The Encyclopedia of the American Revolutionary War: A Political, Social, and Military History.* Gregory Fremont-Barnes, Richard Alan Ryerson, editors. Santa Barbara, Calif.: ABC-CLIO, 2006. II: 504–508. André, Major John, *Major Andre's Journal: Operations of the British Army under Lieutenant Generals Sir William Howe, and Sir Henry Clinton, June 1777, to November 1778,* edited by Henry Cabot Lodge, Boston, 1902; Tarrytown, N.Y.: William Abbatt, 1930. Black, Jeremy. *War for America: the Fight for Independence.* Stroud, UK: Alan Sutton, 1991. Carrington, Henry B. *Battles of the American Revolution 1775–1781, Including Battle Maps and Charts of the American Revolution.* New York: Promontory Press, (1974), originally published in 1877 and 1881. Conway, Stephen. *The War of American Independence, 1775–1783.* London: Arnold, 1995. Higginbotham, Don. *The War of American Independence: Military Attitudes, Policies, and Practice, 1763–1789.* New York: Macmillan, 1971. Jackson, John W. *With the British Army in Philadelphia, 1777–1778.* San Rafael, Calif.: Presidio Press, 1979. Lengel, Edward G. *General George Washington, A Military Life.* New York: Random House, 2005. McGuire, Thomas J. *The Surprise of Germantown, or the Battle of Cliveden, October 4, 1777.* Philadelphia: Cliveden of the National Trust and Thomas Publications, 1994. Mackesy, Piers. *The War for America, 1775–1783.* Lincoln: University of Nebraska Press, 1993. Reed, John F. *Campaign to Valley Forge: July 1, 1777–December 19, 1777.* Philadelphia: University of Pennsylvania Press, 1965. Taafe, Stephen. *The Philadelphia Campaign, 1777–1778.* Lawrence, KS: University Press of Kansas, 2003. Tallmadge, Benjamin. *Memoir of Colonel Benjamin Tallmadge.* New York: Thomas Holman, 1858; (Eyewitness accounts of the American Revolution. [New York]: New York Times [1968]. Ward, Christopher. *The War of the Revolution.* New York: Macmillan, 1952. pp. 363–371. Wolf, Stephanie Grauman. *Urban Village: Population, Community, and Family Structure in Germantown, Pennsylvania, 1683–1800.* Princeton, N.J.: Princeton University Press, 1976. Wood, W. J. *Battles of the Revolutionary War, 1775–1781.* Chapel Hill, N.C.: Algonquin, 1990.

107. *The New-York Gazette; and The Weekly Mercury* 1378 (March 23, 1778) p. 2.

108. *The New-York Gazette; and The Weekly Mercury* 1378 (March 23, 1778) p. 2.

109. Scull, G. D. (Gideon Delaplaine). *The Montresor Journals.* Ed. and annotated by G. D. Scull: [New York, Printed for the Society, 1882]; July 1, 1777, to July 1, 1778.; ed. and annotated by G. D. Scull: [New York: the New York Historical Society, 1882]. pp. 474, 485.

110. *The Royal Pennsylvania Gazette* XXIV (May 22, 1778) p. 3.

111. Scull, G. D. (Gideon Delaplaine). *The Montresor Journals.* Ed. and annotated by G. D. Scull: [New York, Printed for the Society, 1882]; July 1, 1777, to July 1, 1778. p. 494.

112. Extract of Another Letter from the Same Place, Dated June 6, 1778. *The New Jersey Gazette* I: 28 (June 10, 1778) p. 3. The *Independent Ledger, and American Advertiser* I: 3 (June 29, 1778) p. 3.

113. The Scull, G. D. (Gideon Delaplaine). *The Montresor Journals.* Ed. and annotated by G. D. Scull: [New York, Printed for the Society, 1882]; July 1, 1777, to July 1, 1778. Edited and annotated by G. D. Scull. Collections of the New York Historical Society, 1881. New York: the Society, 1882. p. 458. *Archibald Robertson: His Diaries and Sketches In America 1762–1780.* Edited with an Introduction By Harry Miller Lydenberg. New York: The New York Public Library, 1930. p. 150.

114. Journal of Captain James Parker. Parker Family Papers. City of Liverpool Library. Diary of Elizabeth Drinker 1: 255–256. Scull, G. D. (Gideon Delaplaine). *The Montresor Journals.* Ed. and annotated by G. D. Scull: [New York, Printed for the Society, 1882]; July 1, 1777, to July 1, 1778.; ed.: [New York: the New York Historical Society, 1882]. p. 478. Diary of Captain Francis Downman. "Services of Lieut.-Colonel Francis Downman, R. A., in France, North America, and the West Indies, between the Years 1758 and 1784" edited by F. A. Whinyates. In *Minutes of Proceedings of the Royal Artillery Institution.* Vol. 25. Woolwich, England: Royal Artillery Institution, 1898. p. 214. NDAR 10: 557–559.

115. Scull, G. D. (Gideon Delaplaine). *The Montresor Journals. Ed.* and annotated by G. D. Scull: [New York, Printed for the Society, 1882]; July 1, 1777, to July 1, 1778.; [New York: the New York Historical Society, 1882]. p. 474. p. 478. Ward, Christopher. *The War of the Revolution.* New York: Macmillan, 1952.

116. Captain Andrew Snape Hamond to Vice Admiral Viscount Howe February 1, 1778. *Hamond Papers, Letter Book (1778–1779).* pp. 9–11. NDAR 11: 261.

117. Master's Log of HMS *Roebuck*, Captain Andrew Snape Hammond. British National Archives, Admiralty 52/1964. Brig. Gen. William Smallwood to George Washington. Wilmington, December 27, 1777. *George Washington Papers.* Series 4. NDAR 10: 816.

118. Drinker, Elizabeth Sand with. Extracts from the journal of Elizabeth Drinker: from 1759–1807. Edited by Henry D. Biddle. Philadelphia, Pa.: J. B. Lippincott, 1889. p. 78. NDAR 10: 816–817. *The Pennsylvania Ledger: or the Philadelphia Market-Day Advertiser* (February 11, 1778) CXXVI p. 2. *Continental Journal* XCI (February 19, 1778) p. 3. I: 2 (February 24, 1778) p. 1. For more documentation on Bushnell's plan, see Jonathan Trumbull to Colonel William Worthington, 4 Nov. Trumbull Papers 6: 167a in NDAR 10: 393–394. Colonel William Worthington to Jonathan Trumbull, 20 Nov. Trumbull Papers 6: 196a in NDAR 10: 548–549. and Jonathan Trumbull to Brigadier-General Samuel H. Parson, 21 Nov. Trumbull Papers 6: 196b in NDAR 10: 557.

119. Extract of a Letter from London, Jan. 10, 1778. *The Pennsylvania Evening Post* IV: 474 (April 1, 1778) p. 143. *The Pennsylvania Ledger: or the Philadelphia Market-Day Advertiser* CXL (April 1, 1778) p. 3.

120. *Documents Relating to the Revolutionary History, State of New Jersey.* Edited by William S. Stryker. Trenton: The John L. Murphy Publishing Co., 1901. Series 2. II: 255. Marshall, Christopher. *Extracts From the Diary of Christopher Marshall, Kept In Philadelphia And Lancaster, During the American Revolution, 1774—1781.* Edited By William Duane. Albany: Joel Munsell, 1877.

121. Scull, G. D. (Gideon Delaplaine). The *Montresor Journals.* Ed. and annotated by G. D. Scull: [New York, Printed for the Society, 1882]; July 1, 1777, to July 1, 1778. Collections of the New York Historical Society, 1881. New York: the Society, 1882. p. 459–460. NDAR 9: 972–973.

122. *Pennsylvania Archives.* Hazard, Samuel; Linn, John Blair and others. [S.l.: s.n.], 1852–? V: 637. Scull, G. D. (Gideon Delaplaine). The *Montresor Journals.* Ed. and annotated by G. D. Scull: [New York, Printed for the Society, 1882]; July 1, 1777, to July 1, 1778. p. 459. *Revolution in America: Confidential Letters and Journals 1776–1784 of Adjutant General Major Baurmeister of the Hessian Forces.* Translated and annotated by Bernhard A. Uhlendorf. New Brunswick, N.J.: Rutgers University Press, 1957. p. 117. Smith, Samuel Stelle. *Fight for the Delaware, 1777.* Monmouth Beach, N.J.: Philip Freneau Press, 1970. pp. 5–7.

123. Journal of HMS *Pearl,* Captain John Linzee. British National Archives, Admiralty 51/675; NDAR 10: 39.

124. Scull, G. D. (Gideon Delaplaine). *The Montresor Journals.* Ed. and annotated by G. D. Scull: [New York, Printed for the Society, 1882]; July 1, 1777, to July 1, 1778. [New York, Printed for the Society, 1882], pp. 463–64. NDAR 10: 102. Journal of Captain James Parker, City of Liverpool Library, Parker Family Papers, Captain Parker's Journal during the American War in the form of letters to Charles Steuart. NDAR 10: 102

125. Scull, G. D. (Gideon Delaplaine). *The Montresor Journals.* Ed. and annotated by G. D. Scull: [New York, Printed for the Society, 1882]; July 1, 1777, to July 1, 1778. Collections of the New York Historical Society, 1881. New York: the Society, 1882. pp. 463–464. Smith, Samuel Stelle. *Fight for the Delaware, 1777.* Monmouth Beach, N.J.: Philip Freneau Press, 1970. p. 13. NDAR 10: 102.

126. Smith, Samuel Stelle. *Fight for the Delaware, 1777.* Monmouth Beach, N.J.: Philip Freneau Press, 1970. p. 13.

127. Journal of HM Armed Ship *Vigilant,* Commander John Henry, British National Archives, Admiralty. 51/1037. NDAR 10: 147–148. Master's Journal of HMS. *Roebuck,* Captain Andrew S. Hamond, British National Archives, Admiralty 52/1964. NDAR 10: 147. Smith, Samuel Stelle. *Fight for the Delaware, 1777.* Monmouth Beach, N.J.: Philip Freneau Press, 1970.

128. Journal of HMS *Liverpool*, Captain Henry Bellew. British National Archives, Admiralty 51/548; NDAR 10: 165. Journal of HM Armed Ship *Vigilant*, Captain John Henry. British National Archives, Admiralty 51/1037; NDAR 10: 166. Scull, G. D. (Gideon Delaplaine). *The Montresor Journals*. Ed. and annotated by G. D. Scull: [New York, Printed for the Society, 1882]; July 1, 1777, to July 1, 1778. p. 466.

129. Taaffe, Stephen R. *The Philadelphia Campaign, 1777–1778*. Lawrence, KS: University Press of Kansas, 2003. p. 116. Scull, G. D. (Gideon Delaplaine). *The Montresor Journals*. Ed. and annotated by G. D. Scull: [New York, Printed for the Society, 1882]; July 1, 1777, to July 1, 1778. p. 466.

130. Journal of HMS *Pearl*, Captain John Linzee. British National Archives, Admiralty 51/675; NDAR 10: 228. Journal of HM Armed Ship *Vigilant*, Captain John Henry. British National Archives, Admiralty 51/1037; NDAR 10: 228. Journal of HM Sloop *Zebra*, Commander John Orde. British National Archives, Admiralty 51/1100; NDAR 10: 228–229. Journal of HMS *Camilla*, Captain Charles Phipps. British National Archives, Admiralty 51/157; NDAR 10: 229.

131. Journal of HMS *Isis*, Captain William Cornwallis. British National Archives, Admiralty L/J/116; NDAR 10: 405. Journal of HMS *Pearl*, Captain John Linzee. British National Archives, Admiralty 51/675; NDAR 10: 405. Journal of HM Armed Ship *Camilla*, Captain Charles Phipps. British National Archives, Admiralty 51/157; NDAR 10: 406. Journal of HMS *Roebuck*, Captain Andrew S. Hamond. British National Archives, Admiralty 52/1964; NDAR 10: 406. Scull, G. D. (Gideon Delaplaine). *The Montresor Journals*. Ed. and annotated by G. D. Scull: [New York, Printed for the Society, 1882]; July 1, 1777, to July 1, 1778. 473.

132. Journal of HM Armed Ship *Delaware*. British National Archives, Admiralty 51/239. NDAR 10: 827. Journal of HM Armed Schooner *Viper*. British National Archives, Admiralty 51/4385. NDAR 10: 827. Captain Andrew S. Hamond, R. N. to Lt. Edward Pakenham, R. N. LB, Hamond Papers, Orders Issued, 1776–1777. Adressed below signature line. "Lieut Pakenham/ — *Viper* Schooner." NDAR 10: 826.

133. Journal of HM Armed Schooner *Viper*. British National Archives, Admiralty 51/4385. NDAR 10: 831. Journal of HM Sloop *Zebra*, Commander John Orde. British National Archives, Admiralty 51/1100. NDAR 10: 839.

134. Journal of HMS *Viper*. British National Archives, Admiralty 51/4385– Captain's Log No. 4385 Part 4 (1778) Commander: Lieutenant Edward Pakenham. Peckham, Howard Henry. *Toll of Independence: Engagements & Battle Casualties of the American Revolution*. Edited by Howard H. Peckham. Chicago: University of Chicago Press, 1974. pp. 51–52.

135. Letter from Lieutenant Colonel Samuel Smith to George Washington, Fort Mifflin 9th. Commodore John Hazlewood to George Washington, *George Washington Papers*, Series 4. NDAR 10: 128–129. October 1777. *George Washington Papers*, Series 4. NDAR 10: 102–103. Taaffe, Stephen R. *The Philadelphia Campaign, 1777–1778*. Lawrence, KS: University Press of Kansas, 2003. p. 116. Downman, Francis. "Services of Lieut.-Colonel Francis Downman, R. A., in France, North America, and the West Indies, between the Years 1758 and 1784" edited by F. A. Whinyates. In *Minutes of Proceedings of the Royal Artillery Institution*. Vo. 25. Woolwich, England: Royal Artillery Institution, 1898. p. 164. NDAR 10: 119.

136. Smith, Samuel Stelle. *Fight for the Delaware, 1777*. Monmouth Beach, N.J.: Philip Freneau Press, 1970. p. 14.

137. Scull, G. D. (Gideon Delaplaine). *The Montresor Journals*. Ed. and annotated by G. D. Scull: [New York, Printed for the Society, 1882]; July 1, 1777, to July 1, 1778. pp. 467–68.

138. Morton, Robert. The Diary of Robert Morton, Kept in Philadelphia While that City Was Occupied. *The Pennsylvania Magazine of History and Biography* 1: 1 (1877) p. 19. NDAR 205.

139. Col. Joseph Reed to President Wharton, Oct. 24, 1777. *Pennsylvania Archives*, 1853 Volume 5: 701. Morton, Robert. The Diary of Robert Morton, Kept in Philadelphia While that City Was Occupied. *The Pennsylvania Magazine of History and Biography* 1: 1 (1877) pp. 1–39.

140. Extract of a letter from an Officer at Camp, Valley Forge, dated December 27. *Connecticut Journal* 536 (January 21, 1778) p. 3.

141. *Revolution in America: Confidential Letters and Journals 1776–1784 of Adjutant General Major Baurmeister of the Hessian Forces*. Translated and annotated by Bernhard A. Uhlendorf. New Brunswick, N.J.: Rutgers University Press, 1957. pp. 166–167.

142. Scull, G. D. (Gideon Delaplaine). *The Montresor Journals*. Ed. and annotated by G. D. Scull: [New York, Printed for the Society, 1882]; July 1, 1777, to July 1, 1778. p. 468.

143. Journal of HM Armed Schooner *Viper*, Lieutenant Edward Pakenham British National Archives, Admiralty 51/4385. NDAR 10: 235.

144. Scull, G. D. (Gideon Delaplaine). *The Montresor Journals*. Ed. and annotated by G. D. Scull: [New York, Printed for the Society, 1882]; July 1, 1777, to July 1, 1778. p. 469.

145. Lieutenant's Journal of HMS *Isis*, Captain William Cornwallis. British National Archives, Admiralty/L/J/116. Journal of HMS *Camilla*, Captain Charles Phipps. British National Archives, Admiralty 51/157. Journal of HMS *Pearl*, Captain John Linzee. British National Archives, Admiralty 51/675. Journal of HM Sloop *Zebra*, Commander John Orde. British National Archives, Admiralty 51/1100. Captain William Cornwallis, R. N. to Vice Admiral Viscount Howe. Isis off Billingsport 25 Oct. 1777. *William Cornwallis Papers, Letter Book*. pp. 64–65. NDAR 10: 286, 287.

146. Lt. Col. Samuel Smith to George Washington. Fort Mifflin. November 3, 1777. *George Washington Papers*. Series 4. Journal of Major Francois Louis Teissedre de Fleury. November 3, 1777. *George Washington Papers*. Series 4. Journal of HMS *Pearl*, Captain John Linzee. British National Archives, Admiralty 51/675. Journal of HM Sloop *Zebra*, Commander John Orde. British National Archives, Admiralty 51/1100. NDAR 10: 385, 386, 387.

147. Scull, G. D. (Gideon Delaplaine). *The Montresor Journals*. Ed. and annotated by G. D. Scull: [New York, Printed for the Society, 1882]; July 1, 1777, to July 1, 1778. p. 473. Brigadier General James M. Varnum to George Washington Woodberry 9th Novr. 1777. *George Washington Papers*. Series 4. NDAR 10: 448–49.

148. Brigadier General James M. Varnum to George Washington Woodberry 8th Novr. 1777. Brigadier General James M. Varnum to George Washington Woodberry 9th Novr. 1777. *George Washington Papers*. Series 4. NDAR 10: 434–435, 448–49.

149. Downman, Francis. "Services of Lieut.-Colonel Francis Downman, R. A., in France, North America, and the West Indies, between the Years 1758 and 1784" edited by F. A. Whinyates. In *Minutes of Proceedings of the Royal Artillery Institution*. Vol. 25. Woolwich, England: Royal Artillery Institution, 1898. p. 211. NDAR 10: 455.

150. Martin, Joseph Plumb, *Private Yankee Doodle; Being a Narrative of Some of the Adventures, Dangers, and Sufferings of a Revolutionary Soldier*. Edited by George F. Scheer, originally published in Hallowell, Me., 1830, anonymously. (Republished, Boston, 1962.). *A Narrative of Some of the Adventures, Dangers, and Sufferings*. (Eyewitness accounts of the American Revolution). [New York]: New York Times [1968]. pp. 89–90.

151. Brig. Gen. James Potter to George Washington. 12th November 1777. *George Washington Papers*. Series 4.

152. Scull, G. D. (Gideon Delaplaine). *The Montresor Journals*. Ed. and annotated by G. D. Scull: [New York, Printed for the Society, 1882]; July 1, 1777, to July 1, 1778. p. 475.

153. Scull, G. D. (Gideon Delaplaine). *The Montresor Journals*. Ed. and annotated by G. D. Scull: [New York, Printed for the Society, 1882]; July 1, 1777, to July 1, 1778. p. 476.

154. Journal of Captain James Parker. Parker Family Papers. City of Liverpool Library. Downman, Francis. "Services of Lieut.-Colonel Francis Downman, R. A., in France, North America, and the West Indies, between the Years 1758 and 1784" edited by F. A. Whinyates. In *Minutes of Proceedings of the Royal Artillery Institution*. Vol. 25. Woolwich, England: Royal Artillery Institution, 1898. p. 211. *Journal of Major Francois Louis Teissedre de Fleury*. November 3, 1777. *George Washington Papers*. Series 4. NDAR 10: 489, 490.

155. Scull, G. D. (Gideon Delaplaine). *The Montresor Journals*. Ed. and annotated by G. D. Scull: [New York, Printed for the Society, 1882]; July 1, 1777, to July 1, 1778. p. 478.

156. Scull, G. D. (Gideon Delaplaine). *The Montresor Journals*. Ed. and annotated by G. D. Scull: [New York, Printed for the Society, 1882]; July 1, 1777, to July 1, 1778. p. 478.

157. *Encyclopedia of the American Revolution*. Harold E. Selesky, editor in chief. 2nd ed. Detroit: Charles Scribner's Sons, 2007. I: 374–375. *The Encyclopedia of the American Revolutionary War: A Political, Social, and Military History*. Gregory Fremont-Barnes, Richard Alan Ryerson, editors. Santa Barbara, Calif.: ABC-CLIO, 2006. II: 428–429. Dorwart, Jeffery M. *Fort Mifflin of Philadelphia: An Illustrated History*. Philadelphia: University of Pennsylvania Press, 1998. Jackson, John. *The Pennsylvania Navy, 1775–1781: the Defense of the Delaware*. New Brunswick, N.J.: Rutgers University Press, 1974. Jackson, John W. *Fort Mifflin: Valiant Defender of the Delaware*. Philadelphia: Old Fort Mifflin Historical Society, 1986. Smith, Samuel Stelle. *Fight for the Delaware, 1777*. Monmouth Beach, N.J.: Philip Freneau Press, 1970. pp. 355–362. Ward, Christopher. *The War of the Revolution*. New York: Macmillan, 1952.

158. Scull, G. D. (Gideon Delaplaine). *The Montresor Journals*. Ed. and annotated by G. D. Scull: [New York, Printed for the Society, 1882]; July 1, 1777, to July 1, 1778. 468–469. Downman, Francis. "Services of Lieut.-Colonel Francis Downman, R. A., in France, North America, and the West Indies, between the Years 1758 and 1784" edited by F. A. Whinyates. In *Minutes of Proceedings of the Royal Artillery Institution*. Vol. 25. Woolwich, England: Royal Artillery Institution, 1898. pp. 42–43. NDAR 10: 224.

159. Scull, G. D. (Gideon Delaplaine). *The Montresor Journals*. Ed. and annotated by G. D. Scull: [New York, Printed for the Society, 1882]; July 1, 1777, to July 1, 1778. [New York: the New York Historical Society, 1882]. pp. 474, 485. *Revolution in America: Confidential Letters and Journals 1776–1784 of Adjutant General Major Baurmeister of the Hessian Forces*. Translated and annotated by Bernhard A. Uhlendorf. New Brunswick, N.J.: Rutgers University Press, 1957. pp. 164–167. Peebles, John. *John Peebles' American War: the Diary of a Scottish Grenadier, 1776–1782*. Edited by Ira D. Gruber. Mechanicsburg, Pa.: Stackpole Books, 1998. p. 175. Muenchhausen, Friedrich von. *At General Howe's Side 1776–1778: The Diary of General William Howe's Aide de Camp, Captain Friedrich von Muenchhausen*. Translated by Ernst Kipping and annotated by Samuel Smith. Monmouth Beach, N.J.: Philip Freneau Press, 1974. pp. 50–51. *The Pennsylvania Gazette* (May 2, 1778).

160. Simcoe, John Graves. *Simcoe's Military Journal. A History of the Operations of a Partisan Corps, Called the Queen's Rangers, Commanded by Lieut. Col. J. G. Simcoe*. New-York: Bartlett & Welford, 1844. pp. 56–61. Charles Stedman, *The History of the Origin, Progress and Termination of the American War*. London: printed for the author, 1794. 1: 372–376. Marshall, Christopher. *Extracts From the Diary of Christopher Marshall, Kept In Philadelphia and Lancaster, During the American Revolution, 1774–1781*. Edited by William Duane. Albany: Joel Munsell, 1877. Ward, Christopher. *The War of the Revolution*. New York: Macmillan, 1952. p. 355.

161. Report of Captain John Henry. *The New-York Gazette and Weekly Mercury* (Aug. 24, 1778). *The Pennsylvania Ledger: or the Philadelphia Market-Day Advertiser* CLII (May 13, 1778) p. 3. *Documents Relating to the Revolutionary History, State of New Jersey*. Edited by William S. Stryker. Trenton: The John L. Murphy Publishing Co., 1901. Series 2. 2: 217, 375–76.

162. Scull, G. D. (Gideon Delaplaine). *The Montresor Journals*. Ed. and annotated by G. D. Scull: [New York, Printed for the Society, 1882]; July 1, 1777, to July 1, 1778.: [New York: the New York Historical Society, 1882]. p. 474.

163. Extract of a letter from an Officer at Camp, Valley Forge, dated December 27. *Connecticut Journal* 536 (January 21, 1778) p. 3.

164. Peckham, Howard Henry. *Toll of Independence: Engagements & Battle Casualties of the American Revolution*. Edited by Howard H. Peckham. Chicago: University of Chicago Press, 1974. p. 47.

165. Parker, James. Parker Family Papers. Journal entry for November 9, 1777.

166. Morton, Robert. The Diary of Robert Morton, Kept in Philadelphia While that City Was Occupied. *The Pennsylvania Magazine of History and Biography* 1: 1 (1877) p. 30. McGuire, Thomas J. *The Philadelphia Campaign*. Mechanicsburg, Pa.: Stackpole Books, 2006–2007. 2: 235.

167. Waldo, Albigence. Valley Forge, 1777–1778: Diary of Surgeon Albigence Waldo. *Pennsylvania Magazine of History and Biography* XXI (1897) pp. 299–303, 308.

168. *Royal Gazette* 149 (December 27, 1777) p. 3.

169. *The Independent Chronicle and the Universal Advertiser* X: 478 (October 16, 1777) p. 2.

170. *Revolution in America: Confidential Letters and Journals 1776–1784 of Adjutant General Major Baurmeister of the Hessian Forces*. Translated and annotated by Bernhard A. Uhlendorf. New Brunswick, N.J.: Rutgers University Press, 1957. p. 157.

171. Baker, George. "The Camp by the Old Gulph Mill," *Pennsylvania Magazine* XVII, p. 423. *Revolution in America: Confidential Letters and Journals 1776–1784 of Adjutant General Major Baurmeister of the Hessian Forces*. Translated and annotated by Bernhard A. Uhlendorf. New Brunswick, N.J.: Rutgers University Press, 1957. p. 157. Ewald, Johann. *Diary of the American War: A Hessian Journal. Captain Johann Ewald*. Translated and edited by Joseph P. Tustin. New Haven and London: Yale University Press, 1979. pp. 121–122. Boatner, Mark Mayo. *Landmarks of the American Revolution*. 2nd ed. Library of Military History. Detroit: Charles Scribner's Sons, 2007. p. 296.

172. *Pennsylvania Archives*. Hazard, Samuel; Linn, John Blair, and others. [S.l.: s.n.], 1852–? 1st Series, Vol. IV. Martindale, Joseph C. *A History of the Townships of Byberry and Moreland: in Philadelphia, Pa., from their Earliest Settlement by the Whites to the Present Time*. Philadelphia: T. E. Zell, 1867.

173. *Revolution in America: Confidential Letters and Journals 1776–1784 of Adjutant General Major Baurmeister of the Hessian Forces*. Translated and annotated by Bernhard A. Uhlendorf. New Brunswick, N.J.: Rutgers University Press, 1957. p. 162. Scull, G. D. (Gideon Delaplaine). *The Montresor Journals*. Ed. and annotated by G. D. Scull: [New York, Printed for the Society, 1882]; July 1, 1777, to July 1, 1778. Ed. and annotated by G. D. Scull: [New York: the New York Historical Society, 1882]. pp. 474, 484. Library of Congress, *George Washington Papers*, Series 4, Reel 48, 17 March 1778–April 1778. Martindale, Joseph C. *A History of the Townships of Byberry and Moreland: in Philadelphia, Pa., from their Earliest Settlement by the Whites to the Present Time*. Philadelphia: T. E. Zell, 1867.

174. Head-Quarters Valley Forge, February 18, 1778. *The New-London Gazette* XV: 748 (March 13, 1778) p. 3.

175. *The Pennsylvania Evening Post* IV: 459 (February 21, 1778) p 79. *Pennsylvania Ledger*. February 21, 1778. *The New-York Gazette; and The Weekly Mercury* (March 23, 1778) 1378 p. 2. Moore, Frank. *Diary of the American Revolution: from Newspapers and Original Documents*. New York: Charles Scribner; London: Sampson Low, Son & Co., 1890, 2: 24–25. Scull, G. D. (Gideon Delaplaine). *The Montresor Journals*. Ed. and annotated by G. D. Scull: [New York, Printed for the Society, 1882]; July 1, 1777, to July 1, 1778.: [New York: the New York Historical Society, 1882]. pp. 474, 495–496.

176. Brigadier General William Smallwood to General George Washington. Wilmington, March 16, 1778. *George Washington Papers*, Series 4. NDAR 11: 663.

177. Brigadier General William Smallwood to General George Washington. George Washington Papers, Series 4. Addressed at foot: "General Washington." NDAR 11: 742.

178. Sparks. *Writings of Washington* pp. v, 368 in Tower, Charlemagne. *The Marquis de la Fayette in the American Revolution*. 2nd ed. Philadelphia: J. B. Lippincott Co., 1901. I: 327.

179. *Encyclopedia of the American Revolution*. Harold E. Selesky, editor in chief. 2nd ed. Detroit: Charles Scribner's Sons, 2007. I: 55–56. *The Encyclopedia of the American Revolutionary War: A Political, Social, and Military History*. Gregory Fremont-Barnes, Richard Alan Ryerson, editors. Santa Barbara, Calif.: ABC-CLIO, 2006. I: 83–84. Gottschalk, Louis. *Lafayette joins the American Army*. Chicago: University of Chicago Press, 1937. Jackson, John W. *With the British Army in Philadelphia, 1777–1778*. San Rafael, Calif.: Presidio Press, 1979. Lengel, Edward G. *General George Washington, A Military Life*. New York: Random House, 2005. Nelson, Paul David. *General James Grant: Scottish Soldier and Royal Governor of East Florida*. Gainesville: University Press of Florida, 1993. Nelson, Paul David. *Sir Charles Grey, First Earl Grey: Royal Soldier, Family Patriarch*. Madison, N.J.: Fairleigh Dickinson University Press, 1996. Scull, G. D. (Gideon Delaplaine). *The Montresor Journals*. Ed. and annotated by G. D. Scull: [New York, Printed for the Society, 1882]; July 1, 1777, to July 1, 1778. pp. 492–493. Taaffe, Stephen R. *The Philadelphia Campaign, 1777–1778*. Lawrence, KS: University Press of Kansas, 2003.

180. Peckham, Howard Henry. *Toll of Independence: Engagements & Battle Casualties of the American Revolution*. Edited by Howard H. Peckham. Chicago: University of Chicago Press, 1974. p. 50. Robertson, Archibald. *Archibald Robertson, Lieutenant-General Royal Engineers: his Diaries and Sketches in America, 1762–1780*. Edited with an introduction by Harry Miller Lydenberg. New York: The New York Public Library, 1930; The New York Public Library and the New York Times & Arno Press, 1971. p. 171.

181. *The Pennsylvania Ledger: or the Philadelphia Market-Day Advertiser* CLII (May 13, 1778) p. 3. *Connecticut Journal* 554 (May 27, 1778) p. 3. *Documents Relating to the Revolutionary History, State of New Jersey*. Edited by William S. Stryker. Trenton: The John L. Murphy Publishing Co., 1901. Series 2: 217, 375–376.

Delaware

1. Letter from Colonel Haslet to the Committee on Prisoners in the *Papers of the Continental Congress, 1774–1789*. Washington: National Archives and Records Service, General Services Administration, 1971, No. 78, XI, folio 29. Cullen, Virginia. *History of Lewes, Delaware: with Guided Tour of Historic Lewes*. Lewes, Del.: Col. David Hall Chapter, National Society of the Daughters of the American Revolution, 1981, ©1956. p. 20.

2. Pusey, Pennock. *History of Lewes Delaware*. Wilmington: Historical Society of Delaware, 1903. p. 26.

3. Peckham, Howard Henry. *Toll of Independence: Engagements & Battle Casualties of the American Revolution*. Edited by Howard H. Peckham. Chicago: University of Chicago Press, 1974. p. 18. Hancock, Harold Bell. *The Delaware Loyalists*. Boston: Gregg Press, 1972. p. 59.

4. *Papers of the Continental Congress, 1774–1789*. Washington: National Archives and Records Service, General Services Administration, 1971, No. 78, XIX. folio 143. Ryden, George Herbert, ed. *Letters to and from Caesar Rodney, 1756–1784*. New York: Da Capo, 1970. pp. 210–211. Peckham, Howard Henry. *Toll of Independence: Engagements & Battle Casualties of the American Revolution*. Edited by Howard H. Peckham. Chicago: University of Chicago Press, 1974. p. 38.

5. Journal of HMS *Perseus*, Captain Charles Phipps. British National Archives, Admiralty 51/688. NDAR 8: 256. Master's Log of HMS *Roebuck*. British National Archives. Admiralty 52/1965. NDAR 8: 257.

6. Pusey, Pennock. *History of Lewes Delaware*. Wilmington: Historical Society of Delaware, 1903. p. 26. Cullen, Virginia. *History of Lewes, Delaware: with Guided Tour of Historic Lewes*. Lewes, Del.: Col. David Hall Chapter, National Society of the Daughters of the American Revolution, 1981, ©1956. p. 21.

7. *Delaware: A Guide to the First State*. New York: The Viking Press, 1938. p. 270.

8. Jno. McKinly. Directed, to the Committee of Safety, Philadelphia. Favoured by the Rev. Mr. Davidson. John McKinly to the Pennsylvania Committee of Safety. Sam'l Miles. Directed, to Col. [Daniel] Roberdeau, or any of the Committee of Safety of Pennsylvania, Thos. Heinberger, Jacob Antony. Colonel Samuel Miles to the Pennsylvania Committee of Safety. Hazard, et al., eds., *Pennsylvania Archives*. 1st series, IV: 748, 749. NDAR 4: 1466. Alexander Wilcocks and others to the Pennsylvania Committee of Safety. Committee of Safety, Navy Papers, Pennsylvania Archives. NDAR 4: 1467. Autobiography of Joshua Barney, Manuscript Autobiography, Daughters of the American Revolution Library, Washington, D.C. NDAR 4: 1467. Journal of HMS *Roebuck*, Captain Andrew Snape Hamond, British National Archives, Admiralty 51/796. NDAR 4: 1470. Journal of HMS *Liverpool*, Captain Henry Bellew, British National Archives, Admiralty 51/548. NDAR 4: 1471. Narrative of Captain Andrew Snape Hamond, Hammond Papers, No. 4 and No. 5, University of Virginia Library, Charlottesville. NDAR 5: 15.

9. Lossing, Benson John. *The Pictorial Field-book of the Revolution; or, Illustrations, by Pen and Pencil, of the History, Biography, Scenery, Relics, and Traditions of the War for Independence*. New York, Harper & Brothers [1860]. Volume II. Chapter XIV. freepages.History.rootsweb.com/~wcarr1/lossing1/chap46.html.

10. Scull, G. D. (Gideon Delaplaine). *The Montresor Journals*; ed. and annotated by G. D. Scull: [New York: the New York Historical Society, 1882]. pp. 444–445. Peckham, Howard Henry. *Toll of Independence: Engagements & Battle Casualties of the American Revolution*. Edited by Howard H. Peckham. Chicago: University of Chicago Press, 1974. p. 39.

11. Scull, G. D. (Gideon Delaplaine). *The Montresor Journals*; ed. and annotated by G. D. Scull: [New York: the New York Historical Society, 1882]. p. 445. Peckham, Howard Henry. *Toll of Independence: Engagements & Battle Casualties of the American Revolution*. Edited by Howard H. Peckham. Chicago: University of Chicago Press, 1974. p. 39.

12. *The Virginia Gazette* 141 (March 10, 1777) p. 1.

13. Journal of HMS *Pearl*, Captain John Linzee. British National Archives, Admiralty 51/675. NDAR 9: 964–965.

14. Scharf, J. Thomas. *History of Delaware, 1609–1888*. Philadelphia: L. J. Richards, 1888. www.accessible.com/amcnty/DE/Delaware/delaware14.htm.

15. *Continental Journal* LXXI (October 2,1777) p. 4. From the *London Gazette Extraordinary*. *The Pennsylvania Ledger: or the Philadelphia Market-Day Advertiser* CXXXII (March 4, 1778) p. 1.

16. Extract of a Letter form Wilmington, dated January 11, 1778. Dunlap's *Maryland Gazette; or the Baltimore General Advertiser* (January 20, 1778).

17. News from Burlington, New Jersey. *Pennsylvania Packet, or the General Advertiser* (January 21, 1778).

18. Naval News from Philadelphia. *Royal American Gazette* (February 12, 1778).

19. Peckham, Howard Henry. *Toll of Independence: Engagements & Battle Casualties of the American Revolution*. Edited by Howard H. Peckham. Chicago: University of Chicago Press, 1974. p. 51. Journal of HMS *Cruizer*. British National Archives, Admiralty 51/218 Cpt. Log No. 218 Part 12 (1776). p. 109.

20. Peckham, Howard Henry. *Toll of Independence: Engagements & Battle Casualties of the American Revolution*. Edited by Howard H. Peckham. Chicago: University of Chicago Press, 1974. p. 18. Hancock, Harold Bell. *The Loyalists of Revolutionary Delaware*. Newark: University of Delaware Press, c1977. p. 43.

21. From the *London Gazette Extraordinary*. Tuesday, December, 2, 1777. *The Pennsylvania Ledger: or the Philadelphia Market-Day Advertiser* CXXXII (March 4, 1778) p. 1.

22. Purcell L Edward, and Sarah J. Purcell. *Encyclopedia of Battles in North America, 1517 to 1916*. New York: Facts on File, Inc., 2000. Stember, Sol. *The Bicentennial Guide to the American Revolution*. Saturday Review Press: New York, [distributed by] Dutton, 1794; [s.l.]: New York Times and Arno Press, 1969. II: 85–87, 90. Ward, Christopher. *The War of the Revolution*. New York: Macmillan, 1952. pp. 338–389.

23. Brig. Gen. William Smallwood to George Washington. *George Washington Papers*. Series 4. Addressed at bottom of second page: "His Excelly Genl Washington." Docketed: "Wilmington 30th decr/1777/from/Genl Smallwood. NDAR 10: 833. *The Pennsylvania Packet or the General Advertiser* (January 7, 1778) p. 3.

24. Peckham, Howard Henry. *Toll of Independence: Engagements & Battle Casualties of the American Revolution*. Edited by Howard H. Peckham. Chicago: University of Chicago Press, 1974. p. 47.

25. William Ellery to William Vernon. York Town Mh. 16th 1778. Papers of William Vernon and the Navy Board, 1776–1794. *Publications of the Rhode Island Historical Society*. New Series. Vol. 8. Providence, RI: Rhode Island Historical Society, 1900–1901. pp. 221–224. NDAR 11: 662.

26. Journal of HM Sloop *Dispatch*, Commander Christopher Mason. NDAR 11: 560. Journal of HMS *Experiment*, Captain Sir James Wallace. British National Archives, Admiralty 51/331 fols. 120–121. NDAR 11: 559–560. Capt. John Barry to Gen. George Washington Port Penn March 9, 1778. *George Washington Papers*. Series 4. Addressed: "On Publick Service/to /His Excellcy General Washington/at/Head Quarters/Near the Valley Forge." Docketed: "Capt Barry/of the Navy/9th March 1778/Ansd 12th" NDAR 11: 560–561. *Revolution in America: Confidential Letters and Journals 1776–1784 of Adjutant General Major Baurmeister of the Hessian Forces*. Translated and annotated by Bernhard A. Uhlendorf. New Brunswick, N.J.: Rutgers University Press, 1957. pp. 154–155.

27. Colonel Pope to C. Rodney, Grog or Whiskey Town, April 14, 1778. in Ryden, George H., ed. *Letters to and from Caesar Rodney, 1756–1784*. New York, Da Capo Press, 1970. p. 259, 263. Hancock, Harold Bell. *The Delaware Loyalists*. Boston: Gregg Press, 1972. pp. 34–35.

28. http://www.doverpost.com/PostArchives/07–03–02/pages/kentfarm.html.

29. Peckham, Howard Henry. *Toll of Independence: Engagements & Battle Casualties of the American Revolution*. Edited by Howard H. Peckham. Chicago: University of Chicago Press, 1974. p. 50.

30. *History of Delaware: 1609–1888: Local History*. www.archive.org/stream/HistorydelawareOOunkngoog/HistorydelawareOOunkngoog_djvu.txt.

31. From Brigadier General William Smallwood. Wilmington May 17th 1778. From Brigadier General William Smallwood. Wilmington 22d May 1778. Washington, George. *The Papers of George Washington*. Revolutionary War series. Philander D. Chase, editor. Charlottesville: University Press of Virginia, 1985–. 15: 146–148.

32. *The Freeman's Journal; or, The North-American Intelligencer* II: XCVII (February 26, 1783) p. 33. *The New-York Gazette; and The Weekly Mercury* 1556 (August 13, 1781) p. 3.

Maryland

1. Allen, Thomas B. *Tories: Fighting for the King in America's First Civil War*. New York: Harper, c2010. Lossing, Benson John. *Harpers' Popular Cyclopaedia of United States History from the Aboriginal Period Containing Brief Sketches of Important Events and Conspicuous Actors*. New York: Harper, 1893. 1: 409. Nelson, Larry L. *A Man of Distinction Among Them: Alexander McKee and the Ohio Country Frontier, 1754–1799*. Kent, Ohio: Kent State University Press, c1999. pp. 94ff. Shallus, Francis. *Chronological Tables for Every Day in the Year*. compiled from the most authentic documents by Francis Shallus. Philadelphia: Merritt, printer, 1817. p. 410.

2. Peckham, Howard Henry. *Toll of Independence: Engagements & Battle Casualties of the American Revolution*. Edited by Howard H. Peckham. Chicago: University of Chicago Press, 1974. pp. 16, 33. Scharf, John Thomas. *History of Maryland*. Baltimore: John Piet, 1879. 2: 306.

3. T. Stone to Thomas Sim Lee, April 17, 1781. *Archives*. 47: 197–8; George Weedon to Jefferson, April 21, 1781; Edmund Read to Jefferson, April 24, 1781; Julian P. Boyd, ed. *The Papers of Thomas Jefferson*. 5: 25 February 1781 to 20 May 1781 Princeton, N.J.: Princeton University Press, 1952. 5: 529, 548. George Weedon to Jefferson, April 21, 1781; Oliver Towles to Steuben, April 14, 1781, cited in Julian P. Boyd, ed. *The Papers of Thomas Jefferson*. 5: 25 February 1781 to 20 May 1781 Princeton, N.J.: Princeton University Press, 1952, 5: 448, 529–30. Letters to Jefferson from Richard Henry Lee (April 13, 1781), James Mercer (April 14, 1781), John Skinker and William Garrard (April 14, 1781), Julian P. Boyd, ed. *The Papers of Thomas Jefferson*. 5: 25 February 1781 to 20 May 1781. Princeton, N.J.: Princeton University Press, 1952, 5: 435, 447, 451; Oliver Towles to Baron von Steuben, April 14, 1781, cited in *The Papers of Thomas Jefferson*. 5: 448; John Taylor to Jefferson, April 15, 1781, in William Palmer, et al., eds. *Calendar of Virginia State Papers*. Richmond, 1875. 2: 41. freepages.genealogy.rootsweb.ancestry.com/~bush22031/Raids.html.

4. Deposition of John Matthews and William Stoddert. *Maryland Gazette*, November 7, 1776. NDAR 6: 1324–1325.

5. Col. Richard Barnes to the Maryland Council of Safety. Red Book, X, *Archives of Maryland*. Browne, William Hand; Hall, Clayton Colman. Baltimore, Maryland Historical Society. 1883–.; NDAR 5: 1066. Lieutenant Colonel Alexander Somerville to the Maryland Council of Safety. Red Book, X, *Archives of Maryland*. Browne, William Hand; Hall, Clayton Colman. Baltimore, Maryland Historical Society. 1883–. NDAR 5: 1080.

6. NDAR 5: 1093.

7. NDAR 5: 1119.

8. NDAR 6: 132. *Essex Journal* 3: 138 (August 23, 1776) p. 3. Mays, Terry M. H*istorical Dictionary of the American Revolution*. Scarecrow Press: Lanham, Md., 1999.

9. Brigadier General John Dent to the Maryland Council of Safety. Red Book. XV. *Maryland Archives*. NDAR, 5: 1163.

10. Journal of HMS *Fowey*, Captain George Montagu. British National Archives, Admiralty 51/378. NDAR 5: 1220.

11. Journal of the HMS *Fowey*. British National Archives, Admiralty 51/375; NDAR 5: 1220.

12. Major Thomas Price to the Maryland Council of Safety. *Red Book*, XV, *Archives of Maryland*. Browne, William Hand; Hall, Clayton Colman. Baltimore, Maryland Historical Society. 1883–. NDAR 5: 1275.

13. Purdie's *Virginia Gazette* (December 12, 1777). NDAR 10: 715.

14. Thomas Ennals to the Maryland Council of Safety. Correspondence of the Council of Safety. *Maryland Archives*. NDAR, 5: 885–886.

15. Master's Log of HMS *Roebuck*. British National Archives, Admiralty 52/1965; NDAR 5: 1172.

16. Baltimore, August 29. *The Norwich Packet and the Weekly Advertiser* 364 (September 21, 1780) p. 3.

17. Peckham, Howard Henry. *Toll of Independence: Engagements & Battle Casualties of the American Revolution*. Edited by Howard H. Peckham. Chicago: University of Chicago Press, 1974. p. 75.

18. John Skinker to Jefferson, April 11, 1781, Julian P. Boyd, ed. *The Papers of Thomas Jefferson.* 5: 25 February 1781 to 20 May 1781 (Princeton, N.J.: Princeton University Press, 1952) 5: 406. John Skinker to Jefferson, April 11, 1781, Julian P. Boyd, ed. *The Papers of Thomas Jefferson.* 5: 25 February 1781 to 20 May 1781 Princeton, N.J.: Princeton University Press, 1952, 5: 406. Daniel Jenifer to Thomas Sim Lee, April 8, 1781. *Archives* 47: 172–3.

Rev. Mathews was a Jesuit at St. Thomas Manor; see Lee. *The Price of Nationhood.* pp. 15, 151. T. Stone to Thomas Sim Lee, April 8, 1781. *Maryland Historical Magazine* 4 (1909). p. 381. Daniel Jenifer to Thomas Sim Lee, April 8, 1781. *Archives.* 47: 172–3; T. Stone to Thomas Sim Lee, April 8, 1781. *Maryland Historical Magazine* 4: 382. Accounts from the Virginia side, which are not first hand, also suggest that a Mr. Neale had his house plundered and was kidnapped along with Samuel Hanson, and that a Mr. Lawson owned the boat loaded with 100 barrels of corn. See Henry Lee, Sr. to Jefferson, April 9, 1781. Julian P. Boyd, ed. *The Papers of Thomas Jefferson.* 5: 25 February 1781 to 20 May 1781. Princeton, N.J.: Princeton University Press, 1952. 5: 393. freepages.genealogy.rootsweb.ancestry.com/~bush22031/Raids.html.

19. Brigadier General Henry Hooper to Daniel of St. Thomas Jenifer. Red Book, XV. *Archives of Maryland.* Browne, William Hand; Hall, Clayton Colman. Baltimore, Maryland Historical Society. 1883–. NDAR 5: 1296.

20. Major Nathaniel Smith to Governor Thomas Johnson. Fort at Whetstone Augt 23d 1777. Brown Books. V, 50. Maryland Archives. Aquila Hall to Governor Thomas Johnson. Red Books. XVIII, 102. Maryland Archives. NDAR 9: 788, 795.

21. Master's Log of HM Sloop *Haerlem.* British National Archives, Admiralty 52/1789. NDAR 9: 834.

22. See Washington to Nelson, Sept. 2, 1777. Washington, George. *The Writings of George Washington.* Ed. John C. Fitzpatrick. Washington, D.C., 1963. IX: 164); and Scull, G. D. (Gideon Delaplaine). *The Montresor Journals.* Ed. and annotated by G. D. Scull: [New York: the New York Historical Society, 1882].

23. *Revolution in America: Confidential Letters and Journals 1776–1784 of Adjutant General Major Baurmeister of the Hessian Forces.* Translated and annotated by Bernhard A. Uhlendorf. New Brunswick, N.J.: Rutgers University Press, 1957. pp. 100–101.

24. Ewald, Johann. *Diary of the American War: A Hessian Journal. Captain Johann Ewald.* Translated and edited by Joseph P. Tustin. New Haven and London: Yale University Press, 1979. p. 77.

25. Thomas Nelson, Jr. to George Washington. Williamsburg, Sept. 5th 1777. *George Washington Papers.* NDAR 9: 884.

26. Journal of HMS *Phoenix*, Captain Hyde Parker, Jr. British National Archives. Admiralty 51/694. Col. Richard Barnes to Governor Thomas Johnson. 20th Decr. 1777. NDAR 10: 753, 766.

27. www.riverheritage.org/RiverGuide/Sites/html/benoni_point.html.

28. Shomette, Donald G. *Pirates on the Chesapeake, A True History of Pirates, Picaroons and Raiders on the Chesapeake Bay 1610–1807.* Centreville, Md..: Tidewater Publishers, 1985. calvert-county.com/Pirates/pirates.html.

29. *The New Jersey Gazette* IV: 173 (April 18, 1781) p. 3.

30. Joshua Beall to Thomas Sim Lee, April 15, 1781. *Archives.* 47: 188. Around the 14th or 15th, there were reports of enemy boats off St. George's Island in St. Mary's County, Maryland and of warnings of attacks up the Patuxent River. Richard Barnes to Thomas Sim Lee, April 15, 1781; Joshua Beall to Thomas Sim Lee, April 16, 1781. *Archives.* 47: 190, 190.

31. Peckham, Howard Henry. *Toll of Independence: Engagements & Battle Casualties of the American Revolution.* Edited by Howard H. Peckham. Chicago: University of Chicago Press, 1974. p. 84.

Virginia

1. *Virginia Magazine of History and Biography* 14: 133. *The New-Hampshire Gazette, and Historical Chronicle.* 20: 994 (November 21, 1775) p. 2. Eckenrode, H. J. *The Revolution In Virginia.* Hamden, Conn.: Archon Books, 1964. p. 60.

2. Journal of HM Sloop *Kingfisher*, Captain James Montagu. British National Archives. Admiralty 51/506. NDAR 2: 665.

3. *The Connecticut Journal* 427 (December 20, 1775) p. 3. *The Pennsylvania Gazette* (December 13, 1775).

4. Peckham, Howard Henry. *Toll of Independence: Engagements & Battle Casualties of the American Revolution.* Edited by Howard H. Peckham. Chicago: University of Chicago Press, 1974. p. 12.

5. Williamsburg, Jan. 27. Dixon and Hunter's *Virginia Gazette* (January 27, 1776). *The Pennsylvania Gazette* (February 7, 1776). NDAR 3: 1019.

6. Journal of HM Sloop *Kingfisher.* British National Archives. Admiralty 51/506. NDAR 3: 1187.

7. Journal of HM Sloop *Otter.* British National Archives, Admiralty 51/663; NDAR 5: 535.

8. Sir Henry Clinton's instructions to Major General Leslie. Headquarters, October 12, 1780. Clinton, Sir Henry. *The American Rebellion Sir Henry Clinton's Narrative of His Campaigns, 1775–1782, with an Appendix of Original Documents.* Edited by William B. Willcox. New Haven: Yale University Press, 1954. p. 467. Cornwallis to Clinton. August 6, 1780. Ibid. pp. 448–449. Extract from the second instructions from Sir Henry Clinton to Major General Leslie. New York, November 2, 1780. Ibid. p. 472. Extract of a Letter from Richmond, Virginia, Dated October 22. *Connecticut Courant* 825 (November 14, 1780) p. 2. *The Independent Ledger, and the American Advertiser* (November 20, 1780) III: 128 p. 3. *The New-York Gazette; and The Weekly Mercury* 1516 (November 6 1780) p. 3. Philadelphia, November 1. *The New-York Gazette; and The Weekly Mercury* 1517 (November 13, 1780) p. 2. Selby, John E. *The Revolution in Virginia, 1775–1783.* by John E. Selby. Williamsburg, Va.: Colonial Williamsburg Foundation; Charlottesville, Va.: Distributed by University Press of Virginia, c1988. pp. 216–221.

9. *Connecticut Journal* 704 (April 26, 1781) p. 4.

10. *The Pennsylvania Evening Post* 1: 121 (October 31, 1775) p. 495. Captain Samuel Leslie to Major General William Howe. Gosport, Virginia 1st Novr. 1775. NDAR 2: 844, 4: 1369, 5: 487, 6: 749.

11. Eller, Ernest McNeill, ed. *Chesapeake Bay in the American Revolution*. Centreville, Md.: Tidewater Publishers, 1981. pp. 76–77.

12. *Boston Gazette* (December 3, 1775). *Essex Journal* 3: 105 (January 1, 1776) p. 3.

13. Journal of HM Sloop *Otter*, Captain Matthew Squire. British National Archives, Admiralty 51/663. NDAR 3: 199.

14. Ibid., 3: 325.

15. *Encyclopedia of the American Revolution*. Harold E. Selesky, editor in chief. 2nd ed. Detroit: Charles Scribner's Sons, 2007. II: 847. *The Encyclopedia of the American Revolutionary War: A Political, Social, and Military History*. Gregory Fremont-Barnes, Richard Alan Ryerson, editors. Santa Barbara, Calif.: ABC-CLIO, 2006. III: 912–913. Blanco, Richard L., ed. *The War of the Revolution, 1775–1783: An Encyclopedia*. New York: Garland Pub., 1993. Mays, Terry M. *Historical Dictionary of the American Revolution*. Scarecrow Press: Lanham, Md., 1999. Montross, Lynn. *The Reluctant Rebels: the Story of the Continental Congress, 1774–1789*. New York: Harper, 1950. Selby, John E. *The Revolution in Virginia, 1775–1783*. Williamsburg: The Colonial Williamsburg Foundation, 1988. Stember, Sol. *The Bicentennial Guide to the American Revolution*. Saturday Review Press: New York, [distributed by] Dutton, 1794; [s.l.]: New York Times and Arno Press, 1969. III: 173–175, 189. Ward, Christopher. *The War of the Revolution*. New York: Macmillan, 1952. 847–849. Wertenbaker, Thomas J. *Norfolk, Historic Southern Port*. Durham, N.C.: Duke University Press, 1931.

16. Journal of HM Sloop *Otter*, Captain Matthew Squire. British National Archives, Admiralty 51/663. *London Chronicle*. April 16 to April 18, 1776. NDAR 3: 622; 4: 38.

17. Peckham, Howard Henry. *Toll of Independence: Engagements & Battle Casualties of the American Revolution*. Edited by Howard H. Peckham. Chicago: University of Chicago Press, 1974. p. 12.

18. Journal of HMS *Liverpool*, Captain Henry Bellew. British National Archives, Admiralty 51/548. NDAR 3: 839.

19. *The Pennsylvania Gazette* (February 7, 1776).

20. Journal of HMS *Liverpool*, Captain Henry Bellew. British National Archives, Admiralty 51/548. NDAR 3: 927.

21. *The Pennsylvania Gazette* (February 21, 1776).

22. Purdie's *Virginia Gazette* (February 9, 1776). NDAR 3: 1187.

23. Journal of HM Sloop *Otter* Friday April 5, 1776. British National Archives, Admiralty 51/663 NDAR 4: 690.

24. Ward, Christopher. *The War of the Revolution*. New York: Macmillan, 1952.

25. Eller, Ernest McNeill, ed. *Chesapeake Bay in the American Revolution*. Centreville, Md.: Tidewater Publishers, 1981. p. 68. Butt, Marshall W. *Portsmouth Under Four Flags, 1752–1970*. Portsmouth, VA: Portsmouth Historical Association and the Friends of the Portsmouth Naval Shipyard Museum, 1971. pp. 9–10.

26. Journal of HM Sloop *Otter*, Captain Matthew Squire. British National Archives, Admiralty 51/663. Journal of HMS *Liverpool*, Captain Henry Bellew. British National Archives, Admiralty 51/548. NDAR 3: 1092. Extract of a letter from Col. Woodford to the President of the Convention, dated Norfolk, Jan, 21, 1776 in *Connecticut Journal* 436 (February 21, 1776) p. 1. Purdie's *Virginia Gazette* (January 26, 1776). NDAR 3: 905.

27. Account of the Operations of His Majesty's Forces in Virginia, Received the 17th Instant by His Majesty's Ship *General Monk. Royal Georgia Gazette* 123 (July 5, 1781) p. 2. *The Freeman's Journal: or, The North-American Intelligencer* VI (May 30, 1781) p. 2. Ward, Christopher. *The War of the Revolution*. New York: Macmillan, 1952.

28. Journal of HM Sloop *Kingfisher*, Captain James Montagu. British National Archives, Admiralty 51/506. Purdie's *Virginia Gazette, Supplement*. Friday, October 20, 1775. Lord Dunmore to Lord Dartmouth. British National Archives. Colonial Office, 5/1353. Captain Samuel Leslie to Major General William Howe. Gosport Virginia 1st Novr. 1775. NDAR 2: 511, 545, 574, 844.

29. NDAR 2: 1309–11, 4: 1369, 5: 487, 6: 749. Eller, Ernest McNeill, ed. *Chesapeake Bay in the American Revolution*. Centreville, Md.: Tidewater Publishers, 1981. p. 18. *Virginia Magazine of History and Biography* 14: 387. Brooke, John. *King George III*. New York, McGraw-Hill [1972]. p. 219. *Maryland Gazette* (November 29, 1781). *The Pennsylvania Evening Post* 1: 139 (December 12, 1775) p. 570. *Virginia Gazette* (January 24, 1776).

30. Eller, Ernest McNeill, ed. *Chesapeake Bay in the American Revolution*. Centreville, Md.: Tidewater Publishers, 1981. pp. 81–82.

31. *Connecticut Journal* 423 (November 22, 1775) p. 3.

32. *The Newport Mercury* 901 (December 11, 1775) p. 1.

33. *The Pennsylvania Evening Post* 1: 131 (November 23, 1775) p. 539.

34. Simcoe, John Graves. *Simcoe's Military Journal. A History of the Operations of a Partisan Corps, Called the Queen's Rangers, Commanded by Lieut. Col. J. G. Simcoe*. New-York: Bartlett & Welford, 1844. pp. 190–192. *Pennsylvania Gazette* (May 30, 1781) p. 3. Paullin, Charles Oscar. *Paullin's History of Naval Administration, 1775–1911: A Collection of Articles from the U.S. Naval Institute Proceedings*: Annapolis: U.S. Naval Institute, 1968. p. 86.

35. *The Pennsylvania Gazette* (May 30, 1781) p. 3. Peckham, Howard Henry. *Toll of Independence: Engagements & Battle Casualties of the American Revolution*. Edited by Howard H. Peckham. Chicago: University of Chicago Press, 1974. p. 84. Account of the Operations of His Majesty's Forces in Virginia, Received the 17th Instant by His Majesty's Ship *General Monk. Royal Georgia Gazette* 123 (July 5, 1781) p. 2. Simcoe, John Graves. *Simcoe's Military Journal. A History of the Operations of a Partisan Corps, Called the Queen's Rangers, Commanded by Lieut. Col. J. G. Simcoe*. New-York: Bartlett & Welford, 1844. pp. 189–192.

36. Journal of HM Sloop *Kingfisher*, Captain James Montagu. British National Archives, Admiralty 51/506. NDAR 2: 1087.

37. Journal of Captain Andrew Snape Hamond. British National Archives. Admiralty 1/487. NDAR 4: 401–2.

38. Peckham, Howard Henry. *Toll of Independence: Engagements & Battle Casualties of the American Revolution.* Edited by Howard H. Peckham. Chicago: University of Chicago Press, 1974. p. 10.

39. Pinkney's *Virginia Gazette* (December 20, 1775).

40. Letter from Colonel Scott to Captain Southall. *New England Chronicle.* 8: 388 (From Thursday, December 28, 1775 to Thursday, January 4, 1776) p. 2.

41. Woodford's letter of December 7, 1775.

42. Ewald, Johann. *Diary of the American War: A Hessian Journal. Captain Johann Ewald.* Translated and edited by Joseph P. Tustin. New Haven and London: Yale University Press, 1979. p. 288.

43. Purdie's *Virginia Gazette Supplement* (November 24, 1775). NDAR 2: 1120.

44. Extract of a Letter from an Officer in the Southern Army. *The Pennsylvania Packet or the General Advertiser* X: 703 (January 30, 1781) p. 3. *Connecticut Courant* 838 (February 13, 1781) p. 2. *The New Jersey Gazette* IV: 163 (February 7, 1781) p. 3. Narrative of the Movements of the Enemy since Our Last. *The American Journal And General Advertiser* II: 102 (February 17, 1781) p. 1. *The Norwich Packet and the Weekly Advertiser* 385 (February 20, 1781) p. 2. Richmond, (Virginia) January 20. *The Independent Ledger, and the American Advertiser* III: 142 (February 19, 1781) p. 2.

45. Dixon and Hunter's *Virginia Gazette* (December 2, 1775). NDAR 2: 1239.

46. Journal of HM Sloop *Otter*, Captain Matthew Squire. British National Archives. Admiralty 51/663. NDAR 3: 663, 686.

47. Journal of HM Sloop *Otter*. British National Archives, Admiralty 51/663; NDAR 3: 1092. Journal of HMS *Liverpool.* British National Archives, Admiralty 51/548; NDAR 3: 1092. Purdie's *Virginia Gazette* (February 9, 1776). NDAR 3: 1187. *The Constitutional Gazette* 61 (February 28, 1776) p. 1.

48. Account of A. S. Hamond's part in Clinton, Sir Henry. *The American Rebellion Sir Henry Clinton's Narrative of his Campaigns, 1775–1782, with an Appendix of Original Documents.* Edited by William B. Willcox. New Haven: Yale University Press, 1954. (Feb. 12–27, 1776). A. S. Hamond Naval Papers, 1766–1825, roll I, Alderman Library microfilm, Foundation Library. Selby, John E. *The Revolution in Virginia, 1775–1783.* by John E. Selby. Williamsburg, Va.: Colonial Williamsburg Foundation; Charlottesville, Va.: Distributed by University Press of Virginia, c1988. p. 86.

49. *The Pennsylvania Gazette* (February 14, 1776).

50. *The Constitutional Gazette* 84 (May 18, 1776) p. 2. *Essex Journal* III: 126 (May 31, 1776) p. 2.

51. Extract of a letter from Chin[c]oteague, May 20. *Pennsylvania Journal* (May 29, 1776). NDAR 5: 174, 321. Wrike, Peter Jennings. *The Governors' Island: Gwynn's Island Virginia, during the Revolution.* Gwynn, Va.: Gwynn's Island Museum, 1995.

52. Peckham, Howard Henry. *Toll of Independence: Engagements & Battle Casualties of the American Revolution.* Edited by Howard H. Peckham. Chicago: University of Chicago Press, 1974.

53. NDAR 5: 939.

54. NDAR 5: 1078–79.

55. NDAR 5: 1147–49. *The Pennsylvania Evening Post* 2: 238 (July 30, 1776) p. 375.

56. NDAR 5: 1150–51.

57. Williamsburg, July 19. Purdie's *Virginia Gazette* (July 19, 1776). NDAR 5: 1147.

58. Master's Log of HMS *Roebuck.* British National Archives, Admiralty 52/1965. NDAR 5: 1194. Dunlap's *Maryland Gazette.* Baltimore, August 20, 1776. Lord Dunmore to Lord George Germain, British National Archives Colonial Office, 5/1353. NDAR 5: 1313. Narrative of Captain Andrew Snape Hamond. Hamond, No. 5, University of Virginia Library. NDAR 6: 173. Deposition of John Matthews and William Stoddert. *Maryland Gazette* (November 7, 1776). NDAR 6: 1324–1325

59. Extract of an undated Letter From Dumfries, In Virginia [July 24]. *The Remembrancer, or Impartial Repository of Public Events.* Almon, John, Pownall, Thomas. London: J. Almon, 1775–1784. III: 334. NDAR 5: 1206–1207.

60. "News of the Yorktown Campaign: The Journal of Dr. Robert Honyman." MacMaster, Richard K., ed. *Virginia Magazine of History and Biography* 79 (1971) pp. 391, 397. Lassiter, Francis Rives. *Arnold's Invasion of Virginia, 1781.* [New York]: Longmans, Green, 1901.

61. Journal of HMS *Perseus.* British National Archives, Admiralty 51/688 – Captain's Log No. 688 Part 2 (1777) p. 76. Peckham, Howard Henry. *Toll of Independence: Engagements & Battle Casualties of the American Revolution.* Edited by Howard H. Peckham. Chicago: University of Chicago Press, 1974. p. 40.

62. Peckham, Howard Henry. *Toll of Independence: Engagements & Battle Casualties of the American Revolution.* Edited by Howard H. Peckham. Chicago: University of Chicago Press, 1974. p. 59.

63. Peckham, Howard Henry. *Toll of Independence: Engagements & Battle Casualties of the American Revolution.* Edited by Howard H. Peckham. Chicago: University of Chicago Press, 1974. p. 73.

64. Journal of HMS *St. Albans*, Captain Richard Onslow. British National Archives, Admiralty 51/828. NDAR 10: 705.

65. *The Pennsylvania Evening Post, and Public Advertiser* VIII: 807 (March 12, 1782) p. 20.

66. *The New York Gazette and the Weekly Mercury* 1411 (November 2, 1778) p. 3.

67. Journal of HMS *Richmond*. British National Archives, Admiralty 51/784 –Cpt Log 784 Part 3 (1779) p. 90.

68. Eller, Ernest McNeill, ed. *Chesapeake Bay in the American Revolution*. Centreville, Md.: Tidewater Publishers, 1981. p. 466.

69. Clinton, Sir Henry. *The American Rebellion Sir Henry Clinton's Narrative of His Campaigns, 1775–1782, with an Appendix of Original Documents*. Edited by William B. Willcox. New Haven: Yale University Press, 1954. p. 122. Henry to John Jay, May 11, 1779. Madison, James. *Papers*. Edited by William T. Hutchinson and William M. E. Rachal. Chicago: University of Chicago Press, 1962–. 1: 282–283. Henry to Jay, May 12, 1779. Henry to R. H. Lee, May 19, 1779. Henry, William Wirt. *Patrick Henry; Life, Correspondence and Speeches*. New York, B. Franklin [1969]. 3: 240; 2: 30. Sir George Collier to Clinton, May 16, 1779. Sir Henry Clinton Papers, 1776–1779. Clements Library. Collier to Philip Stevens, May 17, 1779. Edward Mathew to Clinton, May 16, 24, 1779. Almon, J. *The Remembrancer, or Impartial Repository of Public Events*. London, 1779. Vol. 8 pt. 2 pp. 290–297. Ward, Christopher. *The War of the Revolution*. New York: Macmillan, 1952. p. 857. Selby, John E. *The Revolution in Virginia, 1775–1783*. by John E. Selby. Williamsburg, Va.: Colonial Williamsburg Foundation; Charlottesville, Va.: Distributed by University Press of Virginia, c1988. pp. 204–208. *Encyclopedia of the American Revolution*. Harold E. Selesky, editor in chief. 2nd ed. Detroit: Charles Scribner's Sons, 2007. I: 376. *The Encyclopedia of the American Revolutionary War: A Political, Social, and Military History*. Gregory Fremont-Barnes, Richard Alan Ryerson, editors. Santa Barbara, Calif.: ABC-CLIO, 2006. II: 431.

70. "Biographical Memoir of Sir George Collier, Knt., Vice-Admiral of the Blue" *The Naval Chronicle for 1814: Containing a General and Biographical History of the Royal Navy of the United Kingdom* XXXII (1814) pp. 265–296, 353–400, 360–367. Collier to Stephens, June 13, 1779. Almon, J. *The Remembrancer, or Impartial Repository of Public Events*. London, 1779. Vol. 8 pt. 2 p. 299. Collier to Germain, June 15, 1779. Germain Papers, 1768–1782. Clements Library. *The Pennsylvania Gazette* (June 9, 1779).

71. Ewald, Johann. *Diary of the American War: A Hessian Journal*. Captain Johann Ewald; Translated and edited by Joseph P. Tustin. New Haven and London: Yale University Press, 1979. p. 278.

72. *The New-York Gazette; and The Weekly Mercury* 1529 (February 5, 1781) p. 3

73. MS journal of the Jager Corps; Ewald, Johann von. *Belehrungen über den Krieg: Besonders über den Kleinen Krieg, Durch Beispiele Großer Helden und Kluger und Tapferer Männer*. 2: 169. Eelking, Max von. Die Deutschen Hülfstruppen im Nordamerikanischen Befreiungskriege, 1776 bis 1783. Kassel: Horst Hamecher, 1976, 1863 (*German Mercenaries in Pensacola During the American Revolution, 1779–1781*. [Pensacola, Fla.]: Pensacola Historical Society, 1977). II: 107, 108). Ewald, Johann. *Diary of the American War: A Hessian Journal*. Captain Johann Ewald; Translated and edited by Joseph P. Tustin. New Haven and London: Yale University Press, 1979. pp. 289–291.

74. Peckham, Howard Henry. *Toll of Independence: Engagements & Battle Casualties of the American Revolution*. Edited by Howard H. Peckham. Chicago: University of Chicago Press, 1974. p. 60.

75. Palmer, William T. Description of Henry's Point Raid. *Southern Literary Messenger* (June 1857) pp. 275–277. Wise, Barton Haxall. *Memoir of General John Cropper of Accomack County, Virginia*. Reprinted from *Virginia Historical Collections*. V. XI, 1892. Onancock, VA: Eastern Shore of Virginia Historical Society, 1974. Barnes, Alton Brooks Parker. *John Cropper: A Life Fully Lived*. Onley, Va.: L. Howard Co., 1989. pp. 61–63.

76. Jefferson, Thomas. *The Papers of Thomas Jefferson*. Princeton: Princeton University Press, 1950–4: 399. Ward, Christopher. *The War of the Revolution*. New York: Macmillan, 1952. Eller, Ernest McNeill, ed. *Chesapeake Bay in the American Revolution*. Centreville, Md.: Tidewater Publishers, 1981. p. 463. Extract of a Letter from an Officer in the Southern Army. *The Pennsylvania Packet or the General Advertiser* X: 703 (January 30, 1781) p. 3. *Connecticut Journal* 694 (February 15, 1781) p. 2. *Connecticut Courant* 838 (February 13, 1781) p. 2. *The New Jersey Gazette* IV: 163 (February 7, 1781) p. 3. Narrative of the Movements of the Enemy since Our Last. *The American Journal And General Advertiser* II: 102 (February 17, 1781) p. 1. *The Norwich Packet and the Weekly Advertiser* 385 (February 20, 1781) p. 2. Richmond (Virginia) January 20. *The Independent Ledger, and the American Advertiser* III: 142 (February 19, 1781) p. 2.

77. Letter from Benedict Arnold to Sir Henry Clinton, dated the 21st of January at Portsmouth VA. It's found in "Documents of the American Revolution 1770–1783," (Colonial Office Series), Volume XX, "Transcripts 1781" edited by K. G. Davies, Irish University Press, 1979. *Rivington's Gazette* (February 7, 1781). Simcoe, John Graves. *Simcoe's Military Journal. A History of the operations of a Partisan Corps called the Queen's Rangers, commanded by Lieut. Col. J. G. Simcoe*. New York: Bartlett & Welford, 1844. pp. 168–169. Jefferson, Thomas. *The Papers of Thomas Jefferson*. Princeton: Princeton University Press, 1950–. 4: 399. *The New-York Gazette; and The Weekly Mercury* 1529 (February 5, 1781) p. 3. Eller, Ernest McNeill, ed. *Chesapeake Bay in the American Revolution*. Centreville, Md.: Tidewater Publishers, 1981. p. 466.

78. *The New Jersey Gazette* IV: 163 (February 7, 1781) p. 3.

79. *The New Jersey Gazette* V: 172 (April 11, 1781) p. 3.

80. "News of the Yorktown Campaign: The Journal of Dr. Robert Honyman." MacMaster, Richard K., ed. *Virginia Magazine of History And Biography* 79 (1971) p. 397. (May 11, 1781). Pendleton to Madison, May 7, 1781. Letters and Papers of Pendleton. 1: 354. Simcoe, John Graves. *Simcoe's Military Journal. A History of the Operations of a Partisan Corps Called the Queen's Rangers, Commanded by Lieut. Col. J. G. Simcoe, During the War of the American Revolution*. New-York: Bartlett & Welford, 1844; [New York]: New York Times; Arno Press. *Eyewitness Accounts of the American Revolution*. [1968]. pp. 201–202. *The Freeman's Journal: or, The North-American Intelligencer* VI (May 30, 1781) p. 2.

81. *The Pennsylvania Gazette* (May 30, 1781).

82. Blanco, Richard L., ed. *The War of the Revolution, 1775–1783: An Encyclopedia*. New York: Garland Pub., 1993. Mark M. Boatner. *The Encyclopedia of the American Revolution*. New York: David McKay, 1966. Purcell, L. Edward, and Sarah J. Purcell. "Battle of Spencer's Tavern." *Encyclopedia of Battles in North America, 1517 to 1916*. New York: Facts On File, Inc., 2000. Facts On File, Inc. *American History Online*. www.factsonfile.com. Simcoe, John Graves. *Simcoe's Military Journal. A History of the Operations of a Partisan Corps Called the Queen's Rangers, Commanded by Lieut. Col. J. G.

Simcoe, *During the War of the American Revolution*. New-York: Bartlett & Welford, 1844; [New York]: New York Times; Arno Press. Eyewitness Accounts of the American Revolution. [1968].

83. *Encyclopedia of the American Revolution*. Harold E. Selesky, editor in chief. 2nd ed. Detroit: Charles Scribner's Sons, 2007. I: 453–455. *The Encyclopedia of the American Revolutionary War: A Political, Social, and Military History*. Gregory Fremont-Barnes, Richard Alan Ryerson, editors. Santa Barbara, Calif.: ABC-CLIO, 2006. II: 543–545. Gottschalk, Louis. *La Fayette in America*. 5 vols. Chicago: University of Chicago Press, 1975. Hatch, Charles. "'The Affair Near James Island (or, 'The Battle of Green Spring'), July 6, 1781." *Virginia Magazine of History and Biography* 53 (July 1945): 172–196. Johnston, Henry P. *The Yorktown Campaign and the Surrender of Cornwallis, 1781*. New York: Eastern Acorn Press, 1981. Lee, Henry. *The American Revolution in the South*. New York: Arno Press, 1969. Marshall, S. L. A. *Men Against Fire*. New York and Washington: Combat and Morrow, 1947. Nelson, Paul David. *Anthony Wayne: Soldier of the Early Republic*. Bloomington: Indiana University Press, 1985. Picq, Ardant du. *Battle Studies*. New York: Macmillan, 1921. Tarleton, Banastre. *A History of the Campaigns of 1780 and 1781 in the Southern Provinces of North America*. London: T. Cadell, 1787; [s.l.]: The New York Times & Arno Press, 1968. Wickwire, Franklin, and Mary Wickwire. *Cornwallis and the War of Independence*. London: Faber and Faber, 1971.

84. Stick, David. *The Outer Banks of North Carolina, 1584–1958*. Chapel Hill, 1958. p. 50. MacClenny, "Nansemond County in the American Revolution," MacClenny Mss. Floyd McKnight, "The County of Southampton, 1749–1957," in Rogers Dey Wichard, *The History of Lower Tidewater Virginia*. New York, 1959. II: 289–290.

85. Hughes, Robert M., editor. "Revolutionary Correspondence of Col. Josiah Parker, of Isle of Wight County, Va.," *The Virginia Magazine of History and Biography* 23 (1914) p. 259; MacClenny, "Nansemond County in the American Revolution," MacClenny Mss. Floyd McKnight, "The County of Southampton, 1749–1957," in Rogers Dey Wichard, *The History of Lower Tidewater Virginia*. New York, 1959. II, 289–290; article by Edgar B. Jackson. *Norfolk Virginian-Pilot*. October 10, 1954. part 5, p. 8; MacClenny, Nansemond County in the American Revolution," and "Cargo of the Spanish Ship The Sacred Heart of Jesus," MacClenny Mss. Parker, J. C. *Old South Quay in Southampton County: Its Location, Early Ownership, and History*. by John Crump Parker. *The Virginia Magazine of History and Biography* 83, no. 2, April 1975, pp. 161, 168–71.

86. Calendar of Virginia State Papers, n. 340, 412.

87. Council Journal (1781) p. 250.

88. Eckenrode, H. J. *The Revolution In Virginia*. Hamden, Conn.: Archon Books, 1964. pp. 254–255.

89. Peckham, Howard Henry. *Toll of Independence: Engagements & Battle Casualties of the American Revolution*. Edited by Howard H. Peckham. Chicago: University of Chicago Press, 1974. p. 89.

90. *Encyclopedia of the American Revolution*. Harold E. Selesky, editor in chief. 2nd ed. Detroit: Charles Scribner's Sons, 2007. I: 206–210. *The Encyclopedia of the American Revolutionary War: A Political, Social, and Military History*. Gregory Fremont-Barnes, Richard Alan Ryerson, editors. Santa Barbara, Calif.: ABC-CLIO, 2006. I: 218–221. Clowes, William Laird. *The Royal Navy: A History from the Earliest Times to 1900*. London: Chatham, 1996. vol. 3. Dull, John R. *The French Navy and the American Revolution: A Study of Arms and Diplomacy, 1774–1787*. Princeton, N.J.: Princeton University Press, 1975. Gardiner, Robert, ed. *Navies and the American Revolution, 1775–1783*. London: Chatham, 1996. James, William. *The British Navy in Adversity: A Study of the War of American Independence*. 1926. Reprint, New York: Russell and Russell, 1970. Larrabee, Harold A. *Decision at the Chesapeake*. New York: Clarkson N. Potter, 1964. Mackesy, Piers. *The War for America, 1775–1783*. Lincoln: University of Nebraska Press, 1993. Mahan, Alfred T. *The Influence of Sea Power upon History , 1660–1783*. 1890. Reprint, New York: Dover, 1987. Palmer, Michael A. *Command at Sea: Naval Command and Control Since the Sixteenth Century*. Cambridge, Mass.: Harvard University Press, 2005. Rodger, N. A. M. *The Command of the Ocean: A Naval History of Britain, 1649–1815*. New York and London: Norton, 2004. Syrett, David. *The Royal Navy in American Waters, 1775–1783*. Aldershot, UK: Scholar Press, 1989. Tilley, J. A. *The Royal Navy in the American Revolution*. Columbia: University of South Carolina Press, 1987. Ward, Christopher. *The War of the Revolution*. New York: Macmillan, 1952.

91. Thacher James. *Military Journal of the American Revolution*. Hartford: Hurlbut, Williams & Company, 1862. pp. 280–281. *The Freeman's Journal: or, The North-American Intelligencer* XXVII (October 24, 1781) p. 2. *Continental Journal* CCXCVI (October 5, 1781) p. 3.

92. Tarleton, Banastre. *A History of the Campaigns of 1780 and 1781 in the Southern Provinces of North America*. London: T. Cadell, 1787; [s.l.]: The New York Times & Arno Press, 1968. pp. 376–381. Ewald, Johann. *Diary of the American War: A Hessian Journal*. Captain Johann Ewald; Translated and edited by Joseph P. Tustin. New Haven and London: Yale University Press, 1979. pp. 329–330. Thacher James. *Military Journal of the American Revolution*. Hartford: Hurlbut, Williams & Company, 1862. pp. 280–281.

93. Minutes of Occurrences respecting the Siege and Capture of York in Virginia, extracted from the Journal of Colonel Jonathan Trumbull, Secretary to the General, 1781. In *Proceedings of the Massachusetts Historical Society*. Boston: the Society, 14: (1875–1876) pp. 331–338. Ewald, Johann. *Diary of the American War: A Hessian Journal*. Captain Johann Ewald; Translated and edited by Joseph P. Tustin. New Haven and London: Yale University Press, 1979. p. 334.

94. Popp, Stephen. Popp's Journal, 1777–1783. J. C. Rosengarten, ed. *Pennsylvania Magazine of History and Biography* 26 (1902) p. 41.

95. van Cortlandt, Philip. Autobiography of Philip van Cortlandt. *Magazine of History and Biography* 22 (1898) p. 294.

96. Martin, Joseph Plumb, *Private Yankee Doodle; Being a Narrative of Some of the Adventures, Dangers, and Sufferings of a Revolutionary Soldier*. Edited by George F. Scheer, originally published in Hallowell, Me., 1830, anonymously (republished, Boston, 1962). *A Narrative of Some of the Adventures, Dangers and Sufferings of a Revolutionary Soldier*. Eyewitness accounts of the American Revolution. [New York]: New York Times [1968] 234–235.

97. *The Norwich Packet and the Weekly Advertiser* IX: 423 (November 15, 1781) p. 3. Feltman, William. *The Journal of Lieut. William Feltman, of the First Pennsylvania Regiment, 1781–82, including the march into Virginia and the Siege of*

Yorktown. Philadelphia: Henry Carey Baird for the Historical Society of Pennsylvania, 1853. Eyewitness Accounts of the American Revolution. New York: The New York Times & Arno Press, 1969. p. 21.

98. Thacher James. *Military Journal of the American Revolution.* Hartford: Hurlbut, Williams & Company, 1862. pp. 283–287. Tarleton, Banastre. *A History of the Campaigns of 1780 and 1781 in the Southern Provinces of North America.* London: T. Cadell, 1787; [s.l.]: The New York Times & Arno Press, 1968. pp. 388–389.

99. *Encyclopedia of the American Revolution.* Harold E. Selesky, editor in chief. 2nd ed. Detroit: Charles Scribner's Sons, 2007. II: 1291–1308. *The Encyclopedia of the American Revolutionary War: A Political, Social, and Military History.* Gregory Fremont-Barnes, Richard Alan Ryerson, editors. Santa Barbara, Calif.: ABC-CLIO, 2006. IV: 1382–1392. Alden, John R. *The South in the Revolution, 1763–1789.* Baton Rouge: Louisiana State University Press, 1957. Billias, George A., ed. *George Washington's Generals and Opponents: Their Exploits and Leadership,* 1964. reprint, New York: Da Capo, 1994. Bosnal, Stephen. *When the French Were Here.* Garden City, N.Y.: Doubleday, 1945. Breen, Kenneth. "A Reinforcement Reduced: Rodney's Flawed Appraisal of French Plans, West Indies 1781." In *New Interpretations in Naval History: Selected Papers from the Ninth Naval History Symposium.* Edited by William R. Roberts and Jack Sweetman. Annapolis, Md.: Naval Institute Press, 1991. Breen, Kenneth. "Sir George Rodney and St. Eustatius in the American War: A Commercial and Naval Distraction, 1775–1781." *Mariner's Mirror* 84 (May 1998) pp. 192–203. Buchanan, John. *The Road to Guilford Courthouse.* New York: John Wiley and Sons, Inc., 1997. Chidsey, Donald B. *Victory at Yorktown.* New York: Crown, 1962. Chávez, Thomas E. *Spain and the Independence of the United States.* Albuquerque: University of New Mexico Press, 2002. Clowes, William Laird. *The Royal Navy: A History from the Earliest Times to 1900.* 7 vols. London: Chatham, 1996. Davis, Burke. *The Campaign that Won America: The Story of Yorktown, 1781.* New York: Dial, 1970. Dull, John R. *The French Navy and the American Revolution: A study of arms and diplomacy, 1774–1787.* Princeton, N.J.: Princeton University Press, 1975. Ellis, Joseph J. *His Excellency George Washington.* New York: Knopf, 2004. Fleming, Thomas J. *Beat the Last Drum: The Siege of Yorktown, 1781.* New York: St. Martin's, 1963. Flexner, James Thomas. *George Washington in the American Revolution.* Boston: Little Brown, 1968. Flexner, James Thomas. *Washington: The Indispensable Man.* New York: Mentor, 1979. Fortescue, John. *The War of Independence: The British Army in North America, 1775–1783.* London: Greenhill, 2001. Fortescue, Sir John William. *A History of the British Army.* 2nd ed. London: Macmillan and Company, 1911. Freeman, Douglas Southall. *George Washington, a biography.* by Douglas Southall Freeman. New York: Scribner, 1948–1957. Gottschalk, Louis. *La Fayette and the Close of the American Revolution.* Chicago: University of Chicago Press, 1942. Greene, Jerome A. *The Guns of Independence: The Siege of Yorktown, 1781.* New York: Savas Beattie, 2005. Griffith, Samuel B. *The War for American Independence: From 1760 to the Surrender at Yorktown in 1781.* Champaign: University of Illinois Press, 2002. Johnston, Henry P. *The Yorktown Campaign and the Surrender of Cornwallis, 1781.* New York: Eastern Acorn Press, 1981. Ketchum, Richard M. *Victory at Yorktown: The Campaign that Won the Revolution.* New York: Henry Holt, 2004. Larrabee, Harold A. *Decision at the Chesapeake.* New York: Clarkson N. Potter, 1964. Leckie, Robert. *George Washington's War: The Saga of the American Revolution.* New York: Harper Perennial, 1993. Lewis, Charles Lee. *Admiral de Grasse and American Independence.* Annapolis, Md.: Naval Institute Press, 1945. Lewis, James A. "Las Damas de la Havana, El Precursor, and Francisco de Saavedra: A Note on Spanish Participation in the Battle of Yorktown." *The Americas.* 37 (July 1981): 83–89. Mackesy, Piers. *The War for America, 1775–1783.* Lincoln: University of Nebraska Press, 1993. Mahan, Alfred T. *The Influence of Sea Power upon History, 1660–1783.* Boston: Little Brown, 1890. Morrill, Dan L. *Southern Campaigns of the American Revolution.* Baltimore: The Nautical & Aviation Publishing Company of America [n.d]. Morrissey, Brendan. *Yorktown 1781: The World Turned Upside Down.* Oxford: Osprey, 1997. Padron, Francisco Morales, ed. *Journal of Don Francisco Saavedra de Sangronis.* Gainesville: University of Florida Press, 1989. Pybus, Cassandra. "Jefferson's Faulty Math: The Question of Slave Defections in the American Revolution." *William and Mary Quarterly* 62 (April 2005) pp. 243–264. Rice, Howard C, Jr. and Anne S. K. Brown. *The American Campaigns of Rochambeau's Army 1780, 1781, 1782, 1783.* Princeton: Princeton University Press; Providence: Brown University Press, 1972. Sands, John O. *Yorktown's Captive Fleet.* Charlottesville: University Press of Virginia, 1983. Skaggs, David Curtis. "Decision at Cap Français: Franco-Spanish Coalition Planning and the Prelude to Yorktown." In *New Interpretations in Naval History: Selected Papers from the Thirteenth Naval History Symposium.* Edited by William M. McBride. Annapolis, Md.: Naval Institute Press, 1998. Syrett, David. *The Royal Navy in American Waters, 1775–1783.* Aldershot, UK: Scholar Press, 1989. Thayer, Theodore G. *Yorktown: Campaign of Strategic Options.* Philadelphia: Lippincott, 1975. Tilley, J. A. *The Royal Navy in the American Revolution.* Columbia: University of South Carolina Press, 1987. Urwin, Gregory J. W. "Cornwallis and the Slaves of Virginia: New Look at the Yorktown Campaign." In *ACTA: International Commission of Military History. XXVIII Congress: Coming to the Americas.* Edited by John A. Lynn. Wheaton, IL: United States Commission on Military History and the Cantigny First Division Foundation, 2003. Ward, Christopher. *The War of the Revolution.* New York: Macmillan, 1952. pp. 886ff. Washington, George. *The Diaries of George Washington.* Edited by Donald Jackson. Charlottesville: University Press of Virginia, 1976–1979. Whitridge, Arnold. *Rochambeau: Neglected Founding Father.* New York: Collier Books, 1965. Wickwire, Franklin, and Mary Wickwire. *Cornwallis: The American Adventure.* Boston: Houghton Mifflin, 1970. Wickwire, Franklin, and Mary Wickwire. *Cornwallis and the War of Independence.* London: Faber and Faber, 1971. Willcox, William B. "The British Road to Yorktown: A Study in Divided Command." *American Historical Review* 52 (October 1946) pp. 1–35. Willcox, William B. *Portrait of a General: Sir Henry Clinton in the War of Independence.* New York: Knopf, 1964. Wood, W. J. *Battles of the Revolutionary War, 1775–1781.* Chapel Hill, N.C.: Algonquin, 1990.

100. Eller, Ernest McNeill, ed. *Chesapeake Bay in the American Revolution.* Centreville, Md.: Tidewater Publishers, 1981. pp. 3–242.

101. Eller, Ernest McNeill, ed. *Chesapeake Bay in the American Revolution.* Centreville, Md.: Tidewater Publishers, 1981. p. 242.

102. Eller, Ernest McNeill, ed. *Chesapeake Bay in the American Revolution.* Centreville, Md.: Tidewater Publishers, 1981. p. 243.

103. Peckham, Howard Henry. *Toll of Independence: Engagements & Battle Casualties of the American Revolution.* Edited by Howard H. Peckham. Chicago: University of Chicago Press, 1974. p. 21.

104. Peckham, Howard Henry. *Toll of Independence: Engagements & Battle Casualties of the American Revolution*. Edited by Howard H. Peckham. Chicago: University of Chicago Press, 1974. p. 32.

105. De Hass, Wills. *History of the Early Settlement and Indian Wars of Western Virginia*. Wheeling: H. Hoblitzell; Philadelphia: King & Baird, 1851. pp. 235–236.

106. Extract of a Letter from an Officer in the Southern Army. *The Pennsylvania Packet or the General Advertiser* X: 703 (January 30, 1781) p. 3. *Connecticut Journal* 694 (February 15, 1781) p. 2. *Connecticut Courant* 838 (February 13, 1781) p. 2. *The New Jersey Gazette* IV: 163 (February 7, 1781) p. 3. Narrative of the Movements of the Enemy since Our Last. *The American Journal and General Advertiser* II: 102 (February 17, 1781) p. 1. *The Norwich Packet and the Weekly Advertiser* 385 (February 20, 1781) p. 2. Richmond, (Virginia) January 20. *The Independent Ledger, and the American Advertiser* III: 142 (February 19, 1781) p. 2.

107. Wallace, Lee A., Jr. The Battery at Hood's: an ambitious fortification failed to protect Richmond in the Revolution. *Virginia Cavalcade* 23 (summer, 1973) pp. 38–42.

108. Arnold to Clinton, 21 Jan. 1781. British National Archives Colonial Office 30/11. James Cocke to George Mutter, 18 Jan. 1781. Jefferson, Thomas. *The Papers of Thomas Jefferson*. Princeton: Princeton University Press, 1950–. 4: 395. Eller, Ernest McNeill, ed. *Chesapeake Bay in the American Revolution*. Centreville, Md.: Tidewater Publishers, 1981. p. 461.

109. Jefferson, Thomas. *The Papers of Thomas Jefferson*. Princeton: Princeton University Press, 1950–. 4: 333–34. Wallace, Lee A., Jr. The Battery at Hood's: an ambitious fortification failed to protect Richmond in the Revolution. *Virginia Cavalcade* 23 (summer, 1973) pp. 38–42.

110. Arnold to Clinton, 21 Jan. 1781. British National Archives Colonial Office 30/11.

111. Arnold to Clinton, 21 Jan. 1781. British National Archives Colonial Office 30/11. *The New-York Gazette; and The Weekly Mercury* 1529 (February 5, 1781) p. 3. Eller, Ernest McNeill, ed. *Chesapeake Bay in the American Revolution*. Centreville, Md.: Tidewater Publishers, 1981. p. 462.

112. Ward, Harry M. and Greer, Harold E., Jr. *Richmond During the Revolution 1775–83*. Charlottesville: University Press of Virginia, 1977. pp. 74–83. Eller, Ernest McNeill, ed. *Chesapeake Bay in the American Revolution*. Centreville, Md.: Tidewater Publishers, 1981. pp. 191, 331–332, 462. Bruce, Kathleen. *Virginia Iron Manufacture in the Slave Era*. New York: Century [c1930]. pp. 51–64. Dawson, Henry B. *Battles of the United States*. New York: Johnson, Fry, & Company, 1858. 1: 641–644.

113. Extract of a Letter from an Officer in the Southern Army. *The Pennsylvania Packet or the General Advertiser* X: 703 (January 30, 1781) p. 3. *Connecticut Courant* 838 (February 13, 1781) p. 2. *The New Jersey Gazette* IV: 163 (February 7, 1781) p. 3. Narrative of the Movements of the Enemy since Our Last. *The American Journal and General Advertiser* II: 102 (February 17, 1781) p. 1. *The Norwich Packet and the Weekly Advertiser* 385 (February 20, 1781) p. 2. Richmond (Virginia) January 20. *The Independent Ledger, and the American Advertiser* III: 142 (February 19, 1781) p. 2.

114. Account of the Operations of His Majesty's Forces in Virginia, Received the 17th Instant by His Majesty's Ship *General Monk*. *Royal Georgia Gazette* 123 (July 5, 1781) p. 2. *The Freeman's Journal: or, The North-American Intelligencer* VI (May 30, 1781) p. 2.

115. Lafayette, Marie du Motier, Marquis de. *Memoirs, Correspondence and Manuscripts of General Lafayette Published by His Family*. 3 vols. London: Saunders & Otley, 1837. [6 vols., Paris H. Fournier aîné, 1837–38].

116. Stember, Sol. T*he Bicentennial Guide to the American Revolution*. Saturday Review Press: New York, [distributed by] Dutton, 1794; [s.l.]: New York Times and Arno Press, 1969. 3: 156. Ward, Christopher. *The War of the Revolution*. New York: Macmillan, 1952. pp. 872–873.

117. Paullin, Charles Oscar. *Paullin's History of Naval Administration, 1775–1911: A Collection of Articles from the U.S. Naval Institute Proceedings*. Annapolis: U.S. Naval Institute, 1968. p. 86.

118. Eller, Ernest McNeill, ed. *Chesapeake Bay in the American Revolution*. Centreville, Md.: Tidewater Publishers, 1981. pp. 194–195.

119. *The Pennsylvania Gazette* (May 30, 1781) p. 3. Account of the Operations of His Majesty's Forces in Virginia, Received the 17th Instant by His Majesty's Ship *General Monk*. *Royal Georgia Gazette* 123 (July 5, 1781) p. 2. *The Freeman's Journal: or, The North-American Intelligencer* VI (May 30, 1781) p. 2. Simcoe, John Graves. *Simcoe's Military Journal. A History of the Operations of a Partisan Corps Called the Queen's Rangers, Commanded by Lieut. Col. J. G. Simcoe, During the War of the American Revolution*. New-York: Bartlett & Welford, 1844; [New York]: New York Times; Arno Press. Eyewitness Accounts of the American Revolution. [1968]. pp. 198, 202.

120. *The Pennsylvania Evening Post* VII: 735 (April 30, 1781) p. 70.

121. Account of the Operations of His Majesty's Forces in Virginia, Received the 17th Instant by His Majesty's Ship *General Monk*. *Royal Georgia Gazette* 123 (July 5, 1781) p. 2. *The Freeman's Journal: or, The North-American Intelligencer* VI (May 30, 1781) p. 2. Simcoe, John Graves. *Simcoe's Military Journal. A History of the Operations of a Partisan Corps Called the Queen's Rangers, Commanded by Lieut. Col. J. G. Simcoe, During the War of the American Revolution*. New-York: Bartlett & Welford, 1844; [New York]: New York Times; Arno Press. Eyewitness Accounts of the American Revolution. [1968]. pp. 198–202.

122. Simcoe, John Graves. *Simcoe's Military Journal, A History of the Operations of a Paritsan Corps Called the Queen's Rangers, Commanded by Lieut. Col. J. G. Simcoe*. New York: Bartlett & Welford, 1844. p. 223.

123. Ward, Christopher. *The War of the Revolution*. New York: Macmillan, 1952.

124. *Fluvanna County Historical Society Bulletin*. March, 1967.

125. Ward, Christopher. *The War of the Revolution*. New York: Macmillan, 1952.

126. *Encyclopedia of the American Revolution*. Harold E. Selesky, editor in chief. 2nd ed. Detroit: Charles Scribner's Sons, 2007. 2: 1141–1142.

North Carolina

1. Journal of HM Sloop *Cruizer*, Captain Francis Parry. British National Archives. Admiralty 51/218.

2. Journal of HM Sloop *Cruizer*, Captain Francis Parry. British National Archives. Admiralty 51/218. NDAR 2: 1054.

3. Journal of HM Sloop *Scorpion*, Captain John Tollemache. British National Archives. Admiralty 51/872. NDAR 2: 1149.

4. Journal of HM Sloop *Cruizer*, Captain Francis Parry. British National Archives. Admiralty 51/218. NDAR 2: 1088.

5. Journal of HM Sloop *Cruizer*, Captain Francis Parry. British National Archives. Admiralty 51/218. NDAR 2: 1088. Journal of HM Sloop *Scorpion*, Captain John Tollemache. British National Archives. Admiralty 51/872. NDAR 2: 1149.

6. Journal of HM Sloop *Cruizer*, Captain Francis Parry. British National Archives. Admiralty 51/218. NDAR 2: 1088.

7. Journal of HM Sloop *Scorpion*, Captain John Tollemache. British National Archives. Admiralty 51/872. Journal of HM Sloop *Cruizer*, Captain Francis Parry. British National Archives. Admiralty 51/218. NDAR 3: 1022, 1026.

8. Journal of HM Sloop *Cruizer*, Captain Francis Parry. British National Archives. Admiralty 51/218. NDAR 3: 1026.

9. O'Kelley, Patrick. *Nothing But Blood and Slaughter*. Booklocker.com, 2004. 1: 90. NDAR 4: 316.

10. O'Kelley, Patrick. *Nothing But Blood and Slaughter*. Booklocker.com, 2004 1: 98–99. Boatner, Mark M. *Encyclopedia of the American Revolution*. 3d ed., New York: McKay, 1980. p. 731. NDAR 4: 742–743, 758, 824, 1220, 1258, 1289.

11. *Newport Mercury* 923 (May 13, 1776) p. 1. *Essex Journal* III: 126 (May 31, 1776) p. 2.

12. Journal of HM Schooner *St. Lawrence*, Lieutenant John Graves, British National Archives, Admiralty 51/4330. NDAR 4: 758.

13. Journal HM Sloop *Scorpion*. British National Archives, Admiralty 51/872; NDAR 4: 824.

14. Journal of HM Sloop *Scorpion*. British National Archives, Admiralty 51/872; NDAR 4: 1156.

15. Journal of HM Sloop *Scorpion*, Captain John Tollemache, British National Archives, Admiralty 51/872. NDAR 4: 1220. Journal of HM Schooner *St. Laurence*. British National Archives, Admiralty 51/4330; NDAR 4: 1258.

16. O'Kelley, Patrick. *Nothing But Blood and Slaughter*. Booklocker.com, 2004. 1: 103–104. NDAR 4: 1384; 5: 139, 1411.

17. Journal of HM Schooner *St. Lawrence*, Lieutenant John Graves, British National Archives, Admiralty 51/4330. NDAR 4: 1384.

18. Extract of a Letter from an Officer of the 15th Regiment, to his Friend Here [London], Dated at the Camp Near Cape Fear, North Carolina, May 17." *Lloyd's Evening Post and British Chronicle*. August 5 to August 7, 1776. NDAR 5: 139.

19. Extract of a letter from Wilmington, in North Carolina, dated 13th May, 1776. *South Carolina and American General Gazette* (May 8 to May 22, 1776). NDAR 5: 80. Extract of a Letter from Wilmington, Cape Fear River, (North Carolina,) dated 17th May, 1776. *Connecticut Journal* 453 (June 19, 1776) p. 3. Forster, Thompson. *Diary of Thompson Forster, Staff Surgeon to His Majesty's Detached Hospital in North America, October 19th 1775 to October 23rd 1777*. [s. l.: s.n.], 1938 (unpublished typed copy) p. 50. Lumpkin, Henry. *From Savannah to Yorktown*. University of South Carolina Press, 1981. p. 5. British National Archives War Office. Series 12 5637/2 Company Pay Rolls. Bennett, Charles E. and Lennon, Donald R. *A Quest for Glory: Major General Robert Howe and the American Revolution*. Chapel Hill & London: The University of North Carolina Press, 1991. pp. 40–41. O'Kelley, Patrick. *Nothing But Blood and Slaughter*. Booklocker.com, 2004. 1:105.

20. Extract of a Letter From an Officer of the 15th Regiment, to His Friend Here [London], Dated at the Camp Near Cape Fear, North Carolina, May 17." *Lloyd's Evening Post and British Chronicle* (August 5 to August 7, 1776). NDAR 5: 139.

21. Journal of HM Sloop *Falcon*, Capt. John Linzee. British National Archives, Admiralty 51/334; NDAR 5: 131. O'Kelley, Patrick. *Nothing But Blood and Slaughter*. Booklocker.com, 2004. 1: 106.

22. Journal of HM Schooner *St. Lawrence*, Lieutenant John Graves. British National Archives. Admiralty 51/4330. NDAR 5: 144. Journal of HM Sloop *Falcon*, Capt. John Linzee. British National Archives, Admiralty 51/334; NDAR 5: 131. O'Kelley, Patrick. *Nothing But Blood and Slaughter*. Booklocker.com, 2004. 1: 106.

23. Journal of HM Schooner *St. Lawrence*, Lieutenant John Graves. British National Archives. Admiralty 51/4330. NDAR 5: 144,175.

24. O'Kelley, Patrick. *Nothing But Blood and Slaughter*. Booklocker.com, 2004. 1: 108–109. NDAR 5 175–279.

25. Peckham, Howard Henry. *Toll of Independence: Engagements & Battle Casualties of the American Revolution*. Edited by Howard H. Peckham. Chicago: University of Chicago Press, 1974. p. 19.

26. Journal of HM Sloop *Falcon*, Captain John Linzee. British National Archives. Admiralty 51/336. Journal of HM Sloop *Cruizer*, Captain Francis Parry. British National Archives. Admiralty 51/ 218. Journal of HM Sloop *Scorpion*, Captain John Tollemache. British National Archives. Admiralty 51/872. NDAR 6: 743–744. *Roster of Soldiers from North Carolina in the American Revolution: with an Appendix Containing a Collection of Miscellaneous Records*. Hay, Gertrude May (Sloan). National Society Daughters of the American Revolution of North Carolina. Baltimore: Genealogical Pub. Co., 1967, 1932. p. 444. O'Kelley, Patrick. *Nothing But Blood and Slaughter*. Booklocker.com, 2004. 1: 164–165.

27. Compiled Service Records of Soldiers, Revolutionary War, Army, M881–785. Caruthers, Eli W. *The Old North State in 1776*. Guilford County Genealogical Society, 1985. p. 23. O'Kelley, Patrick. *Nothing But Blood and Slaughter*. Booklocker.com, 2004. 1: 97–98.

28. Saye, James Hodge. *Memoirs of Major Joseph McJunkin, Revolutionary Patriot*. [s.l.]: A Press, Inc. 1977. (First printed in the Richmond, VA *Watchman and Observer* in 1847). *Pennsylvania Packet*. January 17, 1777. O'Kelley, Patrick. *Nothing But Blood and Slaughter*. Booklocker.com, 2004. 1: 167–68.

29. Cornwallis, Charles C. *An Answer to that Part of the Narrative of Lt. General Sir Henry Clinton, K. B. Which Relates to the Conduct of Lieutenant-General Earl Cornwallis During the Campaign in North America, in the Year 1781*. London: J. Debrett, 1783. Davies, K. G. *Documents of the American Revolution 1770–1783*. (Colonial Office Series) Volume XX Transcripts 1781, Irish University Press, 1979. pp. 107–109. Tarleton, Banastre. *A History of the Campaigns of 1780 and 1781 in the Southern Provinces of North America*. London, 1787; Eyewitness Accounts of the American Revolution. [New York]: New York Times [1968]. pp. 270, 280–281. Lamb, Roger. *An Original and Authentic Journal of Occurrences During the Late American War*. Dublin, 1809. Eyewitness Accounts of the American Revolution. [New York]: New York Times [1968]. pp. 359–361. Schenck, David. *North Carolina 1780–'81, Being a History of the Invasion of the Carolinas by the British Army under Lord Cornwallis in 1780–'81*. Edwards & Broughton, Publishers, 1889. pp. 374–375. Caruthers, Eli W. *The Old North State in 1776*. Guilford County Genealogical Society, 1985. pp. 152–155. *Pennsylvania Gazette* (August 15, 1781). Cornwallis Papers. Class 30, vol. 11 p. 85 folio 22. Barefoot, Daniel W. *Touring North Carolina's Revolutionary War Sites*. Winston–Salem: John F. Blair, 1998. p. 136. O'Kelley, Patrick. *Nothing But Blood and Slaughter*. Booklocker. com, 2004. 3: 214–15.

30. Fanning, David. *The Narrative of Col. David Fanning*. Edited with an Introduction and Notes by Lindley S. Butler. Davidson, North Carolina: Briarpatch Press; Charleston, South; Carolina: Tradd Street Press, 1981. p. 52. Caruthers, Eli W. *The Old North State in 1776*. Guilford County Genealogical Society, 1985. p. 46. Clark, Walter. *The State Records of North Carolina*, Volume XXII, Miscellaneous. Nash Brothers, 1907. p. 1047. O'Kelley, Patrick. *Nothing But Blood and Slaughter*. Booklocker.com, 2004. 3: 315.

31. Morrill, Dan L. *Southern Campaigns of the American Revolution*. Baltimore: The Nautical & Aviation Publishing Company of America, 1993. pp. 7–10.

32. DeMond, Robert O. *The Loyalists in North Carolina During the Revolution*. Hamden, Conn.: Archon Books, 1964. Hatch, Charles E. *Moore's Creek National Military Park, North Carolina: The Battle of Moore's Creek Bridge*. Washington, D.C.: Office of History and Historic Architecture, Eastern Service Center, 1969. Meyer, Duane Gilbert. *The Highland Scots of North Carolina, 1732–1776*. Chapel Hill: University of North Carolina Press, 1961. Morrill, Dan L. *Southern Campaigns of the American Revolution*. Baltimore: The Nautical & Aviation Publishing Company of America [n.d.]. Rankin, Hugh F. "The Moore's Creek Bridge Campaign, 1776." *North Carolina Historical Review* 30 (1953) pp. 23–60. Rankin, Hugh F. *The Moore's Creek Bridge Campaign, 1776*. Conshohocken, Pa.: Eastern National Park and Monument Association, 1986. Saunders, William L., ed. *The Colonial Records of North Carolina*. Raleigh, N.C.: P. M. Hale, 1890. Vol. 10.

33. *Providence Gazette* (April 13, 1776). NDAR 4: 185.

34. Kell, Jean Bruyere. *North Carolina's Coastal Carteret County During the American Revolution, 1765–1785, A Bicentennial Project of the Carteret County Bicentennial Commission*. Era Press, 1975. pp. 69–70. Stewart, Robert Armistead. *History of Virginia's Navy in the Revolution*. Richmond, VA, 1933. pp. 5–6. Still, William N. *North Carolina's Revolutionary War Navy*. The O. Davis Sons, Inc., 1976. p. 12. *The Pennsylvania Gazette* (May 8, 1776). NDAR 4 1345–1347. O'Kelley, Patrick. *Nothing But Blood and Slaughter*. Booklocker.com, 2004. 1: 100–102.

35. Kell, Jean Bruyere. *North Carolina's Coastal Carteret County During the American Revolution, 1765–1785, A Bicentennial Project of the Carteret County Bicentennial Commission*. Era Press, 1975. p. 64. Still, William N. *North Carolina's Revolutionary War Navy*. The O. Davis Sons, Inc., 1976. p. 24. O'Kelley, Patrick. *Nothing But Blood and Slaughter*. Booklocker.com, 2004. 1: 194–95.

36. Clark, Walter. *The State Records of North Carolina*. XIV–1779–'80. Winston: Nash Brothers, 1896. p. 418. O'Kelley, Patrick. *Nothing But Blood and Slaughter*. Booklocker.com, 2004. 1: 195.

37. Kell, Jean Bruyere. *North Carolina's Coastal Carteret County During the American Revolution, 1765–1785, A Bicentennial Project of the Carteret County Bicentennial Commission*. Era Press, 1975. p. 69. O'Kelley, Patrick. *Nothing But Blood and Slaughter*. Booklocker.com, 2004l. 2: 297–298.

38. Kell, Jean Bruyere. *North Carolina's Coastal Carteret County During the American Revolution, 1765–1785, A Bicentennial Project of the Carteret County Bicentennial Commission*. Era Press, 1975. p. 69. O'Kelley, Patrick. *Nothing But Blood and Slaughter*. Booklocker.com, 2004. 2: 353.

39. Journal of HMS *Syren*, Captain Tobias Furneaux. British National Archives. Admiralty 51/930. Extract of a letter from Philadelphia, dated 18th March 1776. Enclosure No. 6 in Vice Admiral Shuldham to Philip Stephens, May 20, 1776. British National Archives. Admiralty 1/484. Journal of HMS *Mercury*, Captain James Montagu. British National Archives. Admiralty 51/600. Josiah Smith, Jr. to Mathew Clarkson and Michael Hillegas. Josiah Smith, Jr.'s Lettercopy Book, 1771–1784 University of North Carolina Library. NDAR 4: 358, 399, 530, 552.

40. *The Pennsylvania Gazette* (June 16, 1779; July 28, 1779). O'Kelley, Patrick. *Nothing But Blood and Slaughter*. Booklocker.com, 2004. 1: 303.

41. Extract of a letter from Newbern, August 19. Dixon & Hunter's *Virginia Gazette* (September 7, 1776). NDAR 6: 239.

42. Kell, Jean Bruyere. *North Carolina's Coastal Carteret County During the American Revolution, 1765–1785, A Bicentennial Project of the Carteret County Bicentennial Commission*. Era Press, 1975. p. 68. O'Kelley, Patrick. *Nothing But Blood and Slaughter*. Booklocker.com, 2004. 1: 169.

43. Kell, Jean Bruyere. *North Carolina's Coastal Carteret County During the American Revolution, 1765–1785, A Bicentennial Project of the Carteret County Bicentennial Commission.* Era Press, 1975. p. 70. O'Kelley, Patrick. *Nothing But Blood and Slaughter.* Booklocker.com, 2004. 1: 187.

44. Journal of HMS *Solebay*, Captain Thomas Symonds. British National Archives. Admiralty 51/ 909. NDAR 7: 1148–1149. O'Kelley, Patrick. *Nothing But Blood and Slaughter.* Booklocker.com, 2004. 1: 170–71.

45. Journal of HMS *Camilla*, Captain Charles Phipps. British National Archives, Admiralty 51/157. NDAR 7: 1149–1150. *South-Carolina and American General Gazette* (February 20, 1777). NDAR 7: 1251. Captain George Keith Elphinstone, R. N., to Vice Admiral James Young. British National Archives, Admiralty 51/309. NDAR 7: 1281. Vice-Admiral James Young to Philip Stephens. British National Archives, Admiralty 1/309. NDAR 8: 68–70. O'Kelley, Patrick. *Nothing But Blood and Slaughter.* Booklocker.com, 2004. 1: 171.

46. Kell, Jean Bruyere. *North Carolina's Coastal Carteret County During the American Revolution, 1765–1785, A Bicentennial Project of the Carteret County Bicentennial Commission.* Era Press, 1975. p. 70. O'Kelley, Patrick. *Nothing But Blood and Slaughter.* Booklocker.com, 2004. 1: 187.

47. *The Pennsylvania Packet.* June 25, 1778; August 13, 1778. O'Kelley, Patrick. *Nothing But Blood and Slaughter.* Booklocker.com, 2004. 1: 202.

48. Kell, Jean Bruyere. *North Carolina's Coastal Carteret County During the American Revolution, 1765–1785, A Bicentennial Project of the Carteret County Bicentennial Commission.* Era Press, 1975. p. 68. Clark, Walter. *The State Records of North Carolina XIV–1779–'80.* Winston: Nash Brothers, 1896. p. 482. *Pennsylvania Packet.* November 7, 1778. O'Kelley, Patrick. *Nothing But Blood and Slaughter.* Booklocker.com, 2004. 1: 204.

49. *Pennsylvania Gazette* (July 30, 1777). Griffiths, John William. *To Receive Them Properly, Charlestown Prepares For War, 1775–1776,* University of South Carolina, Department of History, 1992. p. 203. O'Kelley, Patrick. *Nothing But Blood and Slaughter.* Booklocker.com, 2004. 1: 179.

50. Clark, Walter. *The State Records of North Carolina XIV–1779–'80.* Winston: Nash Brothers, 1896. pp. 138–139. O'Kelley, Patrick. *Nothing But Blood and Slaughter.* Booklocker.com, 2004. 1: 301.

51. *The Pennsylvania Gazette* (July 19, 1780). O'Kelley, Patrick. *Nothing But Blood and Slaughter.* Booklocker.com, 2004. 2: 162–63.

52. Clark, Walter. *The State Records of North Carolina XIV–1779–'80.* Winston: Nash Brothers, 1896. pp. 285–286. Still, William N. *North Carolina's Revolutionary War Navy.* The O. Davis Sons, Inc., 1976. pp. 24–27. O'Kelley, Patrick. *Nothing But Blood and Slaughter.* Booklocker.com, 2004. 1: 204–205.

53. *Continental Journal* LXXXVIII (January 29, 1778) p. 3.

54. Davies, K. G. *Documents of the American Revolution 1770–1783.* (Colonial Office Series). Irish University Press, 1977, XX: 54–55. Tarleton, Banastre. *A History of the Campaigns of 1780 and 1781 in the Southern Provinces of North America.* London, 1787; Eyewitness accounts of the American Revolution. [New York]: New York Times [1968]. p. 230. Moultrie, William, *Memoirs of the American Revolution so far as it Related to the States of North and South Carolina and Georgia.* New York, 1802; Eyewitness accounts of the American Revolution). [New York]: New York Times [1968] II: 261. Fanning, David. *The Narrative of Col. David Fanning.* Edited with an Introduction and Notes by Lindley S. Butler. Davidson, N.C.: Briarpatch Press; Charleston, S.C.: Tradd Street Press, 1981. pp. 6, 33. Still, William N. *North Carolina's Revolutionary War Navy.* The O. Davis Sons, Inc., 1976. p. 23. *The Pennsylvania Gazette* (February 28, 1781). O'Kelley, Patrick. *Nothing But Blood and Slaughter.* Booklocker.com, 2004. 3: 61–2.

55. Davies, K. G. *Documents of the American Revolution 1770–1783.* (Colonial Office Series) Volume XX Transcripts 1781. Irish University Press, 1979. pp. 54–55. Fanning, David. *The Narrative of Col. David Fanning.* Edited with an Introduction and Notes by Lindley S. Butler. Davidson, N.C.: Briarpatch Press; Charleston, S.C.: Tradd Street Press, 1981. pp. 6, 33. Still, William N. *North Carolina's Revolutionary War Navy.* The O. Davis Sons, Inc., 1976. p. 23. Greene, Nathanael. *The Papers of General Nathanael Greene.* Richard K. Showman, ed. Chapel Hill: The University of North Carolina Press, published for the Rhode Island Historical Society. c1976–2006 7: 236. British National Archives. War Office. A List of all the Officers of the Army. pp. 158, 315, 317. O'Kelley, Patrick. *Nothing But Blood and Slaughter.* Booklocker.com, 2004. 3: 62–4.

56. This incident, also known as the Rouse House Massacre, occurred at either the end of March or the beginning of April. Brigadier General John Alexander Lillington (ca. 1725–1786) mentions it in his report on April 9, 1781.

57. Caruthers, Eli W. *The Old North State in 1776.* Guilford County Genealogical Society, 1985. pp. 195–196. O'Kelley, Patrick. *Nothing But Blood and Slaughter.* Booklocker.com, 2004. 3: 169–170.

58. Extract of a letter from General Marion, dated April 21st, 1781. *The Connecticut Gazette and the Universal Intelligencer* XVIII: 919 p. 1.

59. O'Kelley, Patrick. *Nothing But Blood and Slaughter.* Booklocker.com, 2004. 3: 61–62.

60. Dickson, William. *Duplin County History to 1810.* The North Carolina Historical Review, 1928. Ezrael House's Statement. Dickson, William. *Historical Sketch of Old Duplin County.* by Col. William Dickson. The Raleigh Star, 1810. O'Kelley, Patrick. *Nothing But Blood and Slaughter.* Booklocker.com, 2004. 3: 237–42.

61. Caruthers, Eli W. *The Old North State in 1776.* Guilford County Genealogical Society, 1985. pp. 197–200. Barefoot, Daniel W. *Touring North Carolina's Revolutionary War Sites.* Winston-Salem: John F. Blair, 1998. pp. 98–99. O'Kelley, Patrick. *Nothing But Blood and Slaughter.* Booklocker.com, 2004. 3: 278–80.

62. Col. Kenan to Governor Burke July 6, 1781; July 15, 1781. Clark, Walter. *The State Records of North Carolina*, Vol. XV: 514, 535. digital.lib.ecu.edu/Historyfiction/document/mcf/entire.html.

63. Caruthers, Eli W. *The Old North State in 1776.* Guilford County Genealogical Society, 1985. pp. 102–103. O'Kelley, Patrick. *Nothing But Blood and Slaughter.* Booklocker.com, 2004. 3: 328–29.

64. Caruthers, Eli W. *The Old North State in 1776*. Guilford County Genealogical Society, 1985. pp. 203. Clark, Walter. *The State Records of North Carolina, Vol. XIX–1782–'84. With Supplement–1771– '82*. Winston: Nash Brothers, 1901. 1896. p. 963. O'Kelley, Patrick. *Nothing But Blood and Slaughter*. Booklocker.com, 2004. 3: 387.

65. Caruthers, Eli W. *The Old North State in 1776*. Guilford County Genealogical Society, 1985. p. 203. Clark, Walter. *The State Records of North Carolina, Vol. XIX–1782–'84. With Supplement –1771–'82*. Winston: Nash Brothers, 1901. p. 963. Barefoot, Daniel W. *Touring North Carolina's Revolutionary War Sites*. Winston-Salem: John F. Blair, 1998. pp. 279–280. O'Kelley, Patrick. *Nothing But Blood and Slaughter*. Booklocker.com, 2004. 3: 388.

66. Ervin, Sara Sullivan. *South Carolinians in the Revolution*. Baltimore: Genealogical Publishing Company, Inc. 1971. p. 48. O'Kelley, Patrick. *Nothing But Blood and Slaughter*. Booklocker.com, 2004. 2: 163.

67. Tarleton, Banastre. *A History of the Campaigns of 1780 and 1781 in the Southern Provinces of North America*, London, 1787. Eyewitness accounts of the American Revolution. [New York]: New York Times [1968]. p. 287.

68. Rankin, Hugh F. *North Carolina in the American Revolution*. Raleigh: State Department of Archives and History, 1959. p. 63. Cornwallis, Charles C. *An Answer to that Part of the Narrative of Lt. General Sir Henry Clinton, K. B. Which Relates to the Conduct of Lieutenant-General Earl Cornwallis During the Campaign in North America, in the Year 1781*. London: J. Debrett, 1783. Tarleton, Banastre. *A History of the Campaigns of 1780 and 1781 in the Southern Provinces of North America*, London, 1787. Eyewitness accounts of the American Revolution. [New York]: New York Times [1968]. p. 287–289. Lamb, Roger. *An Original and Authentic Journal of Occurrences During the Late American War*. Dublin, 1809. Eyewitness Accounts of the American Revolution). [New York]: New York Times [1968]. p. 198. British National Archives. Cornwallis Papers. Class 30, vol. 11 p. 103 folio 29. Hayes, John T. *The Saddlebag Almanac* X (2002) pp. 18–19. Schenck, David. *North Carolina 1780–'81, Being a History of the Invasion of the Carolinas by the British Army under Lord Cornwallis in 1780–'81*. Edwards & Broughton, Publishers, 1889. pp. 264–265. O'Kelley, Patrick. *Nothing But Blood and Slaughter*. Booklocker.com, 2004. 3: 222–23.

70. Barefoot, Daniel W. *Touring North Carolina's Revolutionary War Sites*. Winston-Salem: John F. Blair, 1998. pp. 160–61. Extract of a letter dated at Hillsborough, North Carolina, July 22, 1780. *The Norwich Packet and the Weekly Advertiser* 363 (September 14, 1780) p. 2.

71. Peckham, Howard Henry. *Toll of Independence: Engagements & Battle Casualties of the American Revolution*. Edited by Howard H. Peckham. Chicago: University of Chicago Press, 1974. p. 75. O'Kelley, Patrick. *Nothing But Blood and Slaughter*. Booklocker.com, 2004. 2: 302–303.

72. Peckham, Howard Henry. *Toll of Independence: Engagements & Battle Casualties of the American Revolution*. Edited by Howard H. Peckham. Chicago: University of Chicago Press, 1974. p. 75. O'Kelley, Patrick. *Nothing But Blood and Slaughter*. Booklocker.com, 2004. 2: 303.

73. Draper, Lyman. Thomas Sumter Papers, Draper Manuscript Collection, State Historical Society of Wisconsin. 10VV169. O'Kelley, Patrick. *Nothing But Blood and Slaughter*. Booklocker.com, 2004. 2: 316.

74. Pension application of Joseph Johnston (Johnson) W5033. Pension application of John Dougan W9836. DeMond, Robert O. *The Loyalists in North Carolina During the Revolution*. Hamden, Conn.: Archon Books, 1964. p. 120. Caruthers, Eli W. *The Old North State in 1776*. Guilford County Genealogical Society, 1985. pp. 86–91. O'Kelley, Patrick. *Nothing But Blood and Slaughter*. Booklocker.com, 2004. 4: 40–41.

75. Furches. D. M. *A Leaf of History–A Reminiscence of the Revolutionary Battle of Shallow Ford*. Statesville, N.C.: The Landmark, February 17, 1887. Clark, Walter. *The State Records of North Carolina XIV–1779–'80*. Winston: Nash Brothers, 1896. pp. 421, 429, 580–581, 667, 669, 675, 676, 692–693, 698–699, 700; XV pp. 123–125; XXII pp. 113–114. O'Kelley, Patrick. *Nothing But Blood and Slaughter*. Booklocker.com, 2004. 2: 318–19.

76. Clark, Walter. *The State Records of North Carolina XIV–1779–'80*. Winston: Nash Brothers, 1896. pp. 421, 429, 580–581, 667, 669, 675–676, 692–693, 698–699, 790: XV pp. 123–125; XXII pp. 113–114. Barefoot, Daniel W. *Touring North Carolina's Revolutionary War Sites*. Winston-Salem: John F. Blair, 1998. p. 334. O'Kelley, Patrick. *Nothing But Blood and Slaughter*. Booklocker.com, 2004. 2: 343.

77. Copy of a letter from Major General Smallwood to John Penn, Esq., Member of the Board of War, North Carolina, dated New Moravian Town, October 16, 1780. *Connecticut Journal* 682 (November 23, 1780) p. 1. Furches. D. M. *A Leaf of History –A Reminiscence of the Revolutionary Battle of Shallow Ford*. Statesville, N.C.: The land mark, February 17, 1887. *Pennsylvania Gazette* (November 8, 1780). Clark, Walter. *The State Records of North Carolina XIV–1779–'80*. Winston: Nash Brothers, 1896. pp. 421, 429, 580–581, 667–676, 692–693, 698–790: XV–1780 pp. 123–125; XXII pp. 113–114. Barefoot, Daniel W. *Touring North Carolina's Revolutionary War Sites*. Winston-Salem: John F. Blair, 1998. pp. 323–325. Draper, Lyman. Thomas Sumter Papers, Draper Manuscript Collection, State Historical Society of Wisconsin. 10VV169. O'Kelley, Patrick. *Nothing But Blood and Slaughter*. Booklocker.com, 2004. 2: 347–49.

78. John S. Pancake. *This Destructive War*. Tuscaloosa: University of Alabama Press, 1985. p. 165.

79. *General Joseph Graham and His Papers on North Carolina Revolutionary History*. Ed. Major William A. Graham, ed. Raleigh: Edwards & Broughton, 1904. pp. 50–52. Clark, Walter. *The State Records of North Carolina* XVII 1781–1785. Winston: Nash Brothers, 1896. O'Kelley, Patrick. *Nothing But Blood and Slaughter*. Booklocker.com, 2004. 3: 78.

80. Seymour, William. Journal of the Southern Expedition, 1780–1783. *Papers of the Historical Society of Delaware*: XV. Wilmington: The Historical Society of Delaware, 1896. p. 17.

81. Caruthers, Eli W. *The Old North State in 1776*. Guilford County Genealogical Society, 1985. pp. 116–118. Pension Applications RG 15, microcopy 804. Pancake. *This Destructive War*. Tuscaloosa: University of Alabama Press, 1985. pp. 158–159, 168–169. Batt, Richard John. *The Maryland Continentals, 1780–1781*. Tulane University Dissertation, 1974. pp. 117–119. Greene, Nathanael. *The Papers of General Nathanael Greene*. Richard K. Showman, ed. Chapel Hill: The University of North Carolina Press, published for the Rhode Island Historical Society. c1976–

2006. pp. 267–269. McAllister, J. T. *Virginia Militia in the Revolutionary War, McAllister's Data*. McAllister Publishing Co., 1913. p. 25. O'Kelley, Patrick. *Nothing But Blood and Slaughter*. Booklocker.com, 2004. 3: 79–80.

82. Peckham, Howard Henry. *Toll of Independence: Engagements & Battle Casualties of the American Revolution*. Edited by Howard H. Peckham. Chicago: University of Chicago Press, 1974. p. 76. O'Kelley, Patrick. *Nothing But Blood and Slaughter*. Booklocker.com, 2004. 2: 353.

83. Caruthers, Eli W. *The Old North State in 1776*. Guilford County Genealogical Society, 1985. O'Kelley, Patrick. *Nothing But Blood and Slaughter*. Booklocker.com, 2004. 4: 87–88. Russell, David Lee. *The American Revolution in the Southern Colonies*. McFarland & Company, 2000. p. 314.

84. "Revd. James Fraser's Papers respecting His Claim for Losses during the Late American War" (Sir Thomas Phillipps MS 16605). Perkins Library, Duke University p. 22–23. *General Joseph Graham and his Papers on North Carolina Revolutionary History*. Ed. Major William A. Graham, ed. Raleigh: Edwards & Broughton, 1904. pp. 50–52, 313–318. Jesse Benton's Letters to Col. Thomas Hart. Thomas J. Clay Papers. Library of Congress. Orange County Tax List of 1779. N.C. Division of Archives & History. Raleigh, N.C. Engstrom, Mary Claire. The Hartford Mill Complex During the Revolution. *Eno Journal* 7 Special issue (July 1978) pp. 52–60. www.enoriver.org/eno/Shop/Journals/MillJournal/hartfordmill.htm. www.rsar.org/military/sherm162.pdf. Dan Alexander Pension File #S2905. Extract of a Letter Dated Richmond, March 8. *The Pennsylvania Evening Post* VII: 725 (March 6, 1781) p. 46. Schenck, David. *North Carolina 1780–'81. Being a History of the Invasion of the Carolinas by the British Army under Lord Cornwallis in 1780–'81*. Edwards & Broughton, 1889. pp. 274–277. Caruthers, Eli W. *The Old North State in 1776*. Guilford County Genealogical Society, 1985. pp. 124–125. Clark, Walter. *The State Records of North Carolina XIX–1782*. Winston: Nash Brothers, 1896. p. 960. O'Kelley, Patrick. *Nothing But Blood and Slaughter*. Booklocker.com, 2004. 3: 86–8.

85. George C. Rogers, Jr., ed. Letters of Charles O'Hara to the Duke of Grafton. *South Carolina Historical Magazine* 65: 3 (July 1964) pp. 158–180; pp. 176–177. Buchanan, John. *The Road to Guilford Courthouse*. New York: John Wiley and Sons, Inc., 1997. p. 360.

86. Hairr, John. *Colonel David Fanning, The Adventures of a Carolina Loyalist*. Averasboro Press, 2000. pp. 127–134, 136. Fanning, David. *The Narrative of Col. David Fanning*. Edited with an Introduction and Notes by Lindley S. Butler. Davidson, N.C.: Briarpatch Press; Charleston, S.C.: Tradd Street Press, 1981. pp. 39–43, 54–57. Newlin, Algie I. *The Battle of Lindley's Mill*. Burlington, N. C.: Alamance Historical Association, 1975. pp. 2–3. Caruthers, E. W. *Revolutionary Incidents: and Sketches of Character, Chiefly in the "Old North State."* Philadelphia: Hayes & Zell, 1854; Greensboro, N.C. (P.O. Box 9693, Greensboro 27429–0693): Guilford County Genealogical Society, 1985. pp. 208–25. Caruthers, Eli W. *The Old North State in 1776*. Guilford County Genealogical Society, 1985. pp. 47–54, 86, 89. Boatner, Mark M. *Encyclopedia of the American Revolution*. 3d ed., New York: McKay, 1980. p. 503. DeMond, Robert O. *The Loyalists in North Carolina During the Revolution*. Hamden, Conn.: Archon Books, 1964. pp. 221, 226. Rankin, Hugh F. *The North Carolina Continentals*. Chapel Hill: University of North Carolina Press, 1971. p. 364. *Pennsylvania Gazette* (October 10, 1781). Revolutionary War Pension Applications. RG15, Microcopy 804. O'Kelley, Patrick. *Nothing But Blood and Slaughter*. Booklocker.com, 2004. 3: 359–62.

87. Ashe, Samuel A'Court. *History of North Carolina*. Greensboro: Charles L. Van Noppen, 1925. I: 696. Hairr, John. *Colonel David Fanning, The Adventures of a Carolina Loyalist*. Averasboro Press, 2000. pp. 134–148. Newlin, Algie I. *The Battle of Lindley's Mill*. The Alamance Historical Association, 1975. Boatner, Mark M. *Encyclopedia of the American Revolution*. 3d ed., New York: McKay, 1980. p. 503. Fanning, David. *The Narrative of Col. David Fanning*. Edited with an Introduction and Notes by Lindley S. Butler. Davidson, N.C.: Briarpatch Press; Charleston, S.C.: Tradd Street Press, 1981. pp. 39–43, 54–57. DeMond, Robert O. *The Loyalists in North Carolina During the Revolution*. Hamden, Conn.: Archon Books, 1964. pp. 221, 226. *Pennsylvania Gazette* (October 10, 1781). *Salem Gazette* 1: 1 (October 18, 1781) p. 3. Caruthers, Eli W. *The Old North State in 1776*. Guilford County Genealogical Society, 1985. pp. 50–57, 86, 168. Haun, Weynette Parks. *North Carolina Revolutionary Army Accounts: Secretary of State, Treasurer's & Comptroller's Papers, Journal "A" (Public Accounts) 1775–1776 part I*. Weynette Parks Haun, 1989. pp. 101–104. Barefoot, Daniel W. *Touring North Carolina's Revolutionary War Sites*. Winston-Salem: John F. Blair, 1998. pp. 158, 396–399. Stedman, C. *The History of the Origin, Progress and Termination of the American War*. London: printed for the author, 1794 II: 406. O'Kelley, Patrick. *Nothing But Blood and Slaughter*. Booklocker.com, 2004. 3: 364–66.

88. Caruthers, Eli W. *The Old North State in 1776*. Guilford County Genealogical Society, 1985. pp. 57–58. O'Kelley, Patrick. *Nothing But Blood and Slaughter*. Booklocker.com, 2004. 3: 378.

89. Caruthers, Eli W. *The Old North State in 1776*. Guilford County Genealogical Society, 1985. pp. 173–174. O'Kelley, Patrick. *Nothing But Blood and Slaughter*. Booklocker.com, 2004. 3: 65–66.

90. www.harwich.edu/depts/History/HHJ/ngreenej.html.

91. Orange County Wills, A–53; Clerk of Superior Court, Hillsborough, N. C. Saunders, William L., ed. *The Colonial Records of North Carolina*. Raleigh, N.C.: P. M. Hale, 1890. VII: 734–35, 758–67. Fanning, David. *The Narrative of Col. David Fanning*. Edited with an Introduction and Notes by Lindley S. Butler. Davidson, N.C.: Briarpatch Press; Charleston, S.C.: Tradd Street Press, 1981. p. 35 n56.

92. Hairr, John. *Colonel David Fanning, the Adventures of a Carolina Loyalist*. Averasboro Press, 2000. pp. 74–75. Caruthers, Eli W. *The Old North State in 1776*. Guilford County Genealogical Society, 1985. pp. 37–38. O'Kelley, Patrick. *Nothing But Blood and Slaughter*. Booklocker.com, 2004. 3: 95.

93. Hairr, John. *Colonel David Fanning, the Adventures of a Carolina Loyalist*. Averasboro Press, 2000. pp. 82–83. Fanning, David. *The Narrative of Col. David Fanning*. Edited with an Introduction and Notes by Lindley S. Butler. Davidson, N.C.: Briarpatch Press; Charleston, S.C.: Tradd Street Press, 1981. p. 35. O'Kelley, Patrick. *Nothing But Blood and Slaughter*. Booklocker.com, 2004. 3: 231–32.

94. Hairr, John. *Colonel David Fanning, the Adventures of a Carolina Loyalist*. Averasboro Press, 2000. pp. 83–84. Fanning, David. *The Narrative of Col. David Fanning*. Edited with an Introduction and Notes by Lindley S. Butler.

Davidson, N.C.: Briarpatch Press; Charleston, S.C.: Tradd Street Press, 1981. pp. 35–36. O'Kelley, Patrick. *Nothing But Blood and Slaughter.* Booklocker.com, 2004. 3: 234–35.

95. Hairr, John. *Colonel David Fanning, the Adventures of a Carolina Loyalist.* Averasboro Press, 2000. pp. 83–84. Fanning, David. *The Narrative of Col. David Fanning.* Edited with an Introduction and Notes by Lindley S. Butler. Davidson, N.C.: Briarpatch Press; Charleston, S.C.: Tradd Street Press, 1981. pp. 35–36. O'Kelley, Patrick. *Nothing But Blood and Slaughter.* Booklocker.com, 2004. 3: 234–35.

96. Hairr, John. *Colonel David Fanning, the Adventures of a Carolina Loyalist.* Averasboro Press, 2000. pp. 86–88. Fanning, David. *The Narrative of Col. David Fanning.* Edited with an Introduction and Notes by Lindley S. Butler. Davidson, N.C.: Briarpatch Press; Charleston, S.C.: Tradd Street Press, 1981. pp. 36–37. O'Kelley, Patrick. *Nothing But Blood and Slaughter.* Booklocker.com, 2004. 3: 273–74.

97. O'Kelley, Patrick. *Nothing But Blood and Slaughter.* Booklocker.com, 2004. 3: 304–305.

98. Hairr, John. *Colonel David Fanning, the Adventures of a Carolina Loyalist.* Averasboro Press, 2000. pp. 105–106. Fanning, David. *The Narrative of Col. David Fanning.* Edited with an Introduction and Notes by Lindley S. Butler. Davidson, N.C.: Briarpatch Press; Charleston, S.C.: Tradd Street Press, 1981. pp. 49–50. Draper, Lyman. Thomas Sumter Papers, Draper Manuscript Collection, State Historical Society of Wisconsin. 10VV32. O'Kelley, Patrick. *Nothing But Blood and Slaughter.* Booklocker.com, 2004. 3: 305–306.

99. Hairr, John. *Colonel David Fanning, the Adventures of a Carolina Loyalist.* Averasboro Press, 2000. pp. 168–169. Fanning, David. *The Narrative of Col. David Fanning.* Edited with an Introduction and Notes by Lindley S. Butler. Davidson, N.C.: Briarpatch Press; Charleston, S.C.: Tradd Street Press, 1981. pp. 61–63. O'Kelley, Patrick. *Nothing But Blood and Slaughter.* Booklocker.com, 2004. 3: 405–406.

100. Hairr, John. *Colonel David Fanning, The Adventures of a Carolina Loyalist.* Erwin, N.C.: Averasboro Press, 2000. pp. 170–172. Fanning, David. *The Narrative of Col. David Fanning.* Edited with an Introduction and Notes by Lindley S. Butler. Davidson, N.C.: Briarpatch Press; Charleston, S.C.: Tradd Street Press, 1981. pp. 63–64. O'Kelley, Patrick. *Nothing But Blood and Slaughter.* Booklocker.com, 2004. 4: 24–26.

101. Extract of a letter dated New Providence April 16. *The Pennsylvania Packet or the General Advertiser* 1: 888 (May 23, 1782) p. 2. *Royal Gazette* 588 (May 18, 1782) p. 3.

102. Fanning, David. *The Narrative of Col. David Fanning.* Edited with an Introduction and Notes by Lindley S. Butler. Davidson, N.C.: Briarpatch Press; Charleston, S.C.: Tradd Street Press, 1981. pp. 36–38.

103. *Massachusetts Gazette* I: 5 (June 11, 1782) p. 3. *The New-York Gazette; and The Weekly Mercury* 1600 (June 17,1782) p. 2. *The New-Hampshire Gazette; or State Journal, and General Advertiser* XXVI: 1339 (June 29, 1782) p. 3.

104. Hairr, John. *Colonel David Fanning, the Adventures of a Carolina Loyalist.* Erwin, N.C.: Averasboro Press, 2000. pp. 185–187. Fanning, David. *The Narrative of Col. David Fanning.* Edited with an Introduction and Notes by Lindley S. Butler. Davidson, N.C.: Briarpatch Press; Charleston, S.C.: Tradd Street Press, 1981. pp. 76–77. O'Kelley, Patrick. *Nothing But Blood and Slaughter.* Booklocker.com, 2004. 4: 59–60.

105. Moultrie, William, *Memoirs of the American Revolution so far as it Related to the States of North and South Carolina and Georgia.* New York, 1802; Eyewitness accounts of the American Revolution). [New York]: New York Times [1968] II: 264. Lee, Henry. *Memoirs of the War in the Southern Department of the United States.* New York: University Publishing Co., 1869. pp. 239–243. Caruthers, Eli W. *The Old North State in 1776.* Guilford County Genealogical Society, 1985. pp. 118–120. Batt, Richard John. *The Maryland Continentals, 1780–1781.* Tulane University Dissertation, 1974. p. 120. Barefoot, Daniel W. *Touring North Carolina's Revolutionary War Sites.* Winston–Salem: John F. Blair, 1998. pp. 362–363. Hayes, John T. *The Saddlebag Almanac* VIII (January 2000) p. 78. O'Kelley, Patrick. *Nothing But Blood and Slaughter.* Booklocker.com, 2004. 3: 80–1.

106. www.harwich.edu/depts/History/HHJ/ngreenej.html 905–908. Lee, Henry. *Memoirs of the War in the Southern Department of the United States.* New York: University Publishing Co., 1869. p. 239. www.rsar.org/military/sherm162.pdf.

107. Boatner, Mark Mayo. *Landmarks of the American Revolution.* 2nd ed. Library of Military History. Detroit: Charles Scribner's Sons, 2007. pp. 271–272.

108. Caruthers, Eli W. *The Old North State in 1776.* Guilford County Genealogical Society, 1985. pp. 119–120. Batt, Richard John. *The Maryland Continentals, 1780–1781.* Tulane University Dissertation, 1974. pp. 122–124. Barefoot, Daniel W. *Touring North Carolina's Revolutionary War Sites.* Winston–Salem: John F. Blair, 1998. p. 346. O'Kelley, Patrick. *Nothing But Blood and Slaughter.* Booklocker.com, 2004. 3: 83–5.

109. Drayton John. *Memoirs of the American Revolution From its Commencement to the Year 1776, Inclusive; As Relating to the State of South Carolina and Georgia.* By John Drayton. Charleston, E. Miller, 1821. 1: 386–388.

110. Kentucky Archives. Kentucky Pension Accounts. Frankfort, Ky. O'Kelley, Patrick. *Nothing But Blood and Slaughter.* Booklocker.com, 2004. 1: 253.

111. *Encyclopedia of the American Revolution.* Harold E. Selesky, editor in chief.–2nd ed. Detroit: Charles Scribner's Sons, 2007. I: 495–496. *The Encyclopedia of the American Revolutionary War: A Political, Social, and Military History.* Gregory Fremont-Barnes, Richard Alan Ryerson, editors. Santa Barbara, Calif.: ABC-CLIO, 2006. II: 585–586. Buchanan, John. *The Road to Guilford Courthouse.* New York: John Wiley and Sons, Inc., 1997. Lee, Henry, *Memoirs of the War in the Southern Department of the United States.* New York: University Publishing Co., 1869. Lumpkin, Henry. *From Savannah to Yorktown: the American Revolution in the South.* New York: Paragon, 1981. Rankin, Hugh F. *The North Carolina Continentals.* Chapel Hill: University of North Carolina Press, 1971. Ward, Christopher. *The War of the Revolution.* New York: Macmillan, 1952. pp. 778–780. DeMond, Robert O. *The Loyalists in North Carolina During the Revolution.* Hamden, Conn.: Archon Books, 1964. pp. 135–136.

112. Caruthers, Eli W. *The Old North State in 1776.* Guilford County Genealogical Society, 1985. p. 128. Dann, John C. *The Revolution Remembered, Eyewitness Accounts of the War for Independence.* University of Chicago Press, 1980. p.

203. Clark, Walter. *The State Records of North Carolina. Vol. XIX–1782–'84. With Supplement–1771–'82.* Winston: Nash Brothers, 1901. p. 960. O'Kelley, Patrick. *Nothing But Blood and Slaughter.* Booklocker.com, 2004. 3: 100.

113. Dunaway, Stewart E. and Jeffrey G. Bright. The Battle of Clapp's Mill March 2, 1781: Prelude to Guilford Courthouse. *American Revolution* 1: 3 (October 2009) pp. 32–43. Pancake, John S. *This Destructive War: The British Campaign in the Carolinas.* Tuscaloosa: University of Alabama Press, 1985. p. 175. Peckham, Howard Henry. *Toll of Independence: Engagements & Battle Casualties of the American Revolution.* Edited by Howard H. Peckham. Chicago: University of Chicago Press, 1974. Tarleton, Banastre. *A History of the Campaigns of 1780 and 1781 in the Southern Provinces of North America,* London, 1787; Eyewitness Accounts of the American Revolution. [New York]: New York Times [1968]. p. 234–236. Lee, Henry. *Memoirs of the War in the Southern Department of the United States.* New York: University Publishing Co., 1869. p. 264. Kirkwood, Robert. "The Journal and Orderly Book of Captain Robert Kirkwood of the Delaware Regiment of the Continental Line," *Papers of the Historical Society of Delaware.* 56 (1910) p. 14. Pension Applications, RG 15, Microcopy 804. *General Joseph Graham and his Papers on North Carolina Revolutionary History.* Ed. Major William A. Graham, ed. Raleigh: Edwards & Broughton, 1904. pp. 50–52. Clark, Walter. *The State Records of North Carolina XIX–1782–'84.* Winston, 1896. pp. 960–962. Hayes, John T. *The Saddlebag Almanac* IX (January 2001). pp. 30–32. O'Kelley, Patrick. *Nothing But Blood and Slaughter.* Booklocker.com, 2004. 3: 109–112.

114. Ford, Worthington Chauncey. *British Officers Serving in the American Revolution 1774–1783.* Brooklyn, N.Y., 1897. p. 99. Boatner, Mark M. *Encyclopedia of the American Revolution.* 3d ed., New York: McKay, 1980. p. 231. Joseph Graham's pension application S6937.

115. Buchanan, John. *The Road to Guilford Courthouse.* New York: John Wiley and Sons, Inc., 1997. p. 366. O'Kelley, Patrick. *Nothing But Blood and Slaughter.* Booklocker.com, 2004. 3: 112.

116. Seymour, William. Journal of the Southern Expedition, 1780–1783. *Papers of the Historical Society of Delaware:* XV. Wilmington: The Historical Society of Delaware, 1896. pp. 18–19. Ward, Christopher L. *The Delaware Continentals.* Historical Society of Delaware, 1941. pp. 406–407. O'Kelley, Patrick. *Nothing But Blood and Slaughter.* Booklocker.com, 2004. 3: 112, 124.

117. Hairr, John. *Colonel David Fanning, the Adventures of a Carolina Loyalist.* Averasboro Press, 2000. pp. 78–79. Fanning, David. *The Narrative of Col. David Fanning.* Edited with an Introduction and Notes by Lindley S. Butler. Davidson, N.C.: Briarpatch Press; Charleston, S.C.: Tradd Street Press, 1981. pp. 34–35. O'Kelley, Patrick. *Nothing But Blood and Slaughter.* Booklocker.com, 2004. 3: 159–60.

118. Tarleton, Banastre. *A History of the Campaigns of 1780 and 1781 in the Southern Provinces of North America* London, 1787; Eyewitness Accounts of the American Revolution. [New York]: New York Times [1968]. p. 235. Davies, K. G. *Documents of the American Revolution 1770–1783.* (Colonial Office Series) Volume XX Transcripts 1781, Irish University Press, 1979. XX: 89. Babits, Lawrence E. *A Devil of a Whipping, The Battle of Cowpens.* University of North Carolina Press, 1998. p. 141. O'Kelley, Patrick. *Nothing But Blood and Slaughter.* Booklocker.com, 2004. 3: 106.

119. Hayes, John T. *The Saddlebag Almanac* IX (January 2001) p. 36. O'Kelley, Patrick. *Nothing But Blood and Slaughter.* Booklocker.com, 2004. 3: 123–24.

120. Tarleton, Banastre. *A History of the Campaigns of 1780 and 1781 in the Southern Provinces of North America.* London, 1787; Eyewitness Accounts of the American Revolution. [New York]: New York Times [1968]. pp. 237–238.

121. Seymour, William. Journal of the Southern Expedition, 1780–1783. *Papers of the Historical Society of Delaware:* XV. Wilmington: The Historical Society of Delaware, 1896. p. 19. O'Kelley, Patrick. *Nothing But Blood and Slaughter.* Booklocker.com, 2004. 3: 125.

122. Baker, Thomas E. *Another Such Victory, the Story of the American Defeat at Guilford Courthouse that Helped Win the War of Independence.* Eastern Acorn Press, 1992. pp. 33–39. Newsome, Anthony. A British Orderly Book, 1780–81. *North Carolina Historical Review* 9: 57–78, 163–186, 273–298, 366–392. Newlin, Algie I. *The Battle of New Garden.* Greensboro, North Carolina: The North Carolina Friends Historical Society and The North Carolina Yearly Meeting of Friends, 1977. Rosengarten, J. G. *The German Allied Troops in the North American War of Independence, 1776–1783.* by Max Von Eelking. Joel Munsell's Son's Publishers, 1893. pp. 189–220. Tarleton, Banastre. *A History of the Campaigns of 1780 and 1781 in the Southern Provinces of North America.* London, 1787; Eyewitness Accounts of the American Revolution. [New York]: New York Times [1968]. pp. 270–271. Lee, Henry. *Memoirs of the War in the Southern Department of the United States.* New York: University Publishing Co., 1869. pp. 273–274. Caruthers, Eli W. *The Old North State in 1776.* Guilford County Genealogical Society, 1985. pp. 133–134. Pension Applications RG 15, microcopy 804. Foote, William Henry. *Sketches of Virginia, Historical and Biographical.* 2nd Series. 2nd ed. Rev. J. B. Lippincot, 1856. pp. 140–149. Hayes, John T. *The Saddlebag Almanac* IX (January 2001) pp. 40–45. McAllister, J. T. *Virginia Militia in the Revolutionary War, Mcallister's Data.* McAllister Publishing Co., 1913. p. 209. O'Kelley, Patrick. *Nothing But Blood and Slaughter.* Booklocker.com, 2004. 3: 133–134.

123. Boatner, Mark Mayo. *Landmarks of the American Revolution.* 2nd ed. Library of Military History. Detroit: Charles Scribner's Sons, 2007. p. 267. *Documents of the American Revolution 1770–1783.* (Colonial Office Series), Volume XX, "Transcripts 1781" Edited by K. G. Davies. Irish University Press, 1979. Lamb, Roger. *An Original and Authentic Journal of Occurrences during the Late American War from its Commencement to the Year 1783.* Dublin, 1809; New York, 1970. Lee, Henry, *Memoirs of the War in the Southern Department of the United States.* New York: University Publishing Co., 1869. Greene, Nathanael. *The Papers of General Nathanael Greene.* Richard K. Showman, ed. Chapel Hill: The University of North Carolina Press, published for the Rhode Island Historical Society. c1976–. Mathis, Samuel. *Letter from Samuel Mathis to William R. Davie, dated 26 June 1819.* Historic Camden: Camden, South Carolina. Pancake, John S. *This Destructive War: The British Campaign in the Carolinas.* Tuscaloosa: University of Alabama Press, 1985. Symonds, Craig L. *A Battlefield Atlas of the American Revolution.* Mount Pleasant, SC: Nautical and Aviation Publishing Company of America, 1986. Tarleton, Banastre. *A History of the Campaigns of 1780 and 1781 in the Southern Provinces of North America.*

London: T. Cadell, 1787; [s.l.] The New York Times & Arno Press, 1968. Treacy, M. F. *Prelude to Yorktown: The Southern Campaign of Nathanael Greene, 1780–1781*. Chapel Hill: University of North Carolina Press, 1963. Ward, Christopher. *The War of the Revolution*. New York: Macmillan, 1952. pp. 784–794.

124. *Documents of the American Revolution 1770–1783*. (Colonial Office Series), Volume XX, "Transcripts 1781" Edited by K. G. Davies, Irish University Press, 1979. XX: 108. Tarleton, Banastre. *A History of the Campaigns of 1780 and 1781 in the Southern Provinces of North America*. London, 1787; Eyewitness Accounts of the American Revolution. [New York]: New York Times [1968]. p. 279. Dann, John C. *The Revolution Remembered, Eyewitness Accounts of the War for Independence*. University of Chicago Press, 1980. pp. 209–210. Hayes, John T. *The Saddlebag Almanac* IX (January 2001) pp. 68–70. Draper, Lyman. Thomas Sumter Papers, Draper Manuscript Collection, State Historical Society of Wisconsin. 15 VV185–186. O'Kelley, Patrick. *Nothing But Blood and Slaughter*. Booklocker.com, 2004. 3: 160–161.

125. Hairr, John. *Colonel David Fanning, the Adventures of a Carolina Loyalist*. Averasboro Press, 2000. p. 79. Kirkwood, Robert. "The Journal and Orderly Book of Captain Robert Kirkwood of the Delaware Regiment of the Continental Line," *Papers of the Historical Society of Delaware*. 56 (1910) pp. 1–277. *The Leeds Intelligencer* (June 26, 1781). O'Kelley, Patrick. *Nothing But Blood and Slaughter*. Booklocker.com, 2004. 3: 165–66.

126. DeMond, Robert O. *The Loyalists in North Carolina During the Revolution*. Hamden, Conn.: Archon Books, 1964. p. 220. Caruthers, Eli W. *The Old North State in 1776*. Guilford County Genealogical Society, 1985. pp. 165–168. O'Kelley, Patrick. *Nothing But Blood and Slaughter*. Booklocker.com, 2004. 3: 302.

127. General Wm. Caswell To Gov. Burke July 31st, 1781. Clark, Walter. *The State Records of North Carolina, Volume XXII, Miscellaneous*. Nash Brothers, 1907. pp. 553–554. digital.lib.ecu.edu/Historyfiction/document/mcf/entire.html.

128. Cornwallis, Charles C. *An Answer to that Part of the Narrative of Lt. General Sir Henry Clinton, K. B. Which Relates to the Conduct of Lieutenant-General Earl Cornwallis During the Campaign in North America, in the Year 1781*. London: J. Debrett, 1783. *Documents of the American Revolution 1770–1783*., (Colonial Office Series), Volume XX, "Transcripts 1781" Edited by K. G. Davies., Irish University Press, 1979. XX: 107–109. Tarleton, Banastre. *A History of the Campaigns of 1780 and 1781 in the Southern Provinces of North America*. London, 1787; Eyewitness Accounts of the American Revolution. [New York]: New York Times [1968]. pp. 270, 280–281. Lamb, Roger. *An Original and Authentic Journal of Occurrences During the Late American War*. Dublin, 1809. Eyewitness Accounts of the American Revolution. [New York]: New York Times [1968]. pp. 359–361. Schenck, David. *North Carolina 1780–'81. Being a History of the Invasion of the Carolinas by the British Army Under Lord Cornwallis in 1780–'81*. Edwards & Broughton, 1889. pp. 374–375. Caruthers, Eli W. *The Old North State in 1776*. Guilford County Genealogical Society, 1985. pp. 152–155. *Pennsylvania Gazette* (August 15, 1781). British National Archives. Cornwallis Papers. Class 30, vol. 11 p. 85 folio 22. Barefoot, Daniel W. *Touring North Carolina's Revolutionary War Sites*. Winston-Salem: John F. Blair, 1998. p. 136. O'Kelley, Patrick. *Nothing But Blood and Slaughter*. Booklocker.com, 2004. 3: 214–15.

129. Cornwallis, Charles C. *An Answer to that Part of the Narrative of Lt. General Sir Henry Clinton, K. B. Which Relates to the Conduct of Lieutenant-General Earl Cornwallis During the Campaign in North America, in the Year 1781*. London: J. Debrett, 1783. Tarleton, Banastre. *A History of the Campaigns of 1780 and 1781 in the Southern Provinces of North America*. London, 1787. Eyewitness Accounts of the American Revolution. [New York]: New York Times [1968]. pp. 285–287. Lamb, Roger. *An Original and Authentic Journal of Occurrences During the Late American War*. Dublin, 1809. Eyewitness Accounts of the American Revolution. [New York]: New York Times [1968]. p. 198. British National Archives. Cornwallis Papers. Class 30, vol. 11 p. 103 folio 29. Hayes, John T. *The Saddlebag Almanac* XI (2001) pp. 17–18. O'Kelley, Patrick. *Nothing But Blood and Slaughter*. Booklocker.com, 2004. 3: 221–23.

130. Cornwallis, Charles C. *An Answer to that Part of the Narrative of Lt. General Sir Henry Clinton, K. B. Which Relates to the Conduct of Lieutenant-General Earl Cornwallis During the Campaign in North America, in the Year 1781*. London: J. Debrett, 1783. Tarleton, Banastre. *A History of the Campaigns of 1780 and 1781 in the Southern Provinces of North America*. London, 1787; Eyewitness Accounts of the American Revolution. [New York]: New York Times [1968]. p. 287. Lamb, Roger. *An Original and Authentic Journal of Occurrences During the Late American War*. Dublin, 1809. Eyewitness Accounts of the American Revolution.[New York]: New York Times [1968]. p. 198. British National Archives. Cornwallis Papers. Class 30, vol. 11 p. 103 folio 29. O'Kelley, Patrick. *Nothing But Blood and Slaughter*. Booklocker.com, 2004. 3: 222.

131. Dickson, William. Duplin County History to 1810. *The North Carolina Historical Review* 1928. Esrael House's Statement to the clerk of court in 1811. House-Autry Mills Company. Dickson, William. *Historical Sketch of Old Duplin County*. by Col. William Dickson. The Raleigh Star, 1810. digital.lib.ecu.edu/Historyfiction/document/dit/entire.html. O'Kelley, Patrick. *Nothing But Blood and Slaughter*. Booklocker.com, 2004. 3: 233–34.

132. Hairr, John. *Colonel David Fanning, the Adventures of a Carolina Loyalist*. Averasboro Press, 2000. pp. 84–86. Fanning, David. *The Narrative of Col. David Fanning*. Edited with an Introduction and Notes by Lindley S. Butler. Davidson, N.C.: Briarpatch Press; Charleston, S.C.: Tradd Street Press, 1981. p. 36–37. Caruthers, Eli W. *The Old North State in 1776*. Guilford County Genealogical Society, 1985. pp. 165–166. O'Kelley, Patrick. *Nothing But Blood and Slaughter*. Booklocker.com, 2004. 3: 235–237.

133. Dickson, William. Duplin County History to 1810. *The North Carolina Historical Review*, 1928. digital.lib.ecu.edu/Historyfiction/document/dit/entire.html.

134. Hairr, John. *Colonel David Fanning, the Adventures of a Carolina Loyalist*. Averasboro Press, 2000. p. 109. Fanning, David. *The Narrative of Col. David Fanning*. Edited with an Introduction and Notes by Lindley S. Butler. Davidson, N.C.: Briarpatch Press; Charleston, S.C.: Tradd Street Press, 1981. p. 33. Cornwallis, Charles C. *An Answer to that Part of the Narrative of Lt. General Sir Henry Clinton, K. B. Which Relates to the Conduct of Lieutenant-General Earl Cornwallis During the Campaign in North America, in the Year 1781*. London: J. Debrett, 1783. *Royal Georgia Gazette* (August 30, 1781).

O'Kelley, Patrick. *Nothing But Blood and Slaughter*. Booklocker.com, 2004. 3: 307. Barefoot, Daniel W. *Touring North Carolina's Revolutionary War Sites*. Winston–Salem: John F. Blair, 1998. p. 90.

135. Dickson, William. *Duplin County History to 1810*. North Carolina Historical Review, 1928. digital.lib.ecu.edu/Historyfiction/document/dit/entire.html.

136. Dickson, William. *Duplin County History to 1810*. The North Carolina Historical Review, 1928. digital.lib.ecu.edu/Historyfiction/document/dit/entire.html. Ezrael House's Statement. Dickson, William. *Historical Sketch of Old Duplin County*. by Col. William Dickson. The Raleigh Star, 1810. O'Kelley, Patrick. *Nothing But Blood and Slaughter*. Booklocker.com, 2004. 3: 237–38.

137. Clark, Walter. *The State Records of North Carolina XV–1780*. Winston: Nash Brothers, 1896. pp. 475, 483, 518; XIX–1782–'84 pp. 524–525. O'Kelley, Patrick. *Nothing But Blood and Slaughter*. Booklocker.com, 2004. 3: 272.

138. *The Pennsylvania Evening Post, and Public Advertiser* VIII: 807 (March 12, 1782) p. 20.

139. www.ah.dcr.state.nc.us/Sections/HS/horsesho/horsesho.htm. Hairr, John. *Colonel David Fanning, the Adventures of a Carolina Loyalist*. Averasboro Press, 2000. pp. 94–104. Fanning, David. *The Narrative of Col. David Fanning*. Edited with an Introduction and Notes by Lindley S. Butler. Davidson, N.C.: Briarpatch Press; Charleston, S.C.: Tradd Street Press, 1981. pp. 48–49. Caruthers, Eli W. *The Old North State in 1776*. Guilford County Genealogical Society, 1985. pp. 42–46. Pension Applications RG 15, microcopy 804. Barefoot, Daniel W. *Touring North Carolina's Revolutionary War Sites*. Winston–Salem: John F. Blair, 1998. pp. 388–391. Hayes, John T. *The Saddlebag Almanac* XI (2003) p. 29. O'Kelley, Patrick. *Nothing But Blood and Slaughter*. Booklocker.com, 2004. 3: 303–305.

140. Peckham, Howard Henry. *Toll of Independence: Engagements & Battle Casualties of the American Revolution*. Edited by Howard H. Peckham. Chicago: University of Chicago Press, 1974. p. 88. O'Kelley, Patrick. *Nothing But Blood and Slaughter*. Booklocker.com, 2004. 3: 281–82.

141. Hairr, John. *Colonel David Fanning, the Adventures of a Carolina Loyalist*. Averasboro Press, 2000. p. 109. O'Kelley, Patrick. *Nothing But Blood and Slaughter*. Booklocker.com, 2004. 3: 317.

142. Cornwallis, Charles C. *An Answer to that Part of the Narrative of Lt. General Sir Henry Clinton, K. B. Which Relates to the Conduct of Lieutenant-General Earl Cornwallis During the Campaign in North America, in the Year 1781*. London: J. Debrett, 1783. Fanning, David. *The Narrative of Col. David Fanning*. Edited with an Introduction and Notes by Lindley S. Butler. Davidson, N.C.: Briarpatch Press; Charleston, S.C.: Tradd Street Press, 1981. p. 33. *Royal Georgia Gazette* (September 27, 1781) O'Kelley, Patrick. *Nothing But Blood and Slaughter*. Booklocker.com, 2004. 3: 317–18.

143. Hairr, John. *Colonel David Fanning, the Adventures of a Carolina Loyalist*. Averasboro Press, 2000. pp. 109–110. Cornwallis, Charles C. *An Answer to that Part of the Narrative of Lt. General Sir Henry Clinton, K. B. Which Relates to the Conduct of Lieutenant-General Earl Cornwallis During the Campaign in North America, in the Year 1781*. London: J. Debrett, 1783. DeMond, Robert O. *The Loyalists in North Carolina During the Revolution*. Hamden, Conn.: Archon Books, 1964. p. 61. Fanning, David. *The Narrative of Col. David Fanning*. Edited with an Introduction and Notes by Lindley S. Butler. Davidson, N.C.: Briarpatch Press; Charleston, S.C.: Tradd Street Press, 1981. p. 33. O'Kelley, Patrick. *Nothing But Blood and Slaughter*. Booklocker.com, 2004. 3: 318.

144. Barefoot, Daniel W. *Touring North Carolina's Revolutionary War Sites*. Winston–Salem: John F. Blair, 1998. p. 24. O'Kelley, Patrick. *Nothing But Blood and Slaughter*. Booklocker.com, 2004. 3: 276.

145. Fanning, David. *The Narrative of Col. David Fanning*. Edited with an Introduction and Notes by Lindley S. Butler. Davidson, N.C.: Briarpatch Press; Charleston, S.C.: Tradd Street Press, 1981. p. 45. Caruthers, Eli W. *The Old North State in 1776*. Guilford County Genealogical Society, 1985. pp. 38–40. Hairr, John. *Colonel David Fanning, the Adventures of a Carolina Loyalist*. Averasboro Press, 2000. pp. 89–96. Barefoot, Daniel W. *Touring North Carolina's Revolutionary War Sites*. Winston–Salem: John F. Blair, 1998. p. 393. O'Kelley, Patrick. *Nothing But Blood and Slaughter*. Booklocker.com, 2004. 3: 300–301.

146. Fanning, David. *The Narrative of Col. David Fanning*. Edited with an Introduction and Notes by Lindley S. Butler. Davidson, N.C.: Briarpatch Press; Charleston, S.C.: Tradd Street Press, 1981. pp. 60–61. Hairr, John. *Colonel David Fanning, the Adventures of a Carolina Loyalist*. Averasboro Press, 2000. pp. 167–168. O'Kelley, Patrick. *Nothing But Blood and Slaughter*. Booklocker.com, 2004. 3 p401–402.

147. DeMond, Robert O. *The Loyalists in North Carolina During the Revolution*. Hamden, Conn.: Archon Books, 1964. pp. 120–122, 220. Haun, Weynette Parks. *North Carolina Revolutionary Army Accounts: Secretary of State, Treasurer's & Comptroller's Papers, Journal "A" (Public Accounts) 1775–1776 part I*. Weynette Parks Haun, 1989. pp. 101–104. Caruthers, Eli W. *The Old North State in 1776*. Guilford County Genealogical Society, 1985. pp. 94–98. *Royal Georgia Gazette* 137 (October 11, 1781) p. 1. O'Kelley, Patrick. *Nothing But Blood and Slaughter*. Booklocker.com, 2004. 3: 308–310.

148. DeMond, Robert O. *The Loyalists in North Carolina During the Revolution*. Hamden, Conn.: Archon Books, 1964. pp. 120–122. Haun, Weynette Parks. *North Carolina Revolutionary Army Accounts: Secretary of State, Treasurer's & Comptroller's Papers, Journal "A" (Public Accounts) 1775–1776 part I*. Weynette Parks Haun, 1989. pp. 101–104. Caruthers, Eli W. *The Old North State in 1776*. Guilford County Genealogical Society, 1985. pp. 95–98. Barefoot, Daniel W. *Touring North Carolina's Revolutionary War Sites*. Winston–Salem: John F. Blair, 1998. pp. 138–139. O'Kelley, Patrick. *Nothing But Blood and Slaughter*. Booklocker.com, 2004. 3: 311–14.

149. Peckham, Howard Henry. *Toll of Independence: Engagements & Battle Casualties of the American Revolution*. Edited by Howard H. Peckham. Chicago: University of Chicago Press, 1974. p. 89. O'Kelley, Patrick. *Nothing But Blood and Slaughter*. Booklocker.com, 2004. 3: 316.

150. Hairr, John. *Colonel David Fanning, the Adventures of a Carolina Loyalist*. Averasboro Press, 2000. p. 108. Fanning, David. *The Narrative of Col. David Fanning*. Edited with an Introduction and Notes by Lindley S. Butler. Davidson, N.C.: Briarpatch Press; Charleston, S.C.: Tradd Street Press, 1981. p. 51. O'Kelley, Patrick. *Nothing But Blood and Slaughter*. Booklocker.com, 2004. 3: 316–17.

151. Hairr, John. *Colonel David Fanning, the Adventures of a Carolina Loyalist.* Averasboro Press, 2000. pp. 117–118. O'Kelley, Patrick. *Nothing But Blood and Slaughter.* Booklocker.com, 2004. 3: 321–22.

152. Ashe, Samuel A'Court. *History of North Carolina.* Greensboro: Charles L. Van Noppen, 1925. I: 690–91. There are no contemporary accounts of the battle of Elizabethtown. Most of the story comes from a letter written by A. A. Brown, editor of the *Wilmington Weekly Chronicle* in 1844 included in James Sprunt's *Chronicles of the Cape Fear River: 1660–1916.* "The Coastal Chronicles." August 2000. www.elizabethtownnc.org/History. htm. Hairr, John. *Colonel David Fanning, the Adventures of a Carolina Loyalist.* Averasboro Press, 2000. pp. 115–117. Fanning, David. *The Narrative of Col. David Fanning.* Edited with an Introduction and Notes by Lindley S. Butler. Davidson, N.C.: Briarpatch Press; Charleston, S.C.: Tradd Street Press, 1981. p. 52. Caruthers, Eli W. *The Old North State in 1776.* Guilford County Genealogical Society, 1985. pp. 46–47, 98–103. Barefoot, Daniel W. *Touring North Carolina's Revolutionary War Sites.* Winston–Salem: John F. Blair, 1998. pp. 122–123. O'Kelley, Patrick. *Nothing But Blood and Slaughter.* Booklocker.com, 2004. 3: 319–20.

153. Hairr, John. *Colonel David Fanning, the Adventures of a Carolina Loyalist.* Averasboro Press, 2000. pp. 134–148. Fanning, David. *The Narrative of Col. David Fanning.* Edited with an Introduction and Notes by Lindley S. Butler. Davidson, N.C.: Briarpatch Press; Charleston, S.C.: Tradd Street Press, 1981. pp. 39–43, 54–57. Newlin, Algie I. *The Battle of Lindley's Mill.* The Alamance Historical Association, 1975. Boatner, Mark M. *Encyclopedia of the American Revolution.* 3d ed., New York: McKay, 1980. p. 503. DeMond, Robert O. *The Loyalists in North Carolina During the Revolution.* Hamden, Conn.: Archon Books, 1964. pp. 221, 226. *Pennsylvania Gazette* (October 10, 1781). Caruthers, Eli W. *The Old North State in 1776.* Guilford County Genealogical Society, 1985. pp. 50–57, 86, 168. Haun, Weynette Parks. *North Carolina Revolutionary Army Accounts: Secretary of State, Treasurer's & Comptroller's Papers, Journal "A" (Public Accounts) 1775–1776 part I.* Weynette Parks Haun, 1989. pp. 101–104. Barefoot, Daniel W. *Touring North Carolina's Revolutionary War Sites.* Winston–Salem: John F. Blair, 1998. pp. 158, 396–399. O'Kelley, Patrick. *Nothing But Blood and Slaughter.* Booklocker.com, 2004. 3: 364–66.

154. Ashe, Samuel A'Court. *History of North Carolina.* Greensboro: Charles L. Van Noppen, 1925. I: 700.

155. Graham, Major William A. *General Joseph Graham and his Papers on North Carolina Revolutionary History.* Edwards & Broughton, 1901. pp. 359–360.

156. Hairr, John. *Colonel David Fanning, the Adventures of a Carolina Loyalist.* Averasboro Press, 2000. pp. 153, 155, 157–161. Caruthers, Eli W. *The Old North State in 1776.* Guilford County Genealogical Society, 1985. pp. 200–201. Clark, Walter. *The State Records of North Carolina XIX–1782–'84.* Winston, 1896. p. 963. Barefoot, Daniel W. *Touring North Carolina's Revolutionary War Sites.* Winston–Salem: John F. Blair, 1998. p. 141. McGeachy, John, "Revolutionary Reminiscenses from the "Cape Fear Sketches", NCSU History Paper, 2001. O'Kelley, Patrick. *Nothing But Blood and Slaughter.* Booklocker.com, 2004. 3: 375–77.

157. Hairr, John. *Colonel David Fanning, the Adventures of a Carolina Loyalist.* Averasboro Press, 2000. pp. 89–96. Fanning, David. *The Narrative of Col. David Fanning.* Edited with an Introduction and Notes by Lindley S. Butler. Davidson, N.C.: Briarpatch Press; Charleston, S.C.: Tradd Street Press, 1981. pp. 39–43, 54–57. Newlin, Algie I. *The Battle of Lindley's Mill.* The Alamance Historical Association, 1975. Boatner, Mark M. *Encyclopedia of the American Revolution.* 3d ed., New York: McKay, 1980. p. 503. DeMond, Robert O. *The Loyalists in North Carolina During the Revolution.* Hamden, Conn.: Archon Books, 1964. pp. 50–57, 86, 108. *Pennsylvania Gazette* (October 10, 1781). Haun, Weynette Parks. *North Carolina Revolutionary Army Accounts: Secretary of State, Treasurer's & Comptroller's Papers, Journal "A", (Public Accounts) 1775–1776 part I.* Weynette Parks Haun, 1989. pp. 101–104. Barefoot, Daniel W. *Touring North Carolina's Revolutionary War Sites.* Winston–Salem: John F. Blair, 1998. pp. 158, 396–399. O'Kelley, Patrick. *Nothing But Blood and Slaughter.* Booklocker.com, 2004. 3: 367–68.

158. Letter of Major James Henry Craig to Lieutenant Colonel Nesbit Balfour, October 22, 1781. British National Archives 30/11/6. Hairr, John. *Colonel David Fanning, the Adventures of a Carolina Loyalist.* Averasboro Press, 2000. pp. 150–152. Caruthers, Eli W. *The Old North State in 1776.* Guilford County Genealogical Society, 1985. p. 91. DeMond, Robert O. *The Loyalists in North Carolina During the Revolution.* Hamden, Conn.: Archon Books, 1964. p. 61. O'Kelley, Patrick. *Nothing But Blood and Slaughter.* Booklocker.com, 2004. 3: 369–370.

159. Caruthers, Eli W. *The Old North State in 1776.* Guilford County Genealogical Society, 1985. pp. 43, 86. O'Kelley, Patrick. *Nothing But Blood and Slaughter.* Booklocker.com, 2004. 3: 332.

160. Hairr, John. *Colonel David Fanning, the Adventures of a Carolina Loyalist.* Averasboro Press, 2000. pp. 130–131. Caruthers, Eli W. *The Old North State in 1776.* Guilford County Genealogical Society, 1985. pp. 49–50. O'Kelley, Patrick. *Nothing But Blood and Slaughter.* Booklocker.com, 2004. 3: 362–63.

161. Hairr, John. *Colonel David Fanning, the Adventures of a Carolina Loyalist.* Averasboro Press, 2000. pp. 162–163. O'Kelley, Patrick. *Nothing But Blood and Slaughter.* Booklocker.com, 2004. 3: 373–4.

162. Caruthers, Eli W. *The Old North State in 1776.* Guilford County Genealogical Society, 1985. Draper, Lyman. Thomas Sumter Papers, Draper Manuscript Collection, State Historical Society of Wisconsin. 10VV161. O'Kelley, Patrick. *Nothing But Blood and Slaughter.* Booklocker.com, 2004. 3: 372.

163. Barefoot, Daniel W. *Touring North Carolina's Revolutionary War Sites.* Winston–Salem: John F. Blair, 1998. pp. 321–322. O'Kelley, Patrick. *Nothing But Blood and Slaughter.* Booklocker.com, 2004. 3: 383–84.

164. Clark. Murtie June. *Loyalists in the Southern Campaign of the Revolutionary War.* Baltimore: Genealogical Publishing Company. Inc. 1981. 1: 187. Caruthers, Eli W. *The Old North State in 1776.* Guilford County Genealogical Society, 1985. p. 203. Clark, Walter. *The State Records of North Carolina, Vol. XIX–1782–'84. With Supplement–1771–'82.* Winston: Nash Brothers, 1901. p. 963. O'Kelley, Patrick. *Nothing But Blood and Slaughter.* Booklocker.com, 2004. 3: 388–89.

165. Cornwallis Papers, Class 30, Vol. 11, part 3, folios 203–204 British National Archives. Chancery, Class 106, Volume 88, part 2. Hairr, John. *Colonel David Fanning, the Adventures of a Carolina Loyalist.* Averasboro Press, 2000. pp. 164–165. Davies, K. G. *Documents of the American Revolution 1770-1783.* (Colonial Office Series) Shannon: Irish

University Press, 1972, 1981. XX: 267. Caruthers, Eli W. *The Old North State in 1776*. Guilford County Genealogical Society, 1985. pp. 200–201. Fanning, David. *The Narrative of Col. David Fanning*. Edited with an Introduction and Notes by Lindley S. Butler. Davidson, N.C.: Briarpatch Press; Charleston, S.C.: Tradd Street Press, 1981. pp. 33, 60. Lipscomb, Terry W. *South Carolina Revolutionary Battles Part Eight (With Map), Names in South Carolina*. South Carolina Historical Society, 1980. XXVII (Winter 1980) p. 16. McGeachy, John, Revolutionary Reminiscences from the "Cape Fear Sketches", NCSU History Paper, 2001. O'Kelley, Patrick. *Nothing But Blood and Slaughter*. Booklocker.com, 2004. 3: 396–97.

166. Hairr, John. *Colonel David Fanning, the Adventures of a Carolina Loyalist*. Averasboro Press, 2000. pp. 169–170. Caruthers, Eli W. *The Old North State in 1776*. Guilford County Genealogical Society, 1985. pp. 56–57. O'Kelley, Patrick. *Nothing But Blood and Slaughter*. Booklocker.com, 2004. 3: 409–10.

167. Barefoot, Daniel W. *Touring North Carolina's Revolutionary War Sites*. Winston-Salem: John F. Blair, 1998. p. 83.

168. Russell, Phillips. *North Carolina in the Revolutionary War*. Charlotte, N.C., Heritage Printers, 1965. pp. 286–7.

169. Blythe, Brockman. *Hornet's Nest. The Story of Charlotte and Mecklenburg County*. Public Library of Charlotte and Mecklenburg County, 1961. p. 5. Heitman, Francis B. *Historical Register of Officers of the Continental Army during the War of the Revolution, April 1775 to December 1783*. Washington, D.C., 1914; Baltimore: Genealogical Publishing Company, 1967. p. 368. O'Donnell, James H. *Southern Indians in the American Revolution*. University of Tennessee, 1971. p. 47.

170. Nichols, John L. Alexander Cameron, British Agent Among the Cherokee, 1764–1781. *South Carolina Historical Magazine* 97: 2 (April 1996) p. 109. Saye, James Hodge. *Memoirs of Major Joseph McJunkin, Revolutionary Patriot*. [s.l.]: A Press, Inc. 1977. (First printed in the Richmond, VA *Watchman and Observer* in 1847). Barefoot, Daniel W. *Touring North Carolina's Revolutionary War Sites*. Winston–Salem: John F. Blair, 1998. pp. 220–221, 237, 246. O'Kelley, Patrick. *Nothing But Blood and Slaughter*. Booklocker.com, 2004. 1: 147, 149.

171. Sketch of Henry Rutherford. *The American Historical Magazine* V (1900) p. 225.

172. Saye, James Hodge. *Memoirs of Major Joseph McJunkin, Revolutionary Patriot*. [s.l.]: A Press, Inc. 1977. (First printed in the Richmond, VA *Watchman and Observer* in 1847).

173. Davies, K. G. *Documents of the American Revolution 1770–1783*. (Colonial Office Series) Volume XII Transcripts 1776, Irish University Press, 1973. p. 229. *Pennsylvania Packet*. January 17, 1777. Milling, Chapman J. *Red Carolinians*. The University of South Carolina Press, 1969. p. 253. Ervin. Sara Sullivan. *South Carolinians in the Revolution*. Baltimore: Genealogical Publishing Company, Inc. 1971. pp. 67–77. O'Donnell, James H. *Southern Indians in the American Revolution*. University of Tennessee Press, 1971. p. 471. O'Kelley, Patrick. *Nothing But Blood and Slaughter*. Booklocker. com, 2004. 1:166–67.

174. *Encyclopedia of the American Revolution*. Harold E. Selesky, editor in chief. 2nd ed. Detroit: Charles Scribner's Sons, 2007. I: 202. Dickens, Roy S. Jr. "The Route of Rutherford's Expedition Against the North Carolina Cherokee." *Journal of Southern Indian Studies*. XIX (1967) pp. 3–24.

174a. Boatner, Mark M. *Encyclopedia of the American Revolution*. 3d ed., New York: McKay, 1980. p. 221 Tuskeegee and Overhill Towns (Cherokee War of 1776)

175. William Christian to Patrick Henry, October 27, 1776. *Virginia Magazine of History and Biography* XVII (1909) pp. 51–59. Nichols, John L. Alexander Cameron, British Agent Among the Cherokee, 1764–1781. *South Carolina Historical Magazine* 97: 2 (April 1996) pp. 110–111. White, Katherine Keogh. *The King's Mountain Men, The story of the Battle with Sketches of the American Soldiers Who Took Part*. Baltimore: Genealogical Publishing Company, 1966. pp. 158, 163. Pension Applications RG 15. Pancake, John S. *This Destructive War: The British Campaign in the Carolinas*. Tuscaloosa: University of Alabama Press, 1985. p. 77. Barefoot, Daniel W. *Touring North Carolina's Revolutionary War Sites*. Winston–Salem: John F. Blair, 1998. p. 233. Sanchez-Saavedera E. M. *A Guide to Virginia Military Organizations in the American Revolution, 1774–1787*. Richmond, VA, 1978. pp. 24–25. O'Kelley, Patrick. *Nothing But Blood and Slaughter*. Booklocker.com, 2004. 1: 168–69.

176. Journal of Lt. Thomas Anderson of the Delaware Regiment, 1780–1782. *Historical Magazine* 2nd Series 1 (April 1867) pp. 207–211. Peter Force Collection. Series 7E Item 4.

177. www.tradingford.com/fateful.html.

178. Fanning, David. *Col. David Fanning's Narrative of His Exploits and Adventures as a Loyalist of North Carolina in the American Revolution*. Ed. and annotated by John S. Barnes. New York: Printed for the Naval History Society by the De Vinne Press, 1912. pp. 26–28.

179. Hairr, John. *Colonel David Fanning, the Adventures of a Carolina Loyalist*. Averasboro Press, 2000. pp. 45–49. Fanning, David. *The Narrative of Col. David Fanning*. Edited with an Introduction and Notes by Lindley S. Butler. Davidson, N.C.: Briarpatch Press; Charleston, S.C.: Tradd Street Press, 1981. pp. 26–27. Caruthers, Eli W. *The Old North State in 1776*. Guilford County Genealogical Society, 1985. p. 35. Bennett, Charles E. and Lennon, Donald R. *A Quest for Glory: Major General Robert Howe and the American Revolution*. Chapel Hill & London: The University of North Carolina Press, 1991. pp. 70–84. O'Kelley, Patrick. *Nothing But Blood and Slaughter*. Booklocker.com, 2004. 1: 201–202.

180. Peckham, Howard Henry. *Toll of Independence: Engagements & Battle Casualties of the American Revolution*. Edited by Howard H. Peckham. Chicago: University of Chicago Press, 1974. p. 80.

181. Graham, Major William A. *General Joseph Graham and His Papers on North Carolina Revolutionary History*. Raleigh: Edwards & Broughton, 1904. pp. 300–301. www.tradingford.com/graham.html.

182. Davies, K. G. *Documents of the American Revolution 1770–1783*. (Colonial Office Series) Volume XX Transcripts 1781, Irish University Press, 1979. p. 88. Tarleton, Banastre. *A History of the Campaigns of 1780 and 1781 in the Southern Provinces of North America*. London, 1787; Eyewitness accounts of the American Revolution. [New York]: New York Times [1968]. p. 227. Schenck, David. *North Carolina 1780–'81. Being a History of the Invasion of the Carolinas by the British*

Army under Lord Cornwallis in 1780–'81. Edwards & Broughton, 1889. pp. 248–249. Draper, Lyman. Thomas Sumter Papers, Draper Manuscript Collection, State Historical Society of Wisconsin. 6VV67. O'Kelley, Patrick. *Nothing But Blood and Slaughter.* Booklocker.com, 2004. 3: 76–7. Boatner, Mark Mayo. *Landmarks of the American Revolution.* 2nd ed. Library of Military History. Detroit: Charles Scribner's Sons, 2007. p. 271.

183. Clark, Walter. *The State Records of North Carolina XVII–1781–1785.* Winston: Nash Brothers, 1896. p. 1056. Pancake, John S. *This Destructive War: The British Campaign in the Carolinas.* Tuscaloosa: University of Alabama Press, 1985. pp. 167–168. O'Kelley, Patrick. *Nothing But Blood and Slaughter.* Booklocker.com, 2004. 3: 77–8. Rankin, Hugh F. *The North Carolina Continentals.* Chapel Hill: University of North Carolina Press, 1971. www.angelfire.com/nc/Lockes/Lockes1.html. Sherman, William Thomas. *Calendar and Record of the Revolutionary War in the South: 1780–1781.* 2003. www.usgennet.org/usa/ga/topic/military/argeorgia/wt_sherman_bk.htm.

184. Hairr, John. *Colonel David Fanning, the Adventures of a Carolina Loyalist.* Erwin, N.C.: Averasboro Press, 2000. pp. 175–179. Fanning, David. *The Narrative of Col. David Fanning.* Edited with an Introduction and Notes by Lindley S. Butler. Davidson, N.C.: Briarpatch Press; Charleston, S.C.: Tradd Street Press, 1981. pp. 37, 71–73. Barefoot, Daniel W. *Touring North Carolina's Revolutionary War Sites.* Winston–Salem: John F. Blair, 1998. pp. 381–382. Caruthers, Eli W. *The Old North State in 1776.* Greensboro, N.C.: Guilford County Genealogical Society, 1985. pp. 63–85. Clark, Walter, et al., editors. *The State Records of North Carolina.* Winston and Goldsboro: Various publishers, 1895–1907. 16 (1781): 799–780; 17: 966–967. DeMond, Robert O. *The Loyalists in North Carolina During the Revolution.* Durham, N.C.: Duke University Press, 1940. p. 123. O'Kelley, Patrick. *Nothing But Blood and Slaughter.* Booklocker.com, 2004. 4: 43–44.

185. Remonstrance and petition from a number of Inhabitants of the District of Salisbury, April–May 1782, Joint Standing Committees, Propositions & Grievances—Report and Papers, General Assembly Session Records, North Carolina Department of Archives and History, Raleigh. Lee, Wayne E. *Crowds and Soldiers in Revolutionary North Carolina: the Culture of Violence in Riot and War.* Wayne E. Lee; foreword by Stanley Harrold and Randall J. Miller. Gainesville: University Press of Florida, 2001. p. 179.

186. Barefoot, Daniel W. *Touring North Carolina's Revolutionary War Sites.* Winston–Salem: John F. Blair, 1998. p. 275. George C. Rogers, Jr., ed. Letters of Charles O'Hara to the Duke of Grafton. *South Carolina Historical Magazine* 65: 3 (July 1964).

187. General Richard Winn's Notes–1780. *The South Carolina Historical and Genealogical Magazine* XLIII: 4 (October 1942) pp. 203–204. Hill, William, *Col. William Hill's Memoirs of the Revolution.* Edited by A. S. Sally. Columbia, S.C., 1921. Draper, Lyman. Thomas Sumter Papers, Draper Manuscript Collection, State Historical Society of Wisconsin. O'Kelley, Patrick. *Nothing But Blood and Slaughter.* Booklocker.com, 2004. 2: 189–190.

188. White, Katherine Keogh. *The King's Mountain Men, The Story of the Battle with Sketches of the American Soldiers Who Took Part.* Baltimore: Genealogical Publishing Company, 1966. pp. 145–146. Barefoot, Daniel W. *Touring North Carolina's Revolutionary War Sites.* Winston–Salem: John F. Blair, 1998. pp. 252–253. O'Kelley, Patrick. *Nothing But Blood and Slaughter.* Booklocker.com, 2004. 2: 301–302.

189. Allaire, Anthony. *Diary of Lieut. Anthony Allaire.* Eyewitness Accounts of the American Revolution. [New York]: New York Times [1968]. p. 29.

190. Schenck, David. *North Carolina 1780–'81. Being a History of the Invasion of the Carolinas by the British Army under Lord Cornwallis in 1780–'81.* Edwards & Broughton, 1889. pp. 128–129. O'Kelley, Patrick. *Nothing But Blood and Slaughter.* Booklocker.com, 2004. 2: 346. Ferguson, Nancy Ellen. *Gilbert Town: Its Place in North Carolina and Revolutionary War History With Information on Andrew Hampton, Griffith Rutherford, William Gilbert, and the Death of James Dunlap.* Paper presented at the Kings Mountain National Military Park. 1998, 2003. www.overmountainvictory.org/Gtown.htm.

191. Barefoot, Daniel W. *Touring North Carolina's Revolutionary War Sites.* Winston–Salem: John F. Blair, 1998. p, 152. gaz.jrshelby.com/wahabsp.htm.

192. www.cmhpf.org/S&RR/McIntyreFarm.html.

193. Boatner, Mark Mayo. *Landmarks of the American Revolution.* 2nd ed. Library of Military History. Detroit: Charles Scribner's Sons, 2007. p. 272.

194. Thomas, Sam. *The Dye is Cast: The Scots-Irish and Revolution in the Carolina Back Country.* The Palmetto Conservation Foundation, 1994. p. 35. Clark, Walter. *The State Records of North Carolina XIX–1782.* Winston: Nash Brothers, 1896. pp. 968–969. 990. Barefoot, Daniel W. *Touring North Carolina's Revolutionary War Sites.* Winston–Salem: John F. Blair, 1998. pp. 177, 179–180. O'Kelley, Patrick. *Nothing But Blood and Slaughter.* Booklocker.com, 2004. 2: 319–20. www.carolana.com/NC/Revolution/revolution_battle_of_the _bees.html.

195. Thomas, Sam. *The Dye is Cast: The Scots-Irish and Revolution in the Carolina Back Country.* The Palmetto Conservation Foundation, 1994. p. 35. Tarleton, Banastre. *A History of the Campaigns of 1780 and 1781 in the Southern Provinces of North America.* London, 1787; Eyewitness Accounts of the American Revolution. [New York]: New York Times [1968]. p. 160. Cary and McCance. *Regimental Records of the Royal Welch Fusiliers.* Forster Groom & Co., 1921. *Pennsylvania Gazette* (October 25, 1780). MacKenzie, Roderick. *Strictures on Lt. Col. Tarleton's History of the Campaigns of 1780 and 1781 in the Southern Provinces to Which is Added a Detail of the Siege of Ninety Six, and the Recapture of the Island of New Providence.* London, 1787. pp. 54–55. O'Kelley, Patrick. *Nothing But Blood and Slaughter.* Booklocker.com, 2004. 2: 343–44.

196. Stedman, C. (Charles). *The History of the Origin, Progress, and Termination of the American war.* Eyewitness accounts of the American Revolution. [New York]: New York Times; Arno Press, c1969 2: 225.

197. Blythe , Brockman. *Hornet's Nest. The Story of Charlotte and Mecklenburg County.* Public Library of Charlotte and Mecklenburg County, 1961. pp. 7, 8. Tarleton, Banastre. *A History of the Campaigns of 1780 and 1781 in the Southern Provinces of North America,* London, 1787; Eyewitness Accounts of the American Revolution. [New York]: New York Times [1968]. pp. 166–168. Draper, Lyman. *Kings Mountain and its Heroes: History of the Battle of King's Mountain, October 7th, 1780, And the Events Which Led To It.* The Overmountain Press, 1996. pp. 370–371. Moultrie, William,

Memoirs of the American Revolution So Far as it Related to the States of North and South Carolina and Georgia. New York, 1802; Eyewitness Accounts of the American Revolution. [New York]: New York Times [1968]. II: 246–247. Schenck, David. *North Carolina 1780–'81. Being a History of the Invasion of the Carolinas by the British Army Under Lord Cornwallis in 1780–'81.* Edwards & Broughton, 1889. pp. 180–181. Robinson, Blackwell P. *The Revolutionary War Sketches of William R. Davie.* Raleigh: North Carolina Department of Cultural Resources, Division of Archives and History, 1976. pp. 26–27. Draper, Lyman. Thomas Sumter Papers, Draper Manuscript Collection, State Historical Society of Wisconsin. O'Kelley, Patrick. *Nothing But Blood and Slaughter.* Booklocker.com, 2004. 2: 344–345.

198. Barefoot, Daniel W. *Touring North Carolina's Revolutionary War Sites.* Winston-Salem: John F. Blair, 1998. pp. 177–178. O'Kelley, Patrick. *Nothing But Blood and Slaughter.* Booklocker.com, 2004. 2: 360. Extract of a letter from an officer in the Southern army, dated Camp, near the Waxaws, October 31. *The Pennsylvania Packet or the General Advertiser* X: 697 (January 9, 1781) p. 3. *The American Journal and General Advertiser* II: 94 (January 13, 1781) p. 2. Hanger, George. *The Life, Adventures, and Opinions of Col. George Hanger.* George Coleraine; William Combe. London: J. Debrett, 1801. Thomas, Sam. *The Dye is Cast: The Scots-Irish and Revolution in the Carolina Back Country.* The Palmetto Conservation Foundation, 1994. pp. 33–34. Tarleton, Banastre. *A History of the Campaigns of 1780 and 1781 in the Southern Provinces of North America.* London, 1787; Eyewitness Accounts of the American Revolution. [New York]: New York Times [1968]. pp. 158–159. Kentucky Archives. Kentucky Pension Accounts. Lee, Henry. *Memoirs of the War in the Southern Department of the United States.* New York: University Publishing Co., 1869. pp. 196–197. Schenck, David. *North Carolina 1780–'81. Being a History of the Invasion of the Carolinas by the British Army under Lord Cornwallis in 1780–'81.* Edwards & Broughton, 1889. pp. 106–112. British National Archives. Cornwallis Papers. Class 30, vol. 11 p. 3. Robinson, Blackwell P. *The Revolutionary War Sketches of William R. Davie.* Raleigh: North Carolina Department of Cultural Resources, Division of Archives and History, 1976. pp. 24–26. Clark, Walter. *The State Records of North Carolina XIV–1779–'80.* Winston: Nash Brothers, 1896. pp. 958–959. Batt, Richard John. *The Maryland Continentals, 1780–1781.* Tulane University Dissertation, 1974. pp. 45–46. O'Kelley, Patrick. *Nothing But Blood and Slaughter.* Booklocker.com, 2004. 2: 313–16.

199. Stedman, C. (Charles). *The History of the Origin, Progress and Termination of the American War.* London: printed for the author, 1794. Eyewitness Accounts of the American Revolution. [New York]: New York Times; Arno Press, c1969. Tarleton, Banastre. *A History of the Campaigns of 1780 and 1781 in the Southern Provinces of North America.* London: T. Cadell, 1787; [s.l.]: The New York Times & Arno Press, 1968. Gen. Cornwallis's letter to Lord Germain March, 17, 1781. Graham, Major William A. *General Joseph Graham and his Papers on North Carolina Revolutionary History.* Raleigh: Edwards & Broughton, 1904. Sherman, William Thomas. *Calendar and Record of the Revolutionary War in the South: 1780–1781.* 2003. pp. 845–850. www.usgennet.org/usa/ga/topic/military/argeorgia/wt_sherman_bk.htm. Barefoot, Daniel W. *Touring North Carolina's Revolutionary War Sites.* Winston–Salem: John F. Blair, 1998. Boatner, Mark M. *Encyclopedia of the American Revolution.* 3d ed. New York: McKay, 1980. Boatner, Mark Mayo. *Landmarks of the American Revolution; A Guide To Locating And Knowing What Happened At The Sites of Independence.* Stackpole Books: [Harrisburg, Pa.], [1973]; 2nd ed. Library of Military History. Detroit: Charles Scribner's Sons, 2007.

200. Tarleton, Banastre. *A History of the Campaigns of 1780 and 1781 in the Southern Provinces of North America.* London, 1787; Eyewitness Accounts of the American Revolution. [New York]: New York Times [1968]. pp. 225–226. Graham, Major William A. *General Joseph Graham and His Papers on North Carolina Revolutionary History.* Raleigh: Edwards & Broughton, 1904.

201. Schenck, David. *North Carolina 1780–'81. Being a History of the Invasion of the Carolinas by the British Army Under Lord Cornwallis in 1780–'81.* Edwards & Broughton, 1889. p. 252. Gen. Nathanael Greene letter to George Washington dated camp Guilford Court House, February 9, 1781. Greene, Nathanael. *The Papers of General Nathanael Greene.* Richard K. Showman, ed. Chapel Hill: The University of North Carolina Press, published for the Rhode Island Historical Society. c1976–2006. VIII: 267–269.

202. Gen. Nathanael Greene's letter to General Isaac Huger, Feb. 7, 1781. Greene, Nathanael. *The Papers of General Nathanael Greene.* Richard K. Showman, ed. Chapel Hill: The University of North Carolina Press, published for the Rhode Island Historical Society. c1976–2006.

203. Boatner, Mark Mayo. *Landmarks of the American Revolution.* 2nd ed. Library of Military History. Detroit: Charles Scribner's Sons, 2007. p. 271.

204. Henderson, Archibald. The Conquest of the Old Southwest Chapter XIX. www.worldwideschool.org/library/books/lit/historical/TheConquestoftheOldSouthwest/chap19.html.

205. Seymour, William. Journal of the Southern Expedition, 1780–1783. *Papers of the Historical Society of Delaware:* XV. Wilmington: The Historical Society of Delaware, 1896. p. 19. Caruthers, Eli W. *The Old North State in 1776.* Guilford County Genealogical Society, 1985. p. 132. Tarleton, Banastre. *A History of the Campaigns of 1780 and 1781 in the Southern Provinces of North America.* London, 1787; Eyewitness Accounts of the American Revolution. [New York]: New York Times [1968]. p. 239. O'Kelley, Patrick. *Nothing But Blood and Slaughter.* Booklocker.com, 2004. 3: 125–26.

206. Robert Love's pension papers S18093. Arthur, John Preston. *Western North Carolina: A History (from 1730 to 1913).* Edward Buncombe Chapter of the Daughters of the American Revolution, of Asheville, N.C.; Raleigh: Edwards and Broughton Printing Co., 1914. p. 108.

207. Draper, Lyman. *Kings Mountain and its Heroes: History of the Battle of King's Mountain, October 7th, 1780, and the Events Which Led To It.* The Overmountain Press, 1996. pp. 437–448. Barefoot, Daniel W. *Touring North Carolina's Revolutionary War Sites.* Winston–Salem: John F. Blair, 1998. pp. 214–216. O'Kelley, Patrick. *Nothing But Blood and Slaughter.* Booklocker.com, 2004. 3: 188–89.

208. Landrum, J. B. O. *Colonial and Revolutionary History of Upper South Carolina: Embracing for the Most Part the Primitive and Colonial History of the Territory Comprising the Original County of Spartanburg, with a General Review of the Entire Military Operations in the Upper Portions of South Carolina and Portions of North Carolina.* Spartanburg, S.C.: Reprint Co., 1977, 1897. pp. 360–361. Johnson, Joseph. *Traditions and Reminiscences, Chiefly of the American Revolution in the South: Including*

Biographical Sketches, Incidents, and Anecdotes, Few of Which Have Been Published, Particularly of Residents in the Upper Country. Charleston, S.C.: Walker & James, 1851. pp. 419–420. O'Kelley, Patrick. *Nothing But Blood and Slaughter.* Booklocker.com, 2004. 3: 381.

Glossary

1. *Oxford English Dictionary.*

Glossary

Abatis: Sharpened branches pointing out from a fortification at an angle toward the enemy to slow or disrupt an assault.
Accoutrement: Piece of military equipment carried by soldiers in addition to their standard uniform and weapons.
Bar shot: A double shot consisting of two half cannon balls joined by an iron bar, used in sea-warfare to damage masts and rigging.
Bastion: A fortification with a projecting part of a wall to protect the main walls of the fortification.
Battalion: The basic organizational unit of a military force, generally 500 to 800 men. Most regiments consisted of a single battalion which was composed of ten companies.
Bateau: A light flat-bottomed riverboat with sharply tapering stern and bow.
Battery: Two or more similar artillery pieces that function as a single tactical unit; a prepared position for artillery; an army artillery unit corresponding to a company in an infantry regiment.
Bayonet: A long, slender blade that can be attached to the end of a musket and used for stabbing.
Best bower: The large anchor (about 4,000 pounds) on the starboard side of the bow of a vessel. The other is called the small-bower. Also the cable attached to this anchor.
Blunderbuss: A short musket with a large bore and wide muzzle capable of holding a number of musket or pistol balls, used to fire shot with a scattering effect at close range. It is very effective for clearing a narrow passage, door of a house or staircase, or in boarding a ship.
Bomb: An iron shell, or hollow ball, filled with gunpowder. It has a large touch-hole for a slow-burning fuse which is held in place by pieces of wood and fastened with a cement made of quicklime, ashes, brick dust, and steel filings worked together with glutinous water. A bomb is shot from a mortar mounted on a carriage. It is fired in a high arc over fortifications and often detonates in the air, raining metal fragments with high velocity on the fort's occupants (see Photo VA-2).
Bombproof: A structure built strong enough to protect the inhabitants from exploding bombs and shells.
Brig: A small two-masted sailing vessel with square-rigged sails on both masts.
Brigade: A military unit consisting of about 800 men.
Broadside: 1. The firing of all guns on one side of a vessel as nearly simultaneously as possible. 2. A large piece of paper printed on one side for advertisements or public notices.
Canister or **Cannister shot:** A kind of case-shot consisting of a number of small iron balls packed in sawdust in a cylindrical tin or canvas case. They were packed in four tiers between iron plates..
Carronade: A short, stubby piece of artillery, usually of large caliber, having a chamber for the powder like a mortar. It is chiefly used on shipboard.
Chain shot: A kind of shot formed of two balls, or half-balls, connected by a chain, chiefly used in naval warfare to destroy masts, rigging, and sails.
Chandeliers: Large and strong wooden frames used instead of a parapet. Fascines are piled on top of each other against it to cover workmen digging trenches. Sometimes they are only strong planks with two pieces of wood perpendicular to hold the fascines.
Chevaux-de-frise: Obstacles consisting of horizontal poles with projecting spikes to block a passageway. They were used on land and modified to block rivers to enemy ships (see Photo PA-13).
Cohorn or coehorn: A short, small-barreled mortar for throwing grenades.
Company: The smallest military unit of the army consisting of about 45 to 110 men commanded by a captain, a lieutenant, and an ensign, and sometimes by a second lieutenant. A company usually has two sergeants, three or four corporals and two drums.
Crown forces: The allied forces supporting King George III. They consisted primarily of the British army, Hessian mercenaries, Loyalists, and Native Americans.
Cutter: 1. A single-masted sailing vessel similar to a sloop but having its mast positioned further aft. 2. A ship's boat, usually equipped with both sails and oars. In the eighteenth century, the terms sloop and cutter seem to have been used almost interchangeably.
Demilune: Fortification similar to a bastion but shaped as a crescent or half-moon rather than as an arrow.

Dragoon: A soldier who rode on horseback like cavalry. Dragoons generally fought dismounted in the 17th and 18th centuries. Dragoons in the Southern Backcountry were the equivalent of "light cavalry" in that they fought almost exclusively from horseback and were frequently confronted by mounted militia on mounts equal to or superior to their own.

Earthworks: A fortification made of earth (see Photos VA-5, VA-13, VA-14).

Embrasure: A slanted opening in the wall or parapet of a fortification designed for the defender to fire through it on attackers (see Photo VA-5).

Envelopment: An assault directed against an enemy's flank. An attack against two flanks is a double envelopment.

Espontoon: See **Spontoon.**

Fascine: A long bundle of sticks tied together, used in building earthworks and in strengthening ramparts.

Fraise: Sharpened stakes built into the exterior wall of a fortification to deter attackers..

Gabion: A cylindrical basket made of wicker and filled with earth for use in building fortifications.

Galley: A longboat propelled by oars. These boats had a shallow draft and were particularly useful in rivers, lakes, and other shallow bodies of water.

General engagement: An encounter, conflict, or battle in which the majority of a force is involved.

Grape shot: A number of small iron balls tied together to resemble a cluster of grapes. When fired simultaneously from a cannon, the balls separate into multiple projectiles. The shot usually consisted of nine balls placed between two iron plates (see Photo PA-14).

Grenadier: A soldier armed with grenades; a specially selected foot soldier in an elite unit selected on the basis of exceptional height and ability (see Photo PA-9).

Gun: A cannon. Guns were referred to by the size of the shot they fired. A 3-pounder fired a 3-pound ball, a 6-pounder fired a 6-pound ball.

Gundalow: An open, flat bottomed vessel about 53 feet long, 15 feet wide, and almost four feet deep in the center. It is equipped with both sails and oars, designed to carry heavy loads, usually armed with one gun at the bow and two mid-ship (see Photo PA-12).

Hessian: A German mercenary soldier who fought with the British army. Most of the German soldiers came from the kingdom of Hesse-Cassel, hence the name. Other German states that sent soldiers include Brunswick, Hess-Hanau, Waldeck, Ansbach-Bayreuth, and Anhalt-Zerbst.

Howitzer: A cannon with a short barrel and a bore diameter greater than 30 mm and a maximum elevation of 60 degrees, used for firing shells at a high angle of elevation to reach a target behind cover or in a trench.

Hussars or Huzzars: Horse soldiers resembling Hungarian horsemen. They usually wore furred bonnets adorned with a cock's feather, a doublet with a pair of breeches, to which their stockings are fastened, and boots. They were armed with a saber, carbines, and pistols (see Photo VA-15).

Jaeger: A hunter and gamekeeper who fought with the Hessians for the British army. They wore green uniforms, carried rifles, and were expert marksmen.

Jollyboat: A sailing vessel's small boat, such as a dinghy, usually carried on the stern. "A clincher-built ship's boat, smaller than a cutter, with a bluff bow and very wide transom, usually hoisted at the stern of the vessel, and used chiefly as a hack-boat for small work."[1]

Langrage: A particular kind of shot, formed of bolts, nails, bars, or other pieces of iron tied together, and forming a sort of cylinder, which corresponds with the bore of the cannon.

Letter of marque: A license granted by a monarch authorizing a subject to take reprisals on the subjects of a hostile state for alleged injuries. Later: Legal authority to fit out an armed vessel and use it in the capture of enemy merchant shipping and to commit acts which would otherwise have constituted piracy. See also **Privateer.**

Light infantry: Foot soldiers who carried lightweight weapons and minimal field equipment. They were younger, more athletic and more lightly equipped than the regular foot soldiers. The Light infantrymen and grenadiers were "flank companies."

Loophole: Aperture or slot in defenses through which the barrels of small arms or cannon can be directed at an outside enemy.

Loyalist: An American who supported the British during the American Revolution; also called Tory.

Magazine: A structure to store weapons, ammunition, explosives, and other military equipment or supplies.

Man-of-war: A warship (see Photo PA-16).

Matross: A private in an artillery unit who needed no specialized skills. Matrosses usually hauled cannon and positioned them. They assisted in the loading, firing, and sponging the guns.

Glossary

Militia: Civilians who are part-time soldiers who take military training and can serve full-time for short periods during emergencies.

Minuteman: Member of a special militia unit, called a Minute Company. A minuteman pledged to be ready to fight at a minute's notice.

Mortar: A cannon with a relatively short and wide barrel, used for firing shells in a high arc over a short distance, particularly behind enemy defenses. They were not mounted on wheeled carriages (see Photo PA-15).

Musket: A firearm with a long barrel, large caliber, and smooth bore. It was used between the 16th and 18th centuries, before rifling was invented.

Open order: A troop formation in which the distance between the individuals is greater than in close order (which is shoulder to shoulder). Also called extended order. This maneuver was used to cope with the terrain and to counter the attacks by partisans.

Parapet: Earthen or stone defensive platform on the wall of a fort.

Parley: A talk or negotiation, under a truce, between opposing military forces.

Parole: A promise given by a prisoner of war, either not to escape, or not to take up arms again as a condition of release. Individuals on parole can remain at home and conduct their normal occupations. Breaking parole makes one subject to immediate arrest and often execution. From the French *parole* which means one's word of honor.

Pettiauger or **pettyauger:** 1. A long, narrow canoe hollowed from the trunk of a single tree or from the trunks of two trees fastened together. 2. An open flat-bottomed schooner-rigged vessel or two-masted sailing barge, of a type used in North America and the Caribbean.

Pinnace: 1. A small light vessel, usually having two schooner-rigged (originally square-rigged) masts, often in attendance on a larger vessel and used as a tender or scout, to carry messages, etc. 2. A small boat, originally rowed with eight oars, later with sixteen, forming part of the equipment of a warship or other large vessel. It could also be navigated with a sail (see Photo VA-6).

Polacre: A three-masted vessel with square-rigged sails and pole masts without tops and crosstrees.

Portage: An overland route used to transport a boat or its cargo from one waterway to another; the act of carrying a boat or its cargo from one waterway to another.

Privateer: An armed vessel owned and crewed by private individuals and holding a government commission known as a letter of marque authorizing the capture of merchant shipping belonging to an enemy nation. See **Letter of marque.**

Rampart: An earthen fortification made of an embankment and often topped by a low protective wall.

Ravelin: A small outwork fortification shaped like an arrowhead or a V that points outward in front of a larger defense work to protect the sally port or entrance.

Redoubt: A temporary fortification built to defend a prominent position such as a hilltop.

Regiment: A permanent military unit usually consisting of two or three companies. British regiments generally consisted of ten companies, one of which was grenadiers. Some German regiments consisted of 2,000 men.

Regular: Belonging to or constituting a full-time professional military or police force as opposed to, for example, the reserves or militia.

Ropewalk: A long, narrow building where rope is made.

Round shot: Spherical ball of cast-iron or steel for firing from smooth-bore cannon, a cannon ball. The shots were referred to by the weight of the ball: a 9-pound shot weighed 9 pounds; a 12-pound shot weighed 12 pounds. Round shot was used principally to batter fortifications. The balls could be heated ("hot shot") and fired at the hulls of ships or buildings to set them on fire. The largest balls (32- and 64-pounders) were sometimes called "big shot."

Sapper: A soldier who specializes in making entrenchments and tunnels for siege operations.

Schooner: A fast sailing ship with at least two masts and with fore and aft sails on all lower masts.

Scow: A flat-bottomed sailboat with a rectangular hull.

Sedan chair: A chair or windowed cabin suitable for a single occupant. It is borne on poles or wooden rails that pass through brackets on the sides of the chair. The two or more porters who bear the chair are called "chairmen."

Shell: An explosive projectile fired from a large-bore gun such as a howitzer or mortar (see Photo VA-2). See also **Bomb, Howitzer,** and **Mortar.**

Ship of the line: A large warship with sufficient armament to enter combat with similar vessels in the line of battle. A ship of the line carried 60 to 100 guns (see Photo PA-16).

Shot: A bullet or projectile fired from a weapon. See also: **Bar shot, Canister shot, Chain shot, Grape shot, Round shot, Sliding bar shot, Star shot.**

Sliding bar shot: A projectile similar to a bar shot. A sliding bar shot has two interlocked bars that extend almost double the length of a bar shot, thereby increasing the potential damage to a ship's rigging and sails.

Sloop: A small single-masted sailing vessel with sails rigged fore-and-aft and guns on only one deck. In the 18th century, the terms sloop and cutter seem to have been used almost interchangeably.

Sloop of war: A three-masted, square-rigged naval vessel with all her guns mounted on a single uncovered main deck.

Snow: A small sailing-vessel resembling a brig, carrying a main and fore mast and a supplementary trysail mast close behind the mainmast; formerly employed as a warship.

Sons of Liberty: Patriots who belonged to secret organizations to oppose British attempts at taxation after 1765. They often resorted to violence and coercion to achieve their purposes.

Spike [a gun]: To destroy a cannon by hammering a long spike into the touch hole or vent, thereby rendering it temporarily useless.

Spontoon: A type of half-pike or halberd carried by infantry officers in the 18th century (from about 1740).

Stand of arms: A complete set of arms (musket, bayonet, cartridge box, and belt) for one soldier.

Star shot: A kind of chain-shot.

Tory: A Loyalist, also called Refugee and Cow-Boy. The Whigs usually used the term in a derogatory manner.

Trunnions: Two pieces of metal sticking out of the sides of an artillery piece. They serve to hold the artillery piece on the carriage and allow it to be raised or lowered. The trunnions are generally as long as the diameter of the cannonball and have the same diameter (see Photo VA-19).

Whig: Somebody who supported independence from Great Britain during the American Revolution. The name comes from the British liberal political party that favored reforms and opposed many of the policies of the King and Parliament related to the American War for Independence.

Index

1st Regiment, 206
3rd Regiment, 206
1st Maryland, 230, 231
1st North Carolina Regiment, 169, 173, 178
2nd Maryland Regiment, 230, 231
2nd New York Regiment, 148
2nd North Carolina Regiment, 173
2nd Virginia Regiment, 104
3rd Continental Dragoons, 222
4th Continental Dragoons, 57
4th Maryland Regiment, 42
4th North Carolina Regiment, 176, 189
5th Regiment, 39, 43, 77
7th Company of the First Battalion of Northumberland County militia, 17
7th Regiment, 269
8th Continental Regiment, 200
8th Pennsylvania Regiment, 5, 8, 14
10th North Carolina Regiment, 238
10th Regiment, 52, 83
11th Pennsylvania Regiment, 12
11th Regiment, 11, 13
13th Pennsylvania Regiment, 67
14th Regiment, 114, 119, 123, 182
15th Regiment, 74, 175
16th dragoons, 29, 37, 95
16th Regiment, 39, 95
17th dragoons, 67
17th Regiment, 32, 33, 146
23rd Regiment, 53, 77, 96, 220, 224, 234, 269, 274
26th battalion of the Maryland militia, 89
27th Regiment, 33
28th Regiment, 175
33rd Regiment, 175, 178, 223, 224, 269
37th Regiment, 175
40th Regiment, 29, 42
42nd Regiment, 39, 43, 109
44th Regiment Light Infantry, 175
49th Regiment, 33, 96
54th Regiment, 175
55th Regiment, 23
57th regiment, 175
63rd light company, 63
71st Regiment, 29, 78, 95, 163, 166, 224, 269
76th Regiment, 114, 148, 162, 164
80th (Edinburgh) Regiment, 114, 127, 130, 158, 160, 162, 163, 164, 187, 188, 189, 241, 249
82nd Regiment, 163, 187, 188, 189, 241, 249

Abatis, 25, 31, 149, 192
Abbott's Creek, 198
Abercromby or Abercrombie, Robert, 59, 114, 150, 162
Aberdeen, 94, 239
Aberdeen Creek, 239
Aberdeen Proving Grounds, 94
Abingdon, 156
Accomac, 128, 137, 152
Achison or Atchison, Robert, 181
Actæon (New York schooner), 185
Adams, John, 53
Adams, Sergeant, 159
Admiral Warren Tavern, 33
Adrian (transport), 50
Adventure (Whig merchantman), 185
African American, 4, 76, 91, 105, 106, 110, 111, 115, 116, 117, 118, 119, 122, 123, 127, 137, 143, 148, 180, 196
Aggie (British or Loyalist brig), 183
Agnew, James, 29
Aikens Tavern, 82
Alamance Battleground State Historic Site, 218
Alamance County, 201
Alamance Creek, 205, 218, 220, 222
Alamance River, 218, 220, 221, 223
Albemarle Sound, 136, 238
Alert (British schooner), 84
Alexander, Charles, 77
Alexander, William (Earl of Stirling), 29, 31, 34
Alexandria, 88, 89
Allaire, Anthony, 268
Allegheny Mountains, 87
Allegheny River, 4, 13, 14
Allen, Captain, 154
Allen, Isaac, 166
Allen, John, 91, 158, 218
Alston House, 239 *see also* House in the Horseshoe
Alston, Philip , 209, 239, 240
Alston, Temperance, 240
Althause, Captain, 113, 158
Ambuscade, 39, 40, 59, 113, 117, 127, 146, 161, 216, 236
Ambush, 8, 16, 18, 81, 117, 122, 185, 188, 190, 192, 204, 205, 208, 210, 211, 216, 220, 229, 236, 237, 242, 252, 256, 257, 259, 268, 275
Amelia County, 168
Amelia Courthouse, 168
American Fabius (Whig vessel), 164
American Legion, 114, 164, 167, 270
Anderson, Enoch, 68
Anderson, James, 182
Anderson, Jemmy, 92
Anderson, Thomas, 258
André, John, 26, 40
Andrew Doria (Continental brig), 55
Annamessex River, 154
Annapolis, 87, 89, 98
Anson County, 194, 248, 250
Anson County Militia, 248, 250
Anspach chasseurs, 81
Antes, Philip Frederic, 6
Apollo (merchantman), 164
Appletown, 14
Appomattox River, 157, 162, 163
Arbuthnot, Marriot, 125
Arc en Ciel (French brig), 124
Archer, Thomas, 215
Ariel, 182
Armand, Charles (Charles-Armand Tuffin, Marquis de la Rouerie), 163
Armistead, Major, 114
Armstrong, James, 213
Armstrong, Major, 113
Armstrong, William, 259
Arnold, Benedict, 1, 5, 98, 106, 110, 112, 114, 126, 128, 130, 135, 142, 157, 158, 162, 163

Artillery, 12, 23, 26, 29, 37, 38, 40, 42, 48, 50, 56, 60, 85, 95, 96, 109, 114, 116, 127, 130, 136, 140, 142, 144, 148, 158, 159, 162, 163, 165, 173, 174, 179, 180, 183, 197, 230, 231, 260
Arundel, Dohickey, 122
Ashe County, 275
Asheville, 257
Ashman, George, 15
Athens, 8, 9
Augusta (British frigate), 54, 55, 56, 105
Augusta County, 156
Aurora, 184
Avis, 6

Back Creek, 94
Back River, 106
Baker, George, 2
Bald Head Island, 170, 172, 176
Baldwin's Old Field, 249
Balfour, Andrew, 209, 211, 212
Ball, George, 75, 76
Ballard, Major, 48, 49
Ballendine, John, 160
Balliett, Stephen, 19
Balsam Gap, 256
Bank, Richard, 119
Banning, Jeremiah, 97
Barbeque Church, 234
Barbeque Creek, 234
Barge, 46, 51, 86, 92, 97, 128, 129, 130, 137, 153, 154
Barnes, Richard, 90
Barnwell, Edward, 192
Barras, Admiral Louis, Comte de, 141, 142
Barren Hill, 27, 46, 58, 62, 68, 69, 70, 71, 72
Barringer, Matthias, 254
Barry, John, 84
Bassett, Richard, 80
Bates, William, 276
Battery, 30, 44, 47, 48, 49, 50, 51, 52, 54, 55, 56, 57, 77, 84, 91, 98, 113, 121, 122, 148, 149, 158, 159, 185
Battle of the Bees, 269, 272
Battle of the Clouds, 33, 34
Battle of the Kegs, 43, 44, 46
Baurmeister, Carl Leopold, 25, 31
Bayonet, 26, 36, 60, 82, 106, 134, 162, 175, 189, 230, 260
Bayonet charge, 82, 134
Beal, Reazin, 91
Beale, Dick, 273
Bear Creek, 200, 201, 205
Beatty's Ford, 199
Beaufort, 181, 184, 185, 192, 253, 254
Beaufort Militia, 185
Beaufort Regiment, 192
Beaver, 2
Beaver Creek, 2, 218
Beaverdam Creek, 2, 145
Bedford, 15, 167, 168, 268
Bedford County, 15
Bedford Purchase, 15
Beggars' Town, 25
Bellew, Henry, 49, 108
Benjamin Rush State Park, 38, 67
Benneville, George de, 66
Benoni Point, 96, 97
Bensalem, 58
Benton, 5
Bermuda, 122, 132, 166, 182, 185
Bermuda Hundred, 132, 166
Berwick, 13, 18

Berwyn, Chester County, 34
Bethabara, 195, 196
Bethania, 197
Betsey (sloop), 77, 184
Betsy (British vessel), 138
Betsy Ross House, 43
Big Coharie, 190
Big Glades, 275
Big Juniper Creek, 253
Big Rock Fish, 234
Biles Island, 60, 72
Billingsport, 47, 49, 50, 55
Bird's Tavern, 133, 134
Birmingham Meeting House, 29
Black Hole of the Coweecho River, 256
Black Horse Tavern, 61, 63, 64, 66
Black River, 179, 180, 186, 190, 236
Black, Alexander, 245
Black, Joseph, 156
Black, Kenneth, 239, 244, 245
Black, Mrs., 244
Black's Fort, 156
Blackburne, 206
Blackstone Island, 88
Blackstones Island, 96
Bladen County, 200, 234, 246, 247, 249, 250
Bladen County Courthouse, 200, 246
Bladen County militia, 189, 234, 250
Blair, George, 182
Blakiston Island, 96
Blandford, 114, 161, 162
Blandford Cemetery, 161
Blaxtons Island, 96
Blew Mountains, 16
Blockhouse, 6, 272
Blonde (British vessel), 105
Bloody Rock, 7
Bloomsburg, 13, 19
Bludworth (or Bloodworth), Thomas, 189, 191
Blue Bell Tavern, 52, 53
Blue Ridge Mountains, 168, 211
Blue, Peter, 245
Bogan, Patrick, 244
Bogue Inlet, 184
Bolivar, 5, 156
Bollingbrook, 161, 163
Bombardment, 38, 54, 56, 97, 104, 197
Bombay Hook, 83, 84, 85
Bond, William, 16
Bonetta (sloop), 113, 158
Bonner, Benjamin, 182
Bonner, Thomas, 185
Boone, North Carolina, 275
Boone, Hawkins, 11
Boone's Fort, 11
Boot Tavern, 33
Bordeaux, 184
Borden, Joseph, 45
Bordentown, 21, 72
Bosley's mills, 18
Boston, 87, 100, 169, 181, 186
Boston Tea Party, 100
Bostwick, Elisha, 21
Bottoms Bridge, 112, 113
Bowman, John, 265
Bowman's Folly, 129
Bowman's Hill, 19
Boyd, John, 15
Boyd's Ferry, 213
Boyd's Hole, 88

Index **317**

Boykin's Plantation, 189, 190, 238
Bradley, Francis, 269, 272
Bradley's Plantation, 269
Brady, John, 8, 10
Branchtown, 66
Brandon, John, 270
Brandywine, 5, 22, 27, 28, 29, 30, 31, 33, 35, 36, 42, 70, 76, 78, 82, 95, 96
Brandywine Battlefield Park, 27
Brandywine Creek, 28, 76, 78, 96
Breastworks, 50, 116, 121, 173, 237
Brent, William, 89, 123
Brent's House, 123
Brigade of Guards, 221
Brindletown, 268
Bristol, Pennsylvania, 32, 33, 38, 57, 58, 59, 60, 72
Bristol Ferry, 38
Bristol, Tennessee, 156
British Army, 5, 11, 31, 32, 34, 35, 36, 38, 80, 82, 84, 141, 146, 150, 151, 167, 196, 198, 201, 214, 253, 258
Brittain Church, 268
Broad Axe Inn, 70
Broad River, 268
Broadsides, 46, 84, 113, 125
Broadswords, 60, 180, 181
Brodhead Expedition, 13
Brodhead, Daniel, 14, 15
Brooks, Captain, 86
Brown Marsh, 249, 250
Brown, Thomas, Jr., 4
Brown's Plantation, 209
Bruce, Charles, 212, 213
Bruce's Cross Roads, 212
Brunswick, 77, 169, 170, 172, 173, 174, 175, 179, 181, 252
Brush Creek, 248, 251
Bryan, Daniel, 153
Bryan, James, 196
Bryan, Samuel, 193
Bryan, William, 241
Bryant's Mill, 240
Bryn Mawr, 61, 64
Buchan, David, 244
Buchanan, James, 182
Buck and ball, 234
Buck Tavern, 65
Bucks County, 1
Bucks County Volunteers, 39
Buffalo Creek, 16, 229, 267
Buffalo Ford, 207, 209
Buffalo Valley, 16
Buie, Daniel, 234
Buie, Duncan, 234
Buie, William, 234
Bull Run or Bull Creek, 275
Bull Tavern, 37
Bunker Hill, 100, 231
Burgoyne, John, 42, 57, 135, 150
Burke County, 242, 254, 268
Burke County militia, 268
Burke, John, 268
Burke, Thomas, 192, 203, 241, 247, 248, 249, 254, 259, 261
Burlington, 32, 38, 72, 216, 218, 222
Burnt Swamp, 247
Burwell's Ferry, 112–114
Bushnell, David, 45
Bustleton, 66
Butler, John, 7, 201, 204, 211, 247, 249, 251

Butler, Richard, 133
Butler, Walter, 9
Buzzard's Bay, 176
Byrd, William, 158

Cabin Point, 131
Cadwalader, John, 21, 26
Cager's Strait, 152–154
Caldwell, Captain, 17
Call, William, 134
Callis, William Overton, 106
Calloway, Joseph, 275
Calloway, Richard, 275
Cambridge, Massachusetts, 1, 100
Camden, 76
Camden (South Carolina), 196, 200, 227, 228, 236, 267
Cameron, Alan or Allan or Allen, 87
Cameron, Lieutenant, 146
Camilla (British frigate), 50, 79, 184
Camp Creek, 268
Campbell Town, 179
Campbell, Archibald, 182
Campbell, David, 259, 260
Campbell, Isaac, 196
Campbell, John (d. 1806), 180
Campbell, Richard, 199
Campbell, William, 223
Campbellton, 177, 178, 245
Campen, Moses Van, 15, 18, 19
Canada, 10, 12, 17, 19, 87
Canan, 15
Canandaigua, 14
Cane Creek, 200, 201, 204, 250, 268, 269
Cannon, 2, 21, 33, 46, 48, 54, 55, 56, 70, 72, 78, 91, 94, 97, 98, 105, 107, 108, 110, 112, 113, 114, 115, 117, 130, 138, 142, 145, 148, 150, 152, 160, 165, 172, 178, 181, 185, 188, 193, 215, 237
Cannonade, 30, 42, 45, 77, 91, 110, 113, 122, 145, 148, 150, 176
Canton, 8, 9, 256
Cantwells Bridge, 85
Cape Fear, 169, 183, 184, 241, 247,
Cape Fear River, 170, 172, 173, 174, 175, 176, 177, 178, 179, 180, 186, 187, 188, 191, 192, 204, 236, 245, 246, 251, 252
Cape Hatteras, 182, 185
Cape Henlopen, 75, 76, 183, 186
Cape Henlopen State Park, 75
Cape Henry, 124, 125, 138, 141, 142
Cape Lookout, 182, 184
Cape Lookout Bay, 182, 184
Cape May, 75
Capitulation, 11, 150
Captain Hatch, 130
Captain Johnson, 194, 195
Captain Land, 16
Carberry, Henry, 9
Carleton, Guy, 152
Carmichael, Captain, 83
Carney's Point, 77
Caroline County, 123
Carpenter's Island, 55
Carpenters' Hall, 43
Carr, David, 274
Carr, Patrick, 267
Carr, Sarah, 212
Carr, William, 212
Carrington, Edward, 214
Carson, Andrew, 196
Carter, Charles, 132

Carter's Grove, 112
Carthage, 239, 253
Cary's Mills, 165
Caswell (row galley), 182
Caswell County Regiment of Militia, 260
Caswell County, 204
Caswell, Richard, 178, 179, 180, 182, 193, 204, 237, 241, 245
Caswell, William, 254
Catawba, 220, 227, 231, 254, 256, 257, 272, 273, 274
Catawba River, 227, 254, 272, 273, 274
Catawissa, 18, 19
Cathcart, William Schaw, 43
Catherine's Town, 14
Cathey's Creek, 268
Cavalry, 25, 33, 38, 39, 40, 59, 72, 105, 109, 114, 134, 144, 146, 159, 162, 180, 190, 193, 197, 199, 202, 206, 207, 214, 220, 221, 223, 224, 228, 229, 230, 231, 235, 236, 238, 248, 252, 259, 266, 270, 274 see also dragoons, American Legion and various officer names e.g. Tarleton, Banastre; Washington, William
Cavalry Monument, 224
Cayuga, 7, 9, 14
Cayuga Lake, 14
Cecil Courthouse, 81
Cedar Creek, 75
Cedar Island, 128
Cedar Point, 88, 92, 93, 94
Cedar Swamp, 85, 86
Centre Township, 13
Chadd's Ford, 27–30
Chain, 55
Chalk Point, 98
Champagne, Captain, 146
Chapel Hill, 201, 250
Charles City, 112, 130, 132
Charles City Courthouse, 130
Charles County, 88, 93
Charles County militia, 88
Charleston, 77, 106, 135, 144, 150, 151, 152, 176, 181, 183, 184, 185, 187, 192, 197, 227, 238, 254
Charlotte, 121, 168, 169, 196, 227, 261, 266, 268, 269, 270, 271, 272
Charlottesville, 156, 163, 166, 167, 182
Charming Polly (sloop), 79
Charon (HMS), 148
Chasseurs, 6, 26, 29, 37, 63, 81, 128
Chatham (privateer), 185
Chatham County, 204, 205, 207, 210, 212, 242, 247, 248, 253
Chatham County militia, 205
Chatham County regiment of militia, 210
Chatham Courthouse, 207, 242
Chattanooga, 256
Cheltenham Township, 26
Chemung, 9, 12
Cheraw Hill, 227
Cherokee, 2, 4, 122, 152, 183, 253, 254, 256, 257, 258, 274
Chesapeake Bay, 28, 29, 88, 91, 92, 94, 97, 100, 105, 110, 120, 122, 124, 125, 126, 127, 131, 135, 136, 137, 138, 141, 143
Chesapeake City, 94
Chester, 1, 27, 29, 30, 47, 53, 65, 68, 75, 85
Chester County, 1, 27, 65, 81
Chester River, 85
Chesterfield County, 157, 159, 165
Chesterfield Courthouse, 110, 162, 165
Chestnut Hill, 22, 25, 31, 32, 33, 40, 69, 70
Chestnut Mountain, 206

Chevaux-de-frise, 47, 49, 50, 54, 55
Chew Mansion, 40
Chew, Benjamin, 40, 42
Chickahominy Church, 136, 137
Chickahominy River, 112, 114, 132, 133
Chickamaugas, 276
Chillisquaque, 11, 12, 13, 17
Chimney Top Mountain, 258
Chincoteague, 119, 120
Chinnery, St. John, 185
Choisy, Claude Gabriel marquis de, 146, 152
Choptank Creek or River, 93, 96, 97, 89
Chowan River, 238, 242
Christ Church, 44
Christian, George, 153
Christian, William, 256, 257
Christina River, 75, 76, 78, 83
Christmas, 21, 60
Church Hill, 158, 159
City Point, 114, 157, 162
Clader, Daniel, 18
Clapp, John, 220
Clapp's Mill, 218, 220–222
Clark, George Rogers, 118, 161
Clark, John, 75, 195
Clark, Joseph, 261
Clarke, John, 195
Clarke, Kenneth, 244
Clarkton, 249
Claymores, 180
Cleghorn's Creek, 268
Cleveland County, 267
Cleveland, Benjamin, 275
Cleveland, Robert, 275
Cleveland, Samuel, 47
Clinton County, 6
Clinton, Henry, 40, 43, 57, 68, 70, 76, 77, 133, 135, 136, 140, 141, 152, 158, 163, 169, 173, 174, 175, 176, 181, 227, 231, 240, 274
Clinton, James, 14
Clinton, Richard, 235, 236
Clinton's Crossroads, 235
Cliveden, 40
Clow, Cheney (or China), 84
Cloyd, Joseph, 196
Cobham, 117, 118, 168
Cochran, John, 23
Cochran, Robert, 184
Cochrane's Mill, 177
Cocke, James, 158
Coercive Acts, 87
Coharie Country Club, 235
Coharie River, 189, 190, 238
Cohera Swamp, 190, 235
Cohocksink Creek, 41
Cohorn, 121
Coldstream Guards, 223
Cole's Ferry, 167
College of William and Mary, 114
Collett, John Abraham, 173
Collier, George, 109, 126, 127
Collier, John, 209, 211
Collier-Mathew expedition, 127
Collins, John, 79
Colonial National Historical Park, 134, 138
Colson's Mill, 193, 194
Columbia, 13, 166
Columbia County, 13
Committee of Safety, 75, 77, 107, 178, 181
Committees of Correspondence, 1

Index   319

Concord, 1
Conemaugh River, 5, 6, 156
Congress Hall, 43
Connecticut, 7, 55, 69, 142
Connelly, Henry, 217, 259
Connelly, John, 87
Connoly, Darby, 156
Conshohocken, 62, 64, 70
Constitution (Old Ironsides), 62
Constitutional Convention, 1
Contentnea Creek, 235
Continental Army, 1, 5, 10, 19, 31, 33, 38, 46, 58, 64, 68, 73, 78, 81, 87, 100, 108, 114, 124, 126, 138, 150, 168, 169, 181, 209, 216, 229, 233, 243, 251, 252, 261, 266
Continental Congress, 1, 36, 43, 64, 87, 88, 100, 120, 169
Continentals, 12, 25, 26, 29, 30, 31, 32, 34, 35, 36, 37, 40, 41, 42, 43, 44, 46, 48, 50, 51, 52, 55, 56, 57, 58, 63, 64, 66, 68, 69, 70, 71, 72, 78, 81, 82, 117, 134, 141, 144, 145, 146, 147, 149, 150, 151, 152, 165, 199, 203, 204, 214, 216, 220, 221, 222, 224, 227, 228, 229, 230, 231, 233, 273
Conway, Robert, 89
Conway, Thomas, 31
Conyngham, 18
Cooch's Bridge, 80–82, 96
Cooch's Bridge Battlefield monument, 80
Cooper's Mill, 137
Corbett's Ferry, 179, 180
Core Sound, 182, 184
Cornelius, 76, 173, 208, 272, 273
Cornwallis (British galley), 50, 54, 55
Cornwallis, Charles, 5, 29, 30, 33, 34, 37, 40, 42, 44, 50, 53–55, 63–65, 77, 81, 82, 105 106, 113, 126,133–138, 140–145, 148, 150–153, 161, 163, 165–167, 169, 173–175, 177, 186–189, 193, 197–199, 201, 203, 205–207, 213–215, 217, 220–224, 227, 228, 230–235, 237, 242, 248, 252, 253, 258–260, 263, 265, 267, 269–275
Corporal's guard, 122
Coryell's Ferry, 58
Council of Pennsylvania, 58, 59
Court-martial, 137, 267, 276
Cowan's Ford, 272, 273
Cowee, 256
Coweechee, 256
Coweecho River, 256
Cowpens, 181, 197, 199, 201, 220, 228, 267, 268, 273, 274
Coxe, John, 253
Cox's Mill, 209, 236, 247, 250, 251
Coxe, Robert, 253
Crab Creek, 110
Crafton, Bennett, 261
Craig, James Henry, 177, 187, 188, 192, 237, 238, 241, 242, 244, 245, 248, 249
Craig, John, 25
Crause, John, 195
Crewe, Major, 32, 34
Cricket Hill, 120
Crooked Billet, 57, 58, 59, 66
Cropper, John, 129, 137, 152, 153
Cross Creek, 177, 178, 179, 180, 187, 234, 236, 237, 246, 249
Cross Roads, 211, 212, 224, 229, 275
Cruizer (British sloop), 172, 173, 174, 176
Culp, Captain, 243, 244, 245
Culpeper County, 107
Culpeppers Bridge, 235

Cumberland County, 58, 177, 203, 234, 236, 239, 240, 243, 246, 251
Cumberland County Courthouse, 177, 246
Cumberland County militiamen, 234, 236
Cunningham, Walter, 177
Curle, Colonel, 106
Currie, 178
Currituck, 183, 186
Currituck Inlet, 186
Currituck Sound, 186
Curry, Jane, 17
Curry, Lieutenant, 17
Curry, Robert, 17, 18

Dan River, 195, 198, 199, 203, 206, 207, 213–217, 228, 258, 259
Danbury, 206
Danville, 17, 18
Daphne (HMS), 185
Darby, 46, 52, 53, 59, 156
Dashiell, Joseph, 97, 154
Dauge, Dennis, 183
Daughters of the American Revolution, 273
David (snow), 184
Davidson County, 258
Davidson, George, 270
Davidson, William Lee, 193, 194, 196, 266, 268, 271, 272, 273, 274
Davie, William Richardson, 266, 269, 270, 271, 272
Davis, William, 175, 77, 175
De Forbach, Guillaume Comte, Comte de Deux Ponts, 149
De Grasse, François Joseph Paul Comte, 140, 141
De Lancey, Oliver, 72
Deal Island, 94
Declaration of Independence, 43, 44, 138, 173, 200, 201, 224, 237
Deep River, 165, 201, 205, 207, 208, 209, 211, 212, 222, 228, 233, 239, 240, 247, 248, 250, 251, 260, 261, 275
Deep River Friends Meetinghouse, 228
Deep Water Point, 77, 78
Defence (brig), 76, 91, 153, 154
Defiance (sloop), 176
Deh-he-wä-mis see Jemison, Mary
Delaware (British frigate), 44, 47, 57, 125
Delaware Bay, 75, 78
Delaware Capes, 86
Delaware County, 64, 65
Delaware History Museum, 73
Delaware (militia), 75–76, 82, 83, 85
Delaware Regiment, 79, 85, 221, 224, 229
Delaware River, 19–22, 27, 32, 38, 40, 44–47, 49, 50, 51, 53–56, 62, 68, 69, 72, 76–79, 82–84, 187
Delaware (state), 73, 76, 78, 80, 82, 84–86, 94, 183, 186, 199
Delaware State Museum, 73
Delaware State Visitors Center, 73
Delaware (tribe), 4, 5, 8, 14, 16
Delight (British ship), 105
Denny, Samuel, 122
Dent, William, 177
Department of Conservation and Development, Travel and Promotion Division, 170
Department of Historic Resources, 102
Deserter, 23, 117, 244
Deshon, Daniel, 183
Destouches, Charles René Dominique Sochet, 125
Dewitt's Corner, 257
Diascund Creek, 137

Dick, Alexander, 159
Dickerson, Lieutenant, 176
Dickey's Farm, 216
Dickinson, John, 60, 61, 97
Dickinson, Philemon, 72
Dickson, Archibald, 27
Dickson, Henry, 220
Dickson, Joseph, 270, 271, 272
Dilligente (French frigate), 185
Dillsboro, 256
Dilworth, 29
Dispatch (British sloop), 84
Division of Historical and Cultural Affairs, 73
Dix's [or Dixon's] Ferry, 212, 213
Dobbs County, 244
Dolphin (pilot boat), 120
Dona Creek, 85
Dorchester County, 97
Dougan, Thomas, 195
Dover, 73, 75, 80, 83, 84, 85
Dowdy, William, 212
Doyle, John, 271
Dragoons, 23, 25, 26, 29, 32, 33, 34, 39, 40, 42, 43, 45, 53, 57, 58, 59, 63, 64, 65, 66, 67, 70, 71, 72, 80, 95, 105, 113, 117, 130, 133, 134, 146, 147, 163, 167, 188, 189, 190, 199, 201, 202, 207, 213, 214, 215, 220, 221, 222, 223, 224, 228, 229, 230, 231, 233, 235, 236, 237, 241, 244, 248, 249, 252, 259, 260, 266, 270, 271, 275 see also cavalry, American Legion and various officers' names e.g. Tarleton, Banastre; Washington, William, etc.
Drays Mill Creek, 239
Drayton, John, 216
Drinker, Elizabeth, 44, 46
Drowning Creek, 243, 244, 245, 247, 251
Dry, William, 173
Duck Creek, 80, 85, 86
Duckworth, Jacob, 221
Dudley, Guilford, 130, 236
Dugan or Dougan, Thomas, 195
Duke Power Company's Buck Steam Plant, 258
Dumas, Mathieu, 151
Dumfries, 123
Dundas, Thomas, 106, 114, 117, 146, 159, 220
Dunlap, James, 15, 268, 269
Dunmore (brig), 48, 90, 121
Dunmore, John Murray, 4th Earl of, 87, 88, 90, 100, 102, 107–112, 115–120, 122, 181
Duplin County, 190, 235, 237, 241, 244, 246
Duplin County Militia, 235
Duplin Court, 191
Durham boat, 19, 21, 38
Durham, James, 10
Durham, Margaret Wilson, 10

Eagle (HMS), 55
Eagle Creek, 6
Earthworks, 116, 120, 121, 143, 178, 180, 181, 193, 215
Eastern Shore, 96, 122
Easton, John, 253
Easton, Pennsylvania, 14
Eaton, William, 105
Economy, 4
Eden, James, 91
Eden, Robert, 87, 90
Edenton, 169, 182, 185, 238
Edenton Tea Party, 169
Edge Hill, 22, 25, 31, 32, 57
Edmunds Bridge, 117

Edwards, Edward, 251, 275
Edwards, Richard, 251
Effingham (Continental Navy frigate), 84
Egg Harbor, 68
Elfreth's Alley, 44
Elizabeth (brig), 185
Elizabeth River, 107, 108, 110, 111, 115, 118, 119, 120, 126
Elizabethtown, 180, 187, 189, 246, 247, 248, 249
Elk Hill, 167
Elk Neck State Park, 94
Elk River, 28, 80, 94, 95, 98
Elkton, 28, 80, 94, 95, 96
Elkton Landing, 94
Elrod, John, 194, 195, 248
Elrod, William, 242
Emerald (HMS), 92, 96
Ennals, John, 92
Ennals, Thomas, 92
Eno River, 200, 202
Enochs, Enoch, 4
Enterprize (British vessel), 184
Episcopal church, 253
Eppes, Francis, 118
Erskine, Thomas, 82
Erskine, William, 37, 39, 72, 77, 96
Ethiopian Regiment, 100, 182
Europe (British vessel), 42, 125, 150
Evans, Rev., 145
Everett's Corner, 84
Ewald, Johann von, 34, 70, 113, 128, 133, 147, 148
Ewing, James, 21
Experiment (British vessel), 84

Faddis Tavern, 201
Fairhill, 60
Falcon (HMS), 175, 176
Fallen, Daniel, 94
Falls, Galbraith, 265
Fanning, David, 178, 203, 205, 207, 208, 209, 210, 211, 212, 221, 236, 239, 240, 241, 242, 245, 246, 247, 248, 250, 251, 253, 258, 260, 268
Fanning, Richard, 245, 246
Fanning's Mill, 245
Fanny (brig), 185
Farmar's Mill, 23, 68
Farmer (schooner), 76
Fatland Ford, 32, 35, 36, 37, 38
Fayetteville, 177, 187, 233, 234, 243, 246, 247
Fearnaught (Whig vessel), 154
Felicity (Whig vessel), *92*
Fell's Point, 92
Ferguson, Patrick, 30, 195, 196, 267, 268, 275
Ferguson's Hill, 268
Ferguson's Ridge, 268
Ferret (galley), 72
Fetter, Michael, 15
Field piece, 37, 79, 83, 122, 160, 187, 215, 250, 270
Fincastle (British sloop), 182
Finger Lakes, 14
Finley, John, 8
Fire raft, 49, 175
First Continental Congress, 87, 100, 169
First North Carolina militia, 175
First Virginia Convention, 100
Fisher, Henry, 75
Fisher, Tembte, 136
Fisher, Thomas, 76
Fisher's Mill, 96
Fishing Creek, 14, 15, 18, 235

Index 321

Flag of truce, 76, 97, 120, 209, 211, 238, 253, 267
Fletchall, Thomas, 216
Fletcher, Captain, 236
Fletcher's Mill, 222
Fleur de Hundred, 130
Flour de Hundred, 130
Flourtown, 57, 59
Flowerdew Hundred, 130
Fluvanna River, 166, 167
Fly (Continental sloop), 47, 55
Flying Fish, 153, 154
Folger, Frederick, 92
Folly Creek, 128, 129
Forage, 32, 45, 52, 60, 63, 68, 95, 118, 144, 146, 167, 190, 199, 220, 232, 241
Foraging, 35, 46, 50, 53, 57, 63, 65, 97, 98, 108, 127, 133, 146, 173, 237, 259, 269, 271, 272
Ford, James, 254
Fork Union, 166
Forks of the Yadkin, 194
Forlorn hope, 149
Forman, David, 31
Formidable (sloop), 148
Forster, Doctor, 176
Fort Armstrong, 5
Fort Augusta, 12
Fort Bosley, 13, 19
Fort Bragg, 243
Fort Crawford, 8
Fort Eustis, 118
Fort George, 102, 170, 172, 176
Fort Hancock, 7
Fort Hand, 7, 8
Fort Island, 48
Fort Jenkin, 13, 18
Fort Johnston, 170, 172, 173, 174, 175, 176, 177
Fort McGauhey, 268
Fort McIntosh, 2, 4
Fort Mead, 17
Fort Mercer, 52, 53, 54, 55, 57
Fort Mifflin, 48, 49, 51, 52, 53, 54, 55, 56, 57
Fort Monroe, 102, 124
Fort Montgomery, 15
Fort Mud, 53
Fort Nelson, 109, 126, 127
Fort Niagara, 7, 14
Fort Rice, 18, 19
Fort Rutledge, 256
Fort Trumbull, 142
Fort Washington State Park, 23
Fortifications, 7, 41, 47, 53, 106, 121, 143, 144, 145, 146, 186, 187, 188
Fortune (brig), 184
Forty Fort, 7
Fourmile Creek, 159
Fox, Charles James, 231
Francis, Colonel, 106
Francis, Henry, 196
Francis, John, 146
Francisco, Peter, 157, 224, 230
Frankford, 38–40, 43, 70
Frankford Creek, 38
Franklin (town), 14, 256, 257
Franklin Court, 43
Franklin, Benjamin, 43, 44, 61
Frankstown, 15
Fraser, Simon, 5
Frazier, William, 153
Fredericksburg, 123, 131
Freelands Fort, 8, 10, 11, 13

French, 1, 4, 30, 42, 60, 68, 78, 84, 100, 109, 125, 134, 140, 141, 142, 143, 144, 145, 146, 147, 148, 149, 150, 151, 152, 182, 184, 185
French Broad River, 257, 258
French Jacob's Mill, 16
Frigate, 38, 47, 62, 77, 78, 84, 93, 138, 148, 165, 182, 183, 184, 185, 186, 187
French and Indian War see Seven Years War
Fritz, Wooldrich, 252
Furneaux, Tobias, 183
Furry, John, 19
Fusiliers' Redoubt, 143, 145, 147, 148

Gaddis, Thomas, 4
Gage, Thomas, 87, 169
Galley, 47, 54, 55, 60, 77, 123, 153, 188, 238
Ganey or Gainey, Micajah, 252
Gaskins, Thomas, 15, 17
Gaston, Alexander, 241
Gates, Horatio, 5, 105, 150, 227
Gayton, George, 105
Gelelemind (John Killbuck, Jr.), 4
General Arnold (row galley), 238
General Assembly, 85, 158, 261
General Gage (British armed vessel), 173
General Green, 183
General Monk (HMS), 86
General Nash (North Carolina privateer brig), 183
General Wayne (brig), 30, 36, 64, 185
Geneseo, 14
Genessee Valley, 14
George II, 172
George III, 152, 235, 274
Georgia, 2, 152, 184, 207, 216, 217, 226, 243, 254, 256, 265, 267
Georgia volunteers, 216
Germain, George, 135, 231
German Flats, 9
Germantown, 22, 25, 27, 31, 32, 36, 37, 38, 39, 40, 41, 42, 43, 52, 58, 59, 60, 67, 69, 70, 71
Gholson, Charles, 205, 210, 211
Gholson's farm, 207, 210
Gibsonville, 222
Gilbert Town, 259, 268, 269
Gilbert, William, 268
Gillespie, Daniel, 244, 269
Gillies, James, 212, 214
Gillies, Robert, 241
Gillies's death, 214
Gimat, Jean-Joseph Sourbader de, 163
Gist, Mordecai, 26
Glasgow Packet (British transport), 174, 175
Gloucester, 45, 47, 50, 138, 140, 142, 143, 146, 147, 148, 150, 152
Gloucester Point, 47, 50, 146, 147, 148
Glover, John, 21
Godden, Colonel, 247
Golden Ball Tavern, 161
Goldston, 207
Gondola, 89, 123 see also gundalow
Goode's Bridge, 168
Goodrich, John, Jr., 182, 186
Goodrich, John, Sr., 181
Goodrich, William, 181
Goodrick, Captain, 229
Gordon, Andrew, 160
Gordon, John, 188, 237, 241, 244, 245
Gordon's Ford, 36, 37
Gowen's Fort, 276
Gorham, James, 235, 241

Goshen, 5, 6
Goshen Meetinghouse, 5
Gosport, 108, 109, 110, 118, 126, 127
Gowen, John, 268, 276
Grace Episcopal Church, 140
Grady Monument, 178
Grady, John, 178
Graham, Alexander, 245
Graham, Joseph, 192, 194, 198, 201, 220, 221, 248, 252, 259, 270, 274
Graham, North Carolina, 201
Graham, William, 177, 267
Graham's Fort, 267
Grand Tyger (schooner), 185
Grant, James, 38, 70, 81
Grants Creek, 198, 258, 260
Granville County Militia, 233
Grape shot, 42, 49, 57, 89, 94, 97, 123, 124, 136, 162, 172, 173, 175
Grasshopper, 197
Gravelly Branch, 84
Graves, John, 173, 174, 175
Graves, Thomas, 142, 150
Gray's Ferry, 46, 48, 52
Great Bridge, 100, 105, 108, 109, 111, 115, 116, 117, 127
Great Coharie Creek, 237
Great Fox Island, 152
Great Island, 6
Great Swamp, 200
Great Valley, 29, 100
Green Spring, 134, 135, 136, 137
Green, John, 112, 118
Greene, Nathanael, 22, 23, 29, 31, 41, 52, 80, 88, 152, 158, 166, 167, 183, 197, 199, 200, 201, 203, 204, 206, 213–215, 217, 220, 222, 223, ,227, 228, 230, 231, 233, 234, 236, 241–243, 254, 258–260, 267, 273–275
Greensboro, 201, 207, 212, 222, 224, 250, 258
Grenadiers, 29, 31, 37, 38, 40, 47, 52, 70, 71, 109, 111, 134, 158, 231
Grey, Charles, 26, 29, 35, 70, 77
Greyhound (HMS), 27
Grogan, Henry, 195
Grogtown, 84
Groshong, Jacob, 16
Guadeloupe (frigate), 148
Guard of Light Horse, 43
Guards, 26, 29, 39, 40, 43, 55, 63, 67, 70, 95, 98, 109–111, 117, 119, 151, 163, 175, 177, 178, 197, 204, 221, 223, 224, 229, 231, 239, 242, 247, 259
Gudoin, Captain, 125
Guide to North Carolina Historical Highway Markers, 169
Guide to the Historical Markers of Pennsylvania, 2
Guidebook to Virginia's Historical Markers, 102
Guilford College, 224, 229
Guilford Courthouse, 177, 178, 189, 193, 196, 198, 201, 203, 206, 212, 213, 215, 216, 222, 224, 225, 226, 228, 229, 230, 231, 232, 233, 234, 252, 274
Guilford Courthouse National Military Park, 196, 224
Gulph Ferry Mill, 66
Gulph Mill/Mills, 59, 61, 62, 64–66, 72
Gundalow, 44 see also gondola
Guyon, Stephen, 272
Gwin, Francis Edward, 59
Gwynn's Island, 90, 120

Hackensack, New Jersey, 34
Hackett, Redmond, 136
Haddaway, William Webb, Jr., 92
Hadden, John, 156
Haerlem (British sloop), 94
Hagerstown, 87
Halfway House, 106
Halifax, 181, 192, 193, 209, 213
Hall, Aquila, 94
Hamilton, Alexander, 149
Hammond (brig), 185
Hammond, John, 216
Hamond, Andrew Snape, 75, 76, 78, 91, 114, 119, 121, 123
Hampton, 91, 102, 104, 105, 106, 107, 110, 112, 114, 117, 119, 120, 124, 126, 127, 130, 135, 142, 158, 256
Hampton Bar, 124
Hampton River, 102
Hampton Roads, 107, 124, 135, 142, 158
Hampton, Edward, 256
Hand, Edward, 4, 12
Handy, Levin, 153
Handy, Samuel, 153
Hanger, George, 270
Hanging Rock State Park, 206
Hannastown, 8
Hanson, Samuel, 89, 123
Harcourt, William, 34
Hardin, Jonathan, 14
Harding, James, 205
Harford County, 98
Harlecan (New York privateer), 185
Harlem (British sloop), 183
Harnett County, 234
Harnett, Cornelius, 76, 173
Harrington House, 61, 64, 65
Harris, Robert, 88, 89, 92, 99
Harrisburg, 33
Harrison, Robert, 92
Harrison, William, 89, 96
Hart, Thomas, 9, 12, 201
Hart's Mill, 201
Hartford Plantation, 200, 201
Hartley, Thomas, 9, 12
Haslet, John, 75, 80
Haslett, John, 80
Hatch, Christopher, 130
Hatteras Island, 185
Haverford, 61, 62, 65
Haverford Meeting House, 62, 65
Havre de Grace, 96
Haw Fields, 216, 217
Haw River, 165, 203, 204, 205, 216, 221, 222, 224, 250
Hazleton, 18
Hazlewood, John, 47, 48, 51, 55, 77
Head of Elk, 23, 28, 80, 81, 141
Heard, Charles, 229
Heights of Gowerie, 260
Helltown Ford, 238
Henrico County, 159
Henry, John, 49, 50
Henry, Patrick, 100, 115, 120, 127, 158
Henry, Robert, 273
Henry, Silas, 182
Henry, William, 109
Henry's Point, 128–130
Heroic Women Monument, 178
Heron Bridge, 186, 187, 188
Herrick, Captain, 194
Hershey's Mill, 33
Hessians, 22, 27, 29, 34, 43, 52, 66, 78, 81, 82, 128, 149, 229

Index

Heston, Edward, 63
Hestonville, 63
Hickory Mountain, 248
High Rock Lake, 258
Highlanders, 165, 181, 203, 223
Hightower, Henry, 251
Hillsborough, 165, 200, 201, 202, 203, 204, 207, 211, 216, 222, 227, 228, 249, 250, 251, 261
Hillsborough Division of Duke Forest, 200
Hinchinbrook (HMS), 109
Hinds, John Henry, 208
Hinton, James, 251
Hiokatoo (John McDonald), 11
Historic Landmarks Commission, 102
Historic Preservation Foundation of North Carolina, 170
Historical Society of Delaware, 73
History of Fort Johnston on the Lower Cape Fear, 170
Hiwassee, Tennessee, 257
Hobb's Hole, 119
Hoe's Ferry, 93
Hog Island, 50, 55, 154
Hogg, Thomas, 261
Hoke County, 247
Hokessen's Meeting House, 29
Holland shirts, 123
Holland Straights, 94
Holland, Francis, 94
Holland's Creek, 268
Hollingsworth, Zebulon, 94, 95
Hollis Marsh, 88
Holston River, 257
Hominy Creek, 256
Hood Creek, 186, 187, 192
Hood, Samuel first Viscount, 142
Hood's, 130, 158
Hood's battery, 159
Hood's Creek Bridge, 192
Hood's farm, 157, 161
Hood's fort, 158
Hooker, William, 212
Hooper, Henry, 97
Hooper, William, 173, 201, 224
Hoopers Straights, 92
Hope (British warship), 158,
Hope (schooner), 184
Hope Lodge, 23, 68
Hopewell, 132, 157, 158
Hopkins, 6
Hopkins Island, 92
Hopkinson, Francis, 46
Hospital Point, 56, 127
House in the Horseshoe, 209, 239
House of Burgesses, 100
Houston, Henry, 244
Houston, Thomas, 75
Hovenden, Moore, 58, 67
Hovenden, Richard, 39, 42, 220
Howard, John Eager, 40, 206
Howe, Richard, 54, 70
Howe, Robert, 76, 77, 108, 173, 175, 181
Howe, William, 21, 23, 26, 28, 33, 35, 37, 40, 41, 43, 53, 57, 59, 60, 63, 68, 81, 95, 135
Howitzer, 29, 40, 41, 47, 50, 51, 84, 86, 159
Huger, Isaac, 198, 206, 230, 274
Hughes, William, 27
Humphreys, Jacob, 66
Humphreys, Joshua, 62, 65
Hunter, James, 124
Hunter, Samuel, 11
Hunter's Works, 88

Huntsville, 195, 196
Hussar, 72, 113, 114, 146, 147
Hussar (galley), 4
Hutchings, Joseph, 111
Hyatt, John Vance, 85
Hyco River, 213

Impertinent, 183
Independence Hall, 43
Independence National Historical Park, 43
Independent Company of Carteret County, 184
Inness (Innis), James, 114, 137
Iron Hill, 80, 82, 95, 96
Iroquois, 12, 13, 14
Irvine, James, 25, 31
Irwin Ferry, 215
Irwin's Ford, 199
Isaacs, Elijah, 209, 210
Isis (HMS), 50, 55, 56
Island Ford, 258
Isle of Wight County, 119

Jackson, David, 209, 211
Jackson, William, 253
Jaegers, 26, 38, 53, 57, 63, 66, 70, 81, 82, 110, 113, 114, 127, 128, 130, 133, 134, 147, 164, 165, 223, 230
Jamaica, 78, 184
James Moore Monument, 178
James River, 102, 106, 112, 113, 114, 117, 119, 120, 124, 130, 131, 132, 135, 142, 145, 157, 158, 159, 163, 164, 167, 185
James, Edward, 120
James, Joseph, 123
Jamestown, 112, 117, 118, 133, 134, 138, 163
Janes Island, 153, 154
Jaquett, Peter, 85, 86
Jefferson (Virginia State Navy), 164
Jefferson, Thomas, 43, 88, 105, 159, 163, 167
Jeffrey's Ford, 29
Jemison, Mary, 11
Jenifer, Daniel of St. Thomas, 93, 94
Jenkintown, 31, 32, 66
Jenks's Mill, 67
John Dickinson's residence, 60
Johnson, Jeremiah, 90
Johnston, Gabriel, 170
Jolly Post (tavern), 39
Jolly Tar (barge), 154
Jones Island, 92
Jones, Allen, 254
Jones, David, 189
Jones, William, 188
Jonestown, 14
Jordan, Jeremiah, 90
Jordan's Island, 85
Judson, Joseph, 85
Juniata Valley, 1

Kaigers Strait, 152–154
Kattie (brig), 183
Kearney's Point, 77
Keith, George Keith Elphinstone, viscount, 124, 184
Kelly, Sergeant, 112
Kempsville, 109, 111
Kenan, James, 189, 192, 235, 237, 238
Kenan, Owen, 190, 235
Kenansville, 237
Kendal Plantation, 170, 172, 175, 181
Kedges or Kedgers Strait, 152–154
Kemp's Landing, 105, 111, 112, 126

Kennedy Creek, 270
Kennedy John, 192
Kennedy, Thomas, 242
Kennett Square, 27, 29
Kensington, 38, 44, 52
Kent County, 75, 84, 85
Kent, James, 109
Kenton, 84
Kidd, John, 128, 153
Kidnapper, 154
Killbuck, John Jr. Gelelemend, 4
Killen, William, 80
Kindaia, 14
King George County, 93, 96
King George II, 172
King George III, 152, 235
King Tammany (North Carolina Navy brigantine), 182
King, Elizabeth, 169
King's Ferry, 126
Kings Mountain, 106, 135, 196, 197, 223, 267, 269, 272, 275
Kingsfisher, 105
Kingston, 7, 241, 245
Kingstown, 245
Kinston, 245
Kirk's Farm, 250, 251
Kirk's Old Field, 250
Kirkbride, Joseph, 72
Kirkwood, Robert H., 79, 220, 221
Kittanning, 5, 7, 8
Kitty (brig), 79, 84
Kitty Hawk, 185
Klader or Clader, Daniel, 18
Knotts Island Bay, 186
Knox, Henry, 42, 144
Knox, James, 271
Knyphausen, Wilhelm von, 5, 29, 34, 37, 77, 81, 95
Kolb, Abel, 194
Kosciusko, Thaddeus, 193, 197

Lacey, John, 57, 59, 65
Lady Charlotte (sloop), 121
Lafayette River, 110
Lafayette, Marie Jean Paul Joseph du Motier Marquis de, 30, 62, 68, 80, 125, 133, 135, 141, 144, 161, 163, 165, 166, 167, 168
Lake Mackintosh, 218
Lancaster, 5, 12, 33, 37, 61, 63, 64, 65
Langodoc (Whig vessel), 153, 154
Latchom, George, 129
Laurel Hill, 267
Lauzun, Armand Louis de Gontaut-Biron, Duc de, 146, 147
Lawson, Anthony, 111
Lee, Charles, 109
Lee, Elisha, 34
Lee, Henry "Light-Horse Harry", 199, 213, 217, 220, 221, 222, 228, 230, 233, 252, 275
Lee, Richard Henry, 88
Leggett, John, 245
Lee's Legion, 34, 206, 213, , 214, 220, 223
Legat's Bridge, 236
Legionnaires, 39, 133, 146, 198, 214, 228, 234, 260
  see also cavalry, dragoons, Lee, Henry "Light-Horse Harry", Lee's Legion, Queen's Rangers, etc.
Lehigh Valley, 16, 18
Leigh, Captain, 25
Leonard Creek, 252
Leonard, Colonel, 192
Leslie, Alexander, 70, 105
Leslie, Samuel, 107, 111

Leslie's Expedition, 102, 126
Levering's Mill, 70
Levis, Thomas, 27
Lewes, 75, 76
Lewis, Andrew, 120, 122
Lewis, Micajah, 217
Lewis, Stephen, 214
Lexington, 1, 92, 100, 169, 252
Liberty (schooner), 86
Liberty Township, 12, 13, 17
Light infantry, 6, 25, 26, 27, 29, 31, 32, 33, 34, 36, 37, 38, 39, 43, 46, 59, 63, 66, 67, 68, 70, 81, 82, 109, 110, 113, 114, 127, 130, 133, 134, 158, 162, 163, 175, 188, 200, 213, 215, 221, 222, 223, 229, 230, 266, 270, 271, 272, 275
Lightfoot, 137
Lightstreet, 15
Lilesville, 194
Lillington, Alexander, 177, 178, 179, 187, 188, 189, 234, 237, 241
Lilly (sloop), 182
Limestone Township, 13
Lincoln County, 265, 267
Lincoln County Courthouse, 265
Lincoln, Benjamin, 144, 150, 261
Lincolnton, 261, 262, 263, 265, 266
Lindley, Thomas, 204, 205
Lindley, William, 211
Lindley's Mill, 200, 201, 204, 248, 250
Linzee, John, 175, 176
Little Coharie Creek or River, 189, 238
Little Dick (schooner), 184
Little Duck Creek, 85
Little Fox Island, 152
Little River, 245
Little Tennessee River, 256, 257, 274
Little Tinicum Island, 49
Liverpool (HMS), 49, 54, 55, 75–78, 108, 110, 114, 118
Liverpool (privateer), 184
Livingston, William, 32
Livingston's Creek, 249
Locke, Francis, 198, 260, 266
Locke, George, 271
Locke, Matthew (1730–1801), 271
Logstown, 4
London, 125
London (England), 169
Longboat, 83, 108
Long Bridge, 112, 191
Long Island, 21, 29, 70
Long Island of the Holston, 257
Longstreet Church, 243
Lopp, John, 242
Lord Dunmore's War, 100, 156
Love, James, 188, 189, 191
Love, Robert, 275
Lowe, Robert, 253
Lower Cherokee towns, 177
Loyal American Regiment, 130
Loyal Militia of Randolph and Chatham Counties, 242
Loyalist, 1, 7, 12, 17, 18, 35, 58, 65, 66, 67, 70, 80, 84, 86, 87, 88, 92, 94, 97, 98, 115, 122, 124, 127, 131, 137, 150, 152, 153, 177, 179, 180, 181, 183, 187, 190, 191, 192, 194, 195, 196, 197, 200, 204, 208, 209, 210, 211, 218, 221, 234, 235, 236, 237, 238, 239, 242, 243, 246, 247, 248, 250, 251, 252, 254, 256, 259, 262, 265, 266, 267, 268, 272, 273, 275
Lucas, John, 4
Lumber River, 247
Lunsford, William, 222

Index 325

Lycoming County, 6, 8
Lycoming Creek, 9, 11
Lyles, Henry, 99
Lynchburg, 167
Lynnhaven Bay, 126
Lyon, John, 137
Lytle, William, 217

MacIntosh Park, 218
Mackerel (Royal Navy victualler), 184
Maclaine, Archibald, 247
Magaherty, John, 211
Mahoning, 14, 15, 17, 18
Mahoning Creek, 14
Mallet, Joseph, 84
Mallory, Francis, 106
Malta Island, 21
Malvern Memorial Park, 35
Malvern, Pennsylvania, 33
Manchester, 159, 165, 166
Manson, Daniel, 187, 250
Mantua Creek, 50, 55
Marblehead Regiment, 21
Marcus Hook, 68
Marine Company of grenadiers, 47
Marines, 27, 78, 96, 118, 123, 146, 147, 148, 153, 172, 187
Marion, Francis, 199
Market Dock, 191
Marlin's Knob, 268
Mars (merchantman), 164
Marsh Island, 175
Marshall, John, 26, 117
Martin National Wildlife Refuge, 92
Martin, Alexander, 210, 211
Martin, Francis, 89
Martin, Jack, 206
Martin, John, 13
Martin, Joseph Plumb, 55, 56, 149
Martin, Josiah, 169, 172, 173
Mary Fisher, 136
Maryland Council of Safety, 90
Maryland Historical Society, 87
Maryland Office of Tourism, 87
Maryland Regiments, 230
Mask's Ferry, 194
Mason, Christopher, 84
Mather Mill, 23, 68
Mathew, Edward, 29, 109, 126, 127
Mathews, Thomas, 126, 137, 138
Matson's Ford, 62, 64, 71
Matthewman, Luke, 84
Matthews (Matthewes), John, 89
Maxwell, William, 12, 29, 30, 31, 81, 96
Mayflower (schooner), 97
Mayson, James, 216
McBride, Archibald, 245
McCafferty, William, 272
McCalpine's Creek, 194
McClanahan, Alexander, 122
McConkey's Ferry, 19, 21
McCowan's Ford, 272
McCrea, Captain, 117
McDaniel, Marren, 243
McDonald, Donald, 177, 179
McDonald, John, 11
McDougal or McDugald, Archibald, 178, 203, 204, 211, 248, 249
McDougall, Alexander, 31, 34, 52
McDowell, Charles, 254, 268
McDowell, Joseph, 266

McDowell's Station, 254
McDugald see McDougal
McFall's Mill, 247
McFarling, Captain, 183
McGowan's Creek, 200
McIntosh, George, 175
McIntyre Farm, 269
McJunkin, Joseph, 254
McKay, John, 113
McKay, Lieutenant, 239
McKinley, John, 78
McKnight, Elizabeth Gillen, 10
McKnight, James, 10, 11
McLane, Allen, 25, 26, 40, 43, 46, 70, 86, 124, 131
McLendon's Creek, 253
McLeod, Donald, 180
McMahan, James, 17
McNeal, Ann, 13
McNeal, Daniel, 124
McNeil, Hector, 239
McNeil, Hector (1756–1830), 178, 211, 234, 245, 246, 248
McNeil, Hector, Sr. (d. 1781), 203, 204
McNeill, John, 243
McPhaul's Mill, 247, 248
McPherson, Major, 134
McPherson, William, 133, 134
McQueen, John, 77
McRea, Mary, 269
Mebane, 216
Mebane, Robert, 205, 250, 251
Mecklenburg County, 194, 272
Mecklenburg Declaration, 169
Mecklenburg militia, 271
Melfa, 136
Mennonites, 1
Men-of-war, 77, 78, 108, 110 see also Frigates
Mercer, John Francis, 146
Mercury (privateer sloop), 86
Mercury (HMS), 183
Merion Meeting House, 61, 64
Merlin (British sloop), 54, 55
Mermaid (British transport), 84
Metompkin Inlet, 129, 130
Middle Creek Valley, 11
Middle Ferry, 54, 55, 63
Middle Cherokee towns, 177
Mifflin, Thomas, 53
Miles, Samuel, 75
Militia, 1, 4, 6, 11, 15, 17, 21, 25, 26, 27, 31, 32, 41, 55, 57, 58, 59, 60, 63, 64, 65, 66, 67, 68, 71, 73, 76, 78, 79, 80, 82, 85, 87, 88, 89, 90, 91, 92, 94, 97, 100, 105, 107, 108, 111, 117, 119, 120, 122, 123, 124, 127, 136, 137, 138, 144, 146, 152, 159, 162, 163, 166, 167, 169, 173, 175, 177, 178, 179, 185, 186, 187, 188, 189, 190, 192, 193, 194, 195, 196, 198, 201, 204, 205, 206, 209, 210, 211, 212, 217, 218, 220, 223, 224, 227, 230, 231, 234, 235, 237, 238, 241, 242, 243, 246, 247, 250, 251, 254, 256, 259, 260, 261, 268, 270, 271, 272, 273, 274, 276
Militiamen, 4, 6, 7, 9, 10, 12, 14, 15, 18, 19, 21, 25, 31, 32, 37, 38, 39, 53, 58, 59, 64, 65, 67, 68, 70, 72, 75, 76, 77, 78, 79, 81, 82, 83, 84, 86, 89, 91, 92, 96, 97, 99, 104, 106, 108, 109, 110, 111, 112, 113, 114, 117, 123, 126, 128, 129, 130, 131, 132, 137, 138, 143, 146, 147, 156, 157, 158, 159, 160, 162, 163, 165, 166, 176, 177, 179, 180, 181, 185, 187, 188, 189, 190, 192, 193, 194, 195, 196, 197, 198, 199, 200, 202, 203, 204, 205, 206, 208, 209, 211, 212, 216, 217, 221, 228, 234, 235, 236, 237, 238, 239,

241, 243, 244, 245, 246, 248, 249, 250, 251, 252, 253, 254, 256, 257, 259, 260, 261, 266, 267, 269, 270, 271, 272, 273, 274
Mill Creek or Run, 15, 46, 52, 64, 96, 207, 239
Mill's Station, 276
Miller, Samuel, 8
Miller, Thomas, 214
Mills, Ambrose, 259
Milton, 17
Mingo, 4, 14
Mingo Creek, 56
Minutemen, 107, 108
Mischianza, 40, 70
Mobley, Biggars, 190, 236
Mobley, Middleton, 190, 236, 237, 238
Moccasins, 13, 257
Mohawk, 14
Moncrieff, James, 47, 176
Moncure, 233
Monk (HMS), 98
Monkman, Captain, 83
Monmouth County, 59
Monongahela, 5
Monroe's Bridge, 251
Monroeton, 215
Montagu, George, 91
Montagu, James, 105, 111, 112, 113, 114
Montford's Cove, 268
Montgomery (frigate), 47
Montgomery County, 22, 59, 64, 65, 196, 243, 245
Montgomery, Richard, 1
Montgomery, William, 15
Montour County, 17
Montour, Roland, 18
Montresor, John, 49, 51, 53, 54, 67, 84, 95
Montrose, 201
Moor, John, 15, 265, 267
Moore County, 239, 243
Moore house, 140
Moore, Daniel, 84
Moore, James, 169, 173, 178, 179
Moore, John, 15, 265, 267
Moore, Joseph, 85
Moore, Patrick, 257
Moores Creek, 178, 181
Moores Creek Bridge, 181
Moores Creek National Battlefield, 178
Moorhead or Morehead, Samuel, 5, 8
Moravians, 1
More's Plantation, 186, 187, 192
Morgan, Daniel, 25, 26, 32, 53, 168, 197, 199, 206, 227, 228, 230, 258, 259, 260, 263, 267, 273, 274
Morganton, 254, 268
Morgantown, 195
Morning Star, 164
Mortars, 51, 148
Morton, Robert, 61
Mosquito (British vessel), 96
Mount Airy, 25, 40, 43, 275
Mount Mourne, 273
Mount Olive, 245
Mountain Creek, 266, 268
Moyer, John, 18
Moylan, Stephen, 145
Mud Island, 47, 48, 50, 51, 53, 55, 56 see also Carpenter's Island
Muhlenberg, John Peter Gabriel, 105, 114, 128, 131, 162
Mulberry Island, 118
Münchhausen, Karl Friedrich Hieronymus, Freiherr von, 66

Muncie, 14
Muncy, 8, 9, 10, 11, 19
Muquassee, 257
Murphy, Archibald, 234, 260
Murphy, Daniel, 75
Murray, Francis, 67
Murray, James, 9, 13
Musgrave, Thomas, 42
Myhand's Bridge, 189, 237, 238
Mynheer's Ambush, 187

Nansemond County, 136
Nantes, 124, 184
Nanticoke River, 88, 97
Nanticoke Sound, 92
Narberth, 61
Narsworthy, 119
Nash, Abner, 199
Nash, Francis, 30, 31, 200
Nashameny Ferry, 22
Nash-Hooper House, 200
Nassau Bar, 184
National Park Service, 2
National Portrait Gallery, 43
Native American, 1, 4, 5, 6, 7, 8, 9, 10, 11, 12, 13, 14, 15, 16, 17, 18, 19, 58, 68, 87, 88, 100, 128, 156, 177
Nazareth, 13, 16
Neabsco Mills Ironworks, 123
Neale, Henry, 183
Nedrow, Thomas, 66
Neel, Thomas, 177
Negro Head Point, 186, 191
Nelson house, 138
Nelson, Thomas, Jr., 106, 130, 131, 138, 140, 143
Neowee Creek, 177
Nesbitt, Colebrook, 188
Nescopeck, 18
Neshaming Creek, 58
Neuse River, 240, 245, 247
New Bern, 172, 178, 181, 182, 184, 185, 188, 203, 237, 240, 241, 244, 245
New Castle, 2, 76, 81, 82, 84
New Garden, 29, 228–230, 232, 233
New Garden Meetinghouse, 224, 229
New Hanover County, 186
New Hope, 191
New Hope River, 250, 251
New York, 7, 8, 9, 12, 13, 14, 17, 28, 30, 57, 68, 69, 70, 75, 77, 78, 79, 82, 84, 90, 92, 102, 105, 122, 126, 127, 134, 135, 140, 141, 142, 145, 148, 150, 152, 158, 163, 184, 185, 187, 257
Newark, 80, 81, 82, 96
Newcastle County, 27
Newmarket Creek, 106
Newport News, 105, 106, 118, 130, 131
Newport, Rhode Island, 140, 142
Newtown, 12, 14, 34, 58, 66, 67, 111, 170, 172, 175
Newtown Ferry House, 170, 172, 175
Newtown Square, 34
Niagara, 18
Nicholas, John, 159
Nichols, Captain, 91
Nichols, Jacob, 196
Nicholson, James, 86, 91
Ninety Six, 216, 217, 227, 256, 258, 259, 268, 269, 275
Ninety Six Courthouse, 216
Noel, Ned, 97
Nolachucky River, 257
Nomini Bay, 88

Index 327

Norfolk, 102, 105, 107, 108, 109, 110, 111, 112, 115, 117, 118, 119, 120, 122, 124, 126, 128, 157
Norfolk Naval Shipyard, 110
Norfolk Road, 109
Norrington, 32, 35, 38
Norris, Isaac, 60
Norristown, 38, 65, 69
North Carolina Historical Commission, 258
North Carolina Independent Dragoons, 241, 245
North Carolina Navy, 182
North Carolina Regulars, 175
North Carolina Society for the Preservation of Antiquities, 170
North Carolina Society of Colonial Dames of America, 170
North Carolina State Legion, 261
North Carolina State Navy, 188
Northampton County, 16, 18
Northumberland County, 11, 16, 17
Norwood, 193
Notre Dame (South Carolina brigantine), 184
Nusquepack, 18

Oak Ridge, 212, 224
Oath of allegiance, 85, 111, 237
Occoquan Creek, 91
Ocracoke Bar, 181, 182, 185
Ocracoke Inlet, 181, 182, 183, 184
Ocracoke Island, 182, 184
Official North Carolina Travel Guide, 170
O'Hara, Charles, 150, 151, 197, 203, 213, 215, 231, 234, 259, 267
Ohio frontier, 152
Ohio River, 2, 4
Ohio Valley, 1
Old Mother Covington, 178, 179
Old Richmond, 195
Old Town Restoration, 253
Oldfields Point, 95
Oldham, Edward, 221
Onancock, 152, 153, 154
Onancock Creek, 153
Oneidas, 68, 70
O'Neil's Mill, 216
Onslow, Richard, 124
Onslow County, 204, 241, 244
Orange County, 200, 201
Orde, John, 76
Orton Mill, 170, 172, 174, 175
Osborne's Landing or Wharf, 132, 163, 164
Otter (British sloop), 90, 102, 104, 105, 107, 108, 109, 110, 118, 121, 123, 127
Outer Banks, 182, 183, 186
Over the Mountain men, 195, 269
Overhill Cherokee villages, 257
Owen, Thomas, 248, 250
Oxford, 39, 40, 96, 97
Oysters, 118

Packhorse (British vessel), 192
Pagan Creek, 105, 131
Pages Lake, 239
Paine, Thomas, 55
Paisley, John, 194, 196, 209
Pakenham, Edward, 50
Pallas (British sloop), 76
Pallet's Mill, 127
Pamplico River, 182
Paoli, 33, 35, 36, 217
Parapet, 178
Parker, James, 60, 122

Parker, Josiah, 136
Parker, Peter, 169, 254
Parker, Thomas, 153
Parley, 80, 150
Parliament, 100, 231
Parole, 80, 154, 194, 211, 239, 240
Parry, Francis, 172, 176
Parsons, Captain Major, 276
Passover poles, 254
Patterson, Daniel, 244
Patterson, Samuel, 95
Patuxent River, 92, 93
Pea Patch Island, 76, 79
Peacock's Bridge, 235
Pearl (HMS), 50, 54, 55, 78
Pee Dee River, 193, 194, 204
Pee Dee County militiamen, 234
Peggy Stewart (British brigantine), 87
Pemberton's plantation, 46
Pembroke (British schooner), 60, 119
Pencadder, 80, 81
Pence, Peter, 15
Pendleton, Edmund, 107
Penn Valley, 8
Penn, John, 224
Pennsylvania Assembly, 11
Pennsylvania Farmer (North Carolina Navy brigantine), 182, 188
Pennsylvania Historical and Museum Commission, 2
Pennsylvania Navy, 47, 84
Pennypack Bridge, 33
Pennypack Creek, 38
Perkins, Commissary, 148
Perry, John, 222
Perryville, 96
Perseus (HMS), 76, 124, 184
Perth Amboy, 80
Pest House, 52
Petersburg, 105, 114, 136, 157, 158, 161, 162, 163, 165, 166, 168, 193, 258
Philadelphia, 1, 19, 22, 23, 26, 27, 28, 29, 30, 31, 32, 33, 34, 35, 36, 37, 38, 39, 40, 41, 42, 43, 44, 45, 46, 47, 48, 50, 51, 52, 53, 55, 57, 58, 59, 60, 61, 62, 63, 64, 65, 66, 67, 68, 69, 70, 71, 72, 73, 75, 77, 79, 80, 81, 82, 88, 95, 141, 169, 183, 184, 187
Philadelphia (galley), 60
Philadelphia State House, 43
Phillips, William, 110, 113, 114, 126, 135, 162, 166
Phipps, Charles, 76
Phoenix (HMS), 92, 96
Phoenixville, 36
Piankatank River, 120
Pickens, Andrew, 201, 203, 217, 220
Picket guard, 31, 138, 235, 266
Piedmont, 100
Pigeon Gap, 256
Pilgrim United Church of Christ, 252
Pincers, 130, 135
Pine Creek, 6
Piney Bottom, 178, 243, 244, 245
Piney Bottom Creek, 243
Piney Bottom Massacre, 243
Pinnace, 124
Pipers, John, 15
Pitcairn, Thomas, 188
Pittsboro, 201, 207, 242
Pittsburgh, 2, 4, 5, 13, 14, 87
Planebrook, 33
Pluggy's Town, 4
Plunket, William, 10

Plunkett, David, 57
Plymouth, 70, 75
Plymouth Meeting, 70
Pocahontas Bridge, 162
Point Comfort, 102, 105
Point Lookout, 90, 93
Point of Fork, 166, 167
Point Peter, 186, 191
Point Weyanoke, 157
Point-no-Point, 38
Polk, Thomas, 176, 272
Polk's mill, 272
Polk's plantation, 272
Polly (merchant schooner), 79, 182
Pont Reading, 62, 65
Poor, Enoch, 12, 63, 69
Poor's Creek, 162
Pope, Charles, 76, 80, 84, 85
Popp, Stephen, 148
Poquoson, 106
Port Penn, 83, 84, 85
Port Tobacco, 93, 98, 99
Portevent's Mill, 186, 190
Portevints, Samuel, 186
Portsmouth, 98, 105, 106, 107, 109, 110, 114, 117, 119, 126, 127, 128, 135, 136, 158, 161, 163
Portsmouth Shipyard Museum, 126
Potomac River, 88, 89, 91, 92, 93, 98, 122, 123
Potter, James, 52, 57, 64, 70
Potter, Samuel, Sr, 25, 60
Pottsgrove, 12, 37
Powell's Creek, 130, 158
Powell's Pond, 239
Powhatan, 96
Pray, Captain, 196
Preston, William, 220, 222, 223
Price, Thomas, 91
Priests Town, 96
Prince Edward Courthouse, 167, 168
Prince of Wales (brig), 183
Prince William militia, 123
Princess Anne County, 92, 96, 105, 111
Princess Anne militiamen, 112
Privateer, 72, 86, 88, 92, 97, 105, 124, 163, 182–186, 238, 253
Proctor, Francis, Jr., 183
Protector (Whig vessel), 153, 154
Providence, 137, 184, 213, 233, 270
Providence Forge, 137
Province Island, 51, 55, 56
Prudent (British vessel), 125
Pulaski, Casimir, 25, 32
Pulliam, John, 2
Puncheon Run, 80
Pungoteague, 136, 137
Purgatory Swamp, 82
Pyle, John, 165, 205, 209, 217, 221

Quaker, 1, 58, 64, 205, 224, 232, 275
Quaker Meadows, 195, 254, 268
Quantico, 123
Quebec, 1
Queen Esther, 9, 18
Queen's Guard, 224
Queen's Rangers, 26, 29, 32, 40, 44, 46, 59, 71, 87, 113, 117, 131, 159, 166
Quinn, Michael, 238

Rabun Gap, 256
Radnor, 65

Raft Swamp, 192, 203, 247, 248, 249
Raiford, Robert, 200
Rainbow (HMS), 126, 127
Rains, John, 205
Raisonable (HMS), 126, 127
Raleigh (Continental frigate), 169, 183, 186
Rall, Johann Gottlieb, 22
Ramsaur's or Ramseur's Mill, 261, 265, 267
Ramsey, Ambrose, 242
Ramsey, Herndon, 242
Ramsey's Mill, 204, 233, 251
Ramsour, Jacob, 265
Ramsour's Mill, 261, 265, 267
Randall, 185
Randolph, 100, 204, 242
Randolph (Continental Navy frigate), 77, 78
Randolph County, 204, 207, 209, 210, 211, 212, 260
Randolph County Courthouse, 260
Randolph County militia, 209, 211
Randolph, Peyton, 100
Ranger (British schooner), 119
Rappahannock River, 96, 119, 124
Ravelin, 2
Raven (poem), 61
Raven (British vessel), 173
Rawdon, Francis, 232, 267
Ray, Duncan, 178, 243, 245, 246, 248, 249, 250
Ray's Mill Creek, 239
Read, William, 197, 260
Reading, 37, 62, 65
Red Bank, 50, 52, 53, 55
Red Lion Tavern, 38, 58
Red Springs, 247
Redoubt, 37, 41, 52, 60, 109, 117, 126, 127, 143, 145, 146, 148, 149, 193
Redoubt Number 10, 145, 147, 149
Redoubt Number 9, 145, 147, 149, 150
Reed Creek, 196
Reed, George, 189
Reed, Joseph, 26
Reedy Creek, 195, 196, 199
Reedy Fork, 212, 222, 223, 224
Reedy Fork Creek, 222
Reedy Island, 79, 83, 84
Reedy Tavern, 59
Regiment Prince Charles, 109
Regiment von Bose, 148, 163, 178
Regulators, 169, 205, 218
Reid, Thomas, 177
Reidville, 215
Rencher's Ford, 198
Renown (privateer), 164
Resistance (Continental brigantine), 183, 186
Revell, John, 153
Richardson, Richard, Sr., 75
Richmond, 75, 100, 102, 105, 113, 130, 133, 135, 137, 157, 158, 159, 160, 163, 164, 165, 166, 167
Richmond (HMS), 125
Richmond County, 243
Richmond Hill, 158, 159
Riddick, Edward, 128
Riddle, Thomas, 233
Riddle, William, 275
Riddle's Knob, 275
Rifle, 17, 30, 85, 112, 113, 188, 190, 191, 194, 208, 215, 220, 271, 272
Riflemen, 25, 26, 32, 77, 104, 108, 112, 113, 116, 117, 123, 131, 134, 174, 199, 201, 202, 206, 217, 220, 221, 222, 223, 224, 229, 233, 259, 260, 270, 271, 272
Rising Sun, 32, 60

Index **329**

Rivanna River, 16
Roanoke Inlet, 183
Roanoke River, 105, 193
Robbins, 194, 195
Robert's mills, 166
Roberts, James, 156, 258
Roberts, John, 64
Roberts, Lieutenant, 148
Robertson, Archibald, 25, 26, 44
Robertson, James, 156, 258
Robertson, Lieutenant, 148
Robertson's Creek, 207, 242
Robeson County, 247
Robeson, Peter, 245
Robeson, Thomas Jr., 245, 246
Robeson's Plantation, 245
Robinson, Isaiah, 55, 128, 137
Robinson, Thomas, 18, 75
Robinson, William, 111
Robinson's Ranging Company, 19
Robison, Peter, 234
Robust, 125
Rochambeau, Jean Baptiste Donatien de Vimeur Comte de, 140, 142, 144, 151
Rockfish Bridge, 237
Rockfish Creek, 179, 236, 237, 243
Rockingham County, 213, 215
Rocky Mount, 192
Rocky River, 193, 248
Rodney, Caesar, 84
Rodney, Thomas, 80
Roebuck (HMS), 46, 50, 54, 75, 76, 77, 78, 89, 90, 91, 92, 119, 120, 121, 123
Rogers, Lieutenant, 183
Rohens's Mill, 64
Romulus (HMS), 105
Ropewalk, 109, 159, 166
Roper, Robert, 250
Ross, David, 166, 167
Rouse's Tavern, 189, 186, 188, 191, 252
Row galley, 47, 55, 75, 76, 77, 91, 123, 182, 238
Rowan militia, 271
Rowan County, 254, 258, 259
Rowland, Thomas, 220
Roy, Samuel, 19
Royal Highlanders, 126
Royal Marines, 100
Royal Navy, 76, 108, 120, 142, 157, 173, 174, 182, 184, 186, 253
Royal North Carolina Regiment, 187, 207, 250
Royal Oak, 125
Royal Volunteers of Ireland, 109
Royal Welch Fusiliers, 30, 143, 223, 272
Rudolph, John, 220
Rutherford, Griffith, 192, 196, 248, 251, 252, 254, 256, 257, 266, 267
Rutherford's Mill, 241
Rutherfordton, 268
Rutledge, Edward, 271
Rutledge, Thomas, 244

Sain, Israel, 262
Saint George Island, 89, 90, 91
Saint George River, 91
Salem, 68, 79, 196, 198, 199, 206, 260 see also Winston–Salem
Salem County, 79
Salisbury, 194, 197, 198, 209, 210, 222, 224, 229, 258, 259, 260, 261, 270, 273, 274
Salisbury, Lieutenant, 106
Salter, Sallie, 246
Saluda River, 217
Sandy Hook, New Jersey, 7, 109
Sandy Point, 89, 92, 117, 165
Sanford, 207, 234, 239
Sappers, 147, 148, 149, 150
Saratoga, New York, 42, 150
Sauratown Mountains, 206
Savitz's (Savis's) Mill, 258
Sawickly, 8
Scalping, 4, 5, 8, 9, 10, 11, 13, 15, 19
Scammel, Alexander, 145
Scheffs Ford, 38
Schutz, William, 178
Schuylkill Falls, 32, 58
Schuylkill River, 32, 33, 34, 35, 36, 37, 38, 40, 46, 47, 48, 50, 52, 53, 54, 55, 56, 57, 58, 59, 62, 63, 64, 65, 66, 69, 70, 71, 72
Scobey, James, 18
Scobey, Robert, 211
Scorpion (HM Sloop), 172, 173, 174, 176
Scotch Valley, 18
Scott, Charles, 116, 118
Second Virginia Convention, 100
Seneca, 7, 11, 14, 17, 18
Senf, John Christian, 105, 200
Serle, Ambrose, 54
Seven Brothers, 92
Seven Creeks, 252
Seven Years War, 1, 84, 100
Sevier, John, 258, 274
Sewell's Point, 105
Seymour, William, 224
Shallow Ford, 195, 196, 197, 198, 199, 260
Shepherd, William, 195
Shepherd's Creek, 268
Sherring, Charles, 208
Sheshequin, 9, 10
Shield, Robert, 106
Shirley Plantation, 132
Shockoe Creek, 159
Shockoe Hill, 158, 159
Shuford, John Martin, 262
Siege, 8, 53, 102, 138, 140, 142, 143, 144, 145, 146, 147, 152, 157, 254
Siler City, 251
Simcoe, John Graves, 32, 39, 40, 58, 59, 71, 106, 112, 113, 114, 127, 130, 131, 133, 137, 158, 162, 165, 166, 167
Simcoe's dragoons, 130, 146 see also Queen's Rangers
Simmons, Richard, 201
Simon's Creek, 85
Six Mile Ordinary, 137
Six Nations, 14
Six Runs Creek, 186, 187, 190
Skippack Creek, 31, 40
Skippack Road, 25, 40, 41, 42
Slaves, 77, 98, 100, 104, 108, 111, 112, 115, 116, 118, 120, 127, 132, 137, 153, 158, 167, 173, 184, 192, 239, 244, 268
Sleepy Hole, 128
Slingsby, John, 178, 246, 247
Slocum, Mary, 178
Smallpox, 91, 94, 119, 122, 244, 245
Smallwood, William, 31, 68, 82, 85, 157, 163, 187, 196
Smith Creek, 93
Smith, John, 214
Smith, Lieutenant, 15
Smith, Robert, 192
Smith, Samuel, 48, 53, 55, 268

Smith Creek, 93
Smithfield, Pennsylvania, 38, 39, 58, 59, 66, 67
Smithfield, Virginia, 107, 126, 127, 128, 131
Smoot, William Barton, 97, 124
Smyth or Smith, John Ferdinand Dalzial, 87
Snead, Smith, 153
Snead, William, 153
Sniping, 174, 191, 237
Snow Camp, 201
Snow, Silas, 83
Society of Friends, 1 see also Quakers
Solebay (HMS), 78, 96, 127, 184
Somerset (HMS), 55
Somerset, 88, 92
Somerset County, 88
Sons of Liberty, 169
Sortie, 107, 150
South Carolina, 76, 77, 91, 106, 135, 144, 150, 152, 176, 181, 183, 184, 185, 187, 192, 194, 195, 196, 197, 199, 204, 211, 217, 223, 226, 227, 228, 232, 238, 241, 242, 243, 246, 249, 251, 252, 254, 256, 257, 258, 265, 268, 269, 273, 275, 276
South Mountains, 268
South Quay, 136
Southampton County, 136
Southern Pines, 239
Southport, 170, 172
Sovereign (British transport), 174
Spalding or Spaulding, Simon, 9
Spaniards, 166
Spartanburg, 269
Spedden, 154
Speedwell, 184
Speedwell Furnace, 215
Speedwell Iron Works, 215, 216
Spees, Jacob, 11
Spencer's Ordinary, 133, 137
Spesutie Island, 94
Sphynx (HMS), 125
Spitfire (Loyalist schooner), 97
Spottsylvania County militia, 88
Spread Eagle Tavern, 34
Spring Friends Meetinghouse, 204
Spring House, 27, 46, 58, 67
Sprowle, Andrew, 108, 110
Spy, 35, 68, 70, 71, 128, 209, 259, 270
Squire, Mathew, 102, 109
Squires, David, 184
St. Albans, 124
St. Augustine, 122, 182, 184, 185, 259
St. Christopher, 183
St. Clement's Island, 96
St. Clements Bay, 96
St. Croix, 184, 185
St. Eustatius, 185
St. George Parish, Accomac, 137
St. John's Church, 100
St. John's Episcopal Church, 158, 159
St. John's Island, 192
St. Joseph's Church, 44
St. Lawrence, 173, 174, 175, 176
St. Mary's County, 90
St. Paul's Church, 107
St. Peter's Church, 44
St. Peter's Lutheran Church, 68, 69
St. Pierre, 184
Stamp Act, 100, 169, 172
Stanly, Captain, 206
Stantonsburg, 235
Starret's mills, 11

State (frigate), 165
State Department of Archives and History, 169, 170
State Historic Preservation Office, 170
Staten Island, 57
Staunton, 156
Steele, Mr., 274
Steele's Tavern, 274
Stenton, 60
Stephen, Adam, 31
Sterne, Major General, 29
Stevens, Adam, 29
Steward, Stephen, 98
Stewards Creek, 233
Stewards River, 234
Stewart, James, 106
Stewart, John (ca. 1719–1777), 156
Stewart's Creek, 233
Stidham, Jonas, Jr., 78
Stidham, Joseph, 78
Still, Mr., 7, 194, 195
Stinson, John, 209
Stockade, 17, 121
Stoddert, William, 89
Stokes County, 206
Stone, Thomas, 93
Stoney Creek, 202, 203
Story, Captain, 71
Stratford, 88
Streeper's Tavern, 61
Stuart Monument, 224
Stuart, James, 224
Stuart's Creek, 233
Stuart's Ford, 233
Suffolk, 106, 109, 117, 126, 128, 158, 167, 168
Sugar Creek, 271, 272
Sugar Creek Church, 271
Sugar Loaf township, 18
Sugar Run, 15
Sugarloaf Massacre, 18
Sullivan, John, 7, 12, 14, 22, 29, 31, 34, 41, 64
Sullivan–Clinton Expedition, 13
Sullivan's Island, 181
Summerfield, 212
Sumner, Jethro, 196
Sumter, Thomas, 267
Sunbury, 8, 10, 11, 12, 16
Surrender, 7, 11, 42, 49, 59, 70, 83, 140, 145, 147, 150, 151, 152, 165, 177, 187, 189, 190, 192, 205, 209, 238, 240, 252, 267, 268
Surrender Field, 140
Surry County, 195, 196, 197
Susquehanna River, 5, 6, 7, 8, 12, 13, 17, 18, 19, 96
Sutphin, 200, 201
Swan Point, 88, 94
Swan Town, 94
Swearingen, Andrew Van, 5
Swede's Ford, 65, 69, 72
Swedes' Ford, 37, 38
Swedesford, 33, 34, 35
Swift (HMS), 158
Swift Creek, 235
Swivel gun, 82, 84, 86, 104, 116, 121, 122, 124, 172, 174, 175, 176, 178, 185, 204, 216, 238
Sword, Ensign, 130
Symmetry (British transport brig), 45, 82, 83
Symonds, Thomas, 184
Syren (HMS), 181, 183

Tangier Island, 124, 153
Tangier Sound, 97, 153

Index

Tannenbaum Park, 226
Tappahannock, 119
Tar River, 235
Tarkill Branch, 186, 190
Tarleton, Banastre, 130, 133, 136, 137, 138, 146, 152, 165, 166, 167, 192, 198, 214, 217, 220, 221, 222, 228, 229, 230, 234, 235, 260, 265, 270, 273, 274, 275
Tarleton's Legion, 146, 147, 163, 214, 217, 229, 260 see also American Legion
Tarrant's Tavern, 273, 274
Tayloe family, 123
Taylor, John, 233
Taylor, Thomas, 239
Taylor's Ferry, 105
Tea party, 169
Tempest (Virginia State Navy), 164, 165
Templeton, 14
Terrible (Whig vessel), 154
Thaddeus Kosciuszko National Memorial, 44
Third Haven Creek, 97
Thomas, Captain, 58, 66
Thomas, Evan, 39, 66, 67
Thomas, John Allen, 91
Thompson, Baalam, 211
Thompson, James, 271
Thompson, John, 210, 211
Thompson, William, 124, 216
Thompson's Island, 13, 14
Thomson, Charles, 64
Thoroughfare, 85, 86
Three Mile Run, 25, 71
Three Tuns Tavern, 33
Thunderer (HMS), 142
Timber Creek, 55
Tinicum Island, 45
Tioga, 10, 12, 14
Tioga Point, 8, 9
Toano, 137
Tobacco, 88, 93, 94, 96, 108, 109, 110, 114, 118, 126, 127, 132, 133, 135, 159, 162, 163, 165, 166, 167, 182
Tollemache, John, 172, 173, 174
Tomahawk, 17
Tompkins's Bridge, 106
Topsail Inlet, 181, 183, 185
Torrance, 5, 156, 273
Torrence's or Torrance's Tavern, 273, 274
Tory Hole Park, 246
Tory House, 206
Tory's Den, 206
Tory's Falls, 206
Tottamy's Gap, 16
Touring North Carolina's Revolutionary War Sites, 170
Towles, Oliver, 88
Town Fork, 206
Town Point wharf, 110
Townshend duties, 100
Trading Ford, 197, 198, 258, 259, 260
Trading Path, 258
Trappe, 62
Travis, Champion, 112
Treaty of Paris, 100, 152
Treaty of peace, 152
Tred Avon, 96, 97
Tred Avon River, 97
Trent River, 240, 241
Trenton, 21, 22, 41, 72
Trenton Ferry, 21
Trimble's Ford, 29

Troublesome Creek, 215, 223
Troublesome Iron Works, 215
Trumbull (Whig vessel), 86
Trunnions, 160
Tryon County militia, 177
Tryon, William, 218, 240
Tuckasegee, 274
Tucker, Robert, 194
Tucker, Thomas, 185
Tucker's Point, 119
Tunis Ordinary, 61, 64
Turkey Island, 164
Turner monument, 225
Turner, Ball, 196
Turner, Kerenhappuck Norman, 225
Twitty, Susan, 268
Twitty, William, 268
Two Brothers, 92
Tyer, Thomas, 252
Tygart Valley, 156
Tyger River, 259, 276
Tyre's plantation, 133, 134
Tyson, Cornelius, 208
Tyson's Tavern, 26

U.S. Naval Shipyard, 126
Union, 16, 166, 185, 187
Uwharrie Mountains, 209, 242, 251

Valley Cherokee towns, 177
Valley Forge, 8, 22, 27, 34, 36, 37, 46, 57, 62, 65, 66, 68, 69, 70, 71, 72
Van Cortlandt, Philip, 148
Van Etten, Johannes, Sr., 18
Vanhorn's hotel, 66
Varnum, James Mitchell, 69
Vauban, Sébastien Le Prestre de, 144
Veach, Jack, 195
Venango, 14
Vernon, Richard, 196, 197
Victory (Whig vessel), 129, 130, 153
Vienna, 97
Vigilant (HM Armed Ship), 49, 50
Viper (HMS), 45, 50, 54, 60
Virginia, 4, 5, 18, 19, 75, 81, 87, 88, 89, 90, 91, 93, 96, 98, 100, 102, 104, 107, 108, 109, 110, 111, 115, 117, 119, 120, 123, 124, 126, 127, 128, 130, 131, 132, 133, 134, 135, 136, 138, 141, 142, 143, 144, 146, 153, 154, 156, 158, 159, 162, 163, 166, 167, 181, 183, 185, 186, 189, 192, 195, 196, 199, 206, 213, 216, 217, 220, 222, 223, 224, 227, 228, 230, 231, 232, 238, 241, 242, 248, 252, 253, 254, 256, 257, 258, 259, 260, 269
Virginia (Whig vessel), 126
Virginia Beach, 111, 119, 124
Virginia capes, 142
Virginia Historical Society, 102
Virginia Landmarks Register, 102
Virginia riflemen, 134, 199, 206, 222, 259, 260
Virginia State Tourism Corporation, 102
Volunteers of Ireland, 269, 271
Von Lengerke, 40
Von Linsing, 40
Von Steuben, Friedrich Wilhelm Ludolf Gerhard Augustin Baron, 130, 131, 136, 144, 158, 159, 166
Von Wreden, Carl August, 53
Von Wumb, Friedrich Wilhelm, 81

Wade, Thomas, 178, 243, 244, 245, 246, 247
Wadesboro, 194

Wadmalaw Island, 185
Wahab, James, 269
Wahab's (Wahub's) plantation, 269, 270
Wake County, 204, 251
Waldeckers, 23
Walker, Andrew, 10
Walker, Hugh, 119
Walker, Stephen, 211
Wallace, 6, 232, 236
Wallace, Joseph, 185
Wallace, James, 185
Wallace, Richard, 6
Wallace's Fort, 6
Walley, Zedekiah, 153
Wallis, Lieutenant, 123
Wallop's Island, 131, 132
Walters, Abigail, 275
War of 1812, 123
Ward, Enoch, 182, 184
Ward's Creek, 157
Warlick Monument, 262
Warlick, Johann Nicholas, 262, 266
Warren, 13, 33, 35, 265
Warren County, 13
Warrior Run, 8, 10
Warrior's Trail, 18
Washington County, 156
Washington Crossing Historic Park, 19
Washington, George, 1, 13, 21, 23, 28, 31, 33, 34, 35, 37, 41, 43, 44, 53, 58, 59, 60, 61, 62, 68, 78, 80, 95, 96, 100, 120, 140, 141, 143, 145, 148, 150, 215, 224, 230
Washington, Robert, 93
Washington, William, 199, 213, 221, 223, 230
Washingtonville, 18
Wasp (British vessel), 77
Watauga, Tennessee, 257
Watering party, 91
Watering place, 108
Watson's Creek, 72
Watts Island, 153
Wauchope see Wahab
Waxhaw Creek, 269
Waxhaws, 217, 258, 269
Wayah, 256
Wayne, "Mad Anthony", 30, 36, 64, 113, 133, 135, 136, 168, 241
Waynesville, 256
Webb, Samuel B., 25
Webb's Ferry, 47, 48, 56, 57
Webber's Bridge, 240, 241
Webster, 223, 256, 274
Webster, James, 178, 222, 230, 273
Weedon, George, 42, 88, 106, 131, 146
Weeks, Captain, 117
Weeks, Major, 127
Wells, Benjamin, 118
Weltch Point, 94
Wemyss, James, 31, 77
West Buffalo Township, 16
West Conshohocken, 62
West Indies, 122, 140, 152, 181, 253
West Point, 126
West River, 98
West Virginia, 18, 19, 100
West, William, 23
Westham, 157, 158, 159, 160
Westmoreland County, 5, 6, 7, 8, 88, 156
Westmoreland County militia, 88
Westover, 130, 157, 158, 159, 160, 167
Wetsell's or Wetzell's Mill, 221–223

Whaleboats, 182
Whaley see Walley
Wharton, Thomas, 59
Wheeling, West Virginia, 4
Wheland, Joseph, 97
White Horse Tavern, 33
White Oak, 245, 268
White Oak Spring, 268
White, Joseph, 92
White, William, 211
Whitemarsh, 22, 23, 25, 26, 27, 31, 32, 57, 58, 62, 64, 65, 67, 68, 69, 70
Wicomico, 127
Wicomico River, 98
Wight County, 136
Wilcox Iron Works, 211
Wilcox, James, 176
Wilkes, 164
William Courtney's Yellow House, 201
William Cuningham and Company, 159
William Mast's Ferry, 194
William Penn Inn, 61
Williams Island, 158
Williams, Colonel, 199, 213, 214, 215, 216, 220, 222, 256
Williams, Elias, 10
Williams, James C., 236
Williams, John C., 237
Williams, Joseph, 196
Williams, Osborn, 99
Williams, Otho Holland, 199, 206, 213, 215, 220, 221, 222, 224, 230
Williamsburg, 87, 88, 100, 102, 104, 105, 107, 108, 109, 112, 113, 114, 118, 120, 124, 127, 130, 131, 132, 133, 134, 135, 137, 141, 145, 158, 166
Williamson, Andrew, 177, 216, 256, 257
Willing Lass (merchantman), 164
Willis, William, 134
Willoughby's Point, 124, 126
Willow Grove, 66
Wilmington, Delaware, 73, 75, 76, 77, 78, 79, 80, 82, 83, 85
Wilmington, North Carolina, 135, 169, 170, 173, 175, 177, 178, 179, 186, 187, 188, 189, 190, 191, 192, 193, 194, 203, 204, 205, 210, 222, 231, 232, 234, 237, 238, 239, 241, 242, 243, 245, 246, 248, 249, 252
Wilmington, Pennsylvania, 5, 47, 52
Wilmington Creek (Christina River), 76, 77, 78
Wilmington River, 170, 175
Wilmonski, Captain, 178
Wilson, Benjamin, Jr., 156
Wilson, Susan, 271
Windmill Island, 47
Windmill Point, 122
Winn, Richard, 267
Winnsboro, 272
Winston, Joseph, 206
Winston–Salem, 170, 195, 197, 206 see also Salem
Winters, Robert, 188
Winton, 242
Wissahickon Creek, 22, 32, 71
Wolf Run, 10
Wolf's Den, 275
Woodford, William, 107, 108, 110, 112, 115, 116, 117
Woody's Ford, 204
Wootten, 105
Worcester County, 97
Wormley Creek, 143, 145
Wright, Gideon, 195, 196

Wright, Hezekiah, 195, 196, 197
Wright, Isaac, 213
Wright, John, 182
Wright, Major, 27, 67
Wyalusing, 9, 10
Wyanoke Ferry, 242
Wyoming, 6, 7, 9, 10, 11, 12, 13, 14
Wyoming Massacre, 6, 7
Wyoming Valley, 6, 7, 13, 14

Yadkin, 194, 195, 196, 197, 198, 199, 258, 259, 260
Yadkin River, 194, 195, 196, 197, 198, 199, 259
Yadkinville, 195
Yellow Creek, 15
Yellow Springs, 6
York, 1
York County, 58
York River, 120, 135, 138, 140, 142, 145, 146, 148
York, Pennsylvania, 36
Yorktown, 102, 106, 113, 126, 127, 135, 138, 140, 141, 142, 143, 144, 145, 146, 150, 152, 189, 205, 232, 242, 248, 252, 253
Yorktown Monument, 138
Yorktown Victory Center, 138
Yorktown Visitor Center/Yorktown Battlefield, 138
Youart, J., 84
Young, Captain, 15
Young, Henry, 187
Young, James, 15

Zebra (HM Sloop), 55

Other titles in the BATTLEGROUNDS OF FREEDOM series by Norman Desmarais

Battlegrounds of Freedom: A Historical Guide to the Battlefields of the War of American Independence. 2005. This fascinating travelogue invites readers to re-enact each battle with maps and photos, well-written text, abundant notation of websites, and many other useful references. This comprehensive work covers Maine to Georgia as well as western territories. 260 pages, 19 maps, 109 photos. Paperback. 0-9666196-7-6. $26.95.

The Guide to the Revolutionary War in Canada and New England: Battles, Raids, and Skirmishes. 2009. Follow along as the author retraces every encounter of the Revolutionary War in Canada and New England along geographical lines. 262 pages, 8 maps, 49 photos. Paperback. 978-1-934934-01-2. $21.95.

The Guide to the Revolutionary War in New York: Battles, Raids, and Skirmishes. 2010. Follow along as the author retraces every encounter of the Revolutionary War in New York along geographical lines. 283 pages, 4 maps, 37 photos. Paperback. 978-1-934934-02-9. $22.95.

The Guide to the Revolutionary War in New Jersey: Battles, Raids, and Skirmishes. 2010. Follow along as the author retraces every encounter of the Revolutionary War in New Jersey along geographical lines. 285 pages, 3 maps, 44 photos. Paperback. 978-1-934934-04-3. $22.95.

All titles available at www.buscainc.com or from book vendors everywhere

www.ingramcontent.com/pod-product-compliance
Lightning Source LLC
Chambersburg PA
CBHW030302080526
44584CB00012B/408